Dreams, Creativity & Mental Health

Dreams, Creativity & Mental Health

Glen A. Just

First Edition

© Copyright 2012 by Glen A. Just

Front and back cover photographs by Ruby Li-Just

Formatting by David Hoffman

Edited by Richard DeBeau and Steven Ulmen

Published by Eagle Entertainment USA

130 Teton Lane #2
Mankato, Minnesota 56001

Website: www.eagleentertainmentusa.com

ISBN: 978-0-9832057-3-9

ACKNOWLEDGMENTS

In heartfelt thanks to all the giants
who walk these pages.
And to each my gratitude
for their love of science.

In further dedication to all the minds
that chatter in the night.
And to two friends whose minds chatter most:
Richard DeBeau and Steven Ulmen.

TABLE OF CONTENTS

PROLOGUE

OVERVIEW

I've been a lucid dreamer for over 70 years. I learned to totally program my dreams over 50 years ago. It is from this long-term perspective that I've come to appreciate the many ways dreams inform us about consciousness, self, mental illness, language, mysticism and subjects as esoteric as Free Will.

Dreams inform us as to how communication occurs across various levels of consciousness, and provide a mirror image of underlying physiological processes. But in order to make these observations we must first learn how to interpret dream imagery. Fortunately, science provides many lenses to observe the inner workings of our brains and minds with new technologies and methods in biology, physiology, neuroscience, medicine, dream lab research, developmental psychology and cognitive science.

Analysis of our dreams enhances our understanding of how consciousness and self come into existence. We gain insight into primary image formation, qualia and metaphor that eventually leads to our ability to use language. Dream methodology offers an observation window into our unique human subjective experiences. And when direct dream observation is combined with direct altered state observation this window is enlarged.

I offer a number of interpretations of dreams that are not standard to dream researchers: Dream functions are specified, dream content analysis is expanded, therapeutic mechanisms available through dream analysis are explained, three forms of repression documented, qualia and metaphor placed in operational and researchable contexts, and the concepts of will and free will are explained in terms of body-grounded images.

My long-term practice of self-hypnosis and its implications for dream and mind research and self-observation is discussed from these points of view. Self-hypnosis is stressed as a preferred method of dream and therapeutic intervention versus other person induced trances or therapies. I also discuss the importance of mastering self-control over autonomic brain functions for improved mental health; and the use of self-hypnosis for dream programming.

I've attempted to review major researchers in the above referenced fields of study as aides to a fundamental understanding of dreams, consciousness, self and altered states. We live in an increasingly dynamic world where interdisciplinary research can be brought to bear on previously isolated areas of study. I'm arguing that triangulating interdisciplinary studies with self-observation and self-experiments provides new insights across a number of interrelated fields.

The reader may prefer to jump around the first five chapters after this introduction and spend some time with chapters 6, 7 and 8 for better grounding. How one proceeds will most likely depend on background familiarity with related materials. I've not tried to over simplify scientific works, nor have I introduced wild speculations about the meaning of this research. Research findings from many fields are presented that has helped me personally understand my own subjective experiences. I'm open to comments and criticisms from all readers. I've also built in conceptual redundancy for those less grounded in the mind sciences.

SERIES OBJECTIVES AND GOALS

The three objectives of this series starting with *Autobiography of a Ghost* which documents how mystic experiences became part of my infant mind before the age of two and how I later came to consciously create and control dreams and other altered states.

In *Mind of the Mystic* I challenged traditional religious interpretation of similar mystic experiences. I took the position that both shamans and prophets of world religions use mystic experiences that are natural physiological phenomena to demonstrate their link to God and the supernatural. Altered states of consciousness were defined as modifications of the brain's neural networks; as creations of our own minds and not a form of communication with God or the gods as has been the usual historical assumption.

Historically, manifestations of our religious nature are expressed with creative variation, and each culture tends to assume their interpretation of the supernatural is correct. How the brain and mind create altered states is ignored. Supernatural interpretations assume that the epiphenomenon of altered states is generated outside one's own brain-mind and originates with God or the gods.

In contrast to this historical interpretation, I argued that our biological capacity to experience altered states underlie all religions. This review compared my own ASC experiments with interdisciplinary studies from psychology, neuroscience and neural philosophy. A major theme that runs through *Mind of the Mystic* and this book assumes that belief is a central element in mental health.

This book views dreams, altered states and consciousness as the product of a dynamic integrated brain-mind system subject to circular causation. In accordance with contemporary neuroscience the brain is viewed as plastic, incredibly complex and capable of multiple kinds of malfunction due to trauma, accident or genetic abnormalities.

I use Walter Freeman to lay out the difference between linear and circular models of causation. The benefits of a dynamic systems approach is the elimination of an agent as a concrete part of the mind that sits in judgment or acts as a little homunculus inside our heads or a specific set of neurons that resides in any one spot in our brain. Thus, focus shifts to circular causative processes that drive consciousness and create self.

In effect, I argue that dreams, altered states, self and consciousness are so intertwined that understanding how these three entities arise and are expressed depends on our comprehension of macro integration and functioning across the brain. One must tease out these interrelationships in order to understand the contribution of parts to the whole. This view is compatible with V. S. Ramanchandran's developmental perspective which culminates in his 2011 work.

However, in contrast to Ramachandran's approach which looks at the effects of reduced capacity, my 50 year old subjective experiments review the effects on the brain when capacity is added and functions are expanded. Both approaches require that the brain be viewed as a macro entity: Meta-consciousness comes to consist of control over all variety of brain states from autonomic functions to the range of dreams and other altered states. This approach permits an expanded dynamic brain-mind interpretation of how to realize what Owen Flanagan calls Eudaimonia—a harmonious society.

I believe that careful self-observation and self-experiment, which are placed in the context of interdisciplinary science, is a required methodology for the exploration of self, consciousness, dreams and altered states. And that individual case studies combined with simple experiments can be as fruitful as Ramachandran's simple and effective therapy with phantom limbs. I present these studies as the book progresses.

I demonstrated in *Mystic* how phenomenal states can be altered at will. And I believe that demonstrated control and experimentation with dreams and other altered states sheds light on the various mechanisms involved. I argue that by looking down from the brain's global level we can observe and tease out sub-system effects associated with various states of consciousness.

Great strides have been made in understanding how neurons and neural circuits express themselves, but this physiological level of analysis does not yet explain macro processes such as that of obtaining immediate relief from long-term nightmares. I will attempt to demonstrate that self-observation viewed through the lenses of contemporary empirical research offers new insight into these processes and brain states.

It is from this perspective that I have analyzed dreams, altered states, consciousness, the shaman, shamanism, and various forms of mystic expression, such as visions. And carrying over the central theme from *Mystic*, I believe that traditional religious interpretations of ASC have distorted our understanding of self, consciousness, dreams, and the meaning of spirituality. I continue to argue that neuroscience has advanced to the point where it is a disservice to the public to let mystics dominate discussions of altered states. The gap between science and spirituality no longer exists; but the gap between science and organized religious dogma does.

My personal experiences encompass lucid dreams, numerous altered states of reality and different aspects of mental illness. Integrating an overview of these experiences offers additional insight into each one of them compared to analyzing them separately. In support of this position, Hobson says: "To begin to understand consciousness as a natural process, we must be subjective as well as objective: We must welcome psychology's prodigal child, subjective experience, back into the family of science (Hobson: 1999, viii)."

Subjectivity can be extreme when it is exercised outside the realm of careful observation and related comparative scientific investigation, or when it is guided by unbounded speculation. Careful self-observation combined with thought experiments can help us re-conceptualize our problems and lead to new paradigms. Phenomenological experience, analyzed in the context of neuroscience, provides insight into self and consciousness that is not yet available through reduction techniques alone. A good example is Ramachandran's work on phantom limbs.

The physiological procedures commonly used to research dreams and consciousness meet scientific protocols, but the study of altered states of reality are either footnotes or sidebars to the main topic of consciousness per se. Systematic use of hypnosis still generally lies on the periphery of consciousness and altered states investigations. It is late in the day for me, but I add 50 years of experiments with self-hypnosis into this mix.

The bottom-up approach to understanding consciousness in physiology has made tremendous progress. Antonio Damasio, for one, has gone beyond cells, circuits, and brain architecture by not being afraid to make consciousness a central focus of his research. He continues to refine ongoing work and develop new insights; *Self Comes to Mind: Constructing the Conscious Brain* being his latest book length effort. And it's good!

The black box called the brain is not totally revealed by the mind sciences but former peep holes have become enlarged panes even if the glass often remains semi-transparent. Walter Freeman and A. Damasio have been most helpful with their perspectives of how consciousness emerges at the global level of our brain-minds. This global approach includes Zimmer's observation that "The architecture of the network itself shapes the pattern of activity" in various models of the brain" (Zimmer: 60). Thus, any approach to dreams requires a basic understanding of consciousness, global and subsystem brain states and an evolutionary perspective that takes into consideration qualitative changes in brain-mind functions through evolution.

It is inevitable in consciousness discussions that science tends to overlap with philosophy. After all, philosophers have been interpreting consciousness at least since the ancient Greeks, Buddha and Confucius. A smattering of philosophy is often found in full-length works of neuroscience. One cannot discuss consciousness in any comprehensive manner without considering qualia, for example. Attempts to explain image formation in my own dreams requires consideration of qualia and how qualia contribute to consciousness. In my opinion field workers in anthropology who attempt to explain shamans or shamanic practices without incorporating research findings from physiology and neuroscience are philosophizing in the tradition of the ancients.

I've tried to present my personal dream and ASC history as objectively as possible from crib to adult years. I know that memory is not perfect, but I believe the basic outline of my traumatized childhood and the numerous distortions and pathologies that it produced are outlined with a fair amount of reasoned objectivity in my autobiography. I insert a minimum of this history when I explain nightmares in Chapter 8.

My fifty plus years of active dream analysis reveals patterns and insights generally supportive of professional dream lab research: However, moving from dream lucidity through altered states while controlling consciousness through techniques of self-hypnosis permits me to offer my own sometimes unique interpretations. I give myself permission to think, interpret, and speculate as I integrate interdisciplinary research. I distanced myself from prominent models of self and consciousness in the late 1950's when I rejected Freud's models of self and dreams and reconfigured Skinnerian Behaviorism.

I find it surprising as we tread carefully into the 21st Century to see the physiological basis of religion neglected. Many prominent researchers such as Damasio and Hobson flirt with religious ideas, but are careful not to fully engage these ideas, as one's professional career has typically been diminished thereby. This neglect gives all kinds of religious charlatans an open field from which to run their plays. I believe we are at a level of understanding in the twin areas of dream analysis and consciousness where an interdisciplinary review of our spiritual nature is warranted.

GOALS AND OBJECTIVES OF DREAMS

In many ways dreaming is a parallel process to our waking consciousness, and in my dreaming and altered reality experiences neuronal exchanges between macro and micro levels are constantly taking place. My dream experiences resonate with Steven LaBerge's position that great similarity exists between dreaming and waking states (2009: 12). As we come to more fully understand our dream states we also come to more fully comprehend other states of altered reality. All forms of consciousness are created by the same brain but using different combinations of neural circuits and various combinations of the brain's own chemicals.

Hobson says that: "So far, neither neurology nor psychology has come up with a satisfactory model of the brain-mind. Such a model would specify how many compartments there are, describe each of them objectively, and formulate the dynamics of information interchange among them. Not an easy task" (Hobson: 1999, 6).

I personally know the effects of trauma on childhood, what repression and active repression means, how programming one's dreams can alleviate anxiety and depression, how to develop and control attention, and what is involved in overcoming obsessive behaviors. Throughout this work I attempt to articulate my psychological interpretations with relevant physiological research.

FUNCTIONS OF DREAMS

What are dreams for? Are dreams just epiphenomena of underlying brain processes, static in the black box, and therefore have no real meaning? Are dreams windows to the supernatural? Are dreams manifestations of unconscious processes as envisioned by Freud? No, no, no and no. So, what are the functions of dreams?

Over the past seventy years of lucid dreaming, I have experienced dreams as multi-tasking phenomena. My observations come from the inside-out by subjectively analyzing thousands of my own dreams. And, I believe that consciousness has a qualitative essence that can only be understood subjectively. We can use various brain scanning technologies to watch the brain in operation, but these methods do not permit us to explain the subjective experiences of consciousness, how meaning is created or the steps by which language emerges. Observations of one's dreams can address each of these conundrums.

My initial goals in dream analysis when I was a young university student were to rid myself of nightmares, learn how to control pathological processes in my psyche, and stabilize my relationships with work, school, and others socially. Understanding my dreams and learning how to control and interpret them accomplished most of these objectives. I share my strategies and life-long discoveries in the following pages.

I'll list the functions of dreams as I've come to understand them. These observations are guided by a very practical approach to self-understanding and therapy. Real psycho-physiological mechanisms are operating to bring about observable changes whether I have the interpretation correct or not. At a minimum, I have employed these mechanisms to bring about positive changes in my own life.

Sometimes my personal experiences support existing research and at other times I disagree with contemporary interpretations. I have no special claim to being correct. I offer insight from fifty years of self-experiments in the hope that I'm making a small contribution, and leave it to future researchers to sift the chaff from the wheat. Yes, there is much controversy here.

The functions of dreams as I experience them are:

1. To support memory by enhancing, changing, integrating and eliminating. I view these as old brain functions found throughout earlier mammalian stages of evolution.

2. To support virtual skill practice related to daily activities. This is an efficiency function enhancing motor skills of immediate importance to the organism.

3. To inform the dreamer of negative states and emotions interfering with body and brain homeostasis.

4. To enhance thinking processes and the integration of complex conceptual materials. This function probably emerged with the advent of enlarged cognitive processing centers for humans; what we associate with the new brain and the expansion of the cerebral cortex. Conscious awareness of this level of brain function is probably not attained by most lucid dreamers.

5. To encode and strengthen primary images as the initial evolutionary step in concept development. One can observe the process of primary image formation in dreams that leads to metaphor and qualia as second and third order levels of neural circuit connectivity and integration. These processes support cognitive and language development. I will explore metaphorical expression and symbol manipulation by analyzing dream content.

6. To embed and modify learning processes supporting numerous brain activities occurring below our conscious level of awareness. This function does not directly expose instinctive and automatic nervous functions but it does address dream activity that articulates with these processes.

Although this is not a function per se, dreams are windows through which we watch the construction of consciousness across both old and new levels of evolutionary brain integration. My position is compatible with A. Damasio's evolutionary model that encompasses two major levels of development for human consciousness. A comprehensive understanding of dreams and other altered states requires a basic understanding of consciousness and how it is manifested in dreams and altered states.

FUNCTIONS OF ALTERED STATES

"What are the functions of other altered states of consciousness?" is probably the wrong question. Altered states, excluding a significant portion of dreams, are probably epiphenomena. They occur because unusual circuit and neural network combinations are triggered by oxygen deprivation, stress, drugs or ritual controls. Altered states are given meaning by the socio-cultural groups where they are expressed. And, their meaning historically has been attributed to supernatural causes. Because science has not adequately scrutinized the neural basis for altered states, ASC has been viewed from an occult vantage point or assumed to be pathological.

I assume altered states are normal, but statistically unusual neuronal combinations. In my own self-experiments I've used control over altered states to explore issues of mental health and my spiritual nature. And by expanding consciousness across this spectrum I've addressed the conditions necessary for eudaimonic selfhood as conceived by Flanagan. For eudaimonia to exist in society the individual must be at peace with him or herself; thus society must also account for altered states as we learn to control mental pathologies.

A primary element of the eudaimonic self is a decrease of cognitive and emotional dissonance at both the individual and group levels. Once a meaningful explanation for the altered state person's experience and behavior is accepted by the group the individual again feels in control. And the individual may become more highly valued than those without ASC. Thus a social psychological interpretation is employed by the individual and the group to re-establish harmony. In other words, a major element of a harmonious society depends on our mutual ability to favorably predict each other's behavior. It is not the behavior that is critical, but the interpretation of the behavior.

Nightmare resolution occurs when an explanation is derived externally or internally that is acceptable to one's Interpreter. To be effective explanations that are acceptable to one's Interpreter often go against explanations provided by our social or professional groups: Freud and psychoanalysis being obvious examples. Nevertheless in both of my nightmares there was immediate resolution once my Interpreter connected the dots.

The critical component that is always so hard to pin down centers around how meaning is created in our minds, or how socially created meaning comes to be accepted by our minds. Obviously, early indoctrination plays a key role in this process. On the other hand we often observe the client accepting a professional opinion of his or her pathology only to find that their Interpreter rejects the explanation and the condition persists.

It also seems obvious that evolution has been a less than perfect cobbling together of our three pound enigma. Social construction performs a function overlooked by evolutionary physiology. Our active self (Interpreter) explains everything that happens to us whether it is the simple behavior of eating an apple or the complex gestalt patterning of a bad dream.

Social functionality enhances group survival as much as improved individual functions do when the cerebral cortex is greatly enlarged. Cognitive-emotional dissonance generated through uncontrolled altered states cannot be controlled by the group per se, just the consequences. Historically it has been a form of cultural natural selection to elevate individuals with ASC to that of shamans. And then assume they possess special relationships with the unknown.

Mystic explanations for altered states are collective social constructions that underlie all religions, small and large. The extent and variety of religious social constructions are as varied as our imaginations. Nevertheless, fundamental neural configurations must support each different altered state. Consequently, there are many religious, shamanic and Western therapeutic interventions in altered states that achieve positive results.

Historically, social elevation of shamans (mystics) has permitted role specialization that addresses healing of the body, mind, and social group. Shamans and priests with their special relationship to the unknown became interpreters of the unknown; hence over time they came to explain everything from eclipses to ghosts and spirit possession. Additional social functions include shamans becoming memory libraries for native pharmacies, medical procedures, and what we now think of as psychological treatments. Cultural accumulation of survival artifacts such as native medicines relied on memory through most of human history.

Avoidance of self-alienation that comes from negative group definitions demands redefinition of altered states by the group. The recognition of mental states of illness was a two edged sword in Western Culture. It removed thousands from the dungeons and chained oppression but stigmatized their social lives. In contrast, the shaman or priest with similar hallucinations received elevated status. We free countless souls from our modern dungeons only to continue their stigma.

Viewing the mind as a process that emerges from complex neural anatomy suggests numerous mechanisms that we can learn to activate, direct and control. The mystery of self, consciousness, and altered states is at least partially eliminated when we come to understand through self-directed control that the mind can change brain, and the mind can change mind.

My almost immediate recovery from nightmares, depression and clinical states of anxiety are supportive of these hypotheses. I've previously shared similar observable effects in Native American religious ceremonies; observations which articulate with the shamanic literature. I've provided additional support for each of the above hypotheses in earlier works.

Subjectively, one experiences an inner release and sense of wholeness that emerges with the elimination of negative emotions such as depression and anxiety. The sense of "flow" that M. Czikszentmihalyi discusses emerges. One comes to embrace a sense of wholeness that leads to feelings of happiness, which in turn represent collectively what Owen Flanagan calls eudaimonia.

We must be able to move freely across our brain's architecture to realize our own creativity and enlarged cognitive and emotional capacities. I'm proposing that what group definition has achieved for ASC affected individual reintegration in society, the individual can promote through his or her own ability to direct and control their own altered states.

Techniques by which we remove cognitive and emotional dissonance lie behind freeing our capacity to be all that we can be; to feel all that we can feel that is desirable, to expand our thinking capacity to the next level, and to realize the good state that can be realized when we become the good citizens of which we are capable.

AUTHOR'S ASSUMPTIONS:

1) Self and consciousness are processes.

2) The self as active agent can be taught to control most conscious and non-conscious brain states and functions.

3) Dreams are multi-tasking brain state phenomena that include memory integration and consolidation.

4) Non-conscious fixed action patterns can be observed in lucid dreaming.

5) Primary image formation underlying qualia can be observed in lucid dreams.

6) The brain-mind operates as a dynamic integrated system.

7) Self-reinforcing patterns of neural circuitry underlie addictive and compulsive behavior. Individuals can be taught to identify and modify these circuits through the use of self-hypnosis and self-control of altered states.

8) Brain chemistry at micro and global levels can be modified through progressive use of self-hypnosis.

9) Individual should avoid normal mental health objectives and seek to achieve expanded, positive emotional and cognitive functions instead: Expand do not just maintain.

10) A significant subset of mental health issues such as depression, anxiety, and dissociated states can be effectively treated by teaching individual clients how to self-manipulate these conditions.

11) Mind can control matter (physical brain) and can therefore eliminate nightmares associated with trauma.

12) Self-directed cognitive-behavioral manipulation of brain states can maximize and expand capacities related to attention, brain state balance, and unity of personality.

13) Altered states of reality are unique neural circuit configurations subject to self-control.

14) PTS can be effectively addressed with control techniques demonstrated in self-directed dream programming and altered state self-control.

15) Currently, reduction based technologies have limited value researching global brain states because global state analysis currently requires macro level subjective methodologies. Self-observation currently remains the only methodology available to study subjective states.

I make these assumptions on the basis of personal experience gained over the past 54 years. My autobiography covers the developmental history associated with each assumption. And, this book attempts to bring contemporary research findings together with my personal history to both support and encourage critical review of these assumptions and the exploratory methodologies I've employed.

CHAPTER 1

CONSCIOUSNESS

INTRODUCTION

I've analyzed my dreams almost daily since 1958 when I began to program entire dream scenarios including major characters, plots and outcomes. I viewed dreaming then and view dreaming now as an altered state in which we can be actively involved. At that time I consciously taught myself to enter my dreams while still dreaming and change the plot or characters as my dreams unfolded. I developed total control over my dreaming nights; nights that had been wracked by nightmares from early childhood. Dream programming offered a means to remove the anxiety of nightmares and stabilize my days.

I was forced to think about consciousness as I searched the limited dream literature at that time. Freud was the god of therapy and dream analysis and his conception of the unconscious forced me, as it did others, to consider the difference between what the conscious and unconscious were. His ideas, like those of ancient philosophers, added mystery to dreams, not clarity. He assumed that raging unconscious impulses bubbled up in dreams. By 1958 I was totally controlling my dreams and analyzing their content. My dream interpretations were at variance with Freud. I came to experience dreaming as an active process and exchange between night and day consciousness. This was not a popular interpretation in the late 1950s. What I retained from Freud was the belief that dreams were natural phenomena concocted by the brain that could be understood through self-analysis. This meant that both dreams and altered states were subject to empirical investigation and self-manipulation.

Altered states, starting with a near death out of body experience before the age of two, became a permanent part of my developmental reality. Consciousness at mid-century was debated in the realm of philosophy and not neuroscience. Even worse, religious schemes were used to interpret altered states. Dreams have been the sacred domain of priests and shamans since ancient times. One did not challenge Jesus speaking-in-tongues because speaking in tongues supposedly put one in contact with God or the gods, and for many the assumption remains. If speaking-in-tongues was and is a natural brain activity, then one was indirectly challenging the divine. Thus, I journeyed into philosophy, social thought and the formal study of religion in psychology, sociology and anthropology, including reading the original documents of the Christian Church. These studies have been complimented over the years with new research in the sciences, the discovery of lost sacred works such as the Nag Hammadi Texts, and explorations into Eastern philosophies. A general understanding of consciousness has helped me interpret all the various altered states that I've experimented with.

I discuss a broad range of altered states and dreams in the following pages by comparing self-observations with the findings of neuroscience and physiology In *Mind of the Mystic* I explored what altered states mean for shamanism and world religions once one learns how to control and direct these states. Changing focus from my earlier book on mysticism, I interpret all altered states from perspectives derived from the mind sciences. Thematically, I continue to replace occult interpretations with natural explanations.

Another theme running though this book deals with eudaimonics and the control of brain-mind states that are necessary for human flourishing. The Greek word eudaimonia means flourishing, and my interpretation follows Owen Flanagan. Human flourishing at both the individual and social levels implies an expanded understanding of all our various states of consciousness. Good parenting or any long-term positive social relationship requires basic mastery of brain-mind states including anger control. People do not flourish magically because of the form of government under which they live; they flourish by the impact governments have on their development. Noble people are raised in authoritarian dictatorships and the most heinous criminals emerge in the world's best democracies. We need to understand why.

Models and ideas related to the meaning and interpretation of dreams follows in Chapter 2-5. Chapters 6, 7, and 8 analyze body, symbolic and trauma activated dreams. Chapters 9 and 10 cover form, function and patterns of dreams. Chapters 11, 12 and 13 review altered states of consciousness and their relationship to dreams. Chapters 13 and 14 explore global brain states and self -hypnosis. Dream dictionaries are covered in Chapter 16 because the majority on the market are misleading in that they assume either occult or boiler plate interpretation of dreams. I was diagnosed with three critical MMPI Profile elevations when I was an undergraduate. I used self-therapy to correct these pathologies as a first year undergraduate student. I discuss the relationship between mental illness and altered states in Chapter 17. Chapter 18 represents musings covering philosophical issues related to altered states. Finally, Chapter 19 suggests hypotheses for future consideration. The logic of this chapter order builds on my previous two books, *Ghost* and *Mystic,* with *Dreams* being the last book of this series.

A number of integrating threads run through these chapters: The significance of self-control and self-hypnosis for dream interpretation, 50 years of dream pattern analysis and pattern changes that occurred, how dream and altered state control can enhance mental health, and the value of longitudinal self case study. I have a deep interest in dreams and altered states as natural phenomena. One of my objectives in this series has been and is to debunk occult ideas about dreams and other altered states. Or how characters can feel like someone I know, but look entirely different.

Insight into conscious states and how the brain maps reality provides insight into how dream morph from one setting to another, and why I have been capable of engaging in illicit behavior in my dreams that I would never think of engaging in while awake. These are common questions that naturally arise when we pursue analysis of our dreams. Dream researchers like Hobson and LaBerge offer more insight and detail regarding these issues than I will cover. My goal is to present what I've discovered over the past half century that still seems relevant in the context of contemporary science.

My contribution to dream literature is insight and speculation about dream functions, how we can observe the brain in dreams generating primary concepts supporting language, the brain's use of perception and meaning to reorder reality, and how long-term self case study can reveal dream patterns of a deep nature. Neuroscience is making rapid and significant strides in understanding consciousness and altered states. I've tried to place my thoughts within this scientific context.

If you want to be titillated by the occult or the supernatural, you will not find my words comforting. However, if you complete this book, I am quite sure you will come to appreciate what altered states mean to those of us who experience them naturally. And, just perhaps, you will have one or two new insights into self, dreams, altered states, and consciousness. Let me try.

EXPLAINING CONSCIOUSNESS

I cover some of the major figures researching consciousness and dreams, and occasionally touch on issues of a philosophical nature such as qualia and metaphorical concepts. Although this is not meant to be a beginner's book on dreams and consciousness, I want it to be accessible to the general reader. The logical order that follows is of my construction, and I apologize for any violations of historical sequencing of major research findings, or attribution of significance to one researcher versus another. I'm referencing some of the giants of neuroscience and physiology who have helped enlighten my understanding of dreams, ASC and consciousness per se. And I throw in a few sidebars along the way.

GAZZANIGA

I'll start with Theory of Mind (TOM). According to David Premack: "It is the ability to observe behavior and then infer the unobservable mental state that is causing it (Gazzaniga: 2008: 49)."

This ability is fully developed by age four and partially in place before two years of age (Ibid: 63). The early expression of this capacity appears to be part of the new born infant's brain architecture. Giocomo Rizzolatti's discovery of mirror neurons helps explain what is going on in our brains. When we see others perform actions, similar neurons are firing in our brains. You smile at me and my mirror neurons smile back. This part of consciousness is built into our brain's structure through evolution. It permits us to duplicate mental processes in others that we often think of as limitation and empathy. Pretty neat stuff!

Continuing Gazzaniga on mirror neurons: "It has also been found that they are involved with understanding why the action is being done, its intentions (Ibid: 179)."

Triggering mirror neurons permits us to surmise the intentions of others because a similar brain state is created. Brain states, in my understanding, contain two elements: One element registers something that is without body or substance, a representation of the other's state of being. The second element reinforces my sense of Self as I become aware of being separate from the other. Awareness of other's intentions through our understanding of mirror neurons helps explain how the Self emerges and is maintained as a process. Feelings generated by mirror neurons are mine but they also represent what you are experiencing and feeling. This capacity within us lets us feel the other as an immaterial thing. We now begin to understand the non-corporeal "Other," the spirit world.

Our mirror and canonical neurons permit us to be in two places at one time: self and other. I can be my own character observing myself in my dreams or in other altered states. I can become the bear in a shamanic ritual and still be the observer; I can experience the ghost as the other, or God as the ultimate Other and be conscious that I am also the observer. All this is possible because you and I have this wonderful neural capacity given by evolution. This is not an exhaustive explanation, but an explanation that gets us started on brain-mind explorations. It is a critical component of self physiology that lets use experience God or the gods.

Theory of Mind depends upon our ability to experience, "If I feel it, it is me. I feel, so I am" (Ibid: 193). Quite the opposite of *cogito ergo sum:* "I think therefore I am." The self is always grounded in the body as A. Damasio, Kandel and Llinas argue. The mind and body are not separate things as consciousness and self always depend on the brain-body being united. Break the brain's contact with the body and consciousness and self disappear, sensations (qualia) disappear. This relationship is critical to our understanding of self, consciousness, altered states and dreams. It is also critical to our understanding of what has been called the soul.

Knowing that mirror neurons are duplicating your brain state in my own brain helps me understand more than just my ability to place myself in your shoes. Cognitively I can know your intentions; emotionally I can feel your sensory state. My mirror neurons act as fictive duplicators when I project myself into the persona of the bear, or in reverse feel this duplication when I become possessed by a ghost. "I feel, therefore it is real." I just change my frame of reference and I possess the other, or the other possesses me. Nothing supernatural is needed for us to understand spirit possession, or the shamanic possession of spirits.

I can create a secondary representation of any feeling state at a cognitive or language level. This permits me to self-talk, or be two characters at the same time in my dreams. If I feel in control of this process, I'm defined as being in a normal state of mind. If I lack control, you may define me as being crazy or in a mystical state. How you and I interpret and control feelings is critical to our diagnosed state of mental health.

Gazzaniga on Paul Bloom: "… children are natural believers in essentialism, the philosophical theory that a thing perceivable to the senses can have an embodied unobservable essence that is real. Bloom considers essentialism an adaptive way to think about the natural world (Ibid: 256)." Ancient Greek thinkers, OBE freaks, and Descartes understood this aspect of essentialism well. And to my mother, this interpretation was fact, as she thought ghosts were real. Our perception of what is material or immaterial starts with body embedded feelings. I feel it, therefore it is real. The second step occurs when our social group (culture) provides explanation.

By our very nature we separate the material and the non-material because that is how we experience our world; that is how our brains image the external world and our own bodies. Biology solves a puzzle unanswerable by traditional philosophy: why we experience the material (physical) and the immaterial (mental). Consciousness is a felt physical state and we experience consciousness as being separate from our physical bodies. We must experience body-mind this way as symbolic imaging is derived from feelings that are tissue embedded. This naturally felt separation becomes the source of an assumed homunculus, little man or woman, in our brain who directs activity. The natural process of an emerging self creates a sense of agent or homunculus, the ghost in the machine.

Infant and young children's brains take years to fully develop. We feel this immaterial "other" and become natural believers as children. Ghosts and angels are just as much a part of our child reality as adults are. So are Santa Claus and Howdy Doody. This is not a physiological state created by culture and the world's numerous religions. It is primordial feeling that comes to be written large that we think of as our basic spirituality. It is a natural biological process that is part of our developmental history. Our DNA capacity is manifested this way as we pass into adulthood. Infant memories are adequate enough for me to recall the reality of angels and ghosts when I was an infant, and I recalled them in detail in my autobiography.

Self-consciousness is, according to Gazzaniga:

[T]he left brain interpreter that is coming up with the theory, the narrative, and the self-image from the 'neuronal work space,' and from the knowledge structures, and gluing it together, thus creating the self, the autobiography, out of the chaos of input (Ibid: 302).

The self emerges from a biological process, but once manifest, the conscious self interprets all of our felt sensory input and in turn can provide coordination and direction to this input. Consciousness carries with it an interpretation of what is being experienced. In this sense we do not experience because we are conscious; we are conscious because we experience. Your dreaming brain interprets all of its sensory input in the same way. If the experience seems bizarre to our waking minds, no matter. The dreaming brain will provide its own logic. We constantly experience differences of logical interpretation as we move between dreaming and waking states. Do not expect dream logic to duplicate waking logic.

Gazzaniga presents his understanding of consciousness well, a view of consciousness that represents the general findings of contemporary neuroscience. In that I'm tying altered states and innate moral predilections together, both in *Mind of the Mystic* and in this book, I will support this connection with a related consciousness aside.

Using mirror neurons as our focus, Gazzaniga says:

Olaf Blanke and Shahar Arzy … have done a review of all such phenomena, collating evidence from neurology, cognitive neuroscience, and neuroimaging. They suggest that OBE are related to a failure to integrate multisensory information from one's own body at the temporo parietal junction (Ibid: 192).

A technical reference to our brain's structure, but the point is clear – scramble our brain's wiring and out-of-body experience can emerge. This is the basic position that I took in *Mind of the Mystic.* It is a position supported by my ability to create and direct different kinds of mystic states including out-of-body experiences. It is also central to my criticism of how shamanism is commonly discussed by anthropologists as occult phenomena, and relevant to how the mysticisms of major religions are maintained.

A final comment from Gazzaniga regarding external brain waves: "Jonathan Wolpaw—SUNY: After several years, he was able to show that people could learn to control their brain waves to move a computer cursor" (Ibid: 343).

I believe that I've demonstrated in previous works that one can learn to control brain waves and networks of neurons to create any image or visual narrative desired; to consciously take control of autonomic nervous system functions, and to create mystic states or trances while either asleep or awake: programming dreams and control of normally unconscious (autonomic) brain functions such as heartbeat and body temperature being examples. What is new with Wolpaw is demonstrating this ability through mind-technology interaction.

In my experience of dream programming and active control of ASC, one can learn to consciously control almost any combination of their neural circuitry. Out-of-body experiences are not just a failure to integrate multisensory information from one's own body; they can be a conscious integration and reconfiguration of multi-sensory information that is under our individual control. Multi-sensory information can be orchestrated by the brain in extremely complex forms as I demonstrate in my cosmic shaman adventure to the beginning of time (Just: 2010:180-184), and in Chapter 11 of this book. This was an OBE involving a trance-like state that I consciously induced while sitting in my favorite easy chair on a cold winter's afternoon in Rochester, Minnesota. I demonstrate positive consequences of modifying multi-sensory integration through the elimination of trauma induced by nightmares in Chapter 8.

By creating, directing, and controlling OBE and other mystic states, I gained insight into unconscious and conscious brain processes and functions. Top down control over brain centers that control both conscious and autonomic functions led me to appreciate brain-mind activity as a dynamic integrated whole. My personal experience says that developing control over neuronal processes that are not normally part of consciousness is necessary to maximize optimum mental health. This is particularly true for those of us suffering from nightmares, PTS or other debilitating pathologies called mental illness. I'm suggesting that any philosophical or cognitive neuroscience discussion of morals or ethics is incomplete without consideration of these mechanisms, and that attempts to control these mechanisms by changing laws is ludicrous.

HOBSON

I quote extensively from J. Allan Hobson's numerous writings. He does not stand alone as a dream researcher or student of consciousness, but he does stand tall. Hobson's research has laid bare the religious musings of Freud called psychoanalysis, revealed the significance of brain chemistry for mental health, and created heuristic models such as AIM that simplify our understanding of dreams and consciousness. I offer only a brief overview of what he says consciousness is in this section, but I reference him throughout *Dreams*.

Hobson observes that: "… consciousness can at any given instant concern itself with only a single idea, a single percept, or a single emotion" (Hobson: 1999: 13). Note the focus on the importance of attention; our ability to block out most other stimuli entering our senses and selectively attending to only limited amounts. However, when we think of our second order consciousness, being aware that we are aware, note this

Glen A. Just

thought:

If the brain is capable of creating an abstract or representation of the visual world (and it is), then I do not find it so hard to believe that the brain can create a representation of that representation (as it does when a visual image arises spontaneously or is voluntarily summoned in the absence of an external stimulus (Ibid: 12).

In other words, we map the external world and we can create abstractions of those maps: "maps" of maps, awareness of awareness. And we can create complex maps whole and treat these auto-creations on a par equal to other felt sensations. We experience this mapping of maps, so to speak, when we self-talk or project part of our conscious self outside of our self in the act of the shaman possessing his or her totem. Chapters 2, 4, and 14 will elaborate on the remapping of maps and how we use interpretation of these processes to explain Free Will, consciousness, and our human ability to use symbols.

Our brains are built around modular architecture. Each of our senses feeds information into our central processors so to speak, where this sensory information if sorted, prioritized and given meaning. A hot July afternoon might take conscious precedence for a thirsty hunter-gatherer, but it pales in importance when that speeding lion is headed directly toward us. The modularity supporting consciousness is structured to promote our survival, fortunately. But all kinds of interesting questions are raised about how all the brain's inner work is conducted. The key point is not that modularity exists, but that sensory input is processed through these various brain modules to provide continuity, priority, and selective focus. "Consciousness is a many-splendored thing, a stupendous synthesis of diverse components," says Hobson (Ibid: 17). And, so it is.

The brain puts modular input together differently in our dreams than during waking states. I can mix and match input any way I want in my dreams through lucidity controls; characters can be combinations of people who look nothing like their real life counterparts, but I know who they are because I "feel" their identities. Scenes can morph radically in dreams as the mind is not obligated to provide geographical continuity as everything occurring in our dreams is taken from memory, except for certain stimuli that directly activate dream content. See Chapter 6 for dream activation through external stimuli such as touch.

Knowing that the brain synthesizes input from all its various senses helps me understand how my sleeping brain can so easily mix and match sensory information. I can collate this sensory information in my dreams any way my dreaming brain chooses. Remember, we don't incorporate whole sensory pictures, visual or otherwise, and store them in files for later dream availability. We collate input elements, attach feelings, give it meaning, and organize all these data bytes as our dreaming brain chooses.

Each new area of cell, neural circuit, brain architecture analysis that increases our understanding of global brain states brings us new insights into the substrates of consciousness. In my opinion, it also supports the subjective study of higher levels of consciousness that can only be understood from a dynamic integrated systems model. The chaos of complex systems as we move from the level of cells and neural circuits to complex biological systems continuously demonstrates qualitatively different levels of emergent properties. Consciousness and subjectivity are emergent processes that can only be experienced and known internally. I can't understand what water is by analyzing O and H, I have to analyze H2O as a composite whole.

Reduction as used in scientific exploration of consciousness has provided huge insights and moved our understanding to new levels. But, it must be complimented with complexity and chaos theory that enhances our understanding of dynamic complex systems. Remapping of basic sensory maps frees our minds of reflexive embodiment at the same time that sensory maps reenter the system to maintain self and consciousness. Global effects are the result of more than a simple mix of smaller components. Global effects created by the increasing complexity of subsystems generate qualitative differences in the course of evolution. Neuronal loops, recursive functions, dynamically create you and me. Rejoice!

A. DAMASIO

I present Damasio's own synopsis of consciousness in Chapter 12 that support my dream interpretation. He employs a model that follows development of sentient organisms. Following his lead, my dreams make more sense when I consider this history. Damasio's lays out the evolutionary complexity scale from proto-self and core self to autobiographical self. When I reference our evolutionarily old brain I'm combining what he calls the proto-self and the core self. This older level of consciousness permits the rat to be aware of its surroundings and lets it navigate a maze. Autobiographical self supports a higher level of consciousness: The, I am conscious of being conscious, aware of being aware level. I make this distinction interpreting my dreams and altered reality experiences. If you are a lucid dreamer, you know this difference intuitively. The autobiographical self I call my Interpreter observes what the core self produces.

Consciousness emerges at a simpler evolutionary level as the brainstem evolves. The brainstem as an older evolved structure is home to the proto-Self. At an intermediate level of complexity Damasio sees the emergence of core Self. Higher order consciousness means that the organism comes to experience feelings that are both felt and known.

"Consciousness offers a direct experience of mind (2010: 177)." And, "Dreams do offer, however, direct evidence of mind processes unassisted by consciousness (Ibid: 178)."

In my dreams I report dream dispositions that are fixed action patterns (FAP), and memory routines that usually occur at the non-conscious level. My dreaming brain is fictively practicing bicycle riding which I would not comprehend without making this normally unconscious process conscious. My dreaming brain embeds body images such as balance that are proto-language on their way to becoming symbols and metaphor. Really, interpreting dreams and altered states at this level is a lot of fun.

Damasio likes Gazzaniga's concept of Interpreter "… as a way of explaining the generation of consciousness (Ibid: 204)," and relates it to his own concept of autobiographical Self. This is roughly equivalent to what I have called my Controller for the past fifty years. Damasio assumes that "… the autobiographical self can be constructed only by means of the core self mechanism …" which is "… anchored in the proto-self and the primordial feelings is the central mechanism for the production of conscious minds (Ibid)."

The body felt must be experienced for consciousness to exist. In the paragraph that follows, note the global presence of consciousness as a distributed process.

Consciousness arises not as a set of cells or circuits, but as a distributed process across brain modules; it is always embedded to be experienced, and the highest order of consciousness integration is experienced as our agent. Eliminate consciousness in coma, for example, and self disappears. Hence, consciousness can only exist in dreams or altered states through direct sensory instigation. These states can change quickly in our dreams and create all the bizarre effects interpreted later by our waking brains.

Damasio continues:

[S]elf can be connected to objects external to the organism or objects (images) created internally… recalled or imaginary motor interactions can modify the proto-self instantly. Should this idea be correct, it would explain why we do not lose consciousness when we daydream in a silent room with our eyes closed… (Ibid: 204,205).

I'll later discuss how these processes between proto-self and core self that create qualia can be observed and interacted with in our dreams. Both externally and self-created images can be integral to the consciousness process within dreams or other altered states. Phenomenological support for this position is taken from the sameness of reality experienced in dreams or altered states compared to waking conscious realities. This is not a complete process explanation. I will develop it further as *Dreams* unfolds.

Damasio accounts for different levels and uses of consciousness with three interrelated concepts: proto-Self, core Self, and autobiographical Self. In my previous books, I emphasized the fact that our dreaming brains create fictive characters and realities, and once these images are created, we can store and continue to use this imagery as often as the dreaming brain chooses, just as our dreaming brains use real imagery acquired from the world external to our brains. Personally, I have dozens of these images in complex form that represent dream scenarios that grow and change over time in a fashion similar to my waking history growing and changing over time.

We can have primordial feelings of a dispositional nature derived from the proto-self, and we can have core feelings derived from the core self: Feelings of feelings, or the substrate for dreams within dreams from this point of view. And all of these generated images can be brought into our higher order consciousness and manipulated by our Interpreter. Some such mechanism must operate for us to get layered hierarchical effects in our dreams. Damasio's hypothesis brings focus to the brainstem and its various complexities, as does Hobson's. Gazzzaniga's Interpreter resonates with Damasio's autobiographical self and my former use of the concept of Controller. It is this interlocking set of hierarchical mechanisms that makes sense to me in a Dynamic Integrated Systems Model. Agency as process replaces homunculus; and consciousness as emergent from different evolutionary process levels addresses the substrate from which self-talk is possible as well as our ability to experience self as separate and dual elements.

In the late 1950s when I created the concept of Controller as my managing editor for programmed dreams, Freud was king of the unconscious with all his quasi-religious mystery. His dream interpretations didn't make sense to me. I combined behaviorism and cognitive elements that are similar to what we now call cognitive-behavioral therapy and went about my self-analysis and self-treatment. I added conscious control through self-hypnosis to overcome nightmares and learned how to control various body functions like heartbeat and pain. I refer to Gazzaniga's Interpreter, and Damasio's Autobiographical Self as being similar to my Controller because I used this concept to create dream programs from scratch and redirect my fragmented self to become an integrated whole. I took top-down control over fragmented brain processes that were chaotic and operating on their own at a non-conscious level. .

Salient maps are those images that are given the most value, says Damasio. Salient maps are key images in my dreams that carry the most emotional content and feeling. Salient maps become bridging elements used to interpret dreams. A bridging element is the key image or feeling that brings the entire dream into meaningful focus. I watch for salient elements when I analyze my dreams upon waking, or I sometimes watch for and analyze them while I'm still dreaming: The use of waking consciousness within dreaming consciousness. These salient elements form a gestalt-type core of understanding combining the various sensory elements entering my dreams, or they may be salient because the entire dream episode that I'm watching or reviewing has this fundamental dispositional quality. My Interpreter has learned to move across this hierarchy.

It is now understood in neuroscience that non-conscious processes dominate the waking brain's activity moment to moment, which is about 95 percent of our brains activity. It seems equally logical that non-conscious processes are dominant when I'm dreaming. A quick review of my reported dreams in Chapter 6-8 supports this interpretation.

Damasio discusses the long period from childhood to adulthood when we educate non-conscious processes, thereby calling our attention to the common method of bringing non-conscious processes partly under conscious control (2010:269,270).

In my experience, whether I consciously or unconsciously learn something from childhood on, I can either unlearn or reconfigure most of this history. I go into greater depth in Chapter 9, "Dream Content, Form & Function" regarding this issue.

Damasio's overview of this normal process of educating our non-conscious brains eliminates much of the criticism around the argument of whether or not we humans have free will. We do from his interpretation, but we must consider the time-frame in the feedback loops of our neural circuits. Non-conscious learning and the execution of routines in acquired memories facilitate our survival. FAP, fixed action pattern dreams are a good example of how our dreams help us integrate memories. Non-consciously we walk automatically to get from here to there while our conscious brains are problem solving or just being alert to our surrounding environmental demands. I express a similar conscious-non-conscious relationship when I engage in Zen driving. I leave the driving up to my non-conscious mind and let my conscious mind relax and enjoy the scenery.

I have to account for these mind-brain interrelationships as they are expressed in my dreams and other altered states. My dreams express facilitated action patterns (FAP), dispositions expressed as social discomfort in my spousal relationship, honing my ability to balance when riding a bicycle and other related non-conscious learning that is going on moment-to-moment, day-to-day, in my brain. I find it helpful to view this non-conscious-conscious relationship of brain-mind activity from multiple disciplinary perspectives as each perspective helps me see the process from a slightly different angle. We can master brain-mind control without understanding physiology or neuroscience, but the joy of insight that comes from the "aha" experience is lacking.

EXTENDING CONSIOUS CONTROL OVER NON-CONSCIOUS BRAIN ACTIVITY

I have contended since the late 1950s that extending conscious control over non-conscious brain activity can significantly enhance mental health. I give examples in the first two books of this series, but now I want to be more explicit. As a child I had to deal with obsessive-compulsive behavior when the cracks in my small town sidewalk took control of my mind. This was not a conscious process for me and I didn't understand what was happening; I just wanted the cracks to stop controlling my behavior. I also had to confront bed wetting, nail biting, stuttering and almost nightly fear of ghost possession, to name a few of my developmental burdens; burdens that emerged from being raised in a dysfunctional family.

I know from first-hand experience that Freudian and psychoanalytic interpretations were both distracting and misleading in terms of finding solutions to my problems. Behaviorism and various cognitive approaches eventually became known to me, and I used this new knowledge to control unwanted, non-conscious brain-mind states. Philosophy that separated mind and brain was not helpful either. How does one make operational mind processes that supposedly exist in the nether world? Freud and psychoanalysis were totally rejected by my second year at the university. Religious interpretations of spirits, ghosts and God's divine hand were placed in context with world culture studies in anthropology. The result of all these intellectual contortions left me with science and self-experiments. I was lucky.

Anthropology has generally studied shamanism from a traditional view held by both pre-literate and literate societies. The non-conscious processes behind trance, vision and altered states of reality have not been dealt with from a rigorous empirical level. Freudians practiced at this mystic shamanic level, yet Freud considered his approach to be scientific. His was *the* model throughout most of my formal university days. Freud was embraced as a prophet of scientific stature. Individuals like me had to lift two anchors in order to sail our lifeboat: The anchors of false religions and pre-scientific mental health models presented as being scientific.

Damasio says:

In the end, the relationship between conscious and non-conscious processes is one more example of the odd functional partnerships that emerge as a result of coevolving processes (2010: 270). Moral behaviors are a skill set, acquired over repeated practice sessions, and over a long time, informed by consciously articulated principles and reason but otherwise 'second-nature' into the cognitive unconscious (Ibid: 271).

One of my favorite neuroscientists is presenting the standard model of how conscious control gets embedded in our non-conscious brains. His wording is clear, helpful, and, I think, needs to be modified for my purposes. Practice does not strengthen moral behaviors unless the brain-mind is receptive and fully functional. In fact, practice may intensify negative results if the perceived value is reversed by brains experiencing dysfunctional cultural interpretations. It is not practice that makes perfect; it is integrated practice that is properly directed with personal love and social support over time that makes perfect.

Hopefully, my position is clear that we can learn to consciously take control of our non-conscious processes in a few days or at most few weeks. Self-control of normally non-conscious processes was a critical step for me. Dysfunctional pathologies of my variety typically operate through non-conscious processes in our brain-minds. Traditional models of psychotherapy were not up to this task in the late 1950s. To the extent that mind sciences were sidetracked by Freud's interpretation of the Unconscious, we have delayed scientific exploration of non-conscious mechanisms that support positive mental health.

Anthropologists who continue the mysticism of altered states in their study of shamanism perpetuate the standard model that these processes are beyond our control. The public remains uninformed, and individuals who have my history are left with bizarre interpretations of what is going on in their mind-brains rather than being given insight and understanding, let alone relief or therapy. And in turn, many flock to an occultist for relief. Creating altered states of reality on demand, controlling them, and playing with their expression takes the mystic out of mysticism. Mastery of altered states offers insight into therapeutic aspects of non-conscious processes.

Interview assessment of mental illness, along with paper and pencil tools such as the MMPI, does not distinguish between individuals with uncontrolled versus controlled altered states. A separate category is created for shamans and mystics, thereby continuing to relegate altered states to the black box. Assumptions of conscious brain-mind passivity were unduly strong when the Minnesota Multiphasic Personality Inventory (MMPI) was created; unfortunately, the Unconscious of Freud was the chief doer for many. From my perspective, failure to understand ASC was a major contributor to this oversight. When I watch a shaman/priest return a troubled soul to health in a brief rite of exorcism, I appreciate direct intervention in non-conscious brain processes. Classifying these treatment options as "hokus-pokus" has not been edifying, unless, of course, they are performed by an acknowledged religious leader such as a Catholic Priest practicing the exorcism. Unfortunate! By granting exorcism authority to historical or modern shamans of this nature, we are agreeing to a hands-off science policy.

CZIKSZENTMIHALYI AND FLOW

In his 1997 publication, Czikszentmihalyi presents flow as an intensely satisfying sense of time and place where external sensations are optimally experienced. In flow, we feel a sense of purpose and direction in our lives. Our thoughts, feelings and goals are balanced, we are at peace with ourselves, time becomes whatever we want it to be, and what we are engaged in becomes an end in itself. Goal directed, contented achievers exhibit this state of consciousness. In my interpretation, thought, feeling and purpose are all in harmony and we experience balance and wholeness, a sense of unity with our surroundings. Flow is not necessarily happiness, but a state that better approximates serenity. This is a state comparable to meditation. It is also the state one can enter through self-hypnosis. I've previously described it as approximating what one experiences lying in the warm Hawaiian sun far enough offshore so all one hears is a gentle breeze creating wave action, the sense of floating in timeless space, exerting no effort and totally at peace. It is the sense one achieves going to the center of one's mind and shutting down all distracting sensations: The peace of the meditating monk comes to our horizon of effortless consciousness.

When I compare the experience of how I interpret flow with other conscious states, I have this inner sense of controlling most external and internal input to my conscious mind. For spiritualists, its extended form is joining with the mind of God. For atheists, it is fine tuning a brain state. For the rest of us, it is recognizing that the mind and brain are one, and we can enjoy whatever state(s) we choose. Consciously entering flow states like meditation and other forms of mind-brain control are addicting, seductive, and enjoyable. For me, they represent a Hobsonian state space where awareness of self is maximized, and we are the master of internal and external sensory inputs. A counterpart of flow is experienced in Zen driving.

Therefore, Flow is not like an aminergic or cholinergic brain state of the Hobson type where activity of one sub-system takes precedence over another. It is an intense state of self-awareness accompanied by a sense of mastery and control. Most likely there is a balancing of brain states and brain chemistry that share many characteristics of early trance states or meditation. If Antonio Damasio is correct and it is impossible to separate feeling from self, then this is a state where cognitive processes, feelings, and directed purpose move together seamlessly.

Experientially, control is a critical element in understanding flow and meditation. Whatever may be going on in Hobson's state space model, and I think state space placement is appropriate, my Interpreter remains in charge in a state of flow, meditation or self-hypnosis. At least one of my Interpreter-Controller mechanisms sits outside the Hobsonian AIM box and remains capable of observing and directing these states. One does not reach a deep state of meditation or self-hypnosis by wishing it to be. The state is reached after considerable practice and modification of the neuronal mass associated with meditation. Practiced meditation is documented to significantly increase the thickness of the affected neurons and proliferation of dendrites for select Buddhist monks. Accomplished states of serenity must follow similar neural modifications. The fragmented brain knows not!

I think a similar process and outcome occurs when I practice self-hypnosis and enjoy complete control over mind and body. I have an intense but focused awareness; I'm in control at all times, and like meditation, I have taught myself to enter and exit this state at will. I sit outside Hobson's box and control the micro-states occurring in the box. It is learning this process, I believe, that will be most helpful to others needing to balance micro-circuit states in order to achieve global brain state harmony and balance their brain chemistry. Brain-mind state control is not mystical, but subject to physiological conditioning. Balancing and integrating fragmented selves created by trauma and/or mass media has much to offer dysfunctional individuals.

In the Western World, the church has historically pronounced itself the authority on all matters scientific, from biological evolution to astrophysics with the Earth being flat and the center of the universe. Science has struggled with religion since science has existed. Today, spirituality and all its biological foundation are still usurped by the churches. Speaking-in-tongues is defined as communion with God, hypnosis as the work of the devil, and evolution a hoax for millions of Americans in this 21st Century. Even meditation is lectured against by fundamentalist churches. Science must wrestle with this dogma if truth be known. It appears as though the God of the Fundamentalists is not the author of science. Unfortunate!

Christian interpretations of hypnosis and altered states have delayed understanding of altered state phenomena and hypnosis. But, the island of dogma continues to erode. I argue from experience that therapeutic use of self-hypnosis has much to offer. In my case, learning these techniques and practicing internal brain/mind control allowed me to reclaim emotional balance and unify my fragmented personality. The brains of traumatized children that exhibit wild emotional swings along with anxiety and depression into one's adult years can be quickly overcome by developing extensive control over body and mind. Personally, these controls were self-taught using self-hypnosis.

Self-hypnosis has been inadequately researched by the medical community, and I've suggested the main obstacle to this research has come from organized religion and those affected by this interpretation. I offer my case history as an example, but believe that the type of work I'm proposing must be done under careful laboratory conditions by qualified personnel familiar with neuro-dynamics.

Flow is a concept whose time has come. Flow is balancing the brain's micro-circuits to achieve harmony, centeredness and unity. These strange sounding words, harmony, centeredness, and unity, can now have operational value. They have a very personal meaning to me. When achieving a sense of flow we experience a quality, purposeful, self-directed and meaningful life. Flow achieved individually can lead to a eudaimonic society through our collective well-being. I don't think a drug dependent collective spurred on by profit-at-any-cost motivated pharmaceutical companies will get us there.

Young people who are in a high state of self-actualization are exhibiting characteristics associated with the state of flow. However, most young people are buffeted by demands, stresses, and achievement needs that put pressure on the harmony and unity of flow day-to-day. Conversely, an individual like me who is retired and at peace with himself "flows." And in compatible fashion, my dreams are almost totally void of negative emotions and conflict. My dreams flow and reflect my days. The aging process that leads to contentment brings dreams of resonance, even if they are mostly mundane. The continuous dramatization of everyday life does not promote flow at any age; serenity and peace dwarf the lesser state called titillated happiness. Achieving harmony in one's life is in stark contrast to the young who traverse a road of drama that is misconstrued as being happy.

NEURO-PHILOSOPHY

Lakoff and Johnson represent the new philosophy; one that starts by assuming that the mind is embodied. Old schools of philosophy commonly assumed after Descartes that the mind and body were separate entities. Neuroscience has established empirically that the mind and body are not separate, but that the mind grows out of the body (brain) and consciousness stops when various subsystems of the brain are damaged or destroyed. *Philosophy in the Flesh* is a joyful read for those who may have struggled through college trying to make sense out of disembodied consciousness in philosophy or classes covering the history of social thought.

Embodied philosophy no longer accepts the traditional wisdom of the ancients that one can just think and thereby come to know what is real. (Metaphysics is a fancy word for what is real). We have to be able to demonstrate through research that our working constructs and hypotheses can be accepted or rejected and then move on as we do in any other area of scientific research. This is no small change in the traditional roads to philosophical heaven. Lakoff says:

The idea that pure philosophical reflection can plumb the depths of human understanding is an illusion. [And] All of our knowledge and beliefs are framed in terms of a conceptual system that resides mostly in the cognitive unconscious (1999: 12, 13).

This position is in stark contrast to religious dogma, and much of historical philosophy in the Western World.

Following their reasoning, all of our knowledge and beliefs are framed in terms of a conceptual system that resides mostly in the cognitive unconscious. We don't think about aspects of what we call our common sense; we just know that we have it, as we know who we are. Our common sense understanding of self typically has two parts: the body and the mind. We know this intuitively. So far so good as we follow Lakoff and Johnson. However, the self is oftentimes called the soul and some cultures visualize human beings as having multiple souls. We are not debating who is correct. Do I have one, two or more souls? We are searching for the basis from which these constructs are derived. Traditional philosophers have debated these issues for centuries while scientists use research to accumulate new knowledge and explain real events.

The cognitive unconscious is a good example of this new fork in philosophy's road. It's not an abstract Jungian idea, but represents the collective internal workings of our brains that operate below the level of our waking consciousness; that 95 percent of brain activity that keeps us going day-to-day. Thus, the collective unconscious is not a disembodied thing or semi-religious supernatural construct. The fact that such a large majority of all our mental activity occurs at the non-conscious level is supported by neuroscience. I will later demonstrate how my dreaming brain manifests these non-conscious processes. Analysis of my dreams supports neuroscience research. I can't interpret my fixed action patterns dreams without knowledge of non-conscious processes.

Lakoff and Johnson note that the self is a metaphor and that "There are more than a dozen such metaphorical conceptions of the self (Ibid)." The mind and body are not separate things; there is no dualism in the new philosophy as there is no mind-body dualism in neuroscience. Both the neural philosopher and the neuroscientist want to understand how "… various configurations of neurons carry out the neural computations that we experience as particular forms of rational thought (Ibid: 16)."

The upshot of all this is that the body and brain shape human thought and reasoning. Animal reasoning evolves into human reasoning as a natural evolutionary progression. Thus the two disciplines are in compatible agreement on this point. Organisms have to categorize all the sensory stimuli that they experience. This doesn't mean that simple organisms have to think about these categories. They just do it. It's a mind-body process built by evolution. However, as organisms become more complex, we humans become conscious of these built in categories and come to manipulate them symbolically in the neural circuits of our brains. How our bodies and brains are structured determines the kinds of categories that come into existence (emerge); change the brain's architecture and we change perception. For example, it is hard to imagine an amoeba having a category for the color red. It takes a much more complex set of neural circuitry for color to become a conscious concept or working metaphor, as color does not exist in nature.

Categories are a part of our experience; we cannot get beyond our categories, but use them in constructing thought. Now I'm simplifying Lakoff and Johnson's reasoning, but what I want to emphasize is the natural formation of categories that classify our world, and note that these categories are derived by the particular architecture of our brains and bodies and the sensory information fed into them. Over deep time evolution built this architecture that mostly exists before we exit the womb. It continues to unfold and mature as we age from the crib onward. The world of thought is not based on arbitrary constructs derived from culture. Our language ability is ultimately derived from the architecture evolution has given us, and the primary images that have their origin in primordial feelings – a process we can observe in our dreams. I'm keying off Lakoff and Johnson, but will follow these thoughts more closely with Llinas discussion of qualia, and Damasio's Qualia I and Qualia II conceptualization.

Consciousness at the level of our older brain is constructed from this primitive process of image formation; a process that we inherit from millions of years of evolution. And, when we add higher cognitive centers to the human brain to remap these proto-images we eventually get Damasio's autobiographical Self. Manipulating symbols at a level of consciousness where we are aware that we are aware generates human culture. This is an amazing process that we are beginning to understand through modern mind sciences. It is a process that we can watch intimately in our dreams. Neuro-philosophers might say that proto-language made possible through evolution permits us to create categorical constructs based on our organism's special neural system architecture. The upshot of this seeming digression is that the world of dreams and altered states reflects our place in the mammalian history of evolution. I know why and how my dreams are different from my neighbor's dogs as I watch primary image formation in my dreams.

It's no mystery that all humans have language, experience emotions, feel pain, see the color red, or worship some type of God or gods. Yes, our separate cultures create great variety in the creation of cultural artifacts such as gods, but the categories and metaphors that make the basic elements possible come from the structure of our brains as mind comes from body. We become aware that extreme versions of cultural relativism floating around academic state space have severe limitations. Cultural variety is perhaps a better term than cultural relativism when we consider a basic assumption in neuroscience – brain structure is isomorphic to function. Simply put, my god may be envisioned as different from your god, but we have all had one historically.

Lakoff discusses some of the basic conceptual categories we humans use. Spatial relations are most fundamental, and represent what is near and far; the bounded region we occupy in space is a container from which we construct what is inside and what is outside, and bodily projections can be seen as starting from the front or the back. The point made is that basic categories form because we have the bodies and brains that evolution has given us. Concepts, categories, and subsequent thoughts develop from this most fundamental substrate on which the mind is built. These are first order emergents that can be and are combined in wonderfully different combinations as we move up the ladder of more complex brains enabling complex abstractions, embodied thought, embodied reason, and embodied self.

The concept of metaphor sits in the middle of my subjective treatment of consciousness. Hobson uses a dictionary definition of metaphor that is not research operational and thereby inadvertently can be used to support disembodied consciousness, details of which I'll provide later. I found this an odd use of resources for such a careful researcher. I will skip a lot of detail from Lakoff and Johnson. However, there are four different false assumptions that support their common sense interpretation of metaphor. Let us lay misinterpretations to rest.

1. **Fallacy:** "Metaphor is a matter of words, not thought." The following examples demonstrate that it is thought, not words, which represent metaphor. "Love is a journey can reflect the following metaphors: Our relationship is spinning its wheels, we're going in different directions, our relationship is at a crossroads; hence, these are all metaphors that represent thought and not words representing "love is a journey." (Ibid: 123).

2. **Fallacy:** "Metaphorical language is not part of ordinary conventional language. Instead, it is novel and typically arises in poetry, rhetorical attempts at persuasion, and scientific discovery (Ibid)." Metaphorical language is part of ordinary conventional language because it is created from basic constructs held in the brain-mind.

3. **Fallacy:** "Metaphorical language is deviant (Ibid: 124)." "Conceptualizing love as a journey is one of our normal ways of conceptualizing love (Ibid)."

4. **Fallacy:** "Conventional metaphorical expressions in ordinary everyday language are 'dead metaphors,' that is, expressions that once were metaphorical, but have become frozen into literal expressions (Ibid)." Being at a crossroad is not a dead expression or concept, and I probably don't need to explain this thought any further.

I don't want to unduly extend this interpretation, but note that after you check the dictionary definition of metaphor, that thought as metaphorical concepts are quite different than concrete alternative expressions for a given word or words, or interpretations fitting any of the above four fallacies. Dream content analysis can help us move beyond dictionary definitions of metaphor to the image formation process that underlies metaphor. It is the primary imaging, proto-language process that one can observe in dreams that is my concern in this book.

If our metaphorical thinkers have this right, and I think they do, then treating metaphor as a dictionary item is a major mistake. It's not easy trying to capture the neural basis of thought, but it is something that we try to do. My dreams do not reflect dictionary definitions of metaphor. My dreams contain all matter of metaphorical thought as described by Lakoff and Johnson. When I say my dreams represent metaphor, I'm using the term generally as they understand it. Complex metaphor is a second or third order construction by our new brain supported by primary imaging of the type exemplified by my bike balancing dream Please see Chapter 4.

Metaphor is represented by a former spouse or friend standing in for my current spouse in a dream; metaphor is the symbolic and visual representation of my uncomfortably dry lungs wanting relief. When interpreting my smoking dreams I pay special attention to lung discomfort, and an awareness that I haven't smoked in decades. My memory clearly associates winter dry air with the discomfort of smoking. Dream metaphor uses smoking as a memory referent. Thus, dream metaphor is represented by various gestalt-like configurations that convey meaning to my waking consciousness. And, in this case dream smoking-dry lungs metaphor becomes my bridging element. Complex metaphor of this type lets one observe the mind-brains process of creating abstractions as we lucidly dream. Movement of my organism through space, any complex self-body or self-environment interaction requires a similar form of abstraction. Nothing is mysterious here.

Dynamic Integrated Systems as a model recognizes that the meaning of words changes over time. Language has this dynamic quality, and we understand this readily when talking to teenagers fifty years our junior. Love as a journey is metaphorically expressed differently in a multitude of different American subcultures, but it is still a journey. Our brain-minds will continue to manipulate primary and complex metaphor regardless of how words change over time. Hence, the multitude will dream of their love journeys with compatible thoughts, not the same old "dead" words of my generation. Love expressed in this multitudinous variety is no less beautiful; the heart beats just as fast, the longing remains, and the need to touch demands. Metaphorical concepts can be expressed in endless different ways in the changing words of one's own particular place in history. The brain traffics in meaning, not language per se. And nowhere can we observe this process more clearly than in our dreams. Learn the language of dreams, and you will add depth to this interpretation.

In my opinion, subjectivity, consciousness, and self can only be understood when we understand how thought and metaphor are generated in our neural circuits. Endless study of neural circuits, synapse, dendrites, and brain chemistry are increasingly demonstrating important aspects of how our brains work. Our brains are modular, memory is distributed, dopamine performs a different function than serotonin, etc. I fall in the camp of those who believe that subjectivity must be studied separately as its own unit of analysis. And I believe that we will never understand subjectivity, consciousness, and self until we do. Meaning is not found in a particular set of neurons. Meaning is configured in our meta-consciousness from our ability to abstract relationships that are bound to sensory experiences in endless ways. And meta-consciousness, through our Interpreter, can direct our dreams, control altered states, and heal our psyche with derived meaning. I'll provide examples in Chapter 8 covering traumatic dreams.

SELF AS METAPHOR

I just woke up from an afternoon nap, ate an orange and now sit in front of my computer with a cup of hot tea. The visuals in my two hour nap are rapidly fading into nothingness. But that's OK, this was one of my thought dreams, and the thoughts remain vivid. I got out of bed telling my half-waking brain that I needed to add another section on Lakoff and Johnson that covers self as metaphor. I'm thinking of the following examples generated by this dream. At this moment my wife asks me to go for a walk and I refuse saying that I want to put these nap thoughts in my computer.

This is a common interplay between my dreaming and waking states. I will quickly note the dream's ideas, or contents, and then develop each one before my dream thoughts go out of focus.

Afternoon Nap Dream Content includes Self as both subject and Self as object. Symbolic Interactionism with the I and the Me, love as a journey examples with subject and Self, and three different dream metaphors with dryness, balancing and coprolite, and last, Wilson's use of consilience.

Lakoff and Johnson discuss five different kinds of experiences our inner lives have which cover how we control our bodies, conflict between inner values and outwardly expressed behavior, what we know and believe about ourselves and what other people know and believe about us, taking another viewpoint by imitating another, and last are the forms of inner dialogue and inner monitoring that we engage in. (Ibid; 267). Without more detail, I just want to call the reader's attention to these inner mind machinations.

Lakoff and Johnson state that:

[We] have a system of different metaphorical conceptions of our internal structure. These are certain inconsistencies within the system. And there are a small number of source domains that the system draws upon: space, possession, force, and social relationships. What is perhaps most surprising is that the same system of metaphors can occur in a very different culture, as we shall illustrate below with Japanese examples (Ibid).

In other words, our inner self-processes draw upon common source domains inherent to all people, regardless of their cultures, to create the basic constructs used in thought. I digress with Lakoff and Johnson because I will constantly point out metaphorical symbolism in my reported dreams.

My focus here is not in the cognitive scientists understanding of self per se, but in the manner in which our dreaming brains handle these processes and metaphorical representations. I'll tie this all together in a moment, but first, let's distinguish between Subject as Self, and Self as Self.

This is a basic distinction I derived from Symbolic Interactionism Theory (SI) in my 1970s lectures at Mankato State University. Unfortunately my lecture notes have been lost, and I reconstruct from memory. Nevertheless, the Self was the "I" in my old lectures, and the Subject, the "Me." I made a simple distinction between the two with the Self (I) being a symbolic representation of the physical me, and the physical me treated as Subject (Me) being the actual referent. That was also how I subjectively experienced myself at that time. There was a non-material "I" represented by symbolic processes and a physical "Me" represented by flesh and blood.

Following Damasio, the "I" is the Autobiographical Self, my Interpreter, and the "Me" is a combined proto and core-self. A somewhat crude approach of mine in the 1970s, but a working set of concepts that let me articulate this relationship. The I and the Me provided working constructs to make operational my Interpreter and exercise self-control over dreams and other altered states. I created this operational distinction by 1958 and took the language from SI years later, a reminder that we think with concepts, not language.

The general structure of our metaphoric system for our inner lives was first uncovered by Andrew Lakoff and Miles Becker (… 1992). Their analysis showed that the system is based on a fundamental distinction between what they called the Subject and one or more Selves. The Subject is 'essence,' everything that makes us who we uniquely are. There is at least one Self and possibly more. The Selves consist of everything else about us – our bodies, our social roles, our histories, and so on (Ibid: 268). Further, Lakoff states that "What is philosophically important about this study is that there is no single, unified notion of our inner lives. There is not one Subject-Self distinction, but many (Ibid)."

The Subject and the Self in this conception arise naturally as emergent structures from the type of body, brains, and neural circuitry we humans possess. We all subjectively experience this dualistic self; we have essence and body, and both seem equally real to me, as they probably do to you.

First, I will discuss "love is a journey" metaphor for Subject and Self. My loved one is my soul mate, she makes my spirit sing, she makes my spirit fly to mountain tops and proclaim my love. This is essence speaking. As my body embraces this relationship, it wants to touch, be near, hold, feel and entwine my lover. This is Self as body.

I cannot explain this afternoon's dream without essence and body. Without Subject and Self, without the I and the Me as key elements, this thought-dream must be made concrete. By concrete I mean attached to its essential and bodily referents. And, so I have. I want to understand all the metaphorical elements in my dreams and being a teacher much of my life means that thoughts keep popping up in many nighttime scenarios as well as in my daytime ruminations. I remain a person of thought. A person of metaphorical thought, that is. And so does my dream persona.

In subsequent chapters I discuss three different dream metaphors which are:

1. Dryness inside my body, the container;

2. Overeating and experiencing enough sleeping discomfort to rise and use the bathroom, and

3. The act of balancing on a bicycle.

In what sense are these three dream scenarios metaphors? Love as a journey metaphor might be expressed as having its ups and downs. We all know that the physical directions up and down do not just represent our relationship in space; we know that when a relationship is our focus, it has a different meaning, and we are representing it symbolically and metaphorically.

One cannot study this physical relationship to space and understand the metaphor. We have to study the subjective thought, the meaning of the metaphor. I will later distinguish between embodied metaphor and disembodied metaphor, or stated differently, between primary and complex metaphor, and in this explanation I will distinguish between modal and amodal concepts.

I look for metaphor in my dreams as dreams to use this form of abstraction, or in terms of Lakoff and

Johnson's view, the way they think all of our normal brains work. What is balancing? Is it my relationship in space, and my positioning against the force of gravity that is maintained by constant adjustment of dozens of different muscles, muscle-brain feedback loops, and a mental construction of this complexity, and a proto-concept called balancing that tells me how well I'm doing? I think so. Balancing is imaged by my brain-mind as proto-language, primary image formation at our old brain's level of consciousness, and it can become a very complex metaphor with all its symbolic nuances at our new brain's level of consciousness.

Complex metaphor represents the plastic abilities of our organic neural circuits to form endless combinations. And, these symbolic elements can be expressed creatively when my dreaming brain has me on that fictive bicycle riding over impossible terrain. These symbolic dream abstractions permit me to slide down the tops of stairs or fly out of body. It represents an embedded, body instantiated primary sensation of balance and the brain-mind instantiated metaphor called balance resides in a container moving through space.

This is metaphor that captures my attention. It is Delaney's bridging element that leads me to understand what my dream means. Seeing metaphor this way eliminates much of what is typically thought of as bizarreness in dreams. My cognitive unconscious doesn't have any need to express itself in the logic of an American brain at the beginning of the 21st Century, and it doesn't express itself using language, but my conscious brain-mind does. My evolutionary moments are expressed as recursive interaction between old brain architecture and new brain function. This all makes sense to me as long as I don't forget what metaphor is and the fact that my ancestors have been building these mechanisms for a few million years.

E. O. Wilson's Consilience is a delightful work that reminds us of how important it is to get outside our own specialized areas of knowledge and embrace the convergence of rapidly expanding bodies of new knowledge. Traditional philosophy is mostly like traditional Freudian psychoanalysis and dream interpretation for me. My personal lesson is not to believe in thought only generated belief. I say belief because contemporary knowledge doesn't support the ancient's beliefs. Nor do we continue to believe in Thomas Aquinas, Descartes, or the reality of Mickey Mouse from our childhood fantasies. I know I'm being harsh with historical figures, but freedom from myth demands that we embrace science as an evolving process. We respect historical thinkers for taking us to the next step on the ladder of knowledge, not for their current relevancy.

Thus, I have completed espousing dream ideas from my afternoon nap.

DYNAMIC INTEGRATED SYSTEMS (DIS) AND CONSCIOUSNESS

Looking at the brain-mind as a dynamic integrated system helps me distinguish between what is going on in my brain when I'm awake, when I'm dreaming, and when I'm in other altered states such as trance and visions. Hobson's AIM model is a conceptual tool used to visualize the different areas of state space occupied in these various conditions. I'll give AIM considerable attention later on. Next, an evolutionary perspective helps me consider how the brain was constructed over deep time; the last million years, for example. There is an assumption of isomorphism between brain structure and function. I find this concept of isomorphism helpful thinking about consciousness at various levels, from cells to networks of cells and integrated networks of cells, and finally, to the emergence of synchronized, integrated networks of cells that act as the Interpreter to direct my thoughts and movements through space.

This final set of integrated neural circuits is not a thing or an agent, but a set of processes that we experience as the self. And yes we do experience these processes as an agent or homunculus. I assume that as we move up the hierarchy of complexity from bacteria to humans we observe both quantitative and qualitative changes: Awareness of awareness is a qualitative change and is evolutionarily uncommon in the animal kingdom; and it appears to be most highly evolved with Homo sapiens. Keeping an integrated, evolutionary perspective in mind helps improve my interpretation of dreams. Our dreams do reflect our evolutionary history, and I refer to these hierarchically expressed differences as multi-tasking.

I make a distinction between Controller and Interpreter as I continue to refine the model of dynamic integrated systems. It appears to be that something like a mouse has a controller which processes incoming sensory information and directs the mouse's behavior primarily through reflexive responses. But as we approach the level of human brain complexity, something else happens. The Controller becomes aware of itself (Interpreter) with a memory that can look back into time and project far into the future: A quantitative building of architecture that leads to a qualitative change in function. It appears that as we technologically refine our ability to screen micro-circuits in the brain and their relationship to larger neural networks, we improve our understanding of how brain complexity creates qualitative differences, i.e., the magic of contemporary neuroscience that permits us to understand consciousness, Free Will and self.

Various state spaces are assumed for different altered states using Hobson's three dimensional cube visualizations. It is assumed that different combinations of neural circuits are expressed as trance, OBE, REM and NREM, etc. Dynamic integrated systems assumes that neuronal activity in any of these altered states, including dreams and waking states, is supported by the 95 percent of processes that are non-conscious. Form as neural excitation and patterning drives function. Emerging structural differentiation through the course of evolution generates qualitative changes. Consequently, I'm assuming that dreams at the old brain level of architecture are qualitatively different than dreams are at our current level of new brain complexity: The neighbor's dog has different dreams than I do, but our old brains both dream.

My dreams reflect memory integration and consolidation with fixed action patterns when I'm learning or re-learning new skills. Most of the time my dreaming brain is dealing with mundane day-to-day activity and body-brain maintenance. Basic principles of evolution should be dictating that my FAP dreams, for instance, parallel the dreams of mammals with less complex brains. Watching animals express emotions in dreams, or comparing the duplication of neural circuit activity by rats that have run mazes when awake with the activation of these circuits during REM sleep supports this interpretation.

Mundane activity with less intense emotions increases in frequency as I age. Therefore, when intense feelings enter my dreams, I flag them as bridging elements to analyze when I'm awake. Strong emotions in dreams reflect big events in my waking life, and my dreaming brain pays attention. Feeling, according to Damasio, makes consciousness, hence self, possible. Feelings are always attached to consciousness whether they are mundane or dramatic. Accepting this perspective, I watch how my dreaming brain prioritizes and puts value on all these elements as they emerge in my dreams. I'm using value to mean how our brain-mind prioritizes both abstract and concrete elements to make them more or less important regarding our social, emotional, and physical survival.

I value thinking, and embrace thoughts of the day or thoughts surfacing at night. My conscious thoughts often become so dominant that they occupy the bulk of my lucid dreaming throughout the night and this pattern can be extended over a period of days. Most lucid dreamers don't report dream mentation at this level. Thought dominant dreams mirror my personal history as a teacher, researcher, and practitioner of assorted human services as well as seventy plus years of lucid dreaming. I problem solve in dreams, give lectures, read books, and engage in numerous higher cognitive activities. I'm not unusual in this respect, as many well- known historical figures have reported similar dreams. Deidre Barrett offers many examples.

Practicing lucid dreaming appears to strengthen the feedback loops between conscious and non-conscious brain activity, as with my dreaming awareness of fixed action patterns. My meta-conscious Interpreter watches fictive bike balancing in my dreams and evaluates it. Self-observation offers new insights when it is systematically practiced in one's dreams over long periods of time. Most significantly, dream self-observation that can be combined with dream-experiments permits direct observation without the obstruction of language, which is the philosopher's disadvantage.

Internal symbol processes I'm contending are less adulterated than culturally tainted language. For example, I can relate how it feels to fly out of body to the beginning of the universe, but you will not fully appreciate what it means through words; even if those words are carefully crafted. It is the limitation of language and the limitation of classical philosophers who rely on language. The significance of embodiment takes on new meaning when one can control and direct dreams and altered states while observing these changes from an internal point of view. Without direct access to image and metaphorical brain-mind processes, we limit our creativity. Creativity is limited, as is understanding, as we stumble across words that do not always suffice. Imagine how different our world would be if Einstein had relied on language.

I taught my dreaming brain to change its routines while I was still dreaming in my undergraduate school year of 1957-58. In the same fashion that I'm aware that I'm aware while writing these words, I can become aware that I am dreaming while dreaming, and change the dream characters or outcome as the dream progresses. At my highest level of consciousness, I change my dreams at will. But sometimes at a non-conscious level my brain-mind will change my dream without any conscious effort on my part. Once neural patterns are embedded as fixed action patterns (FAPs) our non-conscious minds can and will execute them when activating stimuli are experienced. That is, internal or external stimuli. It is not a surprise to dream analysts that this is the case. Later I will discuss the Will as an embedded fixed action pattern to elucidate this point. This is an evolutionary emergent, non-conscious ability that I inherit, as you do, from our primitive past. Personally, the pathological equivalent of FAP activation was anxiety and depression.

Let me elaborate on levels of consciousness as I experience these states subjectively. The memory elements that are embedded, integrated, and/or changed when I'm dreaming are accessing some of the same neural circuits I use when awake. I'm in a learning mode riding my bicycle after years of disuse and attempting to improve balance. I'm partially aware of this process while I'm dreaming and later bring it into full consciousness when I'm awake. Waking awareness of having honed my bicycle balancing skills fictively while dreaming takes the form of willing my bicycle to turn right or left without any conscious effort on my waking brain's part. The bicycle turns as if on automatic pilot. Will in dreams, like Will when I'm awake, accesses non-conscious patterns embedded in memory.

We ride our bikes without effort when awake and we fictively ride them over impossible terrain when dreaming. The same neural circuits and networks must be supporting these efforts. I assume isomorphism between form and function. Once I learn how to consciously enter and change my dreams, Will remains part of my landscape – in dreams or other altered states.

However, I'm aware that I'm aware of this process in my dreams, and in my waking state, attach language to the process so I can discuss it here. Balancing on my bicycle as a learning process is not dependent upon my higher level of consciousness. In fact it proceeds better if I don't think about it but just let my evolutionarily derived learning mechanisms operate by themselves. This is a critical distinction that is necessary to an understanding of Zen driving or sleeping birds in flight, which I discuss in later chapters.

Consequently, attempts to make dreams the predictors of the future or something that puts one in contact with the gods, seems a bit strange. Jungian archetypes seem equally strange, and the Freudian unconscious appears to be a total fabrication. The brain is a biological entity with consciousness and thought derived from the processes of our physical substance. Interpretations of dreams must reflect biological realities; dream dictionaries that try to quantify content without consideration of the 95 percent of brain activity that occurs below our level of consciousness confuse the issue. Brain circuits and related brain chemicals vary from a state of dreaming to that of being awake. I assume that neural circuits and brain chemistry are being expressed differently when one is in trance called glossolalia, experiencing visions, or having an out-of-body trip the occultists call astral travel.

Analysis of my dreams and their content generally supports the above outline. Similarly, analysis of other altered states of consciousness adds depth to my understanding of lucid dreams. It is my hope that comparing other altered states with lucid dreams and consciousness will help divorce altered states from occult control and speculation. Neuro-philosophy builds on neuroscience, which in turn can energize a new field of study called neuro-religion, or perhaps more appropriately, neuro-spirituality. Science has been quite effective probing the unseen in the physical world, and now we are probing the unseen in our brains. The future looks brighter for humanity when we bring occult assumptions of brain activity into the light and put it under empirical examination. World education in this respect is just beginning.

Below, I introduce additional elements into this dynamic integrated systems perspective. By combining top-down and bottom-up views of our brain-minds, I can more fully interpret my dreams and other altered states. The expression and function of unconscious or non-conscious memory is an important part of how I understand dreams and altered states. Feelings are always part of any conscious experience whether I'm sleeping or dreaming, and I generally follow Antonio Damasio's interpretations. An understanding of different types of repression in my dreams helps clarify form and function.

Metaphor in my dreams can mask the activating source behind nightmares. Thus, I must understand dream metaphor in order to deactivate my nightmares. In similar fashion I routinely use metaphor in my waking moments to describe common activities. Just as my spirits were lifted this morning by the beautiful roses in our nearby public park, so too the rest of this day my essence that is life itself will soar as only birds can. Why would we expect dream metaphor to be excluded from our dream processes? Abstraction probably starts at the cellular level, and feeling is what it is.

NON-CONSCIOUS MEMORY CONSOLIDATION

I'm aware that many of my dreams are directly related to memory integration and consolidation. For example, when I'm dreaming of riding a bicycle and in effect practicing riding and balancing while dreaming, or fictive activities, there is active support for visual, muscle, and space relational neuronal mechanisms. Functionally, I need to incorporate visual elements if I practice bike riding in my sleep, and the visuals are automatically supplied. Balancing, physical coordination, and scenery are also readily made available by the necessary sensory centers of my dreaming brain. The effects are real in my dreams and other altered states as these processes draw memory resources that are acquired at both a conscious and non-conscious level. In other words, I'm using various combinations of the same neural circuits, brain chemistry, and brain architecture that are available to me during waking consciousness. My dreaming brain just mixes the batter differently.

By analyzing the content of my dreams, I can more fully understand the mechanisms operating at a non-conscious level. I never had a working bike as a child, and most of my bike riding occurred when I was teaching at Mankato State University. Until retirement these past two years, I've not been a bicycle rider for the past 30 years. Hence, I can readily locate the source of dream content that is visually representative of the scenery during this period of my life. The bizarre elements in this dream represent elements from decades of life that get creatively mixed to create a coherent dream story, and in doing so, consolidate and integrate my bike riding ability. Associative memory in my bike dreams takes me back to the place where most of my bike riding occurred. And my modular brain pulls together people, scenery, and visuals from many different associated memories.

My superhuman ability to ride bike over impossible terrain does not matter. What matters is the fictive rehearsal of bike riding, balancing, and pulling visual memory elements into the dream to create a coherent dream story, and in doing so, consolidate and integrate my bike riding ability. It should not be surprising that we have 25-50 dream scenarios nightly. There's a lot of body-mind maintenance going on.

Creating stories that our dreaming brains find logical should also not be surprising. Our brains are constructed to interpret and give meaning to all our sensory experiences. My old brain fictively rides a dream bike, and my new brain does the interpretation. But unless I teach my new brain metaphor, it misinforms me.

I think we miss these interconnections in dream analysis if we treat bizarre dream form in isolation. I identified the bridging elements in this dream (balancing and practice of motor skills) and then looked for related memory content. If you are familiar with dream dictionaries or psychoanalytic interpretations of dreams that are pre-scientific, you will notice sharp distinctions from my interpretations.

An evolutionary perspective must be combined with a dynamic integrated system model for me to understand these non-conscious processes and remove them from being mystical. Putting an evolutionary perspective into a dynamic model of causation produces different interpretations than putting an evolutionary perspective into a linear model of causation. My brainstem, and earlier evolutionary structures that still function in my modern brain, activates a dreaming process that is directly related to my acquiring and maintaining skills important to my everyday activities and survival. I suspect that a dreaming dog or cat is involved at this proto and core self level as well.

But I have a set of higher level cognitive functions that cats and dogs don't have. I can control and program my dreams, thereby demonstrating open neural linkages between these higher and lower brain centers. As I account for these relationships in all the altered states I experience, including lucid dreams, it is necessary for me to take into consideration meaning, intention, and a more complex self that depends on consciousness described as awareness of awareness.

Dynamically, my brain is modular and my dreaming brain will draw upon visual support for bike riding and balancing to enhance functionality. All of this normally occurs below the level of my awareness, but in that I am a lucid dreamer, I bring these elements into consciousness when I choose. As a young man in 1958 I just had to get rid of all the crazy interpretations of dreams that were common in the mid-Twentieth Century world of Freud, psychoanalysis, and super-naturalisms.

I think a dynamic, evolutionary perspective of dreams offers a fairly direct window into our non-conscious brain-mind functions, but first we must learn how to interpret dreams. I use the term brain-mind because both conscious and non-conscious brain-mind functions are expressed in my dreams and other altered states. Self-analysis of other altered states deepens my understanding of dreams, self, and consciousness. Triangulating dreams and other altered states permits internal comparisons of each state, a slightly altered view of self, and a view of consciousness that is not possible to obtain otherwise. Those who have learned lucid dreaming in their adult years understand part of this difference. Those who can direct and control any of their altered states understand my view in this more comprehensive context.

WAKING AND DREAMING DISPARITY

Hobson says that:

At the formal level of times, places, and persons, dream consciousness displays a superabundance of both incongruity and discontinuity. These dream features are both microscopic, characterizing every second of dream experience, and macroscopic, suddenly interrupting one plot and replacing it with another. But what about waking: Is it really so different (1999: 14).

He is addressing the issue of focused attention. We attend to one thing at a time during much of our waking consciousness, and yet much of the time our waking consciousness drifts across many subjects. We seem to drift around in the most disorganized manner when dreaming but on close examination so do our minds during waking hours.

The question becomes: Are these two states of waking and dreaming that much different? His partial answer is that "The data show waking consciousness to be an exceedingly choppy stream, if it is a stream at all (Ibid: 14)."

He thus draws parallel analysis between our dream and waking states. Research by Barth also supports this view. My personal experience over decades follows a pattern of convergence between day and dreaming consciousness. Decades of lucid dreaming which go back to early childhood seems to exercise and strengthen open connections between day and nighttime consciousness. The perspective that emerges is that day and sleep-dreaming states are always supported by non-conscious processes. And there is considerable "drift" in both states.

A major difference between waking and dreaming for most people is an inability to enter their dreams and change actions as they can when awake. But practiced lucid dreamers can enter their dreams and change actions whenever they choose. In my case I started total dream programming in 1958. We can learn to consciously enter and exit our dreams the way most of us let our minds focus or drift when awake. My experience is that I have the same capacities in either state; the initial difference being that I had to consciously learn dream control. On the other hand, focused attention is an acquired habit as well. Ask any infant.

My brain is always busy performing a multitude of non-conscious activities from visual processing, monitoring temperature, and maintaining an active record of my body in space. These and a number of other functions are going on without my conscious attention. But I can choose to observe them in dreams as I do when I'm awake. What I attend to at any moment is dependent upon my environment, mood, immediate goals, and bodily demands on energy and strength. My dreams manifest these different foci too.

We often overlook the fact that our brains automatically control our relationship in space. I report a specific dream in Chapter 6, a space relationship dream, which covers this form of dream metaphor. I remind myself when interpreting dreams that my non-conscious mind has all these functions that it must attend to, and these functions are manifested symbolically in my dreams. To consolidate something as mundane as bike balancing requires that we employ visual realism. When awake or dreaming, my brain-mind is multitasking.

When I first tried to interpret my dreams over fifty years ago, I tried to use daytime logic and Freud's dream model, but either one worked. Dreams have their own language, their own metaphorical meaning, which one needs to learn. My subjective experience with fictive dream learning, memory consolidation, and integration, is quite different from my waking experiences. I watch my dreaming brain pull memory that has been embedded from external or internal sources, from any of my salient memory circuits regardless of time or my age and mix these elements in an almost random fashion, but a fashion that makes sense in terms of memory associations. I watch my dreaming brain practice physical and or mental exercises and know this process is both functional and efficient. I know at the fictive level that these mechanisms are probably ancient and that I share them with dozens of other species. This awareness gives me a sense of brotherhood with all higher life forms, especially across the species we call mammals.

Thus, disparity and discontinuity are in the eyes of the beholder. I'm happy to have my non-conscious brain take care of 95 percent of my needs this way. And, when my conscious mind enters my dreams and offers redirection or interpretation it communicates information of value, which, of course, means that my Interpreter is on the job. I can choose to program entire dreams if I want to, or let the normal dreaming processes take precedence. My choice, but which choice I make determines the kind of information I get back, and therefore what I have available to interpret my dreams.

Most of the learning that my brain has been involved in over my lifetime is of a non-conscious nature. Most of my physical actions are automatic. Language comes out like elements of a computer program, elements that I've formatted over my lifetime. I respond automatically to non-verbal cues accordingly. I'm relatively sure that all of my sensory modalities are involved in these automatic learning processes. I have a modular plastic brain undergoing continuous modification that possesses an inherited DNA architecture. This inherited architecture needs both development and maintenance from birth on. And, my dreaming brain is intimately involved.

I'm also quite sure that simpler brains based on reflexive learning are not like mine. Consciously I choose to attend to salient aspects of my environment with long or short-term intent and integrate select sensory information into my autobiographical self. Autobiographically I can plan my actions into the distant future, and draw upon memories from the distant past. Meaning is derived from these autobiographical processes, which are partly guided by culture, and not determined by the daily needs of a less evolved hunting animal. My neighbor's dogs don't understand this.

My neurons are busy embedding some stimuli and forgetting other sensory information. I'm quite sure we Homo sapiens direct this process with Free Will unknown to most of the animal kingdom. Our dreaming brains are busy at the level of my neighbor's dog – learning, creating new memories, and forgetting old ones. But you and I are different, because additionally we have all these higher order cognitive abilities. We all know these general facts, but what we all don't know is what this means, and how these differences are manifested in our dreams. And further, we often don't know what this means to our mental health.

The relationship between the 95 percent of non-conscious mental activity and the five percent that is conscious permits us to efficiently go about our daily chores. But to what degree do we connect these conscious and non-conscious neural circuits when dreaming lucidly? In my experience, there is considerable variation between individuals in terms of how we communicate internally between our brain's higher and lower levels of consciousness. My ability to think, to abstract and create, can be carried over from my waking moments by my dreaming brain. I must account for this communicative exchange between my waking and dreaming brain or I have an incomplete model of consciousness. And when I account for and understand this exchange I can engage the process to stop nightmares and control pathologies like anxiety and depression.

Many people historically have demonstrated a high level of connectivity between their dreaming and waking states. They solve math problems, see chemical formulae, hear music, and write poetry in their dreams. These higher dream functions are not common for most people. We have yet to determine to what degree non-lucid dreamers, or even lucid dreamers for that matter, can master these higher functions while dreaming. Is an additional step in brain evolution required to achieve creativity in dreams, or is this creativity a quirk of brain wiring? I don't know, but suspect it can be either. I do think however that all of our brains attempt to integrate and problem solve whether we are awake or dreaming.

I'm more aware of how the complexity and levels of consciousness arise when I trace these state relationships between my dreams and waking self. And, when I do so, I've taken another step to understanding how the hierarchy of my neural circuits continues to create meaning from the seeming chaos of dream forms through neural circuit integration called self-organization. The Self that I'm calling my Interpreter seeks to maintain story, or sensory, continuity as I move through time and space. It seeks this continuity whether I'm asleep or awake. My Interpreter gives meaning to elements of my dreams that make sense to my waking consciousness that are not accurate. My daytime Self, my Interpreter, tries to apply its logic to dreams. I have to teach my Interpreter the language of dreams, dream metaphor, or it continues to misinform me. Uninformed intuition cannot be trusted because it too comes from the non-conscious level.

When I add altered states to lucid dreaming, I have upped the integration ante by adding new memories and circuit connections to the total. My brain's complexity is experienced differently at each level in terms of how my old and new brains function and interpret. All levels of consciousness are dependent on chemical-electrical activity in my neural circuits and surrounding tissue, but the processing of meaning at my highest level of consciousness is uniquely experienced. Meaning construction at my highest level of consciousness can immediately stop nightmares, and over short periods of time remove anxiety and depression and bring balance across numerous brain states. Lower neural circuit activity embedding memory and encoding sensory information is thus experienced differently in my dreams than when I'm awake.

Personally, I know that this higher level of integration brings improved mental health. I propose that eudaimonia, a maximum state of well-being and flourishing, is not possible without this higher level of integration. And, as a nod to Owen Flanagan, eudaimonia necessitates that we provide individuals across society with adequate support in order to reach this level of integration. DNA is not expressed in a vacuum.

THE COGNITIVE UNCONSCIOUS AND THE DYNAMICALLY REPRESSED UNCONSCIOUS

I'm going to address three aspects of non-conscious, unconscious states that I think are distinct. Personally identifying these mechanisms in dreams and visions has been a major key bridging element to remove nightmares and childhood trauma. But first a reference to what Hobson calls implicit mental automata. Mental automata "… can never become conscious no matter how hard we try (1999: 33)."

He uses the example of his memory search for the meaning of the Italian words *pesche fresco*. He recounts his search for this meaning as running without supervision at a below consciousness level, thus the process remains unavailable to him. The meaning of *pesche fresco* is culturally derived through early learning habituation as are the meaning of similar words in English, Chinese or Latin. Words are fixed action patterns and are learned the same way we acquire balance on our bicycles.

Language is the final derivative of more primitive imaging processes, which I will elucidate as the book progresses, especially with the concepts of qualia and metaphor. We should not confuse language, or word, acquisition with the meaning of words; one is a process, and the other is a product of these processes. I can observe a sense of balance being embedded below my normal level of consciousness in my dreams and therefore experience primary image formation. I cannot experience the cultural derivations of secondary image formation that I will refer to as balancing my checking account, or balancing the contents of this book. Before we can even try to trace the meaning of *pesche fresco,* we must first keep our levels of analysis clear. I can trace the origin of balance in my dreams, but not the words' origin.

I will not attempt to explain the language aspects of this unconscious process here, but offer parallel examples with repression. But remember that words are learned like any other FAP, and expressions made up of word strings are complex FAPs. Because I can observe FAPs in my dreams, I can explain playing a complicated classical piece by Bach or Mozart in my dreams even though I've never been trained to do so. I don't just play it; I hear it as I play. And my fingers move like magic.

My dreaming brain is busy most nights rearranging neuronal patterns. Some circuits are being strengthened, some weakened, and undoubtedly some new ones are being created. This is an example of brain dynamism in action. We normally do not become aware of the many non-conscious aspects of our dreams such as (FAPs) or soma-based dream elements. I think that very few people are aware of how FAP elements emerge in their dreams and contribute to memory maintenance and development. This is an active, dynamic, and ongoing part of our collective unconscious, and these processes of necessity must be responsible for maintenance of the motor neural circuits that we use daily, both consciously and non-consciously.

The Repressed Unconscious, from my experience, can consist of two distinct types. In Chapter 8, I report two nightmares: A smothering dream, and a sexual molestation dream. The first subtype is an implicit memory created by mother's attempts to smother me. Hospitalization occurred at about one and one-half years of age. I assume brain damage at that time as I lost my early ability to speak and walk. I brought into recall one of these attacks related to my hospitalization over fifty years later. Recall occurred when I was placed into a yoga type sitting position during a second day of individualized management training exercises.

I refer to this type of unconsciousness as representing a distinct type of memory embedding process. The memory that remained was embedded in muscle and tissue neural circuits that physically responded to my mother's attacks. My language development was limited and probably inadequate to describe what had happened, but I was probably oxygen deprived and suffered brain cell destruction that destroyed my explicit memories of being attacked.

Note that the Repressed Unconscious referred to above is best understood as one's inability to access explicit memories. And in my case conscious, explicit memory was probably lost due to brain damage; thus an organic explanation for memory loss at my higher cognitive level while related memory elements were retained at a core level of consciousness. The living computer we call our brain can also have its memory erased through organic destruction. No Freudian unconscious needed for this explanation.

The study of FAPs in dreams tells us how related elements are being integrated and consolidated in memory. Hence, FAPs as primary embedded images become the starting point for my analysis of how image associations are formed, thus, it is the beginning of the process that eventually leads to word associations. When I analyze my dreams or visions, I remind myself that language is not primary, but derived.

Having worked with a few hundred young people in the criminal justice system both in and out of therapeutic environments, I'm quite sure that brain damage with permanent memory loss is fairly frequent. The young person cannot recall the actual trauma, but has been conditioned to react to similar cues coming from their environments, cues that are set off through non-conscious memory associations. Stated another way, embedded somatic memories are no longer connected to the traumatizing event at explicit memory levels of consciousness. But at the same time, one reacts to environmental cues that match his or her previous victimization. We might say it's a form of blind-sight.

As possessors of living dynamic brains that are dependent on plastic neural circuits, we experience disconnect between non-conscious reactions of this sort and the activating stimuli. Segueing off the above example, I know from personal experience that my mind created explanations to bridge this disconnect. The ghost that haunted me during my formative years is such an example.

My conscious brain attempted to explain the missing piece of memory by creating a ghost that I felt, but did not remember. Ghost was a concept inherited from mother through her own cultural indoctrination. The reader knows from experience that imaginary creations of our conscious minds such as ghosts are a common part of human history. When our higher level of consciousness experiences sensations from implicit memory but has no connection with the source, it gets creative. Concretizing sensation as a ghost is a typical creation. In like fashion, concretizing the felt Other becomes a child's Guardian Angel. How can children not be essentialists?

A second type of repressed unconscious is represented by my Sexual Molestation Dream. I can recall the traumatizing event vividly; however, the nightmares and night terrors that it engendered remained unidentified for years. I was not consciously able to will these nightmares to go away as I failed to identify their source. And the nightmares kept recycling. The critical difference between these two types of repressed unconscious is the existence of intact neural circuits and associated memory. In the second type, one can easily make the connections with the right guidance, that is, guidance from one's own self or from a compassionate therapist.

Children with neural circuits that have been damaged or destroyed through something like oxygen deprivation, or various forms of brain damage, often do not have connectivity between higher and lower brain centers. Consequently, their fears and reactions to normal life situations are frequently seen as being defiant, obstinate, or anti-social. In my experience, children with serious delinquent histories, in the majority, have similar kinds of brain damage.

The third type of repression is what I simply call active repression. In my autobiography (2010: 149,150) I created dream programming to bring multiple nightmares under control. When a nightmare would appear, my Interpreter would substitute a preconceived dream scenario of my choosing. I kept this active repression of nightmares for twenty years. When I discontinued active nightmare repression my most immediate realization was the amount of energy I had been spending to repress them. I experienced immediate relief and a significant increase in energy. We can actively repress explicit memories or the products of implicit memories when awake or when dreaming.

It seems reasonable that image formation at these different stages of brain-mind process complexity are subject to errors similar to errors experienced in at least the three forms of repression given above. And in similar fashion, it seems reasonable to assume that studying image formation under conditions of normal and abnormal dream conditions will shed light on associational processes. In a similar fashion to studying various brain functions brought about by brain damage, we can study image formation under conditions of abnormal image formation in dreams and other altered states.

Obviously, I'm attempting to leave the door open to get around Hobson's admonition. Nevertheless, I think my discussion of primary image formation in dreams takes us down this path to new insights. I'll develop these ideas further in later chapters.

From my experience, suggestion plays a critical role in image formation that relies on these non-conscious processes, how memory is embedded, and how meaning is attributed to all of these elements by our central overseer, our Interpreter. My toddler brain created a complete vision of OBE and angels. At 18 months of age, I was transforming figments of cultural imagination on the part of my parents and family into concrete imagery. Stated differently, both primary and complex images were being metaphorically translated by my toddler brain-mind or the vision could not have taken place. Suggestion must tap this hierarchical translation and development of primary images before two years of age or none of this would have been possible.

The use of suggestion in lucid dreaming is often learned in one's adult years. But I think my history clearly demonstrates that the mechanisms are in place to creatively use suggestion before language capability exists. Further, this is an example of fairly complex thought without the use of commensurate language. Ask an 18 month old to describe and angel or an OBE. Yet toddlers of this age image the process well. A question for dynamic psychiatry becomes: Can 18th month old toddlers actively repress memories? Or, are these memories potentially lost when the brain starts serious pruning around three years of age? How could one distinguish between self-pruning and organic damage at this age? Clearly "muscle" memories put in place by our old brains seem to escape the pruning processes. In any case, my "muscle" memories were revived and permitted me to dispense with this associated nightmare.

The muscle sensations in my lower back became associated with a ghost whose reality mother confirmed. My lower back was also the point of her physical attack. But the ghost sensations did not appear until we moved to another old farm house with similar steep wooden stairs leading to my bedroom. Is this repression or creative metaphorical imaging? Or is creative metaphorical imaging a form of repression? Assuming that I suffered brain damage and/or that neuronal cell pruning was involved, I'm left with an active metaphor creating mechanism in order to explain the ghost. And, the metaphorical representation of back sensations suggests that my Interpreter transformed these sensations into an object, the ghost. Metaphorical imaging combined with suggestion represents the complex mechanism that turns sensations into things.

This type of metaphorical imaging of body sensations serves the function of repression by reducing associated anxiety. And in my case, this mechanism of ghost creation permitted me to live with my mother the perpetrator.

I suspect that both of my sisters, who lived through the same hell I did as a child, fall into this second category by failing to remember most of their entire childhood. One sister still refuses to attempt painful recall, and she pays all the penalties of one who chooses to forget. I'm not suggesting that this pattern of forgetting is conscious; it's reflexive and habitual. It's a mind game of one's own creation; a way for children to survive long-term trauma. By creating a ghost, I was able to retain my other associated memories. My sisters simply repressed. And I suspect similar smothering attacks by mother may have wiped-out crib-bound neural circuits as well.

I think Freud's big mistake was to believe his own dogma about the unconscious. Looking for bubbling sexuality or uncontrollable Id urges emanating from the unconscious caused him to misinterpret dreams and everyday psychic events such as those reported above. Implicit memory processes in fixed action patterns or somatic instigated-dreams are outside of Freud's dogmatic schema.

Dream analysis should take into consideration the different types of memory being expressed. Dream interpretation requires that each dream be scanned during our lucid moments for their emotional components. And the dream interpreter is required to recognize that the visual system, which plays such a central role in the dream process, constructs vision in pieces by combining light wave sensations in over 30 different centers to create completed visuals. Vision is not created by the brain as though one were taking a photographic image; images are reconstructed by the brain once the signals from different types of neural circuits are brought together and internally assembled by our brains. Thus, we should not be surprised that our actively dreaming brains will piece together all manner of creative images. Call them bizarre if you will, but look beyond bizarre for the real meaning in your dreams, or you will miss the meaning behind the visuals being created by your dreaming brain.

I may be leaving you with a little confusion about image formation in dreams, how words eventually come to be, and the role of brain-mind processes that stumble over mechanisms like repression. However, I will build on these ideas as we dig deeper into our dreams and other altered states.

FEELING

In my experience, understanding feeling in dreams is absolutely essential. I like Antonio Damasio's model of consciousness in that he insists feeling is always an integral part of consciousness; that is, consciousness in either our waking or dreaming states. Some of my dreams are primarily feeling dreams, and others are mostly cognitively activated. An example of the former is my Discomfort/Conflict Dream reported in Chapter 8. If my psyche has been wrestling with discomfort throughout the day, or maybe even for a period of days, I'm going to experience psychic discomfort in my dreams. During the day I may or may not be aware that I'm in a state of discomfort because I've been preoccupied with various life demands.

My dreaming brain doesn't care if I'm consciously inattentive. It proceeds to process the discomfort and keep it on my brain-mind plate until it is resolved. I experience this phenomenon as a helpful survival mechanism and one that I should pay careful attention to. My dreaming brain calls attention to what is life-salient the same way my waking brain informs me that the hungry bear is headed my way.

I think of feeling expressions in my dreams that are not in my conscious awareness as a subliminal form of communication that comes from that non-conscious 95 percent of my day-to-day brain activity. An experimental example of this process is demonstrated by items flashed on a screen too quickly for conscious identification. When later quizzed, we recall items that we experienced that were below our conscious level of awareness - an automatic type of sensory perception that is processed at a core consciousness level.

Non-conscious awareness is much like the type that occurs when we are walking down a dark street and become bothered by something that is outside of our conscious awareness. Evolution has given us this survival advantage. We are gradually coming to understand how it works. Sensory processing occurs at a non-conscious level before our higher order cerebral cortex becomes involved. Isn't neuroscience fun?

Feelings are non-conscious bullets of stimuli that bring about immediate actions on our part, actions that occur before conscious awareness kicks in. I visualize the most primitive forms of feeling with an amoeba avoiding a nasty chemical. Feelings guided life before consciousness and its common definition emerged. Chemical signalers remain and become more complex as we move up the ladder of evolution. Emotions stimulated by chemicals that become feelings in our evolved higher order conscious brains play a major role in our dreams. Emotional states are primordial and generate feelings that are remapped to become qualia and metaphor.

Sandy at the Enchanted Forest in Mankato, Minnesota, tells me that she never knows the characters appearing in her dreams. We have a long way to go before we understand how associative memories work in our dreams, or for that matter, how associative memory works for much of everyday recall. My wife appears in current dreams not as a picture duplicate but as a cobbled together modular brain construction that usually looks nothing like her physically. However, I know I'm dreaming about my wife because my dream feelings match with my daytime feelings.

This match can be across the whole range of emotions. If I'm upset with her, I have this relationship with the dream character. If I'm especially in a loving mood, I have this relationship with her dream character, etc. My wife can also appear as a picture duplicate in my dreams as do family and friends, and they can appear age appropriate as well. But my dreaming brain generally accesses energy efficient associations. I suspect that energy efficient association plays a major role in embedding memories as well as retrieving them.

LESSONS LEARNED

Dreams can and do reflect whatever is going on in our lives. Dream recall can bring together any combination of time periods from each individual's unique history. Our modular brains construct dream characters, scenes, and feeling elements in any combination relevant to salient events in our active lives.

Most of my dreams are mundane, but reflect my daily life. The brain-mind is one unit. Self and consciousness are processes and not things. Dream dictionaries by those not informed by neuroscience and psychology are bunk. Freudian and psychoanalytic interpretation of dreams that use Freud's manufactured ideas of the unconscious are not helpful but misleading, and altered states of consciousness, with dreams being the most common form, are just another configuration of brain circuitry.

CHAPTER 2

APPLYING BASIC RESEARCH TO DREAMS

INTRODUCTION

My favorite dream lab scientist has this to say about following a top-down approach to understanding and explaining dreaming:

The LABORATORY STUDY of human REM sleep and dreaming promises a direct correlation between specific aspects of dream content and specific aspects of brain physiology. This top-down approach to dreaming begins with dream content and looks down to the level of the brain for its correlate. Such an approach is fraught with conceptual, methodological, and analytic problems: One is the difficulty of obtaining any detailed physiological information from the brain of sleeping humans (Hobson: 1988: 157-158)

Unquestionably, physiological research and data are indispensable. However, the history of dream research supports multiple approaches that permit us to triangulate information across numerous disciplines. Freud's dream analysis was accepted and wrong. Belief in Freud's model may have delayed our modern understanding of dreams as much as a hundred years. Nevertheless, empirical science and reason has prevailed and clearer heads like J. Alan Hobson are heard.

Rejecting Freud's dream analysis and personality theory left me academically isolated in the late 1950s. On the positive side, this isolation permitted me to develop my own methods of inquiry and create an integrated approach to altered states. I've enriched this perspective over the decades by focusing ideas around a Dynamic Integrated Systems Model. Self-observation and self-experiments over the past 50 years provides time depth for pattern analysis and outcome observations.

The following researchers are recognized leaders in their fields. They've informed and enlightened my long-term observations and self-experimentation. Integrating research from physiology, the mind sciences and psychology and dream labs has been somewhat of a daunting task. However, integrating 50 plus years of self case study warrants this attempt. I assume responsibility for selective interpretation of this research body especially in areas where I'm speculating. The reader is encouraged to pursue resources that they are not familiar with.

LLINAS

Rodolfo Llinas in *I of the Vortex* considers human evolution from individual cells to the emergence of self and mind. A key concept is that the central nervous system (CNS) comes into being to allow organisms to predict active movement (motricity). Self is defined as the product created by evolution that coordinates all of the modules necessary for an active organism's competitive survival.

The senses feed information into this central processing unit called the self, and oscillatory activity across this system helps create "mindness." Mindness is a state where the CNS models both the external world, modeling which is important for any actively mobile organism to survive, as well as the internal world of sensory mapping and expression. Not fully explained by Llinas is how this CNS component called self becomes aware that it is aware and conscious.

Two of his concepts that are important to my analysis of dreams are Fixed Action Patterns (FAP) and Qualia. According to Llinas: "The self, the centralization of prediction … cannot, however, orchestrate every feat the body must accomplish from moment to moment in the ever-changing world in which we live (2002: 133).

Facilitated action patterns are a little like computer routines that kick-in with a keystroke, except they can be modified by a dynamic CNS. For example, we don't think about a bug flying toward our eye, we just blink. This is an automatic reflex and it really doesn't require time consuming thought. We just blink. If we had to think about what was happening, the fly would be in our eye.

Embedded action patterns represent the habitual behaviors that are an integral part of our everyday life. We don't think about walking we just walk. It saves the brain a lot of energy and thus offers evolutionarily advantage. We learn to ride a bicycle or play a complicated musical piece on the piano and turn these learned behaviors into embedded action patterns. I observe fixed action patterns being integrated in my dreams and extensively refer to my bike balancing example.

As an aside, these routines are housed in what Lakoff and Johnson call the Collective Unconscious. The Collective Unconscious being the 95 percent of brain activity that goes on below our conscious awareness. Note that learning how to balance on a bicycle is a memory embedding process handled at a below conscious level, as is its execution (See FAP Dream below and Chapters 4 and 6). Note the importance of implicit memory in this non-conscious process.

Observing non-conscious processes in our dreams helps solve the mystery of Free Will. Our higher order consciousness remains in control as lower order facilitated action patterns efficiently do their work. These non-conscious action patterns are a little bit like my computer; the core memory does most of the work, so I can focus on writing. Cognitive scientists who fail to make this easily observable distinction write endlessly about Free Will without understanding its origin or evolutionary history. The emergence of Free Will depends on FAPs.

Qualia are defined by Llinas as: "… subjective experience of any type generated by the nervous system … be it pain … the color green … or the specific timbre of a musical note…" Qualia are mind "states (Ibid)."

For example, the color green doesn't exist in nature. It is created in the brain, as is pain. What the eye perceives is a particular wavelength of entering photons. This energy is categorized by the brain specifically to mean a particular color; hence, the brain is converting an external stimulus into a specific quale, the color green. The meaning of color to us is a mind creation not something found in nature. Creation of qualia by the brain is central to our understanding of human subjectivity. We do not model the external world as it is. We selectively integrate all stimuli entering our CNS to create qualia which we then manipulate in our brain-minds.

Llinas has a lot to say about qualia, but the key for this discussion is its subjective nature. Our evolved minds have preset architecture that turns external stimuli into specific subjective realities: A helpful insight that goes a long way towards explaining how our subjective, internal brain models the external world to create a form of virtual reality. We don't experience the outside world as it is; we selectively process our view of the world and turn various forms of stimuli into subjective units – qualia. The subjective nature of qualia adds an additional element (s) to processed light waves, and in this addition creates a unit of meaning called color. Note that once created, the color green comes to have many specific meanings to the organism as we actively move through space. The quale green also becomes a central associational unit. This suggests that memory associations cannot be studied without first identifying basic units of qualia.

To observe this process of creating qualia while dreaming, we first have to learn to interpret dream content and dream function. I'm not alone in contending that meaning created by our brain-minds is a subjective event that must be studied in its own right. One can understand all the more than thirty visual centers involved in our ability to see color and still not understand the subjective experience. I support the position that self-observation of qualia in dreams is an essential tool to our understanding of how the brain creates meaning.

I don't experience this light wave-color conversion in my dreams, but I experience quale (singular for qualia) being consolidated in my dreams. For example, balancing on my bicycle is a felt body image. When this felt body image is re-mapped by my higher cognitive centers, I experience what Damasio calls Quilia II. Balance is re-mapped as a Quale II element which then becomes available for symbolic manipulation. And symbol manipulation can take on endless variations that we call metaphor. Thus, lucid dreaming permits me to observe fictive bicycle balancing which is integrating and consolidating a primary image at what is normally a non-conscious level. And the organizational unit is a quale called balance.

Re-mapping and manipulation of primary images by my higher cognitive centers creates complex metaphor. Therefore, once I've re-mapped proto-symbols, I can use them in endless creative ways. In Chapter 14, I will review Damasio's use of Qualia I and Qualia II in order to add depth to this interpretation, and continue to elaborate Llinas's ideas.

Primary image formation by our brain-minds may seem a little complex but grasping an overview of this process is necessary if we wish to understand our dreams. And, once we grasp image-qualia-metaphor relationships to the creation of consciousness concepts like Free Will become almost self-explanatory.

We know that the sleeping brain is as busy or even busier during REM sleep as it is when we are awake. Consciousness, subjective human reality, according to Llinas, is created to meet the needs of an active organism moving in real time and space. There is nothing particularly mysterious here.

Our reality is internally constructed. It is not just a duplicated image of the outside world. Thus, as we switch from one form of consciousness to another awake, or dreaming, mind-created reality whether asleep or awake seems to be equally representative of the organism's total relationship to its world and to itself. This is not just Llinas speaking, but standard neuroscience.

Dreaming dogs and other mammals with rapid eye movement (REM) must be processing FAPs in a fashion similar to what I experience in my dreams. Following Llinas's logic evolution builds new functions from old biological platforms. Animals with color vision will exhibit a capacity to form color qualia, at least what Damasio calls Qualia I. Animals are understood by Llinas as using fixed action patterns too, an evolutionary development that he traces in considerable detail. I can't explain my subjective experience of "muscle-vision-balancing" dreams without using Llinas' concept of fixed action pattern. We don't even know where to look in our dreams without thinking in terms of the basic concepts from neuroscience.

By observing primary image formation in our dreams, we can watch the natural evolutionary emergence of mammalian symbol capacity. The functional brain-mind capacity of Homo sapiens slowly emerged one functional and architectural level at a time. The dreaming brain circuit patterns of rats run mazes, and the dreaming brain circuit patterns of dogs chase rabbits. At this level of human old brain functions, we are cousins.

I'm reasonably sure that my dreaming brain is practicing bike balancing, and it does so in a fashion that parallels the neural circuit activity of dogs and rabbits. Damasio's two stage development of consciousness, the old and new brain of Homo sapiens, is a useful conceptual tool that helps me explain FAP dreams, Qualia I and Qualia II.

The self emerges through evolution:

[From] the animal's neurological becoming is the fact that the animal can have an internal representation of itself not only as a set of parts but as a whole entity. It is here, from this germinal metaevent, that abstraction begins and the self emerges (2002: 206).

Our dreaming minds employ a sense of self as a whole entity. My reported thought dreams and dreams based on emotion must use an entire entity for reference.

Modular sensory processing in our dreams makes more sense if we visualize the jerky nature of dreams as managing sensory processing in relationship to this whole entity. I use the term Controller or Interpreter to represent this entire entity. And as the agent of Self, my Interpreter always observes. But my Interpreter as essence (mind) can experience my Self as feeling (body). This relationship of entire self to part self permits self-talk, the sense of being Self and other, ability to be possessed, enter the body of an animal as a shaman, and much more.

Lucid dream windows that permit us to observe FAP generation also permits us to experience the next level or levels of abstraction as we follow the process of how different levels of meaning are created with a primary concept such as balance. Balance is a body instantiated FAP that connects neurons to muscles, and in doing so, depends on vision.

Intentionality is defined by Llinas as:

[T]hat which one intends to do in relation to that object or goal (2002: 227). Intentions represent an internal abstraction for the organism that is directed toward a specific goal. Emotions exist as internal states, they are not something found in the outside world; they are something invented by the central nervous system (Ibid: 227).

Emotions and their derivatives, feelings, are central concepts necessary to understand self and subjectivity; hence, language.

Llinas states further that:

… our ability to vocalize the different aspects of intentionality developed first as the ability to separate the properties of things from the things themselves (2002: 228).

Thus we see how abstraction and intentionality arise from an actively mobile organism that models the external world internally, develops economy of function through facilitated action patterns, and generates self by creating a central coordinating neuronal set that brings all the senses into a functioning whole called consciousness. But note that abstraction, according to Llinas, is a process that begins well down the evolutionary hierarchy as organisms become aware of their environment.

This is not Descartes black box, nor Freud's bubbling cauldron of the Unconscious. Higher levels of abstraction are possible because we re-map primary sensations to have a symbolic representation of any referent either an internal or external referent. Observing this process in our dreams provides a window into the black box. Thus, "… abstract thinking must have preceded language during evolution (Ibid)."

Neural science has clearly placed Homo sapiens in a chain of increasing evolutionary sophistication that we now un-ravel through science. We have an increasingly clear outline of how language, self, intentionality, and abstraction evolved. I have skipped considerable details of Llinas's argument which the reader can enjoy on his or her own time. Nevertheless, his discussion of FAPs, emotions as FAPs, qualia, and language in following Chapters 7, 8, 10 and 11 is central to my interpretation and use of these concepts.

Note my toddler nightmare at 18 months (Chapter 8). I abstract Heaven, angels, and journey to the netherworld without complex language. My brain creates a clear visual experience with all the appropriate feelings. And, abstract meaning is created with a toddler's version of angels and Heaven. This simplistic yet complex imaging is contrasted to my Genesis Journey's meta-complexity when I'm an older adult.

Reviewing basics from Llinas demonstrates how dream triangulation with mind science can help us understand how consciousness and self emerge. Consciousness and self are just as active in our dreams as during our waking hours. In one sense, we can experience an earlier stage of our own mammalian evolution, as we watch our dreaming brains embed memory elements that are later expressed non-consciously.

We lucidly observe fictive re-enactment of skill development in our dreams and then experience its expression during our waking hours. The rat re-runs the maze in its dream and I ride my bike. However, I'm different because the following day I'm consciously aware of how my bike riding skills have improved.

My task at this point is to integrate an evolutionary model into a clearer understanding of dreams and visions. Key aspects that I think must be considered in this process include memory, self, consciousness, human ability to abstract, embedded action patterns and intentionality. I pursue this line of reasoning using these concepts to analyze the internal processes one can observe in dreams and visions. I do not treat dreams and visions as separate events, but as products of parallel brain-mind processes.

FAP DREAM

Dream (8-25-10) Recorded 7:00 a.m. I'm on a college campus, Mankato State University in Minnesota with a group of non-university colleagues from later years. This does not seem strange to me. I leave the campus to walk to my former residence on Skyline. As I walk toward the valley and downtown area the terrain becomes rugged; I see water, a bridge and the river. All of this landscape actually exists in Mankato, but cannot be seen from the top of the hill where I'm placed physically in this dream, nor can this scene be seen from the hill on which the MSU campus sits. My dreaming brain has constructed this scene from scraps of memory. And as it is common in dreams, I'm looking down at the river and valley from a view that would be above the tree line, similar to looking down at my own body as a toddler observing my own death.

My brain integrates a landscape from memory that is not visible from any one geographical location in the real world. This process serves to remind me that my brain's ability to abstract and reintegrate at will is an active part of dreaming. It also reminds me that I integrate stimuli from my world in any configuration that makes meaningful dream sense, not physical sense.

Lucid dreamers constantly experience these internally fabricated realities. My smothering dream in Chapter 8 is an additional example. In this vision I'm above my crib looking down at myself as my mother comes raging toward me – a normal dream or vision fabrication. Looking down at one's self in dreams or visions is common because we are upright creatures whose vision normally looks out and down. No mystery here. This is the position and angle from which we observe the world. This daytime vision duplicates a visual perspective common to my dreams as well as common types of dream reports discussed by Hobson and others.

The hill's grade abruptly drops at a sharp angle and I jump on a cement abutment, slide down, and congratulate myself that I'm able to balance so well. I'm very conscious of sliding on my shoes, arms outstretched, and moving at a rapid pace. I'm also conscious while dreaming that this fictive balancing feels very much like riding my bicycle down neighborhood streets during my morning outings. And it should! After all, feeling is created in the brain-mind, not in the outside world.

As I recall this dream, I'm aware that almost nightly this past week I have recalled physical components in dreams where I am balancing or trying out related motor skills.

Three nights ago, 8-22-10, I was drawing in my dream and realized that my eye-hand coordination was better than I remembered during my waking hours. I also experienced dream surprise and satisfaction at my skill level. The day before, I had drawn heavy dark lines free hand on a print for a new stained glass window. I was fictively honing my ability to cut stained glass in various controlled sweeping motions.

Dream practice is efficient, an energy and time saver, and a great evolutionary invention. FAP dreams and skill reinforcement and integration have greater depth of meaning if one carefully reads Llinas.

Thoughts: I have been paying more attention to my brain-mind recording muscle and skill sets while I'm dreaming. I'm a little surprised to find how extensively I'm practicing balance, drawing and cutting glass in my dreams. These skills have not been used for decades. New skills or long unused skills are fictively practiced in my dreams. Bike riding, glass cutting, and balancing dreams stopped after I reached a point where I just willed the behavior. Like you, I stop observing behavior that becomes automatic, and so do my dreams.

Clearly my procedural memory is being enhanced in this dreaming process. My dreams are supporting memory functions that usually occur below my level of waking consciousness. My more highly developed cerebral cortex, Interpreter, observes from its more sophisticated level of evolutionary development. My Interpreter tries to explain FAP dreams as real life events, and they aren't. I remind myself that my brain-mind is multi-tasking, and I must pay attention to at least two distinct levels of consciousness.

Memory work in our dreams demands visual components, and in turn, the resulting dream scenarios follow our normal world modeling functions. I cover Brooks and Vogelsong's extensive use of world modeling in dreams in Chapter 16. My higher brain centers try to give a daytime interpretation to FAP dream visuals. Remember that lucid dream observation of basic memory functions is not necessary for memory reinforcement to be effective. I suspect that evolution didn't give most people access to this type of fictive dream rehearsals for this reason.

As we come to interpret dreams from perspectives supported by physiological research, dream forms seem less bizarre. Additionally, the information we receive from our conscious dreaming states is not only more easily understood and transparent, but we move closer to understanding other brain states of altered consciousness as well.

A considerable amount of our dreaming adventures are byproducts of memory-related processes, as indicated by FAP dreams. After all we need visuals in our dreams if we are going to fictively practice balancing on a bike. And, our higher order conscious minds try to make sense of all our dream experiences. From Llinas' perspective, an active organism moving through space expressing motricity needs visual input: A logical connection with the dominance of vision in dreams.

In my FAP dreams, I experience a specific causal pattern. The sensation of balance is accompanied by dream visuals, which creates a context for "muscle" memory, which is then followed by cognitive awareness that this sensation is of primary importance. Interpretation of these dreams says that memory integration and consolidation activates the process and visuals are supplied to virtually support our physical orientation in space.

Visual components naturally come into play in motor supporting FAP dreams as they do in all other REM dreams, or dreams that become lucid. Try riding a bike with your eyes closed. In the 1970s when I indulged myself with extensive listening to classical piano and violin, I performed special recitals in my dreams. I played Mozart, Bach, and other classical artists to my own dream amazement.

I questioned my competency in these dreams, but when I sat down to a dream piano or picked up the violin, I was always able to perform effortlessly. In terms of Llinas's presentation of FAPs, I was able to perform in my dreams because I had embedded complex music FAPs in the manner of a true performer. After all, dreams don't need fingers; dream fingers are similar to Ramachandran's phantom limbs. Anyway, I was a pretty decent dream performer.

It is easy to see how someone like Freud who did not analyze his own dreams could interpret my dream piano playing as wish fulfillment. When I stopped immersing myself in music classics, I stopped playing dream pianos and violins.

Shifts in my dream's contents occur concurrently with changes in my daily routines. As I age, my dreams are centered on conversations with people, less action and more talk. Some of my dreaming nights are totally devoted to dream talk, and this dream talk is not just early evening carryover from the day's activities, but represents through-the-night dream activity. This is not surprising, as dream talk isn't as difficult for me as playing Mozart on my dream piano. I never took lessons on either instrument, but I love them both.

As I become more involved writing this book, the visuals that accompany many of my lucid dreams consist of school-type settings with various conversation-engaged partners or placement in lecture settings. Previously, I never had night-long talking and lecturing scenarios of this nature in my dreams unless I was in an academic setting. Apparently this book's demands duplicate enough of my history to activate associated dream patterns and their internalized FAPs. To me a dream lecture seems no more difficult than dream Mozart.

Focus on nightmares in my youth left me hunting for meaning, connections and interpretation in my dreams. My dreams no longer have these intense emotionally salient features; hence, I'm much more attentive to the activation elements behind my ordinary dreams. But I remind myself to pay attention to different levels of brain activity that reflects multi-tasking in my dreams. My dreams represent a dynamic integrated self that is always processing emotion, memory and cognitive elements

EVOLUTION

The single cell felt the other,
was it father or was it mother?
Cobbled eons all asunder,
brought you and me in curious wonder.

GAZZANIGA

In *Nature's Mind* Gazzaniga develops two additional aspects that are central to my understanding of dreams:

1) The infant's brain architecture at birth, and
2) The Interpreter's role coordinating all the modular input of the brain.

All the sensory input coming from our modular brain is coordinated and bound together. We do not just record stimuli, our brains make inferences about what this input means. We are born with this organizational architecture in place, which in turn promotes development of our unique self.

We are not passive recipients of stimuli as originally conceived by early behaviorists; we are active organisms with conscious intentions. We don't observe our entire landscape, but rather, we selectively focus on landscape elements that are important to us. The charging lion is not valued the same way as the tree he emerged from.

Gazzaniga says: "The variation that exists in each of us, the capacity to be unique, to override the rigidity of our nervous system must be addressed. Humans have a greater functional plasticity than other species… (1992: 112)."

What this means is that by nature, our brains are structured to interpret all the sensory data received and turn it into meaning. A creature capable of creating abstract thoughts and meaning only exists if neural patterns can be created and changed over time.

Real creativity emerges with Free Will at the complex metaphorical level, and I'll explain this relationship in Chapter 4. For example, that chocolate donut has a different meaning to thin people than it does to fat people. A piece of steak means one thing to a hungry dog and many other things to Homo sapiens with higher order consciousness and clogged arteries.

However, the modular system used by our brain has gaps that must be filled in; gaps that create illusions that are interpreted as real until we more fully understand the brain mechanisms involved. Infants have a built in mechanism that looks for cause and effect.

"Indeed, infants are born with the processes that automatically allow for this kind of inference already built into the brain (Ibid: 114)."

Gazzaniga details the architecture and function of our modular brains from infancy to adulthood in a wonderfully clear fashion.

The adult visual system has a representative understanding of objects, yet does not always act in accordance with what it knows. This system is prepared to accept even bizarre perceptions in the presence of a sufficient illusion. Our brains have… the ability to detect the inconsistencies, but lack the ability to modify what we see (Ibid: 114).

Modular mechanisms also operate when we dream. Our Interpreter must explain these bizarre features without the continuity and external sensory input from our environment. Therefore, bizarre elements seem more salient during our dreams. Additionally, external stimuli are metaphorically imaged in our dreams. An example that I later use is that of a 1955 Chevy standing in for a cold shoulder. To further compound the issue, our dreaming minds auto-create whole scenarios and store them for future use.

Whether stimuli come from our inside or the outside, it must be assembled, bound together, by its modular subsystems. And once sensory information is bound together and expressed as a dream scenario, our Interpreter must determine the meaning. Our dream Interpreter makes logical what our waking Interpreter finds bizarre.

Our modular brains combine dream character features from many sources. I know who the characters are only from my feelings towards them. Scenes, units of time, and logical progression of events can be and are mixed randomly. Nevertheless, our Interpreter needs to fill in inconsistencies and provide continuity where there is none. This perspective will be more fully developed as the book progresses, but for now, just remember that these mechanisms support what Hobson calls dream forms. Understanding dream forms is one of our first steps to understanding dream language.

Our Interpreter gives meaning to emotions and visual input as is evident with split brain research (Ibid: 121-129). Aspects of dreams seem to parallel split brain processing when select modular input is either heightened or shut down. As Hobson's research details, visual activation is increased and critical interpretive capacities reduced in REM. When our brains shift modular processing in our dreams, we have different phenomenological effects. It just works this way.

Understanding our brain's innate architecture and functioning from Gazzaniga's perspective helps me appreciate the interpretive role of the brain's left hemisphere. My Interpreter assigns meaning by carefully attending to modular stimuli and integrating these stimuli through processes of metaphorical and symbolic abstraction.

From an evolutionary point of view, emotion activates response in our organism before conscious awareness does. This facilitates our survival, but it also enhances the bizarre quality of dreams. As dream multi-tasking unfolds modular input shifts to support memory, express feeling states, or integrate thought. This skipping around quality of dreams is supportive of many dream-brain functions, but feels bizarre to our waking consciousness. However, dream processes come to feel normal once we appreciate the neuroscience behind them, especially with long-term lucid dream analysis.

In The Mind's Past, Gazzaniga reviews many aspects of the automatic processes routinely used by the brain and notes that most human behavior is directed by the brain at a sub-conscious level. Our brain executes action routines before our mind is aware that a decision has been made. As noted above, these sub-conscious routines are an efficient evolutionary mechanism and they do not detract from, but actually support higher order consciousness that we call Free Will.

According to Gazzaniga, the left brain contains our Interpreter. The term I have used for the past fifty years for Interpreter is "Controller." Physiological research clearly establishes that the Interpreter is always on when we are conscious, and continuously does its job (1998: 123-148). It is always making sense of what we are consciously experiencing, even when this sense in retrospect is nonsense.

Our Interpreter also continues to make sense of sensory experiences in our lucid dreams. For example, in agnosognosia, the patient doesn't feel a body part, and when physically shown this part, such as an arm, denies that it is his or hers. If you can't feel it, it's not yours. Conversely, if you feel it, it is yours. Embodied sensation is our reality.

Consciousness ceases when body grounding is absent. This awareness explains why I believed my body and mind flew into space together when I was a child: Without brain-mind grounding, there is no consciousness, and as adults, we still have a realistic sense of body and mind traveling together in dream or vision flight. It is this realistic sense of body and mind traveling together that makes it so much fun. To emphasize this point, in my Genesis Journey to the beginning of the universe, I physically hit the plasma wall. I felt the wall the same way I feel the keys on my keyboard as I type these words. Pain and touch does not occur at the point of contact; it is created in the brain.

When our dreaming or vision-making minds enter other worlds of virtual reality, we are engaged in the same process of reality making. This capacity is given to us by evolution. As we come to understand altered realities, including dreams, we appreciate how normal these processes are. We now smile at occult and ancient interpretations. Ignorance of evolution eventually gives way to human inquiry. And we began to understand the mentally ill.

Gazzaniga emphasizes the importance of body-grounding both for consciousness and the separate maintenance of self. Looking at body-grounding from my mind's internal view, I recognize that consciousness requires this grounding: No grounding, no consciousness. Consequently, body-grounding is experienced in out-of-body and spirit projections by my mind because it is a requirement of consciousness. When I project into the body of the bear as a shaman, I experience a new body fabricated by my conscious mind. This is a simple projection that we experience in parallel fashion every time we cry with a sad friend.

False memories that are totally created in the mind's center of virtual reality can enter our consciousness, and are treated equally to externally-generated conscious events. Our normal world of consciousness is one of virtual reality because we assemble sensory input in our brain-minds. Our unfocused attention sees things that are not there. Auto-created memories emerge and insist what one is experiencing actually exists outside of one's self. We must learn to appreciate how the modular brain works if we hope to have any degree of objectivity, especially in our dreams.

Auto-created false memory occurs when we create real life episodes, episodes that can be movie length, and record them in our memories. Individuals who are not lucid dreamers, and lucid dreamers who have not done their homework, experience these dream vignettes as being real. The degree of "realness" is demanding when the lucid dreamer fails to recognize he or she is dreaming. In waking hours, this mechanism sends innocent people to death row.

Consciousness dependent on body-grounding helps us understand how self-generated memories come to equal the reality of events that we have actually experienced in our external environments. Consciousness is grounded to body at our primary level of awareness and continues to support our secondary level at what we call awareness of awareness. Turn off primary consciousness and the movie stops.

Gazzaniga says that from split-brain research we know that "… our personal narrative for why we feel and do the things we feel and do…" is in our left hemisphere. The left brain's Interpreter is always busy when we are conscious. Therefore, it seems logical to me that when I have thinking or lecturing dreams, my higher cognitive and language centers should be as active as when I'm awake. This is an easily testable hypothesis for the neuroscientist.

Lastly, "The interpreter is only as good as the information it receives …" says Gazzaniga (1998: 137).

Whacky information in, whacky information out is the case from this perspective. But in a similar fashion, the integration of complex ideas and a variety of emotional stimuli presents our Interpreter with ongoing challenges. Dreams are not serving one function but many. Dreams are not localized in any one neuronal network, but reflect the full range of neuronal interactions from single cells to neural networks to higher order exchanges with our Interpreter. Dreams may be primarily somatic or reflect emotions. At higher cognitive levels, my dreams process complex thoughts and give lectures. "Our brains are built to remember the gist of things, not the details (Ibid: 142)."

And we experience how our brains remember the gist of things with the wonderful dream cobbling of characters and scenes. My dream character looks like a number of women in my life, but feels like my current spouse, for instance.

It is inevitable that we consider metaphor in our understanding of dreams. Metaphor becomes a construct that represents a complex of neuronal activities that bring together numerous elements from our senses. Our brains take primary somatic images and add value as these images merge with feeling. This composite becomes re-imaged symbolically and complex metaphor in all its glory becomes possible.

LINDEN

In *The Accidental Brain,* David Linden notes that "The brain is not elegantly designed by any means; it is a cobbled-together mess…" (2007: 3).

What he references is the biological fact that evolution selects functions, in other words, brain structures that help the individual organism survive. This cobbling process goes on continuously, and our understanding of how the brain and mind work must take this long-term evolutionary process into consideration. This process is not particularly elegant, meaning that new functions are created in the course of evolution from old parts.

Brain plasticity has been a debated issue since the 1980s. Numerous reviews such as Begley and Doide's pull together much of this discussion, while Merzenich adds some very interesting research. Linden states: "… while the overall wiring diagram of the brain is laid down in the genetic code, the fine-scale wiring of the brain is guided by patterns of activity which allows the strength and pattern of synaptic connectivity to be molded by experience, a process called synaptic plasticity… (2007: 49).

We are the product of our genes interacting with our environment, which is a dynamic process. Change the environment and the same genes are expressed differently. From this vantage point we begin to understand the importance of a stable, supportive and caring environment for children.

Learning, which means continuous adaptation to our environment and reorganization of memory, helps us make sense of our changing environment, both social and physical, because it is a continuous process. The brain is built to learn and adapt. Our brains are designed to be continuous learners and the process doesn't stop when we switch from waking consciousness to all the activity taking place in our sleep and dreams. It's important to remember that our brains change as we age, and all these changes are reflected in dream content and dream patterns.

Linden's discussion of mirror neuron physiology sheds light on empathy and our ability to duplicate feeling states being experienced by others. He states that "… affective pain centers can be activated by both your own painful experience and those of others, [this] may shed light on the neural substrate of empathy (Ibid: 103)."

We activate compatible neural circuits and neuro-modulators to produce the same brain feeling and chemical states as others. In this manner, our brains become mirror duplicates of other's feelings, and this enhances our individual ability to intuit each other's thoughts - what is referred to as Theory of Mind.

When I project myself into the body of the bear, I experience its size, power, and other qualities. I know that my experience is probably not an exact duplicate of what the bear feels, but it is different from my ordinary feelings. If I'm a True Believer shaman it is the same. My higher order consciousness lets me be aware that I am aware, plus the duplicative process of mirror neurons, permits me to simulate the internal state of the bear while I'm still conscious of being "Me." I can always be in two states, self-awareness, or core consciousness, and aware that I'm aware, or autobiographical consciousness. It is this basic human capacity that the shaman exercises in his or her rituals. Really, it is not that complex.

I identify with the bear, I feel the bear, and I become the bear. A shamanic state that is not common to most people, but a state that is utilizing the same mechanisms, physiologically speaking, as we use when feeling another's pain, laughter or related senses. As we come to understand the neural science behind consciousness and dreaming, we also come to understand these aspects of shamanic experiences and ASC.

experience panic or discomfort from this feeling of somewhere else.

In my dreams, my higher cognitive center, or Interpreter, knows intuitively that it is observing, and often controlling and directing, another part of my brain. My Interpreter knows when I'm awake or dreaming that most of my total brain activity is occurring at a non-conscious level. And my Interpreter intervenes in any altered state when it chooses. Computer-like programs that I've taught my Interpreter can be activated without my momentary consciousness being involved.

If our culture tells us this feeling of somewhere else is the spirit world, we come to believe this cultural fiction. In visions and other altered reality experiences, our conscious brain strives to interpret where these experiences are coming from. The answer as to source is frequently given as The Other Side. And individuals like Sylvia Brown have become best sellers with this mythology. Our higher cognitive centers compulsively seek to explain all the sensory stimuli received. We feel it, we know it must be coming from somewhere, thus, we invent explanation, or go into panic. We can either provide a scientific explanation, or let the occultists have their day.

I'm always expressing a mood as I move about my daily routines. I'm happy, sad, or anything in between. I go to bed and dream with the dominant emotions of the day. These emotions activate neural circuits that become strengthened or degraded as well as setting the stage for all my brain's chemical activity. It is the overall activity of these processes that is important, not specific content that is spawned in my dreams. Nevertheless, content can be used to focus on the salient issues and feelings processing through my dreams. In this sense, feeling and dream content mirror each other. Pay attention to content.

"When Penfield electrically stimulated the motor cortex of his operating room patients, he produced movement that the patient felt no sense of connectedness with (Ibid: 39)."

The dreaming brain in REM is disconnected from its motor system; hence, we don't run in our sleep or perform other acrobatic feats. This type of research clearly demonstrates the brain's modular neural circuit ability to dissociate itself from its sense of body thereby creating a dualistic perception of self. It can free my mind to travel out-of-body, enter the strange world of trance, or enjoy Zen driving. And, I can engage various patterned groups of neural circuit while I'm awake or sleeping. These states are called dreams when I'm sleeping, and visions when I'm awake, and many other things as well.

"Each brain hemisphere processes different aspects of the environment (Ibid: 42)."

This position is well understood in neuroscience; thus, the sleeping brain's selective access to modular input will naturally create a waking sense of the bizarre because the Interpreter is selectively engaged after the fact. As Restak says: "Thinking is for doing (Ibid: 55."

And during dreaming, our brains and bodies are not synchronized as they are when we're awake.

Restak quotes a rubber hand experiment by Henrik Ehrsson where the hand is hit by a hammer and the participant responds as though it were a real hand. "The study shows that the brain distinguishes the self from the non-self by comparing information from the different senses..." You could argue that the bodily self is an illusion being constructed in the brain," says Ehrsson (Ibid: 91)."

Hence, if you feel it, it is real; if you should feel it, it is still real. Belief is the ability to predict what should be. And if it should be it is real. We die for our beliefs.

In my discussion of the shaman becoming a bear, I'm experiencing a similar type of reality. Except it is not just my hand that is involved, it is my entire mind and body. From this perspective, we understand the mechanism involved quite well, even if we don't understand all of its specifics. Neuroscience helps explain these experiences of altered realities as it explains normal realities. In my words, the mechanisms that underlie the reality that is self can be projected to create new realities for the self in any number of social settings: Even the reality of being the bear.

Social reality in this sense is a collective projection of individual reality. And, it relies on mechanisms that we all share but do not all use. Our unused ability to project ourselves as the shamans do often leaves us in awe. We feel this sense of projected self, but are not capable of individually executing this state. But it's such fun!

Restak says: "We have a greater ability than we've previously imagined to become more empathic by including positive changes in our brain (Ibid: 116)."

The sciences have traditionally shied away from exploring consciousness. From an empirical perspective, consciousness has been a death knell for tenure and professional academic status. So has the empirical study that questions major world religions. I think this has been unfortunate. My argument is simply that our brains have the ability to enlarge not only our empathic capacity by fostering positive changes in our brains, but enlarging our psychological capacities across our brain-mind landscape. Political scientists and clergy should ground themselves in neuroscience.

Restak refers to memory morphing when one observes real life events and then adds in their own interpretations. "Moreover, these false memories are incorporated into historical memories for events that actually did happen at that time in their lives (Ibid: 155)."

This process of memory morphing occurs when we are awake, so why should it not occur when we are dreaming? It does. Scientists of necessity stress the difficulty of being objective; dream scientists have a double problem in this regard as centers of logic disengage or are at low levels when we dream.

LEDOUX

Joseph LeDoux observes that cognitive science has tended to explain away emotion as a merely cognitive process (Hobson: 1994: 156). A review of works by Shapiro and Noe drive this point home. Noe's 2009 publication, for example, doesn't reference Damasio or Llinas, and they are two of neuroscience's leaders on consciousness studies. Neuro-philosophers like Paul Churchland are more relevant to an understanding of mind science to the degree that their work is grounded in physiological research.

A. Damasio presents a strong argument starting at least in the 1990s that emotion and cognition cannot be separated and that cognition always contains emotional elements. Damasio's interpretation of consciousness resonates with LeDoux's criticism, and is in sharp contrast to much of mainstream cognitive science.

I will use seven principles from LeDoux's **Synaptic Self** on how self is assembled to support my emphasis on brain plasticity and how sensory systems integration relates to dream interpretation. LeDoux states:

Emotion systems learn by association—when an emotionally arousing stimulus is present, other stimuli that are also present acquire emotion-arousing qualities (classical conditioning), and actions that bring you in contact with emotionally desirable stimuli or protect you from harmful or unpleasant ones are learned (instrumental conditioning) (2002: 303).

What this means to our brains is that neural networks are altered and there is an increase in neural mass when related networks are frequently stimulated, and emotions play a critical part in this process. I don't see how one can discuss consciousness and its correlates independently of emotion any more than one can discuss genetics independent of DNA.

The bottom line is simple: Functions depend on [synaptic] connections; break the connections, and you lose the functions (Ibid: 304).

From my personal history: Meld new connections and you create new functions; or perhaps I should say you can create altered or enhanced states of consciousness when altered synaptic connections are engaged. Subjective experience tells me that this process works both ways: Function depends on synaptic connections; therefore, the potential for altered states of consciousness are embedded in our biology the same as dreaming or waking consciousness is so embedded. These processes exemplify a model of circular causation in which we can learn to actively intervene.

Our brains are "… assembled during childhood by a combination of genetic and environmental influences (Ibid: 307), but we also know that they can be modified continuously throughout our lifetime. This is brain plasticity. In my experience, learning to consciously control and direct much of this modification underlies expanded attention, learning and self-activation on many different levels.

It appears to me that the analysis of our dreams is gradually being standardized for research purposes, and it is only time before a similar standardization is applied to other altered states. Brain plasticity is revealed when we take control of our dreams and nightmares to change our moods, control anxiety and depression, and enter at will whatever altered state we chose.

Below I list seven principles from LeDoux and interpret them as they relate to dreams and consciousness:

Principle 1: Different Systems Experience the Same World.

Although the different neural systems have different functions, because they are part of the same brain they will be involved in encoding the same life events. One system processes the sights, another the sounds, and still another the smells in a given scene (Ibid: 308)."

Sensory information is bound together in our brains so that I don't just see my spouse visually. I know her touch, her special aroma, her softness in bed, her voice, her profile, her walk, etc. My spouse is not just a name or a visual object. She is all of the above and more. Often in my dreams she is only part of this complex of bound elements. My visual dream frequently has a physical presence of Ruby that is either a composite picture put together by my brain or a physical person so unlike her that I recognize Ruby as my wife only by the feelings this dream image brings forth to my sleeping brain.

Remember, in our dreams we may know someone by a singular modular sensation that calls forth an associated feeling. Ruby may become manifest in my dreams as a morphed person because my modular brain is keying on conflict and calling forth a composite of former spouses. My modular brain may key on sexual feelings toward Ruby and make similar associational composites, etc.

We should not expect the characters in our dreams to be photographic duplicates of others. They can be, but more frequently, they are composites put together by a binding process that operates loosely. Do not expect your brain to take pictures like a camera, or process other sensory information like a mechanical recorder, it does not. Once we become aware that sensory binding is experienced differently while we are dreaming, it gets easier to interpret what is going on in our dreams.

Knowing that my brain does not simply take pictures and store them like a camera eliminates the supposed mystery of this process. My brain visually assembles every object that is scanned and taken in, as it also assembles objects that it manufactures internally. And even more confusing is the fact that it mixes and matches this assembly process. Our sleeping brains can assemble any combinations that they want. The bridging element for Ruby in my dreams is usually the emotional reaction I feel toward her dream character.

For dreamers who are not involved, or have not been involved in an intimate relationship for some time, their dream characters will commonly be composites. And, over time the emotional binding elements too will become mixed. If, on the other hand, you've had one or two major relationships with intense emotions, it is more likely that accurate, true to life images of them will emerge in your dreams.

Off the shelf dream dictionaries can be entirely misleading as they typically do not address the physiological basis of how our brains assembly our dream characters, or mix time sequences and scenery. Add in the morphing features as our dreaming brains skip from one function to another, and the language of dreams can become confusing. Even worse, as Chapter 16 on dream dictionaries reveals, these books are usually compilations of manufactured ideas equal to that of the local palm reader. Hobson, LaBerge, Delaney and Brooks-Vogelsong are not riddled with this mythology, so try them instead.

Principle 2: Synchrony Coordinates Parallel Plasticity

How various features of an object are brought together in the brain is called the "binding problem." Another way of stating this is that neurons that fire together wire together. The Ruby example above exemplifies this binding problem.

 LeDoux states that "Unfortunately, little is known about whether changes of this type actually take place between networks in the brain (as opposed to within individual networks) (Ibid: 311- 312)."

 The question is whether or not binding occurs in one network or across networks. Let's see how long-term self-observation in dreams addresses this problem.

 In my balancing dream, my non-conscious brain is bringing together my physical relationship to gravity – I'm honing my ability to balance on a bicycle. Multiple sets of muscles are involved. My inner ear is involved, my visual system is involved, and I may or may not have waking conscious involvement in my dream version of bicycle riding. However, when awake, I'm conscious of balancing when I'm actually riding my bike. Because I'm a lucid dreamer, I do have conscious dream involvement balancing on my bike as I ride down what would be an impossible bicycle route in my waking life.

 In the abstract dream where I am explaining convergence zones, (CZ), I'm bringing together second and third order abstractions from multiple brain areas. The subjective conclusion is this: Binding can occur within one system or across systems depending on the level of complexity. It doesn't make sense to me to see binding as an either or phenomenon, or to see binding as operating at only one level of system complexity. Evolution had to address the binding problem before our higher order cerebral cortex came into being. And during what I've called "thought dreams," complex circuits must come into play across wide portions of my dreaming brain.

Principle 3: Parallel Plasticity is also Coordinated by Modulatory Systems

Various modulatory chemicals are released throughout the brain and impact multiple brain systems. "Parallel processing in different brain systems is further coordinated by modulators (Ibid: 312)."

 Strong emotions that represent significant experiences in our lives release select modulators. In other words, our brains can be and are influenced across multiple systems by these chemical processes.

 Subjectively, what this means to me is that both my waking and dreaming brain can access various past events through more than one of my brain's subsystems. If I had read LeDoux back in 1957, interpretation of my nightmares would have been much simpler. The starting point that seems most important is to recognize that any of our multiple subsystems can connect us back to a bridging element in our dreams. Let's try.

 In my sexual molestation nightmare, I'm captured by the perpetrator and my dreaming brain is chastising itself for being so stupid as to be caught this way. The perpetrator's hold tightens and I'm transported back to the hay farm in Northwestern Wisconsin where the sexual abuse occurred. Reenactment of "muscle" memories in my dream immediately transported me back multiple decades to the actual experience. Muscle memories connected to the actual sex act, which in turn entered my dream consciousness. I awoke immediately and transferred normally short term dream memories to long-term memories of my waking consciousness.

 In this case, the dream's bridging element of physical restraint was so strong that once I brought it into consciousness, I immediately associated it with the molestation. Delaney offers various exercises that are good examples of how one can ask themselves questions that cut across various brain systems to bring us this type of awareness. My experience does not support all of her suggestions; nevertheless, she offers many that I find helpful.

Principle 4: Convergence Zones Integrate Parallel Plasticity

Another important mechanism in self-assembly, especially in humans and other primates, is the existence of convergence zones, regions where information from diverse systems can be integrated (Ibid: 315).

LeDoux provides a detailed explanation as to how these convergence zones (CZ) function; I will skip the details but note that our brain's many neural subsystems are creating memories at both the implicit, or unconscious, and explicit, or conscious levels.

Most of us are unaware that our dreaming brains are practicing bicycle riding and other forms of skill maintenance, for example, and that other neuronal activity is extensively taking place in our brains at a non-conscious level. In your own dream interpretations don't dismiss these non-conscious bridging elements, but learn to explore them.

Principle 5: Downward Mobile Thoughts Coordinate Parallel Plasticity

The process by which a thought can cause the brain to issue certain orders is known as downward causation. We prove that downward causation exists every time we carry out an intention (Ibid: 319).

The big question, however, is how this might occur in our dreaming brain. Hobson demonstrates through careful brain research that this two-way flow of information within our brain's systems is greatly modified when we are sleeping. However, in my experience there is a lot more two-way communication both ways than Hobson emphasizes. I also assume that two-way communication increases in frequency as we age, become better self-integrated, and undergo architectural brain modifications. Individual differences most likely come into play as well.

To continue with LeDoux:

If a thought is a pattern of neural activity in a network, not only can it cause another network to be active, it can also cause another network to change, to be plastic (Ibid).

How we think about ourselves can change our brains. Thus, meditation, concentration exercises, relaxation techniques, and various forms of cognitive-behavioral conditioning have a physiological basis in our brains. If you regularly use suggestion to modify your dreams, you will be shaping select ways that your dreams are expressed. Systematic exploitation of this principle permits behavioral and cognitive change. I assume that not only neural mass is being modified, but the patterned neuronal changes also occur.

I have pushed this example a little further in my autobiography, for example, my 1950s self-experiments with concentration exercises and dream programming. Point made, however, is that this potential of brain plasticity can be systematically developed for self-therapy, self-control, and physiological brain modification that affects both the brain's neural circuitry and neural modulators. Taking control of and eliminating one's nightmares must impact both neural circuits and modulators.

Principle 6: Emotional States Monopolize Brain Resources

Intense emotional states such as fear or anxiety take precedence over other feelings. We note this effect in dream research that generally supports the predominance of negative feelings in our dreams. This is especially true for young people under pressure or those who live dysfunctional lifestyles. I've tracked these effects over 50 years of dream analysis, and note a significant decrease in negative dream elements as I age. This I associate with life security and a considerable improvement in my self-unification.

Let me focus on two aspects of this principle as I think many readers like me experience, or have experienced nightmares and disturbing dreams with different levels of psychological impact. LeDoux says:

Because emotion systems coordinate learning, the broader the range of emotions that a child experiences the broader will be the emotional range of the self that develops. This is why childhood abuse is so devastating (Ibid: 322).

I don't want to leave you with the idea that traumatic childhoods are devastating forever. In my experience, and I think with adequate therapy, rather quickly we can transcend what then becomes temporary dysfunction. As we grow well beyond childhood trauma, the experiences can permit expanded sensitivity to life and other people. Like the monkey's use of adrenaline, we have choices with proper social support.

Disturbing repetitive nightmares are a natural reaction by our brains for self-preservation. Nightmares are sirens in our sleep that demand our attention. They don't go away because we wish them to, and they don't necessarily diminish their intensity with time unless there is active intervention. Nightmares are like food and water to which our bodies demand attention. We must address our basic emotional needs if we wish to improve or maximize our mental health. Balanced emotional homeostasis is not possible when nightmares prevent adequate sleep and release neuron killing modulators.

If you have trouble finding the bridging elements to your negative dreams, read Delaney and Brooks-Vogelsong. If that doesn't work, join a dream interpretation support group or create one. The process of dream interpretation may seem a bit mystical at first, but I firmly believe we can all get the hang of it. For me, dream interpretation got much easier when I started interpreting dreams through the research of the mind sciences.

Secondly, my experience says that our dreaming brains are nightly communicating the state of our well-being or lack of well-being. Pay attention, learn and apply self-knowledge. Simply, personality integration, or that growing sense of self-unity that brings us peace, comes about when we learn to interpret implicit memory that rises to the level of demand in our dreams. Our goal is to make implicit memory explicit.

Principle 7: Implicit and Explicit Aspects of the Self Overlap, but not completely

LeDoux is associating implicit learning with emotions and the role of our amygdale in processing our emotions. It's important for the reader to recognize that our conscious daily focus may be on our jobs or certain relationships such as our spouses, but our non-conscious emotional focus can have another orientation such as creeping anxiety or depression. Thus, conscious focus and unconscious focus are out of sync. Dream analysis is a wonderful tool to contrast these different levels of awareness.

Remember that we each have two levels of consciousness operating at the same time. I must attend to situational demands, walking, talking, job duties, protecting myself, etc. But my Interpreter sits above the fray observing as a form of meta-consciousness. Emotional states that I don't attend to on time, that continue to build rattling noises in my neural networks, are noticed by my meta-consciousness. Dream analysis is a good way to bring this building drama into awareness.

From an evolutionary point of view LeDoux calls attention to the fact that:

Our brain has not evolved to the point where the new systems that make complex thinking possible can easily control the old systems that give rise to our base needs and motives, and emotional reactions (Ibid: 323).

Become aware of FAP-like dreams and how your body's senses are entering your night movies, and you will develop a fuller appreciation of this aspect of your own evolutionary history. The same applies to emotions that we are consciously trying to ignore. Personally, I used self-hypnosis to bridge the gap between these two levels of consciousness.

The critical point for readers who are in the process of discovering this difference between our cognitive and emotional systems is acknowledging the importance of bringing both systems into synchrony. We sometimes call this balance or harmony, but subjectively, we all know how it feels when we have it and how it feels when we don't. In "flow" we have it, in distress we don't.

In my dream experiences, I have become acutely aware that my dreaming brain speaks volumes about my emotional well-being, even when my conscious self tries to ignore this mighty river that runs under what is often my smug cognitive wall.

One last point, don't just focus on emotional elements that are normally unconscious in your waking hours, but also focus on mundane, banal elements like bicycle riding in your dreams. My experience as my life has stabilized with ageing and maturity is that these mundane elements dominate my dreams. If this isn't your situation, then by all means develop a firm commitment to become a proficient dream interpreter: Bumpy roads need attention or your car shakes apart.

LeDoux is a wonderful thinker, researcher and writer. He may offer more detail than most readers want, but he is well worth the struggle if you do not normally follow this type of research. His clarity of writing has been of immense help in my own understanding of self, consciousness, and how it relates to my dreams. Thank you Dr. LeDoux!

CONNECTIVITY

Synapses dance and synapses play
Synapses speak and synapses pray
Synapses make you and synapses make me
But Joseph LeDoux makes synapses sway.

CHAPTER 3

HOBSON'S DREAM RESEARCH

INTRODUCTION

J. Alan Hobson has been a prolific writer with multiple contributions to dream, consciousness, and mind science research. He challenged and then dismantled the Freudian view of self and dreams, especially in *Out of Its Mind: Psychiatry in Crisis,* which he wrote with Leonard. For me, he expresses a degree of honesty in his writing that is a breath of fresh air. He has affirmed my thoughts about Freudianism and traditional psychiatry to such an extent that I think of him as an unofficial mentor. I'm covering primary highlights from his published books to capture many of his key concepts and findings that have relevancy to my own observations and subjective methodology over the past 50 years.

From Hobson's *13 Dreams Freud Never Had* I've extracted 27 characteristics to compare with my own dream experiences. There are a few areas in which my long-term subjective analysis differs from Hobson's. I'm not challenging Hobson as his dream research is top notch. I leave the worth of my observations and accompanying criticisms to the professionals, especially Doctor Hobson. I share my personal lucid dream history since age two and over fifty years of almost daily dream analysis. My dream patterns change over time with ageing; therefore, I propose that brain-mind integration over long periods of time modify dream processes and internal brain-mind interchanges. Additionally, I will throw in comparative observations from active control over altered states.

As a life-time writer, researcher and practitioner, Hobson continues to offer new knowledge and insights year-to-year. He has much to say about many related topics, but I think the scope of his dream knowledge base is best represented in **13 Dreams**. Readers with a serious interest in dreams will be familiar with Hobson's research and know his commitment to solid science. If you are unfamiliar with him start with **13 Dreams.**

HOBSON'S DREAM CHARACTERISTICS

First a look at Hobson's view of consciousness and the brain-mind:

The first is that the brain-mind is a unified system. The brain and mind are inextricably linked: no brain, no mind. Furthermore, when I dream of criminals in a hotel and when Bertal hallucinates dive-bombers, our respective brain-minds have entered states that have common physiological and psychological traits. We can use physiology to predict psychology, and psychology to predict physiology." "Three bold corollaries of this unification principle hold: that consciousness is the brain's awareness of its own physical state; that consciousness is a tool for studying the brain; and that consciousness is a tool for changing brain activity in strategic and healthful ways (1994:26).

I believe this book supports all three corollaries of this unification principle. We can use consciousness phenomenology to study the brain, and we can use consciousness to change our brains. I think one of my better examples is nightmare control and elimination, but others are removal of anxiety and depression. Further, we must not only be changing brain activity, but over time we must be changing electro-chemical patterns and oscillations within this modified neural mass.

Changes should be occurring in a number of different ways:

1) Increasing neural mass through altered selective attention and use which, for example, in my case involved changing attention from 20 minutes to eight hours.

2) Controlling the release of the brain's own chemicals that kill dendrites and cells.

3) Closing negatively self-reinforcing circuits that perpetuate nightmares, anxiety, depression, and others symptoms of PTS.

4) Opening connections in neural nets that enhance positive brain-mind functions such as creative thought dreams.

Overall these changes lead to a sense of balance, positive brain-mind homeostasis, and eventually, a sense of flow.

Hobson's observations are woven though many chapters of this book. His research has impacted how I organize my thoughts on dreams and dreaming more than any other individual. If you are a lucid dreamer, you appreciate Hobson's careful research, historical reviews, and first hand sharing of his own dreams and major life events.

The following list of 27 dream characteristics is from *13 Dreams Freud Never Had,* characteristics which I'll compare with my experiences over the past 50 plus years.

1. The disorientation of dreams is normal, not pathological... This interpretation is in contrast to those who … insisted that dreams were banal and were as well organized as waking mental content (2005: 42).

At 75 years of age, my dreams are mostly mundane (banal) as I note in Chapter 4. Mental content can be well organized as in my lecturing dreams, but dream recall is not at the same conscious, comprehensive level as my university lectures. This type of organized dream is not common to most dreamers. Nevertheless, disorientation in my dreams is common.

2. [Studies] suggest that each REM cluster can generate its own dream scenario (Ibid: 44).

Over the course of a single night we may be having 25-50 dreams. My experience when I'm overly tired, or if I drink excessive amounts of coffee in the evening creates what seems like endless dreams, plot after plot after plot. A single scenario is generally coherent, but sequential dreams usually reflect numerous multi-tasking elements. My body sensations such as being hot or cold can create their own dream scenarios.

3. I speculate that REM sleep dreaming is constantly novel and unpredictable because the brain is running its startle program in an uninhibited way … it might mean that a good way of getting attention, a good way of provoking emotion, and a good way of ensuring learning is by means of surprise (Ibid: 45).

Startle for me is any dramatic element that flags my attention. Startle responses to strong emotions are less frequent as I age. Startle responses to "aha" thought dreams are equally noticeable, but without the same level of adrenaline. In that most of my dream content is of a mundane nature, it is easy to pick out the "blips" on my startle screen. Infrequently, I have full nights of thought dreams that are very transparent. My emotion-laden dreams demand attention, and I believe reflect a dream function that is part of my brain-mind maintaining emotional homeostasis.

4. [T]he autocreativity of REM sleep dreams is important to our view of ourselves as humans." "Society and civilization are built on the creativity that goes with the flow of imagination that comes to the surface in our dreams (Ibid: 47).

The creativity of self flows in my dreams as it flows during the day. However, in our dreams, creativity is unencumbered by daytime distractions. The reader will note in following chapters how much dream creativity occurs for me as I write this book. My dreaming brain constantly seeks inference through symbolic abstraction when I'm involved in extensive writing or academic activities. At least one-third of this book has been suggested by my dreams.

5. Hobson notes that mundane behavior such as sitting at one's desk is not dreamed about, and says: "So much for the theory that dreams reflect waking experience (Ibid: 59)."

Being careful with the definition of mundane, I note that activity such as balancing on my bicycle, or skills associated with drawing and glass cutting are fictive reenactments in my dreams. Sitting at my desk? No, that's too mundane. However, common practiced skills such as lecturing are expressed extensively in my dreams. I assume that highly routine behaviors that are consolidated in memory do not need attention, as they do with newly facilitated action dreams that support complex skills. Thus, I predict that habitual bike riders do not have balancing dreams of my type.

6. [Recent] work by Roar Fosse suggests that the hallucinatory power of dreams increase across the night, while thinking declines early in the night and stays low thereafter. Highly hallucinatory dreams thus are most typical of early-morning REM mentation (Ibid: 57).

I agree with Fosse about the hallucinatory power of dreams increasing across the night. Whatever the multi-task being performed by my dreaming brain, it seems to reach a peak of consolidation and integration in early morning REM. Contrary to Fosse, my lectures and thinking dreams achieve greater focus as morning approaches, often producing new insights and conclusions to extensive chains of thoughts. FAP dream consolidation with activities such as fictive bike riding over impossible terrain reaches crescendo in the morning, and for me, this is Roar Fosse's "highly hallucinatory" element.

I think individuals who have been long-term lucid dreamers enjoy a higher level of communication across their brain-mind subsystems. For example, most people do not lecture in their dreams. However with thought dreams, insight and new ideas reach their peak in morning REM. Fixed action patterns such as bike balancing, integration, and consolidation appear to reach their peak in early morning REM as well. Bike riding hallucinatory power reaches its peak in the morning when I ride like Superman. It is this effect that I associate with memory integration and consolidation. There are many creative people historically in art, literature, math, and science who report similar experiences.

My subjective dream experiences suggest the following sequence: Basic image formation that I observe in dreams such as balance suggests that small steps earlier in the night come before final consolidation. In this example, muscle responses must be bound together with one's vertical relationship to gravity, feeling is added in as a non-conscious guide to correct bike posture, and finally, visuals fictively complete the experience that consolidates another fixed action pattern (FAP). If this interpretation of function is correct, highly hallucinatory dream scenarios should peak in early morning.

Following the above logic, my bike FAP dream reflects the binding process of multiple senses to create something equivalent to Damasio's Qualia I (balance). If I think of Qualia II as primary metaphor, I recognize how instantiated imagery is body derived. When primary metaphor is re-imaged to become complex metaphor, we can move from primary metaphor as balance to complex metaphor as a balanced checkbook. Thus, thought is metaphorical and ultimately derived from body imaging. This interpretation supports Lakoff and Johnson, and identifies how primary images are formatted. Language and words following the logic of this process are derivatives, and thought is metaphorical.

I observe this primary imaging scenario in bike riding and other similar dreams. When I tease out the metaphorical concepts being visually displayed in my dreams, I derive interpretations that reflect underlying dream functions, and when I apply these metaphorical interpretations, my nightmares vanish.

From my experience a considerable amount of dreaming is memory consolidation and reorganization. Highly salient or life-threatening events are going to be strongly encoded in memory. It is logical that our most salient experiences – whatever the brain is most actively involved with, are given emphasis as one nears his or her morning wake state – that's when the information is useful. Transfer of dreams to explicit memory that is accessed in the daytime is turned off when we dream. Dream memory is of short duration. If we are a lucid dreamer, we can pay special attention and transfer dreams to our long-term memories. I see this as a limitation of new and old brain connectivity.

Our library of dream memories is best read during the early morning hours, as evolution would functionally select for this type of sequential dreaming process. In like fashion, the complex integration of fictive bike balancing should follow memory instantiation if smaller memory elements are being integrated earlier in the night.

7. The drive to move and see, not unconscious wishes, is what constitutes the real latent content of dreams (Ibid).

Overall review of basic research in Chapter 2 strongly supports this assumption. In my understanding of brain physiology, modular sensory connections between the limbic system and higher brain centers must retain visual and motor exchange for lucid awareness of FAP dreams to be experienced. This exchange at least occurs intermittently throughout the night's sleep cycle. Hobson's activation-synthesis models and his extensive dream research generally support this position. At least, it doesn't rule out this through-the night sequence.

In terms of what I call thought dreams, I have entire nights of dream lectures and thinking related to this book, hence, there must be continuous exchange operating between my higher and lower brain centers. I change Hobson's wording slightly to "the drive to move, see, integrate, and coordinate not unconscious wishes is what constitutes the real latent content of dreams."

8. Our dreaming minds mimic the waking mind's habit of explaining why things are the way they are. The explanations are as bizarre as the events of the dream world." (Ibid: 61).

This appears to be a universal. Lucidity in our dreams demands explanation as we dream, as do daytime experiences. We are meaning creating animals, and creative explanation never stops until death or coma. In waking moments, we have learned to represent thoughts with words. In dreams, we represent thoughts metaphorically. Representing thoughts with words is a socio-cultural necessity, as complex thoughts cannot be transferred non-verbally. From this perspective, language emerged from our social interactions.

9. Discussing dream confabulation, Hobson notes that: "… the normal brain in REM has altered its memory capacity." (Ibid: 62).

Confabulation occurs when data is missing and the brain-mind adds in the pieces needed for continuity. Hobson references Korsakov's psychosis where brain neurons have been burnt out due to excessive alcohol use. I think part of confabulation occurs because of the brain's modular construction and partially because memory consolidation around activities such as bike balancing is facilitated by imagery not common to or possible during waking hours. If I'm fictively practicing bike balancing in my dreams, why would I need transitional continuity between dream scenarios?

Most of my dreams are activated by memory consolidation and integration that supports my ongoing waking activities, so at least part of confabulation is a byproduct of the processes representing the mechanical work being performed. For me, another part of dream confabulation is the continuous creation and evolution of dream memories that are auto-created. Long-term lucid dreaming creates these scenarios, and they are used just as effectively for my brain's mechanical work as externally derived memories are. When I interpret dream function from this perspective, confabulation has a meaning in dreams that is different from our waking interpretations. My auto-created dream memories are as good as my waking memories, and sometimes better when it comes to embedding skill FAPs which require memory integration and consolidation; dream biking being exhibit number one.

10. The … fact that all vision depends on internal as well as external form (67). Mental imagery might depend on our capacity to activate, at will, the visual centers of our brains (Ibid: 68).

As commonly noted by sleep researchers, our visual centers are active during dreaming and have direct connections with the sensations coming from the brain stem. Those of us who create, direct, and control our dreams do not think about visuals, which are there on command. We are active animals involved in complex motor activities that demand visual support. When I look at a treed lion in the jungle, my brain catches glimpses of its outline and fills in the pieces. This is survival through mechanisms of evolution. I cannot only fill in the pieces; I can fill in the whole picture.

The only times I don't have accompanying visuals are in select altered reality states such as speaking-in-tongues. Visual images are created at will in my brain-mind when I set off on a daytime vision. My Genesis Journey in Chapter 12 is a good example of this complex mental imagery. Not only can we create mental imagery of a visual nature, but we create sounds and music, touch sensations and changes in perceived body temperatures, and the like across our senses. Dream examples supporting other senses are provided in subsequent chapters.

Thus, sensory images or the capacity to reconstruct sensory images must be stored as FAP-like entities that we can call up on command. Qualia are these sensory images. They are the basic sensory units that support consciousness, and without qualia, there is no consciousness or self. The brain-mind not only experiences qualia, but it uses these sensory elements to act back on the body proper. The ability to act back on the body proper also permits our higher order conscious self to dream, vision, and experience simultaneously self and other, mind and body. Isn't it wonderful! The logic being expressed follows Antonio Damasio's use of qualia.

11. Everything in our dreams is based on experiences we have had and identities we have come across in our waking lives. The emotions that are tied to those identities are revealed in dreams, especially the hot emotions. But dreams are de novo creations of the sleeping brain (Ibid: 69).

Let me extend the use of "everything" in number 11. Because I follow dream content and at times past I've extensively programmed my dreams, I'm aware that internally created dream content also becomes part of my memory library, and competes with externally derived dream content in normal dreams. I'm surprised at how much of my auto-created dream content is used over and over again. Thus long-term memory, explicit or implicit, auto-created or externally derived through normal sensory routes, is an evolutionary mechanism that supports learning that is functionally used in both dreams and during our waking hours. Auto-creation not only fills in the outline of the treed lion. It can fill in the whole picture.

The process that supports auto-created memories is necessary in order for our brain-minds to re-image primary images such as balance in the creation of Qualia II or metaphor. Auto-created memories, memories that we create whole, are not given enough attention by dream lab researchers in my experience. Long-term memory associated with my dream "Heaven on Earth" utopia must have association with memories of well-being that I hold in explicit consciousness, or they would not be available to mix randomly in my normal dreams. Evolving dream scenarios that I consciously follow with dream analysis have become a permanent part of my explicit memory.

12. The fact that I had an erection indicates that this dream was driven by REM sleep brain activation, because erection and clitoral engorgement in females are constant features of REM sleep physiology whether or not the associated dream content is sexual (72).

Reviewing my 50 years of active dream analysis leads me to these conclusions: a) My brain is multi-tasking, and I may wake with an erection while my dream is focused on other more salient elements; b) A majority of the time that I have erections in my dreams, there is no dream content supportive of sexual activity; a minority of the time, the two are associated.

Viewing my brain-mind as a dynamic integrated whole leads me to assume that routine physiological conditions do not activate my dreams unless they are outside of my normal maintenance baseline. My history dictates that younger people will differentially experience the frequency of erection or clitoral engorgement due to differences in hormone levels from that of older individuals, therefore, the frequency with which their dream erections and sexual visuals correlate will be much higher. I experience, as indicated by my dream reports, erections that correlate with their dream visuals when my normal baseline of sexual activity is not maintained. At 75 years of age, erections normally occur without any accompanying dream visuals. Conversely, dreams expressing sexual desire or coitus usually occur without an actual erection.

13. [T]he use of sleep and dreaming to advance scientific or artistic endeavors... personally, sleep does seem like a good way to incubate ideas (Ibid: 78).

I believe from experience, and the literature, that this creative interconnection can be actively enhanced through long-term practice of lucidity and conscious control of dreams. Enhancement permitted me to move from dream suggestion to total dream control; enhancement permitted me to move from rhythm induced dance trance and rhythmic voice activated glossolalia to complete control of visions. Thus I suspect that my dream ability to engage in full nights of dream lectures follow from similar dream gymnastics. Creative capacity has been well documented in the dreams of dozens of historical figures (See Barrett). However, the fact that dream creativity at a complex level is uncommon probably means there is a normal curve for this ability, but a curve that can be manipulated.

14. Today, cognitive neuroscientists use the term semantic network to imply interconnections of words and meanings embedded (somehow) in interconnected neural networks (Ibid: 82).

By observing FAPs in dreams, one is observing primary images such as balance being integrated and consolidated. Sensation is being embodied in our neural circuits. The use of balance by a mobile organism only requires implicit, non-conscious learning and memory consolidation. This is consciousness and mindedness operating at a reflexive level; a level my neighbor's dog understands. However, at the human level, I also note that my Interpreter is observing this fictive process of superhuman bike riding and taking full credit. Conscious awareness of our dreaming brains embedding primary images has taken on some form of remapping in order that these tissue sensations can be felt.

The following section has been rewritten following my dream of (10-8-11) which is presented at the end of this chapter. I'm following Damasio's developmental sequence from proto-self to core self and then to autobiographical self. Proto-self and core self together are responsible for our first level of consciousness that integrates and directs the complex behaviors of rats and cats. This is a level where the organism is aware of itself. The autobiographical level of humans steps up one level from that of rats. We are aware that we are aware. This higher level of cognitive ability permits me to self-talk, take the role of another person, and exercise Free Will. Rats can't do this.

An amoeba exhibits a very low level of tissue consciousness when it tries to move away from destructive chemicals in its water world. Life has sensitivity to its environment and a primordial will to live. Evolution creates complex organisms with specialized abilities, and at the human level, we call them our primary senses. To coordinate all this mass of billions of cells, evolution created specialized cells called neurons. But a major problem that must be solved by evolution in the creation of complex organisms is binding of all these sensations together into an operating functional whole. At the dog and cat level, the job gets done with considerable sophistication. In fact, it's even pretty sophisticated for the amoeba.

Qualia are primary sensations where the organism is responding to its environment, such as temperature, need for food, water and oxygen, processing light for vision, etc.

But the fundamental questions become:

1) How do all these sensations (qualia) get bound together to direct human-level activity?

2) How do qualia eventually shift from guiding reflexive behavior of the rat to giving humans Free Will, and the ability to create complex cultures?

Answering these questions permits us to understand how metaphor is used by our brain-minds in dreams, and helps us explain different forms of mental illness.

Llinas refers to any sensations that are imaged by the organism as qualia. Damasio goes a step further and distinguishes between Qualia I and Qualia II. I will follow Damasio's interpretation.

My objective is to review qualia as basic brain-mind sensory units and show their relationship to metaphor. Once this relationship is established, I will use these concepts to explain how images become embedded in tissue as FAPs, how metaphor and complex metaphor are related to thought and the emergence of Free Will, and finally, explain why language is a derivative of these processes.

I use my bike balancing dream as an example throughout this book in order to maintain a consistent referential example for the reader. I've primarily used dream examples from the time period it has taken me to write this book; thereby demonstrating how my brain-mind makes associations, derives dream patterns and themes, and to offer insight into how my dreams can be metaphorically interpreted.

My bike riding dream repeats numerous times, and over a period of days and weeks, I become conscious of a very significant increase in balance. After about five weeks, I just "will" my bike to turn as I ride down the street, and it does. Riding becomes an effortless activity much like walking; it just seems to happen by itself. I've fine-tuned a balance FAP that's been unused for thirty years. And my balance FAP represents sensory binding that is part of a feedback loop between my brain-mind and my body.

This fixed action pattern called balance is fine-tuned by embedding sensory input that orients my body to the vertical (gravity) and coordinates verticality with muscles and vision. FAPs are the circuit embedded entities that guide most of our behaviors non-consciously. We learn FAPs through practice at a non-conscious level and express them without conscious effort. Just as the dog runs, I bike, because both sets of behavior are FAP dependent.

I observe my balance FAP being embedded through metaphorical dream analysis. I'm riding my bike over impossible terrain in the fashion of a Superman. And I do so to the amazement of others, my dreaming self included. I also have related dreams where I'm standing on the edge of tall buildings looking down and being dream conscious of my excellent sense of balance. I am fictively practicing and reinforcing balance in these dreams. In like fashion, an Olympic athlete mentally practices his or her FAP routines before executing highly skilled routines.

Quile that maintain my body's relationship to the vertical are being bound to sensations from my muscles, and all of this is being supported by my sense of vision.

Primary bound sensations, Qualia I, are collectively being re-imaged by our brains to become what Damasio calls Qualia II. When primary sensations, Qualia I, are re-imaged, they are felt. We use these feelings to act back on our body proper. In this example, Qualia II are the brain's working units that are learned and expressed behaviorally at a non-conscious level. I'm referring to these entities that bind our senses as fixed action patterns. An infant learning to grasp a crib toy is learning and embedding qualia that become fixed action patterns. Eventually the child and adult will not think about reaching and grasping any more than one thinks about walking.

Metaphor is commonly thought of as a conceptual unit that represents and stands in for something else. In Lakoff and Johnson's use of metaphor, which I follow, love as a journey is such a representation. In one of my dreams, a Glock pistol is metaphor for my penis.

Primary sensations are Qualia I and their re-imaging by our brain-minds are Qualia II. Recall that in order to be felt, balance as quale has to re-map a primary sensation, i.e., the organism's relationship to gravity.

Qualia II re-imaging permits a dog or cat level of cognitive ability to support purposeful movement of the animal across its landscape. This is an evolutionary stage where reflexes control most of the animal's behavior. From a human perspective, the behavioral repertoire that supports most of the dog's behavior and reflects the 95 percent of our non-conscious mental activity is directed at the level Damasio refers to as core consciousness. At this level of consciousness the organism has mapped its self and its environment. Humans and dogs share this capacity level, which is responsible for almost all of the dog's behavior and our reflexive behaviors, and represents the majority of our daily actions.

I am using the concept of primary metaphor to represent sensory binding that is felt at Damasio's Qualia II level. Qualia I is the sensation itself, and its remapping is Qualia II. Experimental steps for self-observation require us to connect the various steps in cause and effect relationships. I have followed this basic outline.

Qualia II are tissue embedded entities that represent the organism's response to primary sensations; they are the feelings of what is. The feelings of "what is" are primary metaphor; units of analysis that are a second order emergent.

Primary metaphor is embedded in tissue. It is tissue dependent. My balance FAP binds a number of sensory units together and feels them. Balance is now experienced at the level of self as body. (Recall self as mind and self as body). Balance has to be re-mapped in order to become a "minded" entity.

I re-map balance to create complex metaphor, and I can now balance my checkbook or have a balanced life. Complex metaphor from this perspective frees the mind from tissue dependence. I am contending that this is the mechanism that gives us Free Will.

While the dog is being directed by reflexes and is conscious, I move up a level to being aware that I am aware. This higher level of consciousness depends on a new stage of evolutionary development beyond that of the dog. At the level of our higher order consciousness, which is supported by complex metaphor, conceptual units that underlie thought are freed from tissue dependency and reflexive actions. Our Autobiographical self is now present, and being free of tissue reflexivity, we can exercise Free Will.

The reader may object to my putting Qualia II and primary metaphor on the same level of brain-mind process development. My main point, however, is to call attention to the hierarchical stages of imaging and re-imaging that leads to freely manipulated minded entities that I'm defining as complex metaphor. Eventually, physiological and mind science research will refine these observations.

Linguistic interpretation of primary sensory entities or even complex metaphor as language is misleading. One does not derive meaning from words; meaning is derived from conceptual entities that are initially tissue embedded. Concepts are metaphorical, and precede their derivatives – language.

Glen A. Just

Image formation is a complex process. It demands an understanding of image re-mapping stages. Hence, one cannot talk of Free Will at the primary metaphorical stage any more than one can equate Qualia I with higher order thought. In like fashion, one cannot understand how meaning is created in our brain-minds by focusing on language.

I could think before I had embedded word FAPs in my brain tissue. This is obvious when we acknowledge that we can teach an infant to communicate with sign language before it can talk. My 14-18 month old mind experienced an OBE and went off to Heaven supported by embedded conceptual entities, not words.

In this hierarchical model of image formation, we have identified the neural base from which the capacity for language emerges, and at the same time, acknowledge that conceptual units from which thought is derived precede language (words).

The origin of primary image formation and the binding process that creates FAPs can only be observed in lucid dreams. This explains much of the problem linguists and semanticists have coping with primary image formation. How language and meaning is created in our brain-minds requires that we understand these physiological processes.

I find paying a little more attention to basic physiology and neuroscience, especially of the Llinas and Damasio variety, to be helpful. And I'm suggesting that a dynamic integrated systems interpretation of dreams should be thrown into the mix. These physiological processes cannot be understood using technology from outside our skulls. We can only observe these processes at this point in history through subjective case studies. And it is only in dreams that we can experience these processes at the same time we lucidly observe them. Ignoring these early steps in primary image formation keeps a window into our brain-minds shut.

It is also helpful to add a little depth to how human higher order consciousness and the autobiographical self emerge. Both human subjectivity and our ability to manipulate conceptual units that make thought possible depend on qualia. These same basic processes are critical to our understanding of numerous mental health issues. More later!

15. On dream interpretation, Hobson says:

As time goes on … it seems to me that we will be forced to conclude that the chance of falling into error with any formulated approach to dream interpretation is still greater than the scientific benefits of taking the risk (Ibid: 83).

Never having believed in dream dictionaries, and finding Freud's interpretations just another religious scheme, I have spent over 50 years interpreting my own dreams, and thus, I approach the matter knowing the benefits of dream analysis. I agree with Hobson that formulated approaches to dream interpretation are generally a waste of time and often very misleading. However, I also think that approaching dream analysis as a dynamic process that supports basic brain-mind functions holds considerable promise.

Once we get a reasonable handle on the primary activation sources of dreams, it is fruitful to pursue interpretation in terms of the brain-mind processes involved that directly or indirectly support maintenance functions for the organism.

Hobson goes a long way toward correcting the inane assumptions of dream dictionaries with *13 Dreams Freud Never Had.* I think a formulated process approach is in the making and just needs a little more time. I hope that my model of dynamic integrated systems will support this development.

16. As we focus more … closely on the role that sleep plays in learning and memory, we are likely to appreciate dreaming as a clue to the reinforcement of remote associations, to the reorganization of memories, and to the regulation of the psychological self (Ibid: 84).

Not Freud's royal road to the unconscious, which is highly criticized by Hobson, but Hobson's physiological road to understanding dream consciousness appears to form the base for enlightenment.

REM dreams in all other mammals speak volumes about what is going on in our dream states. The human REM dreaming fetus, and the steady decrease of REM frequency as we age, provides observational support for the memory functions performed. And at a higher level, reorganization of the psychological self is made most explicit in my dreams when they consist of day-to-day conflict, tension, or nightmares. I'm also arguing that second order consciousness, being aware that we are aware, adds a dimension to dreams and REM that less evolved mammals do not possess. I'm guessing that elephants and dolphins probably fall somewhere slightly below our dream capacities, but higher than the family's cat or dog, because they too experience a sense of self. The complexity of dream functions must be isomorphic with the evolution of cognitive capacity.

17. Hobson's following definition of memory parallels the interpretation common to mainstream cognitive science.

The distinction between learning, which does not require consciousness, and memory, which does, tends to suggest that language or the capacity to form propositional thought is a watershed in brain evolution (Ibid: 100).

Language capacity in humans is unquestionably a watershed development in evolution when we compare our capacity with other primates. However, other animals possessing self, such as dolphins, communicate with clicks and whistles that we have yet to interpret. Language capacity clearly emerges in stages and is not an either or development. Chimpanzees can learn sign language, even combing concepts to show relationships, but do not have ability to vocalize across the human range of sounds.

A coarse grain distinction between memory and learning can be a little confusing. Implicit memory (learning) occurs without our conscious awareness. For example, embedding a bicycle balancing FAP does not require my conscious awareness. Nevertheless, I can observe and experience this process as I report in my bike riding dreams. And the acquisition of other FAPs related to skill development can be observed in our dreams.

We can be conscious of a normally unconscious brain function through practiced lucid dreaming. Have I turned a normally unconscious brain activity called learning into a memory through this observation? Or is part of the problem one of playing with definitions as I'm implying? Without incorporation of sensations in tissue (memory) there is no learning.

Fixed action patterns (FAPs) are possible because our brains bind sensations, and in the case of balance, they are fairly complex combinations of qualia, such as our relationships to gravity, our muscles relationship to vertical posture, and all the supporting visual imagery that makes balance possible. But remember, qualia are re-mapped to become what Damasio calls Qualia II. At the Qualia II level, primary sensations are felt.

Our organism learns balance by doing, and it is a thoughtless process. It is non-conscious and it is learned. And in this process of repetitive doing, memory is embedded in tissue. Evolution has taken one small step in the creation of consciousness based on reflexes, and one giant step with complex metaphorical concepts to free the human mind from tissue dependency.

Millions of memories are embedded at the non-conscious level and guide our behaviors through FAPs. This includes walking, talking, balancing, performing Mozart if one is an accomplished pianist, and a thousand other habituated activities. Propositional thought strings together previously acquired conceptual units (metaphors) that can later be expressed as words. Conceptual units from this perspective are embedded like any other FAP and are strung together in order for us to engage in complex thought. Language does not create thought, because thought exists before language can emerge. Animals that are conscious of their selves may be executing thought at a primitive level according to human standards, but in their ability to direct behavior, it is thought.

Memory versus learning distinctions made by linguists, and semanticists tend to draw attention away from basic brain-mind mechanisms that are observable in one's dreams. Starting analysis with language confuses the physiological process of primary image formation and subsequent re-mappings from which language is derived. Assuming that meaning arises from words is false. Meaning is associated with conceptual images that come first. Semantic networks are dependent on strings of metaphorical concepts.

Language and words are derivatives of these processes. And words should not be treated as thoughts, because words reflect and represent thoughts. Words are a mechanism by which social animals communicate ideas. Verbal communication in the social group becomes part of our evolutionary environment. The social environment builds language capacity over millions of years in a fashion similar to how an organism with upright posture and grasping hands modifies interaction with this environment.

Memory is not dependent on words or verbal accounts of one's experiences. I have learned and played Mozart and Bach on dream piano and violin. I have never had related music lessons. And my lucid dream self was as amazed at this ability as my waking self was. Why? Because I didn't understand FAPs in the 1970s when I engaged these dream performances.

In similar fashion, my muscles learn and coordinate my entire body through a FAP embedding process to perform flawlessly on my bicycle. And the entire process occurs at a non-conscious level. If we're chatting over lunch, my words flow just as effortlessly as my balance flows when riding my bike. My words and balancing should flow effortlessly, because they are both are built on the same brain-mind architecture that was used to create these fixed action patterns.

I know how bike balance is embedded but I mask this process if I try to understand it with language rather than my knowledge of dream physiology. This distinction seems obvious to the long-term lucid dreamer, but the definitions can become contentious when thought is confused with language. Or, words are treated as disembodied things that originate in the mind without being connected to one's body. The content of our dreams are expressed as thoughts, not in words. We think using metaphorical concepts and we dream using metaphorical concepts. When we try to interpret dreams with words we run into this basic problem of not understanding that the mind thinks with metaphor.

As you read and follow my thought dreams, pay attention to how much is metaphorical and how much is language. Language that is habituated can show up in my dreams as it does in my waking expressions. But most problem-solving in my dreams is expressed using metaphorical concepts. Language in the form of dream lectures and discussions is mostly a set of props. My dream of (10-8-11) is a typical example.

We do not understand the language of dreams as words; we understand the language of dreams in terms of metaphorical thought. Furthermore, failure to understand this distinction makes it difficult for therapists to treat children with my background of trauma. Unless of course one assumes masking symptoms with drugs is treatment.

If I acknowledge that second or third order remapping of images is involved that permits conceptual units to be free of an embodied referent, I then understand what happened in the evolution of the human brain. I'm referring to a re-imaging level that reflects conceptual units that have become disembodied, or the re-imaging of re-imaged units, that now represent complex metaphor. Trying to interpret dreams using words as our primary conceptual units muddies the water of analysis. Thought is a metaphorical process from which meaning is derived. My dreaming brain understands this relationship. If I speak and listen to metaphor, my brain-mind is my faithful servant.

I lucidly watch my dreaming brain practice balancing on my bicycle, or I observe dream enactment of drawing or cutting glass as real daytime skills are being integrated and consolidated in memory while I'm dreaming. And, I observe metaphorical manipulation of ideas for this book in what I call thought dreams. Clearly I am learning, practicing and consolidating a set of fine motor skills which are accompanied by visuals in my bike and thought dreams.

We call conceptual unit manipulation by our brain-mind in dreams, dream creativity. This is no minor point of semantics for me, as making implicit memory explicit is the key mechanism that resolved my nightmares. It is a mechanism that is too often neglected or misunderstood by some therapists. Traditional language use in linguistics and much of standard cognitive science has contributed to this obfuscation.

I directly accessed memories of childhood trauma by duplicating the physical, bodily conditions under which the trauma occurred. I directly accessed memories of childhood trauma in my dreams by identifying the bridging elements that make these associations. I give examples of both in Chapter 8 covering traumatic dreams. And the key point is that these bridging elements are always metaphorical.

Coarse grain analysis using language inhibits access to these fine grained primary images, and their associated memories. From this point of view, coarse grained talk therapy remains ineffective for the treatment of PTS. I'll explain this relationship more fully with consideration of qualia and trauma elimination in subsequent chapters. But here I've tried to lay the groundwork for later development.

18. Hobson references Tom Nielsen who says that:

[Same-day] events can be included [in dreams] but … the peak of memory incorporation in dreams occurs six days after the events that seed the dream (100).

My memory does not work this way, as it mixes and matches time, space, characters, and landscapes in any combination. What holds my dreams together are the bridging elements, the metaphorical keys to interpretation and understanding. I have hundreds, probably thousands, of dreams that do not support Nielsen. We are often too quick to find general principles where none exist. Dynamic brain-mind associations that have existed for over one year as I write this book make this quantification suspect.

19. In contrast to the Freudian explanation of the mind in terms of the perverse habit of disguise—censorship, we are now considering dreams as functioning to reveal, not conceal, personal truth (101).

As young people say: "Right on!" The ease with which I analyze my dreams, the positive feedback I get from behavioral change associated with these analyses, the outright transparency of day activity carried into dreams, and the manipulation of symbols during lucid dreams all speak to this transparency.

20. Hobson addresses our species as a believing species:

[We] can even postulate that our beliefs are a product not only of our percepts but also of our feelings." We must believe as "Belief is necessary in attempting anything out of the ordinary (102).

An organism with a self, neural plasticity, and the ability to remember the past and anticipate or predict the future, must be a believing organism. In *Mind of the Mystic,* I describe this human characteristic as residing in our DNA. Hobson finds it in our cells and physiology. A. Damasio finds this entity in consciousness, in that feeling is always connected with cognition.

The interesting pattern that develops as we come to understand the differences between dreaming consciousness and waking consciousness is the convergence taking place around this theme. Biology and evolution confirms rather than denies this most human characteristic. We can debate types or kinds of belief, but we all must believe that it is worth our while to pursue tomorrow's goals. We must all believe that we are capable of loving and being loved, we must all believe that there is hope for the future, and so the story of belief goes.

21. If the brain is self-stimulating in sleep in a way that even remotely resembles its stimulus-drive activation in waking, the result is a convincing sense of movement of the self or of dream objects in dream space (112).

Hobson is talking about the fact that we engage in all manner of acrobatic stunts in our dreams, called fictive movement. If dream movement depends on the same FAPs as waking movement, which it must, then the mystery is solved. To be executed, FAP-based memories do not need to be attached to muscles. It is to our sleeping advantage that they aren't.

In waking life, it is the job of the vestibular system to track every detail of the body's constantly changing position in space and to integrate that data with the position of the head and eyes (Ibid: 111-112).

Simply put, the mechanisms that account for real movement during daytime consciousness account for fictive movement in our dreams. It would be a dysfunction of evolution if this were not the case. But the constraints of a real time day environment are lacking in our dreams. If my interpretation of FAP dreams is correct, fictive dream movements that are extreme or superhuman help consolidate FAPs.

22. In saying that my dreams amplify and clearly display important themes in my life, I am agreeing with contemporary dream content analysts such as William Comhoff who minimize the differences between waking and dreaming consciousness to press for the continuity of individuals traits across state boundaries; our dreams reflect our waking concerns (119).

My dream reports strongly support Comhoff's interpretation, whether they are FAP or thought dreams.

23. Transmogrification is Martin Seligman's wonderful name for what we call changes in identity by dream characters or objects (120).

Dreaming transformation is a trick of the mind that, I believe, at least partially comes from our ability to take the role of another. We put ourselves in their boots, feel what they are feeling, and engender similar thoughts. Mirror neurons probably play a central role in this process. Hence, when I'm being a shaman and project myself in the persona and body of the bear, I'm using a fairly well understood dream mechanism. It is a mechanism that also mirrors my social being during the day when I'm not dreaming. This aspect of shamanic projection, I believe, is no longer a mystery. And for felt others such as spirits, beliefs expressed in my dreams or trances guide reality construction (See Chapter 11).

24. The brain changes state so dramatically in sleep that we are not always the same people in dreams as we are in waking (134).

A quick look at dream literature reveals this dramatic change. However, as I later note, this dramatic difference has decreased considerably as I age. It is almost impossible for me to do anything to another human being in my dreams that I wouldn't do when awake, the exceptions being the case when I act in a dream as a less mature moral person, a more immature moral me that I pull from memory. Even so, the moral me in dreams has always been able to take more liberties than my waking self could.

The dream drama that is associated with acts such as flying or performing super-human feats is no longer frequent. I generally treat acts of dream levitation or flight as mundane events when they do occur. I only seem to engage in levitation or flying in my dreams when the dream plot demands these unusual responses. However, any permanent memory in my dream library such as flying can be accessed by my dreaming brain to fill in plot continuity, or serve a basic memory function. And my library of self-generated memories from dreams and other altered states has become large.

25. Hobson states that with lucidity training we can introduce voluntary control over emotions expressed in our dreams (137).

In what I've called dream programming, I totally orchestrate the dream, its characters and content, and can redirect the dream, even while dreaming, at will. I describe this process in detail in my autobiography where I banish nightmare trauma for 20 years. Meditation, extended attention, and total control over dreams, including feelings, are all part of this ability. Feeling intensity reaches its maximum in nightmares, yet these feelings can be immediately banished with dream programming. Something we want to duplicate with PTS.

26. Dreaming … provides a very good primer for any naturalistic philosophy of mind. [T]he brain-mind uses its own energy and its own information to create a complex and exciting virtual reality (147).

I have previously demonstrated that my mind is using its internal energy and its own information when I consciously create trance states, self-projections into animals, or move through physical objects, speaking in tongues, and other related virtual reality experiences. We use different combinations of our neural circuitry as we move between dreams and other altered states, which is all we have. Consequently, the study of altered realities, or altered states of consciousness, should be as systematic as the study of dreams.

27. Dream memory failure is more likely a form of functional but entirely organic amnesia (151).

If my interpretation of dream functions is correct, remembering FAP dreams would normally be dysfunctional. Emotion activated dreams are commonly recalled because this awareness supports one achieving emotional homeostasis. However, thought dreams appear to be associated most frequently with cultivated practices we are engaged in during waking hours. Those without a teaching or lecturing history probably have thought dream mentation at a less complex level.

By themselves, FAP dreams appear to be organic and represent integration, consolidation, and reorganization of memory. The evidence seems overwhelming, whether it is my brain's own mood altering chemicals, hormones, or facilitated action patterns that occur below my conscious level. An organic basis for the above types of dreams is made clearer in the following dream chapters.

Below, I discuss three types of repression:

a) Cell destruction;
b) Non-conscious repression of threats; and
c) Active repression as experienced with dream programming.

My fifty years of dream interpretation and self-experiments is generally compatible with Hobson's dream lab research findings. I have been fairly arbitrary about selecting the above 25 items as I picked them in order to compare and contrast my dream experiences with Hobson's dreams and those of other individuals he quotes. My personal dream history sometimes varies with Hobson's interpretations as noted. Usually this means a small modification rather than disagreement with him.

Standard definitions across disciplines usually do not exist, but when I integrate cross-discipline constructs such as qualia, metaphor, and the linguist's use of words, I try to identify specific referents of a physiological nature that are grounded in research and replicable observations.

PRECURSORS: ACTIATION-SYNTHESIS

Using microelectrodes, Edwart Evarts was one of the first researchers to communicate directly with a single nerve cell. "Evarts was able to observe the firing patterns of individual neurons under a continuous series of spontaneously varying states—just as we needed to study sleep mechanisms (Hobson: 1988: 162)."

He noted that cell activity increased in REM and increased in a particular way. "In REM sleep, a motor event could thus become the stimulus of a sensory response."

Evarts said, in essence, that the function of sleep may not be so much to rest the brain as to reorganize its information (Ibid: 166).

Evarts' early work and its later development in the Activation-Synthesis Model resonates well with the subjective dream experiences I report riding my bicycle, balancing, and drawing. My "at rest" brain appears to be busy consolidating and reorganizing experience. Hence, motor events become the stimulus for a sensory response, and I fictively ride my bicycle like a Superman. The reader is cautioned to pay close attention to this aspect of their dreams. I didn't in my younger years, as my focus was on dream trauma, and having fun with programmed dream plots.

71

Hobson follows this developmental line as he builds the case for activation-synthesis: "Dreams are characterized by a sense of continuous movement, and brain neurons concerned with movement fire intensely during REM sleep (Ibid: 171)."

This is a pattern also found in our waking state. One difference is that we seldom have the experience of willing the movements that occur in our dreams. Without dream suggestion, movements just seem to happen. This is a logical cause and effect relationship, as FAPs must be consolidated before they can be willed into expression.

As I note, reacquiring bike riding skills was expressed in my FAP dreams. But another aspect of skill building was related to Will. After a couple months of bike riding, I no longer consciously directed my bicycle around objects in the road or around corners, I just willed the movement. A clear indication that my brain had again embedded an action pattern that didn't require conscious thought. Using the concept of Will action just seems to happen, riding my bike or in dreams. Why wouldn't it?

The corollary to this waking willed action occurs in lucid dreaming when one consciously changes the action pattern being expressed by the dreaming brain. If I choose, I can express the same Will in my dreams to change action directions or outcomes. Without this conscious dream intervention, I just watch the dream unfold in what I refer to as natural dreaming. I can easily tell when my Interpreter is intervening either in my dream or during waking consciousness, as the act is just as focused and specific in a dream state as in a waking state, or conversely, just as non-conscious.

Physiologically, strengthening of neuronal cell mass must occur over a period of time during such learning experiences. The succession of related dreams over a period of days, as in the bicycle riding case, creates extended dream themes over many nights. Hence, sequential dream patterning, having a similar dream over a number of night's sleep, seems to be self-explanatory, as is the bizarre nature of related dream content.

Hobson:

Waking is concerned with information acquisition, catabolic energy expenditure, and action upon the world: REM sleep is concerned with information shuffling, anabolic energy conservation, and suspended animation. Sleep may thus serve development and maintenance of the nervous system, perhaps with reorganization of the nervous system's own information (Hobson: 1988: 194).

Now, over two decades after Hobson wrote these words, we find studies by researchers such as Diekelmann and Born supporting this observation. The specific neural circuits and cortical centers involved are increasingly made known. The crack in the black box has become a window over the past twenty years.

Criticism by cognitive scientists such as Alva Noe that the black box of the brain remains unopened does not seem justified. Neuroscience increasingly unveils the workings of our brains. And, when we consider work by A. Damasio addressing how meaning is created through neural development that elaborates qualia, the window grows ever larger. Noe's either or doesn't exist for me; there's too much grey.

Hobson in *The Dreaming Brain* discusses the functions of REM sleep with unborn babies, who spend most of their time in this state (1988: 291-3). Thus, Hobson sees one of the functions of REM as being integral to the brain's neural development.

In that newborn babies have an active memory for the mother's heartbeat and other sounds in their fetal environment, it is reasonable to suspect that REM and memory of these events are closely correlated.

A related physiological hypothesis keys on the idea of practice. Athletes mentally go over complex routines before they compete, as mental review strengthens their ability to accurately execute learned skills. They are strengthening embedded FAPs this way. As noted by my FAP dreams, I often practice skills fictively; it's an economical way for the brain to strengthen motor skills that I also use during my waking hours.

Dream activity related to balance was not limited to fictive bike riding. During my fifth week of bike riding, I had a related dream where I'm perilously balancing on a narrow beam in an outdoor environment. In real life, this behavior could easily have resulted in my falling and being killed. Dream consciousness was very active, and I found myself not only practicing balance, but being quite good at it. The next day when I was out for my morning ride, I was very conscious of an improved sense of balance. I have no idea how often I dream practiced balancing over the previous five weeks, but I found it noteworthy that my dreaming brain observed the improvement before my conscious brain did.

My dreams do often inform me of emotional states and complex thought outcomes before daytime awareness. This must be an emerging evolutionary function that comes with our complex higher cognitive centers. Much, if not most, of my dreams seem to be activated by body sensations and memory functions, unless I'm writing a book. Evolution still seems to be working to bring emotional states and feelings at our core self level into higher order conscious awareness. Nevertheless, paying attention to one's dreams heightens awareness of feelings and cognitive elements that can continue to swim below our waking level of awareness. Paying attention to daytime moods can likewise enhance dream sensitivity. Conversely, exchange between high and lower levels of consciousness become obvious when daytime suggestions repeatedly enter our dreams.

I gradually increased my biking time to one hour from the initial twenty minutes. In my earlier years I had been a runner, but a blood clot fifteen years ago changed this habit; hence, the biking routine. I must be careful with my left leg not to increase exercise too rapidly. If I increase my exercise level too quickly, the left leg rebels and swells. I increased my biking time twelve minutes per week, and the fifth week proved stressful to my damaged leg.

I awoke early one morning to find my left leg physically pumping as though it were riding the bicycle. In my dream, I was riding bike in Mankato where I used to teach thirty years ago, and the dream ride was actively engaging both legs. This is the geographical site where most of my biking history occurred. Because the large vein in my left leg is damaged, I consciously move it throughout the night. This leg seems to be partially disconnected from the shutoff mechanism that keeps my right leg immobile when I dream.

My experience with skills and physical development demonstrates a rather direct link between my waking and sleeping consciousness. Daytime development and associated memories are integral parts of my dreams, but I have not used technology to test the frequency of this relationship. It does appear to be continuous, however. I can easily follow physical, mental, and emotional aspects of my waking life because they systematically carry over into my dreams.

HOBSON'S ACTIVATION SYNTHESIS MODEL

Hobson's Activation-Synthesis Model was derived from his work as a professional dream researcher. His approach is empirical and formal, and focuses on how we perceive, think, and feel rather than the content of what we dream (Dreaming: 2002). His work is in contrast to earlier psychodynamic approaches which were mostly unscientific. He is Professor Emeritus of Psychiatry at Harvard Medical School and their sleep research lab. Along with his colleague, Robert McCarley, Hobson proposed that neurophysiology controls our sleep cycles and generates the content of our dreams.

His strong position on the importance of physiology was a paradigm shift away from the assumptions about the role of the unconscious in Freud's psychodynamic musings. He states: "We are not saying that dream content is unimportant, uninformative, or even uninterpretable. Indeed, we believe that dreaming is all three of these things…" (Dreaming: 2)

These are my observations too.

Hobson demonstrates the crucial role of dream generation by the brain stem as well as top-down dream activation with before bedtime suggestion. He uses suggestions in his own dreams, and is thus personally very aware of the process. I will continue to make comparison between activation-synthesis and other altered states as this book unfolds.

Addressing self-organization of the developing brain, Hobson says:

In sketching this developmental model, several important new concepts have surfaced that will require continued attention. To the notion that brain-mind states are organizational units of enormous importance, we have added the idea that elemental building blocks of such states are motor patterns. In REM sleep, the automatic activation of motor patterns gets a self-organizing process going that gives the system the capacity for continuous and progressive change (1994:142).

I believe my balancing dream is a good example of the motor patterns he is referring to. Also note that self-organizing patterns are a fundamental characteristic of open dynamic systems. Fixed action patterns support behaviors such as swallowing that babies are born with. Fetuses began to have erections while still in the womb, along with thumb sucking and practiced arm and leg movements: These are obvious survival behaviors that we think of as instincts. REM stage sleep dominates the fetal brain as it nears birth, and continues at this high level after birth. As we age, changes in the frequency of REM appear to be associated with a reduced need to create and maintain fixed action patterns. These ongoing neural processes are specifically manifested and observable in my FAP and memory consolidation dreams. Age means that I have thought dreams, while babies learn to reach and grasp.

ACTIVATION-SYNTHESIS REVISITED

In Chapter 6 under the section titled Muscle-Cognitive Dream, Llinas's concept of a fixed action pattern (FAP) nicely explains my dreams where I'm walking with one stiff leg and pumping the other fast enough to overcome joggers. In this example, I reactivated an embedded muscle complex FAP from lawn mowing that was thirty years old. Content analysis permitted me to identify the origin of this fixed action pattern. The bridging element for interpretation was my walking faster with a stiff leg than my dream jogger competitors. Focusing on this bizarre feature quickly permitted a non-conscious memory to surface that was associated with my thirty year old lawn mowing behavior. Identifying this stiff legged dream walking as reactivation of a fixed action pattern removes its interpretation as being bizarre. As I learned to identify these bizarre dream elements, and associate them with underlying brain-mind function, they stopped feeling bizarre. I now accept that fictive dream actions, extreme or not, are a necessary part of memory consolidation.

Ask yourself how a stiff leg memory can be reactivated and strengthened in a dream? Fixed action patterns are functional before birth (instinctual), and after birth (acquired), and they change in frequency with age. Long-term dream interpretation requires this perspective.

Attempting to explain FAP dreams by only referencing cognitive processes does not work, any more than trying to explain how language emerges by only referencing cognitive processes. Consolidation and integration of FAPs in dreams probably dominates young children's nights. This is an example where following a sample of dream types though the decades can be insightful.

Content analysis expands my use of Activation-Synthesis when fixed action patterned dreams are compared with cognitive dreams such as lecturing or writing on a dream blackboard. I have entire nights of dreams that represent manipulation of ideas. These are not just short vignettes, as they can occur across a whole night of dreams. Hormone activated dreams with sexual content probably range all the way from fetal erections to fictive coitus, thereby giving new meaning to fixed action patterns. (Sorry, I couldn't help myself).

Functions are reinforced and memory consolidated at various levels of dream activation. Vision is our species dominant sense as we physically move through three dimensions. Skill learning that supports fixed action patterns is initiated during our waking hours as we move in three dimensional space assisted by supporting visuals. My dreaming brain supplies any manner of visuals, bizarre or not, to make these dream rehearsals functional, and my higher cognitive centers try to make daytime sense of these visual narratives. We should not expect dream narrative to reflect waking logic.

Once I discovered the source of these bizarre dream elements, and my Interpreter started experiencing them as just another set of feelings, they no longer seemed bizarre. However, I still flag them as bridging elements for dream analysis. And at this analytical junction, one is forced to consider metaphorical imagery in dreams.

Thought dreams are different and more one dimensional with a continuous sense of ideas moving rapidly through my mind. Visuals in thought dreams are a set of props that my Self as the active agent observes. I can be in any number of dream settings with any combination of audiences, but given my teaching background, visuals typically occur in a teaching or lecturing arrangement. I continue to have numerous thought dreams as I write and edit this book. It is now October, 2011, and I've had two related thought dreams in the past five days that are related to this book.

My dream about qualia (2-14-11) is a good example of how I process thought dreams. Random images are rapidly moving through my dream visuals, and these visuals seem to be the main dream focus, but they aren't. Attached to the visual sequence is a single organizing thought, that being Qualia. In this particular dream, at the moment when I awoke, the meaning of qualia in my dream enters my waking consciousness. Thought dreams are typically focused around a limited number of concepts. Most people organize complex thoughts around three to five elements, and my reported thought dreams usually follow this same pattern, although they can be much more complex. I develop ideas about qualia in dreams more fully in the next chapter.

Reinforcing soma-based action patterns requires fictive dream visualization, as balancing is a complex, dynamic relationship between my body and the external world. It is not important that my dreaming brain is grabbing scenes, figures, and interpretations from its memory banks that make the narrative seem bizarre. What is important is the integration and consolidation of memory related to the use of my muscles and posture while balancing on my bike. Our dreaming brains select content through our own associational memories to form story plots. Much of the bizarreness in my dreams occurs because I'm using fantastic dream visuals to embed functional fixed action patterns. Understanding how metaphor is used in these story plots is the key to their interpretation.

The visual imagery displayed in my dreams simply acknowledges the fact that consciousness only exists as a process. Stop the processes that support consciousness, and not only my dreams would disappear, but also my Self. I would enter coma or death without consciousness. I must experience my body's senses over time for consciousness to emerge and be maintained.

Consciousness exists at more than one level in my dreams. I have consciousness of body (core consciousness), and consciousness of mind (autobiographical Self). Thus, I assume that bottom-up and top-down dream activation must be operating as a circular causative process. My dreams reflect activation, either bottom-up or top-down, as multi-tasking dreams activity unfold through the night.

CRITIQUE OF HOBSON'S SCALAR METHODOLOGY

I'm going to criticize two aspects of Hobson's scalar methodology; his scaling procedures, and his use of dictionary definitions. Criticisms of both elements are made because I believe this study has unnecessarily shifted emphasis from the importance of image formation (qualia) in consciousness.

Hobson used the Engine Man to create a scale for the analysis of dream content bizarreness (1988: 259-269). The bizarre in dreams always catches our attention. How could it not! He says:

It is the discontinuities, incongruities, and uncertainties that make dreaming unique as a mental state; and these are the dream features Freud sought to explain by his disguise-censorship theory. They are thus the most central and the most demanding elements to be explained by any dream theory (1988:258).

In other words it's like seeing a flying saucer overhead; it must be explained.

Hobson used Webster's New Collegiate dictionary to define bizarreness. How is Webster's definition related to dream bizarreness? Can it be meaningfully made operational?

When we set up scales to evaluate observational criteria, we want our operational definitions to represent the underlying phenomena. Hobson, in my experience, has taken epiphenomena, second order elements of dream bizarreness, set up a scale for their evaluation, and produced some very careful quantitative data. But what does quantitative data mean if the bizarreness being measured is epiphenomenal? This is not a minor point as Hobson observes that discontinuities, incongruities, and uncertainties "are thus the most central and the most demanding elements to be explained by any dream theory." I agree they are demanding elements, and hence, review of this study.

"Items in the Original Bizarreness Scale" include "Uncertain character, Dead character, Violation of natural law, Time shift," et cetera. Careful enumeration of secondary elements cannot, in my understanding of scalar techniques, get at the underlying qualities and functions that the scaled items seek to reveal.

Let me compare this scale to one of my FAP dreams. Yes, I too believe that there can be direct correlations between physiological and psychological principles, but I think this relationship has not been factored out in this scale. I will use my FAP bicycle dream as example.

I'm reinforcing and integrating balancing on my bicycle. In this dream, the scale elements identified by Hobson, such as time shifts and violation of natural laws, are basically irrelevant in that scale results do not clarify their supposed relationship to function. Thus, no matter how carefully one quantifies these scaled elements, they do not provide a necessary or sufficient explanation of my FAP dream. If a major dream function is memory integration, and I think it is in my bicycle dream, then the scale must measure these underlying elements, but it doesn't. Scaling epiphenomenal dimensions fails to measure primary elements related to function.

Note that this argument only holds if my general interpretation of FAPs is correct.

If, as I believe, my FAP dream is about reacquiring balance on my bicycle, then reinforcement of this long unused facilitated action pattern is the key. All the remaining bizarre elements are secondary, and related dream forms are epiphenomenal. Cellular, circuit integration, and consolidation for bicycle balance requires a visual component.

My brain does not typically record pictures, as we know from physiological studies. It cobbles together whatever is necessary from its visual storage bank, which is drawing upon something like 30 different visual centers of our brains to create coherent visual dream elements.

My dreaming brain flagged balancing as the key bridging element in my bicycle dream, but reduced input from my higher cognitive centers did not provide enough information for logical dream interpretation while I was still dreaming. However, the FAP element was flagged by my dreaming brain for early morning review. At other times, I often conduct these reviews while still dreaming. Analyzing our dreams in a lucid or waking state permits us to transfer information between lower and higher consciousness centers. In agreement with Hobson, interpreting this type of dream is both straightforward and transparent.

Most of the bizarreness in my dreams disappears once I take into consideration learning and memory functions of dreams, as well as my conscious self's need to interpret and create meaning from all of my waking and dreaming activities. Following Hobson's early work, I strongly believe that we must start with physiological processes and build upward, but incorporating his later work, it is equally important that we note the feedback loop from the higher brain centers to brain stem functions within a larger dynamic framework. In most cases when I find myself diverging from Hobson, it is in the realm of imaging, qualia, and metaphor.

I believe my brain is operating much as the Engine Man's brain in seeking a narrative explanation for my dream story. The explanation, for me, is usually not in the story, but the primary activation that generates the story, and this activation can come from either the lower or higher brain centers. In either case, following my dream's bridging elements permits analysis.

I'm not being single minded. My dreams multi-task, learning and memory elements are being embedded, image formation emerges that generate qualia and symbolic abstraction, and my higher cognitive centers remain active. But my higher cognitive centers perform differently, as communication between my old and new brain is a dynamic and sometimes disjointed affair.

HOBSON'S DREAM FORM

The cardinal features of all dreaming—detailed sensory imagery, the illusion of reality, illogical thinking, intensification of emotion, and unreliable memory—constitute its form, as opposed to and irrespective of the content of a particular dream (1988: 230).

Hobson notes that dream stories are seductive, and I would add that the bizarre features of our dreams are equally titillating. And, that we should also not be seduced by titillation. Further, be satisfied with hormone seduction alone, and remember that our dreaming brains don't even need hormones for sex. Older people appreciate this fact.

By providing an alternative view of dream content, the formal method also allows a new approach to interpretation (Ibid: 232).

Hobson goes to argumentative lengths to demonstrate that dreams are not psychologically or historically predetermined as has been the case with psychoanalysis. He further notes that:

The distinction between form and content, while apparently sharp, does not imply absolute independence of the two processes any more than my emphasis upon physiology denotes independence from psychology. Quite the contrary: dream form and dream content, like physiology and psychology, are inextricably intertwined (1988: 230).

With this last quote, I find myself in near total agreement with him. I am arguing that form and content in my dreams rather directly reflects function. Riding my bicycle over impossible terrain (form) necessitates balancing content and I'm arguing provides support for my balance FAP. I support Hobson on form and content, but differ with my interpretation of functions. And to arrive at function, I had to employ metaphor.

AN ALTERNATIVE MODEL OF DREAMING
(Hobson: 2001: 179-181).

Hobson notes in *The Dream Drugstore* that his critics have voiced concern that his Activation-Synthesis Model has:

[overemphasized] the dependence of dreaming on REM sleep. Dreaming can occur in the absence of REM, especially at sleep onset and during Stage II sleep in the early morning hours prior to awakening. Such dissociations of dreaming from REM sleep indicate that the forebrain could enter physiological states capable of engendering dream consciousness without the brain stem's involvement (Ibid: 179).

This is my experience.

It was therefore further proposed that the forebrain mechanisms of dreaming were autonomous of brainstem influence and that REM sleep physiology was incidental to dreaming (Ibid).

Brainstem insignificance is totally rejected in my experience, especially in dreams reported in Chapter 6. Any argument that explains dream activation from a single brain-mind subsystem is rejected.

Hobson goes on: "With respect to the integrated model proposed here, the forebrain-activation alternative to AIM also emphasized changes in activation but postulated a shift toward intrinsic cortico-cortical inputs as the main source of endogenous stimulation."

AIM is a brain state based three-dimensional visual model that supports his update of activation-synthesis. From my experience, thinking and lecturing dreams that dominate whole nights of sleep represent top-down dream activation and facilitated action pattern in dreams represent a brainstem level of activation. Additionally, this model of forebrain activation must have considerable applicability for trance states as I can move quickly from a normal waking state into a Genesis Journey, as reported in Chapter 12, with all its REM characteristics and elements. I think altered states of consciousness share neural circuits with REM, and one size does not fit all.

Continuing with Hobson:

The forebrain activation model was therefore not related either to input-output gating in the periphery or to the changes in the rates of aminergic-cholinergic neuromodulation of the forebrain. A slight change in activation was all that was needed to produce the shift from waking to dreaming consciousness, and a change in forebrain activation was thus necessary and sufficient to produce dreaming (Ibid:179-189).

In the above referenced pages, Hobson presents the original and refined diagrams for activation-synthesis. Originally, I too was critical of activation-synthesis, but find the AIM update helpful to visualize what is happening in REM and altered states. Like all careful researchers, he has continued to generate research with ever larger scope and meaning. To appreciate the implications of his refined model, it is necessary that one follows his research over time.

I can produce altered state dream-like activity through forebrain activation. Visions share visual and motor comparisons with REM, but lack bizarre forms. Those of us who move between altered states and lucid dreams have a different existential reality from what is reported by observers without this capacity. Visions have all the formal qualities and movements common to waking activity in our environments.

Hobson:

I consider it to be a matter of fact that consciousness is a continuum of states, that aspects of two or more sometimes distinct states can coexist, that consciousness can be dreamlike even in waking, and that it is likely to be more so at sleep onset or upon waking (Ibid: 180).

My reports on altered states and dreaming support these assumptions. Hobson goes on:

It thus seems to me quite reasonable to propose that we can explain many of these facts by changes in the level and distribution of activation in the forebrain, and that one forebrain site can become an input source for another (Ibid).

Again, my experience supports his position, and my thought dreams seem to be a good example of forebrain to forebrain exchange. My forebrain is guiding complex thoughts about this books' content while another section is observing. This is my existential reality.

In my younger years, it was common to create a second observer who observed my Interpreter watching and analyzing my dream. In like fashion, an accomplished pianist can be performing flawlessly while observing and critiquing his or her own execution.

Over fifty years ago, I actively practiced what I called dream programming providing plot, characters, and outcome to my dreams. I believed then, as I believe now, that a feed-downward loop has to be extended as I can interpret dream activation from Hobson's model. My interpretation of dreams, especially nightmares, says there has to be a feed-upward loop to my forebrain. Otherwise, how could such instantaneous removal of nightmare trauma be possible? I specifically offer my smothering dream as a prime example.

Mind Science research has made great progress understanding dream physiology and consciousness by generating excellent data in a number of neuroscience related areas: Integration of this diverse research takes place one step at a time. Replicable research always takes precedence over speculation based on one's subjective experience. I've written this book in the hope that long-term self-observation and self-experiments can make a small contribution to our collective understanding of dreams.

PROBLEM SOLVING DREAM (10-8-11)

I've attempted to edit the above material four times over the last four days, and the sections dealing with qualia and metaphor were still contorted. I understood what I wanted to say, but the words did not flow. The "Committee of Sleep" in my late morning dream offered the following advice: Use yourself as reference, because your readers will, and start from the smallest conceptual units and move upwards to the most complex ones. This advice seems terribly simple, but I immediately accepted it as the solution that would make the sections on qualia and metaphor readable. Note how I'm interpreting metaphor in this dream.

Lucid dreamers who ignore metaphor would not find their problem solved in this dream. Hence, part of understanding dream creativity is being able to interpret dream metaphor.

The language of dreams is metaphorical. I solve my problem not with words, but with brain-mind manipulation of raw data – my version of Einstein on his bicycle visualizing space-time.

I'm at a large corporation's central headquarters in this problem solving dream. I could be at Apple or Cargill. The dream starts in the main office between me and a number of lower level staff. A corporate officer enters the scene, and it becomes clear we will all be put through a series of tests to see who is the most creative. The officer asks who has written any material lately that interprets some complex aspect of culture. I think for a moment that I have, but I'm not sure it applies because the material was very brief.

The scene shifts, and we are walking toward a large classroom in another building. However, to get into the classroom, we must duck down and go through a low tunnel entrance that is quite long. The tunnel floor is wet and we must step cautiously over excrement. In the classroom, long discussions ensue, but eventually a picture of intersecting branches is projected on a large movie-type screen. We are asked to envision a straight line dissecting as many branches as possible. People take turns with each one finding additional intersecting lines. I don't want to focus on this silly exercise, but force myself to, as my turn is approaching.

The respondent before me finds 12 intersecting lines, but the facilitator disqualifies him saying one must start with them self as reference. I adopt this posture and quickly find at least 18 intersections. Some of the people in my test group are former co-workers from Rochester, Minnesota. An interesting aspect of dream associations calls my attention to the fact that the Rochester setting was the last work place where I engaged in "brain-storming" exercises.

This is a brief summary of the dream as my test group leaves the test situation at least three different times. The tunnel for our return becomes more difficult to navigate each subsequent time, and the excrement becomes harder to avoid. In the last scenario, everyone returns by a normal hallway and door that did not previously exist. Everyone, that is, except me. I return by the demanding tunnel, which is now at its lowest level and even harder to navigate. Upon awakening, I have the solution to my problem that I've already written down in the first paragraph of this section. I will now go back to the main text on qualia and metaphor and put in the details of this outline. Circuitous reasoning is almost as much fun as metaphorical thought! And, by the way how do they differ?

CHAPTER 4

QUALIA AND MEMORY IN DREAMS

INTRODUCTION

Four aspects are always salient in my dreams: image content, memory elements, feelings and integration; integration being how these three components come together to form abstractions and themes. My brain multitasks over one night, over weeks and over years. Maintaining memory appears to be a major nightly activity. Memories are formed from both external stimuli and auto-created sources.

Auto-created memories have a life of their own, and are updated and integrated over time just like externally derived memories. Both sources of memory are creatively combined in my lucid dreams. Internally generated memories often become serial narratives much like a soap opera. For example, years ago I created my favorite physical setting, which is a slowly morphing version of our family farm in N.W. Wisconsin. This piece of geography matures over time. It is an abstract ideal environment, my Heaven on Earth. One should not be surprised at similar self-created memories; they are much like daydreams of things we wish for.

Construction of internally created dream elements, or entire dream scenarios, seems to follow the same rules of organization as those directing my daily life. The dream elements can be very concrete, like my evolving Heaven on Earth, or these dream elements can reflect the range of symbolism and metaphor of my waking hours.

Jane is an old high school friend whom I dated a few times, but never had a romantic relationship with. Her appearance was true to life in my dreams for decades, and her dream character approximated our actual social relationship. Jane's dream character assumed that I was bent on seduction. I, in turn, played a role where I pretended the same while never having any such intentions. I report the maturation of this long-term, decades old dream soap opera in Chapter 10.

My brain, like the reader's, maps the external world as it sets priorities while I move through time and space. Emotions generated by my body's relationship to its total environment set the stage for my action priorities. Salient feelings which emerge from this emotion generating base enter my higher cognitive centers to provide direct input into my every action. My entire history plays out in my dreams as priorities are set and realized moment-to-moment and day-to-day. Cross-talk between day and night goes on.

This is a general process of living for all of us. We sometimes forget the degree to which feelings drive all of our life's decisions. We often do not realize how daydreams enter this process, and rarely know that our dreams can introduce a non-conscious element to these complex processes. Dream thought may be experienced as having its own separate language, but it draws on the same mechanisms as waking thought. These mechanisms at higher cognitive levels are metaphorical in the Lakoff and Johnson interpretation. Jane in the above example is metaphor for the coy woman, but metaphor based on "em-bedded" experiences. Sorry, I couldn't help that one either.

I experience an active, directing agent called Self, and Self is experienced as the essence of who I am. I know Self is a constantly changing process, but I experience Self only in the now. At any moment in time, I'm just me, even though I use the now to look backwards and forwards in time with extended memory. I still sit in the middle of the "I" of the vortex. My now, like yours, is a composite of externally mapped stimuli that makes sense of my world, and it is a composite of my externally mapped virtual reality plus all the internally generated virtual creations. In this sense, we all live in a dream world of our own creation: A dream world within a dream.

The extent of our virtual creations is more extensive than we often imagine. Virtual dream creations add an additional dimension to our daytime reality. Wonderfully, dreams let us view this process directly. Dreams remind us that reality is manufactured in our brain-minds using external and bodily derived sensations, and that part of this virtual reality is totally auto-created.

If the balance between these two, external and internal, realities tips to far in either direction, we may be considered strange or even mentally ill. I can only become aware of dream generated reality through analysis of my own lucid dreams. And I must observe my dreams over long periods of time in order to have this awareness. Awareness of these processes answers part of the question as to, "Where did that thought come from? Where did that feeling come from?" Dream analysis permits us to observe this internal talk. And, we all do talk to our selves, but at more than one level of consciousness. When Jane appears in my daydreaming thoughts, I know where she has been hiding and why she appeared.

By closely observing how my dreaming brain forms reality, I can identify the mix of internal and external elements that contribute to my total reality. It is only through dream content analysis that I can separate these internal and external elements. I pay attention to the age old question as to what is real and what is simply part of my imagination. The bottom line acknowledges that everything we experience is a product of our imaginations, and here, I'm using imagination to mean the total process of brain-mind reality construction. We never experience the external world directly. How boring that would be.

From this perspective, I wrestle with qualia and how it is experienced in dreams. I can grasp a new concept, or acquire a new awareness, and have an "aha" experience when I'm awake or dreaming. But I can't experience primary image formation in waking consciousness the way I can in dreams. The value of dream observation is being able to quiet extraneous stimuli and noise and observe the mechanisms used internally to practice and embed primary images such as balancing on a bike.

When I'm awake, higher consciousness gets in the way of observing primary image formation. Higher consciousness represents a stage supported by what Damasio calls Qualia II, and what Lakoff and Johnson call metaphor. In waking moments, we think with metaphorical concepts which we learn to express verbally. Thus, many confuse words with thoughts.

In dreams, we think metaphorically, and do not need words. It can get confusing, because words as FAPs can enter our dreams. We talk in our dreams as well as when we're awake, but when words enter our dreams and other altered states, they are often configured metaphorically. Follow my dreams in forthcoming chapters, and you will see how distinct this difference is.

The structure of any language partially shapes our thought processes. Imagine trying to think about dynamic processes with a language that demands linear cause and effect, such as the acquired language that many of our children enter first grade with, for example, or the concrete thinking of rigid people. We will have a conversation with our computers when we program them to think metaphorically.

Circumventing the limits of thinking with words is our first step into creativity. Einstein rode his bicycle routinely because these actions freed his mind of language while he played with spatial imagery. What does space-time look like in words? A potential doctoral thesis lurks in this shadow. Thus, we come to consider alternative methods to teach our self and others creativity.

Some of my repeated discussions on qualia may seem a little technical, but enhancing my understanding of qualia and metaphor has added depth to my dream analysis. It is being aware that we only see what we have been taught to look for. It is becoming aware that one of the first steps for many to think metaphorically is to learn how to analyze their own dreams.

LLINAS: QUALIA-SUBJECTIVE MIND EXPERIENCES

Qualia are subjective experiences of any kind, according to Llinas. "Qualia are fleeting and discontinuous events for the same physiological reason that consciousness itself is a fleeting and discontinuous event (2002: 207)."

According to this interpretation, consciousness is pieced-together and made whole by the mind as it fills in physiological gaps for the active organism. Consciousness is a streaming process with gaps, but a process that feels continuous to our subjective Selves. During waking hours, we fill in these gaps and generate a feeling that the process is seamless. We don't fill in these gaps the same way when we're dreaming; hence, consciousness in our dreams seems to skip around and morph to a greater degree.

An important aspect of this view of consciousness for dreaming is the physiological changes during non-REM sleep. According to Llinas:

When we fall into dreamless sleep, non-REM sleep as it is called, we see this functional state is characterized by slow wave synchronous delta wave activity. This whole brain, rhythmic pattern is in the .5—4 Hz frequency range … when in this deep sleep state, sensory input of all types (modalities) for the most part [is] rejected by the thalamocortical system. Sensory pathways carry the modality-specific information, but this information is not given internal significance; there is in fact no sensory experience whatsoever. Qualia have temporarily ceased to exist (2002: 207).

The key point is that sensory modalities are active, but admission of this input is blocked when we are in deep, or non-REM sleep. He looks at how qualia come and go to create consciousness. Qualia in this perspective are the critical elements at the core of consciousness. Feelings come from and are embedded in body states, our senses, are at the core of qualia and consciousness. If we don't feel anything, we are in coma or dead. Note that Llinas understands non-REM as being dreamless, which it is not.

Continuing with Llinas:

So it is not just electrical activity of neurons that determine qualia, but particular frequency ranges of whole brain activity where qualia may appear and disappear. In simple terms, there are particular types of electrical patterns, global and local, that must be coactivated for feelings to be evoked (2002: 208).

Note once again that consciousness has either a local to global basis or a global to local basis. Consciousness is not a thing; it is not a specific set of neurons firing. Consciousness is a distributed process that occurs through global and local exchange. Distributed consciousness helps explain why consciousness is not lost when one part or parts of the brain are damaged. In my dreams, global to local and local to global communication is observed with thought and FAP dreams for example. What must be varying is the degree of local or global input between dream types; not just between dreaming and non-dreaming states.

Llinas' position supports a top-down and bottom-up exchange during consciousness. It appears to me that the longer we practice lucid dreaming, the more this exchange pattern in dreams begins to approximate the frequency of such exchanges during periods of waking consciousness. The fact that I can enter my dreams at any time, or my Interpreter will enter one of my dreams without my consciously willing it to do so, seems to support this position. I'm interpreting this exchange process as circular causation in a dynamic system.

There is speculation that consciousness occurs due to quantum mechanical effects at a sub-atomic level, and it is these micro-mechanical effects that make consciousness so hard to corral. Without going into detail,

Llinas rejects speculation about quantum mechanical structure in terms of microtubules and microfilaments to create consciousness. For Llinas, quantum effects are not at the core of consciousness, qualia are. Consciousness is thus a psychological state that emerges from physiological processes. I share this interpretation.

Quantum effects at the macro level or the micro-to-macro levels are not closed issues. In the first decade of the 21st Century, research has begun to empirically explore macro quantum effects. I think it is premature to dismiss micro or macro quantum effects on brain-mind functions.

Vladko Vedral is a good starting point to explore quantum effects at the macro level as they might apply to brain-mind functions. But be careful of soothsayers who are using these ideas to sell books that mix spirituality with quantum mystery. However, in the real world of physiology, there is still much mystery about our brain's neurons and neural networks. And for physics, the quantum world is still a mystery too; hence all the speculation by non-physicists.

Qualia seem to be related not only to particular neurons per se, but also more to the geometrical, electrical patterns of activity that neurons are capable of supporting (2002: 209). Llinas doesn't think qualia transcend the neurological substrate of neurons (Ibid). He says: "[I] believe that patterned electrical activity in neurons and their molecular counterparts are sensations (2002: 210)."

His positions seem most logical to me.

Thus, Llinas rejects a quantum basis for consciousness, and locates consciousness in the global to local distribution of neuronal electrical activity. Qualia originate as body-dependent sensations.

Llinas: "For all intents and purposes, the question of qualia or feelings is the question of conscious experience (2002: 209). He then goes on to argue that "… qualia must arise from, fundamentally, properties of single cells … amplified by the organization of circuits specialized in sensory functions (2002: 212). Furthermore, "… neuronal activity and sensation are one and the same event (2002: 218).

He is saying the larger mystery of the black box is gone; this is how qualia arise and consciousness comes into being.

From this point of view, qualia are a necessity. Qualia that are re-imaged between the brain-mind and body represent the mechanism that creates Self. Qualia facilitate the operation of the nervous system by providing well-defined frameworks, the simplifying patterns that implement and increase the speed of decision and allow such decisions to re-enter (the system) and become part of the landscape of perception (2002: 220).

From the first two chapters, the reader will be aware that Damasio follows this line of reasoning too.

Qualia represent judgments or assessments at the circuit level of the information carried by sensory pathways, or sensations. They are the 'Ghost' in the machine and represent the critically important space between input and output, for they are neither, yet are a product of one and the drive for the other. And all the while they are simplified constructs on the part of the intrinsic properties of the neuronal circuits of our brains (2002: 221-222).

Whew! Llinas has just given us a naturalist's interpretation of consciousness: No Descartes, no Aristotle, no Kant, and no Freud. And, I am saying from a phenomenological perspective we can watch image formation in our dreams as primary process such as bike balancing, and feel the products of this process executed as "Will."

The feeling element of qualia are integrated in FAPs and executed on my bike without conscious thought. After a few weeks of practice, I ride my bike as effortlessly as I walk. Habitually engaging this non-conscious process seems to require no effort or conscious thought. I don't think about walking, I just do it. I don't think about turning my bike as I navigate down local streets, I just will it. We call this non-conscious execution of embedded FAPs Will. And as mental health practitioners, we want to teach people how to control unwanted non-conscious processes. How to will them away.

Will is experienced in my dreams when I ride my dream bike over impossible terrain, or will my Self to fly. Once we embed fixed action patterns, they can be activated at and by Will. From this perspective, once

I'm on my bicycle and the appropriate context for bike riding occurs, I control my bike with these feeling elements alone.

Our waking consciousness knows we can't fly, but our dreaming brain-mind simply executes flying the way it executes fictive bike balancing. No mystery here. Lucid dreamers teach themselves to enjoy superhuman abilities through suggestion. Suggestion is a conscious brain-mind event, and Will is the non-conscious execution of FAPs.

What we call "Will," assumes the existence of a non-conscious mechanism at the core level of self-development. Will coordinates reflexive behaviors; FAP dependent behaviors.

When I first taught myself self-hypnosis, I started with small suggestions: "Your fingers will begin to twitch, you will feel a tingling in your left foot, your left foot is beginning to rise on its own, etc." I transferred body actions that are normally under conscious control to control by Will, following the above logic.

My conscious mind made the suggestion but did not follow through by activating muscles. My core self took over this action. When my core Self executes actions, the actions feel like they just happen on their own. Thus, I established a new relationship between my core and autobiographical Self. Once this relationship was established, I built additional FAPs that my autobiographical Self could execute through suggestion. In this way, I came to control and program my dreams and eliminate my nightmares. I came to have the capacity to immediately execute daytime visions, and I came to control non-conscious reflexes called anxiety and depression.

As newborns, all we have operating is a set of automatic mechanisms that operate without conscious thought: We suckle, breathe, cry and burp. We laboriously learn to control one action after another. In my use of self-hypnosis, I go back to this core self level and assume control.

We all have a body relationship with gravity. This relationship can come under our conscious control in our dreams, which enables us to fly and ignore the force of gravity. When this disconnection occurs during waking consciousness we can easily panic. But in dreams when our muscles are disconnected and we can fictively practice motor skills, flying can be a lot of fun. We use suggestion before bedtime to make all this happen. But in my case, I first tapped this mechanism using self-hypnosis, and then applied it to whatever actions I wanted to in dreams or daytime activities.

The concept of Will at its playful best becomes endless putty for the philosopher pot thrower. Will at its generalized peak underlies the sensation that we can move matter with our minds. We feel that we move matter with our minds, and in my example of actual bike riding, we do. Will generalized to the ultimate "Other" permits God or one's gods to create the universe with "Its" will. Intuitively, this process of Will feels logical, it should.

Will is a common brain-mind mechanism supported by FAPs that direct complex behaviors. It seems just this simple to me. Evolving brain physical complexity creates new functions, and the autobiographical self emerges. However, this whole process is a cobbled together mess. Core self functions continue to support the rat, cat, you and me. But we need to teach our core self a thing or two. In terms of the above discussion, Will keeps cats and rats going, and historically, philosophers would have benefited by observing them.

Philosophers have discussed Will endlessly over the ages. But as a tissue embedded mechanism, we can use it to go flying in our dreams or visions, we can use Will to change our neural circuits to remove nightmares and anxiety, and we can know that as an embedded mechanism, Will can be used to control matter, the neurons of our brains.

Philosophers have traditionally discussed will as a disembodied thing without understanding how images arise from primary processes. Abstractions such as the Will of God or the Will of Mankind only muddy the waters further. From my interpretation, Will cannot be understood without basic familiarity with qualia and FAPs.

The philosophical question "What is Will?" has traditionally been an exercise in word play. To understand any phenomenon derived from physiological process, we must understand what initiates or causes the process, and how the process is expressed.

Neuro-philosophy is embodied philosophy, and it recognizes that the conceptual entities of thought arise from tissue processes. And the use of embodied entities like metaphor lead us down the road to a naturalists explanation of self, consciousness, Will and Free Will, and maybe, a deeper understanding of language itself.

LLINAS INSPIRED DREAM

I was editing the above section (9-14-11) and sometime around 4:00 a.m. the following morning, I had a thought dream. None of the content in the dream could be called a bridging element, nevertheless, my dream character was agitated and uncomfortable. I got up at 6:00 a.m. and went through my normal breakfast preparation routine. As the fog of night lifted and the coffee was beginning to perk, two thoughts became dominant: "You just had one of your typical metaphorical dreams, which are packed with symbolism, and you have not explained the operating principles. My Interpreter didn't say: "Put this in your book!" But it did remind me to be more thorough. And so I have.

In last night's dream, I'm back in a university setting as a student taking some kind of advanced placement test. I'm in a large classroom setting with 50-100 other students and the test is timed. The first set of questions on page one is easy and I breeze through them. The test is unique as it has a word, math formula, or symbol that each test taker has to decide how to answer. Examples: an algebra equation, the term Lorentz, which appears twice, a multi-character gargoyle, and then two pages of mostly incomprehensible terms. There is one exception on each page of incomprehensible terms, the word Palestine. I answer: "next to Israel."

As I struggle to finish the second example, the proctor insists that I turn in my test. I print my name on it, but the paper has turned into a statue-like object. My pencil penetrates the object and it begins to leak fluid. I tell the proctor to hold the statue face up so it doesn't leak more. I'm frustrated at finishing so few of the test items and my agitation continues. The proctor announces that the second part of the test will be given tomorrow. I'm only partly relieved, because if it's more of the same, I'll never get into this new Ph.D. program.

INTERPRETATION

This is one of my classic thought dreams. Significant agitation throughout the dream test is my bridging element. What is bothering me? All the gobble-de-gook on the test is metaphorically representing material in this chapter.

When I wake up, Llinas and qualia are tapping at the underside of my awareness and asking to be let in. I left the above section unedited yesterday as my wife interrupted me repeatedly. I finally gave in and went for a walk with her in the park. As I write these words, I remain frustrated by the lack of clarity surrounding the term qualia between neuroscience and cognitive science. Throw in all the musings from linguists and semanticists, and feelings of suicide rapidly approach.

Fact I: My thought dreams are structured around metaphor, and symbolic abstractions are exemplified by the dream test.

Fact II: Complex metaphor is dominant in my dreams when my brain-mind is processing conceptual units with high levels of ambiguity. The principle at work seems to be this: Conceptual units must have a body to be manipulated, and the physical references in my thought dreams take on this form.

DAMASIO ON QUALIA

Damasio was my hero when I wrote *Mind of the Mystic,* as he was the first neuroscientist that helped me make sense of consciousness as it applied to my dreams and altered states. His treatment of qualia resonates with my dream observations of how consciousness emerges. I can watch primary image formation in dreams from the inside-out. Dream observation permits me to feel this process of primary image and FAP formation, and experience the substrate from which Will emerges.

Damasio notes that when we look at a beautiful sunset, we not only see the wavelength variations entering our eyes, we also feel the sunset, and it often creates a sense of joy within our brain-minds that is felt throughout our bodies. Damasio asks: "Why should the construction of perceptual maps, which are physical, neuro-chemical events, feel like something? (2010:254)"

How do physical entities become feelings? His answer is that "No set of conscious images of any kind and on any topic ever fails to be accompanied by an obedient choir of emotions and consequent feelings (Ibid)."

Emotion is this physical, chemical response by the organism's tissue, and feeling is the mind's response to this emotional state: This is standard Damasio. There are two tracks that are always being played in one's mind. First, there is the actual sunset which we perceive, and second is our reaction to, and internal mapping of, that sunset.

Damasio sees this process as being straightforward, and believes there is no longer a mystery in what he calls this process in action; it is qualia I:

There is constant signaling going on between the brain's image-making regions and its emotion-triggering regions. A cascade of events takes place in the back-and-forth signaling process creating a continuous readout of the emotion as a feeling (Ibid: 255).

Qualia II shifts focus from the construction of perceptual maps to the feeling of perceptual maps. "… why should perceptual maps, which are neural and physical events, feel like anything at all (Ibid: 256)."

Feelings always accompany perceptual maps, and the origin of those feelings must be explained. The answer is that "… the body communicates to the central nervous system and the latter responds to the body's messages (Ibid: 257)."

This is a dynamic, bonded unit according to Damasio. We don't distinguish between primary sensations and our reaction to these sensations (feeling) as separate entities. Instead, they are experienced as an integrated whole, or Qualia II.

"Neurons … imitate life so thoroughly that they … become one with it (Ibid)."

Simple unicellular organisms have attitudes even though they do not have brains. Cell irritability, from this point of view, a term which is borrowed from Rodolfo Llinas, continues to retain this irritability when they become collectives in more complex organisms and animals. In our case, as a species with a complex brain, signaling between our brain and body is carried out both with chemicals and electrical excitability within our neuronal circuits. These signals both cause and modulate our feelings.

To make a complex problem shorter, we have neuronal loops between the brainstem and the body and the brainstem – the limbic system and our higher cerebral centers. The success of these interconnected circuits in the brain-mind bring together sensory maps from throughout the body. These maps from the surrounding sensory portals are of a secondary nature, such as the feelings that accompany visual percepts located around the eyes supporting tissue, and maps of the emotional-feeling reactions to these maps.

[Q]ualia is part of the contents that come to be known as the self process, the self construction illuminating the mind construction." "But somewhat paradoxically, Qualia II is also the grounding for the protoself and thus sits astride mind and self, in a hybrid transition. The neural design that enables qualia provides the brain with felt perception, a sense of pure experience (Ibid: 262).

And, it is wonderful!

One should really follow Damasio's logic by pursuing his own words, as his language is eloquent compared to mine. Nevertheless, his approach adds insight to what I've referenced from Llinas's *I of the*

Vortex. Damasio's focus on emotions and how feelings are mapped and come to represent a cascade of reactions within our brain-minds and body help me understand my dreams, altered states, and mental illnesses a little better. Disturb the process by which feeling becomes integrated with body imagery by any means, and problems emerge.

I must always analyze my dreams in terms of attached feelings, and my dreaming brain's reaction to these feelings. I can't just focus on the bizarre nature of my sleeping brain's forms compared to my waking brain's logic and ability to string sensory data together in consistent ways. I have to respect the different neural and chemical systems operating between waking and dreaming, and how these system mechanisms create and string together qualia, with all their gaps, to form different states of consciousness.

FAP DREAMS, QUALIA AND SYMBOLS

If you become a long-term lucid dreamer, your virtual dream world will expand and become richer. It can and does create its own history. My waking consciousness is still amazed at my impossible bike riding feats, even though it understands the necessity of my core consciousness to perform these feats in order to properly hone and embed actual bike balancing.

In other dreams, I may be sliding down stairs by riding on their outward edges from top to bottom as if I were riding a sled. Or I might jump feet first on the banister and perform the same downward sliding action that I could never perform when awake. I experience the goal of my dreaming brain in these scenarios as the consolidation of balance. My muscles are coordinated, vision is involved, and there is a feeling of mastery as well. This fantastic dream scenario supports a very mundane process that is embedding balance. So much for Freud!

The sense of balance mastery in my dreams is expressed as Will during my daytime bike rides. I become aware over a number of bike-riding days that my balance has significantly improved, and further, that fictive bike balancing in my dreams reflects this daytime improvement. My sleeping, dreaming brain is as much involved in my life as my waking brain is. How could it be otherwise?

After a few weeks of bike riding, I no longer consciously focus on balance, I just will the bike to turn and it does. My dreaming brain has fictively helped me embed all the visual and muscle elements supporting balance. This composite gets coordinated with my higher cerebral centers directing bicycle riding in the act of Will. It would be dysfunctional, energy consuming, and time wasting for my higher cognitive centers to ride my bicycle without Will.

Dream practice riding my bicycle under impossible conditions, or performing balancing feats of a superhuman nature, all help embed primary images, or sensations, into a FAP called balance. Most of our brain-mind operations are performed at a non-conscious level by organizing this complex of sensory images (qualia); that 95 percent of our non-conscious brain-mind that is called the collective unconscious.

The Collective Unconscious as used by Lakoff and Johnson is our brain-mind's non-conscious program that directs most of our daily behaviors. This non-conscious form of learning and associated memories dominates our behavior moment-to-moment and day-to-day, as it must for behavior underlying the developmental history of all mammals. Before we mammals had higher cognitive powers, evolution provided for our survival with these basic mechanisms. It still does.

I access this learning to memory embedding process in my dreams by making normally unconscious dream elements become conscious. In terms of Damasio's, *The Feeling of What Happens,* once FAPs are honed and efficiently expressed, I experience a feeling called mastery. My sense of mastery exists when my actions become effortless, when they are directed by Will. This is true for bike riding or university lecturing. This is accomplished intent.

To quote Damasio:

[T]he brain makes neural patterns in its nerve-cell circuits and manages to turn those neural patterns into the explicit mental patterns which constitute the highest level of biological phenomenon, which I like to call images. Continuing he says: Solving this problem encompasses, of necessity, addressing the philosophical issue of qualia. Qualia are the simple sensory qualities to be found in the blueness of the sky or the tone of sound produced by a cello, and the fundamental components of the images in the movie metaphor are thus made of qualia (1999: 9).

And I add the joy of effortlessly balancing as I guide my bicycle with Will on a warm, sunny day, a ride mixed with clean air, the sound of birds, and the chatter of children. At the pre-image stage of development, there are no words:

Whatever plays in the nonverbal tracks of our minds is rapidly translated in words and sentences. Curiously, the very nature of language argues against it having a primary role in consciousness. Words and sentences translate concepts, and concepts consist of the nonlanguage idea of what things, actions, events, and relationships are. Of necessity, concepts precede words and sentences in both the evolution of the species and the daily experience of each and every one of us (Ibid: 185).

One would have to be language-centric to assume that words precede thought, or be oblivious to the findings of neuroscience. I have an overwhelming sense of how accurate Damasio's observations are, as I watch these normally unconscious processes play out in my dreams.

I more fully appreciate why cognitive science oriented individuals like Shapiro do not seriously engage the works of Damasio. To engage Damasio requires that one considers feelings. Understanding how primary sensation becomes Qualia II makes much of the cognitive science literature on language obsolete. Fortunately, we have whole areas of neuro-linguistics and neuro-philosophy developing that are gradually replacing speculations that are not grounded in physiology..

Our bodies are interacting with our environments at a non-language level, and in this process, the very beginning of Self, proto-Self, comes into being. We experience these non-language processes rather directly in dream content analysis as outlined above. And at the macro level, as an entire Being, I interact with you in similar fashion. We evaluate the stranger in seconds or split-seconds. We like or dislike others for no apparent reason. We fall in love in the moment. We are self-to-feeling, feeling-to-feeling, feeling-to-others Beings. Our non-conscious activators of Self are always busy. And Self sits at the center of the vortex directing our actions.

Damasio continues: "The word image does not refer to 'visual' image alone, and there is nothing static about images either. The word also refers to sound images … and to the somatosensory images that Einstein used in his mental problem solving – in his insightful account, he called those patterns "muscular images" (Ibid: 318).

Einstein didn't get hung up on language, but went directly to the bedrock of mental processes with unusual visual clarity, a clarity he expressed in his thought experiments, and a clarity my teen mind found lacking with most other adults. Einstein became my academic hero when I was fifteen, and I discovered thought experiments, general and special relativity. And I eventually came to know why I loved Einstein's thought processes. It is because I visualize in a similar fashion.

The term "representation" is bandied about in cognitive science, but for me, clarity comes with Damasio's use when he says: "I use[d] representation either as a synonym of mental image or as a synonym of neural pattern (Ibid: 320)."

Straightforward use of image ties the phenomenon to the mind and to neural circuits. The goal of explaining mental activity, or thinking, in terms of activity in neural circuits is moved forward when we empirically identify primary images with the formation of qualia. It is also a major step toward understanding how matter becomes mind, and brings us a step closer to understanding how mind controls matter; our neural matter, that is.

Lucidity in my dreams permits direct contact with the neuro-muscular processes which support images that are being embedded in my unconscious brain. Content analysis lets me focus on bridging elements such a bike balance to more fully understand what my dreaming brain is about. The idea of primary images that are tissue embedded helps me understand pre-metaphorical image representation of brain-mind memory consolidation and learning processes. How qualia are being processed to create FAPs explains away a lot of the bizarre events occurring in dream forms. We can observe this process of image making and memory consolidation in our dreams, but not in our waking moments. I feel balance in my daytime bike rides, but I observe the process of it becoming in my dreams.

Minus all the specific physiological mechanisms of image formation and representation in our brains, I think we have a pretty good general handle on how higher order consciousness emerges; being conscious of being conscious.

As I watch FAPs being embedded in my dreams, I come to recognize that this lower level of consciousness permits me to engage in Zen driving as it permits the wolf to stalk its prey. And at the next level of consciousness, re-mapping of mapped primary images makes possible the awareness of being aware. This seems rather straightforward to me, and I think partly answers the question asked by Ramachandran of how the neural basis of metaphor occurs (2004: 57).

Fictive dream expression also helps explain cross-modal abstraction processes. Ramachandran gives an example of asking subjects in different cultures to connect the words Booba and Kiki with visual shapes, and reports a 95% plus consistent responses, thereby demonstrating that cross-modal abstractions seem to be of a universal nature (2004: 77).

Once we stop considering metaphorical concepts as language, as propositional language structures, we identify image making processes that can be studied empirically.

Qualia and their metaphorical counterparts are cross-modal by nature. Chinese from this perspective do not dream using Mandarin or Cantonese. They dream metaphorically the same way you and I do. Our ability to think is directly tied to our body's ability to form images. And re-imaging primary input from our senses creates Damasio's Qualia II, and lays the basis for the protagonist he calls the Self.

I'm speculating, but I think all that has to occur is a little rewiring of primary image processing, and we have synesthesia, a condition where one might see red every time they see the color 5. The mechanism that supports re-imagining of primary sensations just needs one of its wires to be connected to the wrong circuit, and we change the number 5 into the color green. Reality construction occurs in our brains; change the wiring, and reality changes. We must discover our own biology in order to discover our self.

The hierarchy of re-imaging primary sensations that eventually leads to the construction of the Self addresses a number of conundrums in many different areas, from philosophy to neuroscience, and from mental illness to dream flight. And how we come to feel is central to cracking these traditional nuts.

Our minds experience some level of consciousness in brain states associated with daydreams, night dreams, or other altered states. Engaging these processes through lucid dreaming allows us to bring what is normally unconscious into consciousness. Our brains operate on two levels of consciousness: one associated with our old brain, and the other with our new brain. Awareness at both levels can be enhanced through the careful observation of our dreams. Altered states of consciousness are just different combinations of how our circuits are connected at any particular moment. Uncontrolled or controlled states of consciousness rely on the same neural circuits. All I had to do to regain mental health was to teach my Interpreter how to take control of these processes.

From this perspective, when the primitive, old brain executes its programmed routines out of synchrony with our newer brain, all manner of modified consciousness and potential conflict can arise. Conversely, establishing new circuit configurations can eliminate self-activating neuronal expressions we call nightmares. I provide specific examples with traumatic dreams where two different nightmares are eliminated through insight.

Operationally, insight occurs when new neural connections open information exchange between the old and new brains, or between brain subsystems that were not previously communicating. A nightmare example supporting each type of information exchange is given in Chapter 8. New circuit connections bring closure to the trauma causing the nightmare by providing a meaningful interpretation of what is causing the nightmare.

Nevertheless, note that the embedded feelings in our cells must be quieted by identifying the actual event that created our nightmare, or the nightmare will return. We can trick our Interpreter short term, but it eventually catches up with the scam. Freudian dream interpretations would not have produced this quieting effect for me. And if you read his works, it didn't produce positive effects for many of his patients either.

By accurately identifying the element(s) activating our nightmares, our Interpreter must be able to close a self-activating circuit. In terms of my nightmares, muscle memories at the core self level are brought into communication with my higher order thought processes. The result is both circuit closure and establishment of a meaningful interpretation that satisfied my higher order self.

My sexual molestation nightmare is a good example of nightmare iterations that are repeated so many times that each version requires its own removal of feeling in order to become extinguished. Control of feeling can result from accurately identifying the activation elements in one's nightmares or by simply using self-hypnosis to control the feelings, which was my 1958 solution. In my experience, talk therapy that does not address this relationship is of limited value.

We are not able to explain all the specific physiological mechanisms underlying insight elimination of nightmares. I just know how it works psychologically. That is, once the activating stimulus is identified, and the self-reinforcing neural connections are broken, the nightmare vanishes. And in my case, spot on identification with the nightmare spawned by mother's attempts to smother me apparently occurred, as the nightmare never returned even in part.

Intuitively, I suspect that highly traumatizing events that lead to PTS continue to activate fear or flight responses until our new brain is satisfied that the threat is gone. Insight that results from killing the lion or transcending the trauma of war is necessary to reset memory circuits in our old brain.

PTS that many of us experienced stem from severe childhood trauma, which approximates the intensity of war experienced by combat veterans. Related memories creating anxiety and stress can be activated by many different environmental factors for the traumatized child grown up or the combat veteran. Activating FAPs from this perspective have nodes that must look like a bunch of octopi arms, thus the extreme resistance to talk therapy alone.

Traumatic effects of PTS often accompany us to the grave, but they need not. Multiple traumatic events multiply the number of neural circuits involved, the number of auto-created memories, if my two major nightmares are representative examples. With my sexual molestation nightmare, I experienced multiple nightmare scenarios where each seemed to represent a separate experience. After I successfully identified the original nightmare's activation with the deviant farmer in N.W. Wisconsin, I had to separately eliminate each of the other nightmares.

A key point to note is how one traumatic experience can lead to multiple nightmare sequences, with each separate dream in the sequence needing its own resolution. This is a pattern that I believe is not adequately taken into consideration with war victims, or even with rape trauma. For rape and war victims, dream trauma recycling can take on its own life and become endlessly self-perpetuating. My method of breaking this cycle was with self-hypnosis.

The mammalian modular brain cross references sensory information constantly, continuously combines and recombines input into unique configurations, and in this process of pattern construction, comes to define what the total value of this information means to the animal. We each have a physiological mechanism that allows permanent learning with one event. We don't get a second chance to learn that the lion is hungry. But for that thing we call PTS, this basic survival mechanism spreads permanent ink on our neural circuits.

DAMASIO ASIDE

Without question, brain states, both physiologically as well as psychologically speaking, must be kept within fairly strict parameters, or limits. Maintaining, updating, and reorganizing neural circuits are a major part of what dreaming is all about. I think we are safe making this assumption, because so much research is converging around this perspective. The lucid dreamer can become a self-therapist to the degree that he or she understands these processes. In my years as a first year university student, I became a self-therapist by just accessing the relevant brain-mind mechanism that permits reconfiguration of neural circuits and neural networks.

My personal experience expressed in previous writings is that the active, conscious self plays the critical role in reacquiring or sustaining homeostasis, balanced mental health. In effect, we teach our own brains how to control discharge in its electrical circuits and chemical pathways. I approached this problem rather naively as an undergraduate student in the 1950s and took the following steps:

1) I used self-hypnosis to gain control over normally autonomic system functions such as pain and heart rate;

2) I extended my attention span from 20 minutes to eight hours;

3) I stopped and controlled nightmares, thereby interrupting whatever cascade of events were occurring in my brain to keep it off balance.

Additionally, these interventions probably stopped neural circuit damage that was occurring from my brain's own chemical output.

Central to this entire process was active intervention on the part of what I called my Controller, what Damasio calls the Autobiographical Self, and what Gazzaniga calls the Interpreter. It is this central, active process in our mind-brains that is so critical to positive mental health; a sense of control that leads to actual control. In my experience, therapists who attempt to make their clients comfortable or stabilize their thoughts and behavior around some normative perception of consciousness miss this critical difference.

Our goal should be to maximize brain-mind capacity by teaching the Self new forms of control. It is this process of enlarging brain-mind capacity – modifying neural circuit connections and controlling neuro-modulators at will – that brings out the best in each one of us.

I don't think we can approach dreaming, consciousness, or an understanding of how mind can control matter unless the mechanisms underlying self-processes are incorporated in our model.

Dreams and other altered states express different forms of consciousness. Discussing consciousness purely as a state rather than a process puts us back at the level of Descartes or even the Ancient Greeks. Once we elucidate the hierarchical development of consciousness Damasio-style, we can begin to follow the building block processes that lead from primary image formation to qualia and metaphor and eventually to language.

In no way do I want to diminish the importance of cell physiology, or the multiple contributions of neuroscience at so many different levels. But consciousness is a qualitative state which supports self and both are built around qualia. Thus, the feeling of what is, subjectivity, becomes its own unit of study.

As evolutionary complexity gradually emerges over time, successful organisms refine their ability to react to, control, and dominate their environment. Electro-chemical mechanisms come to use multiple cues from one's environment to enhance speed of reaction and survival value. These mechanisms evolve with life, and become a fundamental part of our species history and ongoing life expressions.

Feeling is and has been an integral part of life's history from single cells to complex organisms like us. Feelings enhance survival, and are so fundamental to biological evolution that we often overlook them as we seek to objectively study language or social structure. Surprisingly, many people treat and think about animals as though they have no feelings. This is an anti-evolutionary perspective that doesn't include life. It is an anti-evolutionary perspective that might even be challenged by self-assembling crystals.

Once and agent emerges called self, an agent that in Damasio's words is a protagonist that exists separately in the mind, we have a level of control and ability to direct our futures to a degree possessed by no other earthly animal. We build a world based on culture, with all the potential of empathy, love, and support of mutual interest envisioned in the most satisfying utopias. This is our capacity. It is in our DNA, but it is also a dream not permitted by the power brokers of humanity who seem to live in a world modeling paradigm of the 19th Century.

THOUGHT DREAMS

Referring to the Engine Man's Journal, Hobson says:

Since it is not possible to know the kind of sleep from which the Engine Man's 233 reports are derived, we cannot distinguish between those that fulfill all of the usual formal characteristics of hallucinoid dreams, and those that simply describe thought-like activity occurring in sleep (1988:238).

Thought-like activity occurring in my dreams is often packaged with all the formal characteristics of hallucination. I can be lecturing or holding individual conversations with dream characters about aspects of this book, and the characters and scene settings can morph the same way they do in my other normal lucid dreams. Numerous dream scenarios can occur over the entire course of one night, but the ongoing dream activity in scenario after scenario is the lecture or academic discussion. And I must later interpret these academic activities metaphorically.

Like the Engine Man, I now let my dreams occur naturally, and follow along with dream lucidity and analysis. I have lots of thought-like activity in my dreams. I read extensively and go to bed with new materials that need to be embedded in memory, with new materials that need to be integrated with old memories, and with new research findings that need to replace old ideas.

In terms of memory functions, I don't think this learning-memory process differs significantly from learning to balance on a bicycle. But shifts do occur between core and autobiographical self.

I may wake multiple times during the night to find these streams of thought continuing in one dream scenario after another. Thoughts are manipulated in my dreams in many different scenarios: lectures, discussions, taking tests, or reading a book. Thought dreams mix scenes, characters, and time frames just like any other dream. My brain continues to process at night what is important to me during the day. I balance on my dream bike, and I lecture to my dream students.

In the morning before I get out of bed, I often have explicit thoughts on the same topic or theme that I had when going to bed. These thoughts often reflect progressive analysis and understanding. There is continuity here; I'm mentating in two systems that are in resonance. I'm responding to my world of interest and survival, and my brain's circuits are doing what they always seem to do, that is, consolidating and integrating input from both my internal and external worlds, and forgetting what is no longer important.

My sleeping-dreaming brain goes through cycles like everyone else's – lucidity in REM, and, I think, at least partial lucidity in N-REM. But I'm always aware when I analyze my dreams that I'm not just supporting one function such as memory. I'm multi-tasking. If the salient task is thought, that is my dream's major focus. If it's honing a skill like balancing on my bike, that is my dream's focus. Multi-tasking in my dreams can shift over the course of one night or night-to-night.

SENSORY MODES

Hobson states:

Activation synthesis assumes that sensory—channel selection, as well as the nature and intensity of stimulation—as represented in dream consciousness—will parallel the pattern and intensity of REM-sleep sensory-system activation. Thus, if the visual sense dominates dream reports, there is likely to be visual-neuron activation in REM sleep ... (1988: 238). If audition is less prominent than vision and sensation of movement, and reports of pain are rare, then we can expect to find correlates of the dream 'forms' at the neuronal level (Ibid: 239).

Dream form for Hobson correlates sensory expressions in dreams rather directly with related neuronal sensory activity. I'm not questioning this relationship, but interpret dream forms as being epiphenomenal derivatives of underlying physiological processes. I equate physiological processes with dream function. For example, balancing on my dream bike is a strong visual experience, and undoubtedly there is prominent visual-neuron activation taking place.

Riding my dream bike over impossible terrain as Superman is a bizarre act to our waking consciousness. This is an example of Hobson's forms. This highly hallucinatory dream activity supports memory integration and consolidation according to my dream function interpretation. Hence, dream form is epiphenomenal.

We don't have the same capacity when dreaming to fill in the consciousness gaps as Llinas' says. But filling in gaps is the job of our higher consciousness. Core consciousness is attending to a primary survival function in my dreams. And dream forms of bizarreness and illusion are physiological manifestations of core brain functions. I'm also using the bizarre features of dream form to identify the underlying neuronal activity that is being referenced by dream content.

At one time in my life as a young university professor, I had the leisure to indulge in great music. Violin and piano being my favorites, I spent an hour or two listening to the world's best practitioners daily. My dreams were filled will piano and violin, and my daily walks to and from campus were filled with humming and whistling long and convoluted renditions of my most loved instrumentals.

Day-to-day activity is always represented in my dreams, and those were my days of musical dreams and fictive concert performances. I can no longer recount these dreams in detail except that I'm actually playing the instruments proficiently and the music of a Bach or a Mozart is true to form. And my dream friends are as amazed as I am perplexed at having this ability.

To me, pain is like other ordinary, repetitive bodily sensations occurring daily. It is instinctual and part of my genetic makeup, coming in degrees during the day as I pick prickly cucumbers. Why should it be singled out in my dreams? It is only singled out in my dreams when it represents extreme or life threatening events. It is singled out in my dreams when my normal baseline for pain tolerance is exceeded.

Pain can be either physical or psychic. The two nightmares reported in Chapter six support this observation. One can learn to turn off both types of pain through self-control. For example, Ramachandran has demonstrated a similar technique with phantom limbs.

Movement and accompanying visuals are central to balance, to maintaining our position in space. Maintenance of these functions is required daily as we grow from infancy to adulthood with our physical size changes. Consolidation and integration of muscle and neuronal memory follows suit, and innate genetic expressions such as our sex drive flood the brain with hormones. All these stimuli support active expression in our dreams. Thus, lack of movement is not part of dream expression. That is, unless one assumes motricity is not part of life.

I assume that fictive movement in dreams is efficient because it permits FAP maintenance and/or consolidation of muscle routines. Motor modules are disconnected, or we would be thrashing about endlessly in our dreams. Secondly, visuals are part of the memory consolidation process related to an active organism moving through space along any given trajectory. I'm in tune with Hobson here.

Referencing McCarley and Hoffman's findings regarding REM and N-REM reports, Hobson says:

This result is consistent with physiological evidence of high levels of motor activation in REM and lower levels of motor activation in non-REM sleep (1988:254,255).

My experiential sense when I compare my cognitively-focused thought and lecture dreams with fixed action pattern dreams is to experience my mind-brain operating at different modular levels.

With thought dreams, I'm thinking when I go to bed, and these thoughts continue into early stages of sleep and may continue throughout an entire night of lucid dreaming. Multiple lucid dreams throughout the night center on this thematic train of thought. Later in REM sleep, I create visual images of lectures and conversations that support these thoughts, and upon waking, I often experience insight.

Dream lectures, I'm reasonably sure, represent complex mentation that reflects integration and consolidation of thoughts. With insight, I assume that newly formed neural connections are being supported. Following this subjective interpretation, N-REM is less visual because it represents an earlier formative stage of memory integration and consolidation. REM is more visual as all the pieces are put together, and I ride my dream bike over highly hallucinatory terrain.

Hobson makes clear distinctions between sleep and dream stages as he identifies physiological differences. With the above analysis, I'm suggesting that a functional relationship exists between N-REM and REM forms.

In thought dreams, I also experience the stages of sleep as engaging ideas and concepts in a sequential process of increasing complexity. Something newly learned or brought back into working memory is reviewed and then integrated into a larger working association of metaphorical abstractions. Consolidation of thought dream materials can lead to a morning "aha" where I experience insight or where I'm given directions. Morning "Aha" does happen out of the blue.

My understanding of dynamic integrated systems agrees with Hobson, as stated above, that:

Activation-synthesis suggests not only that each of the imagined movements corresponds to a real motor command, but that the sequence or flow of events in the dream is compelled by such commands. When these commands change suddenly and/or are incongruous as a sequence, a scene change may occur (Ibid: 256).

My bike riding dreams squares with his interpretation.

Hobson's emphasis on the physiological basis for scene changes includes people. Motor impulses are "fixed acts, the behavioral readout of the so-called instincts (Ibid: 256)." My FAP dreams speak directly to this interpretation. The true bizarre elements of our night stories are Freud's dream wishes, not fixed action patterns.

Using the Engine Man's dreams, Hobson continues:

Such elemental motor programs are also available for the enactment of more 'sophisticated' repertoires, such as swimming, flying, spinning, and golfing. And, whatever the nature of the dreamed act, it will often seem to just happen to the dreamer, as if one were a wind-up toy! Or an Engine Man (Ibid: 256).

Non-conscious expression of these repertoires depends on embedded FAPs. And my earlier discussion of Will allows the dream act to occur "as if one were a wind-up toy." The dream act just happens, but it happens for a functional reason. And when we come to understand the metaphorical basis of thought, our front lobes can provide interpretation.

Research supports the forgetting aspects of memory, and individually, we can probably trust our own experience. Forgetting is a process that is also well known to our conscious states, however, what does forgetting mean to the 95 percent of our non-conscious mental activity? A lot! It is one thing to forget the name of an old high school classmate 55 years ago, but another to forget fine motor skills riding one's bicycle.

Does the reader have a conscious memory of how his or her brain gradually forgets fine motor skills? We know when these skills diminish and often feel them sliding into the history of days gone by, but to experience this type of memory loss more directly is currently not possible. Like most of our brain's work, forgetting occurs below our radar screens. As we age, we just notice that something is gone. Neural circuit maintenance and forgetting processes says it must be this way. Forgetting is a natural part of plastic brains.

The only way I knew my bicycle riding and general balance had lost robustness was to get on my bicycle, or stand on the edge of a roof and look down, or try to unconsciously skip over the tops of rocks as I traversed a river bed. Use it or lose it is an apt directive. The use of young people in dream research does not capture these ageing changes, if they show up at all. Physically and cognitively slowing down has its dreaming counterparts in my personal experience.

How memory is recorded in individual cells will probably be known someday, but now it is only hinted at. What we do know is that neuronal mass increases with practice for any skill, and tends to get smaller when skills are not exercised over long time periods. These documented changes are worth noting in our dreams. If you are an older person like me, change your routines and challenge yourself with new skills, learn a new language, study that math you never liked, and watch what happens in your dreams. Like riding on a bicycle, your brain will rebalance. The biggest mistake we make as we age is to seek to have normal thought and behavior for our years, and thereby reduce our mental and behavioral capacities. Ugh!

If you are past the mid-century of life, pay attention to the mundane and banal in your dreams, as you will probably find ageing written large. If you use suggestion extensively, or dream programming, you may "write over" these mundane aspects of dreams and probably miss them entirely.

It is my experience discussing dreams with others that even when we do not actively try, suggestion enters our dreams. Even though I don't dream program any more, or actively use suggestion to change my dreams, or consciously enter them while I'm dreaming, they change on their own. And changes that occur while I'm lucidly dreaming reflect my dream mood at that moment. I remind myself that dream scenarios reflect whatever is going on in my life, and my dreams multi-task.

I don't will my hormones or neuro-modulators to be expressed at any specific level; they are expressed according to how my DNA has come to interact with my environment over time. I don't normally control my heartbeat or body temperature; these aspects of body maintenance are part of the physiological program I was born with and modified over many decades.

In similar fashion, suggestion is expressed at a non-conscious level in my lucid dreams. As an aside, Brooks and Vogelsong explain dream suggestion well both in terms of individual and socio-cultural influences. If I dislike something that is happening, the dream scenario can change itself instantly. This is the type of automatic expression at a mid-level of consciousness that so bedevils the mentally ill. It is this level of control that can be so helpful to extend our concentration, remove anxiety and depression, and generally improve our sense of mastering life's demands. I personally know how beneficial manipulation of these non-conscious processes can be.

My learning how to control and manipulate core memory functions occurred before my ability to program dreams through auto-suggestion and self-hypnosis. Nevertheless, manipulating memory to stop my nightmares was a simple transfer of new capacities that followed learned manipulation of automatic functions such as heartbeat and pain.

Control at this level permitted me to expand my normal brain-mind capacities in dreams and other altered states. To reach this level of control, I first had to practice controlling autonomic body functions such as heartbeat, changing temperatures in my hands and feet, opening clogged sinuses with thought, and shutting out pain. Once these neural channels were open, total dream programming was available of demand. Next, control over unwanted states of anxiety and depression followed with minimum effort on my part. I had enabled my Interpreter, my active Self, to move its normally restricted control over higher consciousness activities to active control over normally non-conscious and autonomic functions

Emergence

Core self yearned to be me,
could only sit at Skinner's knee.
Consciousness embraced becomes
Self with qualia set free.

CHAPTER 5

APPROACHING DYNAMIC INTEGRATED SYSTEMS

INTRODUCTION:

Why do we dream? This question has been asked throughout history, and the answers have commonly been supportive of mystery. Dreams are messages from the gods, dreams foretell the future and dreams put us in contact with other dimensions; or more recently with Freud, dreams are windows to our unconscious. What we humans didn't understand about our own minds, dreams, consciousness, or self, we attributed to other-worldly entities. Dreams as states of consciousness are now understood from a scientific perspective. Dreams are not shadows in the caves of mysticism, but creations of our dynamic integrated brains and minds.

Francis Crick and Graeme Mitchison proposed a different physiological theory of REM – we dream to forget (Hobson, 1988: 296). Their hypothesis has received considerable research support over the intervening decades. Expanding on this dream function, David Linden adds that "... my own guess is that holistic explanation is more accurate: it's likely that something about the cycling between REM and non-REM stages throughout the night is particularly beneficial in memory consolidation and integration (2007: 201). Thus, we have moved from other-worldly explanations for dreams to researchable functions. Holistic explanation is also my guess.

Dream lab researcher Hobson has a professional lifetime that supports this developmental history, and goes on to consider higher order brain functions that are expressed in our dreams. Dreams, consciousness, and self all come under consideration as researchers attempt to fathom the depths of our brain's activity during the night. Dreaming is a required brain activity if we are to achieve positive mental health. Denying sleep and dreams for an extended period leads to death.

A major theme in my interpretation of dreams is that we can achieve improved mental health by learning to interpret and control our dreams. For example, mastering our nightmares brings immediate physiological relief by improving sleep, and mastering nightmares that improve our physiological well-being greatly improves our psychological well-being. In the spirit of neuroscience, we establish a direct link between control of a brain-mind state and mental health.

Historical understanding of dreams through self-observation is referenced below with Hobson's review of Brooks and Vogelsong. I've followed this tradition of self-observation for the past fifty years. I add to self-observation methodology an increased measure of control through the use of self-hypnosis and active manipulation of other altered states of consciousness.

I've explored image formation and qualia in my dreams as elements of embodied cognition. From this perspective, dreams become tools to access non-conscious processes that make up most of our brain's activity day and night. From an integrated, dynamic perspective, I'm focusing on dreams being influenced bottom-up from the "old" brain and top-down from our "new" brain. Evolution cobbles together working architecture in our nervous system to create new functions, and in my experience, interchange between the old and new brains needs a little help to achieve balance, unity, and positive well-being. This help can be gained through active dream control.

Conscious control of dreams and other altered states helped me eliminate negative self-cycling that supported anxiety, depression, and other pathologies. The intervention mechanisms proposed are only partially speculative on my part. However, the results I've obtained are not speculative. Thus I offer correlations and self-observations, not hard empirical research, to support my claims. Nevertheless, positive results from control of these processes seems evident, and at the very least, laboratory manipulation of brain-mind interventions similar to mine under controlled conditions is warranted.

Let me start with pre-scientific thoughts on the unconscious in order to bring this argument into relief. History's lessons imply that the chance of stumbling on the brain's operating mechanisms without carefully executed technology and empirically driven research is next to nil. At least that's been the case for a few thousand years.

PRE-SCIENTIFIC APPROACHES

Freud and his psychodynamic model based on the unconscious are thoroughly critiqued by Hobson (1998: 50-51). I found Freud's *Interpretation of Dreams* totally misleading in the 1950s and not at all helpful. In 1958 he was still the god of dreams and the unconscious. The mental health fortress that his adherents commanded locked out my kind of country bumpkin ideas. And, the lockout came with scorn.

My early studies in anthropology and religion offered schemes that ran parallel to Freud's musings and to those of the then contemporary psychiatric community. It was shamanism disguised in language that seemed, at first blush, to be scientific. As Hobson so clearly points out, Freud was following in the footsteps of ancient, biblical, shamanic, and related traditions. When I tried to discuss these similarities during my early university student and teaching days, my teachers, colleagues, and local psychiatrists were appalled.

Hobson has done a nice job of cementing over Freud's crazy construction of the unconscious, especially in *Out of Its Mind: Psychiatry in Crisis*. The unconscious of Freud is a fabricated construction that is not based on research or even on analysis of his own dreams. Hobson says:

Freud complicated matters further by dividing the un-or sub-conscious into a segment that has access to consciousness (the "preconscious'") and one that does not (the "dynamically repressed unconscious") Freud based his whole theory on mental life, including dreams and psychosis, on this conception. All these categories are just that—artificial constructs (1994: 207,208.

Physiological and dream research has destroyed this pre-scientific model, although there are still adherents. In a similar vein, the last time I looked, there were still flat earth believers, along with out-of-body remote viewers and astral travelers. Hobson calls all the memory that exists in our brains below the conscious level, the non-conscious mind. Here reside all the elements we call instincts, and a multitude of learned action patterns. My non-conscious mind is busy learning, changing, and integrating sensory information constantly. Ninety-five percent of my brain's activity goes on below the conscious level; hence, my non-conscious mind is supporting most of my behavior day-to-day. We watch part of this process in our dreams, and in doing so, open another window in the black box.

However, practicing moving from one altered brain state to another demonstrates that I can consciously engage my non-conscious mind both in sleep and while awake. I would have a lesser sense of wholeness if I was unable do this. I would have less enjoyment in life. I would have a more limited understanding of who I am.

Classical conditioning associates something like a ringing bell with an electric shock, until the organism comes to associate the bell sound alone as the shock, and then seeks to avoid it. We understand this type of conditioning well from past research. What do we call a similar type of conditioning when it is all conducted in one's brain, when the brain comes to administer its own internal shock that perpetuates our state of anxiety, depression or hallucinations?

Uncontrolled fear of leaving one's home is a similar type of conditioning, and it can be corrected through fairly simple behavioral reconditioning or unlearning. Now let's take another step and ask what we call our inability to control hallucinations. This is a form of mental activity that goes on totally within one's mind and is not so easily manipulated. Why?

In my experience, one can learn to manipulate the relevant neural circuits to stop hallucinating. I can redirect my dreaming brain to do the same. I taught myself dream control in 1958, and have had a lot of nighttime fun with it. I also eliminated nightmares, anxiety, and depression with this level of control. My interpretation is: We expand brain-mind functions through self-controls that form new neural connections to override dysfunctional circuit self-reinforcement. "Meta-consciousness" can override micro-circuits and self-reinforcing neural patterns that lead to pathologies such as depression. At least, this is my experience. Permanent organic damage probably limits one's control options.

Following Hobson's research, I assume that when we learn lucid dreaming, we alter our brain chemistry to modify the balance between aminergic and cholingergic systems. Once we learn to desensitize and control the in-mind, mental startle reaction, we have taken a major step to controlling certain unwanted brain-mind states. Before I developed this capacity for self-control, I couldn't stop my brain from sliding into anxiety or depression. In this sense, the startle reaction triggering anxiety is self-primed. This learned, self-primed startle reaction becomes automatic and self-triggering.

Let me provide a specific example. My authoritarian father conditioned me to become hyper-vigilant whenever he assumed a threatening voice or posture. When he assumed an authoritarian voice, my conditioned FAP response to threat immediately surfaced. This response generalized to older men in authority, which in turn left me in a state of learned helplessness. This father conditioned FAP still resides in the interior of my brain, but it has long ceased to control my behavior. If I'm in the presence of authoritarians who attempt similar controls, I just pause, concentrate, and call forth a competing FAP that overrides the threat. I perform this maneuver so quickly and with practiced composure that my father's conditioning is no longer observed by others.

Once I developed controls between my old and new brain, I used my new brain Interpreter to control old brain functions such as heartbeat and pain. I say new brain Interpreter controls because I applied them to mental or body states at will. Traumatic dreams were eliminated along with anxiety and depression. And selectively, I stopped pain in any targeted part of my body, open clogged sinuses, and engaged in Zen driving.

As an undergraduate at the University of Minnesota, I approached tests with ever increasing anxiety. Time lost extended as much as 40 of the 60 minutes allotted. I was conditioning myself to fail. Behavioral self-conditioning of this type doesn't involve conscious decision making, any more than going for a walk involves conscious thought to place one foot in front of the other. Old brains are set to run reflexively on automatic

I interpreted my responses as self-activated behaviors. Thus, I just needed to learn appropriate interventions to gain control. I didn't have contemporary knowledge of the brain. I simply created what we now call cognitive-behavioral intervention, and it worked. However, in the therapeutic world of the 1950s, I was non-Freudian, probably crazy, and definitely not eligible to enter any of the professional or graduate schools at the University of Minnesota. This amounted to sour grapes on my part, but probably was a lucky break, as I went on to experiment outside the box of ancient metaphor and shamanism. The black box called the brain responded to behavioral conditioning, and I eliminated all of my major pathologies. Freud's concept of the unconscious didn't work, nor did his ideas about dreams. And for me, the two were not grounded in science, as I had first-hand knowledge of myth and thought I understood the difference. I still do.

POST FREUDIAN THOUGHTS

As Scott Grafton notes, definitions of embodied cognition address how our memory systems encode knowledge of our physical world, how physical cues are coupled with emotional inference, and possible explanations for the origin of language (Grafton: 2009). I have dealt with all three of these definitional possibilities thus far, and feel quite strongly that self-observation of dream phenomena provides insight into each one of them.

Going beyond artificial computer simulations, Grafton focuses on how people "relate knowledge of their own body to understand other people's movements." Basically, study of athletes demonstrates "that physical experience can improve perceptual ability…interference effects such as these provide indirect evidence that some knowledge about action is embodied, and furthermore, that there may be some form of simulation taking place during action observation." Grafton then speculates that simulation may be occurring through "pure mentalizing." Or, the person may be "matching perceived actions with internal models of the same actions." Grafton's analysis focuses on "how action understanding is achieved through simulation within a framework of embodied cognition."

In my experience, watching this process in our dreams provides us with insight into this process, for example, bike balancing. My Genesis Journey vision is an example of auto-created simulation through pure mentalizing.

I've included Grafton as his analysis represents current research going on in cognitive science. My dream analysis says that simulation is taking place during fictive dream practice, and nightmare resolution also demonstrates the role of pure mentalizing in this process. The difference between Grafton and my analysis is separated by 50 years. We therefore have converging evidence over half a century that supports the dream phenomena under discussion. Add mirror neurons, embedded image formation in bike riding dreams, and conscious awareness of these processes in lucid dreams, and the clarity of pixels in the picture multiply.

We start dreaming in the womb when external stimuli entering the fetus's brain is very limited. It is assumed that our developing brains are laying down neural and cellular structures – neural architecture, that is necessary for our survival. We must be ready to breathe on our own, suckle and swallow milk, process the light entering our eyes, and dozens of other activities necessary for a functioning human baby. Why would nature create a neural support system for learning and use it only in the womb? Clearly, at a level of old brain's development, we share this dream capacity with many other species.

Development is not something that happens until we are born, or until we are teenagers or adults. Rather, development is a life-long process. As we age, the amount of time spent in REM steadily decreases from the womb, infancy, to our aged states. Therefore all the related changes in brain development and functioning are closely related to our age, from prenatal to death. I experience constant changes decade to decade in my dreams, as I think we all do. Dreams content and themes age with our bodies. Our dreams reflect embedded FAPs and qualia that support mentation, and dreams reflect changes in the body-mind connections that support consciousness and self. How could it be otherwise?

I didn't need to learn how to ride a bicycle last year, as I learned that skill when I was 13, but I did need to reacquire the fine motor skills associated with balance of a more accomplished bike rider. I no longer need to learn basic language skills, but I did learn new words one at a time early in my childhood. Language plasticity, like all other forms of brain plasticity, has survival advantage. The demand on my "unconscious" dreaming memory as it consolidates and integrates various learning elements changes through time, as it does for all of us.

I have a typical ageing brain in that my memory is not as good as it once was, with foreign language learning being a good example. On the other hand, integrating my life history in simple, meaningful vignettes is much easier now than when I was twenty or thirty. Various forms of experiential integration are much easier in my dreams, and it's much easier during my waking moments as well. These comparative, historical vignettes surface more frequently in my years of retirement than they did when I was younger. Professional periods in my life, as well as two former marriages, continuously emerge in my dreams much like the music Mozart listened to in his own brain.

Understanding our dreams improves with self-understanding. The greater the insight into our basic personalities, the more fully we understand our dream life. The relationship between understanding our dreams and personalities is critical, since we are all unique in our histories and personality configurations. What are the most important items that you bring to bed each night? What are your conflicts, your struggles, your mundane routines? All of this shows up in my dreams. There is not necessarily direct input from one day into each night's dreams. If I have a major long-standing conflict, this conflict over weeks or months may override less salient emotions from the current day, and mix time events in any combination. .

Our human ability to abstract permits any manner of combined elements to emerge in our dream scenarios. And all of these elements can be and are integrated in wonderfully creative combinations by our dreaming brains. I envision abstraction on the part of our brain-minds as a complex schematic with thousands of patterns laid out on a flat surface, patterns that are of different sizes and are constantly joining, separating and reconfiguring. What a marvelously dynamic thing is brain plasticity.

We discover changes in values and life preferences as we document what is important to both our waking and dreaming states. Lucid dreaming for me was more revealing then waking consciousness until I was somewhere in my fifth decade. Integration of experience that results in new levels of self-awareness comes slowly to most of us. Day-to-day awareness is like bumps in the road. The journey of life that gives us insight and wisdom comes from remembering and integrating the entire journey. Increasingly with age, I have frequent dreams of my life's journey as my brain-mind keeps consolidating and integrating my history. Partly, I assume, because I've been writing books that demand this kind of recall, and partly because this is a natural part of growing older. It's a natural extension of maintaining continuity of self in each day's integration of experiences. My dreaming brain reflects this natural human capacity to project into the future and dip into our history of days gone by. My brain doesn't stop this process just because I'm dreaming.

Use your dreams to find the day's bumps in the road, but also use your dreams as you age to discover why that two thousand mile journey was either mundane or profound. For most of us, it is both. How many windows into self-knowledge does each of us have? In my experience, dreams provide insight nightly that is extremely difficult to get from any other source. Even if your therapist is god-like in his or her insight, they are not available daily. But, your dreams are.

SHAMANIC/OCCULT: SOUL AND NETHER WORDS

In *Mind of the Mystic* (156-162) I reference Shamanism in the Interdisciplinary Context by Leete and Firnhaber, Papers from the 6th Conference of the International Society for Shamanistic Research. In this collection, out-of-body experiences are commonly viewed as immaterial parts of Self, of the soul actually leaving the body and engaging in various different types of activities, flights, and movement in nether world dimensions. No scientifically verifiable model or technology is presented. Material is not simply put in the context of ethnographic reporting, but is left for the reader to interpret from an occult perspective.

In one case, a drug induced out-of-body experience is treated as a means to unlock creativity, and three businessmen are taken to the Amazon Jungle for such a drug induced trip (Narby in Leete & Firnhaber: 14-

20). One can only question the quality of peer review that goes into selection of papers for this conference. This pre-scientific genre of anthropology helps perpetuate the occult musings so popular in American culture. I wonder if academics actually get tenure with these articles.

Ancient and shamanic experiences based on altered states of consciousness (ASC) are viewed by many modern people and select professionals as representing a still unknown and valid reality. The assumption is being made that ASC put us into contact with other dimensions, the spiritual realm, and occult nether worlds where our immaterial soul takes flight from the body and has its own experiences. Failure to prepare oneself through interdisciplinary research drives these musings.

I have been arguing in this three book series that altered states and out-of-body experiences must be interpreted within the context of modern psychology and the neural sciences. Phenomenological inquiry should not be left to occult musings alone.

Today in scientific models, we can account for ASC and OBE experiences by using modern technology in the neurosciences and experimental psychology. I will continue to tie these interdisciplinary threads together in later chapters. Generally speaking, scientifically oriented anthropologists tend to ignore this sub-field.

SUGGESTION THEORY: BROOKS AND VOGELSONG

J. Allan Hobson has this to say about these authors:

It is my pleasure to encourage your careful consideration of the unique body of data that forms the scientific base of this book" *The Conscious Exploration of Dreaming].* "Authors Janice Brooks and Jay Vogelsong provide an admirably detailed set of results from their meticulous and systematic study of the conscious control of dreaming. Their work situates itself in the strong tradition of self-observation of one's dreams (Forward: xiii).

I follow a parallel process of self-observation and self-experiment to these authors with the exceptions of experimenting across altered states and using dream control more explicitly for therapeutic purposes. Brooks and Vogelsong argue that the conceptual model employed by lucid dreamers affects one's observations. This is true in my experience as well.

Brooks and Vogelsong's theoretical stance:

The suggestion theory is grounded in a 'world modeling' of how the mind works, as presented in detail by William James in his 1890 **Principles of Psychology,** and as recently articulated in the work of such researchers as Robert Ornstein of Stanford University (Brooks, 2000: 44).

The model recognizes that we do not interact with the world directly, but our brains form mental maps through our various senses. We always perceive selectively as our senses cannot possibly process all stimuli bombarding us from our larger environment. Simply put, we construct our world through this modeling process. In my experience, world modeling occurs in our dreams as well as during our waking hours; it just draws on a different set of sensory inputs.

What this means concerning dreams is that:

The dreaming brain in effect projects an imaginal environment in which its fancies can play out, an inner staging ground configured from past experience of all kinds by the world-modeling function (Ibid: 50)." And, "Any factor reaching awareness should be able to influence the content of an unfolding dream exactly like a hypnotic suggestion. Our "...shifting thoughts while dreaming can play a major role in directing content (Ibid: 51).

Also,

The most basic tenet of the suggestion theory asserts that while the dream state may be determined by physiology, dream content is determined from moment to moment by awareness interpreting and coordinating various suggestion factors through the world modeling function (1999: 173).

Their most basic tenet resonates with Hobson's early emphasis of dreams being primarily activated by physiology. In context, I'm quoting Brooks and Vogelsong from their 1999 work, and in this historical period, the three authors are in general agreement. I agree with their basic world modeling assumptions, and that conscious suggestion to our dreaming minds while we are in a lucid state can be used to change, direct, and control the dream process. I diverge from Brooks and Vogelsong in three ways:

1) The therapeutic value of dreams;
2) Use of dream content for analysis; and
3) My stress on multi-tasking functions of dreams.

Brooks and Vogelsong provide substantial details about their lucid explorations of dreams, as well as documenting considerable research in support of their theory. Their exploration of dreams, as influenced by suggestion, is objective and well written. For readers who have not learned to control their own dreams and are not familiar with the dream literature, I recommend this book along with Gayle Delaney's method, and Hobson's *13 Dreams Freud Never Had.*

Personally, I used self-hypnosis to gain total control over my dreams in 1958 (Just, 2010, 2011). The reader can realize shortcuts to creating and directing their own dreams and visions by using hypnosis. However, you may prefer Brooks and Vogelsong's gentle approach to dream control as they carefully take you through their suggestion model. Or, practice lucid dreaming techniques for self-awareness and therapeutic purposes as Delaney proposes.

However, from a dynamic integrated perspective, suggestion can play a very creative role in our dreams, either using suggestion while our dreams are in process, or as a before bedtime pre-suggestion that is either of a priming or hypnotic nature. Within the larger systems model that I'm proposing, use of suggestion can further our basic understanding of dreams because it permits endless self-experiments. Dream suggestion only addresses one altered state, but we can use active control in any altered state.

Brooks and Vogelsong's focus on lucid dreaming provides considerable insight into their experiences. My goal in this book is a little different in that I want to address the larger and related questions between all major altered states of consciousness and mental health. Self-observation, especially when it is combined with conscious manipulation of brain states, offers a unique window from which to explore altered states and consciousness. In my case, conscious manipulation of altered states was extremely important to my mental health. I will come back to Brooks and Vogelsong in Chapter 16.

However, before I turn to Delaney, Brooks and Vogelsong have this to say about long-term lucid dream practitioners:

They "… may find that sheer repetition habituates certain characteristics of their individual approaches to lucid dreaming into the rest of their dream lives (2000: 27)."

Dream characters, special settings, and what I might call dream history cocoons, are part of my dream repertoire that continues to be elaborated as I age. The Inner Voice in my dreams that frequently gives me advice, interprets my dreams while they are in process, or helps direct the writing of this book has been active many nights. I'll add the following section on "dream sanctuary" at my Inner Voice's urgings.

DREAM SANCTUARY

On May 6th, I woke about 5:00 a.m. dreaming about being at Mankato State University where I used to teach. I was talking to old friends and reminiscing about our younger teaching days, life, and all the changes that have occurred over the years. There were elements in these discussions that covered various programs that my old department sponsored, and I was thinking about the various contributions I'd made to most of them. When I got up to use the bathroom, my Inner Voice was telling me that I've not adequately dealt with this aspect of dream history, and my Inner Voice labeled this and similar dream scenarios that are often repeated as "sanctuary."

There are comfortable and familiar sanctuaries that I go to any given night, many nights in a row, or a few times each month. But the one thing that is clear is that I go to my dream sanctuaries more often as I age, especially when I'm alone, which is my case at this moment of writing. My wife is in China for seven weeks, and I feel the loss of her comfort in many different ways.

Today, May 7th, I woke at 4:15 a.m. from a dream visit to my home town of Cumberland, known as Island City, Wisconsin. I lived in or near Cumberland for 12 of my first 18 years, and have always referred to it as my home town. It is the one geographical place on Earth that my body recognizes. I relax and feel in harmony with both people and nature once I'm within a few miles of my home town. When my dreaming brain searches for geographical sanctuary, this is where it goes.

In this dream, I'm talking to my brother and others whom I recognize and some who are unfamiliar. This discussion takes place on his farm. The scene morphs, and I'm in Cumberland itself, walking down the street and observing what has changed. Actually, in this dream I'm mentally changing the community more than it has physically changed over the years. But, I have a sense of belonging, and being with people who have no other motive than a shared history. I don't pay attention to most of the details in my sanctuary dreams anymore; I just enjoy the sense of being in a friendly cocoon.

I got up at 4:30 a.m. as I was wide awake, and my Inner Voice was telling me to include this dream in the Brooks and Vogelsong section. I got up, ate breakfast, and read while waiting for delivery of the morning paper. By 7:15 a.m., I felt sleepy, the house was quiet, and I went back to bed for a nap. I returned to Cumberland again in my dreams, and had an extensive conversation about the community's infrastructure repairs. My conversation was with a nondescript person who questioned whether or not new water and sewer lines were actually in place. I assured them that I had visited while the work was being done and observed the replacements personally.

I woke up a second time at 9:00 a.m. and recalled that I first had this repair dream in the middle of the winter. I visited a friend living across the street from the now removed old sewer plant in January. Following this trip to Wisconsin, I re-visited Cumberland in a dream and observed repairs being made. The same in-dream ageing pattern happens with Mankato State University; I return for academic discussions on current topics, but also reminisce about actual historical events.

Twelve of my first 18 years of development took place in or near Cumberland, and my beginning professional years as a teacher occurred over 13 years at MSU. These are dominant periods of time in my life that I use repeatedly in my dreams, and they grow and change over the years. Changes are ongoing, characters age, and dream discussions are put in historical context as they are in real life encounters. I often reminisce with old friends and colleagues in these dreams and have focused academic discussions as well. But dream sanctuaries are different from waking use of memory, as dreams can and do mix and match any combination of memories that suits one's ongoing plot or emotional needs.

DELANEY

I will review two aspects of Delaney's approach to dreams:

1) How she uses bridging elements to interpret dreams, and,
2) How she uses metaphor to shed light on dream functions.

Delaney's model is critiqued in the Forward of *Break Through Dreaming,* by Hobson. I'll borrow a number of his empirically supported observations:

1."And when we enter the rapid eye movement (REM) stage of sleep—and we dream--brain activity is as high as when we are startled during waking (xiii)."

2. There is a high level of electrical activation in the system which "…could support the very rapid and extensive information processing that might be involved in memory search for the most appropriate image, metaphor to interpret the disparate (and/or emotionally conflicted) elements that the mind is trying to combine in a coherent dream plot (xv)."

I'm being redundant, but in my experience, the process of forming dream plots is critical to understanding the functions supported by dreams. Using my bike balancing dream as an example, my brain is "grabbing" elements from recent day-to-day experiences as well as older memories to create a coherent bike riding plot. Most of my bike riding occurred in the 1970s. Thus, my brain brings together a thirty to forty year time span.

In lucid dreaming, my Interpreter is always active and attempts to explain the dream according to what makes sense to my waking consciousness. Waking consciousness seems to be somewhat of a misnomer; meta-consciousness that cuts across dreaming and waking states seems more appropriate.

Memory selections supporting dream biking are rather arbitrary. My dreaming brain grabs any memory element that supports the function of embedding related fine motor skills. In this dream, memory elements covering a span of forty years adds numerous bizarre features to this dream. Interpreting this dream in terms of the skill function it serves helps me explain much of the bizarreness of Hobson's dream forms.

3) There is a high level of electrical activity associated with this process. My dreaming brain must be scanning "tons" of circuits to provide visuals in real dream time. Hobson notes from a neural physiological perspective that: "Both sensory input and motor output [is] actively blocked by specific brain mechanisms. Thus there is no need … for the system to be 'realistic' in the way that it must be to function effectively in waking (xvi)."

Meaning that our dreaming brain is in a world of its own, is highly active and accessing a multitude of available sensory elements. However, it is also engaged in a process of plot formation that constantly tries to derive coherent meaning from all of these activities. Dream plot scenarios are required to provide internal continuity to sensation when the external environment is missing. I think there is little doubt that we humans always try to create meaning from our total sensory input whether awake or dreaming. I couldn't get downstairs to breakfast without this mechanism.

4) Emphasizing the strong visual nature of dreaming, Hobson says: "… it does seem reasonable to assume that there is an active, instantaneous, and ongoing collaboration between the brain's highly activated and self-stimulated visual centers and the language area that identifies the imagery, names, and organizes it—as best it can—into a narrative (xvi)."

My dream experiences resonate with the visual-language collaboration addressed by Hobson. But I want to distinguish between "motor" dreams such as balancing, and "thought" dreams like those of my dream lectures. Image formation in skill acquisition dreams such as fictive bike balancing is basic, and I assume common to all mammals, but symbols at the level of abstraction that Lakoff and Johnson call complex metaphors, are experienced in my dreams as representing higher order abstractions.

Metaphorically, qualia have feelings and value attached: A rose is not just a plant on our landscape, but one that evokes feelings of pleasure. Metaphorically, a rose can be that lovely woman sitting next to me on the airplane, or Shakespeare viewing Juliet as the morning sun.

Metaphorically, bike balance is not just an embedded physical posture. At my higher cognitive level, it can balance my checkbook or balance my life. And consciousness at various levels is almost always accompanied by supporting visuals.

Thought occurs through the manipulation of complex metaphor, and as a derivative language, can be used to describe our thoughts. However, primary image formation at its most basic level does not require the new brain of Homo sapiens. I'm guessing that basic image formation is the same process for other mammals as it is for me. However, as a big-brained primate, my dream interpretations require consideration of at least three levels of brain-mind states.

In thought dreams, my brain is free to use metaphorical concepts as abstractly as it does in my waking moments. Thus, the three distinct dream states represented are basic image formation, primary metaphor, and complex metaphor. I caution the reader to think in terms of three different levels of image formation, as the terms used vary across disciplines. I will continue to address these distinctions throughout this book. Dream logic does not have to reach the level of waking logic, even though it does at times. Embedding skills in dreams does not require logic, even though my brain tries to impose it.

When I visualize this process physiologically, I see complex neural connections being made as dendrites and cells communicate in all manner of creative interplay. Basic image formation by our old brains forms the substrate to help shape complex neural circuits in our new brains. Secondary re-imaging of primary images becomes Qualia II, and secondary re-imaged images can themselves become re-imaged as cognitive levels of abstraction increase.

Thought dreams must require internal communication across these three levels as I assume waking thoughts do. At least, thought dreams require manipulation of simple and complex metaphor. This assumption necessitates exchange across the brain's hierarchy during lucid dreams that are filled with metaphor and abstractions: Hence, my derived assumption that the brain-mind functions as a dynamic integrated whole when we are awake or dreaming. And from my reported dreams, the degree of communication across brain states increases with age.

The new brain of Homo sapiens does not seem to be fully integrated with our mammalian old brain when we dream. A process of ongoing brain state integration as we age runs through this book as a theme. It is self-apparent to me that brain-mind integration is facilitated through lucid dreaming and conscious control of altered states.

I did not have this awareness 50 years ago when I started dream programming. Dreams are part of my holistic survival, and reflect my unique history as a sensing, cognitively active person. Dreams provide a window into our species evolution, from planning and action based on non-language images, to complex metaphorical thought dreams.

Therefore, I agree with Delaney that dreams are metaphorical in nature, and with Hobson that dreams "… are uniquely valuable tools of self-understanding (Ibid: xv)."

The dreamer must be taking perceptual, cognitive, and emotional elements from across the mind's total landscape to create plots, stories, and emotional reminders of what is important to us at any moment of dreaming. As an older person, I find it easy to locate Delaney's bridging elements in my dreams, because bridging elements become increasingly prominent with practiced analysis. They also stand out because most of my dreams are devoted to memory or mundane functions. Bridging elements are like bumps in the road, and with dream analysis practice, they become larger and hard to miss.

Hobson refers to these bridging elements as "huge inferential leaps: Such leaps are likely to reveal our psychological biases, our fears, and our hopes, which might, in the interest of efficiency, be best represented in a symbolic or metaphorical way (xvii).

I make these leaps when awake as I often make them while dreaming. I think Delaney details this process well with her bridging techniques of dream interpretation. The process has worked for me for the past fifty years. It has been an essential mechanism to remove long-term nightmares, or simply used to interpret ordinary dreams. Most bridging elements in my dreams are not huge, but for major fear-driven nightmares, they are.

Bridging elements emerge in my dreams from both old brain and new brain activity. Balance on my bicycle that is of a highly hallucinatory type is basic old brain image formation associated with learning and memory. Bridging elements in my nightmares were triggered by muscle memories. However, bridging elements of an abstract nature such as my dreams telling me to pay attention to certain ideas to or change parts of this book, operate at a higher level of consciousness. And my higher consciousness observes all of these bridging elements.

All bridging elements do not represent the same level of consciousness. Highly hallucinatory dream actions where I ride over impossible terrain are bridging elements for my FAP dreams. Loneliness reflects my need for association with loved ones. The "aha" sensation is my reaction to complex problems that I solve in my dreams. Thus, dream bridging elements may represent basic image formation, keys to emotional states, or complex metaphorical concepts that have been successfully manipulated.

Normally non-conscious elements, muscle memories allowed me to resolve my nightmares. Metaphorical cognitive elements such as "sanctuary" represent higher order abstractions, as do reported dream manipulations of CDs and CZs. Note that basic tissue embedded nightmare images must be bridged to a symbolic level in order to remove the nightmare's power. Opening communication between our old and new brains becomes complicated when we are required to bridge two levels of consciousness. In my nightmare resolutions, I bridged muscle memories that were related to metaphorical abstractions.

Identifying where dream content comes from helps me understand the "… associative and representational nature of information processing (xix)."

I do this by identifying the source of dream content, and recognizing that my dreams are multi-tasking by serving different purposes that address ongoing needs being processed by different brain modalities.

I agree with Delaney that metaphor is a picture-type language. That, "Every night we take a sort of CAT scan of our psyches and examine the dynamics of the problems and challenges we face while awake (1991: 4); and that "… many dreams reflect a form of sophisticated thinking, problem assessment, and problem solving (1991: 6)."

Delaney emphasizes the dreamer's unique history and individualism, and helps guide her readers through a process to learn the language of dreaming. Right on!

I use language to communicate socially, as I'm doing with this book. But I use Delaney's picture language, metaphorical concepts, to explore my subjective Self and all its dream products. When I travel to the beginning of time in a vision such as my Genesis Journey, picture language says it all, even though I know that complex metaphorical processes make the journey possible. In this journey, I not only visualize 14 billion years of cosmic evolution, but I also physically hit the plasma wall of its birth.

Visions are vivid, visual journeys that can exceed our real life daytime experience. I suspect my neighbor's dog doesn't have visions of Mother Mary or of my Genesis Journey. Dreams I share with the dog are those of old brain functions, as it too must embed FAPs. Visions that create God or the gods, I suspect, are also quite dependent on my higher order cognitive centers. Language is involved in neither. This suggests two different pathways to neurologically based pathology: old brain and new brain.

Hobson critiques Delaney from a researcher's perspective, and says that she is not in conflict with neural physiology. His critique helps highlight basic dream processes for me. Delaney's therapeutic work demonstrates how one's mental health can be improved through dream analysis. I find her work resonating well with my own self-experiments over this past half century. Her dream interpretation techniques are especially helpful to those who are exploring new dream discoveries. Nevertheless, I find a few differences between Delaney's interpretations and my dream programming and therapeutic experiences, which I address below.

CRITIQUE OF DELANEY'S DREAM DICTIONARY

The back flap of her book *In Your Dreams* provides this quote:

"At last, an intelligent dream dictionary—by an internationally renowned dream expert! No one-size-fits all dream formulas here: Gayle Delaney provides simple, personalized tools to uncover the unique meaning in your dreams." And, Delaney says: "This is why I have written a new kind of dictionary—one that, like the old fashioned kind, lets you go straight to the theme or image you are curious about. But unlike those rigid books, this dictionary will show you how to discover the very personal meaning of your dream in an engaging, interactive, and informative way (1997: 3)."

I find her dream interpretation methods to be helpful, but her discussion of dream themes and elements offers a narrower interpretation than my experience dictates. Delaney says:

Yet deep down we know our dreams must mean something, and when we dream the same dream more than once, we can't help but think that our sleeping mind is trying to tell us something important. In fact recurring dreams signal recurring situations often indicate that we are stuck in a rut in our personal or work life. In most cases, our common dreams represent a recurring theme or problem in our lives (1997: 6).

I often interpret themes in my dreams this same way. But long-term dream analysis through the decades offers some refinement.

Conflicts and myriad life problems of my youth and young adult years have been replaced with contentment and a very stable lifestyle. It is rare to have a theme dream filled with conflict, but I occasionally do. The larger gestalt patterns unfolding in my life reflect contentment and stability. Delaney works in a therapeutic setting with her partner, and uses dream analysis for insight and therapy. Her work environment supports therapeutic client interventions; thus dream themes in this setting vary considerably from my uneventful days devoid of stress.

Most of my theme dreams reflect changes in my emotional well-being that generally deviate from a baseline of contentment, or what Delaney calls being "stuck in a rut in our personal or work life."

My Chapter 7 provides examples of both types of dreams. The Conflict dream addresses my emotional well-being. Theme Dream I is a reflection of my efforts writing this book. Generally I'm in agreement with her analysis. Nevertheless note that environment changes dream themes considerably, as do the effects of ageing.

However, consistent elements in my dreams tend to be memory related, such as those in my FAP dreams. My thought dreams are highly metaphorical, and this type of dream is not discussed by Delaney. I interpret dream content by triangulating it with dream function, with my bike balancing dream being a good example. Thematic dreams like my "Heaven on Earth" scenarios have their own evolutionary history as do dream characters like Jane.

The above paragraph stresses the importance of age and type of setting as these influences have major impact on dream themes. Therapeutic settings for dream analysis will generally involve people without my present level of contentment. Dream labs or home dream hookups will introduce body sensations into dream differently. And each of these two settings subtly introduces suggestions about what one should expect. That is, if I'm reading the literature correctly.

In my experience, dream elements represent the mind-body-environment totality. Elements range from balancing on my bike to segments of dream lectures; from physical stimuli of the moment entering my dreams, such as temperature changes, or my wife's touch. I interpret dream elements in terms of three major underlying brain-mind functions: emotion-feeling, memory, and symbolic processing at higher cognitive levels, or any combination of these three. I cannot interpret my dreams without these contextual considerations: Meaning is subjective and contextual.

Elements in my dreams can be very concrete or highly abstract. The same element, such as a gun, can be either. Interpretation depends on the context of the elements and their accompanying feelings. And, I'm also stressing that activation source related to function must be addressed in any dictionary treatment of dream elements. Nevertheless, my dream interpretations have considerable overlap with Delaney's.

In terms of themes, there are as many themes as there are ways to think and organize one's world, both our inner and outer worlds. Creating dream themes is a process of an active brain with higher integrative capacity and its own unique history. Each of us learns organizational schemes from our culture, parents, and educators.

Knowing one's preferred manner of organizing his or her world is a starting point to understand dream themes. Themes from this point of view, like dream elements, are as individual as our DNA. To Delaney's credit, she employs case histories to address these issues, as does Hobson.

Religiously oriented people may organize around gods, God, or spirits. Atheists organize differently. Trained scientific minds have their own organizational schemes. Themes will reflect all of these differences. Animals are now so infrequent in my dreams that they are basically inconsequential. However, when I was eight years old, they were prevalent. Now I'm without pets. I don't even own goldfish.

In her scholarly presentation, Delaney often references dream interpretations of the ancients, and sometimes similar rigid interpretations by Freud and other psychoanalysts. Both ancient and Freudian approaches generally depended on artificial constructs, which were then interpreted from a rigid framework. Chapter 16 on dream dictionaries covers some really bizarre interpretations of content that easily compete with Freud's analyses.

As I age, major prior life events from marriage, university, jobs, and salient events in my life keep churning and reorganizing in terms of their evolving importance, and in this process take on new meanings and values. I experience my brain-mind engaging in an ongoing dynamic integration. I sense the dynamic circular neuronal loops as neural circuits modify, change and become something new. Life's meaning is invented, reinvented, and ever changing. It is an expression of my total Being, which is experienced throughout the day and the night. And all of this is built on the plasticity of my brain-mind.

DYNAMIC INTEGRATED SYSTEMS

I've placed Hobson's theory of activation-synthesis and its update at the top of this review. Unquestionably, physiology plays a critical role in dream generation. Through his professional career and retirement, Hobson continues to add new insights to his model to account for higher order cognitive elements in dreams, and the use of dream interpretation for therapeutic purposes. I'm trying to pay proper tribute to his evolving insights and research without ignoring significant changes in his perspective over time.

What I'm calling waking dreams, or visions, must use a similar combination of neural circuits that are active in REM, along with other neural circuits and networks that are active during the day. The effects I experience in visions have the sensory feel of REM along with the reality and continuity of daytime consciousness.

Visions and hallucinations are probably employing similar auto-creative mechanisms. It appears that mechanisms supporting dream consciousness and those that support waking visualization are distinct and can be activated simultaneously. Actually there is not much speculation involved as I report this type of double imaging from personal experience. If I control visions during waking hours on command, why should I not be able to control spontaneous hallucinations on command?

In my Genesis Journey, I closed my eyes and almost immediately set off to explore the beginning of time. This suggests that I might have employed the same movie making mechanisms that I use in REM. In the vision where a departed soul returns in the Native American honoring ceremony (Chapter 11), visual and auditory sensations from my surrounding environment are true to life, while the vision of the young man is superimposed on this normal reality. Again, this suggests two parallel visualizing mechanisms are operating simultaneously.

The smothering nightmare reported in Chapter 8 offers an opportunity to watch these processes in slow motion. I'm sitting in a yoga position when the entire room and two other persons begin to fade. Gradually a vision of my mother starts to appear. As she approaches my crib, her distraught appearance dominates the mixed visuals, and after a few seconds, her image totally commands my senses. The room I'm sitting in and all its contents disappear. I then experience the pillow mother is carrying blotting out all my senses, and all the visuals in my mind yield to total blackness.

These examples suggest to me that dream visualizations operate on a separate set of neural circuits/networks than normal visual sensory input received from one's external environment. In my examples the two networks, as I shall now refer to them, can operate in part or in whole at the same time. They can fade in or out like the orchestration of a Hollywood movie. One can dominate the other, and this pattern can change momentarily. This morphing feature in visions is typically experienced in slow motion, but in dreams, bizarre forms morph instantly.

Homo sapiens at our current level of evolution have developed extended memories of the past which we project as far into the future as we desire. Feelings derived from emotional states are embedded as qualia. We feel everything or we are not conscious, and as Damasio says, feeling establishes the protagonist which makes consciousness possible. Mobile creatures require action priorities, thus, emotions are given differential meaning and value as they are normally attached to motor activity.

In that the vast majority of brain-mind behavior is controlled at the non-conscious level, we recognize that two levels of consciousness exist, and are differentially made available between waking, dreaming, and trance states. Ability to hallucinate seems to be a universal human capacity which is normally regulated by non-conscious mechanisms; that is, unless we are dreaming. The fact that a shadow in moments of extreme tiredness can become a "vision" of an intruder speaks to this common capacity.

Early Behaviorists such as Skinner failed to provide for the conscious role of the mind in the creation of meaning which supports the interpretative process of an organism that is active in a dynamic environment. Skinner's Behaviorism helped me learn how to directly intervene in non-conscious processes, but was wanting in terms of understanding higher order aspects of Free Will or any of the full range of ASC under my control. In the 1950s, I had to fill in these pieces on my own. And in my personal history, employing an active Interpreter in multiple states of consciousness, the only thing that made sense was to think in terms of a Dynamic System.

A physiological-psychologically integrated model must account for brain stem activity with a feedback loop to the frontal lobes, our active prediction of events in the future, the role of sensation and feeling in a mobile organism, as well as our ability to create meaning – that process that interprets an active relationship to our total environment. I must account for all of these phenomena as I bring together my sense of self and consciousness both in dreams and waking states, especially when I play with the extremes of visual-motor phenomena called altered states.

Hobson has outlined two major neuro-modulator systems that operate at the physiological level – the aminergic and cholinergic. Brain chemicals, functions, and neuronal network activation are all changed as one system becomes more or less active in REM compared to when we are awake. Hobson's extensive work documenting the operation of these two systems was a major initial step beyond Freud in the creation of a real science of dreams. It was a major step that eventually put the Freudian unconscious out of business.

Once Freud's ancient, myth-based dream interpretations were put to rest and his interpretation of the unconscious corrected, what were we left with? Perhaps the answer is parallel universes called altered brain states. Hence, a physiological understanding of dreams is a large nail in the coffin of mysticism. A physiological interpretation of dreams and other altered states is one step closer to the conquest of mental illness.

DYNAMIC SYSTEMS ASSUMPTIONS

1. The limbic system represents an earlier stage of evolutionary development that gives animals enhanced survival ability. Fear or a more basic equivalent is even found in bacteria and simple life forms. Non-conscious processes in my brain-mind control 95 percent of my waking behavior. Our brains maintaining and updating these neuronal processes can be observed as is the case with select fixed action pattern dreams.

2. Higher order cognitive processes that enhance my survival can be observed as conceptual metaphor in my dreams. Both metaphor and primary images supporting FAPs are experienced as bridging elements in my dreams.

3. Communication between lower and higher brain centers occurs primarily at a non-conscious level. This form of intra-communication is observable through dream analysis, especially in terms of how one's dreams employ complex metaphor and symbolic abstraction. I experience insight in a dream, or upon waking, or I simply become aware through dreams that I know something that I've not consciously thought about during waking moments. The metaphor and symbolic abstractions in REM get translated into waking logic late in the night's dreams, or immediately following moments when I wake up and clear the cobwebs.

Lucid dreams put me in touch with preconscious abstract processes and related dream machinations. There can be an "aha" awareness in my dreams that parallels the "aha" of daytime discovery, or the "aha" can occur after waking as I reflect on the nights dreams. It is an efficient and energy conserving mechanism for my brain to continue its work at night. Long-term lucid dreaming seems to facilitate communication between different brain-mind subsystems. Muscle memory is tuned, cognitive awareness sharpened, and emotional states articulated with consciousness.

4. Dream content is unique to each person, and the symbolic interpretation is context and culture dependent. For example, ghosts don't appear in my dreams because I don't believe in them, but angels did when I was two years old. Focusing on imagery and symbols in dream content requires that I acknowledge how feelings and cognitive elements are being physiologically processed. Feelings are typically expressed metaphorically as with my spousal conflict dream. Abstract dream elements can be bridging elements such as "Sanctuary," or strung together in what I've called thought dreams. Complex metaphor can be an abstraction of feelings and metaphorical abstractions can represent a composite of cognitive-emotional elements.

5. Elements in dreams seem bizarre when we use interpretations common to daytime consciousness. Riding a bicycle over impossible dream terrain no longer seems bizarre to me when I consider what function this dream is supporting. I'm quite sure that this fictive rehearsal is related to improved bicycle balance day-to-day. Visual cueing is part of balancing, and it is the feeling of balance in this type of dream that identifies it purpose.

6. Most dreams do not represent repressed feelings or wish fulfillments. My dreams permit me to bring functional elements that lie behind dream imagery into awareness. Thus, feelings in my dreams are often more representative of what is going on in my core consciousness than my daytime consciousness is paying attention to. And this evolutionary mechanism supports our survival much as FAPs do.

7. Highly charged dream elements (emotions) can be repressed at either a conscious or non-conscious

level. Trauma in infancy, which is one of my case examples, can be repressed through brain damage, or controlled by making the acts of trauma concrete, as I did by creating a ghost.

8. Traumatic events that occur in an infant or child's life before they have adequate language to express what has happened to them represent special problems for the therapist who is language dependent. My nightmares serve as examples of non-language trauma resolution. I believe there is a whole area of childhood trauma that is best accessed and treated by teaching both adults self-analysis and self-interventions. A Delaney "picture" approach to dream analysis is helpful with children.

9. Dream analysis can be a significant contributor to positive mental health. Resolution of nightmares and PTS are obvious examples, however, day-to-day analysis permits one to get in touch with primary emotions at a level not possible with daytime only observations. Teaching combat vets to turn off nightmares is a good starting point from which one can generalize control over non-conscious processes.

10. Understanding how the mind-brain processes dreams provides considerable insight into the historical interpretation of visions, religious dogma, and occult musings. Altered states of consciousness are just different neural configurations, and these configurations can be brought under conscious control without employing shamanic rituals.

11. Controlling, directing, and interpreting dreams, nightmares, and other altered states contributes to our knowledge of brain functions and consciousness beyond information that one can obtain with intrusive methods. Analysis of each separate altered state makes its own contribution, which can be enhanced through controlled self-experiments.

HISTORICAL CONTRIBUTIONS TO DYNAMIC INTEGRATED SYSTEMS

I became familiar with Henri Beaunis (1830-1921) after reading Hobson's *The Dreaming Brain.* I was somewhat surprised that my personal observation paralleled those of Beaunis. I was even more surprised to discover how insightful Beaunis was compared to the later Freud.

Hobson's summary of Beaunis' research represents an early form of Activation-Synthesis Theory. Key ideas from Beaunis that resonate with my experience are presented below.

1. By taking the necessary precautions, one can be confident in the memories of dreams available upon awakening.

2. There must be three phases of the dream generation process:

> A) The first phase is a primary excitation which can be either external or internal; this leads to the secondary elicitation of a memory as the excitation spreads to the 'cerebral centers.

> B) The second phase, the excitation of memory, can sometimes occur without any primary sensation due to a single change in the pressure or chemistry of the blood, which may act directly on a cerebral center so as to trigger the occurrence of a memory as the starting point of a dream.

C) In phase three, the activity then spreads to other centers of the brain: the sensory, the motor, and the association centers where the full dream experience is elaborated.

3. Dream memories can be recent or remote or both mixed together.

4. In general, dream content corresponds to current wake-state activity, but there are remarkable exceptions to both the sensory and the motor representations of these (Hobson: 1988: 76).

5. The order of clarity in dreams is visual, auditory and then tactile.

6. "[D]ream content was determined as much by intrinsic factors as by the nature and quantity of previous experience."

7. There was a "… predominance of what he called motor images."

8. He noticed that dream content changed as one ages.

Hobson notes that:

Between the ages of thirty and thirty-five Beaunis had a great preponderance of what he called visual motor content, including flying; whereas after the age of fifty, he no longer experienced these magical movements. Likewise, at fifty, 'grotesque' content stopped, and he more commonly experienced what he called intellectual dreams with subjects more directly linked to his professional activity (Ibid: 74-76).

Beaunis was impressed that he never drew or wrote in his dreams, even though his waking life was full of this activity. As reported in my muscle dream, common day-to-day activities are not reinforced at a level that enters my consciousness. However, re-activation of long unused action patterns do, as exemplified by my bike riding and drawing examples.

Two other figures that speak to rediscovery of historical dreaming elements come from J. Mourly Vold and Mary Arnold-Foster. In the case of Vold,

He believed that in sleep an abnormal muscle state could excite the motor cortex, thus causing a central motor command." The nervous signals produced by the motor stages go not only to the motor cortex but also to the visual centers to produce an image (1896), (1988: 77).

Lastly, Arnold-Foster experimented with autosuggestion and dream control. "She found, as have all those who have attempted to replicate Hervey's methods, that following self-arousal, it is possible to return to the same dream on going back to sleep. (Ibid: 79).

Arnold Foster thought that dreams can be controlled and represented a "… psychological concomitant of a distinctive physiological state, and thought that Freud's emphasis on the psychopathological aspects of dream formation was exaggerated, if not completely erroneous (Ibid)."

Hobson muses that it is odd that these early dream researchers are so seldom cited in dream literature. I know from my days as a university student and later during my early days as a university professor, anyone who questioned Freud was denying the truth of the Ten Commandments. My professors, when I questioned Freud, acted horrified, and simply used their authority to shut the discussion down. Consequently, I spent decades on my own simply pursuing what seemed like a logical progression of dream analysis.

A positive aspect of this hiatus was my consideration of all altered states as researchable phenomena. Rejecting Freud and psychoanalysis also gave me freedom to explore my own theoretical ideas. Hobson's research offers hard empirical evidence for the demise of Freud. Dream lab research and physiological studies of the brain have permanently buried Freudian misconceptions, and science continues on its often slow and arduous ways. The thumb of authoritarian thought cannot forever squelch the voices of inquiry.

WAKING-DREAMING COMPARISONS

By 1958 I had rejected Freud and embraced behaviorism. Behaviorism at mid-century was applied to numerous areas of conditioning, but offered little insight into higher order pathologies such as schizophrenia, which the MMPI said was one of my problems. I had to add an active, thinking agent to behaviorism to explain how I could program dreams and control altered states. It was a paradigm shift for me that no one else seemed to embrace. I added model features from Symbolic Interactionism, social psychology, some perspectives from Gestalt and Humanistic Psychology, and then "winged" it. All of these ideas mixed to form an applied approach to resolving nightmares, anxiety, depression, and my poor attention span.

Over the years, I incrementally added new material from neuroscience and developmental psychology to my understanding of dreams, altered states, and consciousness. However, the basic model was functional by 1958 as I applied it to eliminate nightmares and debilitating emotions.

My dream dictionary interpretations are shared in greater detail in Chapter 16. But, I have a strong bias against popular dream dictionaries with their bizarre emphasis on the occult. As a preview to forthcoming dream interpretations and dictionary dissection, I address five trends over my fifty odd years of dream analysis:

1) Waking-sleeping consciousness,
2) Dream dictionary interpretation,
3) Long-term changes in dream content,
4) Emotional expression while dreaming, and
5) Effects of dream programming.

A dynamic integrated systems approach to dreams and consciousness is supported by these interpretations.

WAKING-DREAMING CONSCIOUSNESS

My nightly dreams have been lucid for my entire life, and early on as a small child, they were dominated by nightmares. I rarely wrote them down; in fact, I just wanted them to go away. I generally have three to five lucid dreams nightly, and at least one more, now that I take an afternoon nap. I haven't had nightmares for years, thus, I use traumatic dreams from my autobiography for examples.

Different types of dreams are presented throughout this book. For examples, I select ongoing dreams day-to-day as I write. In one year I could record well over 1000 dreams, and that I find tedious. Major examples of dream types are found in Chapters 6, 8 and 10.

Theme dreams closely resemble what is going on in my daily life over longer periods of time. I'm retired and indulging myself with writing and reading, activities that I've not previously had enough time for. Mundane dreams dominate my nighttime parade of inner movies. My dreams are rarely titillating, and, just maybe, they seem less titillating through long-term habituation. You the reader will decide.

I have a professional work history of being a teacher and administrator, meaning that I lectured, taught, and directed others most of my working days. These life-long activities carry over in my dreams.

I have a dream bank of favorite people and scenes that pop up automatically, including scenes from what is now the University of Minnesota at Mankato, my years developing the first ten million dollar base for the regional Minnesota Nexus Treatment Programs, and time as a multi-county community corrections administrator in Rochester, Minnesota.

My favorite dream characters are family, close friends from these various work sites, and difficult employees who left a lasting impression. Other common elements come from emotionally arousing events in my life, such as divorce, and my personal history with parents. This is the long-term repertoire of memory that my dreaming brain dips into, mixes and matches, and morphs away in patterns that often seem bizarre.

In my day-to-day dreams (Chapter 6), readers will note that images from any given day will be mixed with long-term memories. Emotions of the day are usually carried over into that night's dreams, and scenes and characters in an earlier dream from the same night can be used again in the night's later dreams. By paying attention to content, I can follow dream element origin and patterns of use, and thereby track the emotional elements attached to the overall dream and its characters as well.

There is a strong, consistent carryover of conscious elements and activities from most days into that night's dreams. If daytime activity continues for a number of days, or a few weeks, this pattern will be expressed repeatedly in my dreams. For example, the discomfort dream reported in Chapter 6 where my wife and I experience sustained tension. This is unusual for us as our day-to-day relationship is comfortable, close, and loving. When tension arises between us for any reason, it is always expressed in my dreams, for one night or many nights. And it continues until I deal with it.

I experience most dream dictionaries as being bizarre, and dismiss their occult interpretations. Below are a number of dream categories that I find meaningful. If I'm engaging in new activities or strengthening skills such as riding a bicycle, I look for facilitated action patterns. For example, I may be sliding over the edges of steps as I move from top to bottom of the stairway as though I were on a pair of skis. I may be riding my bicycle down an impossible incline and be conscious that this is a difficult feat, yet feel very comfortable with the dream scenario. I'm even aware that I'm "showing-off" to my dream audience. Obviously, my Interpreter is taking credit for work being performed at the level of my core consciousness. Interpreter: "That poor guy doesn't get enough credit."

I pay special attention to various chemical states while dreaming. But note that hormonal activity related to sexual expression is not particularly associated with having an erection. I assume the same applies to female vaginal engorgement, although I have not tested this assumption in a dream laboratory. Sexual dream encounters when I was a young man could lead to orgasm and a sense of active copulation with fictive partners. Orgasm in dreams with fictive partners stops as one ages, if I'm a typical example. I assume this depends on the individual's hormonal levels and rate of decline. In like fashion, thinking one's self to orgasm becomes difficult with significant hormonal decline.

When my adrenaline levels are high, and this high level can occur through story telling or actual external stimuli before bedtime, I sleep lightly, wake often, and have dreams that flit around with a mind that seems to be on speed or copious amounts of coffee. Characters and scenes from frenetic dream nights are the most bizarre in terms of morphing scenes, character changes, and supernatural powers. But always, my Interpreter attempts to make sense of my dreams

The third category of long-term changes in dream content has been quite dramatic in my personal history. I was severely traumatized as a child, and my nights were filled with night terror and nightmares. It was rare for me not to have at least one nightmare each day, and often two or three. Nightmares stopped if I was so tired that my dreaming consciousness was wrapped in what seemed like fog. For example, in my last two years of high school, I tended bar for my father until 1:00 a.m., cleaned up, and went to bed on site about 1:30 a.m. or later, only to rise at 6:30 a.m. for school. Exhaustion over this two year period of time is my most common memory, with mostly foggy and bizarre dreams.

I spent a year in the Army stationed in Honolulu, which was the happiest time of my life up to that age. Dreams were mostly free of nightmares, but nightmares returned when I entered the University of Minnesota after an almost three year tour of duty. I controlled nightmares for twenty years thereafter with dream programming.

Dream programming permitted me to live in a world where I totally controlled my dreams. I used self-hypnosis to preempt all of my nightmares. Readers can use dream control this way, but if you do, most of your lucid dreams will come to reflect your dream programming. I stopped dream programming in my 40s because I wanted to experience my dreams naturally. In consequence, the nightmares of my childhood returned, and I had to eliminate them through self-analysis.

As my life has become stable over the years and my dreams have increasingly become mundane, traumatic dreams activated by battered emotions no longer exist, and haven't for many years. If your early years were traumatic, you will especially benefit by keeping a dream journal. Most people are not on the high end of lucid dreaming, but for some of us, it just happens. I usually analyze my dreams nightly. It's a fifty plus year old habit. Major changes tend to occur in the amount of conflict we experience in our dreams as we age, which is also the case with hormone levels and erotic dreams.

I think of emotional expression while dreaming in terms of Antonio Damasio's assumption that everything we do has an attached feeling element. Colors and music often have attached feelings that can bring me to a point of near rapture. A beautiful sunset, or a spectacular show of Northern Lights, or the power of great opera can trigger these sensations. But to a lesser degree, I feel everything that is happening to me, as I think you do when you stop and reflect. The words I write are not just words; they either have an emotional impact, or you stop reading, or I stop writing.

I especially watch for the feelings that represent salient dream elements. The symbolism of dream elements is very personal, and I don't believe any dream dictionary can tell you the meaning of a specific element that remains the same from dream to dream, or from person to person. The same dream elements can have any number of meanings in my dreams, depending on the context in which they are expressed. I can be fictively practicing balancing in a dream by riding a bicycle over impossible terrain, sliding down the top of fictive stairs, walking along the edge of tall buildings, etc.

What is consistent is not the content of any one dream, but the context associated with this content and the feelings elicited. Contextual elements such as riding my bicycle like Superman call my attention to dream function, not just dream form.

Find the dream elements that have the strongest or most consistent feelings attached to them, and see if they are bridging elements to your daily life, your emotional state when awake, or major concerns about tomorrow. You will start seeing a different you, especially if you have been trying to follow the interpretations in the typical dream dictionaries that are currently marketed. If you come from a family brought up on narrow religious or cultural dogma, you will notice a mirror form of rigidness in your dreams. The opposite case also seems to apply.

Effects of extensive dream programming will distort your ability to get in touch with your inner feelings and nuances occurring in your life-cycle. A rigid personality ordered around dogma will tend to act as suggestion to shape your dreams. If you enjoy flying in your dreams, or creating favorite stories or plots that you follow nightly, these will tend to become your focus. You will forget to notice mundane action patterns, lose touch with smaller situational elements in your life and the changes that you can make to improve it. You will probably fail to eliminate nightmares, and wind up suppressing them to various degrees rather than eliminating them. You will also diminish the integration of self that occurs between conscious states of waking and dreaming that can facilitate a wonderful sense of wholeness. At least, this has been my experience.

This is a longitudinal self-observation study by one person. However, I believe that my history reflects that of others who have not only survived childhood trauma, but have created a lifestyle that transcends trauma. Further, I have never used chemicals or pharmaceutical drugs to achieve stability or mental health. And, my test scores on mental health scales such as the MMPI have been normal since my mid-20s.

By now, dear reader, you should be experiencing considerable redundancy that I've attempted to build over the first few chapters. I will slow this pace of repetitive imagery as *Dreams* unfolds. Nevertheless, my history and language use is unique enough that I've felt compelled to revisit basic concepts and examples. Forgive me if I've abused your intellect.

CHAPTER 6

ORDINARY AND BODY INSTIGATED DREAMS

INTRODUCTION

My lucid dream recall goes back to the age of two and active analysis, interpretation and programming of dreams have been part of my life for over fifty years. Dream patterns change over time as we age. Dream content is dependent upon our physical location, what we are doing, and the dominant emotions being generated in our total environment. We influence our dreams with non-conscious suggestion and belief. And we can learn to influence our dreams through active suggestion, or we can totally program our dreams content and outcomes if we choose to. I started total dream programming in 1958 and offer this long-term perspective.

Lucid dreaming started after I was hospitalized with a near-death and OBE experience before the age of two. As a young child, I did not distinguish between different altered reality states and dreaming. Specific recall until I was about five years old is sketchy. I covered this history in my autobiography, and elaborate some of the detail in the following chapters.

Shortly after entering the University of Minnesota, I programmed and directed my dreams for two decades the way a movie director orchestrates his films. I then totally stopped premeditated dream programming. I compare twenty years of programmed dreams with thirty years of natural dreaming. However, once one becomes adept at lucidly entering his or her dreams and using suggestion to change them, casual thoughts during the day have a greater probability of becoming suggestions that enter one's dreams. I caution the reader to catalog their own dream patterns, as there is no rigid formula or dream dictionary guidelines that always apply.

We humans enjoy unique variation in how the dynamics of our brains play out in dreams and other altered states. What appears common to all dreams are the processes which include dream activation by environmental factors, emotions, memory integration, and consolidation and manipulation of higher order abstractions. At least these are the processes that dominate my dreams.

Dream influences over time include our changing values, emotions, feelings, plots and dream content, especially those associated with hormones and ageing. Ability to interpret our own dreams and develop ability to use suggestion means that we can learn to enter any given dream and change its outcome. Fun with flying in dreams, which seemed exotic and reminiscent of superhero feats when I was a young man, has long lost its excitement. From my experience, extensive dream programming can interfere with normal dream activity and what this means to our nightly sleep cycles. I will continue to elaborate on this relationship as it applies to conscious and non-conscious repression in later chapters.

My reported waking, daytime conscious Genesis Journey to the beginning of time is much more impacting and exciting than virtual dream flight. If I had been sleeping when my Genesis Journey occurred, P. D. Ouspensky would call it an extraordinary cosmic dream. He said:

… such dreams 'disclose to us the mysteries of being, show the governing laws of life, and bring us into contact with higher forces'. These dreams have the capacity to change our life (Craze: 60, 61).

The feelings are extraordinary, but the neural circuits creating these experiences are just performing their ordinary tasks. Taking the mystery out of Ouspensky's "higher forces" still leaves us with many unanswered questions. Learning how to interpret one's dreams removes many mysteries while adding new ones.

The reader will discover that with long-time practice, they can move in and out of altered states with dramatic visuals at will – whether sleeping or awake. For individuals without personal control over altered states, these "cosmic events" are frequently interpreted as being of supernatural origin. We experience something well beyond the normal, something that our brains configure only under unusual circumstances. We appreciate how people historically came to believe that they were in contact with supernatural forces, because the psychological effects are so dramatic.

My most frequent dreams are mundane. They are dreams instigated by memories associated with changes in physiological activity needed to maintain brain and body functions. The following dreams represent fictive practices like balancing, honing muscle coordination, processing external stimuli associated with cold, heat, or touch, overeating, and former bad habits such as smoking. Other writers like Deirdre Barrett in *The Committee of Sleep* share similar interpretations.

Long-term dream analysis will make readers aware of dream elements and contents from their own memories that are used over and over again. In our waking consciousness, we remember parts of our history that we tell and retell over the years. In like fashion, our dreaming memories do the same. I have a 1965 red Pontiac that is my favorite memory of all the cars I have owned, and it pops up repeatedly in my dreams. As I age, physical skills such as balancing change, and I notice attempts to improve these skills as I practice them in the virtual reality of my dreams.

Dream elements over the months I take to write this book include smoking and dry lungs, skipping or sliding over the edges of steps with superb balance, riding an imaginary bicycle over impossible terrain, practicing balancing on impossible ledges, loss of physical prowess when confronted by threatening dream characters, feeling cold when my bed covers slide down, having "potty" dreams when I've overeaten the night before, or appearing naked in public.

These are typical actions in our dreams that many people find perplexing. This is not a complete list of my ordinary dream actions, but it does exemplify mundane elements in my day-to-day dreams. Most of my dreams are mundane, but some can also be profound. Is the dream help I receive writing this book mundane or profound?

Dream literature is filled with speculation about why dreams occur. The dominance of mundane dreams, those that naturally occur when one is not dream programming or using suggestion, dominate my nights as I believe they do for the average dreamer. However, there are other dream types that occur depending on our larger life's circumstances and age. In nightmares, we are processing demanding emotional material and confronting ongoing problems that need resolution. Through my decades of lucid dreaming, external environmental influences change, and elements in my dreams, dream patterns, and themes change accordingly.

If you are a beginning lucid dreamer, or if you are not in the habit of systematically analyzing your dreams, you will find that the distortions and bizarreness of dreams demand your attention. As you begin to identify the activation stimuli for most of these bizarre dream forms, I believe you will come to experience them as not being quite so bizarre. Dream scenarios such as impossible bicycle riding and balancing no longer have the same bizarre or amazing sense as they did in my early dream history. As I identify the activation sources for these bizarre dream elements, I come to appreciate these strange dream features as dream form variation that mirror underlying brain function.

Dream forms that previously seemed bizarre, such as instant time, scenery, and character shifts, now just seem like shifts in different brain subsystem processing modes. Nevertheless, bizarre forms in my dreams are something I watch closely. Dream form analysis provides clues to the functions that activated the dream scenario. By correlating dream form and elements, I can identify bridging elements that are keys to the dream's interpretation.

Hobson notes that: "When we're dreaming the neural circuits responsible for physical activities are being reinforced in memory but there is no direct connection to muscles. (1999: 171)."

We practice and reinforce motor activity in our dreams this way. Fictive movement in dreams parallels what the sportsperson is doing by cognitively rehearsing tennis or skiing movements prior to competition, which is an efficient way for our brains to consolidate fine motor skills, and this work can be done while we sleep. The following sample dreams demonstrate all of these forms and elements.

If on the other hand, you are a new lucid dreamer playing with fictive flight, creating exotic dream partners, or having a stressful or anxious lifestyle, you will probably pay little attention to mundane dream content of the kind I detail. But don't skip these examples as they tell us much about how our sleeping brain is working. As a traumatized child, I was acutely aware of how dominant anxiety, fear, and negative emotions were in my dreams, and I provide a few personal examples for your comparison in the traumatic dreams chapter. Nevertheless, if you are a long-time practitioner of dream suggestion, I encourage you to stop and compare natural dreams with those influenced by suggestion or programmed with self-hypnosis.

Hobson says that:

In humans, it is very difficult for experimental stimuli to enter and label dream content. This fact has frustrated attempts to study dreaming using the behaviorist stimulus-response paradigm that works so well in other areas of psycho-physiology (1999: 167).

I think part of the problem is trying to apply a behaviorist's stimulus-response methodology to one's dreams. Physical stimuli enter my dreams as directly as they enter my waking consciousness. I experience a direct stimulus-response effect, but it has a metaphorical translation as the exchange takes place between my old and new brains.

In Chapter 9, I discuss cross-modal body maps of both internal and external stimuli. Synesthetes, for example, create the color red in their minds when they see a number like a seven. I'm looking at this process as a cross-modal body map that is hard wired. One image is being substituted for another. To use Damasio's term, it is being re-mapped. My dreams do this consistently as one image is substituted for another as metaphor. A 1955 dream Chevy substitutes for a real cold shoulder. Actual dry lungs are metaphorically represented in my dreams with their original environmental conditions.

Synesthete-like image substitutions are a normal part of dream metaphor. Hence, I'm suggesting that synesthesia is a hardwired form of our normal capacity to re-image primary sensations metaphorically. It would be interesting to explore the possibility of using a Ramachandran-type exercise to modify or correct this abnormal color-number substitution. And such studies should also shed light on how our brains form and use associations overall. But going back to the main topic, I will report a number of dreams where environmental stimuli enter and influence my dreams content.

I admit considerable ignorance of Hobson's procedural and methodological attempts to employ external experimental stimuli to study its impact on dreams. But, his methodology aside, I often experience external stimuli entering my dreams as you will soon discover, especially stimuli associated with motor activity, touch, temperature, and my physical relationship to space and gravity. Dream experiences of this nature are common, and similar dreams are also reported by Barrett.

"Sleep researchers who have applied tactile stimuli to the skin, played recordings of distinctive noises, or shone colored lights on subject's closed eyes, have found that these may be incorporated into dream content (Barrett: 7)."

In accordance with Barrett's observation, I too incorporate all these naturally occurring elements in my mundane and not so mundane dreams. My wife does too.

The autonomic nervous system's name dates from the notion that its processes cannot be brought under voluntary control. Richard Restak says that: "... modern biofeedback techniques disprove this... thousands of people with hypertension and migraine headaches have learned to control the physiological mechanisms responsible for these disorders (1994: 5, 6)."

Many of us have learned to control autonomic functions decades ago, and historically this type of control has been practiced by individuals in non-Western cultures for hundreds if not thousands of years. Personally, learning how to incorporate control of autonomic functions into one's behavioral repertoire is fun, and at the same time, it can be a door opener to controlling dreams and ASC.

Be aware that orchestrating one's dreams or creating altered realities is a construction process that is internal and not external to our brains. We are not entering another dimension. You will find dream objects shape shifting, dream characters that have combined features from any number of memory sources, and times randomly mixed together in seemingly endless ways. When we shut out light during dream time, we give our brains permission to employ all of these processing mechanics of time, space, and characters in wonderful new combinations.

I no longer think of dream morphing as being bizarre. I understand that what is normal for my dreaming brain is often experienced as being bizarre by my waking consciousness. Too much focus on the bizarre draws attention away from functions that are being reflected in our dreams.

Our brains assemble light rays entering our eyes with support from specialized neurons. Specialized neurons and brain centers integrate these complex transmissions into a seamless whole, and in this process create a sense of color. Color as we experience it does not exist in nature, even though our brains interpret color as coming from outside our senses. A similar seeming sense of continuity and unity exemplifies our sense of consciousness.

Without understanding all the details, we assume isomorphism between our brain's subsystems, and the larger integrated processes that create consciousness, and the unity called Self. In other words, complex brain-mind processes create a complex qualia configured entity called Self.

Complex evolved brain-mechanisms create Self as they create color, by integrating input from multiple sources of sensory input. Self is the product of multi-modal integration. Create enough stress or organic damage to alter this integration, and we have multiple Selves or fragmented personalities. Shift focus internally, and we understand why people of some African cultures assume we have multiple selves. My unified sense of Self has long silenced the chatter of the fragmented "me."

Our brains create a sense of unity from many different interacting parts. We create our sense of unified experience as we construct and integrate qualia from multiple senses through what appears to be parallel processing at the micro to macro levels. We experience Self as a unitary agent by filling in whatever is necessary for sensory continuity. But in our dreams, this sense of continuity can change quickly, as we do not have an external landscape that our senses are always attending to.

Following Zeki, Restak says that: "... the integration of visual information is a process in which perception and comprehension of the visible world occur simultaneously (1999: 171)."

This is a profound observation that perception and comprehension occur at the same time. In my words, Self and Consciousness are created instant-to-instant. Self and Consciousness are not things, but processes that bind all our sensory activities into an experienced whole. These brain processes can be interrupted many different ways through trauma, defective DNA, womb damage to the fetus, chemical modification of the various brain states, and so on.

Consciousness and Self are not things in the brain, but rather, they are processes. Access or integrate these processes differently in sleep, and you experience bizarre dream scenes and people and time shifts, that is, according to how your waking brain sees things. For me, bizarre exists primarily because we assume Self is an object.

Our understanding of the modular brain increases our understanding of Self and consciousness. It also helps clarify how the bizarre effects in our dreams come to be. Consciousness and Self in dreams must then be created simultaneously from various modular inputs.

Our visual system is very active in dreams, and the mechanics of sleep visualization affect the phenomenological effects we experience. Visual construction of people, places, and things can morph instantly in our dreams, and these rapid changes seem logical to our dreaming brain. Our minds create a meaningful story when we dream, just as we create continuous meaning of our experiences when we are awake. But when we are awake, dream logic with all the modular changes that goes on often seems illogical. My Interpreter understands this difference; hence the sense of the bizarre in my dreams does not really exist.

Hobson's dream research has teased out the effect of major neuro-modulators when we are awake and when we are dreaming. The aminergic system dominates our wake time, and the cholinenergic system our sleep time. Memory and physical movement are processed differently by our brains during REM sleep. We move fictively in our dreams while brain connections to our muscles remain disconnected.

But let me backtrack to Mountcastle and consciousness:

To Mountcastle the brain is a 'distributed system' where the command cannot be pinned down to one area, but function resides in different brain areas at different times depending on the circumstances. Rather than employing a single central control center, the brain operates as a complex of reciprocally interconnected systems, and 'the dynamic interplay of neural activity within these systems is the very essence of brain function (Ibid: 34).

So, what does Mountcastle mean?

Our brains operate as a distributed system whose functions reside in different areas that constantly exchange information. All the electro-chemical business going on in our brains looks much like sheet lighting walking across the outer cortex. When we are sleeping, some parts of our brain are as active, or more active, than when we are awake. The old idea that the brain turned off when we sleep has been totally discredited. If you are a lucid dreamer, or become one, you will know just how busy your sleeping brain really is. But, sleeping or awake, we always have this sense of unity and a sense being our self. Self turns back on with consciousness. Without consciousness, there is no Self, as our sense of self is created moment-to-moment.

Self doesn't rest like our physical bodies. Instead, it winks out, and is recreated moment-to-moment when consciousness is returned. Consequently, dream morphing is experienced as being logical moment-to-moment as well. It can't be otherwise, because that is how consciousness emerges and is maintained. If you've ever had anesthesia, you know what it feels like to come back from nothingness. If you've ever been in a coma, it's the same affect – coming back from nothingness.

For dream interpretation, each moment-to-moment conscious state feels like me and it is me, but these states can change instantly as my modular brain shifts processing and my dream progresses. Memories that reside in my autobiographical Self maintain the continuity that is me.

As I write these words, I feel younger than I am. My autobiographical Self mixes younger memories of me with my now, and creates this hybrid age that I subjectively experience. You know the feeling well if you are older. I look in the mirror, and barely recognize that old guy. Observe this ability of the autobiographical Self that lets us regress to any age that resides in our memories. In this sense, our dream Self is whatever age we want it to be.

Discontinuity and bizarreness is a common experience as our sleep cycle unfolds on its ninety minute rounds; a cycle which creates dreams for all of us. Inputs from our modular brain vary, as does differential expression of our brain chemistry throughout this cycling.

Our lucid self during dreams interprets each episode logically, even though movement from one dream scenario to another is illogical to our waking consciousness. Dream bizarreness only seems bizarre when we forget how our brains work. In order to interpret my dreams, I must look beyond the momentary logic of my sleeping brain and remember what function it is reflecting.

Glen A. Just

My modular brain is binding all kinds of sensations together when I'm awake or dreaming. It just does it differently in either of these two states. And, from my perspective, my sleeping and dreaming brain has its own specialized functions to perform.

Brain modules are plastic, Self is not a thing, consciousness is a process, and all of these components change through time. This is a crucial awareness as we come to understand how the brain dynamically integrates all of its information into a unified system that becomes conscious of itself. Stop thinking of Self and consciousness as things and embrace them as processes, and much of the mystery of dreams evaporates.

I use language terms that stand in for my Interpreter, Controller, or Self in order to give focus to my thoughts. This is a limitation of my use of language. I take control of brain-mind states, dreaming or when awake, in order to achieve certain outcomes. The construct of Self creates a protagonist, to use A. Damasio's term, which I use to think about normal brain functions.

I control pain, dreams, and various altered states through this contrived construction. But, it is the same mechanism of Self that you have, even if I might be using my conception of it differently.

This contrived mechanism of Self allows me to reconfigure neural patterns, which in turn permits control over autonomic functions, control over my dreams, control over other altered states, attention, or various pathological states. Self is contrived by our brains with the advanced complexity evolution gives us. And, our human level of autobiographical Self offers Free Will.

This process view of consciousness helps me visualize how my brain works. It explains a lot of what is going on when I'm dreaming, and it takes the mystery out of altered state experiences. I no longer get caught up with dream suggestion games, although I have in past years. I don't focus on the bizarreness of dream content, but look for bridging elements that best reflect their underlying messages in my dreams. I recognize that most of my natural dreams are of a mundane nature. I experience the effects of ageing on dream content and style. And because I have this focus, I'm in a position to more readily identify the hidden meanings being processed by my dreaming brain. Neuroscience always increases our insight depth.

Intra-psychic trauma falls to the sword of insight. I come to understand how entire nights of dreaming can be dominated by creative processing and integration of complex materials, and at the same time enhance my understanding of Self. And, a great many of humankind's mysteries related to altered states disappear.

Albert Einstein remarked that some of his best thoughts occurred while riding his bicycle. In my experience, he was calling attention to the relationship between body and brain functions. In one sense, he was thinking three dimensionally as he physically moved through time and space and enjoyed the geometry of his own space-time. From an altered state of consciousness perspective, the rhythmic motion of bicycle riding, like jogging, permits information flow between conscious and normally unconscious states of the brain. Rhythm always seems to harmonize cross-modal states. Inducing trance with dance or chanting goes back well before biblical times.

A reminder to the reader how stimulating access to normally unconscious aspects of our brain-minds can be. Creativity and insight can emerge from these interconnections whether we are awake or dreaming, so dream on. I believe that each one of us must find the unique brain-mind links to our own creativity as Einstein did, although no easy formulae are available.

As I move on to specific dreams in this chapter, I want to emphasize a few of the common dream activation elements and patterns that I experience. Tactile images commonly enter my dreams, and dream sequels may repeat in one night or go on for days or over years. I may be two people in scenarios where I'm engaging in a kind of self-talk. I am able to read and think in my dreams, and my dreams reflect whatever is going on in my daily routines. I sometimes write poetry in my dreams, and I may reread complex materials related to this book in my dreams.

The emphasis on sensory modes expressed in dreams varies over time, for instance, creating new songs or lyrics versus practicing glass cutting, and all of these elements and patterns are expressed in their own dream forms. What fun are the magic movies in nature's most magnificent black box!

No wonder dreams can be as confusing as they are enchanting. A lesson classical philosophy and religion offer over the ages is that when stimuli and information become complex enough, even thousands of years of

122

musings will fail to unravel the underlying meaning. And, the logic that speaks most directly to the moment's cultural interpretation, or to the most salient, culturally acceptable feelings wins. Such is the wisdom of the ancients.

Barrett's *The Committee of Sleep* is a fun read which reviews famous people throughout history who have used their dreams for creative purposes. She presents examples of artists, writers, scientists, mathematicians, composers, and numerous others, and their methods of using dreams to enhance their creativity. You will discover, as I have over the years, that we can all have similar creative bedfellows in our dreams, but they are not all of Einstein's quality.

There is a committee of sleep waiting to meet each one of us. The Committee that can transcend our fragmented self becomes operational through what I've called brain-mind expansion, which, by the way, one never gets to by being normal; statistically normal, that is.

The non-lucid dreamer's brain must be more fragmented than mine is. I've practiced opening channels between my old and new brains at least since age two. If you are reasonably sure that you are a healthy, integrated personality, you must still confront this old-new brain dichotomy. Add in other aspects of the fragmented self and the problems compound.

Barrett offers some interesting statistics that support how unique each one of us is in terms of what and how we dream, and in this review, adds additional weight to how bizarre traditional dream dictionaries are. For example: "Only 5 percent of the population has the ability to block out the real world and daydream with hallucinatory vividness (Barrett: 189)."

Personally, I was surprised by a percentage this large, as I've never met another person who can do this at my visual level. So, if you think your "dreaming" ability is bizarre, think again. I'm not referring to mentally ill people hallucinating during their waking hours, but to those of us who can create, direct, and control these effects on demand.

The following dreams bring focus to how our sleeping brains are processing stimuli from our environments, reinforcing memory, facilitating action patterns (FAP) that we use day-to-day, and conclude with a section on qualia. My discussion of qualia demonstrates how images are being formed from various sensory inputs. Image formation is initially viewed as primary sensory constructions. I then speculate as to how metaphor and meaning arise from this initial stage of creating and integrating memory. This is an introspective interpretation and is not technologically rigorous.

How the brain creates primary images is of fundamental interest to multiple disciplines, from neuroscience and philosophy, to cognitive science and linguistics. Our ability to symbolically represent primary images lies at our center of core consciousness. And, processes of re-imaging primary images lies at our center of autobiographical consciousness, or being aware of being aware. It is this capacity that gives us free will, and our human capacity to manipulate symbols in endless ways.

MUSCLE (FAP) AND COGNITIVE DREAMS

Dream recorded 7:08 a.m. (10-22-10). I noted upon waking at 2:10 a.m. that this dream would be a good example of a "muscle" dream and that I should record it. Upon rising, I made coffee, put out some hot cereal to cool, and typed these initial words. Even though the dream continued on during the night and I have some vague recollections of its morphing content, I made no effort to follow the evolving scenarios. The school theme setting is continued from (10-20-10).

I'm walking along a highway on a bright sunny day headed for Mankato State University. The road is a four lane freeway that gracefully bends across an open landscape. It is nothing like any highway that approached MSU at the time I taught there. There are many other people walking toward the campus, but I'm walking faster than any of them. This was a typical practice for me, as I was a runner and fast walker during the time I spent at MSU.

Two people are jogging ahead of me, and I purposefully walk faster to overtake them. I note that by holding my left leg stiff I can pump my right foot as fast as I want to, and maintain a walking stride to overtake the runners. I do this consciously and watch the runner's expression as I pass them.

The scene morphs and I find myself in a house, and I'm thinking about writing a take-home exam. I'm talking to a friend whose identity remains unclear. In my dream of (10-20-10) it was Jim K from high school, but this person is nondescript. My companion has another version of the take-home test that has three interrelated questions just like my copy, and a fourth question that is totally different. The fourth question is one paragraph about the length of the immediately preceding paragraph of this book. I tell my companion that this won't do; we'll have to call the department and see which one is correct before we can begin writing.

I have a cup of coffee in my hand, move some items on the couch to make room, and sit down, preparing to start writing. I tell myself that I must review all my lecture notes and the text in order to write this test, and I must first make an outline from both that captures the essential items, and then order them in a meaningful way. This is the thought in my mind as I wake up at 2:10 a.m.

While I'm awake, and before returning to sleep, I note that the strange walking stride should be remembered and analyzed. This is my bridging element; an element that gives focus to the physical, muscle-related, nexus of this dream. And, this strange walking stride seems rather directly to support a process of memory reenactment and integration of an unconscious (implicit) memory.

During the course of sleeping between 2:10 a.m. and before wakening, I analyze the meaning representing this strange walking element, and I'll write it down as soon as I prepare a breakfast that I will now eat, as my cereal has cooled and my first cup of coffee downed.

After 50 years of practice, it has become easy for me to move between sleeping and waking consciousness, and in doing so, employ cognitive capacities that are not common to dream states alone. Barrett also gives many examples of others who mix-and-match awareness between waking and dreaming.

ANALYSIS

The cognitive part of this dream is a carryover from the previous two nights. Its theme focuses on integrating and organizing material from various disciplines for this book. Much of my life has been spent in school, both as a student and a teacher. No mystery here as to why school imagery should appear frequently in my dreams. It is imagery with highlighted pathways through my neural circuits.

I believe that dreamers who do not carry over work elements from their waking lives have either not developed their capacity for dream lucidity, or are misinterpreting their dreams. I find carryover normal, and in fact, I would have to dream program waking elements out when I'm dreaming in order not to experience them. I agree with Deirdre Barrett that this psychological carryover effect is common.

The muscle part of the dream may seem bizarre to the reader, but for me it is a common memory reproduction by my sleeping brain. It is a type of fixed action pattern (FAP). I paid special attention to this FAP as I consciously increased my walking speed to overtake the joggers. This focus took me back to the fixed action pattern's origin, and this long forgotten memory came into my conscious mind as a primary image.

Thirty years ago, I had a rotary lawn mower with a rear bag. This mower did not have power to either the front or rear wheels. As the bag filled, I'd lean the left side of my body into the handle to provide steady pressure on forward movement. This mowing effort was necessary for me as I had previously injured my back, and leaning over to push the mower was both uncomfortable and capable of moving one of my vertebras out of alignment. Pay attention to dream elements that seem strange or bizarre, and their interpretation is often just this simple.

Because I always analyze content in my dreams, it is easy to make these bridging connections. I focused on the feeling of walking stiff-legged, and the old lawnmower routine emerged.

Yesterday when I mowed my lawn, I made one round with my new mower and the front wheel power stopped. I wanted to finish mowing as this is probably the last mowing of the season. Without conscious awareness, I automatically pushed my left leg and body into the mower and continued. At that time a little "blip" went off in my head, a blip that was clearly associated with my physical relationship to the mower. This awareness returned in last night's dream with the strange walking behavior, and was analyzed automatically by my brain before I woke up about 6:40 a.m. This FAP element in the dream is a good example of how our sleeping brains access non-conscious memories. This fixed action pattern re-emerged through association with my recent mowing activity.

FAPs are a common and sometimes frequent dream form for me. Here I'm diverging from Hobson's use of form. Fixed action patterns represent an underlying brain function, and thus, I'm connecting function and form directly. The bizarre nature our dreams take as things morph and change unexpectedly are reflections of this process.

We all have waking experiences where there is a feeling of déjà vu, but we can't put our finger on what it means. Stored memories that are mundane, like the above example, play out whether we are conscious or not conscious of them. The memories may be of little significance or they may be salient. As we gain practice identifying similar elements in our dreams, it becomes easier to examine them in our waking consciousness. This "muscle dream" exemplifies how our dreaming brains refine and interpret everyday memories. Sorting out the chaff of mundane dreams makes it easier to identify the themes and significant feelings that remain.

FAP memories activated in my dreams are often experienced this way. My bicycle riding dream is another example of how physical skills are practiced and recorded in our memory during dream time. Many story vignettes are experienced in our dreams, probably dozens in any given night. Do not try to view all these disparate vignettes as one story, as many functions may be supported by different dream vignettes throughout one night. Remember that we probably have 25-50 dream scenarios over the course of one night. Sequencing dream vignettes is a separate study itself.

If you focus on the cognitive elements of your dreams, thereby forgetting that the brain is responsible for your entire body-mind operation, you will miss this level of dream awareness. Staying at a cognitive level of interpretation is equivalent to a classical philosopher explaining consciousness without physiological knowledge. My dreaming mind is also attending to cognitive processes, and entire body operations that have relationship to learning and remembering. This multi-tasking view of dream functions is central to interpretation of how my brain is dynamically integrating and maintaining itself.

What seems a bizarre element in last night's dream turns out not to be bizarre at all. My non-conscious mind was reactivating a 30 year old unused, but embedded memory. This reactivation took on accompanying visuals, and my need, which is always the meaning making part of consciousness, took over to make sense of this visual-muscle scenario. Remember that learning any physical skill involves many different visual and motor cues. I can't physically move in open space without visual references; references that become part of my embedded fixed action patterns.

One can say that the recalled FAP element of a long unused embedded neural pattern for muscle control is bizarre, but then I think we fail to understand our own mind-body relationship. I simply make the assumption that mind is always grounded in and to body, which is a basic understanding from consciousness studies. This is my reference and one I think to be unquestionable.

A. Damasio does a masterful job of tying consciousness and self to our body states. Don't skip his referenced works if you're not familiar with them.

A challenge to those who believe in occult-focused dream dictionaries: Take my lawn mowing fixed action pattern dream and find its interpretation in one of these dream dictionaries.

As we gradually gain insight into muscle memories and fixed action patterns in our dreams, we gain insight into non-conscious brain functions. These dream elements are not just random; they are a specific kind of image embedded in memory.

Recalling and strengthening FAPs in dreams is a common occurrence for me. The hallucinatory aspect of FAP consolidation in my dreams calls attention to visual element integration. And, all of this dream activity places focus on the necessity of metaphorical imaging.

To me, much of this metaphor, as discussed by both professional and lay dream researchers, fails to interpret this two-stage relationship of image formation and metaphor. Lakoff provides additional insight into this metaphorical process (1993: 77-98).

Adding dream observations to their work enhances my understanding of metaphor. Unfortunately this is another book unto itself. Observing FAPs in our dreams is one piece of self-observation methodology with broad implications. In this case, I'm required to rewrite Chomsky's generative procedures for Universal Grammar. I'll refrain. Just possibly by the end of this book, readers will be able to do this on their own.

Dream content and integration expresses itself according to our unique histories. As we come to know our individual histories and how we express them in dreams, the interpretive pieces do come together. We must look past secondary or tertiary interpretations of these elements, epiphenomenal elements, to their primary expression. Balance involved in fictive dream bike riding is an example of my interpretation at the primary level.

If we try to give a secondary level interpretation of this memory and skill reinforcing process, we miss the boat. We wind up calling fictive bike riding over impossible terrain bizarre, or we treat dreams as useless brain residue. Fictive bike riding in this dream is a direct expression of balance being incorporated in memory. Self-observation directs me to the primary processes my dreaming brain is manifesting. I always ask myself after I identify the dream's meaning, "What is the function being represented?"

Consequently, dream metaphor is not something that comes from the other side as occult interpreters assume. It is not an altered reality that takes us to another plane or another world. It is not from Freudian and traditional psychoanalytic schema that represent repressed elements, but rather, it is a reflection of various electro-chemical processes supporting consciousness and the memory behind consciousness. Dreaming brains are busy doing their everyday job of supporting brain-mind functions.

As an undergraduate student at the University of Minnesota, I experienced dreams as representing a two-way flow of information. I learned to program my dream content into complete stories as I learned to control and direct nightmares, and as I learned to bring autonomic functions of pain, heart rate, and breathing under conscious control. I came to interpret Freudian dream analysis as just another form of religious dogma. I learned that psychologists of the day had very little understanding of any of this. I now know from neuroscience why my half educated, intuitive ideas made sense over fifty years ago.

SPACE RELATIONSHIP DREAM

I woke up this morning at 6:00 a.m. and began writing by 6:30 a.m. (12-27-10). I have not been exercising enough, and my blood clot damaged left leg has been swelling with noticeable discomfort. After lunch, I read for half an hour and took a nap in which I had the following dream.

I've been driving my dad's car, return it late, and he is angry with me. My dad is 50ish and I am a teenager. He orders me to get into the car, and as I barely close the door, he speeds off and makes a sharp turn. I do not have time to put on my seat belt and I'm thrown about the car, but I am tossed about in an unusual manner. I don't bump the seats or the sides of the car, but rotate lengthwise as if I were being turned on a roasting spit. I think in my dream that this is a strange way to be tossed about, but focus and stabilize myself in an upright position.

My dad's expression is one of rage, and he continues to speed down the road. Rage of this nature was common to dad, and could be set off by the slightest provocation, thus, this part of the dream is an accurate representation of a real life event. However, seat belts didn't exist when I was a teenager. Note that physical motion in bed probably activated this dream.

The scene suddenly morphs, and I'm at a shooting gallery in some type of amusement park. I prepare to shoot at a half-dollar sized target that has a string running through its middle. I hit the edge of the target and it spins. A person standing next to me who is nondescript comments that those targets can spin in five different directions. I think this is an odd statement as it can probably spin up or down, and if reoriented, left and right. I'm wondering, though, how can it spin five different ways. I then began to wake from a one-and-a-half hour nap.

As I wake up with this last dream scene still on my mind, I recognize the fifth type of movement is up. The spinning target can be moved up and down as well as spinning vertically or horizontally in its present location to create five different types of spinning. Moving the disk vertically in space solves the problem. Also note the symbolic and metaphorical complexity exemplified in these dream scenarios.

ANALYSIS OF DREAM (12-27-10):

In the middle of dreaming, I recall waking enough to roll over on my left side. One of my discs is about half the normal width and often requires me to shift positions in bed for discomfort to disappear. I was conscious of back pain that was speaking louder than usual, as well as a sore left leg. Nevertheless, I quickly returned to sleep and the above dream. As I returned to dreaming, my conscious mind noted that the turning motion in the dream backseat of dad's car exactly duplicated my turning motion in bed.

The reader will note how frequently external stimuli enter my dreams, as I believe it enters yours. It also becomes obvious that this external stimulus is modified by my dreaming brain to fit into an unfolding dream story with all of its internally instigated dream imagery.

My dreams rapidly integrate external and internal stimuli. The impingement of external stimuli on dreams has a noticeable effect on my dreams, and must partially account for my dreams rapidly changing content.

Consciousness within my dreams acts much as consciousness does when I'm awake. If I'm walking across my lawn in bare feet and step on a thorn, I have instant sensory input. Researchers who emphasize dreams being instigated from internal sources only do not resonate with my experience. Dream imagery is unquestionably being generated internally, but it has elements that are also instigated from external stimuli. These external sources can activate an entire dream scenario, or simply be one of its elements. And my dreaming brain will make it all seem logical.

Brains are designed to flag stimuli that diverge from our various sensory baselines. And all of my senses are tuned to notice such divergence. Primitive humans probably moved through sleep cycles with N-REM and REM dreams as we do. Body awareness of environment during these cycles has survival value. This mechanism must be ancient and one we share with other mammals. Once again I pay attention to sensory baselines. Familiar sounds in my house mean nothing during the night; it is the unfamiliar sounds that catch my dreaming attention.

LaBerge discusses lucid dreaming induction devices (LDIDs) that were developed at Stanford University in the course of their research. Flashing lights are used to cue lucidity, and the process demonstrates how external stimuli can enter our dreams. He says: "You may have noticed that occasional bits of sensory information are filtered into your dreams in disguised form, like a clock radio as supermarket music or a chain saw as the sound of a thunderstorm (2009: 29-30." This is my experience too, and I refer to the translations as one type of metaphor.

My dreaming brain mostly receives informational input that is internal. Common external stimuli tend to be camouflaged at a lower level of consciousness that is fit into my dream's sequence and its developing story. A modular brain, which draws most of its imagery from internal sources for dream content, is compatible with this interpretation. And, experience says that multi-tasking day brains are also multi-tasking sleeping-dreaming brains.

The scene at the shooting gallery is just as easy to interpret as the car scene. That the target can spin in five directions is the central focus of the dream, and seemingly represents something that is not true. My sleeping, half-waking brain made note of this strange element; the element that became my bridge to interpretation. As I get out of bed and stand up, the realization hits me that my movement in three dimensional space is being represented by the five types of spin in my dream shooting gallery: Right-left and up-down spin that can be placed higher or lower at the end of the shooting range.

My entire afternoon dream is at least partially instigated by physical discomfort and my relationship in space. When I laid down for a nap, I was lightheaded from a five hour writing mini-marathon, and this lightheadedness cleared during the nap. My lightheadedness was similar to the effects I get from hard exercise that requires subsequent rest for physical recovery. I made a mental note that breaks should follow two or three hours of steady writing, because my stamina has diminished with age.

I was overly sensitive to my back and leg discomfort, and these physical stimuli were incorporated in the dream. I reminded myself that the holidays are not an excuse to ignore exercising, which is doubly bad considering the extra calories I'm consuming.

I recall more than once how my father's raging moments could be expressed behind the car's wheel. I have a blurred visual in his Graham when I was about two years old where I hit my head hard against the side door during a similar rage, and many later examples where his rage was expressed both driving and elsewhere. Somehow the combination of daytime events called forth this imagery. Perhaps lightheadedness or body discomfort is the association, but I do know that my dreaming brain has little respect for the logical ordering of time. It does, however, have great respect for its own method of creating memory associations, especially feeling-based memories.

Somatic dream instigation calls attention to the two different levels of consciousness that we all possess. I'm conscious of learning to rebalance on my bicycle or feeling discomfort from my leg or back. This awareness is expressed directly in my body's tissue as an element of core consciousness. I'm also aware that elements at my core level of consciousness are being observed at my higher level of autobiographical self.

Making this distinction helps me analyze my dreams and simplifies my understanding of them. A. Damasio's different levels of Self articulate with different levels of consciousness: proto-Self, core Self and autobiographical Self. Being conscious of my dream bike balancing as primary image formation is contrasted with being conscious of elements in a thought dream. In contrast to somatic sensations entering my dreams, thought dream elements originate in my higher cortical centers and are expressed as complex metaphor.

I find it helpful to view dreams from these different levels of consciousness, upon which the "I" (autobiographical) and "Me" (Core-body self) aspects of Self rest. In my subjective experience, consciousness must be distributed and not localized in a small set of neural circuits, as sensory stimuli from all of my senses is being bound together to generate these different phenomenological experiences. Binding of sensory information must occur in both waking and dreaming states for consciousness to "wink" on. My Self as Interpreter or Controller can direct this conscious process whether I'm awake or asleep, but by observing primary image formations at the core level of consciousness, I'm aware that most of what is going on in my brain is taking place at a non-conscious level.

Once again, dreams are highly individualistic. I notice body element dream instigation more as I age, because I have more discomfort and less tolerance for items in my environment such as cold and heat. Bridging elements to dream interpretation are not always this easy or automatic, but they are also not difficult to locate once one becomes familiar with his or her own body sensations, and how we process our thoughts and feelings.

My first out-of-body experience occurred before the age of two. I have had over seventy years of dream experience with flying, levitating, and daytime out-of-body excursions such as my Genesis Journey. Subjectively, flying in dreams or daytime visions is just unhooking my brain's gravity monitoring mechanism and visualizing myself in flight. This seems like a simple enough exercise, and one that requires only small changes in how my neural networks are configured.

I want to detail the difference between dream flying and flying in daytime consciousness. Researchers and therapists usually treat daytime out-of-body adventures as hallucinatory and beyond our individual control. This is a subjective interpretation on their part. I don't think of conscious flying that is under my control as being hallucinatory; for me, it is just another brain state configuration that I exercise. In my opinion, traditional mental health definitions for these states create labels that obscure our understanding of altered states, especially when the element of control is not considered, and especially when the element of control can be acquired.

Flying or levitating represents my relationship to gravity. We all have brain mechanisms to coordinate our movement in physical space. Learning to detach our body's gravity bond with space is fun, and for the beginner, something that is often played with extensively. It is more difficult for most people to perform this separation while awake and still keep the separation under conscious control.

In a daytime altered state of consciousness where I'm flying out-of-body and keeping the flying experience under my conscious control, I have a sense of direction and movement that duplicates similar flying experiences in my dreams, or for that matter, flying in an airplane. But, there is an additional component. My Genesis Journey also contained a sense of self-expansion that went outward in all directions. It can be described as 360 degree exponential expansion. But, when I focused on moving outside our solar system and galaxy, the sense of self-expansion stopped and directional focus took over: Newly configured neuronal combinations offer me this option of directional movement or physical body expansion.

This repertoire of memory options exists in my childhood to adult memories. The sensation of change in physical size is a phenomenon that many of us have experienced over the years. I don't know of any other reports where one's physical expansion can occur without limits. I give an example in my autobiography where I physically grow in size equal to half the distance between the Earth and Moon. I've never tried to fill the entire universe with my Self, however, I often do so with my non-material essence.

Our unique learning histories determine how we mix-and-match neural circuits to create different altered realities. Calling daytime, conscious, out-of-body experiences hallucinations tends to mystify them. Softening the meaning to hallucination-like is better. I think referring to them as controlled or uncontrolled neural configurations is preferable. Learning how to control unusual neural configurations has much to offer the mental health practitioner. Learning control over altered states has been a major step into improved mental health for me.

As a traumatized child, I had a sense of being physically larger and smaller that was beyond my conscious control. When verbally belittled by my parents, usually my father, I had a strong sense of shrinking. Subjectively, I would shrink to half my normal size in terms of how I saw myself in relationship to others my own age. This subjective shape shifting has been under my conscious control for decades, but most of my young life it occurred at a level that was non-conscious.

Autobiographically, mechanisms such as shape shifting and altered states flying could be and often were brought into my lucid dreams. In younger years, my dreaming or visioning mind did not differentiate between internally created imagery and that which came from the outside. I left my body when awake or asleep when I was a small child. A history of trauma gives one a different set of dream experiences from those who have had comfortable developmental histories. Cars as traumatizing instruments, for example, have a different meaning for me than they do for most people. This is another reason why dream dictionaries that provide specific meanings for a specific object or event in our dreams can be nothing other than figments of the inventor's imagination.

Our visual senses are dominant in that more sensory information enters our brains through the eyes than any other way. We do not just take pictures like a camera and record the content in our brains. Light wavelength entering our eyes gets visually interpreted by our brains. Our visual perceptual system creates continuity of imagery even when there is none. Consciousness is highly dependent upon a sense of visual continuity when we are awake, and we maintain this sense of visual continuity in our dreams with any specific dream scenario, but not necessarily between scenarios. Remember that visual elements that may be lacking when we are awake are filled in by our brains. For example, I may convert a shadow into a perceived intruder because I'm overtired. I see a ghost or a person where none exists. Or, I may feel the presence of a ghost or person that does not exist.

We fill in sensory elements even more easily when we're dreaming then when we're awake. We construct images and create feelings in both states of consciousness. We create visual reality of continuity and feeling about our external world. When we stop creating this sense of continuity, our life feels out of control, and when this feeling of lost control intensifies, panic results.

However, when I scan the room in which I'm writing these words, my brain does not see jerky motions as I pause and look around or look out the window. My brain's perceptual scanner operates as though the images coming into it were continuous and fluid.

Dream continuity of vision is different. Visuals in our dreams can change abruptly, because all the sensory input is internal. You will note these differences in my dream stories as I speak of scenes and people morphing into toy-like transitions from one shape to another. If you are a lucid dreamer, you have similar dream experiences. It becomes easier to interpret our dreams as we become more fully informed by basic neuroscience. In fact, it is impossible to interpret our dreams with any degree of accuracy without basic neuroscience.

SMOKING DREAM

I'm in a large school with different levels, and my wife is teaching classes. I'm waiting for her, and smoking filtered cigarettes. I smoke one after another and notice that her two hour teaching period is not yet up, and I have smoked over one-half pack of Kents. My mouth and lungs are uncomfortably dry. I think I should stop smoking, and place one unlit cigarette back in the pack. There are two other people sitting with me, and I'm having a conversation with a man I have not previously met who is about 60 years old.

I look around, get up, and begin to walk out the front door. I pass one of the classrooms, and my wife is clarifying her age to a man whom I've never met. They both appear to be in their early 30s. I overhear the discussion, and find it peculiar that my wife keeps bringing the discussion back to sex. The man keeps changing the subject, but my wife keeps returning to the topic. I walk towards the door, and think that she is not a very good counselor and finds her counselee a little too attractive.

The scene changes and I'm outside. A man is sitting at a picnic table at about 20 or 30 yards distance smoking a cigarette. I note that he has come outside to smoke, and recognize that I should not have been smoking in the school. I think, "they let me smoke in the school because I'm new here." I experience a twinge of guilt for being insensitive.

As I start to reenter the school, my wife walks out. She wants to stop at a large nearby grocery outlet before we go home. I think to myself that it doesn't matter if we arrive home late, as she is my former wife and we're divorced anyway. I have no intention of spending extra time with her. I wake up, note that it is 3:35 a.m. and use the bathroom.

ANALYSIS

I haven't smoked for decades, and find smoking distasteful and unpleasant. My first wife smoked, and so I started smoking one cigarette daily to deaden my allergic reaction. That was a bad idea, as I eventually became addicted. I recall that winter smoking usually led to sinus infections and raw throats. This is an image that exists perpetually in my waking consciousness that is apparently shared with my dreaming self.

My dream's content is interesting, as the dream's school is a distorted combination of one where my current wife teaches Chinese, and a former university setting. The man I'm talking to who is 60ish resembles someone I met three days ago at a neighbor's year-end party. My wife counseling a young man, and both of them being in their 30s was a rough copy of a conversation I overheard thirty years ago between my former wife and a construction worker remodeling our house's lower level.

Smoking is the bridging element to the stimulus that activated the dream. The winter air in our house is dry, and I especially noticed being sensitive to the dryness when I got up to use the bathroom and reviewed this dream. My present house has electric heat, which causes the moisture level to drop during cold winter months. I forgot to turn down the heat when I retired last night and this exacerbates the dryness. Smoking is a memory associated with dryness, and this memory of discomfort is triggered by the dry winter's air. This association between dryness and smoking has entered my dreams for the past thirty years.

The counseling episode with my former wife who is remembered as being in her 30s represents a sense of concern about my current younger wife. Ruby went through a rough period of adjustment to American culture about the time I started writing this book. She struggled with her sense of gradually losing Chinese culture with her increasing immersion in America's. This struggle period was overt for about three or four months, and is referenced in one of my dream reports as "conflict."

The reader will note how easily time elements can get mixed. Characters are pulled from three day old or thirty year old memories, and scenes can morph suddenly. My dreaming mind is supplying what seems like logical interpretation during the dream, but various elements seem bizarre when considered together. Scene-to-scene continuity is lacking. The near chain-smoking action in the dream is dealt with logically in the sense that I'm smoking too much, even though I haven't smoked for decades. This logic is followed by what normally is a waking thought – how I can chain smoke one day, and the next day not smoke for long periods of time. Various versions of the smoking dream are part of my dream history over 30-odd years.

It appears that our dreaming brains are not designed to recall events that are too mundane unless discomfort occurs. Keeping such banal stuff in consciousness would be inefficient in terms of psychic energy and neuronal space. Most people have to learn to dream lucidly, and some people have trouble recalling any but a few dreams.

However, dream specialists such as Delaney offer rather straightforward procedures to gain dream recall. In that lucid dreaming is not common, suggests that our evolutionary history does not require lucid dreaming for us to enjoy most of the benefits such as memory integration and consolidation. I've come to believe that a good share of mammalian dreams support the brain's housekeeping functions. In the human evolutionary sense, cobbled on higher cognitive centers try to interpret this lower level of memory function as though it represented waking volition.

Why should you or I be conscious of how our brains are recording, strengthening or eliminating memories? Non-conscious processes perform this function with less effort. It is just as functional for my waking Interpreter not to concentrate on walking, thus, why should dream consciousness expend extra energy associated with conscious thoughts on FAPs or dry lungs? If being conscious of all the processes that support our survival was required, evolution of human abilities would never occur.

The architecture of the human brain requires me to expend considerable effort to interpret dream processes as well as learn the language of dreams and dream metaphor. Nevertheless, my dreams communicate volumes about all my internal brain activities and states every day, both from autobiographic and core centers of consciousness. And by interpreting dream functions in terms of these two levels of consciousness, I can eliminate nightmares, help stabilize emotions, and enhance my creativity.

I recognize that cognitive dreams where I'm giving detailed lectures represent a fairly high level of cortical functioning. Evolution gives me the capacity to think when awake and continue to support these processes when I'm dreaming. Under normal conditions, thinking seems limited for most people when they're dreaming. And if my assumption that the sleep, N-REM and REM sequences is correct, this is the case. However, end products of these processes are realized as FAPs and "aha" solutions to complex thoughts.

OTHER BRAIN ACTIVITY

In the experiential sense, my dreams reflect how my brain-mind is sharing information at multiple levels at the same time that my brain is performing various memory and maintenance functions while I sleep. This awareness comes to me from many different levels, from the concreteness of a facilitated action pattern, to the abstractions that define my recent preoccupation with writing this book.

I awake from a Theme Dream, chapter seven, on the 20th feeling clear headed without the sense of preoccupation that has been with me for a number of days. Whatever was driving my preoccupation has been effectively resolved during the night.

The Theme Dream has cleared my head. It is a habit for me that problems that I'm trying to solve or issues that I'm sorting through in my personal life are dealt with in my dreams in a similar signaling fashion. My below conscious, dreaming brain lets me know that there is an unresolved "something" that is being worked on. The theme itself becomes my bridging element. Abstractions can occur at various levels in my dreams, just as they do during my waking hours.

One other marker that I'm aware of consists of a spot in the back upper right quadrant of my brain. I visually experience a dark spot in this part of my brain when I'm awake, and it doesn't go away until the problem or solution to what I'm trying to understand is reached. I think of it as a personal "somatic marker" that creates conscious awareness in my psyche with this visual attached to a feeling of unfinished business. This marker only appears to me when I'm wrestling with large amounts of complex materials.

Solutions to complex problems must involve input from multiple brain circuits and networks. Dream problem resolution feels very much like complex resolution when I'm awake. It is as though problem solving neurons remain in an excited state until my Interpreter is satisfied; hence a sense that "static" is dominating my neural circuits. My Interpreter decides when a critical level of integration is reached, and as a result, I have a feeling of comfort and mental clarity. This was true with my nightmare resolutions, and is true for any cognitive or emotional state of excitation.

This process must embrace a two-way feedback loop that reaches a satisfactory level of closure for my Interpreter. I'm agreeing with Walter Freeman that the brain's ability to create meaning must be a fundamental part of consciousness. I'm not saying deterministically that meaning creates consciousness. I'm saying that a level of consciousness that satisfies my Interpreter requires that sensory stimuli from all sources be integrated.

Neuronal processes that support the creation of meaning and problem solution to the organism are enhanced functionally if these processes continue during the night. Active dream participation is logical for FAPs, and the carryover or amplification of this mechanism by our higher cognitive centers seems to be a logical and qualitative emergent.

Meaning from this perspective is the integration of external and internal stimuli into complex circuit patterns that are acceptable to one's Interpreter. We all know and experience these feelings – "That solution feels right," or, "I've got a feeling we're on the right track." My most abstract thoughts and thought processes, as well as simple ideas follow this rule. However, the longer one struggles with a problem, the greater is one's sense of relief when a solution is reached. There is a parallel sense of relief for everyday problems that to a small degree feels like resolution to one's nightmares. It is the positive response an infant expresses when a toy is grasped for the first time.

Until I provide for basic life needs such as food and water, my brain will keep focus on these goals. And at a higher level, until I solve whatever problem is being processed by my brain-mind, it will keep me preoccupied. Physiologically in my life needs hierarchy, each level of circuit closure permits attention to the next level of life's demands. Vacations feel good, meditation feels good, and retirement feels good when demands on my brain-mind are processed with feelings that are unencumbered. Kant's idea of pure thought seems ridiculous once we come to embrace the physiological basis for image formation.

Awareness of the importance of meaning in dreams first came to me when successful analysis of childhood nightmares immediately brought relief. Awareness from dream analysis tells me that the mind's search for meaning is a central element of dreams, as it is a central element to our waking consciousness. I'm suggesting that this mechanism at least partially supports our creation of dream narrative. My new brain scans dream scenarios for meaning, even when a FAP function is being performed. Why not? That's its job. My brain works this same way when I'm awake. And, this assumption correlates well with Walter Freeman's dynamic systems view of consciousness.

For me, there is a clear exchange going on between my brain's non-conscious and conscious systems. This circular loop of information exchange operates when I'm awake and when I'm asleep. Sleeping on a problem and finding that it's been solved during the night is a common experience for many of us. My sleeping-dreaming brain's obsession with solution to a major problem that I've been wrestling with during the day, or over days, can occupy an entire night or nights with one related dream scenario after another. A theme or set of interrelated themes becomes the thread that knits together the cloth of meaning weaved whole.

I suspect that the greater facility one has with lucid dreaming, the larger is the amount of information exchanged across brain sub-systems during the course of any given night. Creativity in one's dreams probably follows a normal curve much like most other human abilities.

I don't know what it's like not to have this exchange. I think there is another doctoral thesis here: Train a number of college students over a four year period of time to create, direct and control dreams and other altered states, and see what happens to their problem solving ability.

I'm concluding this point by noting that communication between problem solving neural circuits when one is dreaming must involve extensive exchange across feedback and feed-forward loops . Circular communication between higher and lower brain centers accounts for multi-tasking functions of my dreaming brain more fully than unidirectional signaling. Brain-mind processes at the level of core Self seem to be extensively related to maintaining FAPs necessary for the survival of an organism moving and acting in three dimensions.

I'm suggesting that increasing the information flow between higher and lower levels of consciousness puts the kid's hand in the cookie jar. Consciousness at the human level of complexity where we have Free Will appears to be highly dependent upon complex neural arrangements that have specific meanings to our Interpreter. Increase the plasticity and availability of these circuits at ever higher levels of complexity, and we begin to discover the road to creativity. That's how it feels to me.

Looking for consciousness in single or a few neural circuits ignores the role of meaning and intentionality in my dreams. As we follow the evolution of human brain complexity, it would appear that consciousness, hence the neural capacity and range of our Interpreter, is increasingly more distributed and complex. For me, a FAP dream is engaging a relatively limited number of neural circuits. An agitated state of preoccupation with a complex set of feelings and cognitive elements represents a more complex level of neural integration.

Until this emerging and complex neural pattern reaches an acceptable level of integration, read meaning, a sense of preoccupation prevails. There is a pressure behind the dam of emotion that drove our historical organism before evolution gave us a cerebral cortex. Neural circuits and conscious actions by our evolutionary ancestors were necessary to remove this tension and reorient the organism's self. Why would this mechanism cease to exist at our higher cognitive levels? I don't think it did.

SPOUSE ACTIVATED DREAM

Last night's dream (1-3-11) was an atypical dream for me as it involved fear. I know that fear is a common element in dreams, especially for younger people, along with anxiety and other negative feelings. But in my aged years, fear experienced in dreams has become increasingly infrequent. Consequently, my conscious brain quickly flags fear and anxiety in my dreams and pays close attention.

In my spouse activated dream, I'm in a car that I owned before I went to China in 2006. The lot in which the car is parked is large and mostly dark. I'm with my wife Ruby, and we are both aware that bad people are stalking us. We crouch down in the car to get out of sight, but can hear the voices of our pursuers. I think the doors are locked, but Ruby insists that they aren't. I feel in the dark and flip the lock switch, but there is no sound of the door locks working. Ruby asks what I'm doing, and I tell her that I'm trying to lock the doors. She tells me they are locked, so I reach up and push the lock switch back to its former position.

I realize this act unlocked the door. One of our pursuers opens the door, but I can't tell if he has come in or is just looking. Ruby begins to scream and I ask her what is wrong. She doesn't answer, just screams more. I'm trying to decide what to do, and reach around in an attempt to find who or whatever is causing her to scream. At this point in the dream, I wake up.

As I wake up, my wife is moaning softly in her sleep, and appears to be having a bad dream. I listen and note her behavior. She has fear arousing dreams that I notice every few months, and she always expresses herself by moaning as if in some degree of pain, although at times her sleeping vocalizations can be stronger. If she becomes too agitated, I will wake her and ask for a dream report, or sometimes I just pat her gently, and tell her that everything is okay. Either way, my actions and this additional input will stop her bad dream.

Last night's dream did not require a high level of intervention. I just made a note that my dreaming brain was activated by her moaning and went back to sleep. Concern for her well-being does not stop when I'm sleeping, and this concern was turned into pursuer generated dream fear. Should I call this example of my dreaming brain's translation symbolic or metaphorical?

Fear is such a generic state and probably has ancient correlated evolutionary markers starting with single cell withdrawal from a changing chemical source threat. I think the feeling of fear in this dream represents activation of a primary emotion which is expressed by her moaning, and for me, the dream scenario of victimizing pursuers is my metaphorical dream response. This dream is also very transparent. Ruby has been adjusting to a new culture, America, and her adjustment is modeled around a gradual lessening of fear, which she expresses in her dreams.

I would normally define my reaction to Ruby's moaning in her sleep as concern. But, my concern is her fear, and the two are separated by a fine degree in her dreams. The first few times I noticed her bad dreams that bordered on nightmares was during our early months together in China.

Ruby grew up during Chairman Mao's Era of Young Revolutionaries, and has many stories of family persecution from this period. Old imagery from her experiences in the Cultural Revolution continued while we were in China, but now gradually become less frequent month-to-month as she adjusts to the safety of American culture.

I asked her in the morning if she had another nightmare, and she said she couldn't recall her dream. The dream pattern was evident for me, but her dream recall was zero. She has made major strides in the last few years by unlearning traumatizing memories at both the conscious and non-conscious level. Now she rarely speaks of traumatic incidents during her youth, unless motivated by other similar stories. And dream trauma no longer sets her upright in bed in the middle of the night.

Acquiring deep security in one's non-conscious or conscious mind requires time and reconditioning. This is a good example of how our unique histories are expressed in our dreams. Reassurance, without dramatic emphasis, is a major part of her reconditioning. Dramatic emphasis and deep discussion in the middle of the night would probably have the opposite effect by strengthening related neural circuits and memories.

It is this differential reinforcement of embedded trauma that often unwittingly gets reinforced in therapy. It is this differential effect that is best controlled by the individual him or her Self. I know from self-therapy that I feel fear with an immediate awareness and sensitivity. The therapist often takes time to adjust to and interpret client responses, but with the wrong focus, can unwittingly reinforce what the client is attempting to eliminate.

AUTOMATIC MOTOR ACTS

Hobson says that: "REM sleep guarantees the running of instinct programs so that they will always be practiced and thus available when needed (1994:164)."

Furthermore, REM sleep allows these programs to be updated with new experiential data. This is why dreaming so clearly reflects the where, when, and with whom aspects of our instinctively driven emotional interactions within our respective social worlds.

Newly learned action patterns that are becoming fixed are clearly being created and maintained in some of my dreams. Most of this memory "fluffing" must occur at a non-conscious level, and only some of this activity that is highly hallucinatory breaks through into my lucid dreams. Thus, becoming sensitized to these subliminal memory processes can be of great help when we wish to eliminate uncomfortable aspects of our histories that keep us awake at night.

Much of my dreaming reflects the state I'm in during the day, or the last few days, as I carry these feelings and thoughts into the night. Last night, for example (12-1-10), I awoke when my wife got up for the day. I was dreaming of being in a large, brightly lit area that was transected by roads and parking areas. Over my right shoulder was a car slightly newer than my old 1952 tan Chevy, probably a 1955 model, or that is what my waking brain brought into my morning dream thoughts. The rectangular image of the tan Chevy was exactly placed in my dream where a rectangular hole in my crumpled blanket left my left shoulder exposed to the cool bedroom air, and it was a perfect match. Often my dreams are filled with these encroaching sensory elements instigated by temperature, toilet urgings, or an overfilled stomach. The line between our states of consciousness grows thinner as our awareness increases.

Hobson says: "...to suggest that dreaming is as banal as waking is retrograde with respect to cognitive neuroscience (2005: 121)."

In my later years, my dreams are dominated by these banal elements. This does not mean that my dreams overall are banal, just that the majority of their content is. And, in agreement with William Domhoff, differences between my waking and dreaming states are minimized by this awareness. This was not the case when I was a young man. If I had been in Hobson's dream lab in my teens or early 20s, dream patterns and content would have been dramatically different.

PRESSURE ACTIVATED DREAM

I finished revising part of this chapter and laid down for an afternoon nap (2-10-11). I'm dreaming lucidly, and from a standing position, I look down at my feet, only to find that I have placed my slippers on the wrong foot: left on right, and right on left. I can feel slight discomfort from this mismatch, but before I take dream action to change the slippers, I partially wake up. I'm sleeping on my back, the top layer of blankets is folded back thereby doubling the weight on my toes, and this pressure is causing discomfort. I mentally note the dream symbolism and continue dreaming.

As the dream continues, I'm looking through my slipper covered feet at Tahrir Square in Cairo. The enlarged vision of the square with thousands of people in it shrinks to a small tent section that has been set on fire. I look closer and see that it is a type of field hospital that is burning, along with bandages and medicines. I wake up with an uncomfortable feeling in the pit of my stomach, thinking that Mubarak has escalated the Egyptian confrontation of 2011.

The above dream is typical of my day-to-day banal dreams. Whether or not daily activity is brought into my dreams will depend on my mood, and everything else that has been going on before I enter sleep.

There is no simple formula that directs my memory in dreams. There is no simple rule that says that my dreams must be dramatic or mundane, and there is no simple interpretation that explains the level of imagery and symbolism in my dreams. I note that the correct multiple choice answer to what activates my dreams is all of the above, and more.

SWEATING DREAM

(4-1-11)

I woke up at 2:30 a.m. sweating. But in my dream, I'm at a former place of employment, the Government Center in Rochester, Minnesota. I'm no longer an employee, but I'm engaged in completing some kind of knowledge survey. Time is up and I'm to turn in my answers, but I have two unfinished pages. I quickly mark answers, and announce that I'll probably get at least one extra point for doing so. I turn in my answer sheet to find that my score is 34. I'm given a stack of answer sheets by my former boss and asked to compile their scores. I notice that the average score is 11 or 12 and think that I did pretty well after all.

Along with the stack of answer sheets, I receive financial forms and official reports that should be turned into central administration. I also receive an object wrapped in a shirt. Un-wrapping the object, I note that it is a statue from my former boss's office. The statue is wet, and I think how strange that she has given me all of this material and left without comment. I discover from others present that this is her last day of work, and she has now exited employment.

As I mull over compiling the test data and what to do with the financial spreadsheets. I again open the shirt and look at the statue. Yes, it is wet – my original perception was correct. My sleeping brain makes note that I have observed the wet statue a second time, and I mentally flag it as my bridging element.

ANALYSIS

I woke up with my nightshirt soaked in sweat, and immediately associated the wet statue and nightshirt. I became aware in my dream that the wet statue was my bridging element when I opened the shirt a second time. The manner in which body signals are experienced in dreams suggests that cross-modal input, which includes visuals, is an integral part of dream consciousness. For example, balancing on a bicycle requires visual components as do most body actions when one moves in space.

My brain has been sorting ideas about dream function hypotheses, and thinking about the relationship between physiological processes and psychological functions. I surmise that thoughts related to writing this book are reflected in my dreams with tests, knowledge quizzes, and note preparations. The visuals that enter my dreams are the contextual images formerly associated with similar real life activity. All of this sorting process is occurring mostly at a subliminal level, and it all gets interrupted by a little sweat.

From an evolutionary perspective, my old brain, which runs on reflexes, uses visuals in dreams to integrate and consolidate skills. This re-imaging of primary sensation is an integral part of the binding process that integrates sensory input. Once our new brain emerges at the human level of complexity, we continue to re-image (re-map) qualia at this higher level. Mentation process at the level of core Self has been freed from embedded qualia at the level of complex metaphor; hence, visual imaging in my dreams takes on the bizarre forms that I commonly report.

I'm not interpreting sweat as the primary activation element in this dream, but think instead that multiple subliminal activities are being processed by my dreaming brain. Sweat, or being overly warm, is creating sleeping discomfort, and my dreaming brain incorporates these physiological elements. The reader will note that dry air, physical and eating discomfort, sexual longing, toilet duties, and temperature, are all physical states that get incorporated in my dreams.

These sensory elements are always represented metaphorically. I notice physical stimuli entering my dreams when I pay close attention to dream content, and look for bridging elements with their symbolic representations. The above referenced multi-tasking dream was processing materials for this book as well as paying attention to my body's physical needs.

Thus, I'm aware that considerable subliminal brain activity is going on which is represented by two metaphorically expressed dream segments. One segment associated with sweat is primary metaphor, and the other associated with images free of their embedded elements is complex metaphor. I have an old brain that keeps abreast of my physiological needs, and a new brain that engages higher cognitive functions.

Maintaining physiological homeostasis must be an old brain mammalian function that visually enters our dreams. When higher order cognitive processing of abstract symbols occurs simultaneously in my dreams, I assume it is being supported by new brain architecture. My brain-mind is a complex dynamic whole that constantly performs these multiple tasks, and they are reflected in my dreams. This is how dreams feel. And I always try to note feelings, body sensations, and abstract thoughts when I look for bridging elements. And looking for these bridging elements requires that I pay close attention to their metaphorical representations.

FAP DREAM

(8-4-10)

I'm at a group dinner in a casual setting that has various kinds of food and drinks available. I'm talking to one of the other dream characters, and explaining how I'm regaining my balance riding bike and going barefoot. As I explain the improvements taking place, my brain duplicates bicycle balancing at the appropriate moment of my dream explanation and off I go; dream suggestion in dreams in action. Did the dream explanation morph me onto the bike, or was the dream explanation the instigating factor for my dream discussion? Does it matter whether the answer is A or B?

I think what activation elements determine the direction of dream causality varies; therefore, dream narrative can be very situational. I find it easier to interpret my dreams when I first focus on dream function. Are my dreams informing me of emotions, body needs, memory, or cognitive functions? I suggest that the direction of causality in my dreams is determined by the function being performed.

I'm acutely aware that a real balancing act on my bike just occurred in my dreaming brain, and that I'm experiencing an improvement in balance during this mental rehearsal. My dream rehearsal, I think, is comparable to what athletes are taught to do before competition. The only difference is that I recognize my brain is rehearsing balancing while I'm dreaming. Paying attention to your mundane dreams will put you in touch with many similar body maintenance and skill development functions, and if I'm typical, will mix these elements in multi-tasking ways.

I've not paid much attention to dream activation factors of this type in recent years as my focus has usually been on more dramatic aspects. However, I'm acutely aware that ageing has decreased many of my physical skills. Nevertheless, the exact duplication of balance with the exact sensation of actually riding a bicycle was a little surprising to my conscious mind. Riding a dream bike over impossible terrain felt like an accomplishment that my waking self had achieved.

A quick déjà vu aside: I experienced my first airplane ride when I was in the army. I was contemplating going to flight school, and was taken on an aerial flight of loops and rolls and fairly complex aerobatics. The pilot was checking out my responses after each maneuver. I was in Heaven and wanted to take the controls, but this was not possible for a neophyte. What the pilot didn't know is that I had been flying in my mind since age two. Nothing seemed new or strange; it was just fun.

I realized later as I analyzed this experience that I had mastered each spatial maneuver flying out-of-body over the years. And being above the Earth a few hundred feet was not as complex as flying half-way to the moon. Combining fictive practice from daytime or nighttime out-of-body flights felt the same. How could it be otherwise?

ANALYSIS

I reported another skill activated dream in Chapter 2 when I discussed Llinas's use of facilitated action patterns. In the above dream, the cognitive element was the first element to enter my consciousness. I'm telling another dream character about my improvement in balance from riding bike, and as I explain this change, the actual sensations of bike riding and balancing are executed. With years of lucid dreaming, dream suggestion is just this easy. Thought in the dream itself becomes the activating element to make it happen.

In the FAP dream reported in Chapter 2, the reverse sequence occurs. I experience the sensation of balancing, and notice improvement in my bike riding, and then conscious awareness of what this means emerges. These two dreams with different sequential directions of cause and effect reinforce my perception of the two-way dynamics occurring between lower centers of consciousness and higher cognitive centers.

I don't think this awareness of communication between different levels of consciousness means that I'm in a hybrid state of consciousness that approximates hypnotic trance. Using definition to explain conscious states seems to be the problem, rather than explaining states of consciousness from the perspective of what is being experienced. In a similar fashion, once Freud defined his version of the unconscious and convinced others that it accurately stood for unconscious activity, an artificial, non-existent construct became truth. Careful observation of one's subjective reality states has more credibility than this.

CHAPTER 7

SOMA AND SYMBOLS IN DREAMS

INTRODUCTION

Hobson reminds us that we have 25 to 50 dream scenarios nightly and we remember only a fraction of them (2005: 44). I experience multi-tasking across these extensive dream scenarios. Our brains are busy with memory housekeeping tasks, keeping focus on salient emotional states, and engaging in a myriad of cognitive operations. I'm acutely aware of this scope when I pull up dream vignettes from one night's dreaming that cover multiple sleep cycles. Additionally, if one has been severely traumatized by dramatic events such as rape or torture the accompanying nightmares may cycle throughout the night, night after night as these emotions remain salient until resolved. Our complex brain is about as active at night as it is during the day. Dreams are not mundane, meaningful, supportive of memory functions, metaphorical, or sorting through our feelings; they are all of this and more.

Our personal histories, memories, and degree of control over various brain activities have considerable variation between individuals, and this all changes over time for each one of us. Do not be surprised to find your dream content, thematic patterns, or how your memory accesses stored information is different than what you read in any source book.

I'm a good example. I used self-hypnosis to control autonomic processes such as heart beat, pain and changes in feet and hand temperatures back in the 1950s. I used self-hypnosis extensively to eliminate nightmares. I've also actively initiated and controlled various forms of altered realities. My dreams reflect all of my history, as your dreams do; consequently, our dreams are as unique as our personalities.

The idea that each one of us can quickly learn body and mind controls that include dream programming was considered radical in the 1950s and '60s. Attempts to discuss these techniques with university professors and professional members of the medical community were automatically rejected. I learned to live with this rejection and simply followed my own path to self-discovery and improved mental health.

Restak lends partial support to my 1950s efforts by addressing our ability to learn control over autonomic nervous system functions: He says:

> [At] centers in the brain stem and spinal cord are the elements of the autonomic nervous system. Its name dates from the notion that its processes cannot be brought under voluntary control. But modern biofeedback techniques disprove this; thousands of people with hypertension and migraine headaches have learned to control the physiological mechanisms responsible for these disorders (1994: 5-6)."

By the beginning of the 1960s, I had learned how to control any body or mind function desired. My sequence of learned controls moved from autonomic functions such as pain to extending my attention span for focused learning, and then on to nightmares and other altered states. I was interested, as I think most readers are, in controlling my total relationship to my environment. I labored under this simple idea fifty years ago and I retain this same assumption today. I don't need to know all the mechanics that keep a car running, I just need a basic understanding of how to maintain and drive it. I taught myself to control all these various brain states, and after 50 years of exercising these controls, I experience no major negative repercussions.

Following the winding paths through my dreams, and learning to interpret dream form and function, permitted me to sort out the mundane, symbolic, and profound. The reader may not agree with my procedures, but they worked for me. I knew by the late 1950s that operational procedures could work even if causative factors are misinterpreted. This is a simple lesson one gleams from the study of shamanic practices in world ethnographies.

Like other lucid dreamers, I find object shape shifting in my dreams, characters that combine features from any number of memory sources, and randomly mixed time elements. I don't claim to fully understand all the mechanisms operating to create these features, but dream researchers like Hobson and LaBerge have added considerable insight to our general understanding over the years. I simply experimented with dream control until I got the results I wanted.

By shutting out light during dream time, our brains have permission to employ all of its processing mechanics to create wonderful new sensory combinations. I do not experience these seemingly strange dream shifts as being bizarre as I have come to associate these changes with underlying function. My goal has been to understand the meaning of my dreams, and what the underlying functions being addressed by my brain-mind are. As I increased my understanding of brain physiology, I also increased my understanding of dreams.

Seventy years of lucid dreaming tells me that there can be a significant two way flow of communication between our dreaming and waking states of consciousness, and that there is considerable two way flow of communication between higher and lower brain centers as we dream. I experience, as we all do, a sense of self that exists through time; a unity of consciousness when I'm awake or sleeping. These most fundamental aspects of our humanity are always present in lucid dreams or waking hours. How our brains create this sense of self and unity of consciousness is a fundamental quest for both neuroscience and psychology.

As a reminder from the previous chapter, perception and comprehension of the visible world occur simultaneously as consciousness and Self emerge. Knowledge of the modular brain increases our understanding of self and consciousness. We experience modular input to dream consciousness differently than during waking consciousness. My waking consciousness fills in the continuity gaps that create a sense of "flow" as I move through space and time when awake. My dreaming brain doesn't fill in the gaps this way, because it doesn't need to. My dream focus is on function maintenance versus my waking moments of active movement through space.

Modularity helps me understand dreams better, because consciousness and self in dreams must also be created simultaneously from internal modular inputs.

Restak says:

The brain is a complex of widely and reciprocally interconnected systems. The dynamic interplay of neural activity within and between these systems is the very essence of brain function (Ibid: 33).

The dynamic interplay that occurs in our dreams is primarily an internal process. My dreaming mind dynamically mixes modular exchanges moment-to-moment to create what seems bizarre to my waking consciousness. Subjectively, I experience dream effects, but must make extraordinary efforts to tease out the mechanical underpinnings. A considerable amount of my dream activity is supportive of memory and brain-basic body housekeeping tasks. Why should I be conscious of this banal stuff? Dream forgetting is an efficient evolutionary mechanism that supports brain plasticity. Nevertheless, I can learn to watch some of the mechanics and activation modes as they are being expressed in my dreams.

Discontinuity, bizarreness, and limited logic in our dreams represent the basic brain-mind states of dream consciousness. Dream bizarreness only seems bizarre when we use the waking brain as our default setting. In order to understand and interpret my dreams, I must look beyond how my modular brain's expressions feel, or how illogical dream content is to my waking consciousness. An expanded understanding of brain physiology permits me to sort out how the different brain processing features operate between sleep, dreaming and waking.

Brain modules do not represent fixed modes of interaction; they are dynamic. Self is not a thing, consciousness is a process, and all of these components change through time. My dream content and brain-mind maintenance functions are changed daily as focus shifts from learning to ride a bicycle to writing a book. Changes in social and environmental relationships are reflected in my dreams. And, on and on it goes. It is this awareness that reminds me how dynamic and plastic our brain-minds really are.

I speak of my Interpreter or Controller by using these concepts to give focus to my thoughts and organization to my brain's higher level cognitive activity. This is a limitation of language, as second order symbols of this nature are not pure representations of primary image formation.

Second and tertiary concept manipulation by classical philosophers too often begins with artificial referents. Knowledge of physiological processes permits me to look at primary image formation in dreams and permits me to look past the bizarre manifestations that occur in dreams.

For me, more than any other researcher-writers, Damasio and Llinas have provided additional scaffolding to improve my observations of primary image formation in dreams, and help clarify operating levels of dream consciousness and self.

Viewing the self as process permits me to take control of brain-mind states, either dreaming or when awake, in order to achieve desired outcomes. Following Damasio, the emergent self creates a protagonist, and I use this felt relationship with my protagonist to transcend normal brain functions. I use this moment-to-moment constructed self to control pain, dreams, and various altered states even while I'm aware that it is a mechanism of the moment. It operates like an agent, or thing; it feels like a homunculus, and it gives me the results of a concrete "something."
It helps me to visualize brain processes as occurring at various levels of complexity as I move from proto-Self through core-Self to autobiographical Self.

I need these distinctions in order to visualize modular input, integration, and feedback between the different system levels ranging from those that support primary image formation, to complex cognitive processes.

I recognize that I can use higher cognitive processes to control autonomic functions of the proto and core Self levels. I can use higher order dream suggestions to create and direct dream scenes associated with core-Self, or I can use higher order cognitive processes, meta-awareness to observe these interrelationships. I no longer get caught up in dream suggestion games for the sake of novelty, although I have in past years. I don't focus on the bizarreness of dream form, but look for bridging elements that best reflect the underlying source of their instigation in my dreams. I recognize that most of the content of my natural dreams come from convenient associations that my brain-mind uses to create story narrative. And, I'm very conscious of ageing effects on dream content and dream styles.

INTERPRETATION OF MEMORIES IN DREAMS

We don't have to be conscious of learning for it to occur, as any good parent knows. At the most basic level of learned behavior, we embed implicit memories of activities such as bicycle riding. I don't need to think consciously about improving my balance while riding, but I do need to practice. Unconscious learning occurs as we become habituated to everyday routines.

Our memories hold huge volumes of encoded information that we are never conscious of: Think of the vast number of behaviors you execute without consciously willing these actions—ducking a flying object, hitting the ball in tennis, riding a bicycle, or just walking. What I call mundane dreams reflects this level of memory activity. Long-term lucid dreaming and analysis increasingly makes us aware of these banal elements. The previous chapter is full of examples.

As we improve our ability to analyze dream content, we become more aware of how the dreaming brain processes primary image formation such as balance. And with improved awareness of image formation in dreams, we develop a different understanding of metaphor and how symbolic abstractions are manifested in our dreams. I pay more attention to dream function than dream form. I also ignore occult dream dictionaries as they distract me from observing fundamental processes such as memory integration and consolidation. My early attempts to explain the fluidity and bizarreness of dreams with all their incredible dynamism tended to impose a linear interpretation of cause and effect. Currently, my awareness of the dynamic interplay between brain-mind sub-systems shifts focus to that of circular causation.

Higher order brain functioning has to be taken into account as in Freedman's use of how interpretation of meaning can change brain function. For example, my decades old nightmares disappeared immediately once I understood their activation sources. They were my same neurons, and same neural circuits, and same neuro-modulators, but all of their activity changed in minutes once the source of the nightmares was identified. Physiology tells us so much about dreams, self and consciousness, but physiological reductionism does not explain how these processes use meaning to change outcomes.

As Owen Flanagan would say, "This is the really hard problem. Fortunately, we do not have to explain all the mechanics of this mechanism to use it."

In the words of Restak: "We know but don't know that we know (1994: 89)."

I find it necessary to identify what and how body sensations enter my dreams. I want to change Restak's quote to read: "We know but don't know that we know, but dreams can help us know why we don't know what we know." I want to understand how changing meaning modifies my neural circuits, how it changes my feelings, and how my cognitive processes are altered thereby. I find it necessary to incorporate how meaning, a mind activity, can change dream and mental health outcomes. I want to understand the mechanisms linking meaning, brain structure and function. I'm also well aware that I controlled some of these brain mechanisms fifty years ago without fully understanding them.

Most dreamers in my experience do not look across these various levels of dream expressions, but are more fascinated by the bizarre forms their dreams take, or remain fixated on new abilities to actively create and control their dreams. I think this is a mistake. If we are to know our self, who we really are, and what were capable of, we must crack the nut of how physiological processes generate a mind that creates meaning, and how meaning reenters the system recursively to change physiological processes. I want to be ever more conscious of my role in humanity; to become more not less loving, as well as knowing that this knowledge has permitted me to contribute something to our collective future. Research through reduction is wonderful, but I believe we must try harder to generate knowledge construction from both directions.

Social psychology has a lot to say about the vagaries of memory. We adamantly believe we remember something that never happened, or we adamantly deny something that actually did happen. A little reflection for most of us provides the necessary examples. But memory operates differently in our dreams, and these differences are critical to our understanding of dreams and consciousness.

Dream generated experiences can take on the same realities as real life experiences. When we fail to identify the origin of dream content and mix internally generated images with those from our external environment, we enter a state of dream craziness. And this dream craziness can be carried into our waking moments. And, it can enter our waking moments consciously or at a non-conscious level. Which is most harmful?

Analyzing our external and internal virtual narratives permits us to observe the mechanism driving dreams, consciousness and the formation of self. And it becomes impossible to ignore the role of self as the central agent controlling what is meaningful to the brain-mind in total. I provide dream examples with nightmares, but there are other examples. My dreams are constantly experimenting with complex social arrangements and evaluating outcomes. In like fashion, my dreams are also constantly experimenting with the interrelationships of complex thought.

Yesterday my spouse hosted some Chinese women friends for lunch. Last night my dreaming brain experimented with second wives, a common practice in historical China, and this was at my "dream wife's" suggestion. I give many examples of complex cognitive manipulations in my dreams. My dreams explore socially complex situations as well as complex thoughts, much as my mind does during the day.

Déjà vu is a sense of something happening now that has happened before. I've been in this building before, I visited this location before, or I've met this person before, and so on. We sense that something is known, but can't quite put our finger on it. Déjà vu may actually represent previous happenings, but often, it is just a feeling. Where does this feeling come from? I often have this sense of déjà vu in my dreams as well as during waking moments, and it is in my dreams that I find answers.

Engaging embedded memories need not be conscious. I don't think about moving my feet, but rather, I just walk as memory FAPs do the work. I don't think about picking up that grape as I write these words, I just do so thoughtlessly. Various elements of memory are accessed by my dreaming brain just as automatically. And memory integration in my dreams often means that many elements seem jumbled as times, places, and people are all mixed together to form a momentary story.

My dreaming brain searches for a car and through long held memory associations selects a variation of my 1965 Pontiac Lemans or my 1952 Chevy. It searches for a university setting, and more frequently than not goes to Mankato State University of the 1970s, and it takes liberty to modify all of these elements as the momentary scenarios of my dreams unfold. Any number of different physical characteristics can represent someone who has been or is real in my waking life. I often only understand who this dream character is by the feelings associated with him or her, and so it goes. But, déjà vu can occur from self-generated dream memories as well as from real environmental experiences. Ho, ho, ho! Déjà vu on déjà vu it seems. Dream analysis improves as our ability to observe improves. The virtual elements that are our individual realities are often more virtual than we suspect.

Déjà vu can give me a sense of knowing, because the feeling associated with person, place, or thing activates this sense. The person, place or thing may be real, but often it is a total auto-creation. It's just the feeling associated with composite characters, the similarity of my physical and postural state in space, the similarity of voice, clothing, or walk that makes it déjà vu. A sense of déjà vu emerges because an associated memory is activated. This occurs in my dreams as well as my waking life. My brain accesses memories from real life experiences and memories that are totally auto-created and mixes them across waking and dreaming states. Do you suppose perhaps there's another doctoral dissertation here?

I identify the source of memory elements because I consistently analyze dream content. It's easy to understand how confused Freud must have been, because he did not follow his own dreams. He looked through the microscope, but forgot to clean the lens.

When my dreaming brain creates a scene, character, or emotional attachment in one of my dreams, I may use any of these elements repeatedly in future dreams. It doesn't matter if these are my conscious dream creations, or whether they emerge through non-conscious processes. Remember, self-created elements in dreams can be used over and over again, and they are. In my case, I know that some of these dream conscious experiences enter my waking life to become déjà vu.

It's a two way street. It doesn't matter if the dream elements are auto-created in my dreams, or if the dream elements come from real life experiences. This is part of the magical exchange between brain conscious states when we are sleeping and when we are awake. In my experience, elements from my dreams can break into daytime consciousness as easily as waking elements from the day can enter our dreams.

This relationship is more fully appreciated by those of us who have experienced daytime hallucinations. One can think of déjà vu dream elements flirting with consciousness as shadow hallucinations. Shadow hallucinations can be as much fun to play with as their sister daydream counterparts. What does the reader suppose the difference is?

As an aside, note that if you consciously use suggestion to guide part or all of your dreams, these elements and learned patterns of inserting material into your dreams may follow you forever. I have a dream farm that I visit. The farm is run by a warm, accepting couple, a large house, and extensive lands. It is my land of OZ; it is an extension of my ideal physical setting, ideal people, and ideal life. I never dream programmed this farm and I never even used limited suggestion to create any of its content. Yet, year to year it evolves. This utopia was initially created between my 12th and 14th years. I keep it tucked away in my dream library the way most people keep their special fond memories of childhood.

This week, new characters were added (2-28-11), and the dream plot was once again modified. Similar auto-creations are common to the dream literature. They are common to both historical and contemporary literature, and when we re-enter these dreams repeatedly, they can and do become elaborate.

Brooks and Vogelsong report similar dream creations. Shamans and mystics who re-enter these dreams often build elaborate edifices of supernatural stature. Astral travelers can have favorite planets and civilizations that they visit, or special periods of history that they bring to life. Reality is such an easy thing to create that we do it constantly. When we repeatedly enter these dream worlds in waking states called visions, we may become known as prophets.

Our brains are not movie cameras capturing exact pictures from our daily lives. Instead, our brains are modular, and reconstruct visuals, emotions, and thoughts from smaller chunks of neural circuitry and chemical modulators. And, we perform these constructions differently when dreaming than we do when awake.

Fictive bicycle riding in my dreams is déjà vu in the sense that I've been there and done that before in my waking hours. As I practice balancing on my bicycle during daytimes, I benefit from dream balancing practice where I've skipped down the top of steps, walked along the edge of a precipice, or performed aerial acrobatics on or off my bike. My waking balance practice has none of these delightful elements; I just peddle on down the street. But lifelong I have performed amazing acrobatics in my dreams as we all seem to do.

Balancing is a day-to-day mundane activity, one that I will reenact in a couple minutes as I go down stairs to have lunch. Skipping down the tops of steps or riding my bicycle along an impossible precipice is not symbolic, in that it doesn't hold some deep Freudian unconscious meaning. It is entirely transparent, supporting learning, fictively expressed modifications, and integration of memory in neural circuits.

I find overlapping memory mechanisms operating between dreaming and waking. These common mechanisms call my attention to memory processes that are operating across my entire brain, and its various states. Twenty years ago, being placed in a yoga position by my management trainer activated a long lost visual memory of my mother smothering me. It was the physical position and lighting in this environment that I believe triggered this recall. In the sense of déjà vu, I was there before as my "muscle" memories were once again called forth. Duplicating this yoga-like position activated the vision of mother's attack.

Vision constructions like dream creations exemplify the creative role of our Interpreter. The whole scene must be constructed virtually in our mind, which is most conspicuous when we note the physical position we occupy in dream or vision observation: Observation of my dead infant body, for example, occurred from a position of adult height, thereby indicating my infant observation post when held by an adult.

A memory unavailable to my waking consciousness was visually brought forward in a trance-like state. It was an embedded memory activated by an unconscious déjà vu, which must have been associated with my infant child's crib posture, and most probably encouraged by the subdued lighting.

Memory embedded in one's tissue is easy to comprehend; just walk down the street having a conversation without thinking about picking your feet up and putting them down. You know what I mean. Watch children or teenagers unconsciously mimic the actions and voices of people they admire.

My brain holds memories that are mostly beyond my immediate recall. When social psychologists play with this edge of memory, they typically look at the effects and skip analysis of the physiological memory mechanisms.

My infant brain converted mother's crib attacks into a ghost. Whenever I approached steep steps in old houses as I went up to bed in dim light, the ghost appeared. Memory embedded in neural circuits associated with mother's brutal acts of smothering remained intact. Talk about feelings of déjà vu, it doesn't get much better than one's favorite ghost trying to become manifest. But, my daytime conscious mind only interpreted the accompanying feelings as a "concrete" something, the ghost. I don't think the term repressed memory is adequate. In this case, it is a non-conscious memory brought back to life through a muscle retained memory element that was activated by special posturing and lighting. And for emphasis, I'm not saying repressed memory doesn't happen.

My conscious memory of smothering, which led to a near-death experience, was probably made inactive through oxygen deprivation. Nevertheless, my non-conscious, tissue embedded memory was still intact, and it dutifully replayed once I was placed in an appropriate physical position and environment. This memory mechanism suggests that core self can generate complete visuals without direct activation on the part of our autobiographical self. To what degree auto-generated vision scenarios come into play is not determined by this recalled incident. However, once the autobiographical self gets the general idea, it can and does produce a product called trance vision or hallucination.

The replay occurred more than fifty years later. Being aware of different types of memory, how memory is accessed when we dream, and our dream's conscious and non-conscious characteristics all help in interpretation. Using Damasio's terms, the active role of core and proto-self in dream scenarios does not appear to require autobiographical self for the complete dream scenario to be re-enacted. Only subsequent interpretation of the dream or vision requires this involvement.

Unconscious memories of this nature expressed themselves in my dreams as nightmares with creative symbolic narratives, and in my waking hours as entities that were concretely manifested as ghosts. Physiological processes can explain the difference between memories being non-conscious or conscious, not traditional psychoanalytic interpretations. I can appreciate how crazy-making Freud's dream interpretations must have been to his more resilient clients. Nevertheless for me, my Interpreter had to connect implicit and explicit memories to resolve the nightmares.

Our dreaming brain, as well as our waking brain, attempts to make sense of these sensations and attributes meaning to them. And as with the sexual molestation nightmare, my Interpreter's search for meaning created endless variations of the nightmare over decades. We attempt to explain any sensation that comes into our waking consciousness or lucid dreams. My brain in either state is always trying to explain, interpret and make sense of my relationship to the total environment. And, I'm very aware that this process of attributing meaning to life's events was present before the age of two.

Our concept of self depends on relationships to others. It is a history of self-others that resides in our memories. Challenge our memory, and we challenge who we are. Self has meaning because others attribute worth to us. Thus, self-worth of positive value is highly dependent on our social relationships. Change our relationship to others and we change our conception of Self. Self is robust in a strong, loving set of social relationships, and it is fragile without this support. Observing someone being unexpectedly divorced or losing his or her job highlights how fragile our self-concept can be.

Now to the main point: Self and consciousness are created and recreated in our brains as long as we live, or avoid coma. Self in lucid dreaming tries to make sense of its auto-created inner world one streaming vignette after another. Our 25 to 50 nightly mini-dreams bob and weave like boats on choppy water. Of what benefit would it be to bring all this noise into play and have it compete with our morning cup of coffee? I don't need to remember that my fictive bicycle riding is consolidating balance in memory. But, I do want to remember that my nightmare is telling me that I have an unresolved emotional knot from being sexually molested that has never been untied.

We notice that our dream self can be fragile, or it can be strong. Our dream self is constantly creating meaning out of everyday events, even though this creative process may seem bizarre to our waking minds. Our sense of self feels the same in our dreams, as it does in other altered reality states, because the same supporting processes are necessary for it to exist. This also means that what we call "ego," which is fundamental to our well-being, is maintained in our dreams. I note with dream pride, for example, that I can walk faster than others can jog, or I can be a superhero taking out any number of opponents.

Dream elements that I reuse over months or years provide continuity to my dream Self, just as elements from my waking life provide waking continuity. My waking and dreaming worlds run parallel to each other much of the time, but they also frequently intersect. And, the older I get, the more they seem to communicate. When I interpret my dreams, I recognize the importance of people, places, and things and the role they play in the maintenance of my dream Self. This process parallels what is happening in my waking moments. Both my sense of dream and waking Self change through time along with my memories.

My dream self is ageing, but not as fast as my waking self. The fantastic feats of my dream self are no longer revered to the same degree by either my sleeping or waking self. And as I age, the two senses of self continue to converge. This convergence is part of my growing sense of unity as a person. It also speaks to the interchange of information across my entire brain.

But, a major difference between my dream and waking selves is my dream ability to return to and become any of my former selves age-wise. I can be thirty again in my dream, and being a dream-thirty year old permits me to engage in activities permitted by my conscience at that age. My aged Self can play out the fantasies of my thirty year old Self in my dreams in a manner that my real thirty year old Self couldn't. Ho, ho, ho! Who says we can't step into the same river twice?

Being able to distinguish false memory from real experiences is difficult, and there is a lot of research documenting these difficulties. Most analysis of false memory observes memory functions in the waking state. Dream analysis adds another dimension to my understanding of false memory, and helps me sort out additional dimension, especially the recognition that dream elements can affect waking sensation. Traumatic incidents in our environment can shock our brains into altered states or near altered states. We experience a milder form of creating false imagery when over tiredness turns the shadow into a potential prowler. I don't think we can develop a good understanding of false memory until self-generated dream memories are examined in relation to waking consciousness. Careful self-observation of dreams and other altered states is a good starting point. Perhaps there's a good Ph.D. thesis here too.

I keep track of dream content, identify elements that I create whole, and follow the use of these elements in future dreams. Most people do not distinguish between what their beliefs are and what their external social reality is. For example, tests of self-perception versus how others see us vividly point out this difference. The match between self-belief and how others see us is typically quite disjointed. We are often not the person we believe we are when it comes to social perceptions.

If our understanding of self diverges too greatly from that of others, we are considered bizarre, or even crazy. But most of us never undergo these marketplace tests, and live life-long with our illusions. And, this is just the surface stuff: We haven't included dream contributions to the development and maintenance of self-perception at this level of analysis. Now, add in self-perception for those who experience visions, and we begin to understand why popular cognitive interpretations of spirituality are so distorted by either theists or atheists.

In contrast to the social maintenance of Self, our dreaming brain can be almost totally free to have sex with whomever it chooses, beat up its enemies with impunity, or fly out-of-body to other worlds. This was true for me as a young man, but as I age, my dreaming self increasingly employs a set of ethics comparable to my waking Self. My dreaming Self historically had a higher sex drive and a more liberal sense of morality.

Through time, my dreaming conscience continues to evolve on a parallel course with my waking conscience. Some of our ageing conservative nature appears related to the integration of self-fragments. And self-fragments can be understood as complex role sets acquired in dynamic social settings.

Two basic instincts are always present in my dreams as they are in my waking consciousness: self-preservation and making actions meaningful. I know that when these two instincts wink off, my will to live disappears too. Thus, there is an intuitive awareness of self-preservation at my highest cognitive level that seems to communicate directly with my DNA. And, generating meaning at higher cognitive levels seems to have a direct impact on my instincts.

Self-maintenance and self-preservation are bedrock states supporting consciousness. If my dream character is experiencing fear, or life threatening situations, it will quickly go into action, or change states that wake me up. Our dreaming consciousness provides the wildest explanations to make sense of all the bizarre modular changes it is experiencing.

We act in a similar fashion when awake. We interpret our world to make it meaningful. But, when awake, we add in transitional materials to make experience flow. The fundamental process of self-preservation and creation of meaning remains, but what changes is our physiological capacity to integrate stimuli and make fluid transitions from one dream state to another.

A final comment on memory as a modular event: As my dreaming brain is activated, regardless of the phenomena or epiphenomena being visualized, my modular brain remains modular. It uses emotion to trigger a dream scenario, or it may use a physical stimulus such as heat, cold, or fictive memory consolidation such as balancing. My dreaming brain is also activated by thoughts as much as sleeping discomfort might. I often recall four or five dreams that are spread across the night that are focused on academic discussions, lectures, or even philosophical musings.

Activities such as writing this book can activate dreams that dominate my entire night. It's equivalent to others who write stories or poems in their dreams, or solve math problems, or contemplate the structure of organic chemicals. If you follow TV shows or films with famous actors, you will most likely include them in your dreams. I think all of our dreaming brains engage in similar activities, but at different levels of complexity. It depends on how we've trained and used our brains over the years.

Our dreaming brains access elements of memory that look and feel like pathology and mental illness to our waking selves. Do not be afraid of or shy away from these dream elements, as they are a fundamental reflection of how self and consciousness are created and maintained. In one sense, dreams are half of the bricks and mortar that make the waking self whole. Self and consciousness needs input from all our brain's complex structures if it is to be continuous and consistent. Access to select modular centers of our brains during dreaming creates the bizarre, but the bizarre experientially is a byproduct of our brain's modular, multi-functional development and self-maintenance. I accept these working mechanisms for what they are, and use this awareness to help me interpret my dreams.

Some of the unconscious learning that normally goes on below our awareness becomes more visible in our lucid dreams. Improving understanding of unconscious memory processes creates insight into and respect for the mechanisms that support self and consciousness. In dreams, we approach the mirror of non-conscious processes and image making obliquely, and must know where to look in order to see more than shadows. We know when we identify meaningful bridging elements by the results we get.

No other person can know our subjective realities as we can; that is, if we pay careful attention to the processes creating our subjective reality. I look closely at how my memory works, and how my dreaming and waking consciousness differ, and I gain insight into myself that cannot be obtained in waking states alone. Memory like Self and consciousness is part of a modular brain engaged in modular processes. Understanding this modularity enhances all aspects of my self-understanding when awake or when dreaming. It helps take the mystery out of mysticism and all the ancient and contemporary occult interpretations. At least this has been my experience.

THEME DREAM I

(Recorded 8:42 a.m., October 21, 2010):

Thematically, last night's dreams were made up of three specific episodes that were recalled approximately at 1:30 a.m., 4:00 a.m. and 7:00 a.m. The main character was a composite of one of my high school classmates whose name was Jim Kellerman.

1:30 a.m.: I'm in a new town, attending a new school, and am unfamiliar with my classmates except for the morphed Jim. I attended 12 different schools by the time I entered seventh grade.

One of our classmates carries a holstered pistol, and whenever he is losing at any game, he points the pistol at the person about to win and takes over the ball. None of my other classmates have a personal, recognizable identity, and the game image is vague as it can be either a baseball or basketball. My focus is on the pistol being carried openly and used repeatedly by my unidentified classmate. I think that he must be 18 years of age in order to have a gun carrying permit. It doesn't dawn on me until I wake up that carrying a gun on school property and using it in this fashion would be illegal. The reader will note that my mind is focusing on a stream of action, or theme, using the gun to control the ball, and I only recognize how illogical my interpretation is when I consciously review these elements after waking.

4:00 a.m.: The scene shifts. I'm still in a new school with new classmates, but I'm aware that I'm living just outside of town. Jim also lives outside of town, and I announce that we live about one and one-half miles apart. Hence, we often ride our horses back and forth to visit each other. Jim in real life lived in town, and I varied my living residence from town to country and never liked to ride horses. To my knowledge, neither did Jim, although he did have a gun I admired.

I realize that I'm older than most of my classmates, and should take some leadership role in dealing with our gun-toting classmate. I propose that we begin to make his life uncomfortable through a strategy where we sabotage his personal items. We smear feces on the handle of his school locker. Other students begin to worry about what will happen when the gun totter finds out who is making his life miserable. I inform them that I'll take responsibility, and model my exact words.

7:00 a.m.: There are some gang members looking for me, and I step into a shed and watch cautiously for their appearance. One of the school's teachers, an Afro-American, comes by and approaches the house next to the shed. She notices me, offers a greeting comment, and enters her house. I recognize that the house is in a run-down area, small and inexpensive. I attribute this state of affairs to the fact that she seems to be supporting a large number of extended family members.

The scene changes again, and I'm in a classroom setting. The teacher is giving instructions about a report that is due the following day. I have no knowledge of this report and ask Jim what he is using for resources.

Again, the scene shifts, and we are in the cafeteria. I go through the lunch line, and realize that everything I want is already on a plate at the end of the line. I move to the end and take the plate. I motion to Jim that I want to sit with him, and suggest a table that has two chairs. He motions to two chairs without a table and sits down. I agree and join him. In this dream, like other similar dreams, I never recall actually eating or tasting food. I interpret this fact to eating being such a common, everyday activity that it doesn't need memory reinforcement. I wonder if chefs taste food in their dreams the way some of us play music?

I continue to quiz Jim about the project that is due tomorrow. He is reluctant to share his resources, saying that they are very specific to his report, including a section of complicated statistics. I assure him that I will pick a different topic, if he just clarifies the assignment: He refuses. I realize that I'm not familiar with the statistics involved, but confidently plan to review them before I write my paper.

INTERPRETATION

The theme of being in a school and having problems to solve and papers to write passes through my dreaming brain in at least three different dream scenarios from 1:30 a.m. to 7:00 a.m. The classmate with a gun and gang members don't fit, and make the overall story seem bizarre. The writing assignment, my being older than the other students, and having a problem writing my paper are central to my dreaming consciousness. Are these dream images just random elements popping into consciousness, and making it necessary for my conscious mind to knit them together and give them meaning? I don't think so. Much of the dream imagery is epiphenomenal, but there is an underlying theme that exists throughout the night.

This is the third time in the past five days that I recall having dreams where I'm back in school, in a new geographical setting, being confronted with tasks that are immediate, and requiring knowledge about which I'm uncertain. Are these dreams simply elements from the brainstem? Or, as Linden notes about the view of some neurobiologists: "… the content of dreams has no meaning whatsoever …: The byproduct of some other important process, such as memory consolidation (Linden: 208).

The thematic essence of these dreams covers a number of vignettes which are carried from one day to the next, and were repeated in different forms last night. There is meaning to be had! I am wrestling with the process of writing this book and how to present and integrate materials, and recognize that I can't keep all my resources in conscious awareness concurrently. My most salient thought upon waking is that I have a modular brain, thus, I will modularize my approach to organizing this material. And, I realize that modularize means breaking larger chunks of material into smaller units for easier handling. These dreams occurred after my incorporation of materials from Restak on the modular brain.

I'm aware that waking-consciousness and dreaming-consciousness are wrestling with the same problems and reinforcing each other. However, my dreaming brain doesn't have a complete view of what the book will look like when it's finished, and neither does my waking brain. Hence the struggle is at a general and not a specific level. It is thematic in nature. I'm thinking about this book's contents and organization, but there are too many parts still unorganized for my dreaming brain to provide specific direction. There is just a vague notion that modularity (smaller units of organization) needs attention. I review the above section on meaning, find that it is an incoherent mess, and rewrite it.

I often take direction from my dreams. Dream advice may be general or specific. Transfer of elements that become conscious in my dreams to waking application has a long history for me. Many of us transfer the creative products of dreams to waking consciousness. This transfer and exchange has been reported by different writers, artists, scientists, and others throughout history.

From an evolutionary perspective, an efficient brain keeps focus on the main survival elements in our life. This requires ongoing integration of what's most important to us at the moment, balancing our emotional needs, and giving attention to ongoing memory functions.

A holistic view of my brain clarifies the main point for me. I have a modular brain, distinct brain states exist between waking and dreaming, and these two brain-mind states reinforce each other by helping me sort out what is important day-to-day, prioritize meaningful elements in my life, and interact with each other systemically in terms of ongoing goals and personal objectives. This human hierarchy of needs seems to be constantly expressed in my dreams as it is during my waking moments.

Elements in my dream are only bizarre if I insist on interpreting them the same way in both waking and dreaming states. Lucid dreaming can be just as thematic and metaphorical as my conscious moments. Conversely, watching basic image formation in my dreams takes me to an awareness level that I can't reach when awake. I don't think dreams are meaningless, even though they often reflect maintenance of basic brain-mind functions. My dreams represent multi-tasking activity that ranges from basic image formation, memory integration and consolidation, to meta-cognitive processes. One size interpretation does not fit all dreams.

I don't have solutions to all the organizational details of this book as I write these lines. I'm not sure of all the resources that I will include, or how best to present them. My dreaming brain is wrestling with these issues along with my daytime consciousness. Dream issues that I'm struggling with range from specifics, such as image formation, to meta-consciousness. Some mornings I get specific directions, and others, only a vague sense that processing is continuing. In either case, my dreaming brain reflects activity that runs parallel to my waking consciousness.

Integration of past and present experience is a necessary part of life. Integration of the whole gives me a sense of unity, and this sense of wholeness is reinforced when I bring together materials from the past fifty to seventy years of dreaming in combination with related research.

Nightmares and lucid dreams have been a significant part of my history. And this history weaves like a tapestry through the trauma of child abuse and all its ramifications. My brain abhors a vacuum, which is to say it abhors fragmentation. Greater brain-mind integration means clarity, improved self-understanding, and an increase in focused energy. Clearly the role of dreams and nightmares has varying significance for each one of us, nevertheless, dreams and other states of altered consciousness are integral to what Self is, and what Self becomes.

Why shouldn't my dream elements morph, spit neuronal energy in multi-tasking ways as dendrites play mating games with neurotransmitters, or repeat night after night and throughout any one night? There obviously is work to be done.

Solutions to problems are not always quick and automatic. My brain works like yours most of the time, and we are both capable of thinking abstractly, as abstract thinking is a process of holding multiple elements together at one time and viewing their interrelationship. These complex interrelationships are often expressed in my dreams as themes. In one sense, themes become organizing schema around which complex thoughts rotate. And I am quite sure thematic content can be spread over an entire night and mixed together with a lot of other brain housekeeping activities.

Activation-synthesis, according to Hobson, has key elements that include the brain being activated during sleep, at which time higher visual centers come into play. We have a loss of working memory, or delusional belief, and there is hyper-associative synthesis, or bizarreness, with primary activation of the limbic system, i.e., emotion, accompanied by organic physical amnesia. Meaning is transparent or salient, and interpretation is not needed (2002: 18).

The above reference compares Hobson's activation-synthesis model with Freud, and lays out the model's key elements.

Hobson is criticized for interpreting dreams as occurring one way, which is from brain stem activation upward. This criticism seems legitimate for his early attempts to explain dreams and consciousness physiologically. He either neglected or deemphasized circular exchanges between brainstem and higher order cognitive functions. His later work, at least starting with the time period associated with **13 Dreams Freud Never Had**, corrects this earlier impression and views dreaming and consciousness as a much more dynamic activity. To Hobson's credit, it was still necessary to confront the ghost of Freud at the time of his earlier research.

THEME DREAM II

(12-23-10)

Last evening, I spent three hours talking with my stepson. He was curious about my early life experiences, especially those associated with my growing up as an underclass kid. I explained to him that my youthful environment was one where the new boy always had to prove his physical prowess by fighting. I lived in 20 different places by the time I was fifteen, and almost always, had to fight the cock at the top of the pecking order every time I moved

My stepson is Chinese, and grew up in an environment where boys engaged in simple confrontations such as throwing water on their best friends. He was confronted by a black man in San Francisco a few months back while walking in a neighborhood park. He did not understand this man's actions, and was asking me for clarification. He left for graduate school a month later, and apparently had some concerns about social contacts in his new culture.

We were joined by his mother who informed me that it was bedtime. My wife and I continued to talk in bed until after 11:00 p.m. About 12:00 a.m. I woke up, aware that I had been dreaming about confronting three men who seemed to have hostile intent toward me. I looked at the clock and thought to myself that I had not been sleeping long enough to have had such a vivid dream. I rolled over and went back to sleep.

I later woke up about 3:00 p.m. dreaming that I'm in the company of a former employee who is ranting about my behavior. I recognize him as someone named P whom I once fired. I'm holding an empty beer bottle, and place it on a shelf next to the entrance door. Both the door and adjacent window are glass. P threatens to throw his empty beer bottle at me, and I'm confronting his pending actions. He pretends to throw the bottle in a very realistic manner and I duck. Next, I notice that he is still holding the bottle and his face is full of rage. I'm thinking of how best to take the bottle from him when the scene changes.

Next, I'm walking across a large open field with small groups of people scattered around different locations. I have a growing sense that this is an unsafe environment, and look around for a safer location. The scene changes again, and I'm on top of a hill overlooking the same open field in the earlier part of this dream sequence. The hill slowly morphs into the top of a tall building, which I'm now standing on.

Looking down, I see my grandson, half smiling, half-smirking at me from the ground below. I tell him that one should not trust investing in bonds, because they are not safe. Further, that on the end of a spear, one can never tell whether or not they are safe. Note how these dream elements are riddled with metaphor.

I wake up about 6:00 a.m. as my wife gets up for the day. I stay in bed in the hope that another hour of sleep will visit me. From 6:00 a.m. to 7:30 a.m. I drift in and out of sleep. I'm very aware that the night's sleep has not been restful. The early part of the night was dominated by adrenalin dripping energy. The progression of dream and half-dreaming thoughts from 12:00 a.m. to 7:00 a.m. moved from human confrontation to being dominated by a grandson smirking at me.

Thematically, the night's dreams and semi-waking thoughts all fit together. The bizarreness of thought, scenes, and actions is rather immaterial in terms of understanding this dream. I had been discussing physical confrontations for over three hours before I went to bed, and fight response adrenaline coursed through my sleeping brain activating the above related series of combative events.

No repressed elements are needed to understand and interpret this night of dreaming. It is quite transparent. I loaded myself with adrenaline before retiring as I told various stories of conflict and fighting to my stepson.

SCATTERED MEMORIES DREAMS

Dream (10-25-10) Recorded 9:30 a.m. Dream recall is taken from 1:10 a.m., 3:40 a.m. and about 7:00 a.m.

Erotic Theme: Time 1:10 a.m. I'm in large room that might be either a school or workplace setting. I'm talking to a younger woman who begins to divulge private information about her personal life. Other people are attempting to listen to our conversation, so she moves closer to me and speaks in a lower voice. I become aware of her physical attractiveness and note sexual overtones in her voice.

Erotic Theme: Time 3:40 a.m. I'm at a former place of employment and moving throughout the building discussing technical matters with a number of other employees. I ask for my boss' location, and I'm informed that she is home sick. I receive a call from her informing me that she has just showered, is in her nightgown, and is having a glass of wine. There is a clear invitation to come and join her. An invitation that is historically accurate except for the nightgown and shower elements.

Day's Activity Dream: Time 7:00 a.m. I am walking through an area of recent rainfall, and notice a number of small creatures. One is like a snail, another is an angle-worm, and a third is in a container and known to be poisonous. I stomp the container, killing the poisonous creature, and throw it away. I'm studying the snail like specimen when the scene changes.

A cat that looks like a young, half-grown cougar appears, and is facing me in a crouching position. I'm tempted to pet it, but notice the cat's attack position. I grab an aluminum lawn chair and hold it facing the cat, and notice it is a female with steel-blue eyes rather than the normal yellow eyes of a cougar. I think this cat must be a hybrid. My brother appears and informs me that the lawn chair is not adequate to hold off a cougar. I tell him that cats react to size and are unable to tell whether or not such items are sturdy. He accepts my explanation. End of scene.

INTERPRETATION

The first two dreams are simply erotic dreams that reflect my body's emotional state as I drift off to sleep. Such dreams can have any number of characters or scenarios. But, what I recognize in these two dream segments is a lack of sexual fulfillment. In the 1:10 a.m. dream, the young woman's looks are vaguely familiar; however, I recognize her by my emotional reaction. She is someone that I dated years ago, and have always retained fond memories of. In the 3:40 a.m. dream, the woman is a former boss who occasionally made sexual overtures to me such as asking me to her house to drink wine.

I note in this dream and other dreams I've had in recent years that permission to have sex with dream partners is usually not permitted by my conscience. Values expressed in my dreams are now overwhelmingly values that I hold when awake. I associate this change in dream behavior with the integrated sense of unity I've achieved as I age; that is an increased integration between dream and waking consciousness, and dream and waking conscience.

My dreams, as I believe is the case for all of us, often selects people, scenes and elements from any of my memories irrespective of time elements and mixes them around a theme that can be either cognitive, emotional or a mix of the two. The erotic content dreams are straightforward expressions of mild sexual longing. The characters in these dreams are from 15, 20 and 30 years ago.

HORMONE ACTIVATED DREAMS

The above erotic dreams appear to be activated by rather transparent sexual feelings. My daytime state of being sexually unfulfilled is carried over into my dreams. My Interpreter is aware of these feelings, as it is a common rather demanding state for most of us. I'm assuming that my elevated hormone level is carried over from the evening to create an erotic dream; and any combination of visuals can suffice to create the dream narrative. This is a common pattern for me.

What should I call testosterone and its fictive cognitive component as a dream activator? Surely it is not something I've found in dream dictionaries. Hobson calls it an emotion, and it is surely as basic as fear or anxiety. Hormones associated with lust demand the entire attention of my brain during moments of waking coitus; however, the fictive representation in sleep is more pliable as my dreaming brain can move in and out of these simulations instantly. The fictive emotions of dream sex are totally enjoyable, yet they place no demands on my physiology. Fictive sex is like flying out of body – very enjoyable. Older folks appreciate this more than younger folks.

Lust is a physiological metaphor that represents a complex of internal routines activated by the brain's architecture and hormones. One can observe an infant boy's sexuality developing as he exhibits erections while still in diapers. Sexual desire is expressed in our dreams as all other emotions are. And, we can guide and direct expression of any emotion in our dreams through suggestion or dream programming.

From my point of view, Hobson comes closest to explaining erotic dreams with his Activation-Synthesis Model. Other narrative or story aspects of erotic dreams reflect one's larger social environment with its many directives and influences. Fictive or wet dream sex depends on age, level of arousal, and how one's dreaming or waking conscience interprets sex. There can be as much dynamic interplay between higher and lower brain centers as one chooses, thereby giving new meaning to the old adage that men don't think with their brains.

I've noted elsewhere that as I age, I'm not capable of committing acts in my dreams that I wouldn't commit when awake, e.g., having sex with erotic dream characters. These ageing elements need clarification, however.

On (4-14-11) my dreams contained three different female partners of three different ages: (16-18), (35ish) and (55-60) years of age. I compared the sensuality in these dreams while I was sleeping, and returned to the youngest woman and engaged in sex a second time. I found the dream series a little strange, as I've not had a similar dream since I stopped dream programming years ago. Repeated sex with the younger partner served as my bridging element.

How can I claim moral maturation in my dreams, and then report this type of dream adventure?

My age during this coital dream series was 30-40 years. I can be a pugilist in my dreams if I age regress, but not when I'm my current age of 75. I can perform similar physical feats that are age appropriate in my dreams as well. I'm clearly aware that my moral expression is age dependent. This awareness supports my hypothesis that morality depends on integrating various roles into our developing conscience as the Self matures with ageing. It is not an either or thing. Morality is contextual, socio-historical, and self-integrative around our developing level of conscience and maturity of self.

In 2011, at the age of 75 years, I find it morally reprehensible to think of having sex with a 16-18 year old toward whom I should be acting as a parent, teacher, or guardian. A logical, cognitive level of enlightenment, however, I can bypass this level of enlightenment in my dreams through age regression. In effect, I'm not having sex at age 75 in my dream, but rather, a former, younger, more immature me is.

The feedback loop that opens as I begin to write this book about dreams brings me to ask many different questions about morality in dreams. This particular dream manipulation occurred after reading Patricia Churchill's *Braintrust*. She does not address this type of issue in her new book, but my integrating brain was stimulated by her discussions of morality and created the scenario on its own. Why, what, and how always seem to be active in the recesses of our minds. I'm almost compulsive about revisiting previously contemplated waking issues in my dreams.

What does this say about the role of hormones interpreted by conscience? What does this say about daydreams and daytime consciousness? What does this say about the feedback loops, circular causation between waking and sleeping consciousness, and what does this say about the role of reflecting on Self in the construction of Self? Enjoy!

MEMORY REVIEW DREAM

In the 7:00 a.m. dream, I recognize the rain element and the angle-worms. I went walking yesterday morning in the rain through a nearby park with my spouse. Mostly light rain from the night continued at various intensity levels as we walked. My spouse kept commenting about the dozen of worms squirming on the walkways as we passed by. This scene was duplicated well enough in my dream to be recognizable.

I've recently read *In Search of Memory* by Eric Kandel in which I followed his memory discoveries with aplysia. His work is famous for discovering how neurons and neural circuits control behavior. His autobiography and his firsthand accounts of numerous discoveries in neuroscience are enjoyable. In my dream, one of the creatures is aplysia. The physiological discoveries of Kandel's book are swirling through my waking and dreaming brain looking for new connections.

Various researchers have debated the time lapse needed for daytime experience to enter our dreams. After 50 years of lucid dreaming, I can say with certainty, at least in my case, that mixing and matching daytime elements in my dreams can occur in any combination. I sometimes take stimuli from the moment of dreaming, and mix it with stimuli from my environment the day before, the week before, or thirty years ago.

In my experience, associational memory accesses compatible memories across our recorded landscape of total memories; dream or daytime memories that is. My life is uneventful and routine most days. However, a dramatic event such as a death in the family or close friends who had been diagnosed with cancer will set off memories that quickly reach across my entire history. In this way, if one has an uneventful daily routine that is suddenly punctuated by some form of drama, associational memory will call forth related elements from any previous time period. Associations in dream are not bound by speculative timelines – at least in my case.

Always, my ongoing mental activity is reflected in my dreams. My emotionally arousing dream content can mix over any combination of time dimensions and draw upon any number of emotionally representative elements. Cognitive-based elements reflect ongoing readings, study, or research. And, both my dreaming and waking brain are processing Kandel at the moment in time that I write these words.

The erotic-content dreams speak to my conscious mind rather directly. Dreams with strong emotional content enter my dream consciousness whether they are erotic feelings, fear, or any other strong emotion that is salient.

When I laid down for my afternoon nap today, I reminded myself that I should add a section about erotic dreams and their activation. When I woke up, I noticed that additional, related mental activity had occurred while I was sleeping. My dreaming mind was telling me to elaborate on the chemistry of emotion and write a section on fear, its activation, and relationship to dream dictionaries. This is another good example of the interface between my dreams and waking consciousness. I'll decide later whether or not to follow this advice.

My life has been filled with study, research and teaching, and it is a habit for my dreaming brain to process and integrate cognitive activity from the day or previous days. My pre-conscious brain is often aware of how my study material is being integrated before my conscious brain is. In the past, I would often wake up and proceed to change my lecture notes or power slides according to ideas generated in my dreams.

It is now well understood that non-conscious processes in our brains often achieve integration and initiate various actions before our conscious minds are aware of this activity. By following my dreams over time, I experience these non-conscious processes occurring at various levels of abstraction. Levels noted as being both metaphorical and abstract in my dream reports. A majority of my dream elements are concrete and represent a single function such as memory consolidation. On the other hand, concrete elements often represent the tip of the iceberg for themes or more complex abstractions, and I have to reflect on function to sort out the difference.

When normally concrete elements take on a metaphorical interpretation, they are frequently bridges to my dreams meaning. Visual elements from a lifetime of memories can be mixed and matched in any combination as associative memory plays out. And, the pattern of dream element integration can be at various levels of abstraction and represent a wide use of creative and complex metaphors.

Abstract and metaphorical dream elements are combined in a creative, individualistic manner. Writers of dream dictionaries cannot claim that any one dream element has a specific meaning as was the case with Freud's *Interpretation of Dreams,* and this is true of most popular dream dictionaries such as Browne's. This creative, interpretive dream process and related individual awareness will vary for readers. The degree of self-discipline you have imposed developing your cognitive abilities and integrating your emotional world will be reflected in the kinds of dreams you have and the level of abstraction your dreaming brain exercises. In similar fashion my decades of dream patterns reflect these changes over time.

Another observation that dream analysis must take into consideration is the two-way loop between dreaming and waking consciousness. Story elaboration in my dreams varies by the intensity of my feelings and by the degree of cognitive or social complexity I'm experiencing. Concentrated study, or an emotionally arousing incident, will enter and change my dreams. Even little events such as a cold shoulder, will enter my dream and become a dream element such as a 1955 Chevy.

SYMBOLIC DREAM

(10-27-10, 2:35 a.m.), Recorded 9:39 a.m.

I'm in a zone of conflict, a type of war zone but there is no actual shooting or destruction. A soldier with a rifle slung over his shoulder approaches me with a pistol wrapped in cloth. He tells me that it is a Carter weapon, has 40 rounds, and that it should be sufficient for my purposes. I examine it carefully, and think that it actually looks like a Glock. The cloth wrapping is a set of under shorts, BVD by brand. I think that this is an unusual wrapping, but the BVD is clean, and after all, this is a war zone.

The scene morphs and I am informed by a friend that one of the psychologists nearby would really like to own this weapon. I show it to him, and he is visibly impressed and wants it. I just chuckle and move on. I'm still in the same setting, as I can see the psychologist putting test material into a machine and scanning it. I note that the scanned material is much like an MMPI test where the client simply fills in answers with a number two pencil or dark ink. I remain in this setting and continue talking to other people.

One of the individuals tells me that he is a teacher and has been preparing to teach math. However, his math scores aren't very good, and he is concerned about his teaching performance. His recent math test score is 95 and this is the highest score he has ever achieved on a math test. I'm impressed. Then he adds that the test determines what percentage of six grade math he has mastered. I'm no longer impressed. I think to myself that this guy should never be a teacher with such limited knowledge.

SUMMARY OF DREAMS

I have presented dreams spanning several days to demonstrate how content, themes, and interpretation come together for me. These are ordinary dreams, as there is nothing special going on in my life at the moment. I did not consciously influence any of these dreams through suggestion before or during sleep. Nevertheless, my dreams clearly reflect ongoing daily concerns in my life. They are natural dreams that reflect my current physical state, and how my memory is operating to create themes and metaphor that integrates my day-to-day experiences.

Note that when I say I did not consciously influence my dreams through suggestion, that I assume there is always interplay over a nights dreaming between higher and lower brain centers. Hence, a non-conscious form of suggestion, such as my emotional state, may enter my dreams. I think a broader incorporation of daytime emotions and cognitions occurs for those of us who have a long dream history of consciously using suggestion.

If the reader is familiar with dream interpretation by sources such as Delaney, or Brooks and Vogelsong, he or she will often discover different interpretations from those I've given in my ordinary dreams. I believe that understanding what is going on in our own dreams necessitates non-interference in dream processes. If you regularly use suggestion to influence your dreams, the content, themes, and stories will be different from dreams free of these influences. Further, dream lab environments are a bit artificial, as are home hookups with dream lab technology employed. The bias I'm expressing says that our total environmental stimuli impinge on our dreams.

Those of us who permit natural dreaming have different experiences when our internal environment is left undisturbed. The reader will note in my dream reports how frequently environmental influences enter my dreams. For me, dynamic system integration means that our dreams vary according to our total environment and this includes suggestion. How could it be otherwise?

The brain-mind is a dynamic integrated whole and, I think, must be studied, analyzed and understood in its various normal states, which includes altered states for me. I also think that long-term subjective dream analysis through self-observation offers different insights than group lab studies do. This statement is not meant to diminish in any way the importance of dream lab methodology. Obviously, work by dream researchers has been of immense help in moving us away from the mythology of the ancients and Freudians. Brooks and Vogelsong are an excellent example of how dream lucidity can be achieved and suggestion used to alter one's own dreams. However, if you consistently use suggestion in your dreams, keep a record and compare its effects when you dream naturally.

I know from decades of experience the fun one can have playing with and programming dreams. I also know that memories created internally through suggestion can take on a life of their own. This I believe distorts our understanding of how memory is consolidated, changed or reinforced during dream time. Suggestion has to alter the natural two-way flow of communication between the dreaming and awake states of consciousness. The hundreds of neuro-modulators influencing our brains must be expressed differently with conscious dream manipulation through suggestion. And, I'm more effective at interpreting my contemporary dreams when I isolate auto-created dream memories, which are fairly extensive.

Suggestion used in lucid dreaming distorts the stories derived and dream content in two ways.

First, dream elements are consciously created and mask or partially mask the emergence of natural day-to-day elements. I have hundreds of auto-created dream memories that originated from daytime associations such as my dream farm utopia. Life-long lucid dreaming must increase the frequency of these elements in my dreams, but again, this is speculation born from long-term self-observation.

Second, the derivation of abstract themes and naturally emerging metaphorical elements are altered by introducing conscious dream characters and activities. Long-term dream analysis by a single individual, over an extended period of time, brings these insights into relief. I don't think there's and alternative methodology to self-observation that can offer these same insights.

Those who believe they have engaged in astral travel, remote viewing or other occult activities have become what I've called True Believers. Interpretations of this extreme distortion of subjective processes, I am quite sure, will never lead to improved understanding of the brain-mind mechanisms involved. These subjective games of manufactured virtual reality are just that: manufactured virtual reality that has been disconnected from external stimuli.

Formal dream lab research, along with the findings of neuroscience, increasingly demonstrate that the island on which True Believers of the occult live gets smaller and smaller with each new addition to the larger research base. New research with new methodologies confronts the True Believer's dogma.

Dream suggestion and programming alters our dream experiences in a way similar to how the mystic alters his or her subjective reality. Whatever degree of our total dream elements, characters and plots we alter to that degree we must change our interpretations of reality. Our manufactured dream elements guided by suggestion or auto-created altered states of reality can have major impact on our beliefs. If we analyze dreams altered by suggestion, we will often come to different conclusions than when we dream naturally. And with visions, the reality seems undeniable.

Partially or totally controlled dream content and stories are not true representation of the dreaming brain's normal expressions. And in my experience with nightmare suppression, total dream programming interferes with brain-mind functions. This must be the case when I experience relief from nightmare trauma. On the flip side, the psychic relief I experienced after stopping two decades of nightmare repression being another example. The True Believer fails to distinguish between auto-created experiences and stimuli coming from the external world: Internal stimuli in altered states is stark and compelling and can easily come to dominate the reality of self. Tell the person who is possessed by an evil spirit that his feelings are just illusions.

Following the processes by which auto-created realities come to dominate the True Believer's perceptions is critical for both religious and secular interventions. Historically, the shaman wore both hats. Following these processes also speaks to the futility of a Richard Dawkins trying to suppress these most basic mechanisms of human spirituality in the name of ridding the world of religion.

INTERPRETATION

In *Break Through Dreaming* Gayle Delaney states:

While dreams sometimes show us repressed feelings, they also help us recognize unrealized potentials and bring to our attention creative solutions to daily problems (1991: 11).

I generally agree with her position. Some of my dreams are more symbolic than others. In my erotic dreams, the feelings are not so much repressed as they are unrealized. The dream does not represent a major problem or issue in my life, nor does it directly offer a solution to the dream's main theme. Unrealized potential of my hormones is much like experiencing physical discomfort of temperature of body being flagged to my dreaming brain.

I watched a movie before going to bed last night (2-26-10) that depicted a number of people wandering around a northern Minnesota forest and landscape. Interpersonal conflict was superficial and funny, and all ended well. Some of the forest scenery from this movie was brought into my dream as well as the overall sense of conflict; and the conflict being expressed in my dream was equally harmless.

The bridging incident, using Delaney's term, was the pistol. I didn't think much of the dream when I became aware of it at 2:35 a.m. and didn't plan to incorporate it into this book. However, after waking, I thought what a good example it is of how Delaney interprets dreams using the concept of bridging. I had to focus for a couple minutes in order to return the dream to conscious awareness, as I had decided to discard it during the night.

Scanning my dream, I found the Glock-Carter gun wrapped in a BVD to be very unusual. My spouse recently bought a pair of Carter shoes, and kept talking about what a bargain they were. Carter as a name brand was salient in my current memory. The physical appearance of the gun in my dream was that of a Glock. The symbolism of the gun wrapped in a pair of BVDs goes back to my army days of basic training. "This is your rifle, this is your gun." The gun reference was to one's privates, hence, the sexual theme and overtone, along with a sense of erotic longing that has been swirling through my dreams the past few days.

By identifying the dream's content and its origin, I easily focused on the bridging element and its interpretation. I think the Freudian/ psychoanalytic interpretation of repression is the wrong term to explain this dream; unfulfilled, temporary emotional state seems better. The symbolism is very transparent and reflects my current emotional state, which is an awareness that has been building in my dreams this past week, and randomly mixes with other life elements of current concern.

The testing part of the dream uses a scanning machine that I was exposed to in a TV advertisement yesterday. Test scores are associated with my stepson's recent acceptance into graduate school, but denial of financial aid or an assistantship because his undergraduate academic performance was not high enough. Again, the thematic and metaphorical dream quality seems apparent. I found the gun metaphor humorous as I haven't consciously thought about this symbolism for decades. Associative memory has many interesting and sometimes humorous ways of being expressed. But, let me go back to my (2-26-10) dream.

CONFLICT DREAMS

(2-26-10)

I recalled two separate dreams in considerable detail as I have three hand-written legal pages of notes. I'll present dream number one from my notes and abbreviate dream number two.

Dream 1: Military forces are moving into my area and are not defined by group or country, but clearly a threat. Our military has been creating secret weapons that have gone astray. Cars are fleeing the city, and the highways are packed. I'm on a hillside looking down onto a four lane highway when giant bug-like robots appear. They dwarf the cars, and are moving much faster than the fleeing traffic, maybe twice as fast. As the robot bugs pass over the cars, their knife-like appendages, much like giant ants, pierce the vehicles, disabling them instantly and killing the vehicles occupants. Within seconds the robots race down the road leaving death and destruction. I know that more traditional military will follow mopping up loners like me. I can just see them coming now. I scurry along the hillside, expecting to be shot at any moment, but manage to get out-of-sight.

I enter a cave opening, and think that this would be a good place to hide food. I want to hide supplies before the main war starts so I can be prepared to survive. The cave turns into a large room and I discover that many people are with me. The cave turns into an institutional building I renovated for a treatment program in Hennepin County in the late 1980s.

We are on the street, and a man runs by in shirt sleeves as it is summer. He is covered with blood and looks terrified. I ask him what is wrong, and soundlessly he mouths, "look behind you." I turn to face a giant man, maybe seven plus feet tall, bald, huge body and arms, holding a gigantic knife, which looks more like a machete than a knife. The knife is capable of slashing, stabbing and decapitating.

The man laughs as he raises the knife in front of the bleeding victim and then turns to me. He raises the knife again, and then in a swift movement seems to run it into his stomach. He laughs again and turns sideways. I can see that the huge knife merely passed next to his stomach—a faked stabbing.

A smaller version of the giant magically appears who is about five-and-one-half feet tall, but with the same bald/fat appearance. A little brother, I wonder. They walk away arm-in-arm laughing. (End of dream).

INTERPRETATION

The fantastic images are from science fiction movies that I have been watching the last few days. The large bald man is an image of someone I saw last week in a local mall. The knife is from the Big 5 sporting goods store where I recently bought fishing equipment. The cave in which I hid first turned into a tunnel similar to an underground passageways in the former TB sanatorium turned treatment center in Hennepin County that I renovated.

The two dreams are long and detailed, and represent my total recall from this night. Image content was pulled randomly by my conscious brain's day activity, and knitted into a story that made sense to my dream consciousness. I remember the dreams in great detail as I reviewed them in the middle of the night when I got up to use the bathroom.

Part of the notes I left out included a long, convoluted section with an ex-spouse with whom I was angry and in conflict at the time I renovated the treatment center. I realized that she was filling in for my current spouse, who made me angry and upset during the day. Conflict is often expressed in my dreams through association with science fiction scenes, as I enjoy this genre, or from emotions that I associate with various characters from my personal history.

Emotional conflict with my spouse during the day is being expressed in this dream, and reminding me that I need to pay more attention to what is currently my most important social relationship. I've been too compulsive about writing this book.

Okay, what do I call these electro-chemical processes swirling inside my brain, disturbing a restful night's sleep, and necessitating all this exchange between my waking and dreaming states of consciousness? How do feelings that are normally expressed at an unconscious level get turned into symbols that are then processed at a higher cognitive level?

Feelings of conflict in this dream are associated with my current spouse, a former spouse, and a movie I watched the night before. What emerges is a primary feeling image in my body. This sensation is identified by my core consciousness as Qualia I. The Qualia II translation, or primary metaphor, then becomes defined as conflict by my higher cognitive centers. And at this higher cognitive level, the final association with both my former and current spouses occurs. There must be a complex set of neural circuitry that comes into play to create this particular meaning. It is this last step of meaning creation that is the tough nut to crack for cognitive science.

I'll speculate: Meaning is derived by holding complex sets of metaphor in abstract space while these sets are compared to similar image sets in one's history. In this process, outcomes of complex metaphorical sets are contemplated. This process requires complex metaphor that has been freed of immediate bodily referents, or sensations. Thus, I'll suggest that any mammal, dolphins, and elephants that have a sense of Self have some capacity for metaphorical thought. Self from this perspective depends on complex metaphor, which in turn depends on re-imaging of primary metaphor or Qualia II elements.

Returning to my dream, the final associations are made between my former spouse and current spouse at higher cognitive levels. I derive this interpretation because meaning attribution attached to this hierarchical imaging process occurs at my highest level of symbolic abstraction. Complex metaphorical elements must be compared to a fairly large set of alternatives by my Interpreter, which then selects the most logical alternative. Logic or common sense as we routinely call this end product is the most functional alternative compatible with the organism's history. Thus, in clan or tribal societies, individual logic has a group interpretation, as similar environment and social life creates common sense interpretations.

I can appreciate that a parallel imaging process is occurring with mammals with less sophisticated cerebral cortexes. However, with humans at our highest level of image processing, what I'm referring to as complex metaphor, the images or sensations are divorced from their bodily referents. Thus, meaning can be attributed that is totally auto-created. The image construction can be totally fictitious, such as a ghost, an angel, or the devil. It is at the highest level of metaphorical abstraction that you and I part company with our mammalian pets. It is the level of referent-free abstractions that permit auto-created realities and our human forms of mental illness.

Emotions that trigger my sense of conflict and discomfort must be reflexive and instinctual in nature. The images associated with my feelings of conflict appear to blend the two separate brain functions of memory consolidation and emotional homeostasis. Images derived from my last few days seem to be floating at the top of my explicit memory, and get combined with images associated with feelings toward my current and former spouse. Feeling associations with spouses cover thirty years, and content images are blended over this time period as well. Qualia I derived from primary sensations gets turned into metaphor, Qualia II, which I then identify as conflict and a Glock pistol. This process has end focused meaning as its product, which is conflict with my current spouse. I note as I analyze this dream that I need to resolve these spousal feelings soon.

Our higher cognitive centers can re-image and combine primary metaphor in ever higher degrees of complexity, because complex metaphor has been freed of its bodily references. This seems rather straightforward to me, and partially addresses the hard problem. Meaning is the end product of complex imaging, which is held in higher order neuronal space where it can be manipulated endlessly. Thus, moving from proto-Self and core Self to autobiographical Self, I'm following image formation and re-imaging, according to Damasio's conceptual model.

The emotional activation of these two dreams integrates brain chemistry output with higher level cognitive processes. At least, that is the interpretation that seems the best fit for me.

Discomfort builds a lesser response in this dream than a fear response of nightmare quality would. The bridging element is my ex-spouse, whom I associate with a high level of interpersonal conflict in my personal history. And this most salient memory of interpersonal conflict becomes associated with my current spouse, as do all the random but interrelated scenes that are related to conflict. My dream is using a primitive, body-based derived image that is represented as Qualia I. If the image remained at this level, it would drive reflexive actions, but it does not just remain as a feeling.

Following this line of reasoning, Free Will emerges with complex metaphor, which supports our ability to manipulate symbols in higher order relationships called thinking. Metaphor is derived in a process whereby symbols come to represent other symbols at the Qualia II level. For me, this takes the mystery out of Qualia, Free Will, and higher order consciousness.

Dictionary definitions of metaphor are inherently shallow, as they do not support operational research procedures. The content of the dream with its various elements of conflict are not especially important. The content could and would vary depending on my immediate preceding day's history, for example, whether or not I had watched a sci-fi movie. Thus, the dream form contains the bridging clues to interpretation, and content is analyzed for its metaphorical value.

The feedback loop between my Interpreter and brainstem, so to speak, localizes the key element, conflict with my current spouse, and motivates me to pay more attention to an uncomfortable social situation that I'm responsible for. Day is carried into night as dreaming and waking consciousness communicate.

Interpretation Using Damasio:

Damasio uses the term dispositions to describe the most basic awareness states of an organism. To use one of my dream examples, when I attempt to pick up a worm and skewer it on a hook, the worm wiggles and tries mightily to get away. It's very primitive neural system has this survival mechanism. It surely is not thinking to itself: "This guy's is going to skewer and drown me." In similar fashion, my primitive body dispositions still direct me to move away from pain and toward pleasure. This is simple species survival. This disposition does not require reflective thought, just reflex action for the worm, or me.

The basic mechanics of approach-withdrawal still exist in my evolved DNA, and the connection between my dreaming and waking states of higher consciousness permit me to process primitive emotions in a more complex manner. Primitive brains don't need a high level of mapping image capacity to move away from conflict. But as we move up to our human level of complexity, fine-scale mapping emerges along with higher order representational symbols and our ability to manipulate them. So, what does this mean for dreams?

In the conflict dream reviewed above, my body is in a state of discomfort activated by spousal feelings. Non-conscious processes are reminding me of this tension through my dreams, and like any other state of need, my body and higher order Interpreter try to move away from this state of conflict. If it were body temperature or cold, I would modify my environment and move towards the other end of the temperature range.

In this dream, tension is first signaled by my dreaming brain, and enters my awareness through dream analysis. I'm aware of a dispositional map to use Damasio's expression, and recognize that the bridging element for disposition is a global element, not a specific image map. The dream's bridging element is a body-based memory that is associated with an ex-spouse. The dream's narrative is created from associational memories that provide continuity of programming. My dreaming brain doesn't start with logical continuity demanded by my waking consciousness. It has its own logic, which is immediate, modular, direct cellular recall.

Damasio and Hobson's models both help me think about what is going on in my dreaming brain. I focus on feeling as the key element for interpretation, and then look for image elements that stand out. The key to interpretation comes from visualizing different states of consciousness starting with normally non-conscious primitive image creation, and moving to higher levels of conscious integration. Critical and scientific analysis always requires me to use the simplest explanation, which we call Occam's razor. And, self-observation as a methodology requires me to compare my interpretations to the research literature. Otherwise, I'm exercising pure subjectivism, which is forbidden.

Damasio says that the brain:

… creates memory records of the sensory maps and plays back an approximation of their original content (2010: 136).

Memory records of sensory maps in my spousal conflict dream remind me that reconstruction is not an exact image copy. The imagery is often symbolic and metaphorical. This makes it easier for me to understand how characters can morph or be composites of more than one individual in my dreams. Spousal conflict in this dream permits hybrid visuals cobbled together by associated memories. The same applies to scenes and complex blending of time sequences. Memory is fluid and dynamic in this dream as dispositions command processes that seem to be reactivating and putting together aspects of past perceptions – to follow Damasio's explanation, that is.

CONFLICT DREAM

(5-25-11)

I'm in the Rochester, Minnesota Government Center. An Olmsted County Administrator approaches me and asks that I give a message to a manager. He says that he knows she is at work, but he can't find her. He suspects that she is making herself unavailable and just socializing with colleagues. He has told her to stop socializing on the job, but she continues anyway.

I'm walking through the building and encounter a man holding an open meeting with a small crowd. This man wants to create a new treatment program for offenders. A former colleague of mine from the 1970s at MSU is offering advice, and is monopolizing the discussion. I quickly inject a statement before he can continue his vacuous comments.

I ask whether the man is looking for a single treatment modality or one that is targeted for specific types of offenders. He responds that he is looking for a generic modality. I point out that general treatment modalities have little value and are comparable in outcome to humane incarceration. I compare chemically dependent treatment modalities to those for sex offenders to make my point. This comparison is quite elaborate, and I reference a number of authorities as I explain these treatment modalities.

The man, whom I never identify, insists that he wants a single modality for all offenders. When I wake up about 6:30 a.m., I have been processing treatment comparisons in my dream with Paul Gendreau's research. Research actually supports targeted approaches for different types of offenders, and my dream logic squares with my daytime logic. My dream analysis is elaborate and spans over twenty years of research.

INTERPRETATION

I frequently have cognitively-focused dreams where I present academic or lecture style information to individuals, groups, or students in formal settings. I draw upon my complex academic and work history in these dreams, and piece together various environmental settings appropriate to the time I generated similar lectures or held those discussions. Appropriate settings do not mean true-to-life environmental re-imaging. Mixing and blending of Hobson's dream forms occur, but the daytime logic employed in these dreams is drawn from previous research and lectures.

Upon waking, I'm conscious that this type of discussion frequently occurred during my days as a multi-county community corrections administrator at the Olmsted County Government Center. I recognized the person who spoke to me as an administrator, and the person offering advice as a colleague from the 1970s who specialized in the treatment of the chemically dependent. The reader will note how my memory is busy mixing time frames, personalities, and settings. In this dream, pure thoughts provide thematic continuity, and everything else is supporting elements.

A day or two before this dream, I read an article in the Tri-City Herald, the local newspaper, about offender treatment and also, an article from the New York Times off the Internet that was related to incarceration. I had been thinking about old research topics before going to bed, and musing that Washington State did not even use research from its own institutes. My general frustration with government not using research to positively change offender behavior is a strong theme in this dream and thought sequence.

Frustration with human service systems not being able to use science to solve problems is combined in my mind with the punishment-driven mentality that prevails for political purposes by those who will use any strategy to get re-elected. This dilemma creates a strong agitation and exchange between my emotions and higher cognitive centers, which are clearly reflected in this dream's theme. Hobson gets half the credit for this interpretation.

Aside: My dreaming brain often delivers technical lectures in great detail, but only covering subjects that I have in-depth knowledge of. Newer materials that aren't committed to memory are muddy waters in the clear river of lucidity. Even so, during the process when new material is being integrated and consolidated in memory, my dreams frequently produce new insights.

I frequently take tests in my dreams when I'm wrestling with and trying to integrate new materials for this book, or similar exercises. Metaphorically, test taking in dreams represents my brain-mind's ongoing activity to problem solve. It is my way of making concrete complex concept manipulations. I consciously associate this effort in my dreams with days of blue book exams at the University of Minnesota. That was a time I struggled with test anxiety; a time that remains salient in my memory library.

I think it becomes fairly obvious that our cognitive development can and does gradually exert greater influence over our dream life as we age, and the pattern of our dreams reflects the degree of cognitive complexity realized in our waking consciousness. In a similar fashion, if we extensively use suggestions to shape and modify our dreams, patterns will emerge that would not exist otherwise. I elaborate on this position in Chapter 8 on traumatic dreams.

LaBerge references Ernest Rossi who has proposed that "… integration, whereby the synthesis of separate psychological structures forms a more comprehensive personality, is a major function of dreaming. According to Rossi, integration is the primary means by which personality growth takes place (2009: 45)."

I discuss this process extensively in my autobiography, but my history of self-integration and lucid dreaming strongly supports this interpretation. Following Rossi's interpretation, the first step I took in the late 1950s was to integrate my fragmented Self (selves). The second step was to consciously address the growth of my evolving comprehensive personality. The second step appears to be a life-long effort that is increasingly highlighted with age. Following my dreams adds detail to this interpretation.

MUNDANE DREAM

(11-11-10) Recorded at 11:19 a.m. but initially recalled at 2:30 a.m.

Perhaps I should say this is a very mundane dream. Nightly, the range of my recalled lucid dreams varies from one to six. My dreams reflect salient activities or feelings, and can be dominated by ideas and concepts that play a central role in my daily behavior. Yesterday was uneventful, even though I spent almost the whole day reading and writing. I reviewed familiar material and wrote from extensive notes, and thus, the day was filled with activity more mechanical than new or challenging. I have been writing for three hours prior to recording this dream, and find detail beginning to slip away. Thus, I will need to focus in order to recall the necessary detail.

In this dream, I'm involved in a type of military operation, but everyone is dressed in street clothes, no ties or uniforms. There are five active participants besides me, although I'm often just observing rather than helping with the conflict. Three members of our party are gradually killed off in a manner that remains vague. A woman observer seems to be following the action, and is pleased that we've overcome our adversary and are now safe. She is attractive, tall, and appears to be in the role of overseer. I have no other relationship with her, nor do I have any erotic thoughts even though I notice her attractiveness.

INTERPRETATION

I arose early yesterday, and took my spouse to an auto driving license test. I started writing upon returning home, and except for a couple hours of reading, spent the rest of the day in this activity. By 8:30 p. m. my brain stopped working, and I watched The Red Planet on TV. The above dream is a replay of scenarios from this movie.

Five astronauts arrive at Mars and gradually all but one is killed off. A robot becomes the hunter when it is threatened with having its power source removed; an act which would kill it. The movie was not overly creative, but my tired brain didn't seem to mind. However, I did turn it off before the movie's end.

The military-type events correspond rather closely with the robot hunter and the astronauts efforts to survive. The woman in my dream has a counterpart on a circling spaceship that has brought the astronauts to Mars. The fact that two men survive in my dream, but only one in the movie did not bother my dreaming consciousness. I'm in an observer role much of the time in this dream, which duplicates my role as a passive TV watcher. Logically there must be two survivors as I'm observing.

My conscious mind retains visual images of the spaceship, Mars and the robot. The rest of the movie is gradually sliding into oblivion with its simple plot and rather dull development. Why such a mundane dream? Is it due to an uneventful day, a focus on revising old material for this chapter, or with nothing exciting or out of the ordinary happening?

My interpretation is the opposite. I think my brain was busy integrating all the materials covered yesterday. Memory organization and integration at a below surface level of awareness is occupying my brain. Although I recalled one other dream when I woke up, it quickly slipped away. That is unusual for me. I experience a carryover effect of mental tiredness today as my attention is somewhat forced, as is my ability to hold multiple thoughts in active memory. I need a slower day today, a long walk and some physical exercise. I have two daytime bridging elements connected to this mundane dream: I let my brain relax after a marathon writing period by watching a boring move, and I recalled a dream without any substantial qualities.

Postscript: My awareness of needing a slower day emerged when I reviewed this dream after waking. I'm a compulsive writer until I've completed a final draft, and know that I must then give myself time to regain objectivity before the final work is revised. My dream is telling me that I need to slow down and proceed at a slower pace. This is one aspect of ageing that is difficult to accept. My writing stamina is less than half of what it was twenty years ago.

SYMBOLIC INTEGRTION IN DREAMS

(3-24-11, Recorded 10:05 a.m.)

I'm in a large nondescript room talking to Robin, a therapist whom I formerly employed. We are discussing therapeutic interventions with sex offenders, but the focus of our conversation is on macro approaches to therapy. Listening to this two way exchange is Cindy, a psychologist who worked at the same treatment location in the psychological testing unit. I notice that Robin's nose is much larger than I remembered, and quite pointed. I glance at Cindy and find that her nose is not quite as large, but is sculpted much like Robin's.

The scene changes and I'm walking across an open field toward a long building. The building's side facing me displays a series of open doors about the width of a double garage entrance. There is mud in the bottom of the building, no cement, and wheel tracks go all the way through each of the building units. I understand that this is where the horses are housed, but none is in residence.

I want to walk through the building, but decide that I am going to get my dress shoes very muddy if I do. I think that I should have gone around the building the way my walking companion did. The physical appearance of my walking companion is that of my neighbor Michael. But I'm aware in my dream that I'm substituting Michael's physical appearance for one of the 1990s therapists from Nexus whom I still retain negative feelings for. As I'm contemplating what action I should take, I wake up and use the bathroom. I think this dream is not worth including in this chapter. I eat breakfast, read the paper, and engage in other activities. As I'm reading, I change my mind. This is a good example of symbolism in my dreams, and I should record it.

INTERPRETATION

I have been thinking about brain plasticity the last few days as I review some materials from Ramachandran. One of my research goals when I developed the Nexus Treatment Programs in Minnesota and Illinois was to create a virtual reality simulation for psychopaths committing sex crimes. I wondered then and I wonder now if brain plasticity would permit this type of therapeutic manipulation to activate empathic feeling for psychopaths and character disordered offenders. In the 1990s, I wanted to experiment with virtual reality as a tool supporting cognitive-behavioral therapy, but never generated enough capital to do so.

Robin and Cindy were former employees whom I incorporated into this particular dream setting. Physical movement of this treatment program accounts for the barn setting, as the program was re-located to the center of rural Minnesota. The muddy barn floors are my gardening efforts of yesterday. Robin and Cindy are physical mixtures combined with my neighbors whom I had over for breakfast Saturday. Michael physically substitutes for a social worker on staff who had his own ideas about treatment strategies and organizational structure that often conflicted with mine.

Thinking about brain plasticity and former professional goals called up old memories, and combined dream persons with similar physical characteristics of my neighbor. Physical separation from the social worker in this dream represents my feelings toward him, then and now. Mud on the barn floor, smoothed by drive through ruts, is transparent symbolism. I think of the social worker, and organizational leadership that followed my administration this way. No doubt, sour grapes!

I wrote my autobiography and a book on mysticism before this book, which is taking me into my fourth year of consistent efforts. I often reflect on past events, my professional history, mistakes I've made, and things I could've changed.

Symbolism rises to large scale analysis and is not confined to metaphorical expression. As I deepen my understanding of brain plasticity, complex states of consciousness, and multiple forms of scrambled wiring in human brains, I naturally go back and rethink treatment approaches with supposedly intractable clients.

I included this dream after reading Ramachandran's section on visual perception. It related directly to my dream of last night, and thoughts I've had for over twenty years on methods one might use to change recalcitrant behaviorally disordered offenders. Pattern recognition of macro symbolic representations that integrate my history is common to my everyday dreams. I'm quite sure my neural circuits continuously move up and down this hierarchy of abstraction.

The Vortex's Eye

Dreams mundane, profane, inane,
all embraced without shame.
A night of games, some profane.
Critics lay shame, some say lame;
I see a window to my brain.

CHAPTER 8

TRAUMATIC DREAMS

INTRODUCTION

I shared two traumatic dreams in my autobiography that plagued me for decades. I suppressed both nightmares for twenty years through dream programming, and once I understood their origin, they immediately disappeared. Analysis of my nightmares is a study in what I will call both passive and active repression. How is it possible to be plagued with the same nightmares for decades, and then remove them immediately by simply understanding their origin? Let me calculate the number of nightmares over a ten year period of time assuming just one nightmare daily. It is: 365 x 10 or 3,650. If the dreaming mind is subject to behavioral reinforcement, the neural pathways should look like six lane freeways. I repressed both nightmares for twenty years with dream programming, and then immediately removed them through dream analysis. No psychotherapy, no prescription drugs, nothing but insight was involved.

"David Hartley first suggested that we dream in order to loosen connections in associative memory and thus to prevent the obsessive persistence of over learning. In Francis Crick's modern translation of Hartley's principle, we dream in order to forget (Hobson: 2001: 121)."

I suffered years of almost nightly visitations by these two nightmares, which often repeated a number of times each night, sometimes in the same version and other times with modified plots. How does one connect dreaming to forget with this level of perseverance?

I still recall these dreams vividly when I'm awake, but they no longer have any power over my emotions, and they totally stopped appearing in my dreams once I identified their activation source. Cognitively, I killed the beasts of trauma that threatened me daily for decades with simple insight. Insight made me safe and made me whole. Self-therapy can be this simple, quick and effective. It represents the immediacy of trauma relief that a good shaman offers his or her clients. To be effective, shamanic healers must understand how to manipulate this mechanism. They don't need to understand the mechanism itself.

There was very limited understanding of brain functioning and structure fifty years ago compared to today's knowledge base. But a ray of light was emerging with new control techniques using behavior modification for compulsive actions such as overeating or irrational fears.

I implemented dream control in the late 1950s in what I thought of as behavioral conditioning. I was after the psychological effect, and was unaware then of how neural physiology might be involved. Nightmare resolution allowed me to remove emotional blocks that had been part of my life since before the age of two. In physiological terms, I changed synaptic wiring, regained emotional and cognitive equilibrium, and integrated my work and social life in a few short months. Most of that time, I was teaching myself the appropriate methods.

The immediate positive effect of removing nightmares suggested how words can relieve grief, fear, and anxiety. Nightmares gone meant continuous nights of quality sleep for the first time in my life. New energy allowed me to tackle anxiety, depression, and compulsive anger responses. But, that is another story. In order to get immediate positive behavioral results and emotional relief from insight, there must be a physiological input mechanism that can be directly decoupled from its behavioral-psychological output.

In terms of contemporary neuroscience, I view my 1958 self-therapy this way: Trauma calls forth a complex neural pattern with strong associated neurotransmitters that represents a fixed action pattern (FAP). This FAP represents a perfect storm of fear-driven emotions that will repeat until its activation is interrupted. It is the mechanism that drives PTS. FAPs are contextual and can be activated by any component constituting its complexity – emotional, physical, or social cues. Life events that constitute high levels of stress will call forth this FAP or FAPs in endless cycles.

Primary (Qualia I) and secondary images (Qualia II) are part of this fixed action pattern (FAP) which makes them susceptible to talk therapy. Recall that I equate Qualia II with primary metaphor.

A direct route to self-activating FAPs exists through dream analysis. Once I identified the bridging element connecting nightmare images to their activation source the total sequence was immediately broken. In effect, my Interpreter ascertained the source of the nightmare, and had no further need to search for its meaning. Images remain in one's memory, but automatic triggering of the FAP is removed.

I think it becomes fairly obvious that the higher cognitive abilities of our human brains can and do override automatic reflexive responses of what I've referred to as our core level of consciousness. Nightmare resolution requires that we break the recursive neuronal loop between these two consciousness centers. Our higher order level of human consciousness, awareness of being aware, can be controlled by our Interpreter to perform this function. Without active intervention, self-activated FAPs continue to be expressed by any number of activating stimuli.

From this perspective, traumatic FAPs are expressed on cue much like bicycle balancing FAPs. If you don't ride the bicycle, the FAP remains unused. However, with learned action patterns driven by fear, numerous cues can activate the cyclic response. Such cues are plentiful in a stressful environment, thus, nightmares can continue to build in intensity until they become intolerable.

Primary images (Qualia I), which include emotional elements, can be triggered externally or internally. Fear of one's dreams is enough to trigger the nightmare. If ordinary suggestion can shape our dreams, we must recognize how much more powerfully fear or intense fear can call forth nightmares. I suspect that Qualia II images, or primary metaphorical images, cease to be called forth, and the nightmare stops when our Interpreter breaks the nightmares activation chain.

Clinicians will often use re-definition of a personal problem to break its power and impact on their clients. A similar process seems to be operating with one's self-analysis of dreams. However, with dream self-analysis, the connection to the nightmare's physiological activator is broken, and total relief occurs.

In terms of neural circuits, re-definition must mean re-wiring, creating new circuit connections, and disengaging old ones. Image formation is central to all mental processes, and re-naming the image at a higher cognitive level must change the neural circuit patterning and re-configuration across these two levels of consciousness. In other words, the circuit loops which create meaning are modified.

In my experience, the same process applies during daytime talk therapy. However, talk therapy is more convoluted and takes longer, as access to primary images is more indirect in waking states than in dreams. Understanding this process from the inside-out of dreams and altered states explains how mind controls work. Whether or not I've interpreted this process correctly, the intervention immediately achieves the desired results. At minimum, some mechanism that mimics these processes is operative. I will develop this interpretation more fully in Chapters 12, 15 and 17.

I'm reminded that emotionally driven primary images and their corresponding FAPs are not successfully integrated by our higher cognitive centers until our Interpreter achieves control over them. My modular brain does not perform these integrations automatically. From an evolutionary point of view, it appears that nature has not yet finished its work integrating the human brain-mind's different levels of consciousness, because it's still evolving sub-system integration.

Bridging elements are not minor items for dream analysis. From a therapeutic perspective, for self or therapist that is, they become the key to understanding our dreams, which is required for healing to take place. Intense emotions called fear drove my nightmares. One nightmare was activated before the age of two, and the other when I was 14 years old. Fear recycled in my neural circuits compulsively until the neuronal loop to my higher cognitive centers was closed through insight.

In this view, nightmares repeat because our non-conscious memories are unable to forget. Higher order thoughts and the complex feelings associated with primary images seek integration across brain-mind subsystems according to this interpretation. We are meaning-driven creatures who seek understanding, even if we have to manufacture bizarre supernatural explanations for what is happening to us.

I repeatedly observe this quest to integrate meaning and feeling in my reported dreams, and it is no more evident than how this process works with nightmares. Insert the missing piece that brings feeling and higher order cognitive explanation together and there is resolution.

I'm guessing, but neural circuits that have become self-sustaining are interrupted, and relief ensues, when oscillation-like electro-chemical energy across closed neural loops is removed. The primary, felt images embedded in my infant and childhood memories weren't able to express themselves directly in higher order cognitive processes. To achieve resolution of earlier trauma, I had to bring primary, tissue embedded images into consciousness. Talk therapy can make us feel better temporarily, but primary image identification connected to the trauma can bring about its immediate resolution. The abstraction processes that create meaning and their supportive neuro-circuitry must reconfigure to accommodate previously unidentified traumatic feelings. Stated differently, a new meaningfully integrated Gestalt is created to replace fragmented brain-mind states supporting one's pathology.

As I came to understand states of consciousness and trauma in my dreams, these insights arose almost automatically. In 1958, they were partially intuitive and partially associated with Behavioral Theory. Later, I developed a fuller understanding of talk therapy, dream therapy, and how the Self strives for personal integration.

As I've earlier discussed, this awareness takes the mystery out of the meaning of repression in therapy for me. I understand repression as a process instead of viewing it as a state in the black box. This newly configured, abstract process of neural circuit integration stops compulsive neuronal electrical and chemical activity that is auto-reinforcing. In the late 1950s I thought of this strategy as being cognitive-behavioral, and cognitive-behavioral strategy demanded an operational definition. I now understand, or at least interpret the process, from this modified neuro-psychological perspective.

Addressing the physiological component, Kandel states:

… classical conditioning recruits both homosnaptic and heterosynaptic changes." And further … learning may be a matter of combining various elementary forms of synaptic plasticity into new and more complex forms, much as we use an alphabet to form words (2006: 205):

Thus, to modify a key element in our neural circuits permits both reconfiguration of the circuit, and its relationship to other neural circuits. And what we get is a physiological explanation for psychological treatment effects. Not only can genes be switched on and off like a water faucet, so can neural circuits.

Negative affect is so common in dreams that it usually takes precedence over positive affect, at least for younger lucid dreamers. Negative affect was very much a part of my younger days – through school and into my early professional years. Negative affect is rare in my advanced years compared to my infancy and youth, and is expressed infrequently in dreams like the ones I've presented above. Negative affect in my dreams has always been a flag which calls attention to unresolved conflict. Happy moments don't need attention in terms of evolutionary survival, but fear, anger, and anxiety demand it. I think the answer to extensive negativity in dreams is just that simple.

The age old question as to what degree we control the direction and flow of consciousness, and to what degree we can select its content, is partially answered when one learns to program their dreams and create, direct, and control other altered states. The answer: We control the direction and flow of consciousness and the elements that make up its content to the degree we learn to master our higher order cognitive processes.

I must always conceptualize my inner self as an agent in order to achieve this mastery. Understanding consciousness and Self is not gained through philosophical argument, but rather, understanding is realized individually when we learn to expand, direct, and control the full range of possible altered states.

Internal brain-mind comparisons of altered states are critiqued through self-observation and supplemented with self-experiments. Each brain-mind self-exploration offers its own unique insights. The ancient admonition to know thy-self references this mechanism. It must, as shamanic healing is part of human history.

We can learn to control the flow of consciousness to the degree that we learn how to control our brain-mind states. By my 22nd year, I learned to control altered states and program my dreams. In similar fashion, these control techniques were generalized to eliminate depression, anxiety, and greatly extend my ability to stay focused on one subject for up to eight hours. Control directed by others can easily become dogmatic and authoritarian: Control of consciousness directed by self becomes an ever expanding universe of new insight, meaning, and behavioral capacities. Meditation can be one step in our mastery of self-control.

I'm impressed that 95 percent of our brain's work goes on below our conscious level of awareness. Although I don't need to know every facilitated action pattern or chemical excitation taking place at the cellular or circuit level, I do want to know how to guide and understand these processes in order to enhance my quality of life.

In the 1950s, dream and nightmare control represented the first step toward a new, balanced and integrated self. Without similar control, individuals with severe PTS have lives of abbreviated quality.

Hobson considers "… state boundary blurring and frank dissociations of state components with an eye to appreciating just how easy it is - even without drugs - to create unexpected hybrid states of consciousness (Ibid: 153)."

His focus is primarily on the dream process through which he elucidates the relationship between brain function and structure. I can personally attest to the ease of state changes across most altered states of consciousness. I've presented case histories in my autobiography, and revisit other state boundary issues in Chapter 11, "Altered Realities."

Additionally, Hobson discusses hypnogogic and hypnopompic hallucinations occurring at the beginning and ending of our sleep cycle, and documents well the state changes occurring (Ibid: 153-158).

We have enough evidence from this kind of research to be reasonably sure that other altered state changes are similarly driven. How wonderful it would have been if Doctor Hobson had explained these changes to me when I first entered the university. Wading through the hokus-pokus of monsters lurking in my unconscious (Freudian that is) took a number of years. Psychoanalysis was a path into the desert, but my destination of understanding lay in the mountains of psychology and neuroscience

Out-of-body experiences have a physical quality for me that may be lacking for many lucid dreamers. When I assume the body of the bear, or travel to the beginning of the universe, I have a sensation of physical involvement similar to typing on this keyboard. I feel the bear's body and emotions. I physically hit the plasma wall at the beginning of time (the Big Bang) and I'm aware that I'm aware of these feelings while they are occurring.

Out-of-body physical sensations duplicate the feel of waking experiences. Individuals who become shamans and mystics after such real to life experiences find it hard to deny these realities of the mind. Our capacity to closely duplicate waking state feelings in altered realities is a huge inducement to believe in supernatural happenings. An entire subculture of occult mysticism exists in America that is built around these very natural workings of our minds.

Tell a shaman who has felt the ice-cold interstellar space between Earth and Moon, or the physical hardness of the moon when he sits or stands on it that this experience is not real. Just try. I personally know how the plasma wall at the beginning of time feels. Most people cannot even discuss these experiences. True Believers know. But what True Believers know, they often do not know.

You can tell psychedelic drug-trippers that the iceberg they're sitting on isn't real, and they'll say: "I know that."

The difference is not in the brain circuit or chemicals released in our brains; it is in the perception and sense of control and activation on the part of the shaman or the drug experimenter. The shaman gets visible, sensory results, and thus confirms his or her interpretation. The drug user feels the iceberg and gets relief on a hot summer's day, and takes the experience as another reason to use drugs. I'm arguing that interpreting meaning is as important to understanding altered states as physiology is. In my case, I initiate, direct and control altered reality states; hence, I'm not a True Believer. There is enough mystery in not knowing what is not known.

Alien abductions, astral travel, speaking in tongues, and spontaneous trance inductions all speak to these scrambled neuronal states. They are approximations of hybrid brain states, as Hobson calls them, but each altered state is experienced differently in terms of their particular combinations of hybridization, and the interpretations one makes.

Hobson refined his activation-synthesis model over the years. One of the modifications that I find most helpful is his statement that:

The shift from waking to REM sleep ... is occasioned not only by changes in input-output gating and modulation as previously supposed, but also by changes in regional activation of the forebrain (2001: 193).

My conceptualization of dynamic integrated systems envisions changes in and active output from our higher cognitive centers, Hobson's regional activation of the forebrain referenced in the above quote.

A second shift in Hobson's 2001 updated model notes that: "Four changes in regional activation are particularly relevant to understanding the concomitant changes in consciousness." They are:

(a) specifies how visual images become so intense in our dreams;

(b) focuses on the physiology behind strong dream emotions;

(c) addresses the specific mechanisms by which body emotion is matched with   specific events in one's life; and

(d) emphasis placed on neuromodulators in the brain is modified to include selective inactivation of the dorsolateral prefrontal cortex.

I quote the specific mechanisms involved below for ready reference. We generally recognize how reductive research is continuing to identify complex brain operations. Skeptics, particularly in cognitive science, who challenge neuroscience's ability to build a bottom-up model of consciousness, are increasingly on softer ground.

Below, I provide detail to support this position. The more casual reader may want to tread softly here, but rest assured that Hobson's discussion of the technical aspects of these dream-brain processes are covered more leisurely throughout this book.

(a) "Selective activation of the supramarginal gyrus in REM sleep facilitates the intense and convincing visuospatial imagery in our dreams, a distinctive phenomenological feature that has previously gone unexplained except for speculative reference to the PGO waves..."

(b) "Selective activation of the amygdale in REM sleep is relevant to the phenomenological fact that dreaming is characterized by strong emotion, principally anxiety (but also elation and anger). The apparently primary activation of the amygdale and adjacent paralimbic cortices further suggests that emotion may be a primary shaper of dream plots..."

(c) "Activation of a wide variety of forebrain structures including the hypothalamus and medial frontal cortex may potentiate the generation of emotionally salient memories and of important instinctual repertoires in REM sleep. Significantly, the ventromedial prefrontal cortex is the site hypothesized by Antonio Damasio for the matching of emotional and bodily responses to specific events and scenarios that guide our social behavior."

(d) "Selective inactivation of the dorsolateral prefrontal cortex is a capital discovery that was completely unanticipated by basic sleep research. This data helps our efforts to understand the bizarreness, the loss of volition, the loss of self-reflection, the loss of directed thought, and the amnesia of dreaming that we have previously attributed to the shift in neuromodulatory balance of the brain. Now we can entertain the strong and attractively reductive hypothesis that these two mechanism are both snynergistic and mechanistically integral."

(e) "The central hypothesis linking all four of these integrative propositions is that the regional activation differences may well reflect the differential targeting of the forebrain region by both phasic activation waves (PGO equivalents) and by differential distribution of cholinergic and monoaminergic inputs to the forebrain (Ibid: 193-195)."

The quoted material is a little long, but I wanted to share Hobson's exact words. Dream research that is focusing on specific mechanisms of brain consciousness continues to connect bottom-up and top-down models. Personally, my experience says that inclusion of other altered states in this model will serve to strengthen a more complete understanding of consciousness.

DISCOMFORT/CONFLICT DREAM

I'm observing a river with fast moving water, rapids, and extreme clarity. Next, I'm in a helicopter traveling above the river at considerable height. I notice that the water is so clear that I can see the bottom as the helicopter moves upstream. When I look into the bottom of the river, I have a sense of falling. I repeat looking down two or three times, and decide to watch the river at a distance in order to avoid discomfort. This feeling of looking down into the river duplicates that of my standing at the edge of a very tall building, looking down and overwhelming my senses.

The helicopter lands and I'm in a camping area with other people. I become aware that there are alligators in the area, and I should explore with caution. I'm inside a rough-hewn cabin, and looking out the door, I see a giant alligator of prehistoric size headed toward me. I close the door and peak out the window, but no 'gator. I wait a few minutes and then go to the door, but the door is not visible. I know it has to be there, so I run my hand along the wall where it was previously. I find a slight crack in the surface, prey the door open, and notice that it fits so securely that the door itself vanishes from sight when it is closed.

There are all kinds of dream logic here. Also note that one can create dream elements by wishing or suggesting them to appear as the dream unfolds.

The alligator returns, and is at a distance of about 75 yards and headed directly toward me. I close the door. I'm worried about my wife and daughter who are outside walking. I go to the back door, and they are moving toward me at some distance. I tell them to be careful because there is a giant alligator on the grounds. They smile at me and walk leisurely into the back area of the cabin. Neither my wife nor my daughter has any recognizable characteristics. They are both Caucasian, young, and represent a time when I would be in my middle to late thirties. I just know they are my wife and daughter, as I have similar feelings toward them. My wife also piloted the helicopter when I was flying over the river. I didn't find this improbable feat to be illogical. This wife and daughter are pure fabrications.

INTERPRETATION

When I woke up this morning, my mind was busy organizing two different sections of this book. My mind was telling me to add one dream from Hobson, Delaney, and Brooks-Vogelsong, create a new chapter for these additions, and discuss the helicopter-river projection in the book's section on mental illness. I decided to ignore this dream advice. At 6:00 a.m. I was telling myself that my brain had been busily processing thoughts about dreaming, especially about chemical brain states, and that I did not have full lucidity in last night's dreams. As I completed this thought while putting coffee in the coffee pot, the above dream lucidly popped back into my head.

Yesterday I was telling myself that I don't seem to have flying dreams anymore, or at least not often. I paused and thought a moment and recalled two of recent origin; one flying around the inside of a barn, and another outside flying into airspace normally used by commercial jets. Next, I recalled a number of dreams where I'm walking down the street and jump across the driveway. When I jump, I concentrate and extend the jump as far as I like because I know I can stay airborne by just concentrating. The last image I have is jumping and traversing two driveways before I land. I think this will amaze those watching, but if I continue the jump any further, they will think it strange. My next dream association equates levitation with flying.

The evening before this dream, I watched two TV programs on the Nova and Discovery channels. In the actual movie on space, I started to project into the simulation depicting the expansion of the universe, but before I could fully engage the animation, it changed.

In my dream last night, I projected into the river water in a similar fashion, and experienced a sense of disorientation and falling. My conscious mind was saying: "if you enter the water, you must first fall into it," and I found this to be an uncomfortable feeling. I avoided the discomfort by shifting my gaze upriver. Entering or leaving altered states can be this simple, either in one's dreams or while awake. The self-taught panic of uncontrolled hallucinations can be tweaked.

Imagery in last night's dream was taken from TV programs over the past week. Alligators, rivers, and outdoor scenes were all mixed together in a random associative manner. The dreams, mixed with my conscious waking thoughts, expressed a sense of caution about my interpretation of various books by Hobson, and at the same time, I was left with a sense of accomplishment that I'm actively improving the organization of this book. The first draft was really rough.

Waking thoughts about flying became dream suggestions. Projecting my Self into the TV-universe simulation was repeated from my dream helicopter, but thoughts of entering the river's water were uncomfortable. Avoiding the alligator felt as though I was avoiding an organizational error for this book, and waking with numerous thoughts dominating my consciousness represents a growing sense of organizational mastery for this book. Sharing, waking, and dreaming consciousness, along with accompanying visual imagery, works together this way for me.

The dream reminded me to integrate my ability to project into other mediums, both while dreaming and while awake, into the chapter covering the relationship of dreams to mental illness. Dreams reflect and accentuate what is going on in my everyday life, and frequently this accentuation is dramatic and visual with strong attached feelings.

SMOTHERING NIGHTMARE

I was hospitalized before the age of two, had a near death experience with an OBE, and lost my early speech and walking abilities. Frequent out-of-body experiences and a threatening ghost followed me until we moved to the Lake Stevens Area in Washington State when I was five. A Japanese submarine had been reported in the Sound somewhere near Seattle or Everett. This event took center stage in our home, and we practiced blackout drills with night watchmen verifying compliance.

My Japanese submarine nightmare started and remained vivid for years thereafter. In fact, it remains vivid in my memory to this day. I'm captured by the Japanese and taken to their submarine where they begin drilling a hole in my back, and I know it is with the intention of making me into a flag stand. I free myself, and because I know how to fly, I fly to a hole in the ship and drop into it. As I fall, I concentrate intently, and suspend myself in mid-air. I fall asleep in this position in my dream, and later, wake up in my own bed. I can never escape the submarine any other way.

When I initially wrote this scene in my autobiography, I realized that the hole in the ship was actually a five year old's translation of the hold in the ship. This is a good example of how a five year old brain constructs meaning by translating language into concrete imagery. It's a good example of how language can shape reality in one's dreams, and once the mind creates reality, the brain complies with the necessary sensory configurations.

This process also demonstrates feedback from higher cortical centers. Once my Interpreter assigned the meaning of "hole" to "hold," my auto-creative visuo-motor mechanisms constructed the above dream scenario. And the nightmare became a permanent part of my dream and waking memories.

Constructing the bizarre or fantastic in dreams or other altered realities is just as easy for the brain as recalling and bringing real life features into one's dreams; in fact it's easier. These mental constructions feel just as real, fantastic or not, in various altered states as objective external stimuli. This same process of image construction goes on in waking visions, which makes them even more believable, because we are aware of our immediate physical environment which we can touch, see, and feel. Having a vision, while knowing that other sensory input is coming from one's environment, makes the vision even more credible. Hallucinations or visions, take your pick, but note that one is under our control, and one is not.

I've often thought of the submarine nightmare as being accompanied by intense back pain, but on deeper reflection, I think this is not the case. I feel back pain in the dream, but it is the sense of terror, not pain, that is overwhelming. Terror is the label I'm attaching to the feeling of being unable to breathe.

I suspended this nightmare through dream programming when I was a first-year student at the University of Minnesota. At that time, it was the only way I could think of to make the nightmare stop. And, I kept this suspension for twenty years through active dream repression.

Identifying the source of the submarine nightmare occurred during management development exercises conducted by a trainer who had learned much of her craft in India. Note the importance of the body-based memory. Muscle memories have been the key bridging elements that helped me identify each nightmare's activating source.

The training session started with some warm up physical movements that I experienced as being yoga simulations. My trainer had studied various techniques of integrating mind-body awareness in India. I found her techniques both interesting and helpful. She put her two trainees into a number of different physical positions, and then put me into a cross-legged sitting position. This occurred with the lights partially dimmed, and the only sound was that of softy spoken directions coming from the trainer. Having formal training as a counselor, I'm aware of how much we Westerners typically ignore integrated body-mind awareness that was critical to the final resolution of my nightmares.

I entered a long-forgotten inner-world, and was transported back to my crib within seconds. A life-long image that had been repressed appeared like magic and gradually came to totally dominate my mind. My trainer became a blur behind the screen of action taking place in my brain. At first, my mind was superimposing both the trainer and the internal picture emerging from the depths of childhood; a quirky world in which two scenes and two realities existed at the same time. First, her voice gradually dimmed until her words became inaudible and then totally lost. Next, her visual image faded, and a moment later, I lost contact with her, the room, and all its contents. My total reality became a long lost moment from childhood.

I was in my crib, sitting up looking through the bars into a room that was only partially lit. The vision's view of me and the crib was from an adult standing position behind the side of the crib facing both the crib and my approaching mother. From this vantage point, I had a complete picture of my infant self and mother. Mother was muttering guttural sounds and totally out of control. Her stomach was distended with my unborn sister June, or maybe it was right after June's birth. She had a pillow in her hands, which she held chest high. Her face was distorted and twisted. It was the same mask she wore four years later when my face was forced into the urine soaked sheets in the house by Lake Stevens, and it was the mask she wore when her evil soul went to Hell. My right ear, the one that always got earaches, was pounding, and I was sobbing.

The pillow came first, and then all light disappeared and I momentarily relived her attack in a hole of all consuming terror and darkness devoid of oxygen. The pressure on the small of my back felt like my spine would snap. I struggled to get my breath, but the force of the pillow made breathing impossible.

The sensation of being smothered by mother is still so strong that small enclosed places remain bothersome. I remember waking up in the hospital. I remember refusing to go to Heaven, and I will remember forever the terror I experience when I can't breathe.

The physical movements of Yoga unlocked long suppressed memories that had been too horrible for my conscious mind to entertain for over fifty years. Now they played out like a Hollywood action movie, totally dominating my senses.

The next couple of days, I struggled to understand what my unlocked memories were trying to tell me. The Japanese flag-stand nightmare returned, and when the bad guys started drilling the hole in my back, the drill turned into Mother's hand, and the pain was identified. And I once again relived the experience. I can't explain this nightmare adequately without using the concept of complex metaphor. I'm also impressed with the abstract symbolic substitutions being generated by my higher cognitive centers as the Japanese submarine dream unfolds.

One hand ground me into the crib's mattress while the other took my breath away, and the re-enactment of the crib attack returned in its entirety. The realization that my mother had smothered me and was the cause of my being hospitalized created an intense sense of psychic pain. Now I understood the hospital scene with Mother standing in the background shadows, and my fear when she approached the bed. The image transformation that became the ghost on steep wooden stairs, and later became the Japanese submarine nightmare, had permitted me to nurse at her breast, live with nightmares instead of immobilizing fear, and experience the angels. I only have this awareness by triangulating the nightmare and the vision.

INTERPRETATION

I entered a trance-like state during this training exercise that duplicated the visual and physical sensory experiences of normal dreams, except all sensory modes were expressed dramatically. I witnessed a complete scene, including my Mother when she would have been 23 or 24 years old, a visual of myself sitting up in the crib as though I were an observer standing overhead, and all the sensations that accompany being smothered. This was not a single smothering episode with mother, as I eventually recalled a number of others.

The physical sensation of her hand on my back returned in total. She did not scream at me as she quickly approached my crib, but seemed to utter deep throated sounds that chilled the darkened room. I assumed later, upon reflection, that my earache and sobbing disturbed her attempt to sleep and crossed whatever threshold of patience she had. Her distended stomach meant to me that she was in a stage of advanced pregnancy with my sister, June, or else it was right after delivery and she was recovering. Bringing this awareness of Mother's attack into consciousness permanently erased the nightmare. It also eliminated lingering discomfort from the daytime vision.

The critical bridging element was the physical sensation of Mother's hand on my back, and the related feeling of oxygen deprivation. The nightmare with the Japanese submarine partially duplicated mother's actions, as I was held immobile, pressure on my back was intense to the point that my spine felt like it might snap, and I escaped by entering an altered state of consciousness.

Body imagery instigating this nightmare was selective, and the sensation of smothering remained hidden in the nightmare at a less conscious level. At any rate, my dream bridging elements and sensory triggers only required limited duplication of physical sensations for me to connect the dots.

What this says to me is that traumatic events of this nature can be permanently recorded in our memories with one occurrence, and at a level below our conscious awareness. Oxygen deprivation and related damage to neural circuits must have occurred, as I lost my early ability to walk and talk. Nevertheless, I retained an image or images of mother's attacks, but the specific attack leading to my hospitalization may or may not have been retained.

Attacks of smothering were common enough that I learned to cup my hand over my mouth and curl into a fetal position when she approached my crib. This pattern lasted into junior high school, and was a pattern that used to bewilder my young mind. "Why do I do this?"

My brain recorded the physiological conditions of trauma, and was capable of fully duplicating a visual replay, as well as the correct interpretation in either brain-mind state of conscious dreaming or waking consciousness. The bizarre elements of dreams that I associate with brain modularity are experienced as being normal in my dreams, but seem bizarre when I'm awake.

Trauma resolution through dream analysis is quick and automatic. The bridging element permitted my higher order Interpreter to connect the dots and eliminate the nightmare. In the sense of consciousness residing at two levels, after Damasio, my core consciousness retained the basic memory that was blocked or not available at a higher level. Assuming brain damage, I probably would not have consciously recalled the death related smothering act without multiple attacks by mother.

Hobson's developed dream model considers this two-way flow of information between higher and lower brain centers. Information from non-conscious memories accessible to my core consciousness and suppressed memories from my higher consciousness centers combined to permit nightmare resolution. Note that I'm making a distinction between non-conscious and suppressed memories. Conscious awareness of the nightmare's activation elements eliminated the nightmare permanently.

It is from this perspective that I experience dynamic feedback loops operating across my brain-mind subsystems. I'm not attempting to explain the exact physiological mechanisms involved. The psychological processes themselves seem fairly clear, in that nightmare resolution follows quickly after the source of the nightmare is identified. I assume that resolution of the nightmare occurs because two way communications between higher and lower brain centers is completed, and that this new awareness on the part of my Interpreter rewires the involved neural circuits.

In either a dreaming or waking state, some level of my higher order consciousness had access to this memory. In either a state of waking or dreaming, conscious access to memory is triggered by a specific physical element. Thus, a dynamic theory of dreams and altered states must incorporate two-way communication between emotional and cognitive centers, if we assume isomorphism between brain structure and function. I also assume one of my brain-mind's major functions is to balance feelings and maintain a state of emotional homeostasis.

SEXUAL MOLESTATION NIGHTMARE

I was sexually molested by a farmer in Northwest Wisconsin when I was fourteen. I was subsequently interrogated by a county deputy without the consent or support of anyone. The deputy repeatedly asked me questions, carefully checked his notes, and informed me before he left that I would have to testify in court if the pedophile denied the allegations. My abuse had been set up by a school mate's father who wanted a second witness to his son's molestation by the same sex offender.

I informed my mother about the interrogation, as she had been watching from the kitchen window. She was obviously disturbed by the idea that my being molested would become public knowledge, and my and our family's reputation would be suspect. After all, boys do not permit themselves to be sexually abused unless they consent, or so the questioning went. My mother and the deputy took the same stance.

The thought of going to court and confronting the pedophile face-to-face was gut-wrenching, and I carried this thought around for nine months until we moved from Wisconsin to Washington State. I never heard from the court or the deputy again. In the 1950s, victims coped for themselves – especially victims whose behavior was suspect.

This nightmare had been long-standing with multiple variations. I would be pursued by a gang either on foot or on various types of motorized vehicles. They chased me through woods, along highways, down streets on the edge of towns, and through buildings. In one scenario, a large building is near a dam, and I run into it to hide. Eventually in this rapidly changing scenery, I become aware that the building is full of sexual deviants, and I panic. This nightmare became almost overwhelming when I entered the University of Minnesota at 21 years of age. I suspended the nightmare with dream programming for over twenty years, and then let it reoccur.

A more detailed review exists in my autobiography, hence the abbreviated version here. Nevertheless, the multiple dream versions contain scenery from both Wisconsin and Washington. Content representing the physical terrain from both states is incorporated in different dream scenarios. Characters are sometimes on foot, but mostly on motorized vehicles. Some scenarios have a building with multiple rooms, and when the doors are opened, I come face-to-face with my pursuers. My age also changes from adolescent to adult. For a number of years as a mature adult, I became a superhero and physically beat up all of my antagonists.

I didn't use suggestion or dream programming to become a superhero, because my dreaming brain created this alter ego on its own. However, dream suggestion is a technique that anyone can learn, and use to confront their nightmare antagonists or monsters, tell them they are just fictional dream characters, or physically subdue them. You can do whatever you want to in your dreams. In my case, I beat up the bad guys for years, but as I aged, my physical vulnerability again reentered the nightmare.

Dream programming has a different meaning for me. With dream programming, I stop the nightmare before it occurs and replace it with a pre-programmed dream. I controlled this nightmare, as I did with mother's smothering nightmare, for twenty years with this procedure. Dream programming was directed through self-hypnosis. Partial or less complete dream interventions were instituted with suggestions.

P. Tholey has cautioned against confronting dream characters, as confrontation may make them more monstrous in subsequent dreams (LaBerge: 2009: 55).

Tholey's idea addresses a critical element that those new to dream experimentation should be aware of. If you believe something may be true, this belief can become a non-conscious expectation that is automatically expressed in your dream. If I believe I can control my dream characters, I do, but if you believe they can come to control you, they will.

This is not an either or happening; it is something that happens as a belief product of your mind. Laberge does not make this distinction; however, it is an important distinction for beginners. I believe it is also an important distinction for those with uncontrolled hallucinations.

Your sense of vulnerability, age, sex, and physical prowess are all part of who you are, and you will participate in your dreams as this person. Depending on the strength of your ego, you may require outside guidance to get through traumatic dreams. If you are suffering from PTS, you will benefit considerably by using an outside support counselor or clinician.

That is my experience. I managed alone, but the time frame and active use of repression for decades is not recommended. Many people consider alcohol, drugs, or suicide before they resolve nightmares or frequently recurring hallucinations. Uncontrolled hallucinations for recovering drug addicts can be a major problem, which they may solve through suicide.

In the actual farm event, I'm helping the farmer put up his hay crop, and I spend the day on a tractor. The other adults in the work party are also on tractors, driving trucks, or cars as hay is loaded on wagons and moved.

In the final dream where I gain insight, the gang pursues me, and I'm captured. I'm restrained so tightly that I can't move, and I'm angry with my own stupidity for being caught. I become fully aware that my pursuers are sexual deviants, and I'm their prey. The restraint tightens, and I'm transported back to the desolate hay farm in Northwestern Wisconsin where I had been molested. My dream pursuer and captor is the sick pedophile who used me for group entertainment with his equally perverted buddies. This molestation's terror lasted for forty-four years.

Dream analysis offers so many important insights. Time can morph over decades in our dreams, as can our age and that of other people. All of these modular brain elements can and do mix and match a stream of creative scenarios that help maintain the earlier traumas.

Thematically, this long-term nightmare was quite consistent, but metaphorically, an endless stream of characters, means of transportation, and geographical locations emerged. I continued to age in the nightmare over the decades, went from being vulnerable to being a superhero, and then back to being vulnerable. In terms of trauma, my decades-long experiences speak to the degree to which psychic time is unbounded.

I awoke suddenly when the source of this nightmare was identified. My conscious mind connected with its non-conscious counterpart and the walls between two states of consciousness collapsed. It was a long awaited, wonderfully welcomed recognition. If neurons could shed parks, there were fireworks.

I was never permitted to speak of my sexual abuse as a child, and left with the impression that my forced participation in the act automatically made my motives suspect. My victimization had been transformed into an imaginative series of nightmares with woods, water, vehicles, chases, sexual deviants, and fear of capture. The nightmares ranged geographically from Wisconsin to the State of Washington. The changing dream geography finally made sense to me, as we had moved from Wisconsin to Washington during the time frame in which I waited to hear from the deputy and court.

Self-analysis naturally requires that we pay attention to rapid shifts of emotion in our dreams. Long-term familiarity with my traumatic dreams addresses this conundrum. When my dreaming and conscious mind connected, the nightmare immediately stopped and the traumatizing feelings evaporated. Resolution of this nightmare suggests that with resolution, my dreaming brain immediately shifts to whatever backlog exists in its emotion processing pipeline. In like fashion, once I understand any problem I've been wrestling with when awake, emotional or cognitive, my entire focus and attention shifts priorities. The same effect occurs when I'm wrestling with a new skill or learning complex academic materials; once one required skill or concept is mastered, I automatically move to the next one. Prioritizing actions is fundamental to a mobile creature that moves through time.

I experience this same phenomenon processing emotion in my dreams. If my most serious, traumatizing emotions are dealt with as stacked priorities, why wouldn't those of lesser impact also be dismissed once they are adequately processed in my dreams? Part of conflict engagement and resolution day-to-day must be related to normal memory maintenance. I assume that part of the rapid shift of scenes, characters, and contrived plots in dreams occurs because supporting physiological mechanisms operate in a similar fashion. Once a memory is integrated or a feeling resolved, my brain-mind just skips to the next item. This pattern seems to apply across sensory states.

Some nights I'd wake from one version of the nightmare, return to sleep, and a second or even a third version would continue to wake me. This nightmare had grown into multiple scenarios as my unconscious mind sought relief. Relief from other nightmares had already been realized, and my psyche was free of their torment. Unfortunately, my sexual victimization by the pedophile, re-victimization by the county deputy, and compounded victimization by insensitive parents had created a nearly impenetrable box of repressed, interconnected scenarios; locked boxes beyond the reach of my conscious mind.

Again, an important point to remember is that our memories retain auto-creations and mix them with real environmental experiences. The level of anxiety I felt in Wisconsin went with me to Washington State, and motorized vehicles took on their own creative morphing. I had to work a second day with the pedophile who took extra care presenting himself as a sexually interested person. Ask any sexual victim what it's like to spend time with their victimizer – a problem so common in family pedophilia.

I think nightmares clearly demonstrate our natural survival tendency. If I'm confronted by a physical threat in my environment, I don't shut down, but prepare to deal with it: flight or fight.

I do the same in my dreams. Why would my dreaming brain not be interested in survival as much as my waking consciousness is?

Mark Solms' idea that the brain and mind are completely dissociated in dreams is directly refuted by my experiences. My dreams are overwhelmingly driven by body, brain and emotional needs. This is in agreement with Hobson who says: "The sensations of dreams are the direct result of brain activation, not a secondary psychological response (2005: 174)."

Wishes play a part in my dreams through suggestion or outright dream programming. Our higher cognitive centers are an additional layer of evolutionary development that can be used to support our psychological well-being. Emotions guided our behavior before higher order consciousness evolved. Integration of feelings into higher order cognitive processes is critical for us to maintain balanced emotions and a complex social life. My brain is turning various levels of consciousness on and off in sleep and dreaming as it engages in basic, fundamental maintenance functions and experiential integration of sensory happenings from the day. Sometimes it just needs a little help.

After connecting this series of dreams with being sexually molested, I'd identify one version of the dream in the woods, by the dam, on motorcycles, or being chased on foot through the woods, and the traumatic power of each dream version was removed. Eliminating all the versions of this nightmare took some months as the capture scene that led to my awareness was not repeated in the other versions of the dream. And the nightmare versions appeared sporadically, not daily as they had previously. I think the lesson learned is how multi-layered traumatic memories can become through auto-created scenarios. Add in daily trauma from highly dysfunctional families when one is a child or adolescent, and the involved neural circuitry must be very complex.

I want to emphasize that this nightmare took on multiple versions, and unfortunately I never wrote them down. I recall about five or six distinct versions, but the combination of characters, scenery and type of vehicles could morph in very creative combinations. In my experience, PTS victims are subject to this complex self-reinforcing process. In effect I'm suggesting that each repeated version becomes its own FAP of complex metaphor. Hence, the difficulty experienced long-term by traumatized victims to rid themselves of the initial trauma may be compounded through similar types of auto-created versions.

When victimization occurs over the formative years of a child, the embedded memories, frequency with which the trauma is relived, and potential auto-created versions of the original trauma become overwhelming. A multitude of stimuli from one's environment can activate the nightmare (s) endlessly. This was my experience as a first year student at the University of Minnesota.

A critical point for individuals suffering from PTS is the auto-creation of endless nightmares or daytime hallucinations. Unresolved trauma expressed in my nightmares didn't stop with time. The self-building-cycling process reaches a point of no return. Sleep loss reduces one's energy, and anxiety seems more intense with the resulting fatigue. Finally, one begins to question their ability to cope.

A critical juncture is reached for many who resort to alcohol or drugs. This downward spiral can either destroy significant numbers of brain cells, or the affected person takes their own life. If they are strong enough, life may be maintained by extremely rigid daily behavioral routines, religious dogma, or expressive violence. Obviously, these are not good options. Enter the modern psychiatrist with his or her bag of pharmaceuticals and what do we have?

INTERPRETATION

The reader will recognize creativity in the different versions of this nightmare; its bizarre nature, shifting characters, shifting scenery, and the other formal qualities of lucid dreams. I was misled initially by trying to focus on the huge variations in the content of the various dreams. The multiple variations of this nightmare seemed to represent separate origins, but once I identified the pedophile's strong grip in the nightmare, I was on my way to identifying each dream version and full recovery. Each of the sexual abuse nightmares stopped immediately, and never returned once their activation source was identified.

Resolving these nightmare versions taught me two valuable lessons. Once my Interpreter identified the nightmare's activation elements, it used this awareness to modify how the neural circuits supporting the nightmare were expressed. To be effective, psychotherapeutic intervention must close or somehow neutralize neural circuits that support related memories. This suggests that a great variety of psychotherapeutic models can be effective if they tap these basic mechanisms. For me, this is one of the shaman's lessons. It seems obvious to me that insight, or meaning, can be realized by our higher cognitive centers through use of a large number of metaphors and abstractions. All of my nightmares have been eliminated immediately once their source was identified: The many roads lead to Rome syndrome.

Of particular importance to a basic argument in cognitive science is the role of meaning. Nightmare resolution occurred in two dream analysis steps for me:

1. A bridging element was identified (physical restraint by the pedophile; and

2. My conscious brain connected this bridging element with the molestation and its causative relationship to the nightmare.

Being aware of sexual deviants in my dreams was not enough; consciously I had to connect the bridging element, a type of muscle memory, with higher cognitive processes.

To be effective, analysis must use actual triggers related to the trauma. A mistake is often made when therapists attempt to impose their own models of therapy, with Freud's attempts to impose his dogmatic dream interpretations being a good example. I know that over a period of years, with suggestible clients, a therapist has enough time to create endless internal models of reality: Create them and remove them. Of course, this is unethical. Occultists are particularly good at this game if they are ruthless enough.

The second essential insight is associated with the dream trigger, or what Delaney calls the bridging element. The nightmare was unconsciously programmed into my dreaming brain around the physical restraint that made the molestation and subsequently the nightmare possible. It was a physiologically coded memory in a separate circuit built from fear, a neuronal circuit built from intense fear during the molestation, and reinforced throughout the following day when I still had to work side-by-side with the pedophile. This intense fear was exacerbated by the subsequent trauma created by the insensitive adults in my adolescent world. Bridging elements for ordinary dreams, or dramatically impacting nightmares, are commonly metaphorical constructions derived from primary body imagery such as restraint, balance, or fear.

Meaningful dream dictionaries must identify actual elements, or triggers, and their metaphorical representations. Contextual analysis by Hobson and related attempts by Delaney address this expanded view.

For me, dream analysis parallels how I attribute meaning to my experiences during daytime consciousness. I'm not like a computer that sees a speeding car just as a speeding car. I see the speeding car bearing down on a child as having a specific meaning and take action. The computer must be specifically programmed or it just watches. My brain has learned contextual meaning from day one. My brain is like yours; meaning is derived from context.

Dream analysis and dream dictionaries must reflect real life experience. If not, they are functioning comparably to Freud's dream analysis by adhering closely to a set program – an artificially manufactured schema. Mental health practitioners are most effective when appropriate meaning is derived from context. Meaning takes precedence over specific symbols. And this lack of contextual meaning is a major shortcoming in most dream dictionaries.

THERAPEUTIC INTERVENTIONS

Hobson refers to a technique used by some therapists to rid the client of nightmares and fears:

This can be an effective treatment for nightmares that is to be preferred to pharmacology (which has side effects) and to long-term psychotherapy that may neither uncover nor quell the hypothetical traumatic nightmare stimulus. The dreamer simply says to the fear, 'Hey look, this is my dream, get out and let me enjoy it!' (2001: 94).

In the late 1950s as a university student, I started dream programming. In these orchestrated dreams, I created the whole dream sequence through self-hypnosis including characters, plots and scenery. This programming was continued for over 20 years, during which time I maintained complete control over nightmares. Intervention in my dreams was automatic. If I became bored with the story or erotic dream partners after a few days, I just changed them. Over time, habitual, lucid intervention in my dreams changed the role of my Interpreter. My Interpreter came to intervene in my dreams on its own accord.

I lost almost all of my personal and academic notes in a spring snow melt that turned into a flood, so I cannot say exactly how long I programmed my dreams before I could enter and change them while sleeping. My conscious recall tells me it was within one university 12 week quarter. I no longer practice dream programming, but occasionally my conscious mind intervenes and changes dream characters, scenes, or outcomes on its own volition. For the last two decades I've committed to natural dreaming. I simply monitor the global themes, feelings, bridging elements, and cognitive nature of my dreams. Recording three to five dreams nightly is too tedious.

I appreciate the dream suggestion technique used by therapists but think it is incomplete. By discovering the activation stimuli, or triggers behind my nightmares, I was able to immediately eliminate them. Kandel reports the discovery of a number of principles that underlie learning and memory in terms of cell biology. He states:

[W]e found that the changes in synaptic strength that underlie the learning of a behavior may be great enough to reconfigure a neural network and its information-processing ability (2006: 204). A second related point is that synaptic changes … occur at several sites in the neural circuit… memory is distributed and stored throughout the circuit, and not a single specialized site (Ibid).

This work was done with aplysia, but the implications are clear for circuit modification related to trauma removal. Following these circuit findings, distributed memory suggests that one or more small changes in the circuit's strength can reconfigure the entire network. The answer as to how dream trauma can be immediately and permanently resolved may be this simple.

One of the fundamental features of memory is that it is formed in stages and continuously modified. Circuit and neural network changes built around distributed memory support the neural plasticity we experience daily. Dream analysis tells me that my old and new brain memory structures have overlapping but distinct memory functions. Distinct memory functions at two different system levels add to this plasticity, while it also makes possible self-perpetuating dream trauma.

My old brain integrates and consolidates visio-musculature elements related to balancing my bike. My new brain's higher cognitive centers are responsible for re-mapping these embedded primary images, which permit secondary images, a.k.a. Qualia II and primary metaphor. At the secondary level, balance as a Qualia II concept can be re-mapped as complex metaphor; I'm a balanced person, balance those books, and that's a balance beam. From this perspective, the reduction method of cell analysis provides the base from which we come to understand the emergence of language.

The two helpful insights that emerged when I learned to eliminate my nightmares were the discovery that memories embedded in motor circuits are bridging elements that can lead to higher order conscious awareness. And nightmares can be immediately dispensed through insight. A third awareness acknowledges that self-therapy can be available to anyone who pursues these insights.

Body tissue embedded memories can last a lifetime without our becoming aware of their origin. My younger sister June, for example, suffered claustrophobic reactions to closed space the same way I do. I know my reaction came from attacks of infant smothering by mother, and suspect the same was true for June and my older sister. It seems reasonable that therapists should benefit from special training in this area. For me, using suggestion or dream programming is just one step toward resolving our nightmares. The second and most important step involves identifying the activating triggers.

What I experience when triggers are identified is a sense of immediate emotional relief, which I think occurs because neural circuits close or reconfigure as new meaning emerges for our Interpreter. I assume from an evolutionary perspective that my brain-mind is programmed to keep threatening elements from my environment in my awareness, both when awake and when dreaming. This is a holistic approach to brain-mind isomorphism; part of what I call Dynamic Integrated Systems. When the saber-toothed tiger is killed, or the cave bear pummeled with killing stones, the threat is gone and we can relax. Identifying my triggers kills the neuronal cave bear. I think this is a more effective method to that of just trying to make the bear disappear over the hill. The most modern version of making the bear disappear over the hill is called pharmacological intervention.

My waking consciousness enters my dreams to positively reorient me to my external environment. What I experience is a circular loop of causation between my higher and lower brain centers in this process. Dream consciousness is shared with waking consciousness, and in this exchange, abstract integration occurs that generates new meaning. I have to envision my brain and mind as a working whole, or I can't account for phenomenological experiences and related modifications.

In my undergraduate university days, I married Skinnerian behaviorism with cognitive controls introduced through self-hypnosis; an approximation of what we now call cognitive-behavioral therapy. It worked well for me, but was outside the loop of Freudian determinism in the 1950s and '60s. It is amazing to me, 50 years later, how closely many therapists still cling to the old religious dogma. On the other hand, when I look around the world at major religions, I can appreciate the power of either sacred or secular indoctrination. Traditional psychoanalysts are not alone.

DREAM HALLUCINATIONS, MENTAL ILLNESS AND EPILEPSY

The relationship between dream hallucination and mental illness and epilepsy is often noted. "Epileptic fits" is a term used by my mother to explain the seizures I was experiencing after I came home from the hospital. I was probably 14-18 months old; however the seizures lasted at least until I was eight. My first OBE happened in the hospital, and ability to fly out of body in dreams or during waking hours occurred after this hospitalization.

I was diagnosed with critical scale elevations on paranoia-schizophrenia, obsessive-compulsive disorder, and psychopathic personality my first year at the University of Minnesota as an undergraduate. I was never officially diagnosed with PTSD from childhood abuse, but my sister June was diagnosed by the University of Washington, Seattle, when she was more than 60 years old. The examining clinician stated, according to June, that he had never observed a more severe case of PTSD in a military veteran.

As children, we were never permitted to talk about fears, nightmares, voices, OBE or any other such phenomena by our parents. Luckily, this probably kept us out of the "loony bin" which was how our parents referred to people with similar episodes.

Damasio notes that "… in some situations, brain damage can also lead to seizures, and during or after which altered states of consciousness are a prominent symptom (2010: 236)." And, "When autobiographical self disturbances appear independently, with an otherwise intact core self system, the cause is some aspect of memory dysfunction, an acquired amnesia (Ibid: 237)."

Loss of brain oxygenation, the effects of smothering in my case, most likely lay behind my memory loss. Most of my sister June's childhood memories were lost and never regained in her adult years. In her history, major recall emerges about the time she entered puberty.

I didn't distinguish between leaving my body in either a dreaming or a waking state between the ages of two until sometime after eight years of age. This distinction never seemed especially important to me, as I continued to use this capacity to leave my body at will into my mid-sixties with my reported Genesis Journey. I still use this capacity as I occasionally project myself into a movie simulation.

Hobson talks about the caution needed when interpreting brain-lesion data:

An individual suffering from **epilepsy** may have a well-defined 'focus' in the brain: that is, the abnormal electrical activity is seen most prominently at one point in the brain, which is considered to be the starting point for the seizure; hence, the term focus. Neurosurigcal removal of the tissue in which this electrical focus resides does not necessarily cure the epilepsy: rather, there have often appeared several new foci in the surrounding tissue. This finding suggests that gradients of excitability normally underlie the spread of excitation from one point in the brain to another. The whole system normally undergoes a progressive excitability change so that when one presumed focus is destroyed, others become prominent. Thus, a consequent behavior (as REM sleep) or a disease (as epilepsy) is not eliminated (Hobson: 1988: 176). Also,

We know that seizures become more probable when REM sleep is prevented; and that epileptic discharges may be released in non-REM and suppressed during REM sleep. These observations indicate that changes in the excitability of the brain are common to both conditions. Dreaming may thus be viewed as the conscious experience of a normal nocturnal brain seizure which helps the brain avoid the excessive excitability that plagues epilepsy victims even during the waking state (Ibid: 176).

If REM is the stage for memory integration and consolidation as I've suggested earlier, then this repair and maintenance work at the neural circuit level would most likely interfere with or override epileptic seizures. I prefer to think of dreaming as an integral process for the maintenance of brain-mind health. Dreaming is fundamental for the maintenance of body-mind homeostasis from this point of view.

The repetitive, uncontrolled expression of nightmares as an undergraduate interfered with my cognitive functioning as a student, my social relationships, created sporadic sleeping patterns, and most likely helped maintain the above referenced pathological elevations on my MMPI. Controlling my nightmares immediately began to reverse these negative effects. Stopping my brain from poisoning itself with its own neuro-modulators had to play a central role in my recovery at that time.

The parallel with epileptics seems obvious to me. As with nightmares, the brain is trying to correct the firing of out-of-control neural circuits but gets caught in a self-reinforcing loop. Localized neural circuit removal doesn't address the source of seizures as discussed by Hobson, because nearby foci in surrounding tissues take over. This pattern suggests that fits, or seizures, are a symptom of our brains responding to a distributed source of uncontrolled excitation.

Embedded, self-reinforcing neural circuits are part of our brain's plasticity. Thus, enabling macro-controls top-down would seem to offer a superior strategy to disable the most excited circuits, versus a bottom-up approach using surgery or targeted drugs. My Interpreter can take charge of anxiety, depression, attention span, or the willful execution of a Genesis Journey vision. My Interpreter can't control all the stimuli that create a seizure. If I continue to watch flickering florescent lights, I will lose control. But my Interpreter knows better, and I just move to another setting.

A speculative comparison between epileptic fits and nightmare trauma seems in order. Identifying parts of the nightmare do not stop it. The central trigger from which meaning is derived must be identified for the nightmare to stop. Removing a central locus for epilepsy doesn't address the larger neural network causing fits. In both cases, one must restructure elements in a distributed network to achieve positive results.

Restructuring elements in a distributed network seems straightforward with resolution of nightmares. The bridging element is identified, thus enabling the entire network to reconfigure. Removing a "hotspot" from the neural network without identifying the critical element doesn't work, and focus removal of tissue with epileptics doesn't work.

Brain functioning always runs on neural circuits and neuro-modulators. That's just the way it is. The lesson learned is: Always consider the brain as a dynamic entity we call the brain-mind. Tissue does not operate in a vacuum. Mind can not only change brain functioning, it can also be the causative factor.

As we've learned to artificially turn REM sleep on and off with chemicals, we have also become sensitive to how little chemical is necessary to move from one brain state to another. Hobson says: "If even a minute imbalance of chemicals in a minute region of the brain can influence the whole system and change its state, our conceptual model is important in understanding not only normal conditions such as REM sleep and dreaming, but abnormal ones such as mental illness (1988: 2002)."

My self-taught ability to turn anxiety off must at least modify brain chemicals at this micro level.

The causal direction of wishes (Will) and dream activation seemed clear to me fifty years ago. Hobson says: "Once REM sleep and dreaming have been cholinergically triggered, wishes may be expressed and may even shape dream plots, but they are in no sense causative of the dream process (Hobson: 1988: 202)."

The brain stem may activate the dreaming process, and once this activation has occurred, we can consciously intervene. Practice can permit almost total control of the dream, even to the fine points of movie-type scenes and sequences. In like fashion, epileptic attacks and mental illness scenarios with hallucinations, obsessive-compulsive behaviors, and the like, must be triggered by changes in brain states that are expressed in similar fashion.

Activation of various altered states, as well as hallucinations, usually occurs at a non-conscious level. However, over my long history, I have been able to gain control after activation; at least in the early stages of onset, which is my point of intervention.

In my case, active control of the dreaming process, attention span, and many functions of my autonomic nervous system must initiate alterations in brain circuitry and chemistry, which in turn reflect an isomorphic structural-functional relationship to experienced psychological states. I contended in *Mind of the Mystic* that mental health could be facilitated by taking conscious control of attention, anxiety, depression, and dreams, and thereby, altering one's brain chemistry.

In all cases, no. Once enough damage to neural circuits has occurred through one's own brain chemistry, it appears that only chemical intervention, surgery, or combinations of these interventions with behavioral control can do the job. Intense anxiety over long periods of time appears to play havoc by poisoning our brains with its own chemicals.

On the other hand, in my case, I speculate that by taking control of my nightmares, anxiety and depression, I changed micro-chemical states in my brain that led to recovering stable emotions, and in turn, facilitated improved cognitive functioning. My personal motto has been: save time, save money, by learning self-control and dream programming.

What surprised me at the time was how rapidly these changes occurred. Over the years, working with young people in various behavioral treatment programs, has left me with the impression that long-term drug use for therapeutic purposes decreases the brain's ability to self-balance and self-regulate. I also believe that neuroscientists and medical practitioners like Hobson are saying the same thing. However, removal of pharmaceuticals must occur under medical review.

Hobson says that:

Temporal lobe epilepsy is caused by the phasic discharge of intrinsic neuronal circuits whose excitability has been altered, usually owing to damage to neighboring neurons—presumably those normally exerting an inhibitory influence on the epileptic progenitors. The general hypothesis that we now wish to consider is that this disease process (which is the reciprocal of stroke damage) causes the temporal lobe more readily to enter a condition of phasic excitability increase akin to that which normally occurs only in REM sleep (2001: 195).

Mark Solms says that a corresponding increase in the intensity of dreaming occurs in patients with temporal epilepsy (Ibid). Thus, Solms offers a possible reason for my being a lucid dreamer since age two.

I do not have adequate recall from the early months of my life to a degree that I can claim easily retrieved memories from waking to sleeping to epileptic states. Below, I restate the similarities between pathological dreamy states of epilepsy and normal dream states which I've taken from Hobson:

1. There is a loss of contact with the outside world and a retreat into the virtual reality of the dream(y) state.

2. Hallucinations are quite common and often consist of vivid and sharply detailed visual imagery in both dreams and seizure states.

3. Bizarre cognition occurs frequently in both conditions and is characterized by discontinuities, and incongruities of imagined times, places and people.

4. One may experience strong emotion, especially fear, elation, and anger.

5. The subjective experiences are evanescent and difficult to recall at their termination (Ibid: 196).

I'm agreeing with Hobson who says:

For the cognitive neuroscientist, the analogy serves simply to bring the two apparently diverse phenomena into the same brain-mind state space (Ibid: 196-197).

The contrasting view for neuro-psychiatrists such as Arthur Epstein: This "analogy is strongly supportive of such psychoanalytic constructs as the release of libidinal impulses, primary process thinking, and dreaming as the symbolic manifestation of the same (Ibid: 196)."

My epileptic episodes were first manifested before the age of two years, and I later came to strongly associate them with mother's smothering. I had my first OBE at their onset, probably between 14 and 18 months of age, intensely vivid dreams of flying over the countryside, and a near total loss of fear. I did not differentiate between flying in dreams and daytime flying. Reality was mixed continuously to a degree that I especially recall my father's harsh voice frequently bringing me back to the here and now, and my mother telling me not to say such things, or people would think I was crazy.

CONTRAST: A COLLAGE OF ONE NIGHT'S DREAMS

Last night (3-7-11) is a typical later in life set of dreams that were generated by an uneventful week. The night began with extensive hypnogogic images, some faint and others quite vivid. Figures and background swirled through my mind as I quickly fell asleep; perhaps two or three minutes of relaxation and I was gone. It is now 8:57 a.m., and I'm sitting down at my computer after breakfast and a long chat with my wife. I will let last night's dreams surface naturally.

DREAM SEQUENCE

I'm with my teenage son, Steven, his brother, and a non-descript person who feels like my wife. My son is disagreeing with my instructions and does not want to leave. I forcefully insist that he get in the car so we can return home. He gets in the back seat from the driver's side, lays down with his feet out the door, and makes unpleasant noises. I'm angry, tell him to get out of the car, give him some change and a few dollars, and tell him to find his own way home. I notice as he leaves that it is cold, and he is only wearing a light T-shirt. Wracked by guilt, I follow him down the street and around a corner. He is sitting at an outdoor counter with a hot cup of coffee. I approach, sit down next to him, and he disappears, literally. I'm left with the coffee, which is black and about one-third consumed. I think coffee would be helpful for my drive home, and debate if I should order another one, but think: "No, I'll just get a takeout cup and drink Steve's."

The scene shifts.

I'm visiting various for sale houses with my current wife. The house I'm in is larger, and I think more expensive than what I can afford. However, it is full of beautiful plants. One of the plants has been placed in an odd grouping by my wife, and is a little out of type for the group. I comment to her, but she informs me that it needs to recover its vigor before it can be moved. I talk to the woman of the house, who is pleasant and says we are welcome to return as often as we like.

The scene changes.

I'm visiting my brother on his farm in Northwestern Wisconsin, and I'm in the barn watching him milk cows. As he finishes milking each one, the cow is released and leaves the barn for the yard. I notice that my shoes are collecting residue, and think that I'm tracking manure. A calf comes my way and I pet it. It is affectionate and jumps up, placing its front feet on either side of my shoulders. I push it down and away. The calf acts as though it is somebody's pet.

The scene changes.

I've returned to the above referenced house. The owner is still congenial and welcomes my return visit. My wife and I walk around looking at the interior, but especially spending time with the plants. The plant she had previously placed in a special group in order to allow its recovery is still there. Now, however, the plants have multiplied in number, and are so tightly packed that it is impossible to move freely amongst them. I lift my wife's plant and move it. The owner looks on approvingly, and makes some comment which I've forgotten.

The scene changes.

I'm parking my car in a difficult space. It is narrow and on a rough road. I decide not to leave the car in this location, as it will probably get damaged by other cars that will careen into it. I start backing up, and interrupt an attempt by another car to enter the parking area. This car stops and is immediately mired in a hole surrounded by snow. I realize my error in creating this problem for the other driver. I get out of my car and help him and two male passengers push his car out of the hole. I apologize and the other driver says that it's okay, he understands. I head back toward my car to drive away and the scene changes.

I am driving around a city area that I'm unfamiliar with. I'm not lost but I can't find my undefined destination. I drive down different streets, turn numerous corners, but do not recognize any of the landscape. This part of my dream is vague and I do not have complete recall. I wake up at 7:00 a.m. and decide that I will record this dream series as another example of my normal dreaming. I woke up once last night at 11:50 p.m., but I'm no longer sure of each dream scenario's sequence. I recall visiting the house early in the night before 11:50 p.m. and then again sometime after this waking interruption.

INTERPRETATION

I did not detail all the content of these dreams nor their origin, but just provided a quick overview. There is nothing special about this night's dreams except to illustrate how mundane most normal dreams are, and to contrast them with the preceding nightmares.

The house in the dream looks, and even more so, feels, like one that my wife and I visited yesterday for the first time. She has a new friend that lives in Canyon Lakes, Kennewick, and we visited there most of the afternoon. The dream house has high ceilings, ornate furniture imported from China, and a large number of Chinese items and the woman is Chinese.

I probably repeated visiting this house in my dream for memory functions. This was my first visit and many items reminded me of my own years in China.

It is ten weeks later (5-22-11) as I review this section, and the visual imagery from the house is still very distinct; that is, my memories are fully embedded.

The calf in my brother's barn dream filled in for a new puppy I played with at yesterday's afternoon luncheon. The driving scenes represent daily practice by my wife who will be taking her driving test tomorrow. The rough parking space with an uneven surface is representative of a hole in the parallel parking area of the local testing offices practice space. The dream confrontation with my son is a long ago association with our hosts of yesterday's 15 year old boy, except that the boy is extremely well behaved and played a short piano recital.

In real life, my son Steven never acted out as he did in last night's dream, either. However, a nephew who spent a year with our family while still in Junior High School did occasionally act out this way.

Mundane, uneventful and transparent – such are ordinary dreams. I've been a lucid dreamer for more than 70 years, and every year my dreams become more mundane. Note the contrast between ordinary dreams and those that are traumatic, or reflect strong emotions. Consistent dream analysis helps me quickly locate key bridging elements from which we can derive the dream's meaning. If, on the other hand, one's focuses is on fantastic fictive items such as flying, we lose awareness of normal dream patterns. And, if we infrequently analyze our dreams, we will not notice these patterns at all.

If you follow dream dictionaries with all their bizarre interpretations, you will not have a clue to your dream's meaning. Bizarre dictionary interpretations force one to accept the offered logic, or interpretations that follow from this logic are lost. If we follow Freud's dogma of the unconscious or Jungian archetypes, it will be like trying to look at the bottom of a lake through dirty water.

Our dreams can be as fantastic as our imaginations, as dramatic as our most intense emotions, or as mundane as everyday life. Dreams can be an irreplaceable window into the inner life of our brains and minds, as well as being a free resource to gain and improve our mental health. Don't be afraid of your dreams, but learn to control and understand them. And if you experience other states of altered reality, you'll find the science behind dreams most helpful.

The historical market is filled with trash masquerading as useful dream information. If you have been influenced by any of the many charlatans of the night, go back and make a fresh start with something like Hobson's *13 Dreams Freud Never Had,* Brooks and Vogelsong or Delaney.

CHAPTER 9

DREAM CONTENT, FORM AND FUNCTION

INTRODUCTION

Throughout this book, I'm treating the brain-mind as a single working entity, whether I'm awake, or involved in an average 90 minutes sleep-dream cycle. I understand my dreaming brain to be engaged in a number of different tasks. Multi-tasking includes memory functions such as those associated with fixed action patterns, maintenance of emotional and physical homeostasis, and higher order cognitive activities. I always experience these three functions as being central to dream interpretation.

Dream form as discussed by Hobson is a reflection of how our brain-mind's processes are expressed. I give dream content more emphasis than most dream researchers. Dream content is critical to my locating the bridging elements that are central to dream interpretation. I've already discussed the importance of content from this perspective, plus, I've used content to analyze auto-creative elements related to dream memories, belief, and déjà vu.

Consideration of Damasio's use of convergence-divergence zones (CDZs) and convergence-divergence regions (CDRs) bring this chapter to a close. The hard problem for neuroscience as well as cognitive science is how meaning is created by a bunch of chattering neurons and brain chemicals. This is not just an esoteric problem of philosophical import, but a critical area of analysis for mental health practitioners. I personally think most of the problem is solved, and its solution resides in the realm of what we call subjectivity.

BETWEEN TWO CONSCIOUS STATES

It is (12-4-10) and I'm having an afternoon nap. My dream space is large and open with other people scattered throughout my visual area. I notice the area has considerable garden produce, especially unpicked cucumbers. I begin to pick and carefully put them in a sack that I'm holding in my left hand. As I pick, they become zucchini, and I concentrate on picking the larger ones. Yes, I do garden.

The numbers of zucchini multiply as I pick, and there is an endless supply. I come to the edge of a vehicle and reach under to pull out a large one, only to find that it is a clump of three, not just one. I separate and place them in my bag. I'm on my knees reaching for more zucchini, but find that this is not adequate, and I began to crawl under the vehicle.

The discussion around me focuses on enemy troops approaching, and I think I should crawl entirely under the vehicle and hide: I attempt to do so. However, my feet are sticking out so I pull them in. My back is on the edge of the passenger-side of the vehicle and feels exposed. I try to crawl in farther but have difficulty moving. I reach up and pull the flap down that runs along the lower part of the vehicle by my back. This flap didn't exist when I first crawled under the car. All of this seems logical to my dreaming brain.

As I pull the flap down, I'm aware that my hand is clutching my bedcovers, and I'm pulling them over my cold shoulder. I realize that I haven't just been dreaming, and that I'm in two states of consciousness. I don't know if my sleeping cold shoulder activated the dream, or if I created the car's flap in the middle of the dream. I woke up because I needed to use the bathroom, or I might not have made the connection between my cold shoulder and the dream's content. I returned to bed for a few minutes, couldn't sleep, got up and typed these notes.

INTERPRETATION

My lucid dreams often incorporate physical stimuli from my surrounding environment. External stimuli can activate single dream elements or whole dream scenarios for me, or environmental stimuli can enter my dreams as a single element. I suspect that reading seed catalogs activated the cucumber scenario, and then my cold shoulder activated the car flap component. Body stimuli of various kinds enter my dreams this way, an effect that is probably common to all dreamers.

My conscious mind frequently identifies sensory elements entering my dreams from my body while I'm still dreaming. For example, potty dreams enter my conscious awareness and tell me that I need to get up and use the bathroom. Over the years as I've analyzed my dreams, body stimuli is identified this way while I'm still dreaming.

I sometimes find that I have an erection when waking from an erotic dream. Other times, there is no erotic dream content that accompanies the erection. Decades old analysis of this pattern tells me that erections are a normal part of how my brain and body naturally work together. This pattern also reminds me that if I'm not enjoying a normal baseline of sexual activity, erotic content will emerge in my dreams. If my erotic life is normal, an erection will occur without any dream imagery.

Overeating can create stomach discomfort that leads to an endless variety of dream scenarios. It is not the content of these images that is telling, it is the sensations they create. Eating a large meal late in the evening, which is unusual for me, often leads to a toilet dream. I can be sitting on a dream toilet in public, which is common, or I can be unsuccessfully searching for a restroom. Emerging awareness is first triggered by bowel discomfort that creates a toilet search scenario. This awareness gradually moves into my higher order consciousness, and I get up and use the bathroom. Semi-naked or naked potty dreams are just this transparent. If I'm sleeping in the nude I'm also nude in the dream; if I'm semi-nude, I'm also semi-nude in the dream. There is no mystery regarding my dream nudity.

I interpret primary imagery generated by an uncomfortable bowel as Qualia I. Re-imaging Qualia I as Qualia II at a higher cognitive level becomes dream metaphor for toilet use. Thus, I find Damasio's qualia terminology helpful to visualize this multi-stage process. Dreams where I search for toilets in various stages of nudity are as transparent as my dream reactions to nudity as well as other dream characters being unconcerned about my nudity. My Interpreter understands toilet needs.

Dream researchers like Hobson note that the forms within our dreams are major keys to their understanding. In the above dream, the cucumbers morph into zucchini, a flap grows on the side of the car, and a calm, sunny afternoon environment turns hostile, and I need to hide. I often use the term "morphing" to describe what is going on in my dreams; cucumbers become zucchinis, and cars grow flaps. This is not just scene change; it is creative transformation. And, our dreams are capable of endless creative transformations.

We transform dream content at will while still dreaming.

I'm not totally sure what activated the zucchini dream, most likely garden and seed magazines that I've been reading, but I do know that a cold shoulder created the last part. Dreams can be activated by any of my senses, but once body sensations enter my sleeping brain, they can create one vignette after another. Of the 25-50 dream scenarios we have each night, our sleeping brain must also be attending to a lot of housekeeping chores such as memory functions, emotion processing and maintenance of body homeostasis being most common.

The bridging element was the flap on the side of the car was mundane and trivial, but enlightening. The military part of the dream came from a movie that I watched just prior to retiring. It is common for my dreaming brain to mix elements that appear to be part of memory integration and consolidation, and it mixes these environmental stimuli with many other multi-tasking elements and themes. It is this mixture that occurs over the course of any given night that confused me when I was younger. Especially with nightmares, I would remember the nightmares and totally ignore other dream scenarios; that is, unless I programmed the dreams.

MAINTENANCE FUNCTION OF DREAMS

My sleeping brain continues to process waking elements that are important to my everyday existence, and dream consciousness reflects the salient activities supporting my daily routines. Traumatic dreams are created by strong emotions, whereas cognitively focused dreams emphasize activity devoted mostly to thought and wrestling with concepts and symbolic elements. Mundane dreams are probably mostly cobbled together elements that come from brain stem activity devoted to maintaining my bodily needs, and erotic dreams appear to be activated by hormone and sexual activity levels. And what I've called theme dreams reflect complex interrelated activities such as writing this book. Theme dreams can continue over one night or many days.

LaBerge reminds us that unresolved emotions in dreams are carried over into our waking day (2009: 6). And, that we can learn to relieve anxiety in lucid dreaming in order to keep negative moods out of our day activities (Ibid: 35). He quantifies what happens when he works through his fearful dreams:

I noted that anxiety preceded lucidity onset in 36 percent of my first year's lucid dreams (60 percent during the first six months); ... second year 19 percent ... third year 5 percent ..., and in 1 percent or less during the following four years (Ibid: 34-35).

I have not quantified negative emotions in my dreams this way, but my pattern parallels his. And, segueing off LaBerge, my waking emotions are carried over into my dreaming nights.

I like Hobson's dream forms in his activation-synthesis model, as elements found in the bizarre tell me a lot about dreaming itself. However, when I look at my various dreams, I identify numerous functions that my brain is carrying out: FAP-like dreams seem to be integrating and consolidating memory through fictive practice, and mundane dreams represent ho-hum body activity such as bathroom use. Thinking dreams emphasize concept manipulation going on over a 24 hour period in my higher order brain centers.

Nightmares continue until our higher cognitive centers are satisfied that the threat is removed, and key to this analysis: The threat is not removed until higher order consciousness, our Interpreter, is satisfied.

This process can take one day or twenty years. Nightmares act like self-maintaining oscillations in our neural circuits that can continue indefinitely, but once our Interpreter understands what activates our nightmares, they are automatically eliminated. Instead of being enemies that bring terror and ragged sleep, nightmares understood become tools that we can use to achieve balanced mental health.

Freud's emphasis on unconscious wishes driving our dreams seems totally absurd from my personal experience. How could Freud have entertained his strange notions of the unconscious if he had analyzed his own dreams? Evolutionary tinkering says that my cobbled together brain engages in multiple functions to enhance my survival.

Content analysis helps me identify the different patterns of memory associations that occur in my dreams. I can watch facilitated action patterns being maintained in my dreams by focusing on the emergence of primary images and qualia related to dream content. Finding pattern in dream content also lets me identify themes and broader aspects of abstract concept manipulation. And, an overall view of content from these perspectives tells me that traditional dream dictionaries are a lot of hooey.

Hobson's analysis of form emphasizes the lack of logic in dreams, their time shifting nature, and character transformations. Much of the bizarreness associated with form fades away for me when I look at the activation of processes that underlie form and focus on function. Thus, by identifying the sources of my dream content, I come to understand dream form and function more fully. I start with all three – content, form, and function in my dream interpretations, and through this triage, identify bridging elements that let me make functional correlations.

Dream function, if function and brain states are isomorphic, must cover all the psychological elements I experience. My emotional states and needs are identified; cognitive and memory components are integrated; mechanisms of repression, both overt and covert, are dissected; and the dynamic interface between dreaming and waking consciousness becomes clearer. Subjective brain-mind states are constantly being analyzed by my Interpreter, either in dreams or when I'm awake. Introspection demands explanation of internal processes as does one's overt waking behaviors. From this perspective, what is meaningful to my Interpreter can only be understood subjectively.

Physiological explanations for cell and circuit functions do not explain how meaning is created, stored, and changed by our conscious and non-conscious selves. Damasio comes closest to explaining how higher order consciousness is able to create meaning for me. But, I'm greedy and want to understand the complete process.

I need a dynamic integrated model of dreams and altered states along with Damasio's two stage model of consciousness to explain my dreams. But for me, the interrelationship between content, form, and function has its own special twists. Let me review what I call a multi-tasking dream that cuts across a number of these different components.

MULTI-TASKING DREAM

It is Saturday, February 19, 2011. I have slept soundly and only have vague recall for dreams earlier in the night, but these earlier dreams involved material that I have used in my writing the previous day, as well as thoughts about treatment programs I have administered or developed over the years.

The following dream is my last dream of the morning. It is representative of the multi-tasking that goes on in my dreams as dream elements morph from one scene to another.

I'm in a nondescript treatment program setting for chemically dependent offenders that I evaluated in the 1980s. I'm observing one of their groups. I smile at their group procedures and emit a low chuckle. The client who is the focus of group is offended by my chuckle and says his situation is not funny. I immediately respond that I am not laughing because it's funny, I'm laughing because it's serious and sad. I explain why this is the case and detail five different processes taking place in the group.

The scene morphs and I'm visiting my old job as Tri-County Community Corrections Administrator in Rochester, Minnesota. Many social workers are revising files, cleaning out records, updating logs, and putting all this information in new record jackets. The copy machine is busy with complete files including their jackets coming off the printer. In my dream, I think this copying procedure is a little weird. I compliment the staff for their efforts, and the scene changes again.

I'm talking to one of the local judges. I inform him that I will be temporarily filling in my old job and will be happy to screen all the print material coming through the department for him. I hand him a bunch of material that I've sorted and tell him I've disposed of the remaining trash. He informs me that this will not be necessary; he will do the sorting himself. I agree and he looks at me over the top of his glasses as I go about other business.

I inform the staff that my filling in temporarily for the absent administrator should not last more than a couple months and that I'm pleased to be back with them. I look around the office, it is open, large and entirely different from the physical setting I left years ago. I look past many desks to the open windows to the West. On the right side of my visual field is my wife sitting on one of the desks. She has a coy smile and is studying me. I think: She is clearly suggesting her availability. No one else seems to notice her but me.

INTERPRETATION

As I wake up a number of thoughts enter consciousness. My wife is softly cuddling next to me and being very affectionate, thus, I understand her coy smile in the dream. The five different elements come from an article I've been reading by M. P. Walker on "The Role of Sleep in Cognition and Emotion." Walker states:

[Accumulating] evidence for the role of sleep in associative memory processing [is] discussed, suggesting that the long-term goal of sleep may not be the strengthening of individual memory items, but instead, their abstracted assimilation into a schema of generalized knowledge.

My dreaming brain is contemplating this idea. As I wake up, my conclusion is that it is not either or, as my dreaming brain does both. The judge in my dream was one of my strongest critics, and he did have a habit of looking at me over the top of his glasses, both in the courtroom and in private conversations. It was his way of emphasizing his position.

Former employment scenes frequently enter my dreams. It was my habit to introduce innovative programming in previous human service settings that I administered. I introduced a number of cognitive-behavioral programs, including some that were created whole, in Rochester. My dreaming brain often associates cognitive-behavioral interventions with my prior work settings.

As I get out of bed, seemingly random concepts running through my waking brain include qualia, metaphor, Noe's cognitive science hypothesis, which I'm thinking needs total revision, Damasio's concept of consciousness, and the idea that I should organize all of my soma-based material into one chapter. This is a jumble of thoughts that my dreaming brain associates with material I've been trying to integrate for this book, and with former treatment modalities in Rochester.

I recognize that scene morphing accommodates dream multi-tasking. Not only do dreams serve more than one function such as memory consolidation, but as Walker suggests, dreams involve abstracted assimilation of generalized knowledge. My examples of themes in dreams generally support this view as well.

I had been thinking about Noe's hypothesis before I went to bed and how it seems to be built around a social-psychological model that explains social behavior rather than a model from neuroscience that explains consciousness. A careful treatment of qualia, I think, would make his use of consciousness, body, and environment clearer. My waking brain is stuck on the idea that Noe is using linear causation to explain a dynamic model. My dream seemed to think that Damasio's use of Qualia I and Qualia II would be helpful in this effort. I ate breakfast and sat down at my computer, and later incorporated Damasio's interpretation of Qualia I and Qualia II.

I'm interpreting rapid scene changes in this dream with multi-tasking, and much of the multi-tasking centers around cognitive elements that are being integrated from multiple sources. Part of the dream follows Walker's ideas about the assimilation of abstracted memories. But the dream also seems to be entertaining single elements in memory integration – Damasio's qualia for example.

Various levels of complexity are being addressed throughout this night's dreams. And, following Walker's argument, memory consolidation in my multi-tasking dreams seems to support strengthening both individual memory items as well as the assimilation of general knowledge. My subjective dream experience of multi-tasking supports all five components of his argument:

1) Sleep's role in memory processing,
2) A "mechanistic model of sleep-dependent plasticity,"
3) Abstracted assimilation of generalized knowledge,
4) Regulation of emotional brain reactivity, and
5) Sleep-dependent affective brain processing.

My dreaming brain did not recall all five of these components in detail. I used the abstract itself to construct the above sentence. My sleeping brain had simply flagged five components and brought this idea into my waking consciousness. Although as I got up, ate breakfast, and sat down at the computer, I realized the five components had been sorted out by my dreaming brain with considerable clarity. But the five elements weren't on the tip of my tongue when I woke up. I often access knowledge this way, but don't know that I know until I sit down and let my thoughts spill themselves on paper or through my keyboard.

Logically, I would have to take complete control over my dreams through dream programming to eliminate this morphing set of sequential scenes. I could create a coherent and logical dream story that focused on Walker's material only, and I could prime my brain to do this while I was sleeping. If I did, however, I would lose normal dreaming and miss the other tasks of this multi-tasking cognitive-focused dream, which also involved Noe and Damasio.

I point out this difference as extensive use of dream suggestion alters natural expression in my dreams. Besides, I find it helpful to let my sleeping-dreaming brain process the day's conceptual materials and engage non-conscious problem solving abilities.

Sudden changes in my dreams seem logical, necessary and supportive of my dreaming brain performing many tasks during the night. My sleeping-dreaming brain is shifting scenes and characters as it moves from thinking about material for this book and making associations with former cognitive elements from my professional history.

Cognitive-behavioral memory associations related to treatment modalities connect my "now" with my "then." My dreaming brain doesn't have to go through a conscious sorting process that follows the logic of my waking mind. Through the night I experience varied metaphorical images swirling through numerous dream scenarios. I may be in a student test situation, writing on a blackboard, giving lectures, or reading metaphorically depicted materials of the sort I've already reported. I also have numerous complex discussions with others and myself in these dreams.

My dreaming brain seems to directly manipulate abstract concepts. By this statement I mean I'm not just manipulating the language, I'm actually manipulating the concepts, the conceptual units themselves. I'm not just manipulating words or language in my dreams, but also their embedded referents.

Recall that complex metaphor permits primary metaphor to be remapped at our higher levels of consciousness, thus, one level of metaphor can be used as a referent at the next level of metaphorical use. This process adds a bizarre quality to my dream images as well. I'm suggesting that these complex processes underlie much of the manifest expressions Hobson calls dream forms.

The central Controller in my dreams goes directly to memory elements that can represent different levels of complexity such as CDZs and CDRs to emotional brain reactivity, and as Walker suggests, these abstracted memories are then assimilated into general knowledge. My multi-tasking dream includes physical stimuli from my wife, complex abstractions from Walker's article, and criticism of both Noe's and Damasio's use of qualia. Viewed from the perspective of multi-tasking, the bizarre features of Hobson's dream forms seem less bizarre.

Although physical contact by my wife entered my dream, I'm quite sure her cuddling did not activate a dream that was dominated by this level of abstract concept manipulation. The abstract concepts being manipulated by my dreaming brain were also producing outputs and conclusions.

I'm forced to conclude that our brains operate as dynamic parallel processors or I can't adequately explain this dream. I also assume that the complexity of content in our dreams varies with one's background and current activities prior to entering sleep for the night. In any case, Walker's observations apply if I've interpreted this dream correctly.

DREAM CONTENT

For a number of months my dreams have been dominated by conversations. I've been dreaming normally for years without consciously using suggestion or dream programming techniques. Dream conversations can and do occur in any number of time frames, locations, or with individuals from all walks of professional life. The form may contain the usual bizarre elements of dreams, but there is an added consistency in that the dream content is associated with my brain processing materials for this book. My ebb and flow of feelings is consistently expressed in my dreams.

One short dream vignette may seem illogical to my waking consciousness, but takes on a logical meaning when I tease out the different tasks my dreaming brain is working through. By following dream content over the course of multiple dream scenarios in one night, or even over multiple nights of dreaming, I note that dream themes address complex tasks that can take hours or days to reach closure. Arriving at $E=MC2$ is not a one night affair.

Complex thoughts are not brought into my dream consciousness the same way they are when I'm awake. In waking consciousness, I've learned select approaches to integrating complex cognitive materials. My dreaming brain doesn't have to follow the rules of language the way my waking brain does. Thus, my dreaming brain integrates concepts differently than my waking consciousness does.

My dreaming brain integrates material the way I provide corrections to this chapter on my computer. I just go to the sections I want to change and change them. I don't need to go back and rewrite the whole chapter. In my waking consciousness, I go back and reformulate entire sequences of thought word for word. It often amazes me how directly my dreaming brain can access a specific memory and derive new meaning before I wake. Change the C in $E=MC2$ and...oh you get the idea.

I recognize the same mechanism operating in a FAP-like dream. I'm honing balance on my bicycle or reactivating leg and body motions with my lawn mower as I cut grass. Both action patterns were embedded at least thirty years ago, are fictively being brought up to speed in my dream re-enactment, and are strengthening, integrating, and honing already embedded memories. Learning to lucidly analyze our dreams adds insight because we are one step closer to basic sensory image formation and memory processes. Language can be a cumbersome nuisance. Just ask Einstein!

In my December 6, 2010 dream, I'm in a nondescript location explaining how memory works according to Antonio Damasio. However, my dream focus is on convergence-divergence zones (CDZs) and convergence-divergence regions (CDRs), and the exchange between the two that creates recall in memory. As I discuss the detail of this memory process to other dream characters, my wife physically gets up to use the bathroom. At that moment, I'm both lecturing in the dream and aware of her activity in my conscious brain.

The reader might suspect that my thinking dreams are just a combination of waking-dreaming states of the above nature. However, I have whole nights of thinking dreams with one related dream scenario following another.

Note that with long-term lucid dream analysis, we are aware that the dream continues as we observe; we are aware that we are aware that the dream continues as we observe. We also become sensitive to our dreaming brain's processing of external stimuli. Pretty transparent stuff!

In the dream visual, I am looking at an actual diagram in Damasio's *Self Comes to Mind*, but in the dream, I think it is on page 197. My dreaming brain is positive the page number is 197, and I tell my dreaming self I should remember the page number and check it when I get up. I check the page number later and it is 142.

Furthermore, my sleeping memory is playing tricks as it has the diagram of CDZs and CDRs on the right side of the two page open book and the narrative on the left. I reversed the page order in my dream and changed the page numbers. In actuality, the diagrams of CDZs and CDRs are on the two facing pages of 146 and 147. I have mixed these two sections of Damasio's book. Even my dreaming brain's memory is ageing.

Before I return to sleep, and the clock tells me it is 1:00 a.m. and I have been processing this dream for two or three minutes, I make a mental note that I should fully explain Damasio's use of CDZs and CDRs in my then draft Chapter 2.

In my experience, the more lucidly we dream and the more sensitive we become to what activates our dreams and how to interpret content, the clearer these processes become. I think professional dream researchers miss some of these patterns by not following individual subjects through longer periods of time. But one must be careful not to inadvertently change their dreams through this subtle form of suggestion.

I'll add some related comments on dream multi-tasking before proceeding. When I was a full-time professor, I often taught five different courses in one day. My mind would be processing materials for the day's lectures in a seemingly jumbled mixture of elements if one viewed my mind from the outside. Multi-tasking has this quality of dealing with many things in quick but disordered fashion, or so it seems to an outside observer. The mind in actuality fits the pieces together as though it were a chess master playing a dozen different games simultaneously. My dreaming brain skips one level of this sorting process and hence, the jerky quality of my dreams is multiplied. That is, until I more fully employ the language of dreams.

SYNESTHESIA IN DREAMS

I wake from an afternoon dream of approximately one hour (3-25-11) with the following concepts floating through my waking mind. I'm excited about an awareness that dominates this vague dream and focus on the following swirl of concepts: synesthesia, Ziaoli, little cold, 1955 Chevy, and cross-modal processing. As I wake up, an additional bridging element comes to mind: My dreaming brain uses cross-modal body maps of both internal and external stimuli the way certain synesthetes create the color red when seeing a number 7.

My dreams frequently manifest cross-modal processes like this by using a concrete form, such as a 1955 Chevy, for a body state, like a cold shoulder. A message from my limbic system, core consciousness, is displayed in my dream in billboard form. The 1955 Chevy in my dream is in the exact location and size of the cold spot on my shoulder. At this point in the process, my Interpreter is aroused from dream observer to body caretaker. My body sensation of cold is turned into a visual which my lucid dream observer, Interpreter, immediately notes as being odd; and thus takes action.

I'll skip lengthy speculation on how my brain decided on the image of a 1955 Chevy, however, the visual form of the car and its exact location in this dream in relation to my cold shoulder matched perfectly. The Chevy had no other function in the dream. If a similar object occurred in my visual field when I'm awake it would simply be part of my environment. But, the Chevy is auto-created from memory and immediately flags my conscious awareness. It is a bridging element that focuses my waking attention on an uncomfortably cold shoulder.

I have been reviewing synesthetes in Ramanchandran's *The Tell-Tale Brain* and thinking about cross-modal symbolism in dreams. My dreaming brain configured the above cross-modal link while I was sleeping. This is a good example of how easily waking thoughts get processed in my sleep-dream cycle. In this example, I believe my dream Interpreter identified a process that is common in many of my dreams, but

I don't believe the review of Ramachandran's material created this relationship *de novo*. It just made a comparison with synesthesia.

Ziaoli is a woman friend of a former colleague and she lives in Paris. My friend and I exchanged emails about her yesterday. My brain seemed to be processing this conversation and this processing activated imagery entered my dream and waking recall.

Synesthesia-like, cross-modal processing in dreams makes their interpretation more complex. But common renderings in my dreams include the difference between winter, being part nude, summer, being full nude, night clothes, and how these stimuli instigate dream content. I'm simultaneously processing body stimuli using two separate levels of consciousness: Core consciousness reflects primary sensations, and autobiographical consciousness is more abstract and representative of complex metaphor.

Dream awareness of my physical state of being partially dressed or unclothed enters my dream and seems bizarre. Core consciousness in my naked or semi-naked dreams is processing an actual physical state, and my observing autobiographical self feels compelled to explain my nakedness. As I edit this section (6-30-11) I note that this summer's first naked dream occurred during my afternoon nap.

Cross-modal processing in dreams explains a lot of Hobson's dream form to me. I wonder how it could be otherwise. Fifty thousand years ago when my ancestors lived in caves, they must have responded to real life circumstances that were life and death critical. A multi-tasking brain has survival advantages, and being aware of environmental stimuli is one of them. Today's evolutionary development permits my cerebral cortex to explain this relationship while my old brain does its work as usual.

DREAM FORM

Dream form for Hobson focuses on the lucid dreamer's experiencing sudden changes and unusual variations of time, space and characters. Characters can be composites, time can shift quickly, and one can be in different locations in a split second of dream time.

In the above dream (12-6-10), these morphing qualities are there but limited. I'm in one location, the time is now and does not shift, the scene is nondescript and seemingly unimportant, and I'm focusing on thoughts. I'm fully aware that I'm searching through Damasio's book for specific text. Although Hobson's forms are found with the text as page numbers and material changes: The dream page changes each time I look.

Content that is not memorized typically changes each time I look away from written material in my dreams. In the Damasio CDZ example, content and concepts remain, but page organization and formatting changes. I've never had total recall like my father, but I can usually see sections of written materials, financial spreadsheets, or diagrams. But with age these images grow dimmer. It seems that my brain is now happy just retaining ideas and concepts, and I'm satisfied that my dreaming brain is still capable of integrating old and new concepts before I wake.

However, in thinking dreams, focus on concepts remains and the material can be manipulated similarly to what I do when awake. My dreaming brain doesn't morph around with memorized concepts the way it does with characters, feelings, and scenery. But, my dreaming brain does move from one concept to another without providing logical transitions.

It seems logical to me that as language becomes habituated we impose structure on thought that interferes with our natural creativity. Following children K through 12 informs us as to how much of this creativity is lost. I suggest that the form of picture languages, Chinese for example, is closer to primary image formation. Think about 1.5 billion people thinking with picture images.

I note while dreaming that the number of CDZs necessary to create an image in a CDR is probably seven as I process dream-talk. I pause in my dream and think: No, it probably takes ten CDZs, I then proceed to look in my dream book of *Self Comes to Mind.* My eyes quickly scan the page and I say: "No, not seven but ten CDZs." It is at this point of the dream that I realize I'm looking at two pages of text with the schematics on the right hand side. All of this dream work seems just as realistic as one of my waking reading experiences. I assume that my lack of total recall, and not having memorized Damasio's text, complicated checking these sections in my dream.

DREAM FUNCTION

The 1:00 a.m. images begin to fade rapidly as I wake up with my wife's exit from bed. I remind myself to check the page numbers in Damasio's book. I'm also aware that the conversation I'm having in this nondescript dream environment is with me. I'm engaging in self-talk, and nondescript characters work well in self-talk.

My brain is busy with its housekeeping functions of memory integration and consolidation. In idea dreams I pay particular attention to the non-descript characters as they frequently represent another me. Another "me" creates a second protagonist, to use Damasio's term, which can hold and exchange ideas and concepts.

Separate thoughts are much like our individual social roles that can be complex and evolving. And from an evolutionary perspective, the need to hold complex social roles in working memory must have been instrumental in the creation of an ever larger cerebral cortex; the new brain.

For example, five actors, each performing complex interlocking roles, provides a template upon which complex symbolic abstractions can be laid. Once the brain's architecture is in place, we can use this structure for new functions. It is the way of evolution. Thus, cognitive complexity evolves with social complexity.

Memory processing, idea sorting, and mastery of the material I've been reading seems to be the central function of this dream. I'm not only consolidating memories, I'm connecting the dots between abstractions and actually gaining insight and procedural awareness. My dream reminds me to check the page numbers in Damasio, then include these ideas in Chapter 9, be sure to clarify dispositional memory, etc.

I wake from an afternoon nap (4-24-11) and vaguely remember that my dream has me in an educational setting. I have three thoughts blended like long noodles in spaghetti: hypnopompic thought images I decide represent one element, a second is sensitivity to nuanced communications, and the last one focuses on the absurdity of most dream dictionaries. As I get up, I decide to include these ideas.

Dream consolidation and integration of memory means integrating and consolidating these elements creatively. But, there seems to be a meta-awareness operating that places these multiple dream elements in the context of this book. My dreaming brain is being supportive, as I had planned to spend the rest of the afternoon and evening writing before I had my nap.

The second thought is associated with the department secretary when I taught at Mankato State University. A feeling reconstruction of her appeared in my dream this afternoon. I use the term: "feeling reconstruction" as her dream image was different from her actual appearance. She was experiencing marital problems with her husband and suffering in quiet isolation. I noted that she had not been herself for the previous week or so, and asked her if there was something bothering her. She immediately came to tears, confessed her problem, and asked me why no one else noted her distress. I simply replied that I didn't know.

A common phenomenon with people who expand self-sensitivity is that it carries over into one's everyday relationships. Increased awareness of our own feelings makes us more sensitive to similar feelings in others; hence, the nuanced effect.

It's an interesting non-conscious association on the part of my dreaming brain as this incident occurred over thirty years ago. A feedback loop seemed to be operating that helped my dreaming brain connect associated memories. Increased self-awareness neutralizes much of the extraneous social stimuli that we are confronted with daily and permits a more focused "now." Our mirror neurons become more finely tuned. We often just call this process by the word sensitivity, or social sensitivity. But from a subjective point of view, we have conditioned ourselves to think, see and feel a little more deeply, we see greater detail. It is this evolutionary march to being more fully human that offers humanity hope.

The third thought in this series addresses dream dictionaries. According to Freud, I probably still have lustful thoughts for my former department secretary. Sylvia Browne would likely say that I traveled to the other side during my dream, and received this insight directly from God. J. LeDoux's view: Synaptic energy perseverated. But there's a problem with quantifying thoughts this way. Traditional cognitive neuroscientist X: There is no such thing as hypnopomic thought images, as thoughts are language-based, and have not been empirically verified as coming from the body proper. My former department secretary: "You're a kind man, and thank you for noticing."

In dreams, I refine concepts, assimilate abstract imagery, and mix these activities with my past, present, and future. My dreaming brain is naïve in the sense that it often doesn't understand the difference between being awake and sleeping. My dreaming brain, like my waking brain, tries to find meaning and purpose in all that it's experiencing.

I rejected Freud over 50 years ago because his model could not account for my dream experiences. And, as I came to understand how easily we reify our own conceptual creations, considered Freud a purveyor of dogma not scientific fact. There comes a point where patterns in phenomenological experiences can only be twisted so far. Reality creeps on little cats paws.

DREAMS AS EPIPHENOMENA

(12-27-10)

Dream form typically includes bizarreness of time shifts, character morphing, and improbable phantasmagoria such as flying. I'll review a common dream from late this morning which occurred just before rising at 6:00 a.m. I'm in an expansive park that is open with roads intersecting near the picnic area. There are mature tress scattered throughout the park with a large open area containing picnic tables, water faucets, and outdoor cooking stoves. The stoves are of a fireplace type made of cement block with bar steel tops. They have closable ovens with metal grates that one could use to bake a pie or roast.

I'm talking to a former colleague from Mankato State University who teaches anthropology. His wife and daughter are watching as he prepares a wooden fire under the oven. Mike places a large soup kettle over the wood fire and the pot quickly begins to boil. As he makes these preparations, we are talking about the anthropology program and his current duties. This is a casual conversation without any specific academic focus.

His daughter is approximately five years of age and we're playing, I think, peak-a-boo. She comes over and sits on my lap. I notice that she is wearing the same outfit she had on the day before. She has been playing hard, and I think her mother should have given her a bath last night and changed her clothes. Then I remember that they live in a small town nearby, and think that it's not necessary for kids to change clothes every day, especially if they're camping out.

My colleague disappears from the scene, but the kettle is still boiling on the outdoor stove and I check to make sure it's okay. As I perform this act, I become involved in a conversation with an older woman whom I think is my colleague's mother-in-law and the little girl's grandmother. I make some comments to her about her granddaughter being so outgoing and she confirms this observation.

I think it's time for me to go home and look around, but can't find my car. I think to myself: *I must have walked to the park, so I'll just walk home.* At his point I wake up. It is 6:00 a.m., I dress and get up to make coffee and have breakfast.

INTERPRETATION

This is a common, mundane dream that holds no special insights, and reflects no unusual emotions. The little five year old girl has a counterpart from a Christmas Eve afternoon party that I attended two days ago. The soup pot is a carryover from a dish my wife prepared three days ago. The outdoor wood cook stove in the park is a morphed version of an antique looking wood stove that our host of last night used to create a warm and cheery ambiance. The older woman in my dream was the grandmother at this party, except her real granddaughter is 16 years old. My former colleague is a stand-in for a young man and his girlfriend with whom I had a long talk at last night's party. The park is a reasonable version of one that is nearby, one that my wife and I often enjoy.

I identify all the characters in this night movie from their physical appearances, and although the appearances are not exact, they are reasonable facsimiles. The young, couple at last night's party are university students who plan to teach overseas in about another year and a half. I offer to introduce them to the Graduate University Chinese Academy of Sciences in Beijing, and suggest that with their degrees in writing and linguistics, they would fit into the GUCAS curriculum very well.

The reader will note the limited amount of unusual forms in this dream, the casual manner in which my dreaming brain selects content, and the everyday themes of friends, scenes, and activities. Good shares of my dreams day-to-day have these mundane qualities.

My dreams can be almost entirely free of bizarre logic or highly illogical, depending on the type of dream I'm having. I enjoy science fiction, and my dream scenes, characters and plots will often reflect these elements. This is especially true if I've watched a sci-fi movie just before retiring.

Epiphenomenon is a loose term. My (12-27-10) dream is adding holiday memories to its library of memories and making appropriate associations with my history. It is providing the stream called Glen's Self with meaning and continuity. It appears that I'm primarily experiencing memory integration and consolidation. Therefore, I label the dreams epiphenomenal with the assigned memory functions.

DREAM DISGUISE AND VARIATION

In my 6:30 a.m. (12-6-10) dream, I'm back in my old Rochester, Minnesota, office talking to staff, but primarily I'm interacting with a secretary. It is my last day of work, and she is struggling with a formula to give staff their annual bonuses. In truth, Rochester staff never received a bonus annually or ever. I offer a simple formula, and she still seems perplexed about how to use it. I then quickly apply the formula and give her the results. She thanks me and looks relieved. In real life, this secretary did have trouble translating math formulae.

The scene changes and I'm sitting at a large conference table with the secretary, staff, and one of our regional judges. The judge appears to be questioning the proceedings. Again, I'm explaining some rather technical information to those present and being questioned pointedly by the judge. I inform him that I have no reason to distort the data or misrepresent what it stands for as this is my last day of employment. I go on to state that actually I no longer have administrative authority, and I'm chairing this meeting just to be helpful.

The scene changes, and I'm in bed with the secretary and naked from the waist down as I'm only dressed in a nightshirt. The secretary's husband comes in and asks her who she is with, and I respond that it is only me. I hope he doesn't throw back the sheets or he will see that I'm semi-naked. As I key these words into the computer, I'm aware that this part of the dream occurred when my wife returned to bed from the bathroom. My wife's real life activity puts my dream secretary in bed with me. My brain's circuits are overlapping a bit as they share two states of consciousness. Undoubtedly, analysis by therapists practicing classical psychodynamics is much more exciting than my dream interpretations.

I'm also aware as I continue to wake up that I'm having a dream within a dream. I'm still processing the annual bonuses with the secretary, and holding a meeting at the same time. And, my brain is still busy thinking about Damasio's *Self Comes to Mind*. All of this blends with my earlier dream at 1:00 a.m. as I was reminded while still dreaming to record this multi-tasking dream effect after I eat breakfast.

My wife's activities have entered my dream and are processed the same way that the cold from a dislodged blanket entered my dream as an image of a 1955 Chevy. Consideration of Damasio's work is carried over from the previous day in what seems to be memory integration and consolidation. In agreement with Hobson, my dream is not attempting to disguise some deep underlying meaning or practicing Freudian censorship (2005: 16-25). This is pretty transparent stuff.

DREAM ARCHITECTURE

Dreams with a wide variety of content like those reported above appear to be generated primarily by my old brain. These bottom-up activated dreams are mundane and represent felt body states or are associated with memory functions. Thinking dreams appear to be activated by higher order brain centers. From this perspective, the conceptual units in thinking dreams are abstracted and assimilated into a schema of generalized knowledge.

Dreaming or awake, my Interpreter is always trying to decode and assimilate dream elements and scenarios into a meaningful whole. Once I identify memory functions such as bike balancing as FAP consolidation, further attempts to decode and assimilate cease. My higher order consciousness accepts the necessity of these processes by my limbic system. In effect, I've made my Interpreter aware that it is not responsible for these basic housekeeping functions. It now just observes, and informs me.

I have a subjective sense that evolution has not yet created fluid exchange between my higher and lower brain centers; hence, a little effort is helpful connecting the two through lucid dreaming. And secondly, as I move from lucid dreaming to being awake, snippets of awareness from both levels of consciousness mix. Further, this mix of waking-dreaming snippets is dynamic and complex as multi-tasking dreams cover memory functions, attention to emotional balance, and the integration of abstract thoughts.

Dream researchers have yet to detail all the mechanisms operating in these feedback loops, nevertheless, the advances made in neuroscience keep identifying specific brain-mind functions with specialized neural circuits, networks, and neuro-transmitters.

The transparency of lucid dreams helps me identify the psychological expressions that these physiological processes support. Information that my dreaming brain is processing brings forth new meaning and understanding that can emerge during the dream or the following day.

Non-lucid dreamers who simply sleep on a problem miss all this observational fun. They just wake up in the morning with a solution. And over a lifetime of experience, I'm relatively sure that non-lucid dreamers fail to open new channels to their own creative brain-mind processes, thereby failing to connect the dots as often as long-term lucid dreamers do.

I don't think we should just look at being in one state of consciousness or the other. We must take into consideration the brain's overall activity in any given 24 hour period. We cycle in and out of various mind-brain states continuously, and this includes daydreaming. If our brain's activity was restricted to waking consciousness, we would be dwarfs instead of the giants that we are.

To me, dreams represent the tip of the iceberg called sleep. But, the bulk of the iceberg that floats below the surface represents complex brain functions responsible for memory integration and consolidation, management of our emotional life, and yet to be determined cognitive processes associated with our higher brain center functions. Our brains continuously support all of our body's maintenance and organizational functions.

. How our higher cognitive centers create meaning is one of nature's best kept secrets. Damasio says that:

Emotions are complex, largely automated programs of actions concocted by evolution." "Feelings of emotion, on the other hand, are composite perceptions of what happens in our body and mind when we are emoting. As far as the body is concerned, feelings are images of actions rather than actions themselves; the world of feelings is one of perceptions executed in brain maps (2010: 109).

Images of actions, I like that phrase. We learn to interpret dream imagery to understand the underlying messages that come from both the mind and the body. To me, this is more Gestalt-like, and I've come over the decades to recognize patterns and themes at the tip of my own, personal iceberg. But in analyzing my dreams, I take Damasio seriously when he says "feelings are images of actions rather than actions themselves."

We come into the world with this survival enhancing architecture, and build on it throughout our maturation processes from birth to death. The brain is always busy running an emotion laden program which normally operates at the non-conscious level. In Damasio view, this program is integral to our understanding of consciousness and the emergence of self. To understand our dreams, we must understand the entire iceberg.

I sense connection with the program's a.k.a. iceberg's output when I dream. My body states are constantly influencing my dreams, and revealing the rich non-conscious world that supports my brain and body's well-being, as well as keeping my brain-mind in a state of balance, or in Damasio's terms, homeostasis.

Feelings create awareness of body tissue and states fundamental to the emergence of a conscious self. Feeling helps create the agent we call Self by continuously providing sensory input. Feelings are ubiquitous, all pervading elements in sleeping and waking mentation. Feelings are given value and priority, and are thus a critical part of how we create meaning in everyday life. This is my summary of how consciousness arises according to Damasio.

It helps my understanding of lucid dreaming to know that consciousness must be present either when I'm dreaming or when I'm awake, or there is no Self to interpret the actions taking place. Adding the critical element of feeling into this interpretation enhances my understanding of dreams: Understanding how sensory stimuli created in my body generates consciousness and Self permits me to look for different bridging elements in my dreams. And content analysis of my dreams pinpoints critical bridging elements that feeling provides.

Feelings represent a sensory stream that supports consciousness at Damasio's two levels of core and autobiographical Self. Primordial emotions existed at simple cellular levels before higher order consciousness emerged in human evolution. Emotion guided animal behavior before these elements could be re-mapped into feelings, and it still does.

The old question is whether or not dreams are epiphenomena or support underlying brain-mind functions. Dreams permit me to watch some aspects of memory integration and consolidation. Dreams permit me to identify salient emotions that need attention. Dreams are the tip of the iceberg that supports complex thoughts. Dreams inform me of body-environment interaction such as temperature, and dreams tell me if my internal body-self structure needs attention, as with potty dreams.

How we use the term epiphenomenon can be controversial, so I'll try to detail the process to minimize controversy. I'm quite sure that many FAP dreams require visual re-enactment in order to consolidate and integrate muscle and skill memories. Muscles are disconnected as automatic responses when we dream; hence, my dreaming brain informs my Interpreter of developing needs such as temperature or bowel movements. My sleeping-dreaming brain continues to process conceptual abstraction, which I may or may not become aware of while dreaming, but with long-term dream lucidity, I'm frequently aware of conceptual closure before I wake up.

My experience tells me that abstract conceptual assimilation is facilitated in our dreams as is the integration and consolidation of fixed action patterns (FAPs). Lucid dreaming facilitates one's awareness of conceptual closure. The question becomes: "Does lucid dreaming actually enhance creativity, or does lucid dreaming just make us more aware of the process when conceptual closure occurs during dream conscious states?"

I think there is truth in both positions. However, it is my belief that long-term lucid dreaming improves access to an enlarged store of memories by our higher order consciousness. Thus, lucid dream work enhances but does not generate dream creativity. Lucid dreaming over extended periods of time seems to enhance greater access to our total mind-works.

Damasio notes that the working space for conscious reflection is limited. Unconscious processes support our body-mind's overall performance, thus increasing our survival as a species.

It is my contention that access to non-conscious workspace in our dreams is the mechanism that facilitates creativity. Non-conscious workspace is substantially larger, permits our brain-mind to juxtapose and hold significantly more elements in working space, and thereby facilitate one's creativity. From this point of view, creativity is dependent on dynamic exchange between Damasio's autobiographical and core selves. An, practiced dream lucidity exercises are critical to access and facilitation of our innate capacity. Further, creativity is also advanced when additional altered states come under our direction and control (2010: 267-297).

In a fashion similar to concept assimilation while we dream, emotional prompting is devoid of daytime distractions and offers a cleaner connection to source input. Epiphenomena as a term seems inappropriate to explain emotion-based or thought dreams. If by epiphenomena we mean a mirror image of underlying dream functions, then, okay. As long as we remember that real work goes on in our dreams. If epiphenomenon is defined as some form of static in the machine, superfluous output, then I reject this interpretation.

At the consciousness level where we humans develop awareness of being aware, the complexity of mixing feeling states and creating endless nuance multiplies geometrically. Thoughts become more complex with endless degrees of fine-grained feeling being incorporated. Complex thoughts can in turn generate ever greater feeling complexity, mixed feelings, and feeling states that perpetuate themselves.

On the positive side, this capacity greatly enriches our lives in arts, literature, and complex social structures. On the negative side, auto-generated anxiety and depression can become totally debilitating.

We can and sometimes do learn to disconnect feelings from our body's sensory input: We stop feeling. Traumatized children know this latter sense well as we head bang, pinch, make ourselves bleed, and in endless ways try to feel. Without feeling, we are the walking dead.

For psychopaths, connecting feeling to body states of others does not seem to exist. Theory of Mind says the psychopath's mirror neurons are defective. When body is disconnected from feelings, the self can commit the most heinous acts out of curiosity or self-interest. Normal individuals with healthy mirror neurons find the thought processes of psychopaths incomprehensible.

In our dreams and other altered states of consciousness, we may experience a partial disconnect between higher order cognitive processes called conscience when we perform acts unacceptable to our waking consciousness. When we contrast our dreams to waking consciousness, we come to know that truth and logic are grounded in our feelings. In this sense, we are almost all True Believers and come to the logic of science slowly.

Consolidation of a FAP in our dreams does not require guidance from our conscience. Expression of a dream FAP does not require guidance from our conscience. Hormone driven sexual expression does not require guidance from our conscience. Dreams permit us to exceed the boundaries of daytime conscience, because we do not maintain continuous linkages between old and new brain functions. In my experience, a core consciousness linkage to conscience at our higher cognitive levels is partial, and this partial learning is only consolidated over time with practice.

Truth is written larger the more salient our feelings, and the stronger our feelings, the more obvious Truth becomes. True Believers in the supernatural are not swayed by Richard Dawkins' logic. To be accepted, logic must be accompanied by a salient feeling of correctness. A quantum particle may be in two places at the same time, but it feels illogical. It feels illogical because my waking experiences do not encounter quantum realities. Waking experiences provide the sensory input upon which my logic is based. I have to expend considerable cognitive effort to accept realities I cannot feel. I have to expend considerable effort to understand the language of dreams, which supports functions outside of my waking experiences.

Our brains have ability to process emotion derived feelings and related visual mappings in multiple creative ways. It takes much of the mysticism out of mystic experiences when I come to understand how Truth is created in Self, by Self, and for Self. And in this understanding I come to recognize that my dreaming Self is not the same as my waking Self. I understand Truth, because sensory input is constantly maintaining my feelings when awake or when dreaming. I feel in my dreams as I do when awake, even though the two states are not always experienced the same way. It cannot be otherwise, because feeling is always part of consciousness.

When consciousness is lost, so is feeling. But my feelings are not processed by my dreaming core self as they are by my higher order Interpreter. As I age, my Interpreter seems to continue educating my core self about right and wrong.

An additional insight from Damasio:

In humans, as we have seen, the emotion program also triggers certain cognitive changes that accompany body changes (Damasio: 2010: 116).

I can wake up from my dreams feelings upset, elated or anything in-between, and never have a clue why. Or, I can wake up from my dreams, identify my mood by finding the bridging element, and have greater goal direction for the day or days ahead as I consciously process and interpret the dream's meaning.

Often I'm better at problem solving in my dreams than I am during my thought-struggling daytime hours. Emotion from Damasio's view is always connected to thought. Feelings become part of thought through the bloodstream with hormones, or through our neural circuits with electrical-chemical activity. I am aware that rational thought in our waking moments can be distorted by the form in which dreams are presented. A dream with strong negative feelings can promote carryover of this negativity into my morning hours. We typically refer to this effect as having slept on the wrong side of the bed. It is this larger circular loop connecting brainstem and frontal lobes that I especially pay attention to when interpreting my dreams.

Damasio says:

Some of those thoughts … are components of the emotion program, evoked as the emotion unfolds so that the cognitive context is in keeping with emotions. Other thoughts, however, rather than being stereotypical components of the emotion program, are late cognitive reactions to the emotion under way "Ibid; 119.

For me, it is helpful in interpreting my dreams to use Damasio's explanation of this feeling-emotion cycle. My higher consciousness is informed through this interpretation. My dreams of (12-6-10) demonstrate two-way action in the feedback loop between dreaming and conscious brain states, as well as brain activity that is occurring at different stages of these processes. Multi-tasking clearly seems to be a byproduct of the exchange between Damasio's CDRs and smaller activating circuits called CDZs. Meaning must emerge by enlarging the scope of neural circuit exchange; even though we only partly understand the process.

In my dream-waking cycle of (12-6-10) I'm processing *Self Comes to Mind* in a very conscious lucid dream. I'm considering how to format this book and how content should be presented. In all of this mix, I'm interacting with my wife as bed partner and attending to body functions which are also entering my dreams as content.

If you are familiar with Freud's *Interpretation of Dreams*, it is apparent how bizarre and off base he was with his unconscious dream model. My secretary was a lovely young woman, but my feelings toward her were that of a father and not a lover. Being semi-naked in bed with her was clearly an activated dream sequence based on my usual sleeping attire and the presence and exiting of our bed by my spouse. In my dream, I had no sense of lust toward my secretary, but my Interpreter still needed to find a logical explanation to offer her husband. The shadow of waking logic that enters our dreams this way must speak to the less than perfect exchange between our higher and lower brain centers.

A pattern that often occurs when I am processing technical materials in my dreams is this very overt talking, lecturing and conversation content. First there is a rather direct review of material that is often accompanied by visuals from text, on a blackboard, or incorporated in dream conversations. This seems to be a fairly transparent attempt on the part of my sleeping brain to further process daytime thoughts and their integration in larger abstract wholes. Often this information is manipulated extensively in my dreams, and I wake up with new insights the next morning. I think Walker is right on.

Form and content changes in my dreams seem to represent integration and consolidation of information from the previous day or days, and often there is abstract and symbolic manipulation of information in these dreams.

In the (12-6-10) dream this takes the form of creating a technical formula for the secretary and applying it to determine year-end bonuses. This part of the dream mixes two former employees together in one dream plot. These employees are from two separate time periods and locations. The second employee from a previous job actually had to apply a formula of my construction in order to determine actual year-end bonuses for staff. She had little trouble applying this formula, compared to the secretary, who in real life had difficulty with math. These two employees were support personnel, and they obviously share this association in my memory.

The tip of the thought processing iceberg takes place with the judge questioning me at the dream conference and my telling him that I'm no longer employed and holding the meeting gratis. It is a way of saying that I'm not responsible to him, but do want his understanding.

This was my actual real life relationship to the judge. I had many discussions with judges when I had this secretary. These discussions were usually attempts on my part to share recent research behind effective models of offender intervention and treatment.

Sequential dreams, repeated dreams, dreams within dreams all appear to support the process of creating new memories, consolidating them, and integrating content with the larger landscape of mind-brain processing.

I'm always interacting with both my external and internal sources of stimuli. Hence, I don't experience dreams as devoid of meaning. I don't experience them as simply being symbolic. I don't experience them as just being activation and consolidation of memory. Dreams are all of these processes and more. They are complex, and loop interactive between the brainstem and our higher level cortices as information exchange takes place throughout the night and over the course of days and months. And, all of these facets of dream interpretation contribute to what I call a dynamic integrated brain-mind.

DAMASIO'S CDZs AND CDRs DREAM

As I'm waking up from my dreams (12-6-10), I'm wondering if Wernike and Brocha's areas are equivalent to CDRs. My half sleeping mind recognizes that I've been engaging in self-talk while I'm dreaming, and I wonder if I'm using these two speech areas to access memories in my last dream. I think about this foggy dream thought process as I go downstairs to make breakfast. My dreaming brain is wondering what kind of physical structures CDRs and CDZs are. I decide to check Damasio to see if my dreaming brain is clear about CDZs and CDRs.

Cognitive neuroscientists would probably look at the interconnections between words and meanings as semantic networks (Hobson: 2005: 82). CDRs and CDZs are my dream's concept focus, but my foggy brain is attempting to associate neural processing of meaning with specific brain centers. This foggy state of mind tells me that I'm not clear about the function of CDZs and CDRs in the creation of meaning. And my dreaming brain is trying to connect the dots using Damasio's materials. Note that how meaning is supported by physiological processes has not been determined.

Memory functions are distributed in the brain in different smaller neural circuits (CDZ), of different larger node-like circuits called (CDR) says Damasio. They are processed through various specialized sensory modalities and through various kinds of loops and feedback mechanisms.

My dreaming mind was playing with material that I had been mulling over the previous day. This type of common dream appears to reflect my brain sorting and integrating a multitude of ideas and concepts without my conscious input. I'm thankful for all of these unconscious processes, and remind myself that dream thought often comes in the form of dialogue or lectures, and I must be careful to analyze how complete or incomplete my dream logic is. The dream logic process is not always complete on any given morning.

Real logic may emerge in my dream scenarios, or it may lie masked and surface when I wake. If no solutions emerge over my night's dreams, I will wake up with a sense of heaviness. My mind seems foggy and it takes extra effort to focus on complex thoughts. We all know this feeling called mental overload.

My last night's dream logic was partial; not totally bizarre or off the mark, but not complete. In last night's dream that partial logic made sense. By the time I had my first cup of coffee and checked Damasio, I realized that LeDoux's *Synaptic Self* provides a clearer understanding of CDRs and CDZs. However, my dreaming mind only referenced Damasio. Apparently, LeDoux's material on CDRs and CDZs was not integrated with Damasio's in this attempted dream memory integration. Further, LeDoux was committed to memory a couple years ago, and I just recently read Damasio's new book.

The time difference between LeDoux and Damasio's reviews reminds me that the process of embedding memories that is reflected in my dreams occurs in proximity to learning, and consolidation with associated memory elements occurs separately. I'm guessing, but more complex concepts, more abstract integrations, must wait for embedded memories to be consolidated before larger amounts of related materials can be integrated. Simply put, I must learn to hold the crayon before I can take the next step and draw with it. Memory integration and consolidation in dreams follows this same pattern for me.

So, how do your dream-works work?

CHAPTER 10

DREAM PATTERNS AND THEMES

INTRODUCTION

Most people are not lucid dreamers, and even fewer have a matching history with other altered realities. I have never been medicated for any reason, thus all but one of my altered consciousness experiences have occurred naturally. Learning to totally program my dreams as a first year student at the University of Minnesota in 1957-58 has undoubtedly altered my dream patterns. I continued active dream programming for two decades, but for the last thirty years I've permitted myself to dream naturally. Additionally I've been able to enter and control altered realities such as visions, possession, and speaking-in-tongues at will. I've used self-observation to explore dreams, consciousness, and altered states for over 50 years. .

My position is that long-term patterns of dream and altered state self-observation permits one to observe dream functions in a manner not possible in dream labs or through the use of technology. Through self-observation and self-experiments, I can move bottom-up and top-down across my total range of conscious states.

Long-term dream patterns that are not of the nightmare variety are mostly mundane. By mundane I mean that my dreams are primarily concerned with memory functions, maintaining emotional equilibrium, consolidating thoughts, and reflecting external stimuli that enter my dreams from the outside world. Long-term changes in my hormone levels, physical strength and agility, and how my dreaming brain is activated by environmental stimuli have already been reported. Over the decades, changes in my dreams parallel changes in my waking life.

I started dream programming when I was 21 and continued this practice for two decades. Initially I used dream programming to control nightmares, but very quickly discovered how much fun I could have with dream characters and fictive romances. Controlling dream scenarios in detail naturally brought me to focus on dream content. My initial control of dreams banished nightmares, and restful nights of sleep emerged. Within half of an academic year, my life took on a stable quality that I still enjoy today.

Over seventy-odd years of lucid dreaming gives me confidence that the patterns I report have validity. I don't think the basic functions reported in my dreams are unique, but the dream stories and content are. Dream functions that I report appear to be universal. Below, I recount how sleep arrangements contribute to dreams of being naked, feeling cold, or experiencing dry air. These are examples of dreams commonly reported by others; LaBerge for example. Careful dream observation requires that we watch for these seasonal and environmental patterns.

I'm quite sure that the use of dream programming or dream suggestion over extended periods of time condition one's brain-mind to dream patterns that others either do not experience or do not experience with the same frequency. For example, I have dozens of repetitive dream narratives that are similar to short stories that grow through time and reflect my waking history, with my Heaven on Earth dream being one of them.

The reader may be aware that I am in my third marriage, and spousal conflict themes present themselves in my dreams in interesting ways. I also note the physical changes to my body and hormonal system that modifies dream content and feelings. These decade-long patterns lay waste to dream dictionaries that emphasize the occult, or offer concrete examples for the meaning of anything from acorns to zucchini.

A note on information transfer within the brain seems in order. Restak says that:

Information transfer within the brain … takes place simultaneously in multiple brain areas via a widely distributed network of nerve fibers.' And, "… the motor command to move is spatially distributed throughout the cortical population. Not only that, motor cells are responsive to sensory stimulation, with each cell biased toward light or sound or other sensory stimulus. During the movement, the sensory and the motor components are so intertwined that the old division into sensory and motor neurons no longer makes sense." "In this way, the slightest of sensory signals can initiate activity in a vast network of neurons (1994: 119).

My subjective experience of this distributed activation in dreams is that, indeed, sensory signals can initiate activity in a vast network of neurons as Restak says. Basically, we all get associations in dream combinations, characters, and scenes that are expressed differently in our dreams than they are in waking consciousness. Characters, scenes, and times morph to accommodate dream functions of memory, feelings, and select interchange with higher cortical centers. Sensory exchange while dreaming occurs without the environmental structure and input that normally streams through our portals to the outside world.

Over a lifetime of dreaming, there is greater continuity in a night of lucid dreams than was the case when I was twenty or thirty years of age. Some of this continuity must be associated with a quieter, less hectic lifestyle.

A big difference with dream content over the decades is the amount of auto-created dream imagery that is used and re-used. Dozens of auto-created dream vignettes use the same material over-and-over again by making little sequential changes in characters or scenes. Auto-created dream memories literally have a life of their own.

One can readily see how the use of college students or other individuals who are observed for short periods of time in dream labs would change dream pattern analysis, or how distorting dream dictionary interpretation can be. I would never have noticed these patterns without decades of dream analysis. Dream memories seem to evolve much like a bike balancing FAP. There is an element of change that I associate with a dynamic evolving brain; a brain that is run on neural plasticity.

In dream analysis, I'm not looking for dictionary meanings associated with a specific dream element the way Freud did. I'm looking for the pattern, the feelings generated, and the presence of scenes, characters, and objects that my dreaming brain may have previously used.

Freud assumed dream elements had specific meanings and committed errors of interpretation common to contemporary dream dictionaries. Dogma is dogma!

My dreaming brain will recycle dream elements and forms that were created by the brain-mind itself, or initiated by any of my sensory inputs. It is easier for me to identify dream meaning by placing dream elements and dream form in functional context.

Habituation of dream elements is as much a part of my life as is habituation to routines when I'm awake. I assume that these mechanisms have energy and efficiency value in terms of evolution, as the mechanism is used in both waking and dreaming states of consciousness. Habituation is efficient and time saving. It appears that the architecture of our functioning brain, which supports all of our non-conscious brain work, has parallel expression in the mechanisms that support our dreams.

Understanding brain-mind information transfer from this perspective removes the adolescent desire to find specific meaning with universal symbols down to the level of acorns and zucchini. I am constantly impressed by the metaphorical nature of my dreams. I can actually improve bike balance riding my dream bike over impossible terrain, or I can improve balance sliding down the top of dream stairs, or I can improve balance by jumping on a dream banister, arms outstretched and sliding down to the floor below.

Universality in dreams appears because dream forms reflect brain architecture and function. Consciousness universally depends on sensory processing. Self emerges in the course of evolution from this evolving architecture with its complex cerebral components. Universality in dreams revolves around our being upright animals that move through space. Universality is architectural capacity for language, not the language spoken. And qualia and metaphor are the coinage of consciousness and thought that we humans spend every day of our lives.

Brain-mind mechanisms must be identified and offer the prospect of being researchable; otherwise it's just speculation. When I view the brain as a modular, distributed network of neurons, I better appreciate the reasons for dream bizarreness.

Movement of muscles is disconnected when we dream. Auto-created memories enter my dreams over days and decades. My eyes don't take pictures, but instead, my brain configures sight from over 30 vision supporting centers making composites common. Stimuli can enter one of my ongoing dreams or activate entire dream scenarios. Symbolic and metaphorical images are created such as my gun-penis example, and so on. Why should these examples of dream element expression follow waking expectations? Waking expectations are culturally derived and semi-independent of physiological processes.

Dream patterns and themes reflect these modular, distributed brain-mind operations. In the following section, I begin pattern analysis with nightmares, as nightmares are my oldest remembered dreams. Nightmares were prominent, demanding, and disconcerting well before I was five years old, and their nightly trauma lasted for decades.

I personally know the effects of trauma on childhood, what both non-conscious repression and active repression means, how programming one's dreams can alleviate anxiety and depression, how to develop and control attention, and what is involved in overcoming obsessive behaviors. I will also touch on a few other brain-mind phenomena that suggest specific hypotheses for future research. I recommend that the reader always attempt to connect dream interpretations with brain-mind physiology, and question dream reports that conflict with their personal observations.

Nightmares were the focus of my early childhood starting at age five when I lived in the Everett, Washington Area. It was 1941 and Pearl Harbor had been bombed by the Japanese, and a Japanese sub had been reported sighted in the nearby Sound. Prior to the age of five, what I most remember about sleeping are vague dream recollections and night terrors. I had more fear of being physically attacked in this world than being attacked in my dreams.

I still find the imagination of a five year old intriguing, and note the different levels of abstraction employed. The hold of the submarine becomes a hole that I jump into and levitate in until I go to sleep, but this is all in a dream. At a higher cognitive level, my Interpreter substitutes the Japanese for my mother, and the drill for her oppressive hand. Imagination becomes reality because reality is always a human construction. Without our ability to construct reality, there is no Self. Little mystery here!

My mother's attack occurred when I was about 1.5 years old. In support of Lakoff and Johnson, metaphorical concepts must play a critical role in how one thinks and forms images. Images in this example, (hole-hold), Japanese drill, i.e. Mother's hand, are auto-created and then used in movie-like scenarios. Complex metaphor, the Japanese drill, can substitute for substantive elements, i.e., my Mother's hand. My brain constantly creates complex metaphor, and uses it this way when I'm awake. Balancing on my bike, my physical posture in space, metaphorically becomes a balanced check book or a balanced life. It's interesting to note how well a five year old brain uses metaphor.

Although I don't recall most of my childhood nightmares before the age of five, I've referenced the two major ones that stayed with me into middle age. In terms of age, the second nightmare was my dreaming brain's response to being sexually molested, terrified throughout the following day when I was required to work with the deviant, and being unable to talk about or process the victimization afterwards. This is in contrast to the Japanese nightmare which I eventually identified as symbolic metaphor for my mother's smothering attacks when I was still crib bound.

In its simplest form, metaphor is the substitution of one element for another. This substitution can be purely mental, as with an imagined ghost, or it can become a physical reality, as one feels the ghost begin to penetrate their body in the assumed act of possession. In Damasio's terms, the feeling of "what is" is so closely identified with the object that the two are no longer separated.

Mother's attacks generated night terrors and a ghost that daily followed me to bed. My psyche's creative response to the two victimizations was quite different. The early crib victimization came to utilize a variety of different psychological responses, including night terrors, psychic projection of a ghost, and a strong sense of fear being generated in physical settings resembling the environment of my attacks.

Let me point out what is now most likely a growing reader awareness of pattern analysis between these two nightmares. The submarine nightmare version is a typical metaphorical dream creation. The waking ghost version of mother's attacks turns cross-modal metaphor into something concrete – the ghost itself. Essentialism is inherent to children, who feel, or sense, the non-physical reality of their own minds, and at the same time, know their physical reality. Mother's attacks are manifested in both forms.

The sexual molestation nightmare retains its dream form of essentialism, and morphs over the years into endless creative versions of pursuit. Identification of this nightmare's activation source occurs in a dream when the pursuer captures and restrains my dreaming self. This nightmare has no concrete manifestation comparable to the ghost. Cultural symbolism provided by mother is a critical part that helps distinguish the evolution of the two nightmares.

Early victimization of infants and children creates special problems for us. Without treatment, we are typically seen as difficult, lacking control, and not responding appropriately to adult demands.

I think of a little girl brought into one of my Illinois treatment programs about 1990 or 1991. Her parents were both crack addicts and ran a crack house. Her medical record stated that she was diagnosed with venereal warts by the age of 18 months. She could not tolerate any strange adults in her presence and would bite, kick, and do whatever necessary to make them go away. Imagine this child's future without treatment. Adult versions of this child populate America, especially America's prisons, by the tens and perhaps hundreds of thousands.

Unfortunately, American courts too frequently re-victimize these children with harsh penalties instead of treatment. If the little girl just mentioned was fortunate, she would be placed in a loving foster home by caring social workers. With the typical large caseloads of BA level social workers and their limited training, the little girl would not respond as expected, move from foster home to foster home, and eventually wind up in the correctional system. The criminal justice system generally ignores the history of these children and imposes punishment, including the death penalty, until their behavior changes.

This, in my estimation, is a second act of abuse. The majority of children and young people in treatment programs that I've administered have traumatizing backgrounds. If you ask them to explain their behavior, they can't. Their feelings and actions become as automatic as your or my bicycle riding does.

Let me offer one more example, that of a young man who came into another one of my treatment programs in Minnesota at the age of eighteen. He was in a treatment group that I facilitated weekly. I'm an expressive person when talking, and use frequent hand gestures and arm movements. Every time I lifted my hand to gesture, this young man would flinch or duck. I asked him to explain his behavior, but he couldn't. He was just in the habit of ducking.

The young man's social history indicated that his mother was alcoholic and in the habit of having live-in drunken lovers rotate through her children's lives. She used boyfriends to physically control her two sons. The young man's medical record indicated considerable brain damage from head trauma. He reported numerous childhood beatings about the head that probably caused his brain injuries.

Traumatized youth give spur of the moment explanations for these behaviors which inadequately educated social workers often believe. Even worse, when fear immobilizes or creates fear-based reactions, these children are routinely body slammed in what is called a "take-down." One also observes this take-down practice in highly touted psychiatric wards as well as group homes run by social workers and psychiatric interns.

Working with traumatized children and young adults is an eye opener for most middle class people, who prefer the simplicity of the law over the reality of victimized children's real life experiences. Do these children and adults have bad dreams? Do you know how to make their nightmares go away? What is the reader's reality model?

Nightmares from personal childhood trauma do not go away, but as indicated by my dreams, last forever, and can morph into endless creative plots and scenarios. Most of these nightmares can be fairly easily controlled as my personal examples demonstrate. But nightmares for children involved in America's criminal justice system rarely receive meaningful mental health intervention. They do routinely receive pharmaceuticals, and as they grow into their teens, many find self-medication with street drugs more to their liking. The nightmares and early trauma are forgotten by the CJS, as is brain damage, because punishment is America's preferred method of treatment. Officially according to the law, that is!

There are tens of thousands of these children in America. There are millions in their adult forms in our jails and prisons. Millions sleep on the streets during their pre and adolescent years, and sell their bodies for whatever bargain amount they can exchange. Others have more pride and steal.

The dreams of traumatized children are not trivial. Much of our dream research parallels the polite training of middle-class social workers; it is polite, and of course, civilized. And polite helps fill our jails and prisons as no other world culture does.

ORDINARY DREAM PATTERNS

Many of my dream themes will carry over from day-to-day or week-to-week. As a retired person, my life is patterned with daily activities repeating in weekly and monthly cycles. Dream themes reflect the routines of my daily life. Patterned daytime routines create related dream patterns that emerge on their own. It is as though a parallel dream computer support program is running. For example, I report a dream in Chapter 6 where I'm a student and find myself unprepared. An old high school classmate informs me of a forthcoming test as well as a paper which is due shortly. This dream is a spin-off that reflects materials that I'm covering and will use as references for this book.

It is now a couple weeks later (1-1-11) and I've just finished reviewing some materials by J. Allan Hobson. The same school setting reemerged in this dream, and my high school classmate was there too. He gives me some notes about the type of math problems that will be on our test, and I'm looking at the sample. As I look at the sample, the scene changes, and I'm actually taking the test. The test is very easy, and the sample math problem, I realize, is just simple algebra. These are all lucid dream observations that I place in recall before waking.

In the simple algebra problem, I have to take the square root of 1.07, which I find to be a strange number. The square root turns out to be 1.3 and I realize that I just have to multiply this number by two to get 2.6, which is the correct answer. My sample N is 141, so it all makes sense.

My waking brain doesn't recall most of the dream's detail, but what is recalled is nonsense; nevertheless, while dreaming, my brain found it to be totally logical. When I looked up from my dream exam, I was relieved that the test had been easy, and see that my teacher is smiling at me. My teacher in this high school setting is a former boss from the 1990s. I have the impression from her that she made the test easy for all of us as some sort of year-end present. Further, the sample problem that my classmate gave me and the problem on the test are identical, and taken directly from our text book. I think to myself that this test is so easy. Why did I worry about it?

Next, I realize that the study sheet has the exact problem on it as the test, and quickly slide the study sheet inside the desk out of my teacher's view. I don't want her to think that I've been cheating. I wake up at this point, reflect on the dream, and get up and use the bathroom.

INTERPRETATION

Contrary to the above dream, some of my dreams can be as logical as my daytime thought processes. Sometimes I problem solve in dreams, find new ways to integrate and think about ideas, and often develop creative solutions to problems that I'm cogitating about during the day.

In these dreams, I'm often directed to make certain changes in my writing, and these directions are still logical when I'm awake. The dream reported above was not logical; it was symbolic: The difference being all the illogical mumbo jumbo about square root. An illogical dream structure often flags the dream as being symbolic, and its lack of logic becomes my bridging element for interpretation. Similar abstract or symbolic representations of underlying brain-mind functions or body states are normal products of my dreaming brain.

My brain stores core memory elements from perception, according to Kandel's view, and reconfigures them in an act that fills in gaps or missing pieces in order to maintain sensory continuity (2006: 281). It takes core memory elements and reconfigures them in abstract, symbolic thought.

Perhaps another way to express this idea is that abstract, symbolic elements are more complex reconfigurations of core memory elements. In this sense, the brain acts as a computerized statistical program factoring out underlying dimensions from large numbers of primary images. One factor can be a recombination of several images to create an abstraction. Another factor can be simple or complex image forms that I call complex metaphor. A third factor can focus on a central ideal and be carried throughout a night of dream scenarios thematically. Thought dreams can combine all three factors, and I watch this process in my dreams as the above example demonstrates.

Our brains are constantly making sense and creating meaning of all the stimuli we experience, both external and internal stimuli. Abstract thought must bring together various combinations of neural circuit image elements in new configurations. In like fashion, my dreams combine historical settings that are not time bound, hybrid characters are derived from varied memory associations, and symbolic abstractions are assimilated to enlarge my knowledge base. And in this creative, abstract modeling process, my mind is free in its dreaming mode to generate various hypotheses. It is free to try new neural combinations in its search for solutions. This, of course, is a demonstration of Free Will.

Sensation is an abstraction. Sense perception is not direct, according to Kandel, but much like an illusion (2006: 302).

Analyzing my dreams means that I learn to read the abstractions, illusions, or metaphors – pick your favorite term. In my dreaming experience, this same metaphorical mechanism is used to help me problem solve. Bridging elements that apply to higher cognitive functions are often symbolic abstractions, the Japanese drill for example. My Interpreter recognizes that my conscious mind is capable of connecting my brain's abstract symbol making processes with their underlying sensory images, the primary images, and brain-mind functions. Brain-mind functions such as emotional homeostasis, memory integration and consolidation, or the assimilation of general knowledge can all be expressed in one dream, separately, or individually over the course of one night.

Dreams with repeated elements are common to my dream history. I might use this classroom setting, teacher image, or Jim K again in a few weeks, months, or even years later. I assume that my dream programming and lucid dreaming history has helped prime my non-conscious dream processes to access and repeatedly use these elements whenever it is convenient, much like a script writer who uses the same plot but changes characters, scenery, and the like for another episode of his serial story. I may use repetitive material more often than some lucid dreamers because I totally programmed dreams that substituted for nightmare over a 20 year period. This is speculation, but it really doesn't matter in terms of the frequency with which I used these props, if our focus is on process. My dreaming brain's use of known, historical materials is the point. Known materials can be auto-created or externally generated, and it doesn't matter to my dream machine. Lucid dream analysis over long periods of time permits me to sort out the difference.

The dream school setting and repeated use of old props represents the culmination of reviewing Hobson's materials on consciousness for this section. My sense of relief in the dream test is my emotional reaction to Hobson's work as being clear and straightforward.

I'm not a neuroscientist, and have concern as I write this book that I may be misinterpreting sources, and this concern enters my dream as feeling, and the feeling gets translated into imagery.

The math problem is my bridging element and is carried over from an earlier dream. The math that I was unfamiliar with in this earlier dream becomes a simple formula that uses square root. My teacher takes on the image of a former boss whose smiling, reassuring presentation of Self simply says that all is well. I realize the meaning of the dream immediately upon getting up. I also recognize that the dream plot itself is a carryover from a previous dream.

Current dream patterns reflect my history as a mature, lucid dreamer. My dream programming history, where I use the same characters and plots repeatedly, seems to have taught my dream machine to use the efficient writing techniques of a paid storyteller. Dreams that represent patterned characters and plots are easier to interpret than single episode dreams; in this sense they are déjà vu. Bridging elements such as the math test almost become highlighted as the serial plot continues. The symbolic meaning of dream patterns is more easily identified when they are repeated. Pattern analysis through decades of lucid dreaming could be a separate study in itself.

If you are a new lucid dreamer, you will notice different patterns and themes emerging over time. My dream programming history started in the 1957-58 academic school year. If I wake in the middle of the night and don't like the ending of a dream, the dream will often repeat exactly as though I were re-showing the movie, but my dreaming brain changes the ending to its own liking without any conscious effort on my part. The effect is similar to watching a movie on DVD where one can select multiple story endings. Every part of the dream movie is a repeat except for this segment. My short-term dream memory that re-runs my dream movies is more exact than my daytime memory as it faithfully repeats the thousands of little visual details.

If, however, I especially like the dream scenario, my dreaming brain may re-run the entire dream without changing it. Erotic dreams are more commonly repeated in whole than are other types of dreams. This is a pattern carryover from my younger years when I substituted erotic dreams for nightmares. A comparison between how my dreaming brain uses favorite characters and scenes is in order.

I've described fixed action patterns riding my bicycle or engaging in some other skill acquisition. My dreaming brain has a store of dream scenario fixed action characters and scenes that it trots out on demand. This is an efficient, time saving mechanism that directly calls one's attention to structural changes in brain architecture as we age. I assume my brain uses this mechanism for the same reason writers re-use themes, plots, characters, props, etc. We pay computer programmers to write routines for us, but our brains create them effortlessly and most of the time without our awareness.

SMOKING

Dream smoking is an annual yearly event for me. Every winter, dreams of smoking reenter my nighttime movies. Shortly after quitting smoking, I thought my dreams were simply reflecting my desire for another cigarette: Very Freudian. If you have never smoked, you may not appreciate how good a cigarette can smell to a former smoker, especially in the first few months after quitting. Later, I came to realize that smoking dreams were activated by winter's dryness, and the effect dryness has on my sleeping senses. Lung dryness enters an ongoing dream or activates an entire dream scenario when related discomfort reaches a tipping point.

Within one week of reporting my smoking dream in this book, I had three other dreams where I'm smoking. As I began to observe smoking in my dreams more closely, and bringing these memories into consciousness during the dream, my smoking dreams stopped. I have not had a smoking dream for the past two weeks and the house is as dry as it gets, because we've had unusually cold weather. So, does dry air just get ignored by my dreaming brain? The answer is no. My Interpreter is now directly informed that my mouth and air passages are uncomfortably dry, so I roll over and take a sip of water. Dream analysis educates my Interpreter about basic bodily functions, thereby changing subsequent dream content and scenarios.

It is the end of May, 2011, and our nights have been cool. I'm sweating from the effects of a winter quilt which I've left on the bed. My mouth is very dry and I wake up thirsty. I wake from a smoking dream with an awareness of thirst. My conscious mind connects the actual dryness in my mouth with smoking in my dream. This is a good example of the circular effect one gets with dream interpretation. I become conscious of what activates my smoking dream, and this awareness emerges while the dream is in progress. This feedback loop of cause and effect also sensitizes me to underlying dream functions.

DAD AND BAR DREAMS

An alternative dry air activated dream also represents a long-term pattern with the central figure being my father, the bartender. I worked as a bartender for dad my last two years of high school. I typically worked 64 hours weekly and closed the bar at 1:00 a.m. The building did not have mechanical ventilation or air conditioning, as both were unusual in the 1950s in Northern Wisconsin. Smoking was permitted, in fact the idea that one could not smoke and drink at the same time would have been considered ridiculous by a majority of the patrons.

Smoke would become so thick in the dry cold of our Northern Wisconsin winters that customers would ask or just take it upon themselves to open windows. My dreaming brain associates winter dry air with smoking and bar settings. My alternative dry air dreams find me visiting my father in a bar. I often take over his duties in these dreams and serve customers. The bar has two levels, which was the actual case in dad's Wisconsin facility. I may be serving drinks, washing glasses, cleaning ashtrays, or tidying up the bar itself, for these are all old bartending behaviors. But, this dream only occurs in the winter if the air is dry.

This alternative dry air dream was not something I understood in my earlier years of lucid dreaming. However, I'm quite sure that activation of this dream occurs only when my throat and lungs are uncomfortably dry. Frequent childhood pneumonia and growing up with an in-house smoker leaves me with this sensitivity.

Patterned dreaming becomes more pronounced as I age. If I had written this book twenty years ago, I would have made no reference to these patterns.

The curious reader is encouraged to keep long-term notes of their own unique dream history. I believe that newly lucid dreamers can come to interpret their dream history as easily as I do mine. If you dream lucidly and recall one or more dreams nightly you might consider keeping a random sample of dream reports as keeping track of thousands of dreams seems too tedious.

NAKEDNESS

I use nakedness in dreams as an example because it is such a common element for so many dreamers. Nakedness has many dream dictionary interpretations, and almost all of them are not representative of my dreams. Internal sensations from our bodies or stimuli from the environment can be activators for specific dream element such as smoking or nakedness. Being naked or semi-naked in my dreams always corresponds with my sleeping attire.

I assume that universal dream elements have common causes even though the specific activators may be of a wide variety. Nakedness in my dreams is caused by sensations on my skin that are experienced while a dream is in progress. If I need to use the bathroom, my dream will typically have me searching for one in a public setting. Once my dream places me in a public setting, my Interpreter notices that I'm naked or semi-naked and is perplexed. My waking modesty meets a scenario concocted by my core consciousness, and the two are usually out of sync. For me, nakedness and "potty" dreams are just this transparent.

The settings in which dream nakedness occur are not important. What's important is a common association that accompanies this type of dream, that is, no one seems to notice the missing clothes. This lack of concern for my nakedness on the part of other dream characters is my bridging element. No one notices, why? Answer: My Interpreter understands the meaning of these dreams, It knows I'm in my own bed and partially or totally nude. Over the decades of my life there is a meta-awareness lurking behind the dream's facade.

During waking consciousness, I would never be found in real life settings naked. My Interpreter is very aware of this fact, and my normal response to nakedness creates discomfort in these dreams. I could dismiss dream nakedness as being bizarre and put it in the category of flying or time morphing, but not so. Dream nakedness must be activated by the way I sleep seasonally. The pattern is decades old and very consistent. Dream nakedness can also occur when a cold shoulder simply needs covering to regain sleeping comfort. Dream nakedness from the waist down only occurs in winter. The same pattern and interpretation applies to total nakedness in my summer dreams.

The brain breaks its surroundings into mosaic maps according to Kandel (2006: 309).

Stimuli such as cold or hot or pain are salient compared to being pleasantly warm or in a comfortable state without pain or anxiety. A cold shoulder was visually experienced in one of my dreams as a 1955 Chevy. The Chevy occupied the exact physical location and size in my dream as my body's relationship to the exposed cold shoulder. Body mapping by my senses occurs in my dreams but takes on this symbolic form. Would a 1955 Chevy, or any car for that matter, have the same meaning for different individuals? What imagined contortions would be necessary in order to put my 1955 Chevy in a dream dictionary?

Spatial maps become unstable after three to six hours according to Kandel (Ibid: 311).

If not, one could imagine a brain that got filled up and stopped working after a few years because it was overburdened by spatial maps. Why should our dreaming brain remember spatial maps any more than our waking brains? I experience a lot of dream content that is superfluous, temporary spatial maps if you will. Most of my dream content represents either physiological or cognitive processes, meaning that only the salient brain-body functional representations are worthy of maintenance or permanent encoding. Use it or lose it leaves room for new episodes. And temporary dream elements, like their waking counterparts, are only useful for the moment.

Memory trash is discarded in our dreams and neural circuit efficiency is maintained. I also believe that our capacity to consciously enter our dreams enhances and facilitates exchange between our new and old brains. Our higher cognitive centers, the Interpreter in our new brain, gradually learn how to interpret output from the old brain. Information processing in both our old and new brains must rely on a substantial amount of memory encoding in the 95 percent of our brain that operates below but influences our higher cognitive processes. The education over time of my Interpreter supports information exchange and circular causation between our higher and lower brain centers. My Interpreter in turn educates my core consciousness.

The reader will experience variations in his or her own long-term dream patterns based upon individual histories. Patterns change for me with geography, seasons and jobs. Keeping dream notes can facilitate discovery of these patterns for individuals with limited lucid dream time.

SPOUSAL CONFLICT

Most of us marry at least once or have long-term relationships with significant others. One must be a saint or incredibly programmed by their child to adult socialization not to experience conflict in committed relationships. We experience conflict in our jobs, social life, with children and with spouses – a common condition for humanity. Dreams parallel our waking lives, and it is normal for marital conflict to surface in my dreams.

In a dream the last week of 2010, I'm being ignored by a former secretary in Rochester, Minnesota. This was not her normal reaction to me, nor would it be a typical response from one's personal secretary; hence, this dream element flagged my attention. To put it differently, the secretary's attitude was my dream bridging element. I recognized that this secretary was a stand in for my current spouse. She was a symbolic substitute for my current wife Ruby. This is a simple dream metaphor.

Typical of this dream and dozens if not hundreds of others, I recognize dream characters by their accompanying feelings. I've used this technique enough that it's probably formula for my dreaming brain. I'm as likely to make this association while still dreaming as I am after waking. The only physical resemblance between the secretary and my Chinese ethnic spouse is their height. But I'll not analyze the possible associative memories between the secretary and my spouse, as they are of secondary importance to the dream message.

Conflict is a normal part of our lives, and increasing one's sensitivity to daily moods and relationships makes it easier to interpret one's dreams. Patterns in my dreams reflect unique patterns in my daily life, as yours do. Make some notes from both your waking and dreaming lives, don't forget your daydreams, and review them periodically. Dream study groups of the type proposed by Delaney can also help.

SEX, CONSCIENCE, AND PHYSICAL PROWESS

I have only known one asexual human being in my life. She was a friend of one of my university students and possessed an uncommon DNA profile. I've forgotten her exact genetic profile, but I can describe her: medium height, fairly masculine but not totally unfeminine, voice approximating that of an adolescent boy entering puberty, and breasts like a beginning young puberty girl. She spoke to a number of my university classes and I got to know her fairly well. The class focus always addressed inter-sexed DNA variations. She was totally open about herself and her social relationships.

She is the only person I have ever known who claimed absolutely, 100 percent, no interest in sex. From her point of view, sex was not even on her radar screen.

Most of us find sex an integral part of who we are. It is a major element in all our adolescent social encounters, the driving force that binds us to our life partners, and the physically demanding hormonal drive that makes marriage seem rational. How could sex not be a recurring pattern and significant part of our dreams?

A common sex theme in dreams is performance with multiple partners without guilt. I found this to be the case as a young university student when I programmed erotic elements into my dreams. I substituted my own dream stories for nightmares. I changed dream sex partners and dream stories whenever I became bored. At times I was a wanton, lustful pursuer of sex, a.k.a. young, healthy male.

As I aged, I found that maturation changed how sex was expressed in my dreams as well as how I thought about women in general. My earlier training as a teenage sexist was gradually replaced in the 1960s and 1970s by a growing awareness of my own prejudice. I have a dream conscience now that never existed in my younger adult years, which slowly emerged over the decades as I progressively moved along the continuum of human morality.

My long-term dream patterns with sex parallels my long-term patterns with dream conflict and violent dream behaviors. Now I usually try to solve dream confrontations with the same conscience I use during waking hours. This is not a pattern of how conscience is typically expressed in popular dream reports by younger people. Again, your experience will be unique to you. Don't be afraid to accept your dream uniqueness for what it is, as our complex brains permit endless variation. Find the common themes and patterns in your younger dreams and watch them change as you age.

Physical strength is very much a part of our self-identity. Acrobatics that I performed in dreams, or waking out-of-body projections when I flew into outer space or cavorted with the Northern Lights are no longer common to my aged dreams. Movement in dreams is now much more representative of my 75 year old body. I rarely have a physical encounter in my dreams, and if I do, it is of a fairly mild nature. I no longer engage in boxing or Kung Fu type dream physicals. This noticeable change began to occur in my fifth decade and has only intensified since then. Expressions of unusual physical prowess in dreams are almost always a bridging element to my dream's interpretation. Power and strength is now only expressed in my dreams if I undergo age regression, like when I return to being 20 or 30 years old, for example.

In like fashion, sexual prowess in dreams is basically limited and reflects my reduced hormonal levels, again the exception being dream age regression. Balance in my younger dreams was many times better than it is now. Heights in my dreams never bothered me, but heights also never bothered me when I was awake either. I was a runner and jogger in my earlier years. I was an exceptional runner in my dreams, much better than in my waking moments. Now I'm lucky if I sprint a hundred yards in any dream, which is about what I would do when awake.

INTERPRETATION

I've reported a number of other dream themes and patterns elsewhere in this book and will not detail them again. Note however that reported dream patterns represent my unique history, just as your dream patterns are unique to you. Whatever I'm engaged in day-to-day becomes part of my dreams. My dreams are very, very transparent at my current age. I'm retired and learning to use leisure as an integrated part of my lifestyle, probably because willed changes in long-term life-styles are slow and come with considerable effort. Besides, I'm now more aware of how these changes enter my dreams.

Writing has preoccupied me these past four years, and the related dream lectures, academic dream conversations, blackboard scribbling of a teacher, university settings and classrooms, students, still taking tests and being challenged by teachers all merge into my dreams. If you are a young reader, your mind is probably flitting about on endless life explorations, relationships, job demands, and job changes compared to mine.

If you are a new lucid dreamer playing with dream characters, love partners, flying and other exotic adventures, you will notice a stark contrast to most of the dreams in this book. I've long tired of flying around in my dreams: Even flying in vision-like trances while awake no longer has appeal. Nevertheless, I still fly in my dreams on occasion, and more often than extended flights, I employ some form of dream levitation. If you take the next step to other lucid states of altered reality, you will probably become bored playing these games over time too. At least this is my experience. However, True Believers never seem to become tired of their adventures as astral travelers, remote viewers, speakers-in-tongues, automatic writers or enjoying dance induced trances. By definition, True Believers make these experiences part of their reality landscape.

Hobson in his book *Consciousness* discusses how banal most daytime fantasies are. "What did surprise us, when we overcame the understandable resistance of our subjects, was how banal was the content of most of their normal daily ruminations (1999: 222)."

If you do not use suggestions or self-hypnosis to program your dreams, you will most likely experience this banal quality in your dreams as well. Ask yourself why your dreams should run a different set of night scenarios from what your waking brain routines are. As I age, my waking days tend to converge with my dreaming nights. If your days are full of troubles, so will your dreams. Conversely, if dreams attend to banal functions like memory, why shouldn't daydreams as well?

If you suffer from anxiety or depression, your dreams will reflect these moods. If you are overworked, the same will occur. At least, this has been my experience. Why would we think it should be different? Unless, of course, we have been influenced by the now-defunct dream interpretations of Freudians, astral travelers, crossing over to the other side adherents, or other similarly contrived schemes.

To continue with Hobson:

Consciousness is thus, first and foremost, eminently practical … one other surprise our study held was the recognition that even very practical imaginings are just barely conscious. They float just below the surface of consciousness in what the psychoanalysts call the preconscious (Ibid: 223).

I'm not promoting psychodynamics with the following observation. Remember, 95 percent or more of what our brain-minds are up to day-to-day runs below our conscious level; much like the core processor in our computer that does the main work while I just keyboard these words. There is however a creative or thinking element in my dreams that seems to be more common than for most lucid dreamers, or at least I seem more aware of these elements.

In my experience, preconscious or non-conscious brain-mind activity goes on in both my old and new brain constantly. I'm making a distinction between Damasio's core and autobiographical Self. My core Self handles functions like memory consolidation, while my autobiographical Self handles higher order thoughts and their integration.

The reader is now familiar with both levels of brain-mind activity in my dreams. To extend this point, my core Self doesn't give lectures in my dreams, but my autobiographical Self does. My core Self appears to handle responsibilities such as bike balancing and related image management. And these mundane functions are only attended to by my autobiographical Self when I so choose.

It's positive that our waking brains can unconsciously perform such myriad functions while we consciously go about our daily business. For me, my dreams keep attuned to my emotional states and well-being. My dreams flag important issues and problems in my life, and my dreams often perseverate through one night or over days on elements that are of critical concern to me.

Historically, nightmares were a major focus of concern for me. Now, it is almost impossible for me to ignore sustained dream themes that represent ongoing salient elements such as conflict with my wife, or the demands of writing this book.

I used dream programming to repress my nightmares over a 20 year period of time. Trauma that is normally expressed in nightmares can be repressed with active dream programming. But, as noted, it has repercussions over years of practice as it demands psychic energy. Psychic energy is defined as conscious control over neural circuits that restricts their normal expression. One type of repression is initiated by our waking consciousness, and the other occurs at a non-conscious level.

From my experience, repression has two sources, these being the core Self and the autobiographical Self. One may define physical damage to neural circuits as a third form of repression. Cellular damage would not typically be called repression, because the memories cease to exist. However, in my smothering example, I'm suggesting that partial memory is retained in core Self mechanisms, but lost in autobiographical Self memory.

In my case, initial nightmare suppression permitted me to stabilize pathological mood swings, obtain a good night's sleep, and have a lot of fun programming interesting dream characters. Don't over-program your dreams with suggestion nightly if you want to discover your inner Self. Instead, let non-conscious processes come to the surface. Learn to meditate and experience the tranquility that comes with it. Periodically skip using dream suggestion or self-hypnosis in order to compare the different patterns that emerge. I assume that one of our lifelong goals is self-discovery, and fine tuning self-discovery requires normal dreaming.

Let me offer an aside comment about overloading one's brain with static, or maybe I should call it brain trash. Constant interaction with artificial media, games, TV shows, et cetera, means that our brain-minds must process all this stimuli. And, this processing becomes an integral part of our dreams as well as higher order neural assimilation into our knowledge base. Garbage in, garbage out is an apt computer phrase. Your memory may contain thousands of simple songs and movies, but this repertoire doesn't help you pass algebra II. Turning off the TV for a week for avid TV addicts will be a stark reminder of this paragraph. Next, try a month, and after three months, notice how your dreams change.

LONG-TERM DREAM PATTERNS AND SELF-HYPNOSIS

I started programming my dreams over fifty years ago and continued the practice for two decades. I taught my dreaming brain to consciously intercept my nightmares in order to stop them. I'm quite sure that my long-term dream patterns reflect a degree of conscious input that the typical lucid dreamer doesn't experience, habituation being what it is.

I give lectures in my dreams that reflect the materials that I'm currently studying, and I write on blackboards and read dream materials. I compose poetry in dreams about as often as I do when awake, and I have endless conversations related to my topics of current study. Increasingly over the past fifty years, the fine line between my waking and dreaming states has become thinner. If you continuously practice fun games while dreaming such as flying and superhero stunts, I don't think you'll experience this pattern.

I grew tired of dream programming and decided to once again experience my dreams in raw form. I discovered that total control over my dream elements required energy. I felt an immediate, noticeable, and sizeable sense of relief when I stopped.

I maintained total nightmare control for two decades. Self-hypnosis permitted me to control my dream processes as it allowed me to control other body states such as pain and tiredness. However, this high level of control carries over into our daytime emotions. Consciously one experiences the world through a narrower window of controlled feelings.

However, the longer and more frequently one uses self-induced methods to control altered states of consciousness, the better we become at it. I rarely engage the mechanism of self-hypnosis, but can feel its effects almost immediately when I do. I use it at the dentists and for five year interval colonoscopies. Now I partially reduce pain, but never totally block it out. Total control makes me feel like a machine.

For many years I've used a milder form of self-hypnosis. It's a bit like power-steering in my car with 50 percent employed versus 90. For me to use a greater degree of control I must employ self-hypnosis frequently. I no longer desire to totally mute or control sensory input or processing as I did in days past. I've achieved a desirable level of sensitivity to self and others, and I prefer to stay in this comfort zone.

I'm guessing, but it would probably take me two or three months to get up to full self-hypnotic speed. High levels of self-control are self-addicting brain states that now seem more like a narcotic than a vitamin.

BUDDHISM AND MEDITATION

Buddhist meditation has been studied extensively over the past half-century by numerous individuals in the Western World. I noticed in the Tri-City Herald, the local paper here in Kennewick, Washington, this past week that Buddhist meditation classes were being offered locally. It is well established that meditation changes and increases neuronal mass in affected brain areas. Practice of any kind changes our brains. Change the mind's activity and change the brain is an established fact. And I think for the typical frazzled, work stressed, media hyped person, these practices are a breath of fresh air in a stimuli polluted environment.

I have never taken meditation classes, but practiced sustained focus through self-hypnosis as a university undergraduate until I could read and memorize college textbooks for eight straight hours without a break. Or, I could just focus on nothing and let my mind go to a quantum point. Turning off stimuli input lets our brain-minds rest. The resulting inner peace contrasts sharply with the overloaded world of stimuli that most of us inhabit.

This training permitted me to stay totally focused on any subject desired for periods up to eight hours without any break. I could drive through the night without experiencing tiredness or loss of road attention. I could meditate, or what I came to think of as meditation by just shutting my eyes and closing out the world. Note that maximizing brain-mind controls takes considerable practice over time. It's not a state one can just enter or leave like our front doors. Situational use of hypnotism by a therapist does not have the same habituating effect.

In my self-created exercises, I'd focus on the empty space between atoms where I visualized nothing. I visualized nothing even though I was aware of force fields moving through this so-called empty space. To me, it was visual emptiness as one cannot be conscious without body sensations. The other type of exercise that was one of my favorites was to flood my brain-mind state with overload. I visualized my entire brain and all its billions of neurons simultaneously. Either exercise produced a similar effect – tuned oscillation.

The effect achieved by envisioning billions of brain cells simultaneously was that of endless little lights filling up all my cranial space: A beautiful, almost uniform but patterned star field. Either of the two effects creates the sensation of being part of nothing or part of everything. It is this sense of being one with God that religious adherents experience. Self-hypnosis was easy for me, and I used it in many different ways to achieve whatever brain-mind state or controls over these states I desired.

Control over my body and mind had long-term effect that I found undesirable. My range of feelings became increasingly dampened down over time. I could withdraw totally from my surroundings by just immersing myself in a book or projecting into the night sky. My concentration was complete enough that physical touch would be necessary to break my mood. Controlled brain-mind states were still so appealing that when I retired in 2006, I thought seriously of entering a monastery. I actually checked out a number of different sites.

However, I prefer the modest level of mental introversion that is presently my comfort zone. Long-term conditioning of brain-mind states creates new options in some life areas and reduces others.

Much like bicycle riding, monkish neural circuits are there for reactivation if desired. However, with long-term practice, daily self-reinforcement becomes totally addictive for me. Practicing Buddhist monks, for example, easily returned to their old ways once their oppression by Chairman Mao's Era was lifted in China. Secular reconditioning did not destroy their enlarged neural mass, which is responsible for advanced meditation. Meditation modifies brain circuitry that can be maintained in the most severe environments. When I had peak control over my body and mind, I could reach this level with a few minutes of concentration before sleeping.

Total mind-body controls that are as extensive as mine were can be totally effective. It represents a level of situational control exhibited by those who walked into the fires of the Inquisition while singing or praying. It is the calm of the monk under threat. It's a temporary mindset most of us can experience in extreme crises such as tsunamis, hurricanes, or auto accidents. And, it is control available on demand.

The mystery of what is real or illusion evaporates once we acknowledge that our brains are not embedding representations of the real world around us, but instead we embed a manufactured perception of both our internal and external world. We only experience what our physical electro-chemical neural circuitry permits us to experience, which depends on the DNA and the socio-cultural filters at its disposal. For example, pain is a neural reflex from that pin you just stuck in my hand, but I've decided not to experience the pain, and so I don't. However, if I want to, I can experience any fraction of that pinprick I desire. What is illusion and what is real? Of course, each is both. Oh the joy of word manipulation employed by historical philosophers who were ignorant of neuroscience.

ANXIETY, FEAR AND NEGATIVE EMOTIONS

Negative emotional states tend to dominate our dreams when compared with states of joy or our range of other elevated feelings. Dream researcher Hobson has observed this pattern over many years of lab research. Long-term dream patterns for me have radically shifted away from negative feelings, fear, anxiety, and various terrors of the night.

Dream programming stopped my nightmares for twenty years. When I stopped dream programming, my nightmares returned, and I had to conquer them with dream analysis. However, over the last thirty odd years my dreams have gradually mellowed. It is rare for me to have a dream that is negative. I never have an emotion of nightmare quality that is strong enough to wake me. Nightly I dream lucidly, and only wake up for necessary bathroom breaks or when external stimuli prod my consciousness.

I attribute this shift in long-term dream patterns to improved self-integration, a happy marriage, and a contended life of retirement. In my case, and I suspect for most people who are able to age with relative security, their long-term dream plots will follow a pattern similar to mine.

I've enjoyed reading Brooks and Vogelsong's dream experiments and those of their friend Ruth. I get an impression that they continue to control much of their dreaming life and have not returned to natural dreaming. It would be interesting reading if they do.

Hobson follows his dreams with meticulous care. I cannot determine from his various writing to what degree he enjoys natural dreaming or how often his dreams are guided by suggestion. My impression of his *13 Dreams Freud Never Had* is that he continues to engage in active dream suggestion. Long-term dream case studies that are similar to mine appear to be rare.

Delaney is another one of my favorite dream reporters. She writes, speaks, and guides dreamers along therapeutic lines as well as being helpful with dream interpretation. I would enjoy reading her long-term pattern analysis over a 40-50 year period of time. I think that closely observing how our dreams age over decades offers insights comparable to that of laboratory studies.

DREAM MOOD THEMES

I'm a person who rarely gets lonely. I love to read and always have hobbies and activities that keep me busy. But mostly, loneliness was something I lost by the time I was two years old. Three years ago while teaching in China, I experienced a sense of loneliness that came out of an ordinary dream. I was surprised, because the dream's content clearly let me know I was missing my family back in the states. Up to that time, I couldn't recall ever having a similar dream.

In late April, 2011 my wife Ruby went to China for seven weeks. I've had a theme dream series nightly that started a few days after her departure. In this dream series I nightly spend time with family and friends.

The following dreams were recorded (5-11-11 at 3:54 p.m.)

(**5-6-11**) I'm fishing with my son and one of his friends who has no identifying characteristics. My son and I are both 20-25 years younger. In real life I occasionally fished with Steve, but never recall having a third adult present, although my son has regular fishing partners. This was an activity that he and I usually conducted in our family canoe, or occasionally in his motorized boat.

(**5-7-11**) I'm talking to my two biological sons in a family type setting. The feeling tone is one I experience when we get together for holiday meals; comfortable.

(**5-8-11**) I'm at MSU with my two sons. I'm about 40 years old and we are in the school cafeteria eating. My now deceased Uncle Eric is with us, and we are having a conversation of no consequence. My Uncle Eric never visited me at the University. His age in my dream was at most 50. In life he was about 30 years older than me, and logically in my dream, if I'm about 40, he should be about 70.

(**5-9-11**) I'm sleeping with my wife Ruby who is cuddling me and being very affectionate. The dream scenario could've been a movie scene in actual depiction of our current ages and behaviors.

(**5-10-11**) An old friend of mine and retired history professor from MSU, is visiting; not talking, visiting. We are in a relaxed setting that is not of any special importance, and I'm aware of just enjoying his friendship. Instigation for this dream probably comes from my daytime thought that I haven't called him for some time.

I'm acutely aware that I've developed a sense of being lonely. It's a pleasant sense, but in some ways life was simpler without these feelings. Give me back my family and friends, whom I always enjoy, and you can keep lonely. I resist removing feelings of loneliness from my dreams through programming as I'm committed to normal dreaming and wherever that takes me. If I programmed my dreams to have exciting characters or plots, I would miss these patterns. As I age into my last decade or two, I want to enjoy every dream stage to its fullest. I want to fully experience who I am becoming.

My wife returned from China on 6-15-11, and this dream series continued until her return. I'm not reporting all my lucid dreams for this seven week period. I just want to establish the patterns and themes. I will however add a few more.

(**5-11-11**) I recall five separate dreams:

Jane is a high school classmate whom I occasionally dated. Our real life relationship was more as friends than that of hormone driven teenagers or young adults. But in last night's dream, we were both teenagers and had exquisite sex. I was surprised at how loudly she emoted during orgasm.

The second dream is also with Jane and we are college students. The encounter occurs in a dorm-like setting. We began to have sex and she stops me, claiming fear of pregnancy. In real life Jane and I were never lovers, but we did have dinner together a few times as adults.

The third dream also takes place in a college setting with two other high school classmates, George and Jim. George is asking for help with math problems, as was the case in real life and I was helping him. Jim was looking on and seemingly impressed. I completed some complicated formulae and made a modest comment to Jim. I was pleased with my modesty. A type of educated elitism students instantly recognize.

The fourth dream includes the old university friend from the History Department at MSU. I'm living at his remodeled barn-house, chatting and just enjoying his company. This period of my life actually existed after my first divorce.

In the fifth dream I'm at a lake and notice a strange shaped boat. It's about one foot higher in the back and shaped like a triangle with the front being the broadest. The man in the boat is moving easily, and I'm impressed that he can paddle so well with this design. The scene morphs and I'm in a similar boat looking for fish. The water is full of large fish, I reach down and grab one just above the tail and pull it into the boat. I move to shore, or I should say the boat moves to shore on its own. When I throw what is probably a ten pound fish on land, it falls amongst dozens of similar fish. I get out of the boat, pick up the wiggling fish and give it to my wife Ruby. I tell her that it's not as big as some of the others lying on shore but it will be fresher. In real life Ruby usually goes fishing with me, but I never catch anything this big, and certainly not by hand.

I often experience theme dreams over long time periods that express my moods and feelings. I'm not using suggestion or dream programming, and I'm acutely aware of my feelings in these dreams. My family and friends come back for my enjoyment, and basically I just savor their company. If I weren't a lucid dreamer I would be all alone for seven weeks. I'm aware of real events in my day-to-day life that trigger much of the symbolism in these dreams. Ruby has been gone for one month as I update this section, and these nightly dreams continue. My lucid recall of last night includes three similar dreams. But, enough! And the final "enough" happens with Ruby's return after being gone 52 days.

Dream suggestion, conscious or unconscious gives us what we desire. Freud would be happy with this theme series that exemplifies wish fulfillment.

DREAM COMPLEXITY

Dream patterns that emerge with ageing are not available in dream labs using younger clients, especially readily available university students. And various dream centers tend to focus on getting immediate results for their clients. Delaney says: "… recurring dreams signal recurring situations and often indicate that we are stuck in a rut in our personal or work life." "In most cases, our common dreams represent a recurring theme or problem in our lives (1997: 6)." Amen.

Embedded memories are part of the hard drive that runs our biological computer called the brain. Learned skills, or any other learned memory that has been embedded, can be and is changed as we interact with our environment throughout life. But what happens to internally generated memories that become part of our ongoing dream histories? Answer: Auto-created memories that are generated internally are not subject to external reshaping, as are externally generated memories such as skill training. Interpretation can be perplexing if one doesn't pay attention to recurring dream patterns that mix auto and externally created memories. Decade to decade auto-created dream scenarios take up an increasingly larger part of my dreams. This pattern is comparable to old guys who reminisce, and use the same stories repeatedly.

My brain has patented favorite dreams scenarios and continues to change, expand and update them through time. I've spent much of my professional life as a university professor, and the second biggest time slice is associated with behavioral intervention programs, related research, and treatment strategies. These are the professional settings for my two favorite, ongoing dream series: A little like Rocky I, Rocky II and Rocky III. My personal family life represents a third dream-theme sequence that also gets expanded and updated. Let me provide an example from teaching.

My early years as a young professor were at Mankato State University in Mankato, Minnesota. Dream content, characters, and scenery were from this setting, and sometimes I include special students. I've now taught at six other universities and colleges either full or part-time. My longest teaching stint occurred at Mankato and the memory related elements of geography and people remains more salient than from other settings.

I mix friends and teaching colleagues from any of these settings, often ignore the time sequences, and mix according to themes or special kinds of associations. I mix buildings, geography, and physical props according to my mood any particular day, and I typically update the dream's content with more recent elements. I add in information from contemporary research findings and discuss this material, or even lecture over it, with former teaching and research colleagues. I sometimes age dream characters and at other times I may mix their ages according to some obscure association my brain is making. These series are ongoing, have become increasingly complex by mixing all these elements, incorporating my evolving understanding of science, and bringing together materials from so many different locations and cultures.

Obviously, I agree with Delaney that dreams represent ongoing themes in my life. The dreams are not necessarily problem focused, although temporarily being alone tends to bring forth fond memories. The only rut I feel stuck in is one that says I'm getting older. Memories are like my bookshelf, they just keep growing, and growing memories add richness and complexity to my life. Auto-created dream memories and short stories evolve without any apparent end point. Comforting memories take us to Heaven if we age gracefully, or …

MEMORY CONSOLIDATION AND LIFE HABITS

In my childhood through early adulthood I experienced nightmares thousands of times. The imagery in these nightmares was as clear as any contemporary daytime scene. Nightmare images and accompanying feelings were burned into my memory. If we engage in repeated activities of any kind such as driving a car, playing a game, riding a bicycle, or even lecturing, ingrained memory patterns become automatic. Ingrained recordings of this nature parallel the learned repertoire of an accomplished concert performer. They express themselves like complex fixed action patterns. Nightmares become patterns with bolded outlines in wide brushed black ink in our neural circuits. The same happens when we have a traumatic experience in war or peacetime, when the imagery and dramatized feelings are reinforced nightly in our dreams.

You and I are flesh and blood recorders, reinforcing and consolidating memories with each repetition. However, we continue to add new program elements as the old ones play out. Soldiers who have been victims of brutal war experiences know this effect well, as do traumatized civilian victims of rape, or children experiencing a multitude of different traumatizing histories. Our minds naturally try to make sense of, interpret, and help us avoid the destructive aftermath of processing trauma. Integrating higher order complex metaphor is a quintessential human activity.

We intuitively understand the importance of ridding our minds of all the lingering ugly feelings of trauma, but how to erase the effects of PTS has been slow in coming to the civilized world of the West. Soldiers were traditionally told to "suck it up," rape victims were told to get over it, and children growing up in brutal families were treated equally to children from privileged homes. After all, the law is the law.

I learned in the 1950s from basic application of behavioral principles that we could control, shape and reshape our behavior in incremental states. And in this reshaping process, we could control unwanted memories and dreams. I rejected early Skinnerian Behaviorism which assumed that we were passive vessels to be shaped endlessly by outside forces. Behaviorism was an effective model for simple behavioral changes such as weight loss, stopping smoking or delivering babies. But I couldn't figure out how to use the passivity of behaviorism to stop nightmares.

Stopping nightmares required modifying Skinner's assumptions by creating an active, interpretive and controlling Self. I made this initial change with dream programming. Today we think of this form of human reconditioning as cognitive-behavioral therapy, which tends to be as effective or even more effective then drug therapy when used alone. I assumed that my mind and my Self as Interpreter could take control of memories and nightmares. I quickly discovered that I could, and that this was true.

There are an increasing number of cognitive-behavioral programs for dysfunctional juveniles and adults in correctional treatment programs. The last one I helped create was in the 1990s. One of the major problems I encountered setting up treatment programs for adolescents and young adults were the traditional beliefs held by consulting psychiatrists and master level social workers. Two major problems centered on their desire to use drugs instead of cognitive-behavior approaches, and basic ignorance of dynamic systems. Fortunately, much of the science behind effective treatment methodology has changed. Now we just need the political will to inform and implement.

I have to introduce an aside to drive the degree of these crazy treatment methodologies home. Hobson shares his own experiences about psychiatry's misadventures in *Out of Its Mind*. The kind of problems he confronted over his professional career pale in comparison to the treatment received by children, adolescents, and young adults who were labeled morally inferior by the judicial system and incarcerated without treatment. Brutality, insensitivity, ignorance and misguided benevolence by semi-trained counselors and social workers are a few of the terms that come to mind. Mismanagement by doctoral level professionals in medical settings pales in comparison to the abuse occurring in large numbers of correctional settings. But typically, medical and psychiatric hospitals refuse treatment to children labeled as correctional clients.

In the early 1960s when I was a young juvenile probation officer, Blue Earth County, Minnesota hired a master level social worker trained in the Freudian model. He announced in court shortly after being employed that he was the only person in Blue Earth County qualified to treat and work with one of the miscreants standing before the court. He had been trained in Freud's model, which was next to being trained by God Himself. Obviously, he didn't know the local psychiatrists as well as I did who were even more deeply seeped in Freudianism.

In the 1980s and '90s, I was bringing young people into my Minnesota based treatment program from 25 different states. Commonly they came from previous treatment settings where they had learned rhetoric of a psychodynamic variety, often committed to a pharmaceutical drug history that they were reluctant to give up. These young people were accustomed to physical takedowns whenever they acted out, having learned that they were not responsible for their behavior. Uncontrollable little homunculi were busy at work in their respective heads.

The last example I will share comes from the famous Mayo Clinic in Rochester, Minnesota. I was delighted to become the tri-county community corrections administrator and being able to work in the shadow of Mayo Clinic. I quickly discovered that adolescents sent to Mayo were ejected the same day they entered, once the staff read their social history and discovered they were clients of the corrections system. *Moral prejudice has no place in the medical community*, I thought, but how wrong I was.

The psychiatrist who headed the juvenile treatment education program at Mayo espoused rhetoric that, in my opinion, could have come from Freud himself. I spoke to his students only one time, and that was to their horror, I think, and to the visual disgust of their professor. I had a busy schedule prior to this speaking engagement, and read his students materials early the morning of my presentation. I was in a state of disbelief by the time I arrived at Mayo. It was also not helpful that as I walked down the hall to the lecture room, a young client was being physically taken down in the old fashioned manner of prison control tactics.

The article being used for teaching purposes was written by a political scientist from Chicago. It had as much relationship to treatment as I have to being an astronaut. I couldn't help myself; I chastised them all. I offered to provide current literature or even write new material for this group. As you probably know, silence, silence, silence was my response. I was never asked to speak to psychiatric interns again.

As bad as this state of affairs was, it has only gotten worse. Incarceration came to be defined as treatment in Minnesota. The Governor removed millions from community treatment programs to build prisons, and positioned himself as a tough on crime advocate as he prepared to run for the U.S. Presidency. Morality! What an issue is morality, and how wonderful it would be if we had a clear definition from the larger medical community that was understood by social services and prison officials.

I've been shaped by these social forces over my lifetime. My dreams are as unique to my history as are yours.

Last night I dreamt that I was at a major treatment conference addressing the status of offenders in our correctional system. I paid little attention to the proceedings, but focused in my dream on the program facilitator. The facilitator asked how many people present were probation or parole offices. A positive response was made by a handful of those present. He then went on to talk about real life experiences and how important they were. I stopped him by stating that he had asked the wrong question.

He said OK, ask the right question, and I did. A majority of hands went up to the question of how many of those present are or had ever been probation/parole officers. He changed the direction of his dream presentation, and I got up in the waking world and went to the bathroom.

I have been reviewing parts of my life history for this book by covering the various chronological time periods from infancy to now, and the sequence when various altered state experiences emerged. My dreaming brain dips into my memories this way. The dreams, traumas, and horrendous histories of many of the people I've worked with within the correctional systems of the Midwest, and young people from across the country always seem to remain vivid. I cannot think of traumatized children without thinking of the nation's approach to services, especially now, as we continue to cut the limited and inadequate services for children in the shadow year of 2011.

DIRECTING AND CONTROLLING OUR INTERPRETER

The patterns that form my conscious states and dreams seem very clear to me. They are unique to my history, but clear. As we practice lucid dreaming and dream interventions, we are learning to control much of what happens over the night's course. It is this control over dreams, and the strengthening of neural pathways between waking and dreaming consciousness that I focus on next.

Control over my nightmares fifty years ago permitted me to understand and eliminate them. But, most importantly control over my nightmares gave me an improved sense of well-being, and greater control during my waking hours. I enjoyed dream programming as most people do for its weird effects and superhero exploits, but I think even more significant than playing with dream suggestion is what happens to our psyches when viewed from a macro perspective.

I experience lucid dreaming like any other altered state of consciousness that I play with. Every altered state I experimented with quickly came under my control. With control of each new additional altered state, my sense of personality integration and well-being improved. I compare this process to what happens to clients as they come to understand themselves and subsequently exercise control over their social, play, and work lives in new and improved ways. Satisfaction, relief, and sometimes joy ensue. The need we each have to control events in our lives is secondary, in my experience, to the positive effects we realize by controlling internal brain states. To control our internal brain states is the bedrock of Free Will. We are never free until we have this control.

As a naïve adolescent, I thought of maturity as something that happened with age. One got older, grew up, and life got better. The idea that I could remain an emotional child or adolescent into old age due to trauma, drug intake, or physical brain damage never really entered my mind until I was a university student. My dad was an alcoholic and emotional adolescent who started growing up when he was 90 years old and unable to drink due to cancer. The flip side of growing up is recognizing that maturity is a progressive process that can and should be experienced throughout one's lifetime.

Control over my dreams, and other altered states, has greatly facilitated my maturation. Maturation, on whatever schedule our individual DNA and environment offers us, can be facilitated and promoted when we learn to control larger amounts of that neuronal mass we call our brain. This is a process of development that should be either promoted within our communities, families and educational system; or, at very least become an integral part of mental health intervention strategies for those experiencing major pathologies and personal lifestyle dysfunctions. Our society spends huge amount of its resources incarcerating and punishing the mentally ill and socially dysfunctional. Legal definitions of morality applied with a stick do not create loving commitment to one's neighbors.

I view brain-mind processes that represent various states of consciousness as mental states to be brought under day-to-day, moment-to-moment control. I'm not unique in wanting to be in control of my life, emotions and feelings; *in toto,* their control is our destiny. The life force we inherit in our DNA stretches back in time to our single cell ancestors, and demands this orientation to our universe. I feel an innate force as I think you do that resonates with a universal drive that has created and sustained us throughout the course of evolution. Why should we deny our humanity with harsh words? Why should we disqualify children's basic services in the name of morality? Any therapeutic model that denies a child's basic humanity is hollow.

I think resonance without nobler potential is much of what the Buddhist practitioner of meditation experiences, the peace that is available to the monk, nun, or serious spiritual practitioner. It is, however, a brain-mind state available to all. It is a state that goes beyond the discovery of a Buddha or his followers. It is a capacity inherent in our DNA.

That is my intuitive understanding. It is an understanding that grows as thought, feeling, and my personal value framework finds room for all life and all humanity. Elitist models of therapeutic services blind us to the needs of our most damaged children. Eudaimonia cries in the shadows of elite mansions.

Thus, the consolidation of one's fragmented self, or continued growth of a healthy self, at any age, becomes central to this view of the future. I feel a deep-seated sense of integration as I move back and forth through dreams and waking consciousness, but I also feel this sense of integrated self as I move around other altered states as well. Historically, individuals who have taken creative inspiration as writers, artists, and scientists from their dreams know what it means to bring this integration of self, or should I say selves, together.

Integrating our various brain-mind states can be facilitated consciously, and in this process change both the functioning and architecture of our brain-minds. We have too much research supporting this view not to take it seriously. My personal experience strongly supports this position. Most animals do not have an awareness of awareness that we humans possess, that is, our second order level of consciousness.

We know from scanning technology that most animals dream. I'm quite sure my neighbor's dog is incapable of consciously integrating altered states, which include dreaming, the way I do. Potential control over the variety of conscious states under consideration is an emergent capacity that I believe is little utilized by my fellow humans and greatly underutilized by the mental health community.

Self-control and self-integration are both strengthened throughout our maturation as we learn the techniques and methods of how to integrate the dynamic system that is the three pound enigma sitting on our shoulders.

IMPLICATIONS OF OUR BRAIN-MIND AS A DYNAMIC INTEGRATED SYSTEM

The long-term use of self-hypnosis permitted me to control my dreams, body, and brain-mind states. We recognize the dynamic potential when our minds can direct strengthening or weakening of plastic neural circuits. Mind can change matter. This intuitive understanding of scientifically documented neural processes has been misinterpreted by those ignorant of neuroscience by their adherence to assumptions of magic. And assumptions of magic include the other side or spirit world, souls without body, and disembodied minds.

The use of priming and various conscious feedback loops between the states of being awake and dreaming represented a first step for me to self-control and integration. If we don't take this first step with dream control, consciousness continues to flit about like a butterfly. Dreams become uncontrollable nightmares, PTS wreaks havoc in our day-to-day lives, and children's social lives and educational progress turns into delinquency, drugs, and hospitalization. Control through superstitious dogma or authoritarian conditioning in our correctional systems is no substitute for the creative controls that can be realized through self-actualization.

Training our dreaming brain to access non-conscious materials can open windows into our own creativity, provide understanding of dream bizarreness, and gradually improve two-way channels of day-to-day dream interface with waking consciousness. My understanding of dreaming and altered states of consciousness has a long history. What I've done in my personal life may not always work or be meaningful for others, but possibly it can be a meaningful example from which others can build.

Awareness emerges regarding brain-mind functions, skills, and changing interest as we mature and age. Ability to control anxiety, depression, and bad habits such as smoking and overeating are not always easy.

Self-control is one of the most essential elements necessary to the good life. And, that means dream control, control of personal habits, gaining control over hallucinations, delusions and other dysfunctional brain-mind states. I'm now aware of my body's needs to a degree that greatly exceeds my young adult imagination. I gained near total control over my body before I knew what this type of control meant to my future. My dreams frequently tell me what my body, mind and emotions wants me to hear, and now, I listen.

Implications for expressing and understanding altered states are multiple. I cannot read historical or biblical literature without noting how major world religious figures interpreted their altered states. I cannot study or interact with the shaman or shamanism without hearing what they hear, see what they see, and feel what they feel. I cannot experience the mentally ill who are defined as strange or bizarre without temporarily sharing the bizarreness of their thoughts and feelings. In altered states they are my soul mates, as you are when I'm enjoying normal consciousness.

But, I keep thinking there are so many suffering individuals on this planet that can benefit from learning to control their altered states as I did.

To recap: Our brains are plastic, and we can learn to control and change our various states of consciousness. In doing so, we modify synaptic connections and neuronal mass, brain chemistry and moment-to-moment control, conscience and morality, moods and thoughts, ability to concentrate and achieve, to grow, to care, and to love. Physiological understanding of the brain-mind is a noble goal of science, and understanding and controlling conscious states, in all their altered forms, is an accomplishment of similar worth. I believe we humans are incapable of destroying each other when we truly come to share our common humanity.

Any moral code that separates us from the realities experienced by others is destructive to humanity's future. And this includes religious, secular, philosophical, or medical community models of reality. We all owe a vote of gratitude for Hobson and Leonard's elimination of one such model.

Humanity

Am I not my brother's keeper?
Am I not my sister's keeper?
Am I not my neighbor's keeper?
Why do you covet my gold,
when I offer you my soul?

Can you taste my tears?
Can you share my joy?
Let us fly together
where time began.
Again!

CHAPTER 11

ALTERED REALITIES

INTRODUCTION

Hobson says: "Normal dream consciousness is caused by chemical and regional brain activation shifts (1999: 154)."

Personally, I notice a slight intensity shift, or heightened consciousness, when I change my dream outcomes while I'm still dreaming. I associate this shift in heightened consciousness as I go from dream observer to dream participant. In similar fashion, one experiences sensory shifts in each different altered state. Self-activated visions represent a heightened visual state, speaking-in-tongues shuts down the visual and intensifies the auditory, trance dancing intensifies body awareness, and projection of self into the body of an animal feels surreal. Thus, modular brain activation-deactivation plays out across my senses. I assume related chemical and regional brain activation shifts must be occurring as well.

Visions like those of my Genesis Journey generate sensations comparable to daytime consciousness, but they are more intense and very clear. The effect is something similar to looking through a magnifying glass in that detail emerges with new clarity. Internally generated sensations do not have to compete with external distractions coming from our environment. Each altered state has its own special sensory focus. For example, speaking-in-tongues focuses sensory processing on the salience of body and sound, and neglects visual input. Intense involvement in glossolalia can come to approximate a state of rapture. I suspect that each altered state is as unique individually as one's dreams. Our expectations in altered states shapes the experience much like suggestion helps shape dreams. Studying individual responses in collective drug trips could provide additional insight into these differences.

Over time, I've come to think of all of these different altered states as being just another brain-mind neural configuration. However, the first few times one enters an altered state, it does feel a little strange.

Individuals using street or pharmaceutical drugs to enter personal or collective altered states must be selectively modifying modular sensory input. Our individual response to drugs of all types represents a drug dosage problem at the medical level. Street drug trippers report similar response variations, and have the additional problem of uncontrolled dosage.

External drug use can easily modify the brain in such a way that personal control is lost. Using one's Interpreter to control altered states permits each one of us to maintain control and avoid brain system degradation. Inducing altered states naturally leads to increased control over time with heightened sensory responses.

Watch individuals who routinely practice speaking-in-tongues. They respond similarly to the gambling addict at the door of their favorite casino. It is much like learning to consciously enter and change one's dreams in that practice improves performance. The street drug tripper, on the other hand, is subject to the vagaries of quality control, and even the pharmaceutical addict experiences body reaction changes to dosage over time. Natural self-control over altered brain states wins the battle every time.

Transition from one conscious state to another can generate a sense of being in two places simultaneously. For example, the visual flashback of my mother smothering me before the age of two was superimposed on my actual physical surroundings, resulting in two complete, equally demanding pictures. The experience was comparable to two movie projectors playing side-by-side, except that the two images were superimposed. After a few seconds the image of my actual physical setting faded, and I solely experienced being in my crib and mother's attack. Creating and controlling similar dual-track states of consciousness in the lab, I think, would shed new insight on possible treatments for schizophrenics.

We are all capable of self-talk, either in dreams or during waking hours. But in my experience, the line between role taking in self-talk and being in two states of consciousness is thin. Retain two role states of consciousness and we have Zen driving, which I discuss in some detail below. Observe an alcoholic in blackout driving 500 miles and having no idea how they arrived at their new destination, and one also flirts with dual states of consciousness. It's the alcoholic's own form of Zen driving. States of consciousness shade into each other, while definitions tend to imply each state of consciousness is a discrete category. The brain is capable of fine nuances, and one can learn to sit on the edges of the transition zones and subjectively observe. Possibly this is a key point for the treatment of mental illnesses.

Normally I guide or pre-direct altered states, hence, I have this sense that they are under my control. The crib attack scene occurred on its own as did the Indian ceremony where my friend's dead brother's spirit returned for his honoring. Moving through various altered states, including lucid dreaming, changes the level and type of sensory input to the image making process.

I'm usually a multi-sensory being integrating input from all of my senses, internally and externally. Consciousness shifts occur in all my altered states. I don't know how I could be aware if this were not the case. In my definition of altered states, we are just mixing and matching normal brain circuitry in new configurations.

Being in two conscious states simultaneously does not seem unusual, as I think we often do this. A dream within a dream, talking to oneself, or changing our perspective as we think about a complex problem over minutes or for longer periods of time are similar examples. Watching a replay of being traumatized in our dreams, or just feeling the experience again when in the presence of physical stimuli of new settings activates these feelings. Lucid dreamers understand that they can watch their dreams and act in them at the same time. Change the interpretation and focus slightly and we have dual tracking. And the line between role taking and brain state shifts grows thin.

Visual intensity changes, like a dream within a dream, may become a vision superimposed on one's actual environment, as was the case with the soul visitation in my reported Native American ceremony, or a vision experience may be totally self-contained as in my Genesis Journey. Speaking-in-tongues can occur with eyes open or closed, but if my eyes are open, the external environment blurs as visual input is reduced or lost. One can let light enter their eyes without seeing in a fashion similar to normal neural processing of a pain response without feeling pain.

I'm fairly unusual in that I've played with and controlled a broad range of altered states. I often have a different perspective from dream lab researchers or anthropologists studying shamanic rituals. In former decades I practiced self-hypnosis daily. With consistent practice, recurrent priming meant that I could fall asleep on the count of five, or enter a trance state like my Genesis Journey in a matter of minutes or perhaps seconds. In my experience, any altered state can be controlled and directed. Altered states become old friends, like habits, whose ease of manipulation increases the way riding a bike does with practice. Training our neural networks, I'm arguing, has many applications, and I think is greatly underutilized by mental health professionals. The reader will appreciate the difficulty of having this discussion fifty years ago.

Hobson talks about the effects of auto-suggestion on lucid dreaming:

This glimmer of critical thought might reflect my persistent activation of my frontal lobe networks, whose strength could conceivably grow and spread by recurrent self-activation, especially if those circuits were repeatedly primed by pre-sleep autosuggestion. In this process, I have loaded the networks—'trained them up,' as the engineers would say—so that when they are later automatically activated in REM sleep, the self-awareness 'program' has a better chance of emerging (Ibid: 155).

From my experience, there is little doubt about strengthening neural circuits through auto-suggestive priming. My ongoing admonitions that active practitioners should discontinue this process, after satisfying his or her self through self-experiments, addresses these habituating effects. After long-term practice of consciously controlling dreams, it is sometimes difficult for me to dream naturally. Whenever something happens in my dreams that I don't like, my conscious mind wants to intervene and change it. This circular feedback loop operates automatically. The effect is much like long-term meditation or mind control. The natural connection between a full range of emotions and one's external environment erodes. Like one's favorite foods, habituation feels good; and like favorite foods, too much pasta is unhealthy if one's goal is to live in the natural world of activity.

Our new default level means that we experience less intensity of input from our own feelings with extensive use of meditation or control gained through self-hypnosis. The advantage is an improved ability to focus more fully on the feelings and thoughts of others. It is as though the mind's filter is shifted from Self to Other, in that there is less emotional static in the circuits.

There are advantages and disadvantages depending on the kind of social world one wishes to live in. Positively, understanding this process permits each one of us to create our own desired level of balance between self and social immersion. Observe the semi-aloof monk watching you watching him, for instance.

After twenty years of controlling dreams through this process of self-programming, I had to work at discontinuing the habit. I had to relearn natural dreaming, but relearning does not completely extinguish old habits: Once established, habituated action patterns remain at some level.

After an additional thirty years, my Interpreter occasionally intervenes and changes a dream scenario on its own. I compare these effects to those that lucid dreamers experience. Just try not to dream lucidly after you've practiced the habit for twenty years, or 70 for that matter. These embedded habits must be supported by neural circuit activity that is different from those who do not dream lucidly. In my experience, the same effects apply with other altered states. I used this habituation process to control anxiety, depression, body temperature, pain, and my attention span back in the 1950s.

The mechanisms involved speak to our potential ability to gain control over hallucinations, unwanted voices in our heads, or brain states expressed during severe panic attacks. Learning self-control over these mechanisms of neural processes can be applied repeatedly to control PTS. However, the permanence of embedded hardwired neural circuits associated with PTS suggests that we should intervene early in the syndrome; or create alternative scenarios in new circuits that neutralize stubborn, hardwired pathology.

As a veteran, it seems to me that the military services have been slow to appreciate the self-reinforcing neuronal loops that servicemen experience when suffering from PTS. Long-term military focus to keep soldiers in combat has driven the military's linear perspective. Knowing that one dramatic incident can hardwire a traumatic FAP means that continuing to reinforce this neuronal modification in combat or war theatre creates an intractable condition. Intervention should be self-taught and applied in the theatre of action by the individual.

As I've noted in my autobiography, effectiveness demonstrated by self-experiments offers too much promise to ignore. Directing and controlling nightmares, PTS symptoms, other altered realities, and normally autonomic functions such as heartbeat, body part temperature, pain, anxiety and depression suggests that we can systematically establish mind altering protocols for almost any brain state. I'm assuming that brain and neural circuit capacities are still intact, which is not the case with heavy drug use, and with severe PTS, neural degradation is probably present as well.

I know that my examples represent a 50 year longitudinal study of one, but case studies of even weeks or months have their place. I've experimented with a wide-range of altered states the way others such as Brooks and Vogelsong or Delaney have experimented with lucid dreaming. In my case, lucid control over other altered states are just as easily learned and executed, and the fun one can have directing their dreams is duplicated time and again with extended altered state control.

I think there is a subset of individuals with uncontrollable altered state pathologies who would appreciate learning this type of self-control. For the un-afflicted, learning to control brain states that are normally not experienced, or not under conscious control, offers enhanced capacity that is generalized in a more complete use of innate brain-mind potential. For those suffering from PTS, civilian or military, learning self-control is liberating; it gives one a new life and potentially rewarding future.

It doesn't make sense to teach someone who is hearing voices or seeing visions that these are just events occurring in their heads, that they can become comfortable learning how to compensate for the annoyances, or just keep trying and they will get the right drug or the right dosage for self-control. Why not teach them how to turn unwanted voices and visions on and off at will?

We all want mastery over our mind and bodies, and to think and feel without automatic tapes playing in our heads. The bonus that comes with learning self-control is that one can then make the next step to expanded use of a fuller range of consciousness. In my case, fifty years ago when I moved my attention span of 20 minutes to eight hours, my life improved dramatically. When I learned how to control anxiety and depression, positive life changes became permanent. Learning to turn-off a startle reaction behind a panic attack is a godsend.

My observations are personal and subjective. But I'm taking Ramachandran's admonitions seriously that case studies of one can lead to paradigm shifts in how we view our world. I can't remove value preferences or feelings from my writing, nor do I want to. To be human, to experience, to evaluate, to love, to be, are all part of who I am and who I think you are.

Subjectivity is a real state of being. Subjectivity is the capacity to be aware that we are aware. This second or third order level of awareness sets us apart from our pets. I'm proposing expanded consciousness as a very concrete, obtainable and useful goal, and it includes expansion and control of all altered states.

Below, I recount my personal experience with altered states starting chronologically at about 18 months of age. At that time, I was hospitalized with a near death experience, left my body, and was visited by angels on my way to Heaven. At least, that is what my immature brain perceived the vision characters to be. I recounted various altered states and how I first experienced or discovered them in my autobiography.

In my second book, *Mind of the Mystic*, I use my ability to create, direct, and control altered states to explain the shaman, shamanism, and the origin of major world religions. I see the origin of human spirituality as a natural expression of our higher order cognitive capacity. Spirituality is a DNA given capacity regardless of how intensely the theists and atheists beat on each other. This is a false debate in terms of understanding who I am. The real debate centers on the source of evolution. The false debates are perpetrated by these various dogmatists.

With expanded memory of the past, we humans can project ourselves into any imagined future. Expanded consciousness requires that we mobile creatures predict what is around the next corner. Prediction requires mapping of self and environment, which in turn requires assumptions about our self and our world. This scenario requires belief. In the history of human ignorance, generalized expressions of belief become co-opted by shamans who become priests who become leaders of dogmatized religions: This has been a natural progression of how humanity has interpreted altered states of consciousness, and one that as a small child I understood first hand.

Ability to project our self into the past or future requires the capacity to take the role of the other. This ability is supported by mirror neurons that let me feel your emotions and your thoughts. It is a capacity, slightly altered, that permits me to be an eagle or a bear. It is a capacity that when modeled in reverse by my

Interpreter permits me to become possessed by demons or angels. Why does this capacity seem mysterious to so many? This capacity permits some to be Jesus in the 21st Century.

CHRONOLOGICAL REVIEW OF ASC

In this section, I'm fleshing out autobiographical material along with speculation about various states of altered reality. My autobiography demonstrates how I came to experience multiple behavioral and mental pathologies. As a university student and young professor, most of my experiences and ideas regarding altered states were considered either bizarre or crazy by other professionals. I learned to keep these ideas to myself and thus came to enjoy a long history of unencumbered self-experiments. And, the idea that a non-professional could employ self-therapy of this nature wasn't accepted. Nevertheless, this has been my history, and I offer it for the reader's consideration.

I'm fairly unique in terms of the number of afflictions experienced, starting with crib memories, and the fact that my treatment was self-generated and directed. Self-therapy became a way of life for me at a very young age, as my father thought that any deviation from normal was due to one's own will. He believed that each one of us could use our own minds to exert self-control over whatever was bothering us, even pain. He experienced intense pain from cancer in his final months, remained home, and only at the very end took pain killers. I never recall him using even one aspirin during the years I lived with him. Thus, I was expected to cure my own stuttering, bed wetting, and head banging between the ages of five and six, and I did. I stopped obsessive-compulsive behavior with demanding sidewalk cracks when I was eleven. All the years of my life have been filled with similar self-interventions. This theme of self-control runs through this and the two previous books of my series.

Trying to discuss the voices in my head with dad was to be immediately shut down. I was totally responsible for my behavior and the thoughts in my head once I left the crib and was able to play outdoors. I would be severely punished for any misdeeds. I was informed when I went to school that any punishment meted out by my teachers would be doubled at home.

Dad told me when I turned fourteen that I was a man and responsible for myself. I no longer had to ask permission to move about the community to find work, visit friends, or engage in school activities; that is, as long as I placed no demands on him such as asking for money. From the age of eight when my brother was 14 years old and placed out permanently to work, I understood the same fate would apply to me. Even the pursuit of a high school degree was not something dad would pay for.

Thus, an unusually strong sense of self-reliance was to be my main inheritance. Mother believed in ghosts, and informed me by the time I was three years of age that all children had a Guardian Angel. Mine spoke to me often and always seemed to be available when I needed him. This interpretation was positive in that the voices in my head were those of my Guardian Angel. And, any paranoia that I experienced was interpreted by my father as coming from real world figures who were greedy, selfish, or power abusers. However, the authors of the MMPI did not appreciate my history, or dad's beliefs.

With schizophrenia, Hobson says that:

We view this paranoia as a natural and inevitable response to the perception of threat and accusation in the hallucinatory voices (1999: 206).

My voices were defined by mother as coming from my personal angel; hence, I never attributed malevolence to them. The ghost was malevolent and physical, not voices. Additionally, I had met angels before the age of two when I was journeying to Heaven.

The physical presence of the ghost as I went up steep wooden stairs at night on my way to bed was a different matter. Outside threat was made concrete in my young mind, and it came in the form of a ghost that followed me to bed and tried to take possession of my body. Ghosts were real, said mother, and I understood them from first hand sensory experience.

Try to tell a small child who physically experiences ghosts that they are not real. It would be similar to telling someone who feels the presence of The Holy Ghost that He is not real. Or try to tell someone who is daily doing battle with the Devil that the Devil is not real. Our senses tell us we are hot or cold, in pain or comfortable, and we all learn to trust our feelings, or there is no reality. Teach a child to identify their own natural sensory experiences with a fabricated Other, Devil, or Holy Ghost, with whom they may interact daily, and that child will attend your lectures and read your books the rest of his or her life. Generally speaking that is.

Dad's response to any personal problem such as stuttering was simply that I should use my mind to change the behavior. Mother's response to voices and ghosts was that they were real, and every child had his own angel. Mother made me responsible for myself starting with daylong excursions outside the house while I was still crib bound. Visits to doctors or dentists only occurred in extreme emergencies. As children, my brother and two surviving sisters were to be self-reliant when our ages were still in the single digits. At age fourteen, we were to be placed-out in a trade, and thereafter be self-supporting.

As I grew into this world view, I gradually became aware that the real threats in life were those orchestrated by my parents. In retrospect, my parent's expectations became my reality before I even left my crib. In each of the following real life dream scenarios, I focus on what the subjective experience felt like and meant to me. I passed through a gradual process of self-discovery, but a process that let me look at other people and other cultures through these very personal colored glasses. I see the world differently through the lenses of the world I grew up in. My world gradually became a place where I controlled mind, body, and all altered states. Traumatized children tend to become rigid, dogmatic, or both, unless they learn to expand consciousness to new levels.

NEAR DEATH EXPERIENCE

Smothering was mother's method of keeping me quiet when she desired time off from childrearing. This was a very effective behavior modification tool that took on new meaning later in university life when I became a student of Skinner's Behaviorism.

I was probably no more than 18 months old when hospitalized as I had just begun to talk and walk. I left my body, floated between my father and the nurse at beside, and then journeyed off to meet the angels. I knew the angels were going to take me to Heaven. I refused their offer, returned to bedside floating between my father and the nurse in the same position I had occupied before journeying Heaven bound. I observed my sheet covered body, heard the doctor pronounce me dead, and saw tubes of some sort stuck in my arm and face. I then passed through the sheet and got back into my body.

This series of images was intense, and the photographic quality of the experience has lasted a lifetime. I learned that I could leave my body whenever I wanted to. At that time, I don't recall distinguishing between dream flying and daytime flying. My sense is that I sometimes went out flying during the day and other times when I went to bed; and flew either before or after falling asleep. This was a dreamy period of reality for my not yet two year old brain.

I didn't fly high or over water, as I was afraid of falling. My subjective reality, as was the case in the hospital out-of-body experience, was that my physical body always accompanied me in flight. There was no such thing as my soul or Self going out by itself and flying around; there was just one me, who was a child's conception of the resurrected body. My 18 month old Self was Catholic. Consciousness only exists, no matter how limited, when body sensation prevails.

FLYING AND ASTRAL TRAVEL

I have been a lucid dreamer and self-trained, self-directed pilot since the age of two. I learned to increase my flying distances and out-of-Earth-orbit trips gradually. The Japanese attacked Pearl Harbor when I was five, and living in Washington State. I would use my flying ability to get free of the Japanese sailors, enter the hole in the middle of their submarine, and levitate there until I fell asleep. I didn't fly off the submarine because I couldn't see land, and I didn't know how to find my way back home.

A logical interpretation emerged between my waking and dreaming consciousness that lasted for months and years. This causal explanatory loop also occurred with my flying episodes. Early on in my young years, I established a conscious connection between these two different states, but if I added in daytime flying, which a therapist would probably call hallucinations, I was mixing three different neural configurations and three different states of consciousness.

The following comments will quickly condense other major self-training that enhanced my earthly flying abilities until I became capable of off-planet flight: My 18 month old brain flew off to Heaven, which might seem like a long trip to some, but for me, Heaven was a non-physical abstraction. However, my 18 month old brain only processed concrete places. In the real world that my small child lived in, I had to gradually learn how to fly higher and over longer distances. Logical? It was very logical to my infant self.

The summer that I finished first grade, age seven, we returned to Wisconsin. I had a distinct sense of flying over and through the mountains as I sat looking out the car window. I rose above the clouds, swooped down into the valleys in a projected dream-like state that I still find pleasant in recall. By sitting just so next to the car window, I could be free of obstructing car body and experience a complete sense of flying. This was early priming for what later became Zen driving and off Earth adventures. At the time I didn't realize that one's flying sensation came from detaching mind from body. A larger problem for me at that time was keeping the two together.

The following year when I was eight, my father attempted to chop my brother's head off with an axe. I was so traumatized by this experience that I decided to leave home and go sit on the moon. I got half-way to the moon, shuddered from the cold in interstellar space, left my soul safety tucked away on an Earth-Moon flyway, and returned to the family farm near Comstock, Wisconsin. I could easily have continued on to the Moon, but experienced space as cold and unfriendly, and I then became afraid of getting lost. I knew intuitively by eight years of age that my flying could take me wherever I wanted to go. But logically, I didn't understand geography.

It was at this same time that I became intrigued with how my body could pass through the ceiling of my bedroom. I practiced moving back and forth through the ceiling but never did understand how I could violate physical laws this way. At age eight I still did not separate the flying me as being separate from my physical self, there was just one of me and body and mind all flew together. In one sense, I've now returned to this understanding. I possess an embodied self.

My next flying (OBE) enhancement occurred when I was between my 12th and 13th birthdays. We were living west of a now non-existent town called Lorraine, about ten miles west of Island City, Wisconsin. Northern Lights were beautiful that winter as it was exceptionally clear and cold, and as I watched the lights, I would become physically transported into them. I twisted and turned in space with the Northern Lights in celestial delight. My interest in astronomy became fixed for life. I often took other fictive flights into space where I felt the grandeur and majesty of those wonderful Northern Wisconsin winters; sometimes with Aurora Borealis, and sometimes with the stars and constellations.

My next out-of-body enhancement occurred when I was sixteen years old and living with a farmer uncle. His farm was open, and I could see the thunderclouds forming in the distance. Lighting and sheet lightning were common companions to these storms, and I found that by standing in the rain and looking into the dark swirling masses of clouds that were punctuated by lightning streaks, I could project myself into the storm and feel its power. The storm's energy became my energy – marvelous! I didn't just have a sense of being visually entwined as with the Northern Lights, I became part of the storm. It is a sense of oneness that is shamanic in power. Projecting into a thunderstorm permitted me to take on its energy and power as well as sharing its visual delights. Projecting oneself into nature, or a shamanic projection into an animal totem, provides a sense of oneness with the object. Those without shamanic capacity will appreciate an approximation when sympathizing with a close friend in dire need.

In addition to conquering space and projecting myself into Northern Lights and thunderstorms, I extended my subjective identification with squirrels, birds, and deer that were common to my environment. I stopped shooting small and large animals for sport by the time I was thirteen. Out-of-body projections into nature gave me an increasingly strong sense of being part of the larger universe.

Enhancement of self this way let me feel the unseen and experience its reality. This is not a cognitive-thinking process; it is a feeling state of being. A distinction dimly understood by intellectuals who think feeling and thought can be separated, or by people who think animals don't have feelings. I think it is unfortunate that traditional mental health professionals viewed these identification states as being only pathological, which is a misreading of native people's experiences when one lives close to nature.

Again in retrospect, I was training my mind to extend its reach. Gradually I learned that mind and body can be separated in altered states and still remain under self-control, and that it was acceptable to fully enjoy the experience – privately, that is. I learned that control over altered states was positive, and permitted me to experience my world and universe at a very personal level. However, I didn't fully understand what this control meant for many more years. I couldn't discuss any of these experiences with my parents as such discussions were not permitted. And I was strongly informed by mother not to discuss such things outside the family as people would think I was crazy. And, of course, she was right.

University professionals were even more condemning, because after all, without tenure, one is toast.

GHOSTS AND MOSES

I'm overlapping some of my growing subjective awareness through this chronology, but I want to be clear about how my subjective world developed: The world around me was dynamic and came to extend to the stars. I think an important point of view that you probably have already surmised is the training I was providing my brain-mind to move through and play with various altered states of consciousness. A basic awareness of these processes is critical to fully understanding a number of views presented in this book. In a similar sense one cannot fully understand controlling and consciously directing his or her dreams without first-hand experience.

I experienced what the psychoanalytic and psychodynamic community of that time described as mental illness. The difference for me was a growing sense of mastery that I controlled these states at will. From my perspective, being in altered states does not meet the criteria of being mentally ill unless these states are uncontrolled. The shaman is not mentally ill nor is the equally state bound priest performing an exorcism. This is a slippery slope of fine definition that the MMPI did not address in my day.

I don't recall exactly when my Guardian Angel, whom I came to call Moses, first appeared. I just have a sense that he was there when I came home from the hospital before the age of two. Moses was a part of my inner life. He was a frequent companion during my childhood days. He was middle aged, tall, and about two hundred pounds with dark hair and penetrating eyes. Moses has followed me through my adult years and would manifest his presence when I was reading alone up to about 2006. He has not sat on my bed or read with me since the summer of that year. Moses deserted me when I went to China to teach. Oh well, he'll just have to get along on his own.

What is amazing about Moses is his physical materialization in one of my university classrooms in the late 1970s. I assumed I was hallucinating until one of my students approached me after class and asked who he was. No one else in class was aware of him. This is the one unexplained Moses visitation in my history. The rest of the times I can explain him away with childhood imagination, hallucinations, or the historical comfort he provided me when I was experiencing trauma and loneliness.

Moses was easy to accept according to my mother's guardian angel explanation. I remember the presence of a threatening ghost by the time I was eight years old. We were living on a marginally developed farm in Wisconsin, and the ghost would nightly follow me up steep wooden stairs as I went to bed. This was a house without electricity or running water; thus I nightly entered a dark stairway of imagination. I could feel the ghost in my lower back, and then its presence would spread up my spine into the lower part of my head. I had to race up the stairs and hop under the bedding nightly in order to keep the ghost from possessing me.

My mother believed in ghosts and said they could get inside one's body and mind and take possession. I was terrified by this prospect. We moved frequently, and every old house we lived in with steep wooden stairs was haunted by this ghost. The ghost reappeared in the mid-1970s in my house on Skyline Drive in Mankato, Minnesota. The ghost only disappeared years later when I stopped dream programming and identified it as a concrete manifestation of mother's smothering attacks. .

My mother's hand had pressed with force on my lower back as she attempted to smother me in my crib. I retain a damaged disc from her attacks. Once I identified her hand on my back as the Japanese drill in that nightmare, I quickly realized who the ghost was, and its apparition has never appeared again, nor has the nightmare. A good example of how a Delaney's bridging element can be used therapeutically.

I learned a number of lessons from Moses and the ghost. Cultural definitions of super-natural happenings become real to our young minds. We search for meaning in all our various conscious states, dreaming, visioning, or any other ASC. I assume that I went off to Heaven and was visited by angels before the age of two, as these conversations were part of death definitions at that time, and for some, they still are.

Cultural definitions of supernatural phenomena such as Moses make a lot of sense to children. Our brains have limited experience, especially when we are crib bound, and logical explanations in our social world are not as easily processed as metaphorical ones with fictitious characters who occupy fictitious worlds when we are older. But most importantly, these are felt experiences, and it doesn't get more real than that.

Superstitious people raise superstitious children. In our will to survive, we transform real threats such as death at the hands of our parents, into ghosts and all manner of imaginative creatures. If I experienced paranoia as a child, it was the ghost, or my father the axe man. But the ghost was real in terms of the earlier threat to life that my mother and later my father came to represent.

Therapists inclined to define my ghost as a hallucination do not address the real problem. Such definitions in the mental health community leave concrete manifestations troubling a child's mind unattended. My university MMPI said that I was a paranoid-schizophrenic when I was 21 years old. However, by my BA graduation and after considerable undergraduate efforts to control nightmares, anxiety and depression, all of my MMPI profile fell into the normal range. As Hobson notes in *Out of its Mind: Psychiatry in Crisis*, the Diagnostic and Statistical Manual of Mental Disorders (DSM) can be very misleading. Having taught from this Manual, I totally agree.

I assume because my parents never permitted me to talk openly about my inner voices, Moses and the ghost, which were feelings made into a concrete manifestation, that socially people continued to treat me with a degree of normality that I would not have otherwise enjoyed. My parent's denial had the effect of normalizing much of my social life, and having lived in twenty different remembered locations by the time I was 15 years old meant that long-term observation by others was limited. In school, I was just a problem child, but the reader can imagine what a Freudian would do with my profile during these years.

By the time I was a university student in psychology, I was learning about mental illnesses, noting that many of the pathologies seemed to apply to me, and further noting that this self-application of pathology was common for beginning students of abnormal psychology. Moses was explained away during these early university studies as just another example of common childhood companions.

I came to my university studies believing that learned university professors understood the inner workings of our minds. In the 1950s our psyches were understood in Freudian terms. Our current conception of brain-mind unity did not exist then. Self-mastery and self-control was my father's expectation. I didn't realize how strongly his influence carried into my undergraduate university days. I gradually became aware over the years of how this influence has played out over my life time.

MIND CONTROLLING SIDEWALK CRACKS

I'm eleven years old and living in a rented house on the east side of Island City on Highway 49. I'm a country hick in bib overalls, no shoes, and usually no shirt in the summer. I'm sent into town on errands by my mother, and become an easy target for kids my own age. Their teasing, laughing, and ganging up on me are common events. I'm extremely lonely, feeling isolated, and experiencing growing dislike, if not hatred, toward the town and kids my own age.

By mid-summer, I experience the cracks in the town's sidewalk taking control of my mind. As I came to the first sidewalk, my attention would be forced downward by the cracks. The cracks demanded that I not step on them. I was forced to skip down the main street this way, but townspeople wanted to know what I was doing. I couldn't avoid the cracks as errands to the stores demanded their transit.

By eleven years of age, I knew better than to tell my parents or others about sidewalk cracks controlling my mind. I knew it was my problem and that it was unrealistic and silly, and if I were to regain control from the cracks, I would have to figure out a solution by myself. My memory of the situation is clearer now than my mind was at that time. I was bothered to say the least, extremely bothered by something well beyond my young understanding.

Out of frustration one day, I stamped a crack with my bare foot. The effect was positive and it felt good to be able to do something to get even with their torment. I stamped again and again and again. My bare feet were throbbing before I finished, but my sense of crack-mastery was growing stronger. After giving my feet a rest, I stamped a few more cracks until I sensed the sidewalk was once more just a sidewalk. This obsessive behavior did not fully return and it was only necessary for me to stamp cracks a few more times in order to have complete control. I can imagine how strong this compulsion would have been if I had permitted the pattern to continue for a year or two. Stamping cracks until my feet throbbed and the problem ceased to exist. It is worth noting that pain from stomping cracks was a welcome relief from their control. Nevertheless, I still had a strong compulsion to keep everything in order by straightening items in the house, or later on the farm, so they held their proper alignment.

In retrospect, I was learning to use behavioral controls to effect mind states. I assume now that what I accomplished by stamping cracks was breaking auto-created motor patterns that were initially activated and reinforced each time I stepped over a sidewalk crack. Later, as a university student when I studied behavior modification, it all made sense. And I came to understand that a child could teach himself B-Mod. An observant shaman would have smiled. Or even a kind parent for that matter.

DREAM PROGRAMMING

Lucid dreaming as an altered state of reality has more bizarre features than other altered states. Time and place can change rapidly, and one can instantly move from one particular physical scene to another. Hobson's dream forms are not expressed in visions, for example, the way they are in lucid dreams. Visions retain the sequential continuity of daytime experience; feelings in trance dancing approximate meditation in that one's entire focus is on mind numbing rhythmic oscillation of feeling.

Frequent nightmares returned when I entered the University of Minnesota. They were accompanied by considerable sleep disruption, anxiety, and depression. All of these factors had a major impact on my studies and grades. I had to find a solution to crippling test anxiety and sleep deprivation. I reactivated a high school interest and quickly taught myself the techniques of self-hypnosis.

Using hypnotic suggestion I programmed my dreams in the academic year of 1957-58. Every time a nightmare would appear, and I was experiencing multiple numbers nightly, I changed the characters and outcomes. Before bedtime hypnotic suggestions thus turned nightmares into pleasant dreams. A major dalliance for this 21 year old student was to replace disturbing characters with exotic lovers. I discovered fictive romance. Within a few days or few weeks, as I did not write down the actual times, my nightmares were replaced by fun and exciting dreams. I was sleeping soundly and enjoying the energy and productive focus provided by a good night's rest.

I used dream programming for twenty years. However, I noticed when I stopped active dream programming that suppressing nightmares required considerable psychic energy. I immediately experienced relief when I stopped and the psychic weight was lifted. After twenty years of dream programming, I was in good physical shape from daily jogging and felt that I was the master of both my mind and body. The nightmares returned but had less impact. My years of study, maturity, and improved mental health led to a type of unconscious dream programming that my sleeping psyche initiated on its own. I became a Kung Fu expert in my dreams and severely beat up tormenting dream characters whenever they dared confront me. I didn't preplan being a dream Kung Fu expert; my dreaming mind devised these responses on its own. Nevertheless, I thoroughly enjoyed beating up my tormenters, and I unconsciously looked forward to these dream opportunities.

Enjoyment of beating up tormenting dream characters lasted until I began to notice physical decline with ageing. Eventually, physical prowess declined to the point where I was captured by my pursuers, the capture turned into an episode of sexual molestation that I had experienced at age 14, and I identified the dream activation element. Always in dreams when I identify the bridging element causing the nightmare, the nightmare stops immediately. Interpreting dream functions may be subjective, but the causal relationships, once established by our Interpreter, have real outcomes. Consciously altering our neural circuit expressions gives us mental control over matter. This is pretty straightforward stuff.

The same effect occurred when I identified the Japanese submariner's hand as my mother's when she attempted to smother me: The nightmare stopped immediately. Lessons learned from dream programming and nightmare elimination are multiple. Conscious or non-conscious repression requires psychic energy. Nightmares must occupy select neural circuits like FAPs that form self-perpetuating cycles. Nightmare perseveration interferes with non-conscious brain-mind functions thereby reducing one's goal directed self-actualization both physically and mentally; hence the felt energy drain we experience. Anxiety associated with sleep and accompanying nightmares carries over into one's waking days, and a vicious cycle is set into motion. Lack of control encourages or initiates depression and one's energy level drops. Anxiety before bedtime can act like suggestion triggering the nightmare that one fears. And once the cycle gets going....

Nightmares represent the extreme effects of an uncontrolled non-conscious dream function. From my perspective, one of our basic dream functions is to maintain emotional equilibrium. But to a less dramatic degree, normal dreams left unexplained also exact their toll. For example, failure to identify ongoing tensions with one's spouse permits emotional state carryover from night to day and day to night.

One enjoys a higher level of emotional balance and tranquility with ability to analyze his or her dreams. Controlling nightmares and ordinary dreams not only provides improved emotional equilibrium, but also strongly suggests that this is a major function of dreams.

I gradually learned to generalize conscious control of dreams to other altered states. It's necessary to be consciously involved while our dreams are underway in order to totally create, direct, and control them. I transferred a similar level of lucidity to all other altered states. It is this self-directed control that I believe is underutilized by the mental health profession. The paradigm shift is to teach clients to direct and control their own therapy versus leaving this control with the therapist.

This is a natural shamanic process that is thousands of years old. The client believes the shaman or priest is removing the unwanted spirit, but in reality, the shaman or priest is most effective when he guides the client through his or her own self-healing process. Studying shamanic practices draws our attention to specific psychological mechanisms being tapped. Freud really did do a lot of damage to this paradigm when he presented therapists as authoritarian figures exercising micro-control. If I'm on the right track, effective treatment for PTS must become self-directed on the battle field.

Our control level over various brain states can be enhanced with the simple auto-suggestion that most contemporary therapists use to address nightmare or post-traumatic stress syndromes. But in my experience, we can gain significant or complete control over any unwanted mental state. Gradually one can learn to control their automatic (autonomic) nervous system activities such as heartbeat or pain.

As my control increased over body and mind, I came to experience a sense of mastery that felt like I could reach directly into my brain and flip switches. Self-mastery of brain states feels wonderful. The belief in ones sense of control is magnified with the instant removal of nightmare trauma or the quick elimination of anxiety and depression.

One can observe similar relief experienced by the shaman's clients. But note that I first learned to control autonomic activities such as heartbeat and pain. Secondly, I took control of nightmares and then generalized this control to test anxiety and panic attacks. As a self-therapist, I could react immediately to the sensory cues activating these responses or reactions. By the time one gets to other person directed therapy, the response has occurred with the associated neural circuit(s) strengthened. In my case, immediate self-intervention prevented strengthening these unwanted patterns; thus my contention that similar techniques should be part of military training. It's also a simple way to avoid pharmaceuticals, and thus, therapy must eliminate the startle response.

Obviously, the level of self-control I'm discussing involves incremental learning, and embedding these controls cannot be implanted with a few therapist induced hypnotic sessions. By tapping basic psychological mechanisms, the shaman can bring almost immediate relief without understanding the process itself. And in the case of the priest-shaman exorcising spirit possession, self-intervention is provided with a cross or some similar magic element to ward off further attacks. It is similar to a doctor prescribing aspirin in days gone by without knowing how the chemistry worked. In fact, in the case of aspirin it doesn't make any difference. In the case of the shaman, it doesn't either.

Let me quickly outline how I taught myself brain-mind state control using self-hypnosis. I started with small suggestions such as your hand will rise by itself. Do not move your hand, but watch it slowly begin to twitch and then rise from its resting position. Etcetera! I then used self-hypnotic suggestion to increase my attention span from twenty minutes to eight hours without a break. The eight hours were spent cramming continuously for exams as I had an overloaded schedule of classes and work.

In retrospect, I was rewiring dysfunctional neural circuits inherited from childhood. Self-hypnosis from this perspective simply permitted my Interpreter to exercise control and rewire the neuronal patterns being expressed by my core Self.

One can teach him or her Self to fall asleep almost instantly; for example, on the count of five. In like fashion, we can enjoy out-of-body experiences during normal waking states within minutes. In my experience, practice with altered states is similar to any other skill development in that continuous practice preserves the skill, and disuse is followed by gradual decline.

I trained myself over the years to create, direct, and control different types of altered states. I engaged my Genesis Journey to the beginning of the universe and time in a matter of minutes when I was past my 65th birthday. We must be rewiring our neural circuits and permanently modifying how brain chemistry is expressed in order to experience life-long effects of this nature.

As I learned to create, direct, and control each altered state from dreams to fully awake out-of-body experiences, I came to think of altered states as just being different brain-mind configurations. I'm as comfortable in altered states as I am writing these words. I remain in control and enter altered states only when I want to experiment with them, or just enjoy their effects.

I think that it's unfortunate that the mental health community doesn't teach these techniques to young people. Individual lack of control is frightening and self-reinforcing. Sensations that precede anxiety, depression, or psychotic states such as hallucinations are felt by each one of us. These sensations come to be associated with the pathology's expression. In a priming sense, whatever creates these sensations becomes the trigger that calls forth the syndrome. And I'm not discounting the possibility of wide variations in individual responses. I experienced this priming association for the first time when I was 11 years old when sidewalk cracks began to control my mind.

Individually, we experience this priming sensation as something that quickly grows beyond our control. Habituation leads to the syndrome's expression becoming permanently embedded in our neural circuits. This process generated my ghost on steep farmhouse stairs, and made concrete mind controlling cracks. Whether self-taught or culturally given, the priming effects of pathology grows. One comes to believe that a genie, evil spirits, or the urgings of Freud's unconscious are at work in their brain's black box, and is something that is beyond their personal control.

This brain-mind conditioning mechanism probably goes back 30-50,000 years or more when we Homo sapiens first developed our larger brain. It is marvelous to watch a shaman, who doesn't understand the mechanics of the brain at all, reach into a mind and flip the appropriate switch.

Another quick aside: It was time consuming in the 1990s working with adolescents and young adults in correctional treatment facilities to get past previous therapist conditioning. As the correctional treatment community shifted to cognitive-behavioral treatment strategies, many of our young clients arrived believing that their unconscious controlled their behavior. They acted out because the demons of Freud were still active. Small wonder that young people taught to believe in Freud's construction of the unconscious came to treatment with an additional burden.

I don't think we will understand the limits of using these techniques of self-control, or the range of individual differences, until sufficient methodology and protocol has been developed under research conditions. Hopefully my experiences and self-observations will be of some help to neglected millions in our criminal justice system.

PASSING THROUGH WALLS, CEILINGS, AND TRAINS

My first experience passing through a solid object occurred before the age of two when I passed through my hospital bed sheet. As I got older, it increasingly bothered me that I was violating natural laws this way. I was not permitted by parents to discuss these supernatural experiences and was simply left to my own thoughts. By the age of eight, I repeatedly moved out of my body back and forth through the ceiling of my bedroom before I went out flying. My eight year old sense was that my physical and non-material body always moved together. Out-of-body projections through solid objects have been part of my experience before my brain was fully formed. This history gives me a different perspective on altered states compared to those who experience altered states later in life or who enjoy such fictive movement in their dreams.

I discovered by accident that I was performing similar out-of-body projections while watching the movie *Ghost* in the 1980s. My wife nudged me as we watched the movie at home and asked me what I was doing. I was so absorbed passing through train walls and solid objects with the ghost in *Ghost* that I lost partial contact with my surroundings. It was just a lot of fun. I watched the movie a couple more times by myself just to enjoy the phenomena, but haven't watched it since. It's just something that I turn on and off at will. It's like enjoying singing or playing a musical instrument. It's the expression of a skill that is both satisfying and calming. It's listening to one's favorite music when the effect moves the soul.

Ability to separate mind and body subjectively has been with me all my life. It's mostly fun and it does give one a different perspective. In a parallel fashion, role playing has always been easy for me too. Out-of-body movement began in the hospital before I was two years old; consciously enhanced when I was eight and able to enjoy interstellar travel, practiced with physical phenomena of Northern Lights and thunderstorm, and carried forward into the 1980s with OBE outings in movies such as *Ghost.*

I can think of my Genesis Journey as a form of out-of-body projection or as a vision. Uncontrolled virtual reality projections are explained by most people as a vision; whereas shamanic projections that are ritually controlled and initiated are assumed to have other worldly meaning. My shamanic ritual expectation is to take on the persona of the eagle or the bear. In visions, we remain who we are and experience a separate reality; in possessing an animal or person, we typically acquire its or their identity. As a phenomenon, the experience of mind-body separation feels almost the same. And after separation of mind and body, the rest of the experience is guided by expectation, training, and environmental circumstances. The automatic tapes in our brain-minds play out.

As I grew and matured cognitively, I experimented with a large number of altered realities, both consciously and through natural self-discovery. Altered realities only seem strange to those who don't understand them, meaning those who are unable to create, direct, and control them. In like fashion, altering one's dreams while dreaming seems equally strange to many people without this capacity.

SPIRIT POSSESSION AND POSSESSING SPIRITS

Spirit possession was a fact, a reality made clear by my mother and accepted by me as being true by the time I was seven years old. Ghosts were common spirits that shared the world of my mother, and I too had a personal ghost to contend with. My childhood ghost was a manifestation of something that could not be seen; something that could pass through walls and yet be physical enough to do me physical harm.

Ghosts required attention. To keep from being possessed meant running up steep wooden steps, jumping into bed, covering myself fully with blankets, lying still, and breathing softly. How cruel is it to teach adults that the Devil is the ultimate ghost?

I became fascinated with world ethnographies as an undergraduate student, and taught a world review course my first three years as a university lecturer. Even a cursory review of preliterate world cultures brings one into contact with ghosts and spirit possession. Unfortunately, these entities and their traditional interpretations still hold sway in the 21st Century for many of the world's people.

My childhood adventures with animals in the wild, and day long adventures in the woods of N.W. Wisconsin made animals into kinfolks. I studied their habits and felt their pain. I suspect these were common feelings amongst hunters throughout the ages, as Native American people often offered prayers to the souls of their killed animals. This level of identification is experienced personally by millions of pet owners who treat their dogs or cats as children. Mirror neurons are projected across species. Now if we could just generalize this process to all humans

My first experience of consciously entering the body of another animal happened by chance. I was showing my students a movie about a N.W. Coast Indian Chief who assumed the character of his tribe's totem, the bear. He went through his ritual of becoming the bear in the film, the lights were turned down, and the classroom could be forgotten. I entered the body of the bear with the shaman and assumed its powers. It felt strange at first, but no one was in a position to observe my behavior as I sat in back of the room. I'm not sure what my physical behavior was, but I'm very aware of my psychic response. I grew in power and strength as possessing the bear became real and the Shaman-Chief disappeared. I realized at that time how easy it was to take on not only the persona, but the felt identity of another, whether animal or human. I watched this movie three times a year for three years, and enjoyed the transformation every time.

I can't imagine my ancient relatives not engaging in animal possession this way. It's a natural capacity that some of us exercise, and a capacity that probably goes back as far as modern human cognitive capacity.

A study of traditional shamanism will acquaint the reader with many forms of spirit possession and transformation that I will not try to explain here. It is a phenomenological exercise that most anthropologists do not comprehend well, if one is to believe their field reports. For me, sharing this native worldview enhanced my understanding of my Self and this basic human capacity.

Dream characters can be just as interesting as we create whomever we want to be or interact with in our dreams. As we play with dream suggestion, we gradually learn that fictive characters are entertaining and enlightening. However, a different sense of transformation occurs when we become the bear, the eagle, or any other animal. I have not experimented with becoming another person, except in play acting, as most of my early years were focused on trying to integrate a fragmented me.

We can be our Self and our dream alter ego at the same time in lucid dreams, and we can alter our character(s) so they possess superhuman powers from flying to passing through solid walls. Why should spirit possession be so hard to understand?

I recall an anthropologist that I worked with at Mankato State University. She was a linguist and devoted follower of Jesus. Some of her favorite stories were centered on how she used the spiritual power of Jesus to overcome the power of native shamans when she was working in the field. In the modern world, we would call her a cultist.

In the 1970s when she taught at MSU, the world of spirits walked out of the pages of anthropology into the minds of eager waiting students: A great story teller and easy grader, she was a favorite of favorites. Her eyes would glisten as she recounted her confrontations with superstitious shamans. I was amused. She taught me to understand mysticism more clearly than any paid professor ever did. She taught me that the cultist was the other guy, not the model of reality that one teaches from. She taught me that shamans were false believers, heathens, and spiritually of a lesser quality than she was. She taught her version of cultural relativity and the meaning of objectivity in anthropology that has so often been taken to the field by Western researchers. I liked that lady. Respect? That is another matter.

Possessing the bear or another human or animal is a simple psychic manipulation for some of us. Being possessed is a frightening experience for True Believers. We know this fact from the Catholic Church's ongoing practice and training of priests to perform exorcisms in the 21st Century. Being civilized means we don't have to burn witches anymore.

As a child, my father was alienated from the church, even though he had been raised in the Jesus tradition and had considered becoming a minister before embarking on a life of pleasure. I lived in twenty different remembered locations by the time I was fifteen, and for a majority of those years, attended any nearby church that friendly neighbors took me to.

My first observed spirit possession was that of a little five year old girl my age who became possessed by demons, as the minister ranted on about them and their coming to possess evil children. Her hysterical outburst was so strong that the service was interrupted while the minister freed her from this affliction, which was a concrete demonstration of his power, the forces of evil, and the redemption of Jesus. Oh yes, my five year old brain was mightily impressed.

Hobson is a wonderful source for anyone interested in dreams. His AIM state space model alone is worth an hour's time to review. But, for me, I like his reminder that we are crazy when we dream and that the line between being crazy and sane is thin; it is also a line that shifts back and forth as our neural circuits morph and create endless interesting configurations while being bathed in multiple chemicals from serotonin, norepinephrine, acetylcholine, dopamine and others.

Our consciousness is created moment-to-moment, reality is manufactured in our brain-minds, and the fine tuning that separates one state from another is just that: fine. But it is this capacity that lets us touch the stars, taste the dew of romantic nights, and pass through solid objects.

SPEAKING IN TONGUES

Speaking-in-tongues is the term I learned from the mouth of the same minister cited above. Another member, or maybe there were multiple members involved, would roll on the floor of this church by Lake Stevens, Washington, and speak-in-tongues. This, I learned, was a form of direct communication with either God or Jesus. I never separated the two at that young age, as I was learning to be a Trinitarian.

It was amazing to me that this strange language existed between God and people, but the minister always seemed pleased to open this channel of communication. Speaking directly to God this way was magic, and after such an experience, the individual who had just spoken to God seemed ecstatic. Their eyes glowed with the power of the supernatural, or at least that's how it seemed to me as a five year old.

Those who speak in tongues still seem to have this True Believer effect. They glow afterwards with an inner vision and light. I discovered my ability to speak-in-tongues at a Pow Wow in N.E. South Dakota. The drumming and chanting entered my mind forcefully, and I began to imitate the performer's chanting. The chanting turned into a mystic language. I enjoyed the experience for a few circles around the dance grounds, noted its effect as one would take notice of their lucid dreams, and then left dancing to join my family and friends in the grandstand. The reader can easily understand how fear of altered states deprives one of such fun and self-exploration.

I practiced speaking-in-tongues alone in the safety of my own home in order to become more fully acquainted with its effects. My voice becomes detached from conscious control in a manner similar to self-levitating arms and legs as one enters a self-induced state of hypnosis. At that time, as now, I assumed ritual was activating similar non-conscious mechanisms that I employed in self-hypnosis. Subjectively, I experienced vocalization occurring on its own, without the control normally provided by my conscious brain. It is a pleasant feeling, and I'm sure that one can attribute any meaning to this trance state that is culturally acceptable, with the minister of my five year old memory being a good example. We often forget how easy it is to explore the primitive in our civilized world.

Through conscious induction of glossolalia, I developed a different understanding of chanting and its relationship to rhythm. Speaking-in-tongues sets up a rhythmic effect that dulls my conscious mind, permitting part of it to gradually slip away as the vocalizations create a self-reinforcing oscillation of its own.

The historical connection seems lost to most Trinitarians. But Jesus and his followers practiced dancing, chanting, and speaking-in-tongues as one deduces this practice from Christian Gnostic writings. This practice is thousands of years old and remains an assumed method by which we can communicate with God. This practice is not a cultural invention. It was created with the evolution of the human brain.

This is an old tradition, an expression of reconfigured neural circuits. Actually it's fun to explore. I'll speculate, but it seems logical that once we have our modern level of higher consciousness, this neural configuration called glossolalia naturally arises given the right circumstance. Most people that I've known who practice these rituals assumed direct communication with the divine. It is an amazing redefinition of civilized behavior to watch modern practices of glossolalia while its adherents place themselves above the supernatural hierarchy of common shaman. This is another altered state that I would like to see assessed by sleep researchers.

This practice, as with many practices of the occult, seems to have more female than male adherents. This is a casual observation on my part, but one that is supported by Dean Radin's extensive review of extrasensory experiences in *Entangled Minds*. Women are generally easier to engage in discussions of feelings and subjective states of all kinds.

CEREMONIAL VISIONS

I reported a group street drug experience activated by hallucinogenic substances in my autobiography, and made a comparison with group ceremonies conducted with peyote in the Native American Church. I don't like mind altering drugs except coffee, tea, wine, or a few beers, as I have an intense need to maintain control over my various brain-mind states. Nevertheless, I found drug induced collective states on the part of my university students interesting back in the 1970s. This was the source of my initial awareness that street drug users could orchestrate a common altered state of consciousness. I report an example in my autobiography where some of my students collectively created an iceberg on a hot summer's day and sat on it to cool off.

Fatigue has always been a way to alter our conscious states, and when one adds in a few hallucinogens, the collective effect becomes more likely. Hobson talks about hypnogogic and hypnopompic hallucinations as one is drifting off to sleep or waking in the morning. If the reader has not paid attention to these hallucinations, just remain conscious enough at these times, and you will experience a background of phantoms and spirits playing with your groggy mind. Many people seem to avoid recognizing these transition states because they find them disconcerting. Being afraid of or uncomfortable with common brain-mind configurations limits one's awareness.

I don't think of hypnogogic or hypnopompic hallucinations as hallucinations, although by definition, they are. I'm aware that my brain always has multiple programs running in the background, much as my computer does. As we drift off to sleep and the world around us fades to shadows, the background programs become more prominent. This view is comparable to what happens in rhythmic dancing that leads to trance, speaking-in-tongues, or creating visions; the background becomes the foreground, and one's normal state of consciousness fades. For me, this interpretation takes the mystery out of these supposedly mystic experiences.

Hypnosis is a very personal brain-mind state that remains under my control. Most people subject themselves to a hypnotist who takes over their control and guides them through a subsequent phenomenological experience. But don't forget that the individual actually creates these altered states with guidance, and in this sense, the hypnotist is relative to the shaman. Mass hypnosis has been used by religious figures and occultists since before the time of Jesus in ancient Egypt, and is a practice that some biblical proselytizers seem especially adept at. We observe it being practiced for amusement these days by various stage performers. We observe the rhythmic language of the evangelist mesmerizing his or her followers. From an historical point of view, what's old is new, and what's new is old.

Brooks and Vogelsong offer good advice on using suggestion in one's lucid dreams. One can safely play with suggestion in the privacy of his or her own home. Or, like experiences can be had in formal ceremonial settings.

In formal or ritual settings, group expectations are established by the leader, a ritual ceremony is presented that draws the entire audience or adherents into a phase of induction, and fatigue, drugs, monotonous rhythms, emotional priming, or a combination of these elements are then used to bring forth the images or feelings desired. Anthropologists and sociologists who have not adequately understood this process often become believers after experiencing their personal transformations. Such is scientific objectivity.

Our brain's ability to create scary fictive characters in dreams is matched by our brain's ability to do the same as it transits from one brain state to another. The shadow becomes a threatening attacker; the moving light becomes an angel in motion, etc. At the end of the day, stare at an object, give the object time to imprint in your consciousness, and then look at a featureless surface and notice that the object's visual is superimposed on this bland background. This is a simple technique to remind our self of how our brain creates and superimposes images that it creates and transforms into new realities.

Images of all kinds are created and pass through various morphing versions in our dreams. We may find this strange or interesting, but we all note such transformations. Ceremonial visions are thus easy to understand in terms of our brain-minds normal and fatigued processing mechanisms. An anxious, frightened person alone in the dark can create endless threatening figures. One can come to expect the appearance and reappearance of such figures and become paranoid about them. It's so easy for our frightened psyches to skip the logic and go directly to the supernatural or mystic feelings of these experiences: Culture teachers us well.

Watch a religious revival meeting and the intense emotional atmosphere created by an accomplished revivalist. The voice mesmerizes, often music and lights are brought to play, and the audience is swept into ecstasy and rapture – not a bad feeling place to be any time. Those who consistently follow accomplished stage artists of many different kinds come for the rush, the release of appropriately effective brain chemicals, and the wonderful feelings of peace and connectedness that come to be.

You may laugh, but the therapy and good feelings are real to those in attendance. And as I've noted elsewhere, attempts to debunk these experiences as being illogical, superstitious, or meaningless, as many atheists do, are doomed to failure. What we feel is real to our psyches. Feelings are things of self that we learn to trust, and without feelings, consciousness stops: So much for the logic of Richard Dawkins.

All people with normal functioning brains appear able to access these brain states, and huge international religious movements are dependent of this shared human nature. We routinely recognize these capacities in ourselves, but what do we do with this knowledge?

ZEN DRIVING

I reported Zen driving in greater detail in my autobiography. My step-mother was dying of cancer, and I was driving back and forth between Southern Minnesota and Northwestern Wisconsin every weekend for about six months. This followed ten months of similar driving as my father died of esophageal cancer the previous year. The trip home usually occurred after dark, and to alleviate the boredom, I would engage in Zen driving for the two plus hour trip.

Zen driving as I know it smacks a little of my jogging days experiences. While jogging, it is easy to let the rhythm of our body come under control of our core consciousness. The mind relaxes, the feet are controlled reflexively by the spinal cord, and we drift off, oblivious to most of the scenery around us. A similar effect is reported by motorcycle riders, but this I only know second hand. Many readers have experienced this phenomenon firsthand. But, what is happening in our brains when this dual state of consciousness comes to visit? What is active—right brain/left brain; or perhaps new brain or old brain? One half of a dolphin's brain sleeps well the other watches, but I'm not a dolphin. However, I think I can identify the dolphin's state of mind.

My subjective experience in a Zen driving trance feels like my body takes over the hard work automatically, thereby freeing my more highly evolved conscious mind to drift off and do whatever it wants. The sensation approximates that of rhythmic jogging where the feet and legs do the work while the brain relaxes: Nothing mysterious so far, as most of us have experienced this effect. With a little self-training, Zen states can be called up on command and directed at will. I don't think playing with altered states this way diminishes consciousness; brain state games of this nature let me explore a fuller range of my brain-mind abilities. And in doing so, I'm able to compare one conscious state or sub-state to another.

I use this as an example of the endless ways we can reconfigure our brain states. I have probably played with more brain states than most readers, but many of you have learned to use different brain states such as lucid dreaming for fun and understanding. I think each time we reconfigure another set of neural circuits, we increase our understanding of Self and the capacities of our fellow beings. And we might even understand dolphins better. I don't need to understand all the physiology behind altered states, but I do want to understand how to create and control their phenomenological expression. In my personal history, this understanding was generalized to intervene in and control various forms of personal pathology.

Zen driving permits me to remain in an alert state for long periods of time. The effect is similar to giving my Self a hypnotic suggestion to stay alert and attentive during long road trips. It always works. In Zen driving, one feels they are flying two feet above the road instead of driving on it. The rhythm of the car becomes one with our body. The rolling hills of Western Wisconsin provide a gentle undulating effect approximating wave action off the sunlit Oahu beaches. Visual processing of the road ahead seems to be directly connected to my hands and the steering wheel, and not to my brain. My hands move effortlessly, reflexively, and require no energy.

One normally senses driving tiredness when the brain signals energy expenditure. This is not the case with Zen driving, or automatic writing. My brain doesn't tire, because it is just along for the ride.

The separation of and selective use of my senses is just being expressed differently in Zen driving than it is in normal driving. Accomplished shamans, revival preachers, mass hypnotists, and trance capable prophets all know how to separate conscious states. Most do not understand the physiology, but instead, they just practice effective ritual. Priests and shamans are after effects which do not require understanding brain-mind states. Engaging automatic brain processes probably accounts for the reported fact that those who practice automatic writing for hours do not feel tired afterwards. This is the effect DARPA seeks, but their usual approaches ignore these basic aspects of physiology.

I no longer think of altered states as being abnormal. One state seems about as natural as another, and I subjectively know the differences between altered states. Most people do not play with brain states this way. I generally experience other altered states like I do lucid dreaming, as just another shift in brain-state space.

I think there will be an increasing number of people learning to control states of consciousness for both recreational and therapeutic reasons as neuroscientists make explicit the underlying brain-mind mechanisms. The point I'm emphasizing is that the critical element in dreams, altered states, and mental illness is learning self-control. And self-control can be easily self-taught, at least for some of us.

My interpretation of how Zen driving is possible recognizes our Old brain and evolutionarily New brain. In dream programming, for example, I experience a dual state of consciousness. I can watch my dream unfold and even direct the dream while I'm dreaming, or I can have a dream within a dream: I'm defining ability to control this dual state as meta-consciousness. Meta-consciousness means that our Interpreter observes, sometimes relaxes, but always remains in control of its various subsystems. Moving across altered states with controls supports this perspective.

We have the ability to be active in two or more states of consciousness at the same time. Lucid dreams exhibit this capacity. However, my Old brain doesn't have the autobiographical abilities of my New brain, to use a term from Damasio. My Old brain tends to live in the moment, and survives like a hunting dog by just doing what is necessary in any given moment. Nevertheless, my Old brain can drive a car quite well without all the normal autobiographical input.

I'll take an example from Ramachandran to help clarify Zen driving. In blind-sight, damage to one side of the visual cortex results in a patient being totally blind on the other side, yet these patients can reach out and touch something they conscientiously state they cannot see. The upshot, according to R.V.S. is that the Old brain still sees even though the New brain is not conscious of seeing. Consciously tap this mechanism, in my opinion, and you have Zen driving.

Zen driving and a raft of similar dual state experiences fit nicely into the research model developed by Ramachandran: "Believing is Seeing" (2004: 24-39).

I have this dual awareness while dreaming, Zen driving, trance dancing, possessing the body of the bear, etc. Dual states are so common when we analyze altered states that they are impossible to miss. For one to miss how the shadows of our brain-minds flirt with dual states, we must be altered state phobic. Fear of losing control over our waking state of consciousness is a major factor in not exploring altered states for most people. Not feeling comfortable talking about altered states is an additional burden. Being socially stigmatized by admitting altered states is a knowledge killer.

THE FLIGHT OF SLEEPING BIRDS

Birds that fly long distances are often observed sleeping while in flight. I'm guessing, but it seems likely that they are duplicating my Zen driving or engaging in brain state control similar to the dolphin. If I were a bird, I would just zone out and cruise the same way I drive. But, my wings are a little frayed. Birds run on neural circuits the same way I do. If evolution gives me this capacity driving on the ground, it can surely give birds a similar mechanism after a few million years of development. My core self is placed on automatic pilot with Zen driving by my more evolved autobiographical Self, but for birds, I suspect the equivalent of core Self is hardwired for flight and performs its activity through evolutionary adaptation. Dolphins with half their brain sleeping, long-distance sleeping flying birds, and Zen drivers – what do we have in common? Evolution, which creates and passes on biological mechanisms. How could it be otherwise?

The US Military's Defense Advanced Resource Project Agency (DARPA) gives out millions of dollars to study research of this nature. And, as I'm waiting for my check to arrive in the mail, I'll spill the rest of the beans from my 1958 undergraduate self-experiments. Self-hypnosis can be used to maximize attention, concentration, and states of alertness. Self-hypnosis permits us to separate and execute activities of the core and autobiographical selves. I've given examples a number of times in two previous books, but the short answer is practice.

I don't know how many days I could last without sleep, which is one of the goals of DARPA, as I've never tried. I do know that staying alert, awake, and performing operations such as driving a car long distance depends on one's physical condition. I don't think two weeks without sleep is reasonable, but somewhere between three and five days with near normal efficiency seems to be. If this effect were enhanced with drugs … who knows? Of course, a critical element in this mix of surviving without sleep is the degree of alertness desired. There's another trick possible, but I'll make DARPA pay for it.

AUTOMATIC WRITING

I have not practiced automatic writing, but I've observed a close friend who uses it extensively. It was in the 1990s when she encouraged me to join her, but by then, experimenting with altered states had lost its fascination for me.

I was aware well before the 1990s that personal expectations and practices with altered states would give me the results I wanted. I'm quite sure that nothing is going to emerge from automatic writing that is not available to me in other states of consciousness. This may seem contradictory to the reader, as I encourage experimentation with altered states. However, once my level of control reached the point of dream lectures and Genesis flights to the beginning of time, I preferred to remain in my normal states of heightened consciousness. I naturally fly now and then in my dreams, project myself into animations or enjoy an occasional trance, but not often.

My comments on observing automatic writing follow an approximation of creating a vision like Huxley's age regression or my Genesis Journey. We detach one set of neural circuits from our conscious control, and let other neural circuits express themselves automatically. Automatic is probably a misnomer, as the writing is still being directed by other sub-systems of one's brain-mind but with less input from our Interpreter.

My friend can write for hours without fatigue even though she is not the athletic type. She has come to channel for a doctor who lives 50 years in the future. She is a True Believer. I conducted two experiments with her. One to find the correct lottery number for mega-millions, and the other to explain an esoteric hypothesis related to string theory. Needless to say, the lottery number didn't work, and the physics explanation was off the wall at a Junior High level of understanding.

Failure to understand altered states is rampant in world cultures. Treating ASC as garbage, stupid, superstitious, reflections of mental illness, or even worse, believing these states to be reflections of normal reality from the Netherworld, perpetuates manipulation by the cultists. My friend is bright, educated, as sane as 99.9 percent of us, and a believer in automatic writing. My hypothesis: Automatic writing is just another form of scrambled neural networks. Note that automatic writing as a human capacity probably existed tens of thousands of years before writing. It is an easily studied form of altered states. I cover it here as an example of one more altered state that reflects neural circuit reshuffling.

WAKING VISION

I have experienced three rather profound waking visions:

   1.) My Genesis Journey where I travel to the beginning of time;
   2.) The vision of a returning soul to a group ceremony given in his honor; and
   3.) My 18 month old near-death experience.

I assume my near-death experience occurred in a nearly unconscious state of oxygen deprivation, hence, the reader might question my classification: Was it a vision or a lucid dream? I must be careful not to get lost with definitions. For example, if I discriminate too closely between dreams, visions, trances, or spirit possession, I miss the main point of creating these varied altered states through altered neural circuit combinations.

When I initiate, direct and control altered states, I have a different perspective than others who can't control them, or go through certain rituals to activate these varied states without understanding them, or usually as the case is, taking on cultural explanations that are thousands of years old. Readers who practice dream suggestion and dream programming understand this difference subjectively. In like fashion, one does not experience the complexity of a great musical composition just by listening. True appreciation requires a deeper level of involvement.

The upshot of my interpretation is that we can mix and match altered states to the extent of our own brain's complexity. I think a good place to start a comprehensive classification of altered states is by expanding Hobson's AIM Model of state space. I believe field anthropologists are remiss for not developing a researchable typology or model in their study of shamans and shamanism that is based on neuroscience. On the other hand, when the academic anthropologist is primarily worried about publications and tenure, it is understandable why the current state of affairs exists in shamanic field research.

A last point: Using drugs to induce waking visions must introduce modifications in how normal brain chemicals are released, and neural circuitry is activated, beyond what occurs when I induce these states without drug assists. I believe that comparisons between these different activation procedures will be helpful in our larger understanding of consciousness and altered states, and perhaps make a small contribution to our understanding of mental illness. I predict that involvement of our higher centers of consciousness will be the main distinction.

Hobson, in my reading, is in general agreement with the above assumption about the multiplicity of states which our brains are capable of. He says:

[Consciousness] is multifocal and is dynamically regulated by brain processes that are subject to myriad controlling and disrupting forces. Even normal consciousness is a balancing act, for madness is never far beneath the surface of our outward calm. [The] wonder is not that so much madness exists, but that there is so little (1999: 205).

It seems to me that we can create just about any combination of brain states that we choose. It may take a little priming and practice, but the opportunities are there and we don't need to use drugs. If we can alter brain states with such ease, and if madness or insanity is never far below the surface, why do we rely so heavily on pharmaceutical drugs?

Each new research finding or insight into the workings of our brain-minds and consciousness reduces the playing field for charlatans. An exposed mind is necessary to create a world free of superstition, hypocrisy, and mutual self-destruction. Neuroscience has become the new source of wisdom, not Socrates or prophets of mysticism.

OTHER WORLDS AND UNIVERSES

Perseveration of activity in our neural circuits is something we all experience. I often have a song going through my head for hours, and sometimes this song will repeat for days. We have just passed through the Christmas Holidays as I write these words, and two different songs kept repeating an endless number of times: "Here comes Santa Claus, here comes …." and, "Frosty the snowman …" My Chinese stepson was practicing these songs and my own mind couldn't ignore the constant reinforcement.

What I've experienced in a number of the above referenced altered states, such as mind controlling cracks and speaking-in-tongues, is something akin to this type of perseveration. My neural circuits seem stuck in an old record's groove, and I can't get the needle out. In a similar fashion, perseveration that approximated facilitated action patterns were expressed when my childhood ghost manifested, or manic-depressive or obsessive-compulsive feelings emerged to control my moods or behavior. This neural activity feels much like my experience with the repeating Christmas songs.

My eleven year old brain learned how to stop and then control sidewalk cracks better than my current brain was able to stop repeating Christmas songs. I couldn't overcome the constant reinforcement of my stepson singing these songs repeatedly. In my experience, self-reinforcement at this level maintains PTS, severe anxiety, and depression.

I only know one gift-of-tongue, or glossolalia junkie. This woman constantly moves from one fundamentalist church to another. She moves every time the minister disagrees with her interpretation of Christianity. But with every new church she finds salvation, and proselytizes as actively for one as another. Her eyes light up with inner vision, a near rapture expression emerges, and she can go on as long as her audience will listen about the wonders of her revelations. She lives in a world of altered states where perseveration of Christmas songs never stops. I'm guessing, but discussion of my subjective altered states would most likely seem bizarre to her. Her reality is an unshakeable altered state fueled by dogma and about-to-happen rapture.

The spirit world of the shaman or major adherents to world religions represents a cultural reality come one's own reality. It is a new universe. It is a universe that is just a real as the one that you and I daily manufacture when we convert external stimuli into continuous consciousness. It is a universe that maintains meaning and continuity when meaning, value, and sensation are mixed in the wonderful ways our brain-minds mix these elements to create our everyday waking illusions. These everyday waking illusions are constructed, as the social psychologist says, moment-to-moment, and day-to-day. It's the same process, just different realities.

When social institutions of religious dogma support altered reality illusions, there is social acceptance, although it is sometimes given begrudgingly. When professionals create similar dogmas, we may call them Freudians rather than shamans, or just support the local priest performing exorcisms.

From this perspective, I think my life is richer, fuller, and more interesting because I have mastered altered realities. In a similar vein, my life became richer and more complex when I mastered dream programming. I enter and leave alternate states at will, enjoy them, but don't become addicted to them as my speaking-in-tongue acquaintance does. I have more compassion for her and for the borderline personality converts she seeks, and for those struggling souls who have not yet mastered their own brain-minds and suffer from uncontrolled brain-mind states.

Buddhist Enlightenment, higher states of consciousness, a fuller awakening, and numerous other terms are used to describe transcendence in dreams and trances. Dream researchers like LaBerge write with affection regarding these terms. I address mysticism and the mystic in *Mind of the Mystic,* and I believe that concepts of enlightenment must be refined. They must be brought into the light of scientific interpretation. Enlightenment through another mystic interpretation is not enlightenment. I have manipulated more mystic states, along with decades of dream control, than most people who define themselves as mystics. My definition of mystic contains an element of the supernatural, i.e., something that is not explained in this world. And here I place the Netherworld mystic assumption of souls by the Dalai Lama.

The source of ecstasy in the Big Event of dreams or other altered states seems obvious. We bring together select neural circuits that connect new neural configurations, which in turn release brain chemicals that maximize our sense of well-being, thereby creating a harmonious relationship between mind and body.

All of these processes occur outside our normal waking abilities. To enter and leave altered states at will provides us with new tools that can be used to understand them. This level of control does not diminish ecstasy, the drama of the Big Bang, or the overwhelming sense of well-being and belonging. How could it, we have to engage the same neural circuits and brain chemistry? What is different is how we use our Interpreter.

I'm still composed of the same elements, the same mind, and the same body; I have just reconfigured neural circuits in my brain to create a different subjective experience. I don't think of it as being on an astral plane or entering another universe of Beings. That line of thought denigrates my capacity as an evolved, sentient being. I believe that true enlightenment means both understanding and mastering these processes. One cannot master skiing through study alone.

ALTERED STATES REVISITED

It seems reasonable in terms of contemporary neuroscience that consciousness is a process and its activation and maintenance is distributed across the brain's architecture. We can identify specific subsystems and locations in the brain that shut down consciousness, but the point I'm making here is the fluidity and distributive nature of consciousness. As Hobson says:

[The] line between external stimulus 'waking reality' and internal stimulus 'dream fantasy' is always thin and always shifting. The line between madness and sanity, however firm, may also be quite thin, as our discussion of disorder of modulation will shortly reveal. Consciousness is a many-splendored thing, but some of its splendors are both terrifying and disabling (1999: 202).

My mother described my involuntary loss of consciousness as epileptic fits. I never read my formal medical diagnosis, but I'm reasonably certain our family doctor never wrote it down. Rural doctors in the 1930s had limited understanding of epilepsy, and knowing my family doctor when I was older reinforces my belief. According to our family doctor, I'm quite sure he saw mother's strong suit being one of child neglect, as he attributed the death of my two sisters to this factor.

Hobson says:

Interestingly, mounting evidence suggests that in schizophrenia, the temporal lobe is dysfunctional in ways akin to temporal lobe epilepsy. Recall that epileptic patients, like schizophrenics, may become quite paranoid as they struggle to explain their strong internally generated perceptions in terms of the motives of people in their surroundings (Ibid: 206).

I don't recall the black-outs I experienced when I came home from the hospital after my near-death experience. Mother talked of them, but what I do remember is petit mal type symptoms that lasted until I was at least eight years old. By the time I was eight, I had learned to sit down and go limp when blackout symptoms became evident, pause, take a break, and let my brain refocus. People would ask me what I was doing, and I would say something like, "I'm just catching my breath." In that most of my early life was filled with hard physical labor, this was usually an acceptable explanation.

As I've noted elsewhere, my University of Minnesota MMPI still recorded critical elevation on its schizophrenic scale. Attention deficit hyperactive disorder (ADHD) is much better understood now than when I was a grade-school child. I was usually bored with school, experienced two schools on average each year, and remember only a blur of different teachers. What I remember most about teachers is they didn't like me, and I didn't like them.

I recall bothering others in the classroom, and I have more memories of looking out the window then looking at the blackboard, drumming on my desk with pencils, and being a problem child on the playground.

Today, the doctors would've filled me with stimulants to slow me down, which was a common approach to treating children with ADHD. I suspect that my behavior was often irritating enough that when I did have lapses of consciousness, teachers were just relieved. But by the time I entered school, first grade as I didn't attend kindergarten, attacks would drop me to my knees, I would struggle to refocus, and seconds later, I would be able to talk.

I recount these interpretations for the informed reader who can place his or her diagnosis and conclusions over mine. My history growing up was complex. When I retook the MMPI as a young BA level probation officer in the early 1960s, my profile was completely in the normal range. Our onsite consulting psychologist interpreted the profile as being normal, and my profile being representative of what he called a complex personality. I lost my copy of this MMPI to a spring snow flood years ago; thus, I cannot go back and provide details. I later learned to give and read this test under tutelage from this psychologist, who was also the MMPI Instructor at Mankato State University.

I've shared details from my developmental history in order to provide background for readers with different perspectives, or for those who wish to pursue their own altered realities.

Sharing Minds

Fly on mystic wings,
And sore to universes unknown.
Fear knows only itself,
Let us be brothers and sisters.

CHAPTER 12

MODEL APPLICATIONS: DREAMS AND VISIONS

INTRODUCTION

I woke up a little earlier this morning at 5:00 a.m. I lay in bed unable to go back to sleep as a vague, undifferentiated dream kept running through my mind. I'm either in a large field or a large room, the scenes vary, and I'm explaining different aspects of these large enclosures to others around me. At 5:00 a.m. these scenes and thoughts are banal and insignificant. I don't like being kept awake by something that is so insignificant.

It's 6:00 a.m. and I give in; might as well make some coffee and read the Sunday paper. But, as I get up, I'm flooded with reference to these large dream spaces. They are state spaces from Hobson's AIM Model. This emerging awareness is outlining the main sub-units for this chapter. I put coffee on and heat some hot cereal in the microwave, sit down and flesh out the rest of this chapter's outline.

Dream metaphor can be confusing. But, the metaphor in dreams follows my brain's daytime use quite closely. I didn't identify the meaning of the dream's spatial metaphor while I was still dreaming. The meaning of the dream's spaces came into my consciousness as I transited into wakefulness, and at that moment, Hobson's AIM Model emerged as reference. At a metaphorical level, space and state space came together. My dream comparison is balance on my bike and a balanced checkbook.

Hobson's three dimensional AIM space was associated with actual physical space in my dream. This is an example of simple metaphor, whereas balance on my bike and a balanced checkbook is more complex. At a less than conscious level in the dream, my mind was considering application of state space to the sections of this chapter. Because my dream's use of space was primary metaphor, my Interpreter did not connect the dots until I became fully conscious.

The subliminal level of analysis was completed without dream lectures or specific state space conversations. I don't solve every waking problem in my dreams by sleeping on them any more than I do when I consider the matter when awake. But I can observe the difference between primary and complex metaphor in my dreams as exemplified by this example. The fact that I woke up an hour early suggests that the dream thought process was completed.

Triangulation of my dreams and waking consciousness is often necessary to complete the problem solving work taking place just below the surface of my autobiographical Self and its metaphorical presentation at the level of my core Self. Dream analysis requires that I pay close attention to brain state transitions, as often it is at this juncture that awareness enters consciousness. The "aha" emerging in my dreams is about equally divided between in-dream and dream transitions. And, in this dream, organizational structure for this chapter took precedence over AIM Model application to chapter contents. My waking logic would normally follow this thought sequence as well.

Symbolically, the reader will note that new information can be gained during transitions from our dreaming to awaking states without the use of any bridging elements. As my waking consciousness emerges, it brings all the subliminal machinations of the night into awareness. Symbolically, the large spaces in my dreams and my attempt to identify their various physical components were directly related to the AIM model. Focus on your dream and let your Self wake slowly and naturally to experience the full effect of this emerging awareness.

Sequentially, over the night subliminal processes have sorted out a problem bubbling just below the surface. I can become aware of the solution while the dream is in progress or at the time of waking. The consistency with which this sequence is expressed in my dreams adds fuel to the idea that intensification of hallucinations in early morning REM are the culmination of complex mental manipulations going on during the course of a night's dreams. In late morning REM, the pieces that have been bubbling below the surface come together.

I earlier referenced this sequence of intensifying morning REM hallucinations with the bike balancing FAP where I ride my dream bike over impossible terrain. Also focus on hypnopompic imagery. But for me, the visuals are often lacking as thought quickly dominates my waking moments.

My interpretation of Hobson's AIM Model and its application to altered states follows. The key point of AIM for me was that state space transitions could be associated with many different conscious sub-states of altered realities. Further, conceptualization of altered states of consciousness in state space deemphasizes pathology. Altered realities may not be common statistically, but when one develops capacity to create, direct, and control them, they become just another alternative expression of brain-mind capacity and consciousness. Although I've used self-hypnosis extensively in the past, I've never used hypnosis to enter altered states other than dreams.

HOBSON'S STATE SPACE MODEL (AIM 2001)

AIM stands for Activation-Input-Output Gating-Modulatory Status. This sounds like a mouthful, but the visual model is quite simple. It's a cube of three dimensions in which one places any particular state of consciousness according to the components of AIM, as you can note the components from the bold type in the label.

The human brain is conscious… it organizes its activities… first through awareness, second through a sense of a self that is aware, and third through the awareness of awareness (Ibid: 6)." "Fortunately for the scientist interested in these matters, the attributes of consciousness tend to be organized in a correlated manner, resulting in what are called states. By states we mean syndromes or clusters of attributes. When we speak of altered states of consciousness, we refer to the tendency of consciousness to be at a higher or lower level, to be concerned with external or internally generated data, and to be organized in a linear logical or parallel analogical fashion, and to be more or less affect driven (Ibid).

The three major components that alter consciousness are:

[Activation], corresponding to the raised or lowered level of consciousness. The second is input-output gating, corresponding to the provenance of the information processed. The third is modulation corresponding to the way in which the information is processed (Ibid: 6-7)."

Factor A is activation, the energy level of the brain and its component parts; factor I is the information source; Factor M is the modulatory status of the brain, which is determined by the chemical systems to which the information is subjected.

Hobson then visualizes a three dimensional cube in which he can physically place the state space occupied by any specific state of consciousness.

Methodologically speaking, it should be clear that waking consciousness is a many splendored thing. That is to say, waking can be associated with an infinite set of conscious sub-states, no one of which is easily singled out as typical, stable, or even normal in a statistical sense (Ibid:8).

Dreaming from Hobson's point of view is superior in its capacity to create virtual reality and is a marvel of auto-creativity. He therefore sets the stage from which to compare different space state types of consciousness, which I find meaningfully adapted to other ASC.

As with V. S. Ramanchandran, I find methodology crucial to any research that pushes boundaries in existing paradigms or models. AIM is a helpful model as it permits typological comparisons between various states of consciousness. State space conceptualizations take away the idea that anything besides normal daytime consciousness has a pathological component. This line of thinking that deviation from normal meant pathology, I believe, was erroneously introduced by Freudian oriented thinkers in the 20th Century. It is unfortunate, as scientific study of altered states has been approached from the position of pathology, or at best, mythology.

I had to dissect this perspective in order to make sense of my own dreams, nightmares, and other altered states. The opposite interpretation to pathology is the curative use of altered states employed by shamans for centuries.

I want to revisit form and content before we move on. Hobson says that: "Consciousness is always about something (Ibid: 9)."

Different channels in waking consciousness can be separated such as the verbal and perceptual nonverbal. We used to think that there was such a thing as "pure reason," until folks like A. Damasio came along and made it impossible to totally separate feelings from cognition.

"Emotional salience is an aspect of content that interacts directly with the form of consciousness (Ibid: 10)."

Emotion is always there with many feelings constantly being generated. I always feel something; my body is felt along a continuum of heightened or lessened awareness as I change conscious states, but it is always there. When it is gone, I am gone; thus, "Til death do us part."

Hobson says:

Without meaning to be confusing, we must distinguish form and content because they are inseparable. As far as altered states of consciousness are concerned, it is often the formal aspects that are emphasized: to have visions, internal stimuli must become predominant; to have intense visions, they must become very predominant, and when visions become intense, they are more likely to become exotic, numinous, or preternatural, and thus to suggest other-worldliness. To understand the visions of altered states, we had better understand how the form of visual processing is altered at the level of the brain (Ibid: 11).

Additionally, Hobson notes that "Most of the zones of the state space are in fact, forbidden (Ibid: 18)."

We can tamper with "… the three dimensions of space boundary," through brain damage, hypnosis, and psychedelic drugs (Ibid: 18-19)."

I do not experience altered states as being forbidden when I enter and leave them at will. We can learn to move between various states as I've presented such movement in this three volume series. I have demonstrated in my autobiography that once one has activated related neural circuits, due to any cause, we can learn to consciously activate, direct, and control these circuits.

The altered circuit configurations that are also known as hypnotic trance that we call visions, that we call lucid dreaming, and all the myriad combinations of entering, combining, or leaving such states. This is another version of the hard problem.

Subjectively, we are just bringing together neural circuits which use different combinations of the same mechanisms from dreams to visions, and so on. Thus, fewer of the zones of state space are forbidden once we consciously learn how to control movement between them. With learned control, normally forbidden state spaces come under our command. Commanding formerly forbidden state space, from my perspective, is an expression of expanded consciousness.

Entrance to forbidden state space is only pathological when control is lacking. What happens to the state space in Hobson's cube if we control all of it and how does this change personality assessment like the MMPI?

My brain is plastic and flexible, and can be activated in many magical, wonderful ways. I leave it to the neural scientists to place these many altered states, along with dreaming, in their appropriate state spaces.

Repeating Hobson: "That is to say, waking can be associated with an infinite set of conscious sub-states, no one of which is easily singled out as typical, stable, or even normal in a statistical sense (Ibid:8)."

I think it will be necessary to duplicate each ASC in the laboratory and thereby configure relevant state spaces as envisioned by the AIM Model. Further, our goal should be to establish therapeutic protocol for entering and leaving each state space through natural means and without drugs.

Placing all altered states within the AIM Model should be just as helpful to our understanding of consciousness as those states modeled by Hobson. Therapeutic methodology suggests that we can learn to control normally forbidden state spaces. Following this argument, a comprehensive review of how to control all altered states seems warranted.

The interested reader can find a straightforward version of Hobson's formal presentation of the AIM model and numerous state space visualizations in *The Dream Drugstore*.

I'VE GOT RHYTHM

When I began to actively experiment with self-hypnosis, I started small with simple finger, arm, and leg movements. As I taught my brain to assume control over these body parts by just thinking about movement, I gradually learned to generalize this capacity to heartbeat, temperature changes in my hands and feet, selective elimination of pain in my body, etcetera. Once these capacities were embedded in my neural circuits, I could move in and out of activation and control in seconds, or at most, one or two minutes when I demonstrated this capacity in daytime settings with friends.

Awareness of altering normal brain functions this way sensitized me to the possibility that I could control any area of Hobson's forbidden state space. However, in 1957/58 I didn't have access to this terminology. I did learn from experience, however, that my Interpreter was capable of creating control through Free Will. My personal history made me receptive to this capacity, and formal education gave me the interpretations that I share with readers.

Rhythm impacts my brain in ways that bring forth state changes. When I was between seven and nine years of age, we lived on a small farm in Northwestern Wisconsin. No electricity meant pumping water by hand. In the winter, I pumped furiously when the temperatures were 20-30 degrees below zero, and in doing so, activated petit mal type seizures. My mind would fuzz-out and I would lose control and drop to the ground, gradually recovering and getting to my knees, and then getting up to return to pumping. Gradually I learned to vary pumping rhythm in order to avoid blackouts. Select rhythmic motion can still activate trance for me.

I've enjoyed the outdoors all of my life, and have camped and traveled much of North America. Dogs running on suspension bridges or bridges with limited anchorage will begin to move rhythmically and start resonating with my brain. The feeling is much like pumping water in Northwestern Wisconsin, or jogging long distances.

I reported in my autobiography how I discovered ability to enter trance while dancing at a Native American PowWow. Focusing on the drumbeat and matching its rhythm puts me into trance. Chanting and dancing on ceremonial grounds or in my living room to recorded drum music puts me in trance. Strobe lights or flickering florescent lights move me to the border of trance; I must exit this stimulus or close my eyes to keep directed focus on the here and now.

My brain is sensitive to this type of stimuli. If I go into trance, any manner of imagery will be produced, just as it is with dreaming. I can control altered state activation or let it occur naturally. I prefer self-control. I did not like the undifferentiated sensations that came from near entrance to the plasma field in my Genesis Journey. My Interpreter associated the plasma field in my Genesis Journey with an uncontrolled trance state. I do not like psychedelic drugs for the same reason.

I do not experience hypnogogic hallucinations at the beginning of sleep or hypnopompic imagery when waking as being bothersome. In fact, hypnopompic imagery is often associated with problem resolutions, but as a child, these phenomena were often experienced as being unpleasant. I don't recall separating these phenomena from night terrors.

Being subject to epileptic fits was uncomfortable, because they set me apart from normal persons, and were a constant reminder that parts of my life were beyond my control. Understanding these phenomena was beyond the ability of my family and social circle. The feedback I got was "don't talk about them;" meaning "you are either crazy or communing with the spirits, and communing with the spirits is another form of being crazy," or so the implications went during my childhood.

Jogging sets a rhythm that can have an effect similar to dancing, chanting or drumbeats: Why not? It's the same brain, same neural circuits, and same history. Neuroscience has a lot to say about brain oscillation in neural circuits. Increase the running distance for joggers or driving fatigue on a motorcycle, and one begins to understand this phenomenon from a subjective point of view: Rhythm takes over.

I practiced Zen driving during the time my step-mother was dying of cancer. The two-lane state roads winding through Western Wisconsin back to Rochester, Minnesota are tree-lined, wooded and offer a very relaxing drive, especially after dark. Flying two feet above the highway at 60 miles an hour approximates the trance-like feeling I get from jogging or dancing. Detaching mind from body, I'd let my mind relax and give conscious control to my body, that is, core Self.

Using the concept of a facilitated action pattern (FAP), I was driving a course from my stepmother's in NW Wisconsin to my home in Southern Minnesota that I had driven many times for years. I was physically tired and somewhat emotionally drained as I watched this very significant person in my life slowly die. Zen driving gave the neural circuits in my brain freedom to reconfigure themselves in a manner consistent with my maintaining a sense of well-being and equilibrium. I couldn't dream pleasant thoughts while driving, but I could enter an altered state that counteracted my growing sense of sadness and forthcoming loss.

Jogging, Zen driving, trance states from dancing or chanting all have something in common: The neural circuits in my waking consciousness are being selectively activated. In Zen driving, one level of consciousness, or neural configuration, takes a holiday while the other part pays attention. It is almost as though there were two of me: One me is driving the car, and the other is relaxing. Am I dividing my brain circuits in a manner uncommon to normal waking activity or am I accessing different forms of consciousness that my brain uses between waking and dreaming? Am I a bird that flies while sleeping or a dolphin with half its brain asleep?

When I concentrate long hours on any complex task, I come away with a sense of mental fatigue. Employing automated fixed action patterns seems to consume almost no energy. At least, the energy consumed is minimal and seems to be replaced while the process is going on. In Zen driving, as for those engaging in automatic writing, enhanced brain-mind capacities are being executed. I consciously select the neural circuits and networks to be employed, activate embedded FAPs, and let my normal waking consciousness relax. With Zen driving, one does not experience normal tiredness. In fact mental tiredness will tend to dissipate.

FAPs are a wonderful invention of evolution – efficient, energy saving, and the mechanism that frees up our higher cortical centers for other activities. In Zen driving, we just put our brains on automatic pilot. An accomplished pianist must be employing embedded action patterns at least this complicated.

What I experience from an inside-out perspective is two distinct parts of me, and I don't mean the sane me and the crazy me. I mean the 95 percent of my brain's non-conscious activity that is coordinated and controlled below my normal waking consciousness. I engage my "autonomic" Coordinator that directs core consciousness to take charge of Zen driving, while my higher order Interpreter basically takes a holiday and relaxes. This is one step up from jogging where the Controller automatically puts one foot in front of the other, and the Interpreter tunes out as one runs in front of an oncoming car. A slight shift in micro-circuits and we have Zen driving.

I'm aware of my Controller performing these functions. I'm aware that my Interpreter is observing and is still in charge, and that my Interpreter is aware of my Controller's role. I'm aware that I'm aware. I think this process is no more complex than self talk.

Evolution has given us this capacity and it is a qualitative difference from being a rat or a cat. I'm not schizophrenic, but if I had related this experience to a therapist during the 1950s, I would most likely have been considered crazy. But what fun it is to play with altered states, and, I think, one step closer to understanding consciousness, our many brain states, and how these states can become scrambled.

Enhancing my normal states of consciousness opens new creative options. In my experience, control of altered states is mind enhancing. Control of altered states permits one to employ consciousness experiments not available to those occupying a single closed state space. Enhancing consciousness permits all the different types of brain sub-system cross communication, and leaves it under our control. And, I suggest that control of altered states open our neuronal spreadsheet to greater processing.

VISIONS

Repeating Hobson:

As far as altered states of consciousness are concerned, it is often the formal aspects that are emphasized: to have visions, internal stimuli must become predominant; to have intense visions, they must become very predominant, and when visions become intense, they are more likely to become exotic, numinous, or preternatural, and thus to suggest other-worldliness (2001: 11).

Other-worldliness is experienced in our visions because our conscious minds know how improbable is the form and content of these visions. We believe the subjective reality of our visions as this is the only reality we know, and the only reality we know is inside our heads. The world of objective reality is just as far out there as is the Andromeda Galaxy.

When one learns how to control altered states, we learn that there are as many realities as our mind wishes to create, including our normal everyday created reality. Our senses don't imprint the external world as it is, but rather, our senses select stimuli, rearrange stimuli, and package it as products of our species evolutionary history.

I'm defining visions as dream-like states of altered realities that occur when one is conscious or semi-conscious; visual experiences that are self-activated and are similar, if not the same as, the visuals in our dreams. In agreement with Hobson, visions are intense and demand our total attention. Visions do not occur when one is asleep, for that is the domain state of dreams. Visions occur during our waking hours due to physical deprivation, trauma, or through conscious will or suggestion, as noted.

But, first I want to note the similarity between dream visuals and vision visuals. Both are as visually intense as waking scenes on a bright summer's day. Both are closed to outside stimuli, meaning without any superposition of competing stimuli from one's environment. It's comparable to hearing an orchestra in a quiet concert hall versus listening to the same production driving with your window down.

Hobson says that "… dream consciousness creates the completely convincing illusion of motion (1999: 171)."

Stated differently, visuals feel like seamless, rapidly moving picture frames. It is this seamless quality that we subjectively experience as the arrow of time, or visual flow. And visual flow moves us through space.

We are mobile creatures, not plants. It is only with considerable training as in meditation that one can experience only one frame or object at a time. Visuals are otherwise always dynamic in that they change from moment to moment. This is our brain's reality.

The motion in a waking vision where one is flying is just as real as in a lucid dream. Astral travel visuals and movement in vision projections are totally real, as is the motion that comes from assuming the body of the bear in a shamanic ritual. In the latter case of possessing the animal or the animal's spirit, the effect of motion builds identification with the power and spirit of the bear. Simply put, what I experience is that the mechanisms that create consciousness and the reality of consciousness work with similar effects in all the various altered states that I experience and practice, although not all senses are active in each one of the different altered states. How can it be otherwise? Same brain, same neural circuitry, just different circuit combinations.

The program, *Ghost Hunters* is rather popular on TV these days. Individual programs offer testimony about ghosts of people and animals. Sometimes one sees them, and at other times, the ghosts are heard. Recall how easily micro brain states can change and how quickly imagery can be auto-created in our brains. Ghosts are universal because this very human mechanism is universal. Go back and watch a ghost show and think about this process. Belief makes reality what it is.

HOSPITAL ANGEL SCENE

I vividly recalled this scene over fifty years after the actual experience of being smothered in my crib by mother. The doctor pronounced me dead and covered me with a sheet. Leaving the bed, I passed through the sheet without awareness of this passage, and stood looking down at my corpse. I was positioned between my father and a nurse with the doctor on the other side of my father. This visual image remains permanently burned into my brain. A moment later the scene shifts, and I'm transported into a nether void made up of just me and some distant twinkling lights. As the lights come nearer, I recognize the lights have faces, and then their entire bodies appear. I know that they are angels coming to take me to Heaven.

I reject their offer, rotate 180 degrees, and return to the hospital room. I'm once again standing between my father and the nurse looking down at my dead body. I don't like being dead and decide to consciously reenter my body and return to life, I pass through the sheet, reenter my body, and then my memory goes blank. It is only later when I think about how I passed through the sheet that passage through a solid object becomes perplexing.

Later when I'm older, my father tells me that the doctor pronounced me dead. Dad asked to have the IV and tubes removed and the doctor complied. I'm then covered by a sheet and apparently ready for the morgue, however, I start moving and avert death in the morgue. These images always remain part of my conscious memory. I don't have to make an attempt to recall them as I do in dreams. The images are so intense, so real, that I became a True Believer in Heaven and Angels as a child.

There is nothing bizarre about this vision. Times are not mixed, and characters are recognizable in the visions except for the angels, which are all about the same age as my father, aunts, and uncles. Scenery doesn't morph, but is totally fabricated by a brain that is no more than 18 months old.

I later assumed that suggestion on the part of adults in my social world created the images of Heaven and Angels, or maybe I should say, the thoughts were placed into my young brain, and my young brain creatively did the real work. I was not permitted to discuss this vision with the adults in my world, and if I tried to persist, I was shushed up as a crazy child and told not to talk about such things.

CRIB SCENE

I'm 53 years old and undergoing management training, which includes a number of Yoga-like physical movements. My trainer was educated in these techniques while studying in India. I'm put into a sitting position with legs crossed in a fashion that can be visually imagined as a sitting Buddha. My trainer begins to blur, and an image of my distraught, raging mother begins to emerge. As the two images change dominance in my visual field, they reach a point of superposition: Both images are distinguishable while neither is dominant. The images approximate two transparencies with one placed on top of the other and held to the light.

The room in which I'm sitting gradually vanishes, and I'm transported back to my infant crib. I'm sitting upright looking through the crib's bars, my raging mother approaches with pillow in hand, her stomach extended either before or after the birth of my younger sister June. The pillow is forced over my head, and my mother's hand grinds into my back painfully. Then consciousness of the vision is lost, and I return to the training setting. My trainer is asking why I'm not continuing to comply with her directions, and I mumble something that I do not recall.

I call her that evening and ask to meet for coffee. She reluctantly agrees after I explain what had taken place during the day's training. I ask for this meeting as my vision has begun to incorporate my trainer in a fashion similar to Skinnerian conditioning. I want to stop this association, and feel that to do so, it is necessary to meet with her face-to-face. The meeting works, she is disassociated, and the vision's intensity subsides. The vision then takes a less demanding place in my brain, and I'm able to return home and dream fitfully. I did not want future encounters with my trainer to reinforce or trigger this vision, as I had ongoing multi-monthly contact with her. This episode led to my first and only experience with a therapist during the following months.

The visual experience of being smothered put me in an observing position above and looking down at myself in the crib. I watched my mother approach with pillow in hand and force it over my head, and her hand against my back stopped me from squirming away. In therapy I recalled a number of similar episodes, and came to realize that these acts on the part of mother were meant to silence my crying. I was also experiencing an intense earache at the time of the attack. Thus, I assumed my crying disturbed an overburdened mother intent on getting some rest.

All the visual imagery is intense, the story or plot is totally representative of a natural infant setting, the characters are just my mother and me, or in other words, bizarreness is not part of the vision. All of this takes place during waking consciousness with the setting's lights somewhat dimmed.

It cannot occupy the same state space as when I dream; in other words, cholinergic and aminergic systems must be operating differently than they are in lucid dreaming. And both of the above visual reports are extremely vivid. This vision, like all of my visions, lacks the bizarre forms common in dreams. In Hobson's research, the dominance of the cholinergic system prevails in dreams. I'm assuming dominance of the aminergic system in visions.

The only time I've had such vivid, dramatic visuals is in the two traumatic dreams reported in Chapter 8, and my Genesis Journey. The smothering vision emerged over fifty years after its actual occurrence. How this vision incorporated similar smothering episodes I don't know, but I did recall multiple attacks by mother during therapy. I'm reasonably sure that attacks continued after my hospitalization, because I routinely cupped my hand over my mouth and hid under the bed covers at night. This was an automatic reflex through much of my childhood that often caught my attention. Hand cupping became a FAP-like response throughout childhood. I gave it up consciously sometime during my late teens and early adult years.

Physical movements play a strong role in my lucid dreams and visions, and the physical sensation of body is always present. Fear and trauma are salient factors associated with our survival, and they easily become permanently embedded in our memories. One experience is all it takes. Trauma of sufficient intensity speaks with its own voice becoming the bandit that controls its own highways.

NATIVE AMERICAN CEREMONY

In the early 1970s, I participated in a Native American religious ceremony where peyote was provided. The ceremony went from sundown to sunup, included a fire pit which was maintained by an elder skilled in such practices, and provided opportunities throughout the night for all participants to speak as the spirit moved them. This was a very cathartic setting, and individual expression was both comfortable and easy, as total support came from both the elder and the congregation.

This ceremony honored the death of one of my Native Indian student's brothers, hence, the invitation to participate. I had spent a number of years actively supporting Native People at the university, on reservations, and in various community settings including ex-offenders.

I was the only white person in attendance and experienced absolutely no prejudice. I felt acceptance as one does with family. I knew that the dead young man's spirit was supposed to return during the course of the evening, and I was expending effort to stay awake through the night so I wouldn't miss his entrance.

It was in the wee hours of the morning before an August sunrise in Nebraska when the young man's spirit appeared. I never met this young man when he was alive, but recognized who he was as he appeared by the fire pit. It seemed logical to assume that stray spirits would not just pop-in for a hello. The collective group focused on the young man's spirit as I did. I was one of the first people to notice his presence, as the majority of congregants were dozing or appeared not to be attentive. Nudging all around brought most people to attention.

The elder, a shaman, leading the congregation performed his duties, and the young man's spirit-image returned to wherever it had come from. Quiet conversations followed the spirit's return. In my case, smiles and nods confirmed that we had all observed the spirit. I tend to be quite sensitive to most drugs and consumed a minimum of peyote compared to most of my neighbors by simply putting half or more of the distribution in my pocket.

I consider this to be a vision, as I was not dreaming. I remained in conscious contact with the congregation throughout the night. We all experienced a vision of the young man, although I don't know if my vision of his physical characteristics were identical to that of others or not. In the dim flickering light of the fire, it didn't seem to matter. Anyway, visualizations can add as much detail as one chooses to generate. In a drowsy, tired state, we all know how easily images can form.

The image is retained in memory, as is the Elder Spirit Guide, as is the fire pit, as is the physical setting and various acts of the participants. Everything happened in real time and there were no bizarre features or mixed scenes or characters, hence, I label the experience a vision. I readily imagine how easy it is for some social scientists and anthropologists to come away from these experiences as True Believers: One is conscious, the setting is one of normality, the actors behave in logical and sequential ways, and the visuals are totally believable and reinforced by the behavior of others. Collectively or individually, visions are seductive.

I'm emphasizing that visions are more representative of real life experiences than dreams. They represent real time, undistorted visuals forms, real characters, and steady-state scenes. Visions must be using different combinations of neural circuits and neural transmitters than are dreams.

GENESIS JOURNEY

It is a cold January afternoon in Rochester, Minnesota. I'm sitting in my favorite easy chair and thinking about recently read materials regarding The Big Bang, space-time expansion and super-luminary travel, quantum entanglement, Einstein's equations, which permit travel backwards and forwards in time, and the possibility of Universal Consciousness. I decide to take a trip back to the beginning of time, concentrate for a couple minutes, and fly out of my body. And I do mean fly, as in rocket motion.

I quickly depart Earth and fly past the Sun. The Milky Way Galaxy comes into view, and my warp speed just keeps increasing. I pass through walls of galaxies and great voids of space, and eventually come to irregular galaxies and giant stars as I approach the beginning of time. I hit the plasma expansion that exists before atomic particles are created. I physically hit the plasma wall, and come to a stop. I don't like the undifferentiated nature of the plasma, and have a sense of foreboding if I venture further and enter it. I let myself experience the plasma, and then return almost instantly to my living room the way quantum entanglement permits. I've abbreviated this description, as the journey through billions of years of stellar evolution was astounding.

The images of this vision remain vivid, and I recall that I was so impressed with the subjective effects and feelings that the vision occupied my mind for a number of days. No people in this vision, no sense of it being cold or hot out there, although I logically knew that the plasma was in the millions of degrees. The vision coincided perfectly with my understanding of the physical and quantum properties of space. I could have stopped along the way to see what other planets and solar systems were like, but I didn't. My objective was to see the beginning of time. I felt that I couldn't explore past the plasma wall and still keep my atoms and molecules intact. And as is the case with dreams, one can travel to any world of the imagination in these visionary projections, and interact with whatever beings we desire. Waking altered states of consciousness can use auto-creativity just as easily as we do in dreams.

When I programmed dreams in past years, I could have created a duplicate of this daytime experience and watched it mature over time. Auto-created dream adventures, characters, or scenes can become so seductive that they become a permanent resource to our dream processes. Religious or secular believers return time and time again to their favorite scripts in dreams or in visions. Returning to one's archived dream scenarios adds credibility to one's belief that they have entered another dimension. This process is a little like role playing, for once we get into the act, it seems normal, and we can easily become Adepts.

But for my Genesis Journey, I just wanted to have a waking vision to see what it felt like to explore the universe first hand. It's breathtaking! Whether one has these experiences in dreams or visions, they are *the* Big Event. I'm quite sure that physically walking on the moon in a spacesuit would be no more exciting. I make this comment for the benefit of hide-bound realists who find hypnopompic or hypnogogic transitions before sleep and after waking to be uncomfortable.

The visuals in visions can appear immediately with a total sense of immersion, or we can experience a gentle slide into induction. My journey was orchestrated after lunch and after I had consumed one or two cups of coffee, so I was wide awake.

As a university student back in the 1950s and '60s, I played extensively with dream programming, but never with daytime visions. My first out-of-body experience occurred before I was two years old. I experimented with many forms of altered states for decades. Playing with other forms of altered states can become just as seductive as dream programming for the young uninitiated adventurer. And for the True Believer or astral traveler, each trip reinforces the reality of other dimensions.

There is a balance between states of consciousness that I live in and prefer. I like the feeling of being aware, engaged, and active with all of my senses fully online moment-to-moment. I live in a comfortable relationship with others and the world, a relationship that took considerable effort as I overcame childhood trauma. Memories of childhood don't haunt me or make me uncomfortable, as they have been properly cataloged in my personal history library. Nevertheless, I gain no pleasure reading old memory books of trauma. I live with a sense of expanded consciousness from all of my altered reality history, and have no further desire for habituation. At 75 years of age, I want to experience myself and the universe as it is, as much as I'm capable of.

Hobson says that:

While we are capable of bringing visual images to mind during waking, we are never able to image as sharply, vividly, and completely as we do in dreams, where complex visual worlds spring to life behind our closed eyes. Only in abnormal waking conditions of mental illness is such hallucinatory experience possible (1999: 133).

As noted, I do not find this to be my experience. This interpretation is common in the therapeutic community, and I believe reflects lack of experience with humanity's history of altered states. Most altered state practitioners keep this information to themselves for obvious reasons.

In my experience, most people in Western culture fail to report altered state experiences because of this bias. I say Western Culture because much of the world such as India, China, and Tibet have a long history of controlling, using, and benefiting from conscious engagement of altered states. Ignorance on the part of Western anthropologists lacking an in-depth understanding of shamanism is a case in point. In my opinion, the Western view of consciousness has made it difficult for many scientists to appreciate the implications of quantum mechanics. For example, consciousness as a documented influence in the quantum world has been studiously avoided by most Western physicists. How can we understand any phenomenon by placing its study off limits?

For me, a major distinction between normal consciousness and hallucinations in mental illness centers on control. I control my daytime hallucinations, as they are vivid, and can present themselves with a complete sense of motor reality. Realistic ideas and observations pop into my head while a vision is unfolding, and these ideas retain their realism after re-entering normal consciousness. For instance, in my Genesis Journey, I hit the plasma wall at the beginning of time. I was very aware of having passed through various stages of cosmic evolution, and arriving at this early time of the universe's formation where only a plasma field exists. I arrived at the point before atomic particles were formed and time itself began.

I can employ logic during a vision or while dreaming the same as I can during waking experiences, which of course adds an additional sense of reality to the experience itself.

The reader might respond: "Yes, you can think during a vision, but you are drawing on a worldview that you took into the vision."

My answer: I agree. Further, I draw on this same worldview during waking consciousness. And, this logical thought process is sometimes expressed in my ordinary dreams. But dream logic is typically more transitory, symbolic and metaphorical.

As individuals, we often have extra-normal experiences that don't fit neatly into any preconceived model. Individually unique brains don't always conform to the socio-cultural norms. Social expectations tell us to conform, but the creativity spawned by brain plasticity does not always comply. Brain plasticity says to me that we can have any manner of experiences that are activated by childhood trauma, accidents, chemical brain state changes and the like that mix-and-match brain-mind circuitry and brain chemical states in seemingly endless ways.

If you have experiences unlike any that you are reading about, or having experiences that your friends don't have, write them down and send them to me if no one else listens. Remember that scientific research, not just religious, shamanic, or philosophical musing about dreams, altered states of consciousness, and consciousness itself is still fairly young, even though this research has made quantum leaps since Freud.

The psychological effects and phenomenological experiences I've had do not always fit neatly into existing worldviews. However, I find writings by Hobson, LaBerge, Delaney and others tremendously helpful, and I constantly gain new insights through comparisons.

I for one have been somewhat remiss not sharing my experiences with professional dream researchers. On the other hand, in my historical time period, university professionals didn't appreciate my interpretations any more than local psychiatrists did. In retrospect, many of these individuals seemed too restricted by their narrow professional fields. Fortunately, scientific research has moved us beyond this primitive stage of proto-science.

MOTHER'S DEATH

My mother medicated herself by secretly getting two incompatible prescriptions from two separate doctors in two different communities. The upshot of her covert activity, according to her deathbed doctor, was that incompatible drug interactions leached the potassium from her body and turned her heart into mush. She knew she had hours or days to live, and asked her children to be with her. My older sister and I were able to free ourselves, and we took turns at her bedside. It was my night shift, she was restless, and I was expectantly observant.

About two or three o'clock in the morning, mother gasped, a pained expression covered her face, and then the pained expression turned into an evil mask-like persona and her heart stopped beating.

As I sat looking at her immobile body and was about to notify the nurse, a strange vision appeared: Up through the concrete floor came four ghoulish figures making creepy guttural sounds that would send one's cat into hiding. The spirits reached into her body, and I knew they were there to take her soul to hell. I was spellbound, unbelieving, and immobile. I watched in fascination as her soul was wrenched free and held in the custody of the ghouls who then retreated downward through the cement floor to what I knew must be hell. Talk about metaphor!

The whole vision was disconcerting, as I didn't believe in hell then or now. All of this happened in real time, nothing was distorted, and the ghouls had a demanding presence in the hospital room. The ghouls' movements were realistic in a ghost-like apparitional form. The hospital room did not change in any way, but the sensory impact was profound with both real life sound and visuals. A major Hollywood producer would have been pleased with the quality.

The ghouls were grotesque, dark forms making low guttural noises. Their movements were precise, quick, and very goal directed. Nothing that was otherwise bizarre entered the visual scene. After they departed with mother's soul, her facial expression relaxed, the evil mask disappeared, and her physical form returned to its normal state. I sat in awe for a long time before calling the nurse.

If I believed in ghouls, hell and non-material souls, I had ample reason to accept this vision as real. I had not slept before this vision occurred, as I had been reading and watching mother's restlessness. I had a strong sense that she was entering her final hours. I was not drowsy or in a semi-dream state prior to the ghouls arrival. The whole scenario was just as real as my infant deathbed vision. And, it reflected my personal view of and history with mother. The majesty of the human mind to see, feel, and hear all that belief makes real.

MOSES

As a child, I had a companion, whom I thought of as a Guardian Angel because mother told me they were real. I came to name him Moses. He is my adult height, similar body build, and has dark colored hair. I don't recall ever noticing his eye color. If I mentioned him during my childhood, mother as a matter of fact would tell me that all children have guardian angels. However, I was not permitted to talk about him in public.

I learned as an undergraduate student that personal spirits are common for children, and found this fact to be a great relief. I didn't know how they came about, real or auto-created, but it didn't matter; I was as normal as other children. One day as I walked into my university classroom, Moses was sitting at the far end of the room by the blackboard in a chair I used when administering tests. I immediately identified him as Moses. My brain just kicked-in and said "that's Moses, what's he doing in my classroom?" No one in class seemed to notice him except me.

I looked up repeatedly as I began to lecture, but he remained sitting in the corner chair staring directly at the center of the class. His features were more robot-like as he didn't move, and I don't recall him even blinking. I reached a point of discomfort where I was going to excuse myself, step outside of the classroom and collect myself, when he finally disappeared. His solid, physical appearance was totally disconcerting. I had dismissed him as a figment of my childhood imagination, but there he was in flesh and blood. I thought as I attempted to start my lecture that something was causing my imagination to be wildly creative, since Moses had not been a conscious part of my life for some years, and if I thought of him, it was with the idea of a comforting, preternatural childhood companion.

I finished my lecture and was putting my notes in order when one of my students approached me. She always sat directly in front of my lectern, was an excellent student as I recall, and said: "Who was that sitting in the corner at the beginning of class?" She also added that she often had these experiences, and didn't seem to be perturbed by this one. She treated Moses' appearance as something that just happens. I asked her to describe him and her description was totally accurate. I told her he was my childhood Guardian Angel, and rather quickly terminated the conversation in order to have quiet time to puzzle through this discomforting turn of events.

I recount this vision with all its corporeal reality, and wonder how Dr. Hobson will fit Moses into AIM and the vision's proper state space. I can't account for visions in this kind of setting when they are selectively confirmed by others while the majority of students in the classroom remain oblivious. I had never interacted with this student other than her being part of the class, and the possibility of suggestion being behind our joint vision seems improbable. My notes from this lecture have been lost, but I recall that it covered symbolic and referential aspects of consciousness. The student seemed totally comfortable with Moses and my explanation. I wasn't comfortable, and never again discussed it with her. Unfortunately!

IN-MIND MOSES

As I consider lucid dreaming, visions, and other altered states, it seems obvious how naturally our brain-minds create all of these phenomena. I can account for my childhood Moses easily, as he is a felt "Other."

Different levels of consciousness that we experience in dreams remind one that the presence of felt sentient beings is part of our human brain-mind capacity. We are felt sentient beings who can project this imagery as we choose. My immature brain as an infant and toddler felt this other spirit and attempted to explain it. Children attempt to make sense of their world as we adults do, and it is common for children to have imaginary friends as they learn to navigate a world that is not always to their liking, and as they learn to take on complex roles.

Children's imaginations play roles and create whole persons with whom they interact. Physiologically, childhood friends with the felt other probably represent an immature state of brain development where our felt self is still under development. From experience, I can say that as children we must learn to separate what goes on externally from what is taking place in our minds. But children must also believe what they feel or the natural world is just a jumble of stimuli.

Conceptually, mirror neurons help our brains identify similar states and feelings in others. We duplicate what others feel in our own brains. And when we use technology to scope the brain, we find similar circuits lighting up and similar brain chemicals being produced that mirror what is going on in the other person. Similar mirror neuron processes occur when we lip read (Damasio: 2010: 148-149).

I read my wife's lips, which are saying: "I love you," and I hear her voice in my head. Under a brain scan, I would expect to find that the appropriate hearing circuits in my brain are lighting up just as though I were actually hearing the words. Mirror neurons and shared brain chemistry help us understand how we can share meaning verbally or non-verbally, even though our brains and neural circuits are isolated in our own skulls. In a compatible sense, mirror neurons help us understand how collective visions can occur. Mirror neurons also explain the ghost dogs on TV programs, that is, if we add in our auto-creative capacities.

As a child, when I felt the presence of Moses or saw his image in my head, I didn't think it odd that he was speaking to me. The felt image or visual image of Moses placed him into my consciousness, and what followed – the messages he imparted as thought-words – seemed totally normal; Just as normal as hearing my wife's voice when I read her lips, or just as normal as speaking to myself as I write these sentences.

The neural circuits activated by Moses were probably the same as those activated by any other adult in my life. We can easily account for these altered realities as brain generated states using the research of modern neuroscience. I can account for all of my history with Moses as self-generated mind-state phenomena, with the exception of the classroom experience that was confirmed by one other student.

CONTEMPORARY SHAMANIC STORIES

If the reader will take time to skim some of the shamanic literature such as *Shamanism in the Interdisciplinary Context* (Leete & Firnhaber: 2004) you will quickly discover that occult interpretations are rampant. Shamanic drug trips are treated as having external reality rather than being self-activated, that is, as drug trips are understood by most of us in the modern world. Shamanic trances induced through dancing and drum beating are used to create out-of-body experiences, which are then given equal interpretation to externally created realities. All manner of hokus-pokus is presented in the name of science, and an interesting branch of anthropology.

I've presented natural explanations for shamanic experiences in my three volume series, and find labels like the above in the *Interdisciplinary Context* to be highly misleading. Clearly, altered states are part of the brain-mind's capacity, and most likely have been around since we have been practicing burial or producing cave art as a species. At best, occult interpretations of ASC as they express our most natural human abilities simply detracts from our understanding of religion, consciousness, and brain-mind physiology. At worst, such treatment of our DNA capacities and their human manifestations, its expression and social structuring, results in hatred and death.

Hobson says when discussing "The Cult of Dreaming and Psychedelic Drug Use" that: "One might come to the conclusion that REM sleep is the physiological basis of religion (2001: 294)."

After all, dream interpretation has been around at least since recorded history, with foretelling the future and communing with God being common interpretations.

If REM is convincing, daytime visions are more so. If individual visions are convincing, group viewing is even more so, and when cultural expectations are met and indoctrinated minds receive confirmation, reality is beyond questioning. REM sleep is an integral part of religion, but it is only one manifestation of altered state consciousness. I don't believe REM sleep alone is the physiological basis for religion, but I do believe that collectively, altered states are. All altered states, including dreams, are manifestations of basic underlying brain-mind functions and capabilities. Ancients tended to put various altered states in the same bag.

VISION INTERPRETATION

My dreaming brain was multi-tasking again last night (7-8-11). It woke me at 3:45 a.m. with two parallel processes running. One was a mundane collection of common memories associated with routine activities over the past few days. The other process was prodding me to clarify the memory function differences between dreams and visions. I was at the preceding chapter section when I stopped editing yesterday, and my Interpreter apparently noted that I had not made this distinction yet. I'll complete some thoughts from Hobson and Damasio and add my Interpreter's admonition at the end of Damasio's review.

Hobson:

If one alters the delicate neuromodulatory balance of the brain, the brain-mind can move out of its canonical trajectory through the state space and enter regions otherwise normally forbidden (Ibid: 257).

Neuroscience does not yet understand all the mechanisms involved in various state changes and the imagery that accompanies these changes. But by using self-observation and self-experiments, I can describe a good share of the phenomenology and compare the differences. I believe that we are just around the corner with formal research that will identify the micro-state differences in altered states of consciousness as well as more global patterns. I think it is critical that we include physiological analysis of altered states in this discovery process. As stated in *Mind of the Mystic* and extending Hobson's related thoughts about dreams, I believe altered states are the scaffolding that individually supports mystic experiences, and are collectively manifested as institutionalized religions.

Visions are daytime experiences that can be easily activated by some of us, or they can occasionally be collective experiences. They are not exclusive to one's own religion or the endless number of interpretations provided historically and across all cultures. Visions are incredibly impactful even when one self-induces them. Child indoctrination, adult reinforcement, and cultural expectations all converge to keep these primitive beliefs in competition. The actors are the same, but the plots vary. It is time to engage form, not content, biology, not dualism, and neuroscience, not mysticism.

I look forward to seeing the physiological evidence that places visions and other altered states in Hobson's AIM, state-space model. I suspect, as I believe Hobson does, that the AIM Model is incomplete. Further, we will need a model based on system dynamics that includes circular causation. Models based on bottom up, reduction approaches to science are extremely helpful to our evolving understanding of dreams and consciousness, but I along with others such as Walter Freeman believe that empirical reductionism alone is not adequate to the task.

In terms of hypotheses, how is it possible that one can enter visions with REM-like lucidity almost instantly, while remaining in a waking state? How is it possible that groups of people can share a vision? Is it just cultural expectations as a form of suggestion, or is shared convergence through some other normal mechanism involved? I know that drug users can share visions that include sitting on an imaginary iceberg in the middle of July, and actually feeling cool by doing so. Expectations programmed beforehand permit collective visions the same way I have often programmed my dreams, which is a practice that goes back to the ancient Egyptians that was later imported by the Hebrews of Jesus' Era.

How do visions appear to individuals like me when our most fundamental beliefs deny them? How do they appear to an 18 month old who doesn't even have a vocabulary for them? What does this mean for autosuggestion? What does this mean for unusual neural combinations? I think most of these basic questions have been answered. Refining the physiological mechanisms begs new technologies from empirical science.

DAMASIO: THE BODY IN MIND

In *Self Comes to Mind,* A. Damasio reviews the brain's mapping process for both the outside environment as well as our internal environment. We map these environments, hold them in memory, and call them into action as we move through time and space. This is clearly a major advance in our survival capacity over what simple organisms such as worms do.

He says: "… map-making brains have the power of literally introducing the body as content into the mind process (2010: 89."

The body is the thing mapped, but it is always in contact with the thing that maps it, which is the brain.

And, "… the mapped images of the body have a way of permanently influencing the very body they originate in (Ibid: 89-90."

This finding is central to Damasio's model of consciousness. The brain is informed by the body, and this information is used to regulate the organism's day-to-day activities. We're hungry, need fluids, stressed, etc.

Damasio continues: "… by mapping its body in an integrated manner, the brain manages to create the critical component of what will become the self. We shall see that body mapping is a key to the elucidation of the problem of consciousness (Ibid: 92)."

The body proper becomes the central object of brain mapping. "… the brain can do more than merely map states that are actually occurring, with more or less fidelity: it can also transform body states and, most dramatically, simulate body states that have not yet occurred (Ibid: 93)."

We see this process most vividly in our dreams.

The body and brain are always communicating with each other: The body informs the brain about its various states, and the brain tells the body what to do about those states. But "… it also tells the body how to construct an emotional state (Ibid: 94)."

And, from the point of view of dreams and visions, the mind-brain is creating the emotional states we experience, whether we are dreaming, waking, or visioning. The self can and does tell the brain to modify its states. My interpretation is compatible with Damasio's that there is constant feedback, or exchange, between body and brain, i.e., circular causation. The body informs the brain about its various states, and the brain tells the body what to do about those states.

A theme running throughout this three book series proposes, as it often demonstrates as well, that the self can learn to control a broad range of brain and body states using self-hypnosis, visioning techniques, and various forms of projection and introspection. We are given this architecture, this scaffold of neural circuitry, upon which we build memory and experience, but we also have the capacity to use our active Self (Interpreter) to move between conscious states, and modify the vary architecture from which Self emerges. As I laboriously keep repeating, it is getting a handle on this control process that is so critical to the mental health industry.

We can learn to control this process without fully understanding the entire cellular, circuit, and system aspects that support it. Nevertheless, as our understanding increases, new approaches and techniques of control emerge.

Obvious controls appear as we develop lucid dreaming and our ability to interpret what is going on in this brain state, as we learn to control automatic body processes such as pain and heartbeat, as we learn to control micro-circuits in our brain that permit visions and trances on demand, or as we learn to control states of clinical anxiety or depression, or possibly entering or not entering psychotic states: This is an expanded application of Will.

Damasio presents brain stem nuclei as an integral player in the creation of consciousness:

It is reasonable to hypothesize that in the process of regulating life the networks formed by these nuclei also give rise to composite neural states. The word feeling describes the mental aspects of those states (Ibid: 99).

Further:

This alteration of cognition is probably achieved by the release of molecules from brain stem and basal forebrain neuromodulator nuclei (Ibid: 100).

Without getting into more technical aspects of Damasio's model, he says:

… the brain can simulate, within somatosensing regions, certain body states, as if they were occurring: and because our perceptions of any body state is rooted in the body maps of the somatosensing regions, we perceive the body state as actually occurring even if it is not (Ibid: 102).

This is a fictive simulation composed by the brain, and it is one that becomes very active in the dream or visioning process. We can simulate a body state without producing it, which is a neat way for evolution to save time and energy. In my experience, we can learn to simulate body states in any number of other altered states of consciousness, and most importantly, we can learn to control them.

Damasio brings his model of consciousness in line with Giacomo Rizzolatti's concept of mirror neurons. We duplicate muscular and various internal states in others by first activating similar conditions, muscle contractions, and brain chemical states in ourselves. Brain scans confirm this mirror duplication. His model assumes that in the course of human evolution, our ancestors first learned to map their external and internal worlds, create brain states called feelings, and then eventually discovered these states existed in their fellow species members.

This process becomes the basis for empathy, role taking, and projection. I confirm your grief over the loss of a loved one by activating similar neurons and neural circuits. I literally put myself in the brain-mind of the other. This leads to two related observations on my part:

1. Living close to nature, we naturally observe the world and life around us. This action is necessary for our own survival. As I child, I enjoyed hours and days exploring the woods in Northwestern Wisconsin and all the wildlife that existed there. I came to personally and intimately feel the pain of animals such as squirrels, deer, and owls. It's a different perspective than that of a child who grows up in the city where dead animals are simply cooked and put on one's dinner plate. A perspective that helps me identify with the shamanic state of possessing animals.

2. As I became familiar with American Indian and world ethnography, I learned that animal totems were common across world cultures. My experience in the woods made the transition to totems simple, obvious, and commonplace. When I learned how shamans took on their totem counterparts, the process seemed clear, non-mysterious, and a simple extension of normal human capacities. It still does.

Much of my early years were spent proportionately with animals and not other humans. They were living creatures that shared my pain and pleasures. Life had continuity across species, and I came by the age of 13 years to respect all life forms; much as Native peoples around the world do when they live close to nature. How could it be otherwise? How natural for a shaman to project into the spirit of the bear, the eagle, or any other totemic animal. How natural our role taking ability is, and it is not confined to our own species. How naturally our mirror neurons cross species lines and project anthropocentrically. How easily we moderns identify with that new puppy or kitten by holding, feeding, dressing it, kissing it, and taking it to bed for its and our own comfort. I assume that in order to travel light years, aliens would also possess mirror neurons. Fear not!

Activation of this totemic instinct through close and long association with wild animals taught me to appreciate the wonder and beauty of nature. It was one simple additional step to project into the energy of Northern Lights or the powerful surges in a summer storm. How natural to explore the larger world of the child and humankind when we understand how universally we anthropomorphize both the animate and inanimate world. Why have we placed so many obstacles between ourselves and those who live in other cultural realities? The answer seems rather simple: Because we remain ignorant of our own brains and the mind within.

Removing degrees of ignorance moves us closer to being united with our evolutionary past and evolutionary future. This is Damasio's autobiographical Self written large.

A final thought from Damasio: Recounting a memory, he suddenly thinks of a colleague he calls B; a person that he has no need for in terms of his ongoing day's activity, and he wonders where this thought came from. After some contemplation he realizes that he had duplicated B's walk and in doing so activated memories of him. He then recalled that non-consciously he had earlier observed B walking by his window. It's a pleasant awareness of how our non-conscious brain operates, and a reminder that memory also resides in our tissue. And tissue memory can be most helpful as a bridging element to awareness.

Mirror neurons in action, memories activated, and the realization that deep within our flesh, as Damasio says, these memories move into consciousness.

And, so it is with many, if not most, of my dreams. A physical act recorded in memory comes to activate my nightmare. A feeling of my body temperature dropping into an uncomfortable range activates a dream scenario, which in turn creates a story within my internal movie machine. Pretty transparent stuff Doctor Freud!

I have to offer one more aside about rhythm and dancing to drums. When I first observed native dancers imitating the prairie chicken in South Dakota, I thought it a bit curious. Why imitate a prairie chicken when one can become something much grander, like a bear or an eagle? Then I realized that the rhythm and body movements were soothing and able to transport one into another brain state, although I didn't think of it as a brain state at the time. I thought of it as just being transported into trance. At the moment that I write these words, I wish I had practiced being a prairie chicken, thereby learning how to embed the soothing relief of this rhythm for relaxation. I don't know how all these different rhythms call forth various altered states and how these altered states are expressed. I only understand chanting and basic rhythmic dancing. Nevertheless, ways to engage rhythm are known in a wide, wonderful range within our human community.

Body in mind and mind in body: What a simple, powerful understanding of consciousness, mind and self. As Damasio says:

The living body is the central locus. Life regulation is the need and the motivation. Brain mapping is the enabler, the engine that transforms plain life regulation into minded regulation and, eventually, into consciously minded regulation (Ibid: 107.

Damasio's insights offer each one of us a more complete understanding of consciousness. And in doing so, he enhances our understanding of dreams and altered states.

Damasio presents his model of how the self is constructed:

… the modified protoself must be connected with the images of the causative object," and: "These steps must take place in close temporal proximity, in the form of a narrative sequence imposed by real-time occurrences (Ibid).

The upshot being that as this complex process unfolds, the functions performed by various brain structures come into play and bring this process of processes together.

Damasio offers the possibility that "… the deep layers of the colliculi are a model of what mind-making, self-making brain eventually became (Ibid: 207)."

I acknowledge the narrative sequence imposed by real-time occurrences as they are duplicated in my dreams and in my visions. My dreams document basic image formation that is occurring within my tissue, and moves me through Damasio's Qualia I and Qualia II to and understanding of how my Self as agent becomes possible.

As I follow his model of self-construction, I realize that image superposition, as he calls it, has not always been synchronized for me. That calling forth images from the recesses of my memory and combining them with images that are moving through my mind in present time creates an altered effect of superposition. When my mind retrieves old file images and places them in my consciousness concurrently, I have a double image – two very distinct images viewed at the same time, images that are connected by associational memory. I recall such episodes clearly as they are rare, value-laden, and demand extra processing energy. The Self in consciousness is being created in both image-making processes. I feel both states of Self and being, and struggle to give meaning to what is happening to me. In reality, without consciousness there are no images. Nevertheless, we can be aware of image mapping and re-mapping of these primary images.

When I was undergoing management training exercises seated in a crossed-legged yoga position, an image of me in crib was superimposed over my conscious presence in the training room. The image of being in my crib gradually came into focus as the image of my present surroundings faded. At the midpoint, both images were clear and demanded equal attention on my part. The imaging holding process in my brain was creating two of me; superposition equal to two of me interacting in a dream, and a form of self-talking. I like Damasio because he reminds me that the self-process is active when we are conscious. The self-process may be active at different levels, it may fade in and out, but regardless of how salient or dim it is, Damasio's constructs of consciousness help me explain dreams and altered states.

As one learns to move across the landscape of brain-mind states with greater understanding and growing compassion for life and each other, we no longer fear the unknowns of our inner-world and mystic selves. We come to appreciate the wonders of our genomic history, the beauty of mind and self, and the joy of our evolving world culture; a culture made beautiful through science, and the shared understanding that can come from the efforts of so many dedicated people of science.

DAMASIO: AS-IF DREAMS AND VISIONS

I'm assuming that brainstem activation is critical to our understanding of dreams and visions.

[The] brain is continuously generating a substrate for feelings because signals from the ongoing body state are continuously being reported, made use of, and transformed at the appropriate mapping sites." "For the feeling state to be connected to the emotion, the causative object and the temporal relation between its appearance and the emotional response must be properly attended to (Ibid: 120).

Stimuli are constantly being fed into the active brain stem and brain. Feeling comes into existence when this activated state is attended to; hence, consciousness exists at our higher cortical levels as feeling, and the source of this consciousness exists at the brain stem level as emotion. At the lower level, we have a body loop operating, which one can observe in our dreams as tissue dependent elements such as fixed action patterns.

Damasio says a second type of body loop exists.

The brain regions that initiate the typical emotion cascade can also command body-mapping regions, such as the insula, to adopt the pattern they would have adopted once the body signaled the emotional state to it (Ibid) and: The insula … configures its firing 'as if' it were receiving signals describing emotional state X (Ibid).

These are self-created emotional states of internal origin.

Damasio says: "As-if patterns cannot possibly feel like the body-looped feeling states because they are simulations, not the genuine article… (Ibid: 121)."

A third type of feeling state "… consists of altering the transmission of body signals to the brain (Ibid)."

The brain can receive a distorted view of the body state at any given moment. This can be caused by drugs or trauma, and they are viewed by Damasio as hallucinations. In an effort to play with the reader's mind, I ask this question: If the distorted view of one's body state is received by one's Interpreter as a distorted body state, is this still a hallucination?

So what does all this mean? Movies of the mind can be rather factual interpretations of our external or internal worlds as indicated by dreams that are devoted to balancing on a bicycle or mulling over material from a neuroscientist. Or, they can be self-created fabrications of a fictive nature that challenges the best science fiction. Or, they can be scrambled beyond recognition by our higher faculties and represent hallucinations if we are awake.

In whatever form they enter our conscious awareness, emotions are a critical part of consciousness. When as-if forms enter our consciousness during waking states, they can appear equally real to our conscious Self. And, in my contention, because the internally mapped images are devoid of extraneous fuzziness, they can be very intense.

This intense imagery can be superimposed on our external environment, which tends to create a sense of total credibility. Examples that I've given include the ghouls at my mother's death, and the arrival of an anticipated spirit to a group of believing congregants. Repetition of nightmares can create vividness equal to visions.

Belief systems from our cultures add to and support this aspect of credibility, and once we come to believe that the gods or God are sending us messages, the significance of visions takes on prophetic importance.

Prophets emerge naturally as products of the human brain's reality states. Religion is not a fiction based on manipulating cognitive thoughts. Rather, religion is grounded in our physical bodies and brains, and how our bodies and brains operate to engage their world; social, physical, and internal worlds of the entire brain. Spirituality, in this context, is tissue embedded; it emerges from DNA architecture. I suggest that religion can only become civilized across society when embedded spirituality is understood.

DREAM AND VISION MEMORY FUNCTIONS

Mundane dreams, thought dreams and visions cannot be engaging the same memory functions. Here I'm addressing the different manner in which memory is recorded and used. Memory function from an internal dream observer's perspective has at least three different support mechanisms. This is the reminder that was prompted by my mid-morning's dream on (7-8-11).

Mundane dreams use the existing memory scaffold and add new memory elements to those already existing, and creating a parsimonious mechanism supporting memory. My dream was metaphorically wrestling with AIM space, but the metaphor was based on a concrete similarity to actual space. When I was waking up, my dream observation in metaphorical space became an approximation of real space in Hobson's state space model.

I interpreted this relationship between space and state space from two sets of cues. One was space as metaphor, and the other was my higher consciousness awareness that state space could be viewed as a form of real space. In other words, my brain had an abstraction called space, which Lakoff and Johnson might call Self as container, around which it organizes associational elements. Mundane dreams employ both primary and complex metaphor as the above example suggests, therefore dream content can seem to morph across different levels of the dream landscape.

My visions are projected as if they were accessing a photographic memory. They feel like real time with continuity and transitions common to one's waking hours. Recall is easier because of this real time quality of visions, and reflects the recall we have when awake. And, like dreams, visions are crystal clear as auto-generation excludes unwanted stimuli from one's environment. This memory mechanism permits me to replay a dream as though I were hitting the repeat button on my VCR. It also permits me to change real time segments in dreams by inserting variations such as changing the dream's ending.

Thought dreams that are expressed in discussions with other interested dream parties or professionals, or given as dream lectures, are drawing on all my cognitive faculties as I would in similar waking activities. I must be creatively bringing together embedded memories of a distributed nature in order to think at this level of complexity in my dreams. The type of thought metaphor is different than that of using primary images as is the case with the space and state space example given above. Primary versus secondary use of metaphor can be distinguished by bike balancing as primary, and a balanced life as a higher form of secondary metaphor use: Damasio's mapping of maps example.

Thus, memory functions in dreams are not just integration and consolidation. Memory functions vary according to the goal or objective supported by the memory element. The reader will note that these distinctions are easy to make from an external logical point of view, that is, if we understand dream language. Nevertheless, these distinctions demand our attention as we analyze dreams and altered states from the inside-out. Obviously this is my plug for self-observation and self-experiments as methodology.

DYNAMIC INTEGRATED SYSTEMS AND AIM

Hobson updated his activation-synthesis model with *The Dream Drugstore*. I like the resonance of this model with my understanding of our brain-minds as dynamic integrated systems. And for me, his state space conceptualization is a dynamic method of visualizing what is going on in dreams, visions, and other altered states. As Hobson is fully aware, it is just a model to help us visualize processes.

If the scientific community had been open to this type of research fifty years ago, I would have been a willing participant. I believe that individuals like me who experience a broad range of altered states can be of significant research value. Dream research and neuroscience have taken giant steps, and are in the process of closing more loops in our understanding of consciousness and altered consciousness. I believe however that top-down, macro analysis has its own unique methodology to add to a comprehensive understanding of these subjects.

Another clear example of the AIM brain state model is found in Hobson and Leonard's, *Out of its Mind: Psychiatry in Crisis* (2001: 119-131). This three dimensional cube permits major types of brain states to be visually mapped. For example, coma states are found on the front-bottom left, while waking states are in the cube on the back upper right, REM sleep is on the right lower front. Physical Moses is outside looking in – or so it seems.

Hobson sees consciousness as following along a continuum that can be mapped within this state space cube. Hobson criticizes The Diagnostic and Statistical Manual of Mental Disorders (DSM-IV) for having 1800 different classifications. Basically the criticism goes like this: Expressions of psychoses change over time and may change throughout the day. Psychiatrists, he says, have become mostly pill pushers who see their HMO clients for as little as fifteen to twenty minutes before writing a prescription. This practice results in great misuse of drugs, a misuse that often exacerbates the condition of the patient or can lead to his or her disablement or death over time, especially death through homicide or suicide. The bottom of the barrel clients in America's correctional system bear the brunt of this malpractice.

By placing REM sleep in his AIM state space cube, Hobson recognizes that REM resembles psychosis where judgment is disabled, bizarreness of time and place exists, and characters can morph in any combination. What type of sensory input occurs, whether from the external or internal worlds of the individual, is reflected in the state space occupied at any particular moment as in the: "LSD tripper's state of arousal … the reduced serotonin tilts the brain toward internal imagery and emotions, and away from judgment and reason… (Ibid: 123) thereby creating visual hallucinations.

In contrast, psychoses associated with amphetamine and cocaine addiction (and also with schizophrenia and mania) do not typically cause visual hallucinations but instead rouse imaginary voices (Ibid).

Oh jeepers, and here I thought Moses was such a good friend!

As one changes the chemicals washing over their brains, the state space shifts accordingly. We hear voices, we see things, or we have a sense of being separated from our bodies. Thus, the AIM Model is a useful tool to help us visualize this process.

This suggest, says Hobson "that there may be two principal kinds of psychosis. In one of these (the REM sleep, LSD, alcohol , and opiate type), the thought and memory systems located toward the front of the brain are so disabled that they cannot make sense of pseudosensory signals processed by the back of the brain, and so they report credible visual hallucinations. In the other kind of psychosis (the cocaine, amphetamine, schizophrenia, and mania type), the forebrain's thought and memory systems get cranked so high that the brain becomes hyperattentive, fails to coordinate properly, hears accusatory or threatening voices, and is prone to paranoia. This suggests that sanity depends on a delicate modulatory balance generating neither too much forebrain activity nor too little (Ibid: 124).

The LSD tripper is having a waking dream in that "… the tripper travels from the back of the cube toward the front, far enough forward for internally oriented sensory processing to bend the truth and create visual hallucinations, but not so far as to abolish all external information (Ibid: 123)."

Thus, Hobson and Leonard are defining psychotic states in state space and according to the chemical modulators at work. When this work was written in 2001 "… well over a hundred different psychiatric drugs" were in use (Ibid: 125).

Conscious experiences vary due to chemical modulators expressed by the brain, and vary according to which neural circuits are being turned on and off, as well as differences in neural circuit sensitivity. This becomes a complex collage of possibilities, to say the least. To me, visions represent high activation in the waking state, moderate to high internal information, and high modulation in the AIM cube.

I can close my eyes and have a Genesis Journey vision based exclusively on internal information. I can watch the ghost-brother of a departed friend appear while influenced by peyote, and have some approximation of an LSD experience. I can call forth a half-century old trauma crib scene being fully conscious initially, and then moving into a vision totally controlled from memory.

It is probably incorrect to refer to all of these slightly different altered states as visions, nevertheless, the visual effects are duplicated in these different states as variations in neural circuits must be changing inputs and outputs as the experiences unfold and change form.

I think what is partially happening in addition to the chemical and neural circuit changes presented by Hobson in *The Dream Drugstore* and in the above quoted text, includes all of the above, as we say in multiple choice tests, plus a shift in conscious control through what I refer to as the Controller and Interpreter. I don't think we can understand all the meso or micro-states involved in REM, N-REM, psychotic states, visions and trances without enhancing the AIM-activation-synthesis model. Linear models of causation can only take us so far; although the AIM Model is dynamic and is probably best referred to as a hybrid. A three dimensional cube moving in a vortex through space could supply the added dimension, but would require depictions of sequential moving visuals.

My Controller seems to be the chief operator when speaking-in-tongues, in dancing or chanting trance states, and during automatic writing. In these states, core consciousness seems to be as involved or more involved than is our autobiographical Self. Visuals are lacking as auditory dominance occurs when speaking-in-tongues, or conjuring up trances through dancing or chanting; and in automatic writing motor control is taken over by automatic processes without sound or vision playing a major role. A dynamic systems model that employs circular causations seems to offer the best route to a comprehensive explanation of these differences.

If I use Damasio's constructs, my Controller as Core-Self and Interpreter as Autobiographical Self seem to have a shared relationship, but not necessarily equal when I travel out of body, enter the body of another such as the bear, or feel an intense state of empathy. A dynamic integrated model of consciousness must include the element of control. And subjectively, I experience this element, agent, of control at both the core and autobiographical levels. For example, when I have a dream sequence that my dreaming brain doesn't like, it may decide to change the sequence or ending by repeating the entire dream. This can happen without any conscious decision being made by my Interpreter.

This awareness helps me understand how easily we can perceive the presence of another sentient being in our quiet, meditative moods. Ever present spirits, God's omniscient presence, our Guardian Angels—all lurk in the shadows of our shared states of consciousness. From a long-term perspective, I can visualize my Controller at the level of core Self orchestrating an entire piano recital as a complex FAP, and from the level of my autobiographical Self, observe my Controller executing this FAP while I enjoy a pleasant state of rhapsody, the pianist's version of Zen driving. How easy it is to create alternative selves says the multiple personality.

In altered states, I remain in control, although this is not the case for many people entering ASC when they turn control over to some other entity such as God, spirits, hypnotists, therapists who plant false memories, or some occult agent. I'm quite sure my possession of the bear's spirit and body does not have the same meaning as it does to a bona-fide shaman, but I do think our neural circuits are fundamentally operating the same way. I have continuous control, where the shaman has temporarily turned his or her control over to supernatural forces once he or she has gone through initiating rituals. I'm aware of this control throughout the shamanic process, and can guide or terminate what is happening as I do when dreaming lucidly. But as one is caught up in the moment while role playing, one is caught up into the shamanic moment regardless of how consciousness is played out. We can't take the role of the bear and feel its power without this transition.

I don't think we can answer the question of what altered states of consciousness are without cracking the understanding of consciousness itself. Dream research and related physiological studies have taken us a long way. I believe the incorporation of ASC into Hobson's model can take us another step in our visual and cognitive understanding of ASC and consciousness per se. Most shamans or people experiencing altered states tend to specialize, but as I've testified, specialization is not necessary. One can expand their own understanding of consciousness by creating, directing, and controlling a wide range of altered states.

THE ELEMENT OF CONTROL

The variables of Activation, Information, and Modulation (AIM) simplify our ability to visualize what is going on in the brain. In fact, Hobson devised the model to help clients understand what was going on in their brains for this reason. But for me, the variable of control is critical to an understanding of consciousness in all its varied states. Shamanic practitioners appear strange or other-worldly when control is left out of the equation. Control is a critical element in pathological states and how we deal with these pathologies. I make this statement from personal experience.

When I practice control in dreams, I can stop nightmares or create any plot, characters, scenes, or outcome that I desire. I experienced a high degree of control with the first dream program that I created in 1958, with the ability to enter and re-direct story plots when awake or when I was still sleeping. This felt capacity greatly improved my sense of well-being and enablement, whereas leaving control with a therapist results in a lesser sense of being master of ceremonies.

Individuals entering shamanic or hypnotic trances also have a lesser sense of control. The traditional shaman enters an altered state by performing a ritual, or undergoing some kind of deprivation, or by being guided by a group process. When one enters trance with total control, props are not necessary, external rituals are not needed, and group or environmental influences matter little. What does this mean?

I believe that we can teach our brain to micro-manage the various circuits involved in altered states of consciousness by mastering self-control. Understanding mental illness must include an element of lost control. Mentally ill people often experience a sense of panic as they slide into their favorite illness, and this anxiety must play a continuing role in the creation of imbalance across the brain's neural circuits. The state of panic resulting from lack of control is so frightening to some drug addicted individuals attempting recovery that they often commit suicide.

In my personal history, I not only developed controls for dreams and ASC, but I practiced behavioral conditioning through which I maintained a particular brain state for extended periods of time. I taught myself to concentrate on academic materials for up to eight hours without a break. For someone who was suffering from anxiety, depression, and an inability to concentrate for longer than twenty minutes, this was a major achievement.

Elimination of nightmares permitted full nights of restful sleep. Concentration conditioning resulted in superior academic test performance and a growing sense of being in control of my social world and my future. My brain's own chemical outputs that were most likely destroying dendrites and probably some cells came to a halt with my newly initiated self-controls. These results occurred within one twelve week quarter at the University of Minnesota. Later testing showed a normal MMPI profile, and extensive testing when I was in my mid-50s indicated a boringly normal personality profile. I am now 75 years old and show no debilitating cognitive or behavioral side effects of my childhood traumas or self therapies.

As an undergraduate student of behaviorism and abnormal personalities, as they were called at the time, I assumed responsibility for my self-therapy. I didn't have money for a therapist, and besides, I had already rejected Freud's interpretation of dreams and had major questions about the value of psychoanalysis. By taking control of my own therapy, I was able to experiment and play with dream programming and various altered states. I taught myself to extend continuous concentration to my physiological limits, and I developed control over my physical body that eventually led to fun activities such as Zen driving.

The reader can understand my hesitation to use drugs for therapy. Hobson addresses the sensitive balance in brain chemistry when he says:

This suggests that sanity depends on a delicate modulatory balance generating neither too much forebrain activity nor too little. And while we normally operate within safe limits, we find that various drugs and mental ills can push the system too far in one direction or the other (2001: 124).

I have no doubt that a system that is too far out of whack probably needs to be pushed back into sync with drugs. But I also believe that people with pathologies who are generally able to be functional day-to-day can learn similar controls without drugs. At minimum, I'm a case study of one.

In any case, individuals can learn to recognize the slippery slopes that lead to loss of control, and correct them before falling over the edge. I learned to control my body and many of its autonomic functions in a gradual process of enhancing self-control through my use of self-hypnosis. If I could control my heartbeat at will or block the sense of pain in my hands, I could control behavioral responses directed by my brain. At least, that's how I saw in back in the 1950s. I still do, but the model is now a bit more refined.

THE ELEMENT OF SOCIAL CONTROL

We study the ancient history of art expression in Homo sapiens in an attempt to understand how our modern brains evolved. We have studied preliterate people around the world in terms of art, music, and dance in order to understand the universality of common brain capacities. In the past, much of this effort has been placed in a biased hierarchy of Western Cultural superiority.

I attempted to remove much of this thinking in my discussion of our religious nature in *Mind of the Mystic*. It has always been amazing to me that we can go to the world's most remote cultures to study altered realities when it is so easy to study the phenomena at home. Here, however, I want to nudge our understanding of altered states of consciousness as social mechanisms.

Let me start with A. Damasio: "At the birth of arts such as music, dance, and painting, people probably intended to communicate to others information about threats and opportunities, about their own sadness or joy, and about shaping social behavior (2010:295)."

He builds his ideas of communication around the concept of social-cultural homeostasis by reflecting the necessity of regulating individual behavior in a social community. I use this example to demonstrate disciplined thinking along the lines of linking our physiological development throughout evolution with our current creation of civilized, literate societies.

Altered states of consciousness can be, and I think should be, viewed from this perspective. When we observe the work of shamans with all their therapeutic and social benefits, we realize that their role in human communities is no less significant at a tribal level than similar functions performed by organized religions operating in more complex social groups. Their functions help knit the social fabric, calm the troubled heart, give meaning and explanation to our existence, and support a worldview that interprets what is going on in their public's mind.

Drums and rhythmic beats resonate with how our brains work. We may not understand all the cascading effects within neural circuits, but today we have a much better understanding of our brain-mind physiology.

Trance occurs through conscious induction or under the control of non-conscious processes, but it occurs commonly across world cultures. Visions happen, speaking-in-tongues takes place as an automatic response to various kinds of priming, spirits come to possess us, and the whole gamut of altered states are expressed as a natural, but not frequent, part of our social world.

It has been common in most preliterate cultures to explain these brain states as putting one in contact with the supernatural spirit world. In *Mind of the Mystic* I described altered states as scrambled neural networks. In other words, they are fairly uncommon neural patterns in our brain-minds that are expressed behaviorally. Nothing mysterious here, but what is really mysterious as we begin our journey into the 21st Century is the continued belief in ancient, pre-scholarly beliefs as to what these mystic states mean.

Shamans and mystics have typically been viewed as possessing special powers or having a special relationship with the spirits, or in the case of organized religion, with God. We all have dreams, and they are remembered best when there is salient emotion expressed in them; an altered state of consciousness, no less, and a state that brought one historically into contact with the netherworld. Incorporating ASC into the cultural fabric solved a number of problems for preliterate people, and one that has been underappreciated by modern medicine and science as manipulation of these states by shamans permitted access to many of the non-conscious processes of the human brain. And in my example of the trauma relief effected with nightmare resolution, we come to appreciate quality shamanic interventions, as we appreciate quality contemporary therapeutic interventions.

Often times, chemicals were used by shamans and their clients to enhance contact with the Netherworld, our brain's non-conscious systems, and for their related therapeutic value. A number of cultures in remote areas of the world such as the Amazon still practice rituals using these chemical inputs. Studying their practices from a mystic-shamanic perspective can be as misleading as it can be insightful. Group drug use can be a positive glue to cement the social group as it can be a means to eliminate and or control anxiety, fear, or culturally induced states such as being possessed by evil spirits.

Failure to study altered states as a normal human capacity from both the individual and social control perspectives has been a loss to modern therapies. It has also been a loss to our understanding of consciousness. Traditional rituals that access non-conscious brain processes help restore both individual and social integration and balance. It supports a sense of self-unity as well as social-unity. I suspect that tapping this route to the non-conscious represents an avenue to better understand what medicine calls the placebo effect. Why should we not expect our human community to discover these mechanisms over a few ten thousands of years? Only geocentricism and cultural snobbery would prevent such understanding.

CHAPTER 13

DREAMS & TRANCES

INTRODUCTION

I will compare a self-induced trance I call my Genesis Journey with Aldous Huxley's Age Regression as reported by Hobson. I've also discussed this trance as a vision. Trances are often activated by shamans using drums, dancing, or various forms of physical deprivation. However, with a little practice, some of us can enter these altered states after a few moments of quiet meditation. State space comparisons using Hobson's model will be discussed along with phenomenological factors related to hypnosis and brain plasticity. An example of speaking-in-tongues, glossolalia, is presented as a non-visual form of an alternate trance state. I envision trance states as involving selective activation of neural circuits while suppressing or reducing input from other circuitry that would normally be expressed when consciously executing visual-motor or speaking abilities.

HUXLEY'S TRANCE: A COMPARISON

Hobson shares a hypnotic trance induced in Aldous Huxley which I will compare with a self-induced trance that I call my Genesis Journey. I'm impressed with the sense of wonder and reality one experiences in these psychic journeys, their vividness, and how magnificently the vision scenarios are constructed by our brains. We create dream-like images and combine them with waking presence, causing a dream that occurs outside of sleep. It's amazing to me that altered states should still be treated as mysterious by so many in the 21st Century, or that these simple, life-like daytime dreams are critical scaffolding used to support major world religions.

GENESIS JOURNEY

It's a cold January afternoon in Rochester, Minnesota. I sit in my favorite reading chair, lean back and engage the recliner, close my eyes for a minute or two, and off I go.

"As I left my body, it felt as though I was riding my brain's electrical pulses. My out-of-body acceleration was increasing geometrically with each subsequent electrical discharge in my brain. I visually moved away from our pale blue dot, continued to pick up speed as I shot past the Sun, watched the Milky Way fully emerge, multiple galaxies come into view, and then I began to move at ever increasing warp speeds. It was similar to watching Star Trek only the warp speed kept multiplying. It was the most moving psychic experience I've ever had. It was not like watching a science fiction film where the viewer knows they are outside looking in; just the opposite, I was aware that I was on the inside looking out. I experienced the unfolding of the universe in reverse of its evolution; I was inside and part of 14 billion years of Big Bang evolution; totally immersed in a reality as vivid as eating dinner. All but my physical body shared this reality, but this sensation of astral travel feels as though one's body is still attached. It was truly wonderful. (Just: 2010: 184-190)"

Experiencing these astounding out-of-body adventures makes it easier to understand how they can be interpreted mystically by so many prophets throughout history. Every Shaman or mystic who uses out-of-body experiences to become the bear, sit on the clouds, the moon, to commune with God or the Saints, or explore the world knows this reality firsthand. It is a reality of the only mind and consciousness we possess, a natural capacity that many of us activate and come to both know and enjoy. Imagine how mysterious this must have been to cave dwellers.

There is little mystery that many of our ancestors and fellow travelers become True Believers. Awe of the universe resides within each one of us. It is the sunset, a special flower, a thought beyond the ordinary, a flight of spirit, the soaring of our souls. Quintessentially, it is being fully human as we come to know ourselves in the Gnostic sense. Only fear, or incapacity, keeps us from enjoying these most natural altered states of reality. Some of us just seem to have more capacity to experience and/or create these mystic boxes that are tucked away in the corners of our minds.

"As I continued to accelerate back in time, the structure of stars and endless galaxies came into focus—voids and walls of galaxies appeared; I was passing through billions of light years of time and space in a matter of minutes. The mature world of modern galaxies gave way to the primeval cosmos of giant suns and chaotic galactic structures. I lost track of time while the subjective speed of my movement through the universe achieved incredible cosmic proportions." The brain must experience a global state of select neuro-modulators for this all-encompassing feeling of elation and wonder to be so overwhelming. It is a sense of quantum wholeness that Rosenblum and Kuttner speculate about in *Quantum Enigma*.

"The trip itself was very different from letting my mind alone go to the beginning of time. Going back through the evolution of time in this manner is to experience the unfolding of the universe from a first-hand subjective point of view. This means, as is the case with normal out-of-body projections, that the traveler experiences his or her body moving as well. Remember, consciousness exists because the brain uses the body as reference in order to activate the processes that constitute self. It is being there, it is a sense of being in the moment.

It is flow compounded a dozen times; or it is the beauty of the rose experienced a hundred times over. There is a wholeness of being and connectivity that one comes away with that transcends mere intellect. It also transcends the flesh and blood of biology; we become a part of the stuff from which the entire universe is created; a oneness that lets us identify with atoms, rocks and trees; we come to identify with the animate and the inanimate, it is a sense of being part of the "All" (Ibid: 186)." It is the force of life itself. How easy it is to mystify these experiences.

I hit a plasma wall that was opaque, and devoid of particles; a time when atoms had not yet formed, a point where time was just beginning—I stopped moving. The time machine in my mind not only permitted me to see thirteen plus billion years of cosmic evolution but to experience it; almost 14 billion years of cosmic history was condensed into minutes. I didn't like the undifferentiated chaos of the plasma, and the sense of total disorientation that it offered. Its incredibly high temperature did not yet permit particles to be formed; total chaos reigned; particle quantum entanglement had not yet come into being. Or perhaps I should say a state of proto-entanglement existed. I experienced that moment in space-time when energy becomes matter (Ibid: 187)." It was that moment in evolution when life and mind were set in motion. A primeval time before giant exploding suns created the stardust that makes life possible. Primordial feeling cannot be written larger.

"I let myself briefly experience the chaos of the plasma, the chaos out of which Everything becomes, and then I moved forward in time, and returned almost instantly to the comfort of my easy chair the way quantum entanglement permits (Ibid: 188)."

Notice how easily one distinguishes between real life experiences and psychic journeys. The comfort of my easy chair remained throughout Genesis even when I hit the multi-million degree plasma. Triangulating trance phenomena with that of dreams helps me understand how body senses enter my dreams, as I've noted elsewhere. Otherwise how could the prophets experience hell?

This was a self-induced altered reality experience. I sat down in my favorite armchair on a cold winter's afternoon and decided to play with some of my favorite concepts from physics, including super-luminary, faster than light flight, quantum entanglement, the Big Bang, and an altered state of consciousness.

Astronomy is a fancy of mine. and I follow it fairly closely, especially astrophysics. What the mind can conceive, the brain-mind can create on demand, include whatever scenery it wants, and play beyond the limits of known physics.

It's exhilarating just to think about how much fun controlled visions really are. Imagine our ancient prophets returning repeatedly to these self-created visions believing that God speaks to them as a favored son or daughter, or the joy of entering the chambers of heaven. One can return to the same scenery and characters in visions just as we can in our normal lucid dreams: Exhilarating, and, so real.

By treating altered states as being mystical or under the control of good or evil spirits, we miss the fun of psychic exploration. But for some, astral travel is a genre written into the cosmos with equal wonder. Worst of all, the virtual reality of dreams and visions become our day-to-day basis from which we interpret our environment. In the same way we can learn and enjoy lucid dreaming, we can learn to enjoy other altered states of reality. Hobson refers to Huxley's altered state as trance, and in like fashion, my Genesis Journey is trance. However, I classify the experience a little differently.

Huxley and I are both enjoying a lucid REM-like dream that is self-created. Consciousness is heightened by the aminergic system while the cholinergic system's input must remain at a moderate level. But this is not a dream, as the altered state is entered and must be maintained with a higher level of input from our aminergic system. Visual trance states emerge so quickly that I assume one need only have slight changes in their micro neuro-modulator balance compared to REM.

In similar fashion, if I'm dancing to rhythmic music, chanting, or being trance induced by flickering lights, there must be a reconfiguration of neural circuitry and probably differential expression of neuro-modulators. Stored memory routines keep my feet and body moving while my brain mostly goes on holiday. I zone out, feel the music, go with the flow, and just experience. Select input-output gating modulation must take place similarly when I engage in Zen driving or speaking-in-tongues.

Those who participate in the Sun Dance of the Dakota-Lakota people, placing skewers through their chest muscles in the hot sun, and dancing until their brains shift states, are experiencing this form of rhythmic trance. Their minds create visions as their bodies enter this cycle of altered brain states. It is a bit like sleepwalking, where motor activity seems to run its own program without conscious input.

The value of a long-term case study like mine is that I can track and compare multiple altered states of consciousness over time. I think these long-term phenomenological experiences offer additional insights that are not obtainable from normal sleep lab research. In this respect, I agree with V. S. Ramachandran about the value of using single strange cases versus large statistical samples: "The criticism is sometimes made that it is easy to be misled by single strange cases, but this is nonsense (2004: xi)."

And in terms of using large samples to create breakthroughs in neuro-physiology, he says that: "… I don't know of even one that was discovered by averaging results from a large sample (Ibid)."

Ramachandran is a unique guy, read his stuff.

Hobson refers to those who sleepwalk as being in two states: "… the upper part of the sleepwalker's brain, the cognitive part, is in deep sleep, while the lower part, the motor part, is awake (1994: 255)."

One can learn to simultaneously enter either of these two states, visual or auditory, and each one feels as though something or someone else is guiding the process. The sense of being guided by a supernatural, or outside source or spirit, is very convincing, especially if one has been taught to believe these sources are real. However, when we induce our own altered states on demand, the sense of another spirit or god being present is modified. If you are a lucid dreamer, you know this sense of doing and watching at the same time. Two different levels of consciousness exist and we are aware of both.

As researchers, I believe we must subjectively experience altered states to fully appreciate them, and we must learn to control altered states without drugs or extreme physical deprivation in order not to be overwhelmed by the trance's seductive reality. You will appreciate this advice if you read the cock-a-mammy written by half the students of shamanism.

In terms of other parasomnias besides sleepwalking, I experienced bed-wetting, tooth grinding, and night terrors as a child. Sleepwalking was fairly limited, but the other three parasomnias were fully expressed. In retrospect, my ability to mix and match brain states of various altered realities were well in place by the age of five.

Aside: I've noted in earlier works difficulty trying to discuss hypnosis and altered states with local psychiatrists when I was a young university professor. The medical community I was familiar with almost exclusively followed Freud's bias against hypnosis. I practiced self-hypnosis, and enjoyed all the fun anyway. I did occasionally use hypnosis to help others with weight loss, or in the case of my spouse, for the delivery of our second child. I was a self-taught practitioner, no formal medical training, and no coterie of followers. I was free to explore the world of altered realities unfettered.

HUXLEY'S AGE REGRESSION

The American psychiatrist Milton H. Erickson … was among those who resisted Freud's injunction because he thought that hypnosis could be used effectively both for diagnostic exploration of the unconscious and for effecting desired changes in behavior (Hobson: 2001: 109).

HUXLEY'S TRANCE

He turned back and noted that the infant was growing before his eyes, was creeping, sitting, standing, toddling, walking, playing, talking. In utter fascination he watched this growing child, sensed its subjective experience or learning, of wanting, of feeling. He followed it in distorted time through a multitude of experiences as it passed from infancy to childhood to school days to early youth to teenage. He watched the child's physical development, sensed its physical and subjective mental experiences, sympathized with it, empathized with it, thought and wondered and learned with it. He felt as one with it, as if it were he himself, and he continued to watch it until finally he realized that he had watched that infant grow to the maturity of 23 years. He stepped closer to see what the young man was looking at, and suddenly realized that the young man was Aldous Huxley himself, and that this Aldous Huxley was looking at another Aldous Huxley, obviously in his early fifties, just across the vestibule in which they both were standing; and that he, aged 52, apparently realized simultaneously that they were looking at each other and the curious questions at once arose in the mind of each of them. For one the question was, "is that my idea of what I'll be like when I am 52?" and, "Is that really the way I appeared when I was 23?" Each was aware of the question in the other's mind. Each found the question of 'Extraordinary fascinating interest' and each tried to determine which was the 'actual reality' and which as the 'mere subjective experience outwardly projected in hallucinatory form' (Ibid: 110).

Now, having been there, inside-out that is, this experience makes perfect sense to me. However, in contrast, Huxley played with drugs, but the only drug assisted vision I ever had was with peyote at a Native American ceremony. And this is speculation on my part as I used very little peyote, and that was early in the evening. The vision appeared late in the early morning of the next day. I don't like drugs period, and prefer to induce and control altered states with a clear head.

Comparison: Hobson makes numerous comparisons with lucid dreaming. In lucid dreams as in trance states, we perform fantastic feats, merge with other characters or animals, violate the laws of physics, assume super-human strength and abilities, and project our self into the minds and bodies of others, to name a few major characteristics of altered states.

I can't do content analysis for Huxley to determine where the imagery came from for his vision, but I can for my Genesis Journey. I will analyze my vision without using Hobson's dream forms. Visions like lucid dreams draw upon our personal repertoire of stored memories. Goat herders or desert wanderers don't have the same content in their visions as modern day users of multi-media do.

Visually, lighting throughout my vision journey was MGM movie quality. I have many pictures in my mind of Earth from space, and I effortlessly shrank the orb dynamically as I sped off to the beginning of time.

The perspective of moving in the vastness of space is something I've acquired both from the media and frequent childhood out-of-body adventures. Shooting out of the solar system, my visioning brain looked back, forward, and in all directions and easily maintained proper perspective in 3D. The Milky Way was probably envisioned more like the Andromeda Galaxy than the Milky Way, but how would I know as an Earth-bound observer?

My dreaming or visioning brain can make space resemble whatever it wants, the same way ancient sages or modern Other-side astral travelers do. Nevertheless physical characteristics of galaxies, galaxy clusters and voids are vivid images that I retain in my mind even as I write these words. The Hubble Telescope has been most helpful in this regard. The ancients entered Heaven, I entered the cosmos.

Since my days as a child, I have always been enamored with the heavens. I played with Northern Lights, Aurora Borealis, as a child in the sense that I physically projected myself into the lights—twisting and turning with sheer delight.

Out-of-body projection has been an at-will capacity for me since the days of my near-death experience before the age of two. Space has always been an emotional, physical, and visual friend from childhood through my adult years. I had no fears on this journey as altered states were familiar experiences, and I had a reasonable background in Big Bang Theory, quantum entanglement, and space-time expansion. In other words, no conflicting emotions were involved to distort my trip's reality, or stop it from unfolding.

My Genesis journey was not role playing, nor was it a type of false memory. It has similarities to dream programming where I decide what I'm going to dream, who the characters are, what the setting will be, and then turn my imagination and archived visuals lose to create the story. Recall that our brains engage these processes automatically when we dream.

The subjective reality of these experiences is that my higher cognitive centers, meta-consciousness, provide the plot and story, and my lower animal level consciousness enacts it. I could duplicate the scenario reported by Huxley if I chose to. However, I had a terrible childhood, which I have no desire to relive. If I fully programmed a lucid dream with similar content, the experience would not be a natural dream. But from either a dream or vision perspective, our higher cognitive centers have the ability to generate visuals to match any perceptions of imagined reality we chose.

I can visualize myself in amniotic fluid, floating around, growing, and assembling genetically programmed circuits. It's too easy to do mentally, and even easier to do in trance or under hypnosis. I'm sure that individuals who believe they have recall of the womb and birth believe with the same fervor of any good shaman or priest. False memory is natural, and the ease with which we create false memory becomes obvious when we analyze lucid dreams or visions, especially when we have engaged in suggestion. And, just maybe, select individuals do retain a bit of original memory. Of course, this is just fun speculation.

Huxley could apparently slip into these trance states in a matter of five minutes or less. For Genesis, I sat in my easy chair reading, decided that an out-of-body trip would be fun, put down my book, closed my eyes, and almost immediately began my journey. It may have been one minute or five, but it wasn't longer. I enjoyed the trip as a first hand observer, and carried with me the comfort of my warm easy chair and living room. My physical body was semi-reclining with feet propped on the footrest. This comfortable posture, and relaxed feeling, physically stayed with me throughout the journey. The only disruption was hitting the plasma wall at the beginning of time.

Observed detail in vision or OBE states can be as specific as the detail one is capable of in their waking life. We are free to interact with the virtual scenes being created, and any of the elements within the trance, as is the case in REM. I was so thrilled at observing the universe unfold that I didn't care to visit any of the other planets or solar systems. I knew that whatever I found would be another creation of my mind. Trance states are not only vivid, but unique for each one of us. We know they are creations of our own mind because there is no universal Other out there. I'm not motivated to go back and continue playing with variations of this vision as I have often done with dreams. As with my history of dream programming, I want to have the experience and the understanding; I don't want to get caught up in drama as some prophets and dream programmers do.

Visions are special phenomenological experiences, but I prefer to spend most of my time in this world. Induced visions or programmed dreams become games for many people. OBE journeyers visit their favorite planet or planets repeatedly and create a world apart, and their dreaming counterparts do the same, as have some prophets historically.

Personally, I don't need or want this repetitive escape from everyday reality. And, I don't think these mind games have anything to do with the supernatural. I am a naturalist. But naturalists don't understand the quantum world any better than super-naturalists do.

Ability to take on other life forms or morph into other characters, including two forms of one's own self simultaneously, is an easy transition for many of us. I have always had this shamanic capacity, which I associate with my mother's smothering and my resulting near-death experience. Talking to our Self? We all do that while waking or dreaming, and nothing is strange about that.

Another variation is to talk to one's Self while projecting entirely into the character of another. When we project into an animal such as the bear, we take on its qualities as we know them, believe we see the world as the bear does, and experience his feelings. The literature is full of such stories: Nothing new here.

COMMENTS ON HUXLEY

Huxley displayed exceptional memory in that he could recall most of his writings at will. I never wrote while in trance, but in a similar fashion as a university student, I could study up to eight hours at one sitting without break and recall 98 to 99 percent of the material. I could test as well over the book's footnotes if the instructor referenced them.

Memory is unhindered by extraneous stimuli in trance states. We have no distractions, and are as unaware of the outside world during these states as we are when dreaming. Every college student should cultivate this capability. Educational systems, such as those in China, stress the importance of memory and self-discipline as part of one's normal education. Memorizing 10,000 written characters is a good starter.

Conscious control of altered states gives me greater control over my entire mind-brain processes. In practice, I could fall asleep on the count of three. When I was on long 20 mile marches in the army, we would stop for cigarette breaks for the smokers. I would sit down, sleep five or ten minutes, and feel refreshed when we returned to marching. My army buddies thought I was strange. Their comments: "How do you do that?" Nice trick, I thought, and marched again with renewed energy. I could easily have completed 40 mile marches this way.

I think writing while in trance can be learned by most people. I report a friend in *Autobiography of a Ghost* who wrote for hours in this state. Give your motor skills systems access to your language center, turn off the conscious controls you normally use when awake, enter trance, and write like crazy. The nice spinoff for most automatic writers is that they do not suffer muscle fatigue even when they write for hours. Wouldn't the military love to do this with legs? Simple FAPs do it.

Huxley may have, and probably did, teach himself these altered states through the use of psychedelics. In my personal experience, once I open up new neural configurations, I can access them at will thereafter. It may take priming, or even considerable priming when one first learns these techniques, but it's doable. For some of us, it's just plain easy.

Hobson says there are probably two routes to trance states: "One is top-down where a hypnotist, shaman or some form of ritual is applied. The other is bottom-up, requiring only a simple but sudden physical stimulus (1994: 24)."

Automatic writing is activated top-down but executed bottom-up. Huxley's regression and my Genesis Journey are executed top-down, the difference being Huxley used a hypnotist, and I used self-hypnotism. Trance can be entered bottom-up and remain bottom up as in speaking-in-tongues, or it can be activated bottom-up as in dancing induced trance. Or one can use top-down control to induce trance dancing. It's much like lucid dreaming where one can consciously decide the degree of higher cognitive input into any specific dream.

Practicing these different altered states, we soon recognize the combinations can become rather creative. This is most obvious when we compare trance and vision states in different cultures. The odd example of the Latah trance state in Malaysia recounted by Hobson represents a slight variation. Malaysians susceptible to this state can fall into it when startled or tickled, and quickly undergo a dramatic state change.

It is as if someone flipped a switch and they suddenly lost contact with reality. They may utter unseemly streams of invectives or become submissively obedient to commands. The Latah trance is a hyper-suggestible state that is self suggested. But unlike hypnosis, it is triggered by a startle stimulus (1994:248)."

This is a startle stimulus that contemporary mental health workers should pay more attention to, although increased understanding would be even better. My Genesis Journey doesn't even require a startle stimulus, because my Interpreter knows the difference.

In my experience, the startle stimulus is learned from one's culture, probably in a fashion similar to one learning to hypnotize him or her Self. The response becomes automatic thereafter. This learning process is easily understood by applying behavioral conditioning techniques, or reversing the products of these techniques as we remove panic reactions from conditioned subjects with phobias, for example.

Belief plays a major role when cultural patterns such as that of the Latah emerge. In my experience, individuals gradually identify a pattern, develop a given set of expectations, and use a form of conscious suggestion in preparation to enter their trance states. The priming comes from one's culture and social group when the syndrome occurs across large numbers of people. Those who fall at the far end of suggestibility succumb. We see a similar phenomenon in our culture for those who come to practice speaking-in-tongues, or in The United States, usually through membership in minority protestant churches.

Some North American Indian cultures have a spirit that manifests itself in dark, wet, and secluded environments. The spirit is detected by its particular odor, which activates a feeling similar to being followed on a creepy street in a large city. Extreme caution must be exercised at this point as the spirit is evil and can cause harm. A snapped twig or branch, the startle reaction of an animal—all can bring the spirit crashing into awareness.

These examples play out expectations that have been acquired from one's culture.

Neuroscience is very aware of the physiological differences and tendencies found in Homo sapiens: I'm a good example of the suggestible, maybe hyper-suggestible. In my experience, expectations become embedded in our memories just as much as behavioral routines are embedded in our motor circuits, and once embedded, they can play out just as easily.

HOBSON ON PARALLEL INTERPLAY OF PHENOMENOLOGICAL FACTORS IN HYPNOSIS AND DREAMING

I like Hobson's Table 5.1 in *The Dream Drugstore* (99). He compares hypnosis and dreaming in his usually clear fashion. However, I approach hypnosis differently than he does, as his focus is on hypnotic states induced by others. The factor of self-control with self-hypnosis creates a different subjective experience than that of being hypnotized by someone else. Trance occurs in either case, but I retain control with self-hypnosis. Further, I can increase the degree of control with habituation.

Table 5.1 on volition:

Hypnosis—volition is voluntarily suspended in the hypnotized state; volition is diminished (at sleep onset) and lost in REM sleep (Ibid).

In contrast, I'm always aware of my control with self-inducted trances, even though the thought of conscious control is not always central when the action is taking place. I know when I enter an altered state trance, or if I program a dream in detail, that I'm in control. I remember the induction, the dream or trance, the process, and my exit from either.

Amnesia is not a factor in these states for me. A neural circuit to consciousness must be open in order for me to maintain control. I can flag action in my dreams that I want to remember, and characters I want to change, or actively enter my dream while it's in process to make these changes. I do not repeatedly recreate trance states as some mystically oriented people do when they visit God or the Other Side, but if I did, I could exercise the same level of control as I do in dreams. As Hobson tells us, trance states use different neural channels and brain chemicals. For me, the degree of lucidity varies with the type of trance induced.

Restak discusses hypnotic instructions and their consciousness splitting effect thus:

Hypnosis and other forms of directed attention produce similar splits in conscious awareness. Elaborate instructions given during the hypnotic trance are later carried out without awareness or memory (Ibid: 183).

The researcher focusing on the hypnotists as the controller, and the key element of split consciousness awareness, draws attention away from the fact that the hypnotized person is responsible for the brain's state change. In my experience, an entire area of therapeutic hypnosis is neglected when control is left in the hands of the hypnotist.

Focusing on an outside controller detracts from the therapeutic potential that can be under one's own control. Self-hypnosis or hypnosis performed by another person must be accessing essentially the same brain-mind mechanisms. Focus on the hypnotist adds an unnecessary level to process interpretation. In like fashion, why would you want me to program one of your dreams, determine its content, characters, and plot when you can control these elements for yourself? That is the difference.

Self-hypnosis offers its practitioner the potential of immediate intervention into brain-mind processes. Try to effect brain-mind state changes with pharmaceuticals on this time scale. In the Freudian Era of psychotherapy, therapists forgot the traditional role of the shaman as guide. They became authoritarian figures operating from the outside rather than guides who helped clients flip switches from the inside. Basically, from my experience, the placebo effect is activated by an internal switch. Hobson's creation of the AIM Model to help clients visualize these processes is a step back into analysis of the shamanic tradition from this perspective.

I don't have to be conscious of so called unconscious processes when I ride my bicycle, because I just balance and Will away. I simply will the bike to go right or left or make small scale fine motor maneuvers. Nobody thinks this has anything to do with an outside controller, unless you are paranoid.

Hypnotic trance behaviors are executed by the person who is hypnotized, not by the hypnotist. Most fundamentally, the hypnotist is just showing the inductee how to use his or her abilities to change brain states. This misconception of control by another person creates fear in many people who refuse to be hypnotized, which is probably a carryover from Freudian ideas that still influences the medical community. Many medical personnel in my history have been as paranoid about hypnotic trance as are major church leaders who perceive evil forces at work.

Fearful individuals often believe the popular cultural rhetoric about being unable to interrupt the hypnotist's controls if they are asked to perform morally conflicting deeds. I've experienced this same naïve interpretation by medical doctors and therapists as much as from lay persons without any medical background. Inability to control hypnotic suggestions becomes a self-fulfilling prophecy. Studying auto-suggestion and external operator suggestions as two separate phenomena helps make the above distinctions.

Most of our motor-based behaviors, including speech, are under control of non-conscious processes. Why should I think that someone else is controlling these processes just because they occur automatically, like walking, hitting a ball, or ducking a missile headed my way? I can let the hypnotist act as my Controller, or I can perform these tasks myself. Either way, I make the decision, because the mechanisms involved are part of my brain-mind. Our response to the hypnotist depends on cultural interpretation. Not much different in terms of belief as when one thinks that shadows in the trees are ghosts. Belief makes it so.

I believe that a two-way feedback loops exist between my dreaming brain, which has access to non-conscious action modules, and my higher order brain-mind functions, and that this two-way feedback loop exists in trance states with or without the participant's awareness. Further, this two-way feedback loop exists during waking moments in order for me to enter and exit various trance states. I provide this interpretation because I can enter, create, direct, and control any altered state. What I believe is different for me is my level of awareness, which I maintain through control.

This is my subjective experience. Trance seems like a mysterious process or state only to the uninitiated. I will my body to do something, and it does so without any conscious effort on my part. My leg raises or my fingers twitch, or my hand stops transmitting a sense of pain. Will is access to body mechanisms that the conscious mind does not normally attend to, like balancing on one's bicycle or walking.

We can learn to consciously control these unconscious commands we call will both in and out of hypnotic trance, or any other kind of trance or dream state. In my opinion, understanding this alternative interpretation of control becomes critical during therapeutic interventions where the client is bothered by auto-created stimuli that are felt to be beyond his or her control. In this sense, self-hypnosis is the strong form of self-suggestion. The weaker form of suggestion is commonly used by lucid dreamers to create desired dream scenarios, which they generally do not enter while their dreams are in process, or fail to use their dreams creatively.

I exercised the same controls over 50 years ago in dream programming. I gave myself the suggestion that when a certain undesirable scene, character, or feeling emerges, the dream suggestion will activate. This seems very straightforward to me.

I'm playing with interrelated neural circuits, and just mix and match them as I choose. It is learned control of these mechanisms that I think can be so helpful to people who are terrified by the effects and feelings they experience when internal or external stimuli drive the conscious brain into dissociated panic or paranoia.

Subliminal awareness, in my opinion, is only confusing because the language of hypnosis implies that control is in the hands of the hypnotist. In like fashion, I may learn that my unwanted voices or visions are beyond my control, and the best I can do is control them with drugs. I argue that the hypnotized person permits the hypnotist this control, and thus almost always has some degree of awareness of the suggestion and related subsequent actions he is to perform, unless he or she willingly agrees to totally suppress awareness. Self-hypnosis can open the black box of non-conscious brain processes and permit us to enter at will.

My experience with hypnotized subjects covers a wide range of controls exercised by either the hypnotized person or the hypnotist. Central to my argument, mental health therapists should stress teaching control to clients who experience voices, visions, and feelings that come unwanted and are considered pathological. In my experience, unwanted phantom visits can be addressed during conscious waking hours when we learn this type of self-control, the same as we confront or bring unwanted dream characters under control in nightmares.

Again, we are forced to consider the meaning of consciousness to the subject in any altered state, and hypnosis performed by another or oneself is no exception. Consciousness falls along a continuum. It is a process, it is dynamic, and in some altered states such as REM sleep, it is partial. By partial consciousness in REM sleep, I'm assuming along with Hobson that only some of the brain's modules are accessible, and that aminergic and cholingeric systems turn on and off differentially in these various altered states, as do other neuro-modulators. We know this pattern of shifting consciousness occurs throughout the night in approximately 90 minute cycles. Consciousness levels change throughout the day as we drift in and out of daydreams. We have busy brains that shift states as different functions, energy levels, and demands occur. We have dispensed with older myths about the brain being turned off when we sleep. Myth busting goes on.

In a hypnotic state, I chose to or not to connect various feedback loops across my brain's sensory modules that generate consciousness and self. What is different for those hypnotized by another person is an inability to change or alter the suggestion while it is being executed. The inductee may terminate the trance, but it is basically impossible to take control from the hypnotist and change the suggestion when the hypnotist has convinced the inductee that he, the hypnotist, is in control. Researchers observing these phenomena from the outside generally miss this distinction and its importance. In my self experiments, this element is critical to therapy related methodologies.

In Chapter 11, I reviewed various altered states that I'm familiar with and made some state-change comments. In *Autobiography of a Ghost,* I refer to these state changes as scrambled neural networks.

Hobson says:

Dissociation is the hybridization of one set of state features with those of another. It has traditionally been seen as pathological... (Ibid: 85).

I have contended throughout this three book series that scrambled neural networks, mixed state changes, are behind the various mystical phenomena reported both historically and in modern times, and further, that these state changes are the driving force behind religion. We can know the mind of the mystic, the mind of the prophet, when we come to understand how neural networks become rewired or form new connections.

The power of the prophet is unmasked when we can duplicate and control these mystic states. Control over altered states leads to understanding that can remove the prophet or charlatan's ability to misuse his or her capacity to control and abuse others. Control over altered states also returns the therapeutic power in the hands of the mystic back to the affected individual who can share this power with the therapist, or use it for self-healing.

Hobson's Chapter 5 in *The Dream Drugstore* is recommended as a concise overview of the chemical characteristics of altered states or as I say, scrambled neural networks. In fact, I would suggest the reader review *The Dreaming Brain,* and *The Chemistry of Conscious States* before reading *The Dream Drugstore.* Enjoy!

BRAIN PLASTICITY & TRANCE

As Doidge notes in *The Brain That Changes Itself*, the ability of our brains to exercise plasticity has been slow in acceptance. However, researchers such as Paul Bach-y-Rita and Michael Merzenich have demonstrated this capacity in both monkeys and humans. Regarding brain exercises, it is demonstrated that education increases the number of branches among neurons.

An increased number of branches drive the neurons further apart, leading to an increase in the volume and thickness of the brain (Doidge: 43).

Brain plasticity is now widely accepted in neuroscience, but when I started my self-experiments in the 1950s, it was considered a radical idea.

Brain plasticity is increasingly less controversial as individuals such as Merzenich create learning modules such as Fast Forward to demonstrate how neurons can be rewired. He is also at the forefront of claims for plasticity with this position:

Merzenich … has made the most ambitious claims for the field: that brain exercises may be as useful as drugs to treat diseases as severe as schizophrenia; that plasticity exists from cradle to the grave; and that radical improvements in cognitive functioning—how we learn, think, perceive, and remember—are possible even in the elderly (Ibid: 46).

Modifying neural circuits that are devoted to specific brain states can occur at any age, but some stages of child development are more critical than others. In my case, I believe my brain was rewired before the age of two when mother's smothering episodes created a near-death experience. I assume oxygen deprivation created cell damage when I lost my toddler ability to walk and talk. Repairs that my brain made restored these abilities, but also left me with epileptic-type seizures. Subsequent neural circuit expression represented new brain-mind functions such as mind-body separation. Neural circuits apparently got rewired at that time. Brain plasticity permits not only change but repair, and sometimes new cell growth, especially for an 18 month old child.

To put another nail in the coffin of early Skinnerian Behaviorism, we selectively encode memory according to our focus and perceptions.

Merzenich discovered that paying close attention is essential to long-term plastic change. Lasting changes occurred only when his monkeys paid close attention (Ibid: 68).

Using self-hypnosis, I increased my uninterrupted study time to eight hours from a baseline of about 20 minutes. What is the qualitative difference between twenty minutes and eight hours? My grade school years of looking out school windows and drumming on desks became a distant memory. Positively, enhancement of my ability to focus carried over into all aspects of my higher cognitive functions. I my case, it seems reasonable that this attention enhancement made conscious control of altered states and ability to enter and change in process dreams easier.

Merzenich's position is that: "You cannot have plasticity in isolation …it's an absolute impossibility (Ibid: 91)."

If you change one brain system you change all those connected to it. If we have 100 billion neurons, each with up to 10,000 dendrites, we have more combinations and permutations than there are particles in the known universe. Even if we only have 20 billion neurons, the complexity of our brains is fantastic. No wonder that a bottom-up reduction approach takes so long. For me, it's more fun to play with 100 billion neurons simultaneously.

In addition to eliminating anxiety, depression, and attention deficits, I had anger issues and three critical elevations on my MMPI. There is considerable professional work currently taking place in the area of brain plasticity, but in my case, I labored in isolation without the guidance of modern neuroscience. The therapeutic community in the 1950s being what it was, it would be decades before researchers such as J. Alan Hobson would expose the mythological fallacies of that generation of psychotherapists.

I viewed my self-therapy as a form of Applied Behaviorism. I was well aware of how behaviorists saw their subjects as passive vessels subject to behavioral modification. I never accepted this assumption of passivity, as my personal approach always provided cognitive control and direction. My 1950s techniques of active-behaviorism were renamed cognitive-behavioral therapy decades later. My key point in this digression is that this was a discovery process in which I came to understand and personally control altered states of consciousness.

I believe that specific protocols that reflect my informal steps to self-control would be of help to significant numbers of clients suffering from syndromes similar to those I've reported. And further, that such protocols carefully implemented would increase the medical communities understanding of underutilized brain-mind mechanisms that permit control of numerous altered states without employing drugs.

V. S. Ramachandran is a delight to read. He has grazed beyond the trampled fields of the herd on what turned out to be greener grass. If I could choose a soul-mate, it would be V. S. R. He has never been seduced by mainstream paradigms in the medical community and neurosciences. He uses his own thought experiments to rethink existing models, as with his approach to phantom limbs. He crafted a careful and effective treatment of phantom limbs by re-conceptualizing what is going on in the brain of individuals suffering from this syndrome. His work fits nicely with brain research that demonstrates adjacent brain areas taking on new neural responsibilities.

"But as phantom limbs show, we don't need a body part or even pain receptors to feel pain. We only need a body image, produced by our own brain maps. 'Your own body is a phantom,' says Ramachandran: 'One that your brain has constructed purely for convenience' (Ibid: 188)."

The results of this research go a long way for me as I seek to explain the relationship between dreams, trance states, and visions. Our self is a virtual construction, and we can do whatever we want with this construction.

The discovery of pain maps has led to new approaches in surgery and the use of pain medications (Ibid: 195).

We have developed the ability to teach the disabled how to move computer cursors with their minds. We have developed new insights into how acupuncture works, and have additional insight into how our minds actually work.

What these 'imaginary' experiments show is how truly integrated imagination and action are… (Ibid: 207).

"Everything your 'immaterial' mind imagines leaves material traces. Each thought alters the physical state of your brain's synapses at a microscopic level," says Doidge (Ibid: 213).

If this were not the case, I never would have been able to remove my nightmares by simply identifying their activation source.

We have much more to learn about how the mind-brain works at micro-levels. But in my case, much like Ramachandran, some of us just re-conceptualized the problem in order to effect the desired changes. Applying psychoanalysis to phantom limbs is a bust, because traditional models obviously do not deal with the brain's physiology. Controlling brain states with drugs alone seems to be another bedfellow.

I don't want to denigrate talking cures, as I've seen their positive effects and personally know the comfort provided by a close therapeutic confidant. Nevertheless, we must distinguish between neurologically-based disorders that can be quickly, easily, and cost-effectively treated by Ramachandran-like technologies, versus ineffective, long, drawn-out talk therapies at exorbitant hourly rates, especially those costly therapies assuming interpersonal dependency and transference. And drug therapy alone is not an adequate alternative.

JUST ON TRANCE:

My near-death hospitalization occurred around the time of my sister June's birth: She is 15 months younger than I am. I assume I left my body and met what I then thought of as angels, because of the brain state change caused by mother's attempt to smother me. Movement out of body was immediate in the sense that I didn't think about it. My recall at this early age is probably quite subjective, even though the visual images remain like printed photos.

After this hospitalization, I often left my body. However, I don't recall distinguishing between OBE while sleeping or awake. I'm stretching my memory as a two and three year old, but I don't think there was a difference. Mother often left me in a locked, darkened bedroom in my crib and left the house for hours. I most likely wavered in and out of sleep throughout the day. I recall watching the light through the window shades gradually change form. I learned to crawl over the cribs sides and inch my way down the stairs to the locked door, where I waited.

As I got older and wanted to fly, maybe five or six years of age, sometimes I added a little running motion to my efforts in order to get airborne. At other times, I just concentrated and left my body. If I experienced falling, I concentrated and stopped myself in mid-air, and then I could move wherever I wanted to by just willing it. As a small child, I never tried flying at high speeds as I found this frightening, just as I did extreme heights.

Rapid change of brain states also occur for me when I project into the body of another, as with the ghost in the movie *Ghost,* or in animal possession when I duplicate shamanic possession of the bear.

When I was about eight years old, and around the time I left my body to travel to the moon, I often practiced repeatedly passing back-and-forth through my bedroom ceiling in an attempt to understand how my physical body could do such a thing. My OBE while dreaming and my OBE during waking consciousness felt the same.

I gradually learned that I could express shamanic abilities at will. I could join the North American Indian Shaman in his possession of the bear, or the actor in the movie *Ghost* by just projecting myself into their frame of reference. Lucid dreams, trances, and visions all became simple exercises. It was from this perspective that I became a student of anthropology and world cultures. As I explored lucid dreaming and various altered realities, I assumed that my ability to enter these states approximated that of others called shamans in world cultures, and I wasn't just observing. I was actively involved.

Mostly, shamanic trance has been left in the black box, and at the same time, mysticism has been promoted through either scientific neglect or overt occult worship. I would like to see the mystery of the mystics put to rest, and a real science of religious experience emerge. I think we can now say rather unequivocally that mystic states, like dreams and trances, are just altered configurations of our neural networks that generate altered realities. And I add, underlie religious beliefs across the globe and throughout history.

Before I move further on with brain plasticity, I want to ruminate about lucid dreaming and its relationship to trance. Lucid dreaming permits us to become conscious while dreaming, and engage in all kinds of fun fictive scenarios. I discovered I could exercise this same capacity with altered states of consciousness. We can have lucid trances. On my Genesis Journey, I could have stopped off at Andromeda, or picked an inhabitable planet and paid the exotic life forms a visit. I didn't do so, as I was enjoying the visual effects of this incredibly vivid lightshow. A similar type of lucidity has been possible for me in other trance states, except glossolalia, where vocalization takes center stage.

Entering trance and remaining lucid parallels entering psychotic states in that we are in two conscious states simultaneously. I don't think between two conscious states is an adequate expression of the phenomenology involved, though. It should be a fairly simple exercise to hypnotize a client prone to psychotic episodes when they are in a normal conscious state and teach them this technique. The therapist might have to teach their client other smaller types of controls first that lead one to master self-hypnosis, such as hand-pain desensitization. Preempting the internal startle response to hallucinatory episodes through suggestion, or priming, and self-hypnotic controls worked well for me.

Hobson says that: "… during lucid dreaming, the cortex has caught up and can begin to direct, or at least watch, the action from a distance, like directing or watching a movie (1994: 173)."

Lucid trance states, like lucid dream states, can permit one to not only watch the action at a distance, but take control. Therapists who are unfamiliar with altered states seem to miss both a lot of fun and considerable insight. Viewing altered states as a variation of normal brain functions is a paradigm shift, and one that exists independent of pharmaceuticals.

This perspective goes beyond the model of the old psychodynamic practitioners or those who would promote drug therapy as a singular approach, but it is well within the reach of Hobson's envisioned neurodynamics. I would love to see researchers determine whether or not my self-control interventions work for others. I know it was simple to learn how to control blood flow to my body parts, change heart rate. and block pain centers. I think I was also controlling microstates in my brain when I took charge of anxiety, dramatically increased my attention span, and subdued the blues.

As a teenager and young adult, the idea of soul as a separate entity from one's physical body never made sense to me: Why would an all-powerful God want to create endless non-material souls with free will, then kill off the body while preserving the soul, wait a few millennium, and resurrect the body, or so my young mind reasoned. If you're into souls, embodied souls make a lot of sense, or evolution is a joke. Consequently, I came to treat my mind as a biological entity by the time I entered the University of Minnesota. Descartes, Aristotle, Kant and the Christian Mystics were all fun to read, but they didn't live in my world.

EXAMPLES OF BRAIN PLASTICITY

My self-experiments as an undergraduate university student in the late 1950s permitted me to greatly improve my ability to concentrate, remove anxiety and depression, and gain control over major life goals. Physiological research on the brain has made great strides since then. Sharon Begley reviews some widely known research on brain plasticity in *Train Your Mind Change Your Brain* (Bagley: 2007), and the reader will find many other similar examples supporting brain plasticity.

A simple list of findings related to brain plasticity from Bagley:

1. Selectively the brain can generate neurons. "… adult mice produced twice as many new cells in their brain's hippocampus as sedentary mice did (Ibid: 66)."

2. Genes do not automatically express themselves as expression occurs from gene-environment interaction. "Michael Meaney, from Montreal's McGill University … has toppled the idea of genetic determinism." He has … showed that the way a mother rat treats her babies determines which genes in the baby's brain are turned on and which ones turned off…(Ibid: 10)."

   Suppression of dominant genes in adolescents due to trauma and neglect show similar results, and the probability of the child becoming delinquent multiplies geometrically. Good nurturing, no problem, but bad nurturing, and we get delinquency: Genetic-conditioning interaction that represents another form of brain plasticity.

3. Studies of Buddhists and their meditation habits show selective strengthening of neural circuits related to meditation.

4. Jeffrey Swartz of UCLA: "… signals capable of changing the brain could arrive not only from the outside world through the senses they could come from the mind itself (Bagley: 137)."

I can personally attest that obsessive-compulsive thoughts feel as though they are coming from a part of mind that is not under one's own control. It feels as though something out there is controlling our behavior.

Therapy alters "… the metabolism of the OCD circuit…an avenue of self-directed neuroplasticity… (Ibid: 140-141)."

And in my experience, self-induced and self-directed intervention gave me the controls I was seeking.

When we conceive of the problem as one of brain wiring, treatment procedures change rather radically. In my autobiography under "Mind Controlling Cracks" I became so angry with the cracks controlling my behavior that I begin stomping them in a fit of anger. The more I stomped, the greater my control. Physiologically, I was interrupting a feedback loop in my neural circuits.

I then adopted an attitude that I was master of the cracks, and just stomped them again whenever they threatened me. I was eleven years old and learning to be responsible for my own behavior. Techniques of cognitive-behavioral therapy employ similar circuit-breaking techniques when interrupting or extinguishing compulsive-obsessive behaviors.

5. Attachment disorders of children that carry over into adult years can be attributed to faulty circuits. Nevertheless, the consequences of such disorders are just as real as if one were experiencing organic damage.

6. One final example from Bagley on brain plasticity that is related to focal dystonia. This is a condition where a pianist has two fingers that become glued together, i.e., the fingers respond together rather than separately. Obviously, if the pianist is on the concert circuit, this is a big problem. Mental reconditioning, as is the case with phantom limbs, can reverse this connection when the proper procedures are followed. The procedure is similar to Ramachandran's therapy with phantom limbs that are painful.

In the late 1950s and through the 1960s, I was not in contact with physiological research as its development is reported in Kandel's autobiography. I found no receptive ears among my professors or the medical community, thus, I just kept active with self-experiments until my curiosity was satisfied and I got the desired results.

Paul Bach-y-Rita developed a system using tactile sensation from the skin to allow blind people to see. His subjects were adults who were relatively non-plastic, but adapted to his system in minutes and hours not days or weeks. Noe uses this as an example of perceptual plasticity versus neural plasticity (2009: 56-58). Noe argues that it is our relationship with the outside world that drives the type of plasticity demonstrated by Bach-y-Rite. At this point, Noe and I part company.

My experience with nightmare elimination demonstrates an immediate change; nightmare explained, nightmare gone. This is a perceptual form of plasticity because my neural circuits, like Bach-y-Rita's experiment, did not have time to change. My interpretation says my master controller, Interpreter, resets communication in my brain's neural circuits, thus eliminating the problem. This reset mechanism operates when I practice vision or trance states, and when I'm awake and fully conscious. It operates when I stomp sidewalk cracks. It comes into play when my waking or dreaming brain interprets a complex set of interrelated concepts, and changes them into a new configuration.

Plastic changes to our brains must be of two types:

1) Neuronal mass and dendrite changes, and,
2) Reconfigurations of circuit connections.

Yes, I believe our perception and consciousness is influenced by our environments, but seeing this change mechanism as being primarily influenced outside of our own brains is to reintroduce mysticism into a brain that is constantly being demystified. In a global evolutionary sense, we mobile creatures developed around our relationships to outside stimuli, but the mechanisms I'm engaging are internal. One of the values of using self experiments over many decades is control of these mechanisms even if we cannot yet explain them from a cellular or circuit point of view.

My experience with other forms of altered states of consciousness provides additional support that an internal mechanism of our higher cognitive centers is responsible for perceptual plasticity. When I possess the body and persona of the bear, it feels as though I am no longer in my body, but in the bear's. No rewiring here. When I leave my body and journey in outer space, there is no rewiring either. When I enter trance through glossolalia or dancing, the effects emerge in minutes. There's no rewiring here either. My sense of control, what I call the Interpreter or Controller, conducts the perceptual shift and reorders the meaning of everything that I'm experiencing, whether these stimuli come externally or internally.

I think my examples of immediate changes wrought by my Interpreter support a concept of meta-consciousness. At the level of core consciousness, we can create beautiful movie scenarios or engage in Zen driving. A rather high level of image abstraction must occur for these processes to be expressed. However, a more sophisticated level of abstraction must be operating for my Interpreter to immediately eliminate nightmares. Abstractions at our core level of consciousness re-imaged and free of body imagery seem the best solution to my concept of the meta-consciousness mechanism.

It seems that evolution now permits Homo sapiens to mentally restructure any or all of the sensory information feeding into our three pound enigma. Our capacity to model the world around us, our ability to use mirror neurons to share the mind of others, and our brain's ability to duplicate the chemical states driving another's feelings, all speak to this conscious capacity which underlies being conscious of being conscious. Placing any aspect of consciousness outside of Self fogs over our sensory experiences, and deemphasizes the dynamic relationship between Self and environment that is under our individual control.

Noe's interpretation takes a giant step toward mystifying consciousness. A little further movement and we begin to embrace the realm of quantum consciousness. This is a violation of Occam's razor. It's a violation of documented perceptual plasticity as I've outlined it. It's a reverse step back into the black box of Skinnerian Behaviorism.

We create altered states and we can control them. This interpretation, I think, is fundamental to the development of new therapies for mental illness and other states of consciousness that trouble us.

CHAPTER 14

GLOBAL STATES, PHILOSOPHY AND COGNITIVE SCIENCE

INTRODUCTION

Hobson's publications are a good example of how researchers accumulate new knowledge over time. The scientific process is like a glacier that slowly creeps across the land. Compared to a hundred years ago, today's scientific findings multiply at a rapid pace, and sub-disciplines proliferate like weeds in an unkempt garden. Interdisciplinary research begs to be incorporated in new paradigms, and newly applied methods add richness to this accumulating knowledge base. And the days of sustained dominance by a Freud or Jung are dead.

I've shared riches offered by many researchers that reflect the struggle of a bottom-up approach to explaining consciousness. Historically, like any complex problem, attempts to explain consciousness have focused on cognitive musings in philosophy and religion. As with most complex problems, we do not reveal complicated structures and functions in physics, chemistry, biology, or psychology by just applying formal logic, which is the fallacy of classical philosophical approaches of an Aristotle, Descartes, or Kant. Understanding basic mechanisms and processes in core disciplines emerges with careful observation, new technologies, methodologies, and sequential ability to remove false premises.

There is a role to play for theoreticians and model builders who look past current paradigms to re-conceptualize what is called reality, with Einstein, Schrodinger, Darwin, and Galileo being common examples. But in all cases, confirmation, integration, and progress are made by applying some version of the scientific method. The more complex the problem, the greater is the challenge and required effort. I have argued in this book that self-observation and self-experiments offer one more window from which to view consciousness. And as Ramachandran has demonstrated, one's ability to conceptualize problems can be as critical as technology in gaining answers. But eventually all must be held to the flame of scientific proof.

In this chapter, I will look across some interdisciplinary approaches to consciousness with a global state focus. Much of the review presented thus far has focused on smaller units of research that have built the basic structure from which to understand consciousness – Kandel, LeDoux, and Restak being good examples.

The scientific process of building bottom-up explanations for basic mechanisms supporting consciousness has been tremendously successful. Llinas and Damasio have been seminal researchers and thinkers in terms of putting the big picture together, as they range from primordial feelings to Self. Now I'll try to combine their research with a global perspective that retains focus on dreams and altered states.

I'll start by briefly touching on Hobson's AIM Model. Damasio and Llinas offer me the most insight into my own dreams and altered states of consciousness, hence, will act as a summary. Dream research, especially Hobson's, will be superimposed on Damasio and Llinas's work. Nunez's research on global electrical brain states will be presented in order to flesh out a combined sense of global consciousness. Shapiro contrasts three models of embodied cognition with the standard model of cognitive science.

I will not provide a detailed review of these works, but criticize them instead from the perspective that is informed by long-term dream analysis. Shapiro sees Lakoff and Johnson's approach with metaphor as being un-testable, while I present the latter's use of metaphor as being highly compatible with a dynamic integrated systems model supported by self-observation in dreams and other altered states. I appreciate Shapiro's *Embodied Cognition* for clearly laying out cognitive sciences current status on embodiment, but find it seriously lacking in use of necessary constructs from neuroscience as set forth by Llinas and Damasio. *Embodied Cognition* serves as a good comparative backdrop to the bottom-up historical research findings and subsequent aspects of global integration by the various researchers and neuroscientists that I've covered.

I've attempted to integrate a broad spectrum of research on consciousness. Each discipline adds its own bricks to this edifice, and each brick has helped me understand my own dreams, consciousness, Self, and altered states a little better. I've left out volumes of detail and have been selective with prominent researchers; nevertheless, this book is twice the length I originally imagined. My goal has been to bring into relief long-term observations and self-experiments with dreams and altered states, and how these observations inform about controversial issues such as dream functions, Free Will, and creativity. I'm grateful to the professional efforts of so many who have opened windows into the historical black box that sits on our shoulders.

HOBSON'S UPDATE: AN ALTERNATIVE MODEL OF DREAMING

(Hobson: 2001: 179-181).

Hobson's 2001 AIM Model update removed lingering criticisms that his earlier work gave too much credit to brain stem activity. For comparative purposes, I included his original model assumptions and their modifications over time. Earlier, I did not fully appreciate how necessary it was to document the bottom-up approach to consciousness in order to put classical psychodynamics of the Freudian-type to bed.

Hobson addresses his critic's concern that Activation Synthesis "… overemphasized the dependence of dreaming on REM sleep." And his update states that:

Dreaming can occur in the absence of REM, especially at sleep onset and during Stage II sleep in the early morning hours prior to awakening. Such dissociations of dreaming from REM sleep indicate that the forebrain could enter physiological states capable of engendering dream consciousness without the brain stem's involvement. It was therefore further proposed that the forebrain mechanisms of dreaming were autonomous of brainstem influence and that REM sleep physiology was incidental to dreaming (Ibid: 179).

Brainstem insignificance is totally rejected as indicated by my dream reports. During waking states, both conscious and non-conscious influences are active, and in like fashion, both are active when I'm dreaming. My awareness of input across brain state varies with the type of dream function being expressed. Self-observation that dreams can be activated by the brain stem or by higher cortical activity is in agreement with Hobson's current position. The ease with which I can enter and leave other altered states also supports this interpretation.

Hobson continues:

With respect to the integrated model proposed here, the forebrain-activation alternative to AIM also emphasized changes in activation but postulated a shift toward intrinsic cortico-cortical inputs as the main source of endogenous stimulation (Ibid).

I've addressed forebrain changes in activation with examples of thought dreams as well as how the brain-mind derives meaning when I discussed various types of bridging elements. From this perspective, I assume dynamic interplay across brain subsystems in dreams and other states of consciousness. Immediate cessation of nightmares when my Interpreter identified their source indicates that feedback loops are operating across higher and lower brain subsystems that contribute to consciousness. Damasio's three concepts of Self – proto-Self, core Self, and autobiographical Self, with two levels of consciousness are compatible with this perspective.

From my experience, activation is not solely brainstem or forebrain. There must be a dynamic exchange across systems. I best explain my thought dreams as being activated by my higher cortical centers. And in a corollary fashion for my Genesis Journey, I move directly from a normal waking state into trance. It appears that altered states of consciousness, including dreams, share different neural circuits that can be activated and configured in more than one way; therefore, one size does not fit all.

Hobson:

The forebrain activation model was therefore not related either to input-output gating in the periphery or to the changes in the rates of aminergic-cholinergic neuromodulation of the forebrain. A slight change in activation was all that was needed to produce the shift from waking to dreaming consciousness, and a change in forebrain activation was thus necessary and sufficient to produce dreaming (Ibid:179,189).

My rapid entrance into altered states or sleep supports this position. Rapid entrance into lucid dreams is most noticeable for me when I'm enjoying an afternoon nap. If I'm tired and woken by my wife for any reason, I may exchange comments about some activity, and while she is making her last statement, I'm already reentering or entering a dream. In this case it feels like the dream never stopped, and I was interacting in both modes. In like fashion, I can get up in the middle of the night, use the bathroom, and reenter my dream world as my head is hitting the pillow. Often this means reentering a dream at the point I left off, much like restarting a movie that was put on pause: There exists a dual level of consciousness throughout these transitions.

For me, entering lucid dreams or other altered states depends on mood, energy level, and the types of internal and external stimuli I'm experiencing. I find myself in total agreement with Hobson when he says:

I consider it to be a matter of fact that consciousness is a continuum of states, that aspects of two or more sometimes distinct states can coexist, that consciousness can be dreamlike even in waking, and that it is likely to be more so at sleep onset (Ibid:180." Hobson continues: "It thus seems to me quite reasonable to propose that we can explain many of these facts by changes in the level and distribution of activation in the forebrain, and that one forebrain site can become an input source for another (Ibid).

Over fifty years ago, I actively practiced what I called dream programming providing plot, character, scenery and outcome to my dreams. I believe then as I believe now that a feed-downward loop is part of dream activation. In similar fashion, my interpretation of dreams, especially nightmares, says there has to be a feed-upward loop to my forebrain as well. The tone of my long-term self-observations harmonizes with Hobson's music. I now believe that brain stem dream activation is mainly concerned with homeostasis, maintaining the body states in a narrow range of variance, alerting the dreamer to emotional threats, and supporting memory functions. I do not mean by this statement that select areas of the brain control different types of dreams or functions. Dynamic integrated systems mean that feedback loops exist across the entire system.

There has been great progress understanding dream physiology and consciousness by dream labs and with research findings in a number of related areas, as integration of these diverse models and scientific disciplines takes place one step at a time. Replicable research always takes precedence over speculation based on thought alone. I provide a brief overview of Hobson's work throughout this volume. A reasonable

AIM Model update can be found in *The Dream Drugstore* (2001:184, 192-195).

DAMASIO AND CONSCIOUSNESS

I've taken Antonio Damasio's twelve steps to consciousness from the December, 2010 issue of *Discover* rather than a synopsis from his 2010 book *Self Comes to Mind*. I appreciate Damasio for clarity of thought and ability to transfer this clearness of mind to paper. His steps to consciousness are abbreviated below.

Step 1: Looking at the brain's complex of neural circuits, he states: "Neurons are organized in small microscopic circuits, whose combinations constitute progressively larger circuits, which in turn form networks or systems. Minds emerge when the activity of small circuits is organized across large networks so as to compose momentary patterns (66).

Step 2: "Conscious minds result from the smoothly articulated operation of several, often many, brain sites. The oddest thing about the upper reaches of a consciousness performance is the conspicuous absence of a conductor before the performance begins, although as the performance unfolds, a conductor comes into being (Ibid).

In other words, neuronal activity occurs before the self emerges to direct subsequent activity. Dreaming from this perspective is activated prior to conscious awareness, hence is not activated by it. This position is compatible with Hobson's A-C Model. The reader will note that the emergence of self from this perspective resonates with self-organization in dynamic systems.

Step 3: "The patterns, or maps, of the mind represent things or events outside the brain, either in the body or in the external world. Ultimately, consciousness allows us to experience maps as images, to manipulate those images, and to apply reasoning to them." "Maps are also constructed when we recall objects from inside our brain's memory banks (Ibid)."

A type of virtual reality is always being constructed by the mind from both internal and external images. We cannot miss this process in our dreams if we identify the origin of dream content, especially when we actively involve our self in the dream process. Dream programming and dream suggestion speak directly to image and story formation in our dreams, where suggestion and cultural expectations are always at play.

Note that primary image formation allows animals without our enlarged cerebral cortex to plan and act with purpose, and to exhibit knowledge of cause and effect relationships even though they do not possess language. Using Damasio's terms, they possess a known self that he calls "me," even though the higher autobiographical Self he calls "I" has not fully emerged. It is across these developmental levels that I focus on primary image formation which progressively becomes complex metaphor. A major problem in cognitive science is how primary images emerge. I'm arguing that one can only observe this process of primary image formation in dreams. FAP dreams such as bike balancing being the example that I've developed in this book.

Step 4: Damasio envisions a slice of brain tissue laid on a microscope: "... in each cortical layer that you inspect, a sheath-like structure that essentially resembles a two-dimensional square grid. The main elements in the grid are neurons, displayed horizontally. "One can sketch patterns onto such a grid..." and, "...the lines in a brain map ...are... the result of momentary activity of some neurons and the inactivity of others (67-68).

Brain maps are distributed across neuronal space as groups of neurons turn on and off, continuously creating consciousness and self. For me, this process helps explain the jerky quality of dreams and their related morphing features. But note that this complex of circuits being turned on and off still maintains consciousness, but consciousness is not an expressed select group of circuits. The jerky transitions we experience in dreams results from the normal expression of how consciousness is created and expressed. During waking hours, we fill in gaps and access so-called memory packets to provide a smooth experiential flow.

Step 5: "Brain maps are not static …" and "Brain maps are mercurial, changing from moment to moment to reflect the changes that are happening in the neurons that feed them…" also: "The images in our minds are the brain's momentary maps of everything and anything, inside our body and around it, concrete as well as abstract, actual or previously recorded in memory (68)."

All of both the internal and external sensory activity is dynamically, continuously being organized by the brain's cartographic skill.

This model of consciousness is highly dynamic, and consciousness itself is dependent upon the constant chattering of neurons. When we are awake, our controller is directing outcome based activity, and we have a sense of being in control. When we are sleeping, the interpretation occurs after the fact as the brain appears to be performing many maintenance functions such as memory integration and consolidation. Hence, we experience bizarreness, rapid changes of scenes, characters, and sensations. In my interpretation, this change while dreaming adds a more pronounced awareness of being an observer in our dreams versus our waking states. When awake, I have sustained moments, periods, when my self is resting or only being casually alert and paying attention. Constant character and rapid scene shifts in dreams does not permit my conscious mind to doze or wander.

Step 6: "Because brain maps are the substrate of mental images, mapmaking brains have the power of literally introducing the body as content into the mind. But body-to-brain mapping has a peculiar aspect, for although the body is the thing mapped, it never loses contact with the mapping entity, the brain. Under normal circumstances they are hitched to each other from birth to death. Just as important, the mapped images of the body have a way of permanently influencing the very body they originate in. "Any theory of consciousness that does not incorporate these facts is doomed to fail," says Damasio (Ibid).

The two way interaction between brain-mind and body stressed by Damasio is basic. It is central to his concept of consciousness. Hence, waking consciousness and dreaming consciousness must include this relationship. My DIS Model of dreaming is in agreement with this emphasis. The intimate relationship in dreams with body states, hormones, brain chemistry, and FAP-like memory speaks directly to this relationship.

Step 7: Discussing "Sensual Windows On The World" Damasio notes that: "The body tells the brain: This is how I am built and this is how you should see me now. The brain tells the body what to do to maintain its even keel (68)."

The brain-mind is using all of the body's senses to stay oriented and direct the body in physical space.

We shouldn't forget that gravity plays a role, and is sensed by the brain as is evident when we jiggle a baby up and down through space and share the giggles. In my understanding, disconnecting this neural network creates the sense of flying and being free of gravity. It is the source of out-of-body experiences that first occurred for me before the age of two. Subsequently, I was able to disconnect this circuit at will and enjoyed flying from toddler age on. Light-headedness after consuming too much alcohol is a chemical form of near-OBE that many people recognize as they approach either coma or circuit disconnect.

Step 8: "Feelings of emotions … are composite perceptions of what happens in our body and mind when we are emoting. As far as the body is concerned, feelings are images of actions rather than actions themselves. (68-70).

Feelings as images of actions are a combination of electrical and chemical activity across the brain, and down the spinal column in many instances. I feel fear and joy before my conscious brain-mind maps it. This cause and effect relationship is explained mechanically by the mapping-re-mapping process that goes on.

Qualia are the instantiated, abstracted images that result. And when re-mapped, feeling images can be and are manipulated symbolically in our dreams. We don't need quantum theory to explain this process. Llinas also agrees.

Step 9: "Consciousness is a state of mind – if there is no mind, there is no consciousness. The conscious state of mind is experienced in the exclusive, first-person perspective of each of our organisms, never observable by anyone else." Further, "Conscious states of mind are possible only when we are awake. Conscious states of mind are felt (Ibid)."

This applies to lucid dreaming as well; conscious states are felt in dreams as they are in waking consciousness. To be free of feeling is to be not conscious. Consciousness also makes what is called the soul a body-dependent entity. Damasio removes mysticism from consciousness.

Step 10: Autobiographical selves "… draw on the entire compass of our memorized history, recent as well as remote. The social experiences of which we were a part (or wish we were) are included in that history, and so are memories that describe the most refined among our emotional experiences, namely, those that might qualify as spiritual. As lived experiences are reconstructed and replayed, their substance is reassessed and inevitably rearranged, modified minimally or very much in term of their factual composition and emotional accompaniment (Ibid)."

From this point of view, the autobiographical Self, or Interpreter, plays a similar role in lucid dreaming. The autobiographical Self uses images that are totally created internally along with images formed from outside stimuli in its consciousness processes. Our dreaming brains are often more creative in rearranging memories as they are less distracted by the noise of our waking environments. Dreaming brains can randomly access memories that are recorded during waking consciousness, or during non-conscious states. Clearly, what I've called FAP dreams is an example of the latter. Note that acquiring a skill such as balancing is non-conscious, and this form of non-consciousness differs from creating dream scenarios whole and building on these scenarios over the years. My little piece of Heaven in N.W. Wisconsin is an example of the latter.

Step 11: Damasio says we have: "… a mind with an autobiographical self that is capable of guiding reflective deliberation and fathering knowledge." This reflective self asks the why, where, and how questions. "That is when myths are developed, when social conventions and rules are elaborated, leading to the beginnings of a true morality (Ibid)."

Consciousness necessitates belief, which is a fundamental part of why and how we navigate our world. From my point of view, understanding these physiological processes permits the emergence of a grounded study for understanding belief systems and religion. We cannot explore consciousness without being confronted with belief, morality, and spirituality, as they are a very personal part of our own brain-mind developmental histories. From this physiological base, they become the basic scaffolding for our socio-cultural past and present. We thus trace the physiological basis of spirituality through various psychological processes to its higher hierarchical expression in cultural institutions of religion.

It becomes fairly apparent that how memory, consciousness, and Self come to be leads inevitably to the universal emergence of what we call spiritual or religious experiences. Triangulating the analysis of dream and other altered states helps bring these processes into focus. I detailed my personal history in this regard in *Mind of the Mystic.*

Reflective deliberation is not just something that happens when one is awake. My dreams are constantly full of reflections that cut-across all of my major life events, especially my professional history and personal relationships. Last night, (8-17-11) is a good dream example. I revisit an old teaching colleague and fellow graduate student. We are at current teaching assignments, although we are also both retired. We are in physical settings that reflect both our major professional work environments, but considerable liberty is taken by the dream to select content of its choosing. Dream content is a mixture that spans a 40 year time period.

We discuss both our current views on our professional histories and how our professional careers unfolded. I am conscious that personal conflicts with this former colleague are to be forgotten and some form of our old friendship renewed.

Step 12: "Traits and functions rise or fall in the history of life depending on how much they contribute to the success of living organism." This is Damasio's way of saying that evolution selects for consciousness and specific types of consciousness because it confers adaptive advantage.

He also says directly that consciousness is not something found only amongst humans or higher primates. It begins at least at the bacterial level. But, that's another story. Read *Self Comes to Mind* for a more complete interpretation.

Both forms of consciousness as awareness and consciousness of being aware that we are aware are expressed in our dreams. It is this higher form of consciousness that lets me have conversations with myself in my dreams, just as I have conversations with myself when I'm awake. The awareness that permits me to make this distinction in waking moments also permits me to suppose this level of communicative exchange when I'm dreaming. Consciousness at a primary and core level of awareness is represented by body state dreams which address balance, hot, cold and gravity stimuli.

From the perspective of lucid dreaming, we can explore how these various levels of consciousness come to be, as well as explore how our innate morality and belief systems emerge. Applying an evolutionary perspective to consciousness and dreams helps me engage this heuristic stepladder of physiological processes to create what I think of as meta-insight. Philosophers and New Age Thinkers are increasingly compelled to include Damasio in their speculative formulations: Attempting to explain consciousness, self, image formation-language, or human subjectivity without including emotion-feeling elements is not reasonable. In fact, it is not even possible.

The degree to which the Self is prominent during consciousness varies, but it is always present to some degree if we are conscious.

Damasio says:

When we are unsolicited by the outside world, our self moves closer to center stage and may move further forward when the object under scrutiny is our own person, alone or in its social setting (2010: 229).

I especially notice the changes in self saliency as I move across levels of dream control and through various altered states. And, to the degree that I initiate, direct, and control a dream or altered state, saliency runs parallel to the degree of consciousness control that I maintain.

Self Comes to Mind continues to refine Damasio's earlier works. I wish, however, to emphasize one of his key ideas: "... the globalized nature of the conscious mind is undeniable (Ibid: 249)." And, "At any given moment, the conscious brain works globally, but it does so in an anatomically differentiated manner (Ibid: 241)."

In lucid dreaming or lucid altered states, we experience various degrees of consciousness, and with practice, we can exercise various degrees of conscious control over dreams and other altered states by an active agent called the Interpreter.

From Damasio's perspective, the brain stem, thalamus, and cerebral cortex are the three critical interacting brain structures that have given us consciousness with human self and awareness over evolutionary time. The conscious self operates globally in dreams or when we are awake. Compatible with Damasio's perspective, I call these patterns of interaction a dynamic integrated system that multitasks when we are dreaming as it multitasks when we are awake. Some of these processes enter our awareness and some take place below our level of consciousness. From my dream reports, I observe the mirror reflection of non-conscious processes. But most importantly if the reader accepts Damasio's interpretation, as I do, the conscious Self when awake or when dreaming operates across this global framework. I can't understand my dreams without this micro to macro perspective.

OVERVIEW OF LLINAS

I introduced Llinas in Chapters 2 and 4 because his basic model helps me interpret FAP dreams. *I of the Vortex* is a seminal work that moves his reader from neurons to self, hence, is a micro to macro interpretation of how consciousness and Self emerge in the course of evolution. Llinas and Damasio's works are central to my interpretation of image formation, feelings and symbolic thoughts in my dreams.

Their presentation of qualia is essential to my understanding of how self and language come into being, and how dreams and altered states are part of my being human. Being human means that my higher order self can observe and interact with REM imagery, and can create, direct, and intervene in dreams and other altered states. And just possibly an expanded understanding of these processes can lead to self-healing for others as it has for me.

That old biological expression: "Ontogeny recapitulates phylogeny" takes on personal meaning as one learns the language of dreams. A series of quotes from Llinas will help clarify some of his key concepts that I've employed to analyze my own dreams, especially those I've called FAP dreams. Revisiting Llinas will also serve to review basic assumptions underlying the evolutionary perspective that takes one from neurons to self.

1) "Fixed action patterns are somewhat more elaborated reflexes that seem to group lower reflexes into synergies (groups of reflexes capable of more complex goal-oriented behavior (2002:134)."

2) "We may look at FAPs as modules of motor activity that liberate the self from unnecessarily spending time and attention on every aspect of an ongoing movement, or indeed on the movement at all (Ibid)."

3) "[T]he expression of FAPs is supported by the interplay among a number of vastly differing parts of the nervous system and the basal ganglia. These nuclei are localized in the center of the brain. They connect synaptically with the thalamus and receive input from both the cortex and the thalamus… (Ibid: 136,137)."

4) FAPs are relatively hardwired and can be considered as reflexes when they are activated (Ibid: 150).

5) "We have a motor system that when driven by global strategies implements contextually appropriate FAPs." FAPs may be overridden…by [the] thalamacortical system, the self (Ibid: 151)."

Okay, I've just accounted for my bicycle balancing dream using Llinas's quotes. I used this dream to explain supposedly bizarre dream behavior such as riding over impossible terrain, sliding down the edges of steps or banisters. Honing FAPs in our dreams nicely accounts for common dream behaviors that are consolidating action pattern in our neural circuits. Now let me focus on emotions:

6) "[E]motions are elements in the class of 'fixed action patterns…where the actions are not motor but pre-motor (Ibid: 156)." "[E]motional states give context to motor behavior (Ibid: 158)."

7) "[W]e may look at emotions as the global sensation aspect of FAPs, if not the FAPs themselves (Ibid: 161)."

8) "[The] sensations we feel during the course of a dream are complete confabulations on the part of our brain (Ibid: 159)." But let us not forget that human subjectivity is a "confabulation" of the

external world that is a form of virtual reality.

Dream emotions such as fear drive nightmares, but as complete confabulations, all we have to do is identify the activating element, and the global response generated in the thalamacortical system, the Self through meta-awareness eliminates it. I've demonstrated how easily and quickly this is possible with my own nightmares, and I've suggested that following this line of intervention, we should be able to generate protocol to interrupt the more intractable FAPs associated with PTSD.

Emotions are primordial and complex. They are the triggers to muscle action before animals were capable of complex thought and nuanced actions. Emotions are a critical part of the troika homunculus that I use to interpret my dreams.

9) Emotional states liberate FAPs (Ibid: 168). And, liberated FAPs are constantly being expressed in our dreams. "In fact, the activity in the basal ganglia is running all the time, playing motor patterns and snippets of motor patterns amongst and between themselves (Ibid: 170)."

Recall that a FAP can only be modified once it has been activated (Ibid: 174). For me, this recognition explains much of what is going on in my mundane dreams. My brain is always busy with maintenance functions, and FAP maintenance requires activation. Why shouldn't evolution create or discover the fictive advantages of dreams? Our evolutionary history gives us neuronal reflexes and supporting architecture. Some of our neuronal abilities are learned and other aspects are inherited from evolution.

10) "We may come to learn the word...'green,' but that we perceive 'green-ness' is not learned ontogenetically; it has been learned and remembered phylogentically (Ibid: 178)."

It seems painfully obvious that green as quale cannot be understood through linguistic philosophizing; green is to be understood as a word from culture and a sensory configuration inherited from evolution.

11) "[Q]ualia, must be primordial in the global organization of the nervous system function. In fact, qualia must represent a significant and influential drive throughout evolution (Ibid: 203)."

12) Sensory experience is localized and contextualized "... into one global functional state—something akin to 'I feel' that acts to mediate decision making (Ibid: 204)."

13) "[T]he effectors of qualia are very similar in their neuronal bases to the neuronal bases of motor FAPs—except that they appear to be internalized FAPs (Ibid: 208)."

14) "For all intents and purposes, the question of qualia or feelings is the question of conscious experiences (Ibid: 210)." "... neuronal activity and sensations are one and the same event (Ibid: 218)."

15) "[I]t is not the code or message coming from the outside world that is being transmitted, but rather it is the neuronal element that responds to the message from the outside that is itself the message (Ibid: 219)."

16) "Qualia represent judgments or assessments at the circuit level of information carried by sensory pathways, or sensations. And these sensations, the integration product of the activation of internal sensory FAPs, represent the ultimate predictive vectors that recycle/re-enter into the internal landscape of the self. They are the 'ghost' in the machine... (Ibid: 221)." Or, I might say—a light in the black box.

17) "Emotions are premotor events that activate FAPs" "[E]motions… are simply invented states on the part of the central nervous system and as such are clearly abstractions (Ibid: 227)." Emotions are represented by mapped configurations in our neural circuits; therefore, only exist as subjective states and can only be studied as such.

18) "[Even] before language was sufficiently well structured to be communicable, its genesis must have had as a prerequisite foundation the nervous system's capacity to generate the pre-motor imagery to abstract the properties of things from the things themselves. That is, it required the pre-motor imagery to make abstractions of universals (Ibid: 228)."

Abstract thinking preceded language. And, "[Language] is simply an element within a much larger, more generalized category of function (Ibid: 228)." This is Llinas 2001.

Below, I have referenced Shapiro 2010 for comparison. Llinas provides a framework to explore the emergence of Self, consciousness, and to explain qualia. Qualia lie at the foundation of cognition. Llinas's 2001 research-based observations speak eloquently to my dream interpretations. For me to get at basic processes such as how the brain derives primary images, I must employ lucidity in dream observation. I think triangulating dream observations and self-experiments with mind-science research and cognitive science offers an opportunity to enhance each one. At least from my introspective methodology, this has been the case. I'm arguing that linguistic and semantic exploration of language and meaning is incomplete without incorporating a Llinas—type understanding of the processes that generate qualia.

19) "[Human] language, arose as an extension of premotor conditions, namely those of the increasing complexities of intentionality as abstract thinking grew richer (Ibid: 242)."

20) "[Vocalizations] became with usage a FAP (Ibid: 243)."

Observing FAPs in dreams, the mapped images that are codes that represent our relationship with the outside world, the elements that create our virtual universe, helps explain dream actions. FAPs are honed and maintained in our dreams, and this process creates dream scenarios one after the other. Dreams actions are disconnected from muscles for obvious reasons. Nevertheless, neural circuits are established and maintained through fictive rehearsal over the course of one's lifetime, and this process must start in the womb.

I'm belaboring Llinas. Qualia are collections of primary sensory experiences that are remapped and reconfigured in the course of human evolution. We understand the emergence of feeling as re-mapped images as core elements in cognition. We understand qualia based on motor activity as FAPs. And from this model, the role of qualia in cognition is understood bottom-up through neural science. Language is a derivative of these processes, and with any derivative, they must be referenced back to primary processes in order for us to have an intelligent discussion of words, language and meaning.

21) "[We] as a species, have evolved to express our internal states more thoroughly than any other species." "[Words] can be generated by an individual whose brain has been damaged to an extent that only the most minimal neurological correlates to the module remain. This indicates that the motor FAP is necessary and sufficient for the behavior of that particular module but not sufficient for other aspects of speech, such as being able to produce the thought behind the words… (Ibid: 244,245)."

Motor FAPs and emotional FAPs are rapidly called forth in dreams and visions, along with related contextual imagery. In visions, real time sensory continuity parallels waking sensory continuity, and in dreams, sudden shifts and morphing elements breaks this continuity. This suggests to me that the dream function changes with these discontinuities as well. And I note that FAP sequencing unaided by daytime consciousness, which fills in discontinuities, contributes to these dream forms.

My ability to lecture in dreams supports the FAP-like nature of words. Talking ability with rapid structuring of multiple FAPs suggests the active role of self as FAPs are strung together in proper sequences. Emotional content of pre-motor FAPs supports the feeling nature of words and language. Proper structure of words, like a beautiful voice or sonnet, can bring us to tears or ecstasy. The musical power of voice or violin speaks eloquently to the physiological logic of Llinas.

Language is word (qualia) FAP dependent and complex patterns are expressed through conditioning that parallels a motor FAP such as bike balancing. The major question for me is how the CNS, cerebral cortex, comes to guide all of these processes. I can control and direct these processes in dreams and altered states, but I can only surmise the mechanisms involved. Nevertheless, neuroscience as reviewed has taken much of the mystery out of self, consciousness, and altered states. Neuroscience has taken much of the mystery out of how the brain and mind create language and meaning as well.

NUNEZ AND EEG

In *Brain, Mind, and the Structure of Reality*, Paul Nunez integrates findings from EEG to explore consciousness. EEG is one of the technologies designed to look at global functioning of the brain, and what this means to the relationship between the brain's subsystems and its global conscious states. Nunez, who is an Emeritus Professor of Biomedical Engineering at Tulane University in New Orleans, gets a little wild in some of his speculations about the possibility of a larger consciousness, which he calls Mind, and whether or not human consciousness can communicate with this cosmic entity. I will skip this part because it is pure speculation, but for me, it is a fun read. I'm interested in his empirical findings using EEG technology.

Consciousness appears to occur in conjunction with large-scale moderately coherent EEG signals, of moderate amplitude and within selected frequency bands, observed mostly in the 4 to 13 Hz range in scalp recordings." A healthy consciousness may also be associated with a proper 'balance' between local, regional, and global mechanisms, perhaps occurring in states of high dynamic complexity (2010: 246).

EEG recordings differ in terms of frequency range depending on the state of the brain's health, and in various altered states such as REM sleep. In epileptics, for example, brain electrical activity is in an elevated, chaotic state that is reflected in various degrees of consciousness loss by the affected individual. We can basically say that a healthy brain represents global electrical patterns that remain in balance.

A disruption of global electrical balance represents loss of consciousness when it reaches certain limits. Thus, from EEG observations, it is not just signaling and electrical output by various circuits and subsystems in the brain, but integration and balance across both subsystem and global circuits is required for both consciousness and good mental health. This finding fits well with a larger understanding of how micro and macro-circuits in the brain operate in waking consciousness, or sleeping consciousness, during REM.

Dreams appear to play an intended role using the brain's architecture to help balance global circuit patterns and maintain mental health. Immediate removal of global brain state imbalance through nightmare resolution or learned controls support this integration-balance hypotheses. Long-term sleep deprivation that results in death speaks to the deleterious effects of critical brain imbalance.

Nunez continues with his model of cortical dynamics:

The model provides a number of approximately accurate predictions of the very large-scale dynamic behavior revealed by EEG. The model also directly addresses the so-called binding problem of brain science by suggesting top-down resonant interactions between global fields and non-overlapping networks. This mechanism may allow brain subsystems to be functionally localized in some frequency bands, but at the same time, functionally integrated in other frequency bands (Ibid: 246).

We know that empirical predictions are difficult in dynamic systems as complex as our brains. But what Nunez is getting at through EEG research and other imaging methods such as fMRI, and what is important for our understanding of altered states as we move from dreams to speaking-in-tongues to other ASC, is the question of how altered subsystem circuits in the brain modify and change the phenomenological experiences of the actor.

We need further study on this matter, however, EEG findings support my altered state experiences with the assumption of scrambled neural networks. Reported dream events with bike balance, heat and cold, sweating and nightmare resolution, are direct manifestations of underlying brain-mind functions, from my perspective. I further assume that dream activity, whether one sees it as phenomenal or epiphenomenal, supports homeostasis, and integrates and provides meaning to our emotional landscape. Defining these processes as phenomenal or epiphenomenal depends on the hierarchical stage from which we initially view these processes.

Nunez says that: "… neither internal nor external observers may have access to the unconscious, which nevertheless receives information from the external world and provides influences on the brain's conscious entities (Ibid: 249)."

I differ from Nunez in that long-term lucid observation of dreams permits one to see primary processes in action. Image formation in the core Self with my balance dream being such an example. I observe active integration and consolidation of memory that underlies my conscious acts of riding and balancing on a bicycle, or executing drawing and glass cutting movements.

I find it very helpful to combine research from dream labs, physiological technology, and self-observation to further one's understanding of dreams, consciousness, and complex communication loops between our non-conscious and conscious states. I assume that further quantification and identification of these dream process elements and dreaming states is a necessary step in understanding how the brain's subsystems support either dream or waking consciousness.

It appears to me that both short-term and long-term memory storage can be studied using these combined methodologies. Consciousness appears in process stages. Memory development and integration appear in process stages. There is no single level on the scale for these multiple stages that leads to consciousness.

Nunez continues:

I see no compelling reason to focus on any single scale as the foundational substrate of consciousness. As each spatial scale is crossed through interactions, new (integrated) information is evidently created together with the attending emergent properties of the larger systems (2010: 267).

Compatible with this view is the fact that various parts of the brain can be physically destroyed without the person losing consciousness.

When we are awake, there is a constant interplay between our non-conscious processes and our conscious processes. Every time I ride my bicycle, I'm reminded of this fact. Waking in the middle of the night, noting dream content and returning to sleep, only to have earlier dream content and plot reenter my subsequent dreams, reminds me of the complexity of brain dynamics.

I sense an exchange occurring between these non-conscious processes and conscious processes throughout my night's dreams. The form of exchange during waking and dreaming obviously varies according to the functions served by my brain's subsystems, but it occurs.

Logic while dreaming is expressed around Hobson's dream forms with sudden scene changes and character shifts, but the overall reasoning process still provides thought integration and discovery. The degree of rationality varies according to the type of dream function. FAP and emotional content dreams must be serving different functions than thought dreams as I've reported them. Dream review of one's life, professional activities, and social intimates must incorporate long-term memories, current social realities, changing values, and a wealth of feelings.

SHAPIRO: EMBODIED COGNITION

I have relied most heavily on physiological and mind science research to evaluate my personal history and self-experimentation with dreams and altered states of consciousness.

Subjectively, we can observe primary images being formed in dreams through content analysis. And most importantly, this primary image formation is a critical link missing in cognitive science as discussed by Shapiro, and much of the field for that matter.

Interdisciplinary perspectives require the triangulation of methods, theory, and the partial explanations each contemporary science provides. Much of what I've written is speculative as I've attempted to triangulate physiological body-brain processes with minded activities of dreams and other altered states. Consciousness as discussed by Damasio and Llinas recognize the emergent and subjective nature of consciousness derived from a base of communicating, interacting cells in our brains and bodies. The marriage between cell and mind research gradually unravels how consciousness and the subjective self come to be. Cognitive science has and continues to move further away from philosophical speculating into the empirical camp we call embodied cognition.

Shapiro's *Embodied Cognition* is published in Routledge's "New Problems in Philosophy." It is a concise, well written account of embodied cognition's current status. However, I have a bias that says models of cognitive science must continuously be passed through a comprehensive caldron of empiricism called physiology and neuroscience. Cognition, language, and consciousness can never be explained without reference to the physiological processes that support them. And as Damasio and Llinas have so eloquently argued, an evolutionary model that details the steps of hierarchical complexity is necessary if we wish to explain self and consciousness.

In my opinion, a good portion of contemporary cognitive science is at a level comparable to Skinnerian Behaviorism of the 1950s and '60s. Skinner ignored the active agent called Self. In like fashion, the contemporary cognitive science of embodied cognition presented by Shapiro fails to adequately incorporate three critical operational constructs: Open versus closed dynamical systems, feelings, and how primary images are formed by the brain. I cannot explain my dreams or other altered states of consciousness without considering these dimensions. After all, dream consciousness is still consciousness.

I think methodological limitations in cognitive science are especially obvious in the area of primary image formation and primary image re-mapping: Failure to operationally link primary image formation with qualia and metaphor results in endless speculation. Early behaviorists of the 20th Century downgraded or ignored volition on the part of Self as agent. Basically, pigeons and humans were treated equally as passive organisms that could to be similarly modified. Skinner ignored the Self as active agent capable of Free Will, and in fact, Free Will was an oxymoron for Skinner when I was an undergraduate student.

In a parallel fashion, contemporary cognitive science as presented by Shapiro does not adequately distinguish between open and closed dynamic systems, as this distinction is relevant for consciousness research. Distinctions between open and closed dynamic systems have been quite well developed over the past 40 years or so. Most telling, however, is the neglect of feeling by Shaprio. And as the work of both Damasio and Llinas demonstrate the role of feeling in the formation of Self, consciousness and qualia is critical. Neglecting feeling in select areas of cognitive science is equivalent to studying quantum mechanics and ignoring particle-wave dualism. One must at least attempt to account for the phenomena observed.

A closed system can be viewed as deterministic if X effects Y in a known, specific way; the Watts Centrifugal Governor being an example (Shapiro: 2010: 119-123).

An open system is probabilistic in that X effects Y with a certain level of chance, but the exact outcome is not deterministically known. I do not find this level of distinction adequately formulated in Shapiro or Chalmers' work. This is especially disturbing when dynamic models are used to interpret consciousness (Shapiro: 2010). Embodied cognition demands that attention be given to primary image formation, feelings, and open dynamic system processes. Analyzing embodied cognition without these necessary conceptual units is similar to looking at the elephant one body part at a time.

Nunez's stress on the relationship between global and micro states calls my attention to the "bootstrapping" process that leads from primary images to metaphor and amodal language, or in parallel fashion, from primordial images to Qualia I and Qualia II. These hierarchical relationships appear to be critical in any analysis of human symbol or language development. These hierarchical relationships are fundamental to our developing understanding of self and consciousness. Dynamically, we are moving across a hierarchy of evolutionary complexity from animals driven by simple reflexes to humans possessing free will.

Shapiro contrasts the competing models of standard cognitive science and embedded cognitive science. In all, I find his analysis to be incomplete because he does not include necessary and sufficient conditions and processes. I cannot make meaningful connections with related research by Damasio, Hobson, Gazzaniga, Ledoux, or Llinas with the analytic limitations imposed by Shapiro's presentation of the current state of cognitive science. This is a very limited criticism of Shapiro, but one that is meant to draw attention to the necessity of including open dynamic systems, emotion-feeling, and primary image methodology in any attempt to explain cognition, self, consciousness, or language. In my experience, introspective analysis which employs dream methodology must be combined with external empirical procedures in order to fully explore human subjectivity. Qualia are at the heart of human subjectivity and critical to an understanding of consciousness. Language is a derivative of these processes.

I believe that a cross-discipline approach to cognition is required that articulates more fully with developments in the neurosciences. Embedded cognition and neuroscience have been most helpful for me to understand my own phenomenological world. Personally, I find Lakoff and Johnson's use of metaphor most helpful as I move from primary image formation to explanations of complex thought processes in dreams, or attempts to explain visions such as my journey to the beginning of time.

My 18 month old toddler self went off to Heaven and met angels. I can't explain this experience without metaphorical concepts. And when I link primary images that I can observe in dreams with their re-mappings at the level of core Self and autobiographical Self, I eliminate much of the speculation contained in *Embodied Cognition*. Self-observation and self-experiments in altered states provides many of the missing pieces for me.

It is not my intent here to critique the whole of cognitive science. In contrast to the level of conceptual development in cognitive science presented by Shapiro, physiological developments in the neural sciences has moved from intra-cellular, to cellular, to neural circuits, to neural networks, to models of representational mapping to consciousness. This bottom-up approach has provided a sound base for each subsequent level of research.

Making researchable concepts operational at each level of cognitive science development seems to be a work in progress. The methods of Lakoff and Johnson as they interpret metaphor, enhances my understanding of neurological processes which support the meaning and function of dreams. My use of dream metaphor has been inspired by their work. The creative re-mapping of primary metaphor is a capacity expressed by a dynamic self operating in an open system that has emerged through evolution. It is this level of evolutionary development that gives language its freedom from deterministic linkages of reflexive behavior driving animal life early in our genome's history.

It is a creative re-mapping process that permits awareness of being aware. Mapping of maps, creating a dynamic Self through the brain-mind's use of secondary and tertiary image remapping, a process where images re-enter the system to create situational, ongoing consciousness, being conscious of our own consciousness; and being the masters of Free Will. The engine of evolution is not only a dynamic integrated whole, it is an engine that recreates itself in acts of continuously emerging levels of complexity. Evolution is not finished!

Shapiro defines Lackoff and Johnson's use of metaphor: "… metaphor is the means by which one comes to understand more abstract concepts through their explication in simpler, already understood concepts (2010: 215)."

305

Basic or primary concepts provide the bridging element to our understanding of dream metaphor. My discussion of primary concepts, Qualia I and Qualia II, is an attempt to integrate Damasio with Lackoff and Johnson. Damasio follows qualia as emergent phenomena driven by evolutionary complexity. The emergence of images and metaphor from body processes is the core of Lakoff and Johnson's metaphorical model. Note the distinction between Shapiro and Damasio's use of metaphor. The two streams of thought processes come together in one river, which supports our higher level of consciousness, Self, and the subsequently derived phenomena called language.

Shapiro defines the use of basic concepts in Lakoff and Johnson's theory of metaphors: "[Basic] concepts are those that are tied directly to properties of the body, and hence do not require understanding through other concepts (2010: 212)."

My example of balance for bicycle riding exemplifies this basic concept as it bridges to metaphor. It provides a direct tie between an embodied philosophical construct and a physiological element critical to memory formation. This conceptualization focuses our attention on specific dream content as these elements are incorporated in memory at a non- consciousness level, and triangulating non-conscious memory elements with functional outcomes permits their observation in dreams. This is one of the unique aspects of dream self-observation and self-experiment methodology.

I think the methodology is straightforward, operational steps are fairly clear and replicable, and the link between a physiological function that I associate with non-conscious memory consolidation and behavioral skill is identified. In terms of interdisciplinary analysis, behavioral psychology is married to embedded philosophy and neuroscience. However, I fail to find these necessary operational links in my reading of Shapiro.

I have attempted to provide operational definitions for basic concepts in my dreams, for example; and believe that these specific operational definitions are necessary in order to avoid what I experience as unnecessary polemics. Discussion of symbols being modal or amodal exemplifies how preliminary the transition is from the standard model of cognitive science to a dynamic operational model. I believe an operational definition, along with the methodological procedures of dream element analysis, helps clarify the distinction between modal and amodal symbols. Definitions must be made within operational terms, or it is just polemics.

Shapiro clearly presents the developmental history of cognitive science to date and I do not wish to retread his review. But, let me take one example of an operational concept derived from my dreams that should help clarify my argument supporting systematic self-observation methodology.

I want to know how my brain is creating representational maps of my world, but I don't want to get bogged down in a comparison of representational map models across neuroscience. I assume we can all accept brain maps as established constructs in neuroscience. Analysis of specific dream elements permits me to identify how my brain is creating representations at a non-conscious level. I assume, given my evolutionary history as a mammal, that a similar process is probably operating across species. Hence, higher and lower levels of consciousness and awareness become part of this discussion, and an evolutionary perspective is critical to this analysis.

My bike balancing dream mirrors a process of how primary images become embedded in what I've called FAP dreams. I suggest that cats and dogs have fixed action pattern dreams when they are embedding supporting images in their neural circuitry. They have mindedness at least at the level of core Self that permits purposeful activity such as hunting. They do not possess brains that can use complex metaphor to balance one's checkbook.

Balance is also a language construct that comes later in mammalian history. The felt, experienced state of balancing must precede the emergence of secondary symbol formation, which requires primary image remapping. The fundamental body-brain-environmental relationship with gravity exists for all mobile organisms, and this relationship is so basic that it is often overlooked in dream analysis. It should not be. My spatial dream relationships are exemplified when I fly. My spatial relationship using gravity is noted when I view my dead body in the hospital as a toddler. My spatial relationship to gravity is dominant in my vision of mother's crib attack. Our relationship to space and gravity is critical to the how and what of dreams.

I am always oriented to gravity at both a non-conscious and conscious level. This is one of my basic sensory orientations to the world as much as touch and sight. I acknowledge balance and my need to practice balancing in my dreams when I engage fictive bike riding, or actual bike riding when I'm awake. Balancing is a non-conscious skill acquisition. Brain-mind architecture to acquire balance is a set of processes inherited from my DNA, as I'm born with a bodily orientation to gravity. Evolution created the DNA that generated the architecture upon which these neural circuits operate, and the process of non-conscious learning that accommodates gravity occurred before conscious learning, that is, before bicycle riding came into being as a learned skill.

Dream analysis helps us understand how primary symbols become embedded in mammalian tissue. Remapped and remapped-remapped primary images are the critical elements that direct thought processes guiding mammalian movement through space. Re-remapping of these secondary images results in language as language is derived from these underlying processes. This entire process includes an overview of cellular evolution and the emergence of complex neural circuits that support non-conscious learning. Continued evolutionary development creates higher order cognitive centers, which eventually lead to you and me being aware that we are aware. But a critical point is that remapping of primary images permits a level of experience guided by mental imagery that we refer to as metaphorical thought.

I'm contending that contemporary cognitive science, as outlined by Shapiro, has considerable work left in order to reach the integrated level of interlocking mechanisms already explained by neuroscience, and that the neuro-philosophical level addressed by Lakoff and Johnson best articulates with this empirical research.

The discovery of mirror neurons provides a specific mechanism by which we can compare the state of one organism with that of another. It seems reasonable that mirror neurons and emotions developed to coordinate social behavior before higher cognitive structures did. When I feel your pain, my brain's synapses and chemistry are duplicating what is going on with similar synapses and brain chemistry in your head. We experience each other's joy and pain by duplicating brain states, which is an embedded physiological process of cognition, a shared state of qualia. This understanding of empathy is derived from fundamental physiological research and leads to new hypotheses based on findings at each stage of the research process.

But I also feel my dog's pain when it is smashed by a rushing car, and the dog seems to feel my pain in reverse fashion. Interspecies empathy seems quite natural from this evolutionary point of view. Hello ET!

Motor programs that run on neural circuits are as automatic in function as Shapiro's discussion of Watt's centrifugal governor (2010: 119-123). If we ignore the fact that the governor was created by a thinking human being and represents a single output from this agent, we can discuss the generator's representational capacity in isolation. This may serve an initial purpose to demonstrate self-regulating processes, but in context, the closed loop non-conscious learning that takes place in my brain when I ride a bicycle also represents a closed loop system between my brain and a specific part of my environment. My focus is not on the agent's capabilities as it creates Watt's centrifugal governor, but the dynamic capacities of an open system that makes these conscious thought processes possible. The dynamic closed system process of heartbeat, breathing, and body homeostasis goes on as my higher cognitive centers focus on reworking this book.

Motor development in the context of my dreams that is experienced fictively, is symbolic at a conscious level, but it is also real motor skill reinforcement as part of my larger organism's functioning. The generator analysis used by Shapiro as a self-regulating process is not adequately integrated with stages of evolution or levels of brain hierarchical development common to research in the neurosciences. The steps between neural network developments from non-conscious to conscious level of cognition are not laid out by Shapiro. In other words, logical analysis of scientific or mechanical processes is not adequately articulated with known neurological findings. Employing open system processes in his analysis would be a step in this direction.

Primary images that underlie metaphorical concepts as presented by Lakoff and Johnson are identified in my dreams. The sense of being gastronomically full, hot and cold, anxious or content, happy or sad, cognitively busy through thinking, etc. are all examples.

Note how easy it is to derive Damasio's Qualia I level symbols from primordial images— balancing, or feeling hot or cold, or happy or sad. Note the specific composition of remapped primary images that Lakoff and Johnson present as metaphor. Observing primordial images and their remapping has a different clarity in the context of dream analysis. Observation of primary image formation in dreams informs us as to how symbols are grounded. Without this linkage, I am contending we cannot hope to explain how our organism derives meaning.

In the above context, modifications of the standard model of cognitive science presented by Shapiro lacks this articulation. To quote Shapiro:

Lakoff and Johnson, and Glenberg find standard cognitive science at fault for relying on an apparatus of amodal symbols and algorithms. Such symbols, they contend, cannot be meaningful, and so cannot acquire the representational function that standard cognitive science assigns to them. Cognitive science must therefore look for meaning elsewhere, e.g., in the properties of the body and the unique styles of worldly intervention that particular kinds of body afford (2010: 204).

However, Shapiro does not agree with Lakoff's position, but generally offers explanations more closely associated with the standard model of cognitive science.

Applying system distinctions, it is noted that at the level of core Self, with proto-Self connections, the fixed action patterns observed in dreams are part of a closed dynamical image forming system. Remapping primary metaphor, or Damasio's counterpart with Qualia I, forms the base from which Qualia II and complex metaphors arise. Metaphor and Qualia II are amodal in the sense that they have become re-mapped and free of primary body-brain grounding. As concepts, modal and amodal are identifying stages of image formation and their re-mapping.

Operationally, one perceives these distinctions in dreams as the process moves from balancing on one's bike to balancing one's checkbook. Dynamic, open system interpretations rely on probabilities, because balance as an amodal entity can have infinite degrees of nuance. Once we give up the notion of a homunculus sitting astride our cerebral cortex, we are forced to give up the notion that complex processes are things, and fully embrace complex dynamic systems.

Process development of human imaging as it develops across complex evolutionary stages accommodates both concepts. Thus, contemporary cognitive science from this perspective should continue to engage neuroscience and neuroscience's evolutionary view, especially those ideas presented by Damasio and Llinas.

In my experience, we have to connect the substrate of primary images with basic concept formation and the derivation of metaphor before we can have a meaningful discussion that leads to an enhanced understanding of consciousness and cognition. Understanding how consciousness arises in human evolution, which centers on qualia conceptions as set for the Damasio and Llinas, enhances our understanding of language. Language is a derivative of these processes. To understand one is a giant step in the direction of understanding the other. In my opinion, that is why linguistics and semantics has an inherent dependency on neuroscience.

Content analysis of dream elements offers me this initial bridging step. And my understanding as set forth above is derived from and supported by works of Damasio and Llinas using these interlocking steps.

Going back to Skinner, I found over 50 years ago that passive models of behavioral conditioning were inadequate to explain my dreams or my behavior. I had to add volition and self-awareness in order to initiate behavioral change. I didn't understand what we now know about brain circuits and brain chemistry. I just wanted to change my behavior, eliminate anxiety, depression, and nightmares. Nevertheless, learning to control internal brain-mind states and processes permitted me to modify my behavior as I desired. And, that meant employing an active agent.

The reader will note how much quicker these changes occur than with standard B-Mod techniques, as well as noting the limitations of behavior modification by itself. Behavior modification with therapist directed cognitive elements is still less effective than when cognitive-behavioral change is directed by the agent him or her Self. Directly altering neural circuits and chemistry is a superior intervention if the individual can learn the necessary degrees of self-control over his or her own neural circuits. All of this changes our view of image formation and re-mapping by a dynamic brain that can be directed by an active Interpreter.

I discovered along the way that a simple paradigm shift that included introducing volition in Skinner's model made a world of difference in terms of methodology and outcome. Precedent can be a terribly blinding light in research or therapy, as we torturously sort through dogmas such as traditional psychoanalysis. Or torturously examine one top-down model of cognition after another without clearly laying out methods of empirical exploration for interlocking process steps. Once neuroscience establishes necessary components to consciousness, as I believe Damasio and Llinas have done, these elements must then be included in cognitive science speculations and research, or the distance to meaningful explanation grows infinitely long.

To summarize dream and ASC observations as they apply to embodied cognition, I offer the following:

a. Cognition is embodied and two levels of consciousness must be considered as discussed by Damasio. Our higher level of consciousness remaps Qualia I, which necessitates incorporation of modal and amodal constructs to reach a level of necessary and sufficient process analysis that lies behind cognition and language.

b. Primary images are not just felt but re-mapped by the time evolution creates the equivalent of Damasio's core Self. Dream imagery supports multistage processes that involve perceptual symbols, affordances and meshing.

c. Higher cognitive levels reflect open system functioning which culminates in higher level abstractions and complex metaphor which is free of embodiment. This level of image complexity is the opposite side of the consciousness and free will coin.

d. Words at the spoken or written level may typically bear arbitrary connections to their referents. However, dream analysis permits one to trace embodied referents back to primary image formation through this intermediate stage. Free Will necessitates this distinction.

e. Modal information does not need to be detached from cognitive processes although it may. Human thought from a dynamic, open system perspective incorporates the entire range of human image making capacities. This complexity as expressed in dreams is perplexing until we interpret dream content from an evolutionary perspective. Hence, thinking that is mostly concrete should be dominated by modal thought processes. The most complex thoughts are amodal even though they can usually be traced back to their modal roots.

f. Glenberg's Indexical Hypothesis states that meaning is embodied (Shapiro: 2010: 102). It seems apparent, now that meaning is embodied, but reaches a stage of development where disembodied meaning emerges with complex, abstract thoughts, even though abstraction initially occurs at a preconscious level. I'm using disembodied meaning when I refer to an abstraction such as Heaven or Hell. Heaven and Hell do not have concrete references, but are second order metaphorical abstractions.

g. Understanding, meaning, occurs before language, as language is a cognitive process derivative.

h. "For Lakoff and Johnson, facts about the body determine basic concepts, which then participate in metaphor, which in turn permeate just about every learned concept (Ibid: 112)." Multistage emergence of image complexity that one can observe in dreams supports their position. I've attempted to demonstrate how the methodology of lucid dreaming permits one to observe processes by which primary images in our dreams are fictively embedded and integrated in memory. Primary image formation in FAP dreams for example, reflect active processes that are generating qualia, and these products derived from primordial sensory integration are correlated with behavioral and psychological states.

    i.   Primary images are connected to what Damasio calls Qualia I, whereas Llinas does not make a distinction between Qualia I and Qualia II. Qualia I such as bicycle balancing is a visual-muscle-feeling entity. Willing one's bike to turn is an example of a pre-motor feeling which is executed non-consciously as a complex motor fixed action pattern.

Hence, meaning to the organism always has some degree of feeling attached even at higher abstract levels. Metaphorical thought is as much about feeling as it is about imagery. Qualia can be the feeling derivative of emotion causing one to jump spontaneously in fright.

    j.   Mirror neurons duplicate feeling states of others because sensory input activates comparable images—maps that are embedded and available on demand. Metaphorical mappings are similarly embedded and called forth by the organism's personal history, genetic potential and cultural conditioning.

Again, this analysis is very limited and presupposes some familiarity with the material on the part of the reader. A more thorough treatment would probably require a Shapiro length book. My purpose, however, is to demonstrate how dream and ASC analysis can inform us about fundamental questions that are currently only accessible through introspective methods.

LAKOFF AND JOHNSON'S METAPHORICAL CONCEPTS

I will take some liberties with Lakoff and Johnson, because my discussion of their metaphorical model will be as limited as was my discussion of Shapiro's *Embodied Cognition.* I've felt for many years that mind-brain research has not adequately dealt with image formation in dreams and other altered states. In the latter part of the 1960s and through the 1970s when I was a young university professor, I wrestled with some of these issues without coming to any conclusions. My main problem at the time was that I did not understand enough brain physiology. The works of Damasio and Lakoff and Johnson in the 1990s helped considerably, as I've noted elsewhere. I will not try to critique Lakoff and Johnson's various works. Instead, I will discuss their treatment of metaphor in terms of a dynamic integrated system of dreams, ASC, and consciousness that is the focus of this book.

I find that Lakoff and Johnson's understanding of embedded cognition articulates well with the various works I've reviewed throughout this book. From Llinas, we can appreciate how universal sensations, qualia, emerge and enter recursively into consciousness and the development of self. Damasio breaks the evolutionary expression of qualia into two levels along with his two stage development of consciousness and the emergence of self. What I find helpful with their formulations is the support it lends to the model of self-observation and self-experiments that I've build dream and altered state analysis around. I've faulted cognitive science generally for not incorporating enough basic research from neuroscience and physiology. This, I suspect, is a temporary situation in process of remediation.

Shapiro's quote states that:

For Lakoff and Johnson, facts about the body determine basic concepts, which then participate in metaphor, which in turn permeate just about every learned concept (Shapiro: 2010: 112).

I belabored Llinas in order to highlight what seems to be unnecessary neglect of basic neurological processes on the part of contemporary cognitive science. I also emphasized the role of emotion-feeling in consciousness and cognition as set forth by Damasio to further drive this point of neglect home.

I've placed embodied cognition into a multistage process that parallels Damasio's discussion of self-development from proto-Self to core Self and finally autobiographical Self. I add clarity to my own thoughts by adopting Damasio's evolutionary progression. Damasio's model of the multistage emergence of image complexity supports a view that metaphor emerges from primary embedded images, and is then re-imaged to generate complex metaphor and subsequent higher levels of abstraction. I've attempted to demonstrate how the methodology of lucid dreaming permits one to observe processes by which primary images are fictively embedded and integrated in our dreams. This is a mirror reflection of active self processes that I correlate with daytime behavior and psychological states.

Considerable support has been garnered for Lakoff and Johnson's view of metaphor since *Metaphors We Live By* was published in 1980. I've presented Damasio's basic thoughts on consciousness and qualia because he incorporates feelings as essential elements in image formation, which are critical to an understanding of his two stage model of consciousness: Acknowledging two stages of image-symbol formation in mapping and re-mapping stages accounts for the emergence of Qualia II and Free Will. Here I want to make clear that primary image formation observed in dreams lies at the base of our human ability to derive complex processes that lead to language. A marriage between Damasio's use of qualia with feeling elements incorporated into the binding processes and Lakoff and Johnson's development of metaphor as basic conceptual units supporting thought seems warranted.

Earlier, I criticized Hobson for discussing metaphor using a dictionary definition. In contrast, I accept Lakoff and Johnson's interpretation that metaphor "… is not a matter of definition… it is a question of the nature of cognition (1980: 246)." Also, "Metaphor … is a matter of conceptual structure (Ibid: 235)."

Complex metaphorical concepts such as love and happiness are grounded in our world experiences (Ibid: 119). Primary metaphors are conceptual structures that represent embedded patterns in our neural circuits.

The emotions of joy or anger are primary images, and the re-mapping of these emotions as feelings become metaphor. Balance on my bike is a primary felt state, while primary metaphor takes us to the next level. Balance that refers to our checkbook can become amodal at the complex metaphorical level. Language is a derivative of these embedded patterns.

Primary metaphor is derived from in-body images that retain their embodied direct linkages. My use of the term "re-mapped" recognizes that a sequential process of derived image arises in our neural circuits. At the core Self level, I'm assuming that conscious subjectivity exists for higher order mammals such as dogs and cats. In related fashion, reflexive behavior is the norm. This is Skinner's early level of theorizing that excludes Free Will: A level of analysis that excludes incorporation of open systems: A level of analysis currently central to the Free Will debate.

Re-mapping of primary images permits primordial images to be felt. Re-mapping of mapped images permits endless nuances of meaning to be felt or to be experienced. Obviously, this remapping includes all sensory modes. Words and language at the end of this process are derived from primordial stimuli that have been converted into qualia. In fact, I assume that our human ancestor probably produced simple vocalizations to represent re-mapped feelings as a first step to full language development.

Human subjectivity results from our remapping of maps that represent primary images as the containers from which meaning originates. The body as a bounded entity, container, to use a Lakoff and Johnson metaphor, fits nicely into this image to symbol progression as outlined above.

Subjective meaning to the organism can only be ascertained by connecting primary images, qualia, to metaphor. It cannot be ascertained through the formal analysis of language alone. By making the distinction between open and closed dynamic systems, Qualia I and Qualia II distinctions, primary metaphor and complex metaphor, I can account for FAP dreams and thought dreams. I can also account for Will and Free Will with this model.

Recurrent human experience generates universal metaphorical concepts. Metaphorical concepts can build in complexity, but primary metaphors are supported by primary sensory experiences. During waking moments of bike riding, I experienced FAP consolidation by willing my bike to turn and navigate city streets while letting casual thoughts float effortlessly. I understand Will as a FAP derivative in this respect, and I understand thoughtless walking, which is effortless, from this respect.

Is it any wonder that a thoughtful philosopher by the name of Descartes should not feel this difference? Even small children feel this difference, especially when they go off to Heaven. Essentialism refers to these felt stages of image formation.

Combining complex metaphors generates gestalt configurations and various levels of abstractions as sensory binding, and increasingly complex neural circuit configurations emerge. Complexity of neural circuits and metaphorical expressions can be as complex as a Mozart recital, or perhaps the memorization of the Old Testament. Always, however, embedded cognition is the basement in the house of consciousness and its Director that we call Self.

Complex metaphor is an organizing term for embedded circuits that can be combined in endless neural configurations. My dream where a glock pistol stands in for penis is an example of complex metaphorical thought. Bike balance is an example of a primary metaphor, which emerges as a representation of my physical relationship in space as I move through time. As a toddler, I went off to Heaven, and on my way, stopped to commune with angels. Angels were simple reconstructions of adults in my small experiential world. But, Heaven and angels at about 18 months of age already represented a level where complex mechanisms supporting metaphor were being employed.

The physical sensation of my OBE was moving toward twinkling lights that eventually took on the shape of adult angels. The sensation was one of moving from dark to light; hence, a tunnel effect that is commonly reported for similar near death experiences. Darkness to light is the obvious progression of consciousness winking back on. Basic physiological processes combined with 18 month old imagery created, or generated, metaphor that incorporated feelings of Heaven-bound happiness with grounded adult images in my limited life experience. Lakoff and Johnson's use of metaphor must incorporate feelings, stimuli that are generated internal to body and self, if I'm to explain my toddler's conceptual journey to Heaven. Llinas accounts for this element in his use of feeling-based FAPs: Emotions are pre-motor FAPs, to use his words.

Emotions expressed as feelings are also embedded in our brain's circuitry, but represent the body's reaction to sensations created through electro-chemical activity in our neural system. The physical impact on our neural circuits is complex for FAPs such as balance, because emotional FAPs can incorporate fine nuances generated by hundreds of different chemicals in our total body-brain-mind system. Nevertheless, along with Damasio and Llinas, emotional FAPs join the mix of FAPs generated from external stimuli. It can't be any other way. As I write these words, a car just passed my open window, and my body tells me I need to do something about all that coffee I've drunk this morning.

From the above outline, mapping feelings is the first evolutionary step on the road to being human; it is the most basic step and the grandfather of language. Feelings are essential elements in metaphorical thought that have not been given, in my opinion, adequate consideration in cognitive science as we address meaning, symbol formation, and language. Dream observation and experimentation offers a continuity to causal linkages not found in external methods of inquiry.

I conclude this section by agreeing with Lakoff and Johnson that "… our conceptual system is largely metaphorical… (Ibid: 3)." But I reject the view that "… metaphor is typically viewed as characteristic of language alone, a matter of words rather than thought or action (Ibid: 3)."

From the work of Llinas and Damasio, metaphor becomes a parallel operational concept to qualia, and understanding either conceptual model entails linkage to primordial processes, primary image formation, and FAPs.

WALTER FREEMAN AND CIRCULAR CAUSALITY

Freeman takes linear models used to explain the brain to task. Central to his argument are the concepts of intention and meaning. How it is that we humans are both conscious and aware that we are conscious? This question has been central to both philosophical and scientific arguments since ancient times. I include Freeman in this analysis for the clarity he offers in terms of circular causality.

In contrast to circular causality, a simple understanding of linear causality is that A occurs, which in turn causes B. For example, I ingest a pathogenic bacterium (A) and get a stomach ache (B). He uses an oft quoted example of a chaotic process where a butterfly flapping its wings in Brazil causes a hurricane in China. Supposedly, this is an example of how chaos operates in dynamic systems. But, says Freeman, this is not the case:

There is no meaning to the question of how individual neurons cause global state transitions, any more than it is meaningful to ask how some air and water molecules or a butterfly can cause a hurricane, or how a few rocks can cause and undersea earthquake and a tsunami (2000: 132).

Once the cause, the butterfly flapping its wings, has been presented, the reasoning becomes linear and one can somehow trace this linear flapping of wings to the hurricane in China. This is false reasoning and an inaccurate presentation of circular causation. In my interpretation of Freeman, the linear reasoning is inaccurate because the dynamics of air turbulence are totally ignored, and our understanding of circular causation, its recursive effects, is lost.

Freeman builds a careful model of neural functioning and interrelationships from micro to meso to macroscopic levels. I will skip most of his detail and focus only on the key elements of his argument as I attempt to translate some of his technical usage into more familiar terms.

Critical neural AM wave-pulse patterns (Ibid: 46-47) depend on the historical meaning previously generated in our brain-minds. Global neural patterns at the macro level represent cooperative processes underlying the unity of perception and action (Ibid: 110).The uniqueness of each one of our brains as we process stimuli and create our inner world of reality is generally assumed across a number of fields from neuroscience to social psychology. Freeman demonstrates how neural AM patterns accomplish this uniqueness. It is not necessary to understand AM patterns to follow Freeman's logic.

His specific arguments supporting this position are based on a dynamic systems interpretation dependent on circular causality. There is no agent, or homunculus, behind awareness, consciousness, and intention: These states are supported by processes that are free of linear reasoning.

Full meaning to the individual arises only at the global level. From this perspective, dream consciousness is physiologically fragmented. This is a different approach than Hobson's, but a model that arrives at the same conclusions.

Stimuli from all of our senses is not directly transcribed from the outside world into our brains, but is synthesized uniquely by each one of us. For example, what are commonly called qualia, concepts such as the color red or happiness, are internal brain configurations that may be similar or quite different for each one of us. Reflection for a moment on the concept of happiness demonstrates the potentially wide variations possible with the quale called happiness.

Chaos, a central concept in dynamic systems, exists in normal neuronal processing, however, the chaotic neuronal fluctuations commonly reported are smoothed out by larger neural circuits. Positively, this process allows active interaction with one's environment without one kind of neural stimulation taking precedent over the others.

Unconscious processing goes on within a dynamic model as it does with linear models. And in Freeman's interpretation, local neural circuits retain a degree of autonomy "... whereas the global AM pattern is self-organizing (Ibid: 135)."

In contrast to unconscious processes, "Consciousness is the process that makes a sequence of global states of awareness. It is a state variable that constrains the chaotic activities of the parts by quenching local fluctuations (Ibid: 135)."

In my understanding, quenching local fluctuations is necessary to maintain the continuity of daytime consciousness, but this quenching process obviously operates less well in our dreams.

In other words, consciousness is part of what Freeman calls an intentional arc. Each of our actions are organized and integrated into meaning, and become part of the new actions that follow. Consciousness thus "… facilitates the enrichment of meaning (Ibid: 135)."

Again note that there is no agent guiding this process, and degrees of autonomy within the global field process become central to our understanding of Free Will. Consciousness at the human level is a dynamic operator process. In this model Freeman rejects arguments against free will as being false, as they are based on linear reasoning. They are a distortion of dynamic models based on circular causation.

"The denial of free will, then, comes from viewing a brain as being embedded in a linear causal chain … the apposition of free will against determinism creates a pseudoproblem (Ibid)."

Hence, arguments supported by linear models of free will presented in cognitive science are rejected, for they are pseudoproblems.

Distinguishing between closed and open systems, Freeman says: "… meaning is constructed within each brain as a closed system… (Ibid: 138)."

This position should be fairly self-evident in terms of how stimuli are processed in the brain. Further, "… living brains are open systems that feed on energy and freely dispose waste and heat. As such they are capable of self-organizing chaotic dynamics that lead to unpredictable and complex new behaviors (Ibid)."

Note the distinction of how we create our virtual realities as a closed system at the same time our brains are open, and "feed on external energy and freely dispose waste and heat."

In summary, Freeman has reviewed how the brain self-organizes competing neural circuits and networks to create awareness and consciousness at the global level. At the same time, he has outlined the processes by which neural circuits at a non-global level retain their autonomy.

Circular causation within a dynamic systems model eliminates the need to have an agent organizing and directing our brain-minds. These are recursive features noted in the above presentations of Llinas and Damasio's work. He demonstrates the misuse of linear causation that he sees as being commonly misused in both philosophy and bottom-up models used to explain our brain's operations and functioning. In this process, he restores Free Will by rejecting false arguments of linear causation. Hobson appears to have made the transition from linear to circular causation as I've presented his work in historical context. Llinas seems to have beat most of us to the punch.

What this means for dreams is that the Interpreter is created moment to moment within the global conscious state. Consciousness at an intermediate level will be patchy and broken. In Damasio's terms, the role of the autobiographical Self will not be fully realized in dreams, with the exception being those individuals who dream lucidly and have learned to integrate waking consciousness with dreaming consciousness. But even then, we are talking about degrees, not absolutes, and must make distinctions between different dream scenarios.

Deirdre Barrett has provided numerous examples of creative people who have developed specific methods to bring aspects of their non-conscious processes into consciousness. I've provided a number of examples in this book that parallel Barrett's, but my examples are of minor significance compared to the scope of her historical review. She provides dozens of examples from artists, filmmaking, literature, music, science, math, and moral organization by individuals such as Gandhi. Barrett is on the psychology faculty at Harvard and approaches creativity in dreams from this level of analysis. My experience supports her research.

Circular causation must operate across various levels from dreaming to waking consciousness and from dreaming consciousness to waking. Dream examples which employ complex metaphor and abstractions are central to the creative processes occurring in my dreams.

Our brain-minds are always supporting circular, integrated, and dynamic processes. Further, analysis of creativity in Barrett's Committee of Sleep exemplifies processes that I also find occurring in other altered states. Astral travel, remote viewing, Genesis Journey visions, and problem solving dreams all smack of this creativity. In all, the brain-mind is involved in multiple wonderful acts of creativity that emanate from our brain-s basic architecture. All are embedded.

LANGUAGE AND MEANING

The Committee of Sleep has me sitting before my computer keyboard this sixth day of November 6, 2011 at 4:30 a.m. I fought sleep admonitions for about fifteen minutes, but finally gave in to a dreaming mind that wouldn't let go. This is the 22nd month that I started recording my dreams for this book, thus, I have nearly two complete dream years of seasons and cycles that have been incorporated. This morning's dream was reviewing the range of sensory input that has been expressed in these dreams, and correlating patterns with language and meaning. Actually, the dream left me with this waking thought: Two years of dream analysis outlined in this book provides a basic outline for an integrated theory of semantics and linguistics. The prod from my Committee of Sleep insisted that I get up and put this outline in my computer.

I typed the above paragraph, and then went downstairs to eat my breakfast and pour my first cup of coffee. These acts let my sleepy brain focus on the collage of swirling elements that follow: Chomsky, Lakoff and Johnson, basic image formation, qualia, metaphor, semantics and linguistics.

The central thought expressed in paragraph one focuses on a comprehensive, integrated approach to how our brain-minds form images and meaning from which language is derived. The physiological substrate supporting these processes has been incompletely formulated by linguists and semanticists. Self-observation in dreams seems to supply this missing information.

I've used my example of bike balancing, and how this FAP is expressed and observed in dreams, as an example throughout this book. However, the Committee of Sleep was reviewing all the basic forms of sensory input that I've detailed in my dream reports over the past 22 months. My reported dreams have covered sensory input from balance, my relationship to gravity, levitation, and flying, relationship to gravity again, temperature, flags that tell me when my comfort zone is violated, dryness of mouth and throat, sweating, my spouse's touch as it enters my dreams, hormone dream elements, internal discomfort from overeating, potty dreams, nakedness, awareness of body in dreams, FAP image formation with balance, drawing, glass cutting, FAP renditions of Mozart on my dream piano, multiple examples of cognitive processing and integration, just to name a few.

Conspicuous by its absence is taste. I have many dreams where I'm getting food, eating with others, and going through all sorts of related habits, but none with taste. I assume that taste is so basic to any organism that it operates at an instinctual level. Even single cell bacteria have taste. They respond to chemical differences the same as amoeba and other single cell organisms do.

Vision is so ubiquitous for us mobile creatures that all my dream consciousness revolves around this, our most primary sense. I move through space with two primary sensual attractors operating; my relationship to felt gravity, and my visual cues. It is this combination that is responsible for my sense of balance. It is this combination that is indelibly manifested in my bicycle riding dreams. It is this combination that directly addresses the sensory binding processes observed in dreams that is identified as qualia.

This quick overview depicts a dynamic integrated systems overview of how our total range of sensory experiences is expressed in our dreams over a complete year's cycle. One is struck by the degree to which basic sensory processing in our dreams results in what I've called mundane dreams. But one is also struck by the extent higher cognitive feedback has entered my dreams this past year to help write this book. I believe the feedback and feed-forward recursive loops between our higher autobiographical Self and core Self operate for all of us.

In that I'm a long-term lucid dreamer, I'm assuming I've greased this process a bit. Further, I also believe that facilitating exchange between higher and lower brain centers opens up neuronal space that facilitates creativity.

Most importantly for language and meaning is the identification of primary image formation in our dreams, and where this method of self-observation takes us. To my knowledge, self-observation in dreams is the only method that permits one to observe primary image formation. We can observe the brain's electro-chemical circuits operating with technology, but we can only observe its meaning through dream methodology. And understanding, which is only possible through subjective experience, is at the heart of semantics. Philosophers may intuit meaning like bees buzzing their hives, but understanding in a definitive sense is only possible when we observe and identify primary processes.

Vision dominates human senses, and is involved with most of our motor movements through space. However, in an evolutionary sense, gravity was dominant before organisms were able to process light in the act of seeing. Understanding that an organism's relationship to gravity is fundamental says that the principle of isomorphism dictates a neural architecture that supports this function. Modify or change input-output from this structure, and we fly, levitate, or get "giddy."

This modification is easy for many people in their dreams, but most people are not able to perform this modification at will when they are awake. Thus, infrequency of daytime, waking flight is given greater import when prophets report such episodes in visions.

Image formation as used here follows Damasio All sensory experience is imaged, such as balance, hot-cold, dry-wet, etc. It is acknowledged that sensory imaging is identified by the organism with Damasio's distinction between Qualia I and Qualia II. There is a re-imaging of primary images that creates the "feeling of what is" to use Damasio's language.

Re-imaging of primary images means that our brain-minds substitute one electro-chemical element for another. It is a basic process of abstraction that is central to our genome. I also refer to re-imaging as primary metaphor. The next step of re-imaging results in complex metaphor as earlier described.

Complex metaphorical schemata can be derived from these primary metaphors. Primary metaphor should be universal across human populations. Primary metaphor is probably universal across higher order mammalian species such as the Great Apes. We should be able to test this hypothesis directly as new imaging technology is employed.

Complex metaphor such as balancing my checkbook, versus primary metaphor balancing on my bike, is the level at which true mammalian creativity comes into play. It is the level at which embedded symbols are free of their body proper. What is modal and amodal is thus outlined physiologically. And self-observation in dreams permits us to observe both sensory binding and image formation. From this perspective, we can follow the emergence and use of complex metaphor throughout our dream analysis. The missing link to language formation and semantics, how meaning is created, is no longer missing.

Damasio's sequencing of proto-Self, core Self, and autobiographical Self moves image formation from Qualia I and II to primary and complex metaphor. The human cerebral cortex permits re-imaging of primary metaphor, which in turn permits freedom from instantiated images that drive reflexes. This is the process that I've previously outlined that supports the emergence of Free Will. From this perspective, primary image schemata operate at the level of core Self, while core consciousness, and secondary image schemata operate at the level of complex metaphor. I don't think this process is mysterious at all.

Complex metaphor schemata are constrained somewhat by their derivation from primary metaphor. However, socio-cultural interaction that becomes increasingly sophisticated can and does drive creative re-combinations of complex metaphor, and for the first time in evolutionary history on this planet, we experience at the level of Homo sapiens the ability to engage a process of sensory recursive processing with our environment that can lead to a scientific understanding of our world.

We are creatures of subjectivity; that is all we know. However, engaging and incorporating the findings of science helps shrink the circle of subjectivity that permits us to grasp nature's fundamentals. How wonderful it is!

Meaning is juxtaposing primary and complex metaphorical images in creative combinations on the tapestry of subjectivity. Everything else is derived, and that includes language.

Undoubtedly the emergence of language followed a path similar to what we observe with trained chimpanzees and apes that have limited, but substantial, image manipulation when they are taught sign language. The Great Apes and dolphins can think, but not speak or use language as we know it. At 18 months, I went off to Heaven and met angels. Think about this ability and contrast it to a Great Ape with a three year old's capacity.

Clearly, socio-cultural conditioning provides structure to different world languages. But this structure is a derivative of physiological capacity and processing. I'm suggesting that a true theory of semantics and linguistics is dependent on a fuller understanding of physiological processes than those currently incorporated into theories of semantics or linguistics. And that the missing piece of this generative process has been available for decades in our dreams.

CHAPTER 15

USING SELF-HYPNOSIS TO EXPLORE ALTERED STATES

INTRODUCTION

I used self-hypnosis to program dreams and control nightmares when I was an undergraduate student. One has a different experience when we are our own hypnotist. Hypnotic states are qualitatively different for me than suggestion, or autosuggestion commonly used with lucid dreaming. The critical difference lies in control. I had a limited understanding of how important self-control was in the 1950s, but my appreciation of self-control in altered states has deepened over the decades.

Using self-hypnosis, I learned to control functions commonly under the command of my autonomic nervous system such as heartbeat and pain. I created the entire content of dreams and substituted pleasant dreams for noxious nightmares. I gave all of these suggestions to myself while awake and executed them while sleeping. It was not necessary for me to wake up to redirect a nightmare, as I pre-programmed this option before going to bed. Subsequently, my Interpreter automatically transferred this command to ordinary dreams that I had not programmed. And even though I haven't programmed dreams for decades, my Interpreter will occasionally enter a dream and redirect it, repeat it, or change an ending without any conscious volition on my part.

I was plagued by nightmares since early childhood, but within a matter of days, I taught myself to use hypnotic suggestion to redirect entire dreams. I called this process dream programming. Thus, I became nightmare free for the first time in my life, and was able to sleep uninterrupted throughout the night. Very quickly I came to enjoy a greater degree of focus, sense of well-being, and energy level.

Dreamers like Hobson or Brooks and Vogelsong report use of autosuggestion to modify their dreams. I first used self-directed hypnotic suggestion to control both body and mind states, and applied this level of intervention to total dream programming. I didn't make a distinction between sleeping and waking conscious out-of-body flight until I was about eight years old. I've been a lucid observer of dreams since about age two, and a lucid observer of other altered states since my early twenties.

IMPLICATIONS OF SELF-CONTROL WITH HYPNOSIS

Hobson states that:

In hypnosis another individual's will and ideas are substituted or transplanted into the now susceptible and plastic brain-mind of the recipient. In the natural state changes taking place during sleep, cortical processes become less active as other parts of the brain-mind become more active. In both sleep and hypnosis, the emerging states are characterized by a relatively high ratio of non-conscious to conscious mental processes (Hobson: 1988: 92).

I'm not questioning that we experience a "relatively high ratio of unconscious to conscious mental processes" in sleep. I believe I have more control over dreams, altered states, and body functions than those who do not use self-hypnosis. The level of individual control over brain-mind states can be increased using self-hypnosis to control dreams, pain, trances, heartbeat, and similar functions. In my experience, those adept at hypnosis perform well in all of these areas. Employing self-hypnosis in altered states increases ones control over these states in a fashion parallel to its use in dreams.

In 1957-58 I was experiencing symptoms of PTS accompanied by extreme test anxiety and depression. I was not aware, until I was ready to graduate four years later that my MMPI profile as a first year university student was critically elevated in three separate areas. I was considered a hopeless case by the University of Minnesota; one ineligible for any of their professional programs. Nevertheless, within my first year at the University of Minnesota, I corrected all of these disabilities. I taught myself to concentrate uninterrupted for eight straight hours and had become very adept at maneuvering within the University.

In historical retrospect, and in terms of my current understanding of how the brain works, I had taken control over negatively self-reinforcing neural networks and related destructive brain chemistry, and brought them under self-control. At the time, I attributed these changes to self-directed behavioral conditioning, which was a cobbled together form of what we now call cognitive-behavioral therapy. It was my approach to self-therapy created by combing Skinnerian Behaviorism with an active self-agent.

I came to define the active agent that is my Self as my Controller. I gave directions to my Controller and He executed them on command. It was my way of visualizing an active Self. Using Damasio's model of Self, my Interpreter, or autobiographical Self, gave commands to my Controller (Core Self). My Interpreter performs this role in all altered states as well as being able to take control of autonomic body functions.

I believe that active control over body functions such as pain permitted me to control negatively, self-reinforcing neural circuits that remain beyond the control of most individuals. I basically thought of neural circuits, using today's language, as brain subsystems that were subject to my control. I thought of anxiety, depression, nightmares and attention span as behavioral manifestations of underlying physiological processes that just needed adjustment. Mind as something that resided outside of my brain never entered this naturalistic conception, except in my reading of philosophy, that is.

Self-hypnosis permitted my Interpreter to remain as an active overseer of my dreams and other altered states. In dream control, my Interpreter intervenes when I give it permission; I can give this permission while dreaming or as a suggestion before I enter sleep. Or, I can usually turn it off totally and permit natural dreaming to occur. I also experience my Interpreter integrating dream elements during the course of an evening's sleep. And, I wake up with new insights that are of an "aha" variety. Macro interpretation of dream processes seems self-evident, and in this case, higher order cognitive functions are supported during sleep, including their manifestation in dreams, as are lower order functions such as fixed action patterns (FAPs). Creative integration of dream elements and concepts is not special to me, as Delaney discusses similar examples. Lucid dreamers also commonly report "aha" experiences.

Pierce Howard has this to say about hypnosis: "Its effectiveness relies on the power of the hypnotic relationship to enable the subject to switch from external to internal sources of consciousness (2006: 891)."

I quote Howard because his view is common. Hypnotism is understood as an induced state by another. In my experience, the power of hypnotism can only be maximized through self-control. With self-hypnotism, internal control can be executed anywhere at any time. The induction process becomes an embedded FAP that can be executed within seconds. Hypnotism experienced through relationship lacks this capacity and insight. All the involved mechanisms are internal to my brain-mind; hence, why shouldn't I control them?

The power of self-hypnosis is commensurate with the degree of self-control one learns to exercise over basic physiological mechanisms. Experientially, one does not feel the mystic hand of an external controller at work. We are aware that this felt hand is our own. Experientially, we do feel a fairly conscious shift in mind-brain state with self-hypnosis. Our Interpreter in this dual state of consciousness can learn to control any body or mind function that it chooses to. There is a sense of growing strength of self and mind as one executes self-directed commands. Why should one not learn to control hallucinations in a manner similar to controlling dreams or nightmares?

By retaining control over this dual state of consciousness, we gain a further insight. The brain-mind's dual state permits action and observation of action simultaneously. This dual state as actor and observer can be generalized to any of our other altered states. It should be obvious that no mystic hand is operating. God or the gods are not fairies that light up our dreams.

Therapists make a huge mistake when they fail to guide their clients in both the use and understanding of these processes. Mastery of brain-mind processes is lessened or lost when control is attributed to an outside agent. The historical lesson of shamanism is that of therapist as guide. Traditional religious healers followed this rule because physiological mechanisms internal to our brain-minds were often the only curative element available to them. In the Christian tradition for example, the cross and special words could be used to ward off demons. This was a simple technique that returned control to the individual. If one got possessed again, they just went back for another exorcism.

The effects obtained with self-hypnosis are similar to conscious control over one's dreams. I can create almost any kind of awareness I want in either lucid dreaming or through a self-induced hypnotic state. I'm aware of my control in either state, and I can intervene while in either state. Control over body movement is different under self-hypnosis versus that of an outside hypnotist, as I can physically direct my body movements through the exercise of Will alone. I assume that related alterations in neural circuits occur under self-hypnosis as when one uses a hypnotist. But there must be some variations due to the self versus other controls exercised.

Referring to Developmental Psychologist Jerome Kagan's work, Hobson says:

Developmentalists assume that the self arises when sensations associated with movement come to be taken as causes of these movements, which they precede. This construct resonates strongly with the idea that mature human thought and consciousness have both motoric and causal aspects (Hobson: 1999: 100).

Self as agent comes into being when a myriad of body sensations are bound together through complex processes. Feedback loops from our higher cortical areas in turn can and do direct goal oriented movement and actions on the part of the organism. Movement requires extensive access to fixed action patterns that we have placed in memory at a non-conscious level. My bike riding dreams fixing balance in memory being one example. Will is used to execute FAPs and our control over actions seems to take place on its own as is the case with walking. From my perspective, Will creates the sensations that are then taken as their cause. How easy it is for the human mind to believe that Will alone can move objects, and when that object is our Self and our body, it becomes an understandable truism.

Contemporary neuroscience sees Self arising as a process of feeling one's body and feeling movement. From feeling body and movement, there emerges a symbolic representation of bodily "some-things." As a young student and unqualified university professor teaching with my BA Degree, I used a Symbolic Interactionist approach and simply saw the relation as being that of symbolic Self to referential body. An active relationship had to exist between body and mind, because I experienced all the effects of mind to body control. But in the 1950s, controlling mind and body this way was considered freaky by most professionals, who were still struggling with Freud's unconscious.

Subjectively, I experience this mind-body relationship when using self-hypnosis. I take conscious control of Self and body by using self-hypnosis to change the normal way my neural circuits are expressed. A dual sense of my non-material Self, or I, controlling my material Self, or me, emerges. Motor functions that are normally under control of automatic, non-conscious processes are taught to respond to my higher order sense of Self. Using Damasio's terminology, my Autobiographical self directs functions normally controlled by my Core self. However, both Core and Autobiographical Self have awareness; and this awareness is felt in much the same way as I feel two of me when I self talk.

Self talk as exchange that occurs within our higher cognitive level differs from the exchange that occurs between Autobiographical Self and Core Self. The difference being that the practiced self-hypnotist has learned to control non-conscious physiological processes. Our Core Self can be taught to exercise direct control over autonomic processes when our Interpreter wills it to be done. We thereby shift control that is normally automatic and put it under the conscious direction of our Interpreter. But I must exercise Will consciously or my Interpreter loses control, and control is automatically returned to my core Self. Obviously, we do not want to trigger debilitating pathologies this way.

Self-hypnotism permits one to move across the entire landscape of brain-mind functions. The question arises, why should this level of control be denied to the mentally ill? A slight paradigm shift from self-talk permits application across levels of evolutionary development with major therapeutic applications. It worked for me in the school year of 1957/58, and the effects have lasted a lifetime.

Conscious control of dreams and other altered states of consciousness are addressed by this or what may be multiple mechanisms. It is this altered relationship between normally conscious and normally non-conscious brain-mind mechanisms that I used to improve my own mental health. It is this mechanism that I think offers considerable potential for the mentally ill who are primarily treated with pharmaceuticals, especially in the early stages of illness before the brain has been too corrupted by its own chemicals such as cortisol, and pathologically embedded neuronal patterns that are expressed like any other FAP.

It is standard neuroscience that says we build neural mass with habit; the neurons that fire together wire together idea. These physiological effects have been established both with meditating monks and laboratory animals. Viewing clinical treatment as application of mind controlling drugs, which starts with grade school children diagnosed with ADD or ADHD, is to equate brain-minds with a piece of meat. Unfortunate, as this equation puts us back with early Skinnerian Behaviorism.

Neural processes controlling positive brain states through mind exercises like meditation become corrupted in various pathologies that can lead to uncontrolled anxiety, depression, or hallucinations. From this point of view, a sub-group of related pathologies are conceived as being hardwired changes in the brain through self-reinforced habits. I did say subgroup. Conceiving of the brain-mind as a functional whole that is subject to plastic modification under our own control, leads us down the path to cognitive-behavioral therapy.

The naturalist perspective suggested to me by behaviorism in the 1950s said that mind was a brain emergent. By the 1970s, I needed a dynamic systems model to interpret the mechanisms I was playing with in self-experiments. Dynamic systems and chaos theory conceptually offered emergent properties that added in the missing pieces.

CONCEPTUALIZING BRAIN STATES

Hobson moves along a continuum of three major brain states: awake, sleeping, and dreaming (1994). Conceiving of brain states on a continuum begs the question of where to place other altered states such as trance and vision. Following a linear model, I would define the continuum as awake, trance-visions, sleep, and dreaming. Other altered states either become hybrids of being awake or dreaming, or occupy a separate category. Hobson's three dimensional cube visualizes brain states placed differently in the cube according to how the state is activated, type of input-output, and chemical modulation (2001: 45). His three dimensional cube is preferred over a linear model as it easily permits visual placement in the cube for other altered states. And the cube moves us one step closer to state space, which lends itself to dynamic applications.

In my personal history, one can learn to experientially mix and match any combination of mind-brain states. In this mixing and matching, we create visions, possession, speaking-in-tongues, etc. In effect, I'm referring to all the altered states that have been historically associated with mystics and shamans. Mysticism only exists in the mind of the beholder. Naturalists use these mechanisms for play.

What I think occurs with lucid dreams we call visions is the role my Interpreter plays; that is, lucidity and recall is increased with visions when compared to normal dreams. Most people are not lucid dreamers, thus, when a vision does occur, their sense of reality is overwhelmed, and they often interpret the vision as a window into another dimension. Hobson acknowledges insight and creativity with higher brain functions during dreaming. Nevertheless, visions occur when we are awake and interrupt the continuity of our social and environmental interactions. In similar fashion, other trance states remain mysterious for most people who report them. Thus, failure to explain altered states empirically has left them under the province of mystics, spiritualists, shaman-priests, and soothsayers.

The active role of higher cerebral processes becomes important when I attempt to explain my altered states of reality. Brain structure and function are isomorphic, meaning that when different structures are activated, different functions are expressed. In like fashion, I assume that when entering a trance state, I activate different brain structures, neural circuits, and networks than those which are operating when I'm experiencing normal daytime consciousness or when I'm dreaming lucidly.

However, trance states are experienced as a combination of sleep-dream consciousness and awake-consciousness. As I've stated in Mind of the Mystic, what we experience are separate combinations of different neural circuits. As we come to document the physiology and brain states when we sleep and dream, we are also in a position to empirically explore what is happening in our brains when we experience other altered states. Through self-experiments, we can create, direct, and control all altered states, thereby gaining insight into the basic brain-mind mechanisms involved. Tracking brain operations in ASC should be as easy as dream lab work.

Suggestion can be used to encourage and direct dreams at a lesser level of control than that which is possible with self-hypnosis. I don't personally know anyone else who can move directly from a waking state into a trance without the use of drugs or a hypnotist, as I only have myself as reference. Huxley's regression is an example of a drug user employing a hypnotist. Most people engaging in shamanic trances go through a special routine to activate appropriate neural circuits and call forth trance, visions, and spirit possessions. The use of physical deprivation, dancing, and chanting are common ritual activators. Active control of brain-mind states just takes practice. One can teach their automatic/autonomic neural circuits to be responsive to Will as I've defined it.

Using special neural circuit activators of this nature helps me understand what is going on with self-hypnosis. We are closing down some aspects of normal daytime consciousness, and opening other neural circuit combinations needed to create trance or vision. This happens to most people spontaneously when the right ritual, drug, or form of brain damage occurs.

In my Genesis Journey, I immediately entered trance due to prior self-conditioning. It's an example of brain state control comparable to teaching oneself to fall asleep on the count of five. It is related to the trance expectation of the religious zealot who is psychologically prepared to speak-in-tongues, and quickly falls into this brain state as the preacher revs up his or her rhetoric. Neurons that fire together wire together; remember?

Equivalent movement into these brain states can be activated consciously to control what must be both electrical and chemical activities of the brain. Hobson presents a beginning approach to brain state regulation that parallels what I do, however, I change brain-mind states without chemical induction (1988: 117-133). With practice, my Interpreter turns these states on and off like a water tap. I parallel the kind of practice that Buddhist monks experience when meditating by shifting my Interpreter's perspective.

I also depart from the behavioral psychologists who ignore and deny the scientific study of phenomenology and subjectivity. I think as a phenomenological researcher, I can and have demonstrated the value of looking at consciousness and altered states of consciousness from the inside out, i.e., self-observation. We do not fully understand all aspects of consciousness, but we can use different existing methodologies such as self-observation to deepen knowledge of them.

I experience the contemporary field of cognitive science as being too restricted when it ignores feeling and emotions as phenomenological aspects of consciousness. Following Skinner's model, or the contemporary standard bearers of cognitive science, I would not be sitting at my computer writing these words. Instead, I would be on meds, or at the "funny farm."

My traumatic childhood required explanation, hence, I created a working model of Self, consciousness, Will, Free Will, brain plasticity, and self-therapy. Without assuming that I could be the active agent in control of my brain and mind, none of my self-interventions would have been initiated.

I see consciousness as the integrative moment-to-moment processing of all the input from my senses, as well as their established memories, that represent my relationship to my total environment, body, and brain. I see the Self as an emergent that arises during our evolutionary history to become the central coordinator and controller of these processes. And like A. Damasio, I think the Self becomes an emergent protagonist sustained by these processes. It is our world of embedded cognition.

Further, arguments about whether the color red exists in nature or not fall into the category of how many angels can God put on the head of a pin if He is omnipotent? The question of the color red cannot be answered unless one addresses the phenomenological and subjective separate category represented by consciousness. And, for that matter, neither can the question of God.

Yes, there is a wavelength easily determined by modern physicists that represent the light entering our eyes that becomes the color red when interpreted by the brain-mind. Does red exist in nature? No. It exists in our subjective selves, and must be understood within the scientific category called subjectivity.

To answer the query of the cognitive scientist, yes there is a direct correlation between wavelength and subjective experience, but we experience light as red after the photons influence a couple dozen brain centers. Red can no more be explained as something that exists external to our brain-minds than language can. Language and the color red remain brain-mind subjective creations.

My brain-mind does not know the wavelength associated with the color red. My brain-mind has added feeling to the color, which I experience every time I watch a sunset, or view a great artist's work, or simply put the color in a stain glass piece that I'm working on. To debate the color red's subjective human meaning by divorcing it from subjectivity is a fool's exercise. It is equivalent to debating if there is a sound in the woods when a tree falls and no one is there to hear it. Absurd! But these are fun brain games for children.

Consciousness is not simply an epiphenomenon of brain mechanics. It is causal and it sustains and directs the larger course of who we are, and what we become. Yes, we embed thousands, and probably millions, of little routines that do not demand our conscious awareness moment-to-moment. But overall, you and I experience free will, and we experience being active agents of Self. We are capable of more than rehashing two thousand year old Greek philosophies. Language, color, qualia, intention, purpose, Free Will and more are all part of our conscious, phenomenological Self. In like fashion, one does not understand water as H and O, it is understood as H_2O. And in like fashion, each is subject to a naturalist's explanation.

COMMENTS ON HYPNOSIS

Hobson says that "… the failure to establish a physiological substrate of hypnosis has hindered its scientific investigation severely (1999: 236)." And, "… so far, it has been impossible to find physiological similarities between the states of sleep and hypnosis using the techniques of surface electrical recording (Ibid)."

He also says that with the development of new brain imaging techniques, this may all change.

Self-observation and self-control of hypnosis provides a subjective technology that should not stand alone. It does, however, give us an approach to brain-mind states that some day may be fully imaged technologically. But I believe a full understanding of the physiological substrate of hypnosis will require a subjective component like the one I have used for over fifty years.

Any combination of internal-external communication can be maintained with self-hypnosis as it can be with lucid dreaming. And, in my experience, practice of self-hypnosis can build almost instant priming responses not available with an outside hypnotist.

Ramachandran employed a simple re-conceptualization of phantom limbs to correct the problem of removing pain from a limb that doesn't exist. His method is that of a subjective methodology. Obviously the pain from a phantom limb resides in one's brain and not the limb. It is a subjective state which needs a subjective intervention for solution. In like fashion, we don't study hypnosis from the outside; we employ a subjective methodology, because that is the state of interest.

Observing hypnotic trance from the outside has severe limitations. First, behavioral cues are equivalent to dream forms that reflect underlying physiological mechanisms, and it is the mechanisms that we want to understand. Secondly, a hypnotized individual is taking cues from the hypnotist who, in effect, is adding static into the machine. Self-hypnotism circumvents these problems. Hence, traditional study of hypnotism has been barking up the wrong tree. The problem is one of methodology.

I haven't followed all the new technology developments. I think it's important to emphasize the subjective aspects of hypnosis from a number of perspectives: brain-mind control, self-hypnosis versus hypnotist induced trances, and long-term practices that permit one to move easily across brain-mind states.

I touch on all of these aspects in this book with specific emphasis in this section. The application of self-hypnosis to create and alter states of consciousness is different from physiological assessment. There is a different focus with subjective self-observation that leads to new understanding. It is similar to trying to understand quale called the color red by printing out numbers and schematics on paper. Combining physiological and phenomenological methods seems to best maximize potential findings.

From a psychological and mental health perspective, it is important to understand the physiology of hypnosis. I never want to detract from basic research, but let me note that Native American people used the chemical in aspirin to achieve medicated effects for generations without understanding it. This has generally been true of natural medicines around the world. Long-term use, often thousands of years of use, without understanding the physics, chemistry, or biology of helpful medications is part of our human history. We still go to places like the Amazon and explore native medicines, or to China and study natural healing in this 21st Century. If the boat floats, I don't have to understand the physics to go sailing.

I used hypnosis with my wife when we had our second son. The nurse refused to give me scrub clothes until the doctor directly ordered her to. The doctor found birthing through hypnosis interesting, took one arm of my wife and I took the other, and we walked her from the delivery room as she carried our new son. Interesting, end of story; the year was 1961. It was a skill not taught in medical school.

My last years in Rochester, Minnesota, often put me in contact with various medical practitioners and doctors. Most through the early 21st Century with whom I discussed such phenomena still saw hypnosis as a curiosity. I have a colonoscopy every five years, and carefully watch the procedure on the screen as the doctor and I discuss the screen's output. He never asks me how I manage without an anesthesiologist. His comments the last (3rd) time he performed this procedure: "You make this look easy." PS, I still get charged for the anesthesiologist.

Part of my being incredulous comes from fifty years of experience with self-hypnosis. It seems so easy and so normal that I have a hard time believing so many doctors can see hypnosis as occult phenomena. Ministers and priests of Christianity often see both meditation and hypnosis as being unacceptable; yet, many can practice exorcism and see this practice as falling within the range of the normal. Reality is such a strange phenomenon.

I understand medical practitioners being afraid of trying new procedures outside of standard practices due to insurance liability and related law suits, but this should not keep medical schools from researching tried and true practices, even if the mechanisms aren't known. The mechanisms will never be known without appropriate research.

I see subjectivity as a legitimate method of study. I can't appreciate reality as being independent of self-awareness or consciousness. Technology has given us a window into the brain-mind that is only possible through science. Technology, I believe, combined with subjective self-experiments will deepen this understanding. It's me, and you, and you, and me. Machines can probably duplicate most human thought at some point in the future, but in today's world, the human level of cognitive mapping with associated emotions is still very much a mystery. Machines should have no problem identifying the electro-chemical elements that make up the color red, but at that level, machines will not experience red as a color. Machine manipulation of data must still be interpreted. Machine imaging of brain-mind phenomena will be enhanced when we triangulate methodology. In my experience, method is as critical to progress as technology is.

Psychiatrists that I have known over the years have been mostly arrogant, mostly Freudians, and often very, very limited in their understanding of interdisciplinary research. All of this is changing as Hobson points out, but much of the change is driven by money from the pharmaceutical companies with their obvious bias.

Religious fundamentalists of my acquaintance only seem interested in their own dogma. Religious or psychiatric dogma that is not based on solid research has always felt the same to me. Dogma can thwart progress for a decade, a hundred, or a thousand years: The scientific study of hypnosis by the medical community being a good example, and 21st Century practice of exorcism being another.

BRAIN-MIND CONTROL

Teaching myself self-hypnosis was easy and quick. I had excellent control over attention and body parts, including pain, within one 12 week university term. I found that with subjects who were reluctant to be hypnotized that I simply broke the induction steps into smaller Skinnerian-type directives: "You will feel a sensation in your hand; your hand will begin to twitch on its own; your hand begins to rise without any effort on your part, etc."

What I learned from early years of using hypnosis with myself and others was how differently our minds are configured in terms of trust and belief. Sometimes I had to deliver a little lecture or explanation about hypnosis before individuals would agree to try it. Although, I must admit, I never tried using hypnosis on anyone who thought of it as witchcraft or occult contact with the evil forces of the universe.

My brain seemed to easily adapt to self-hypnosis. I will never know to what degree my brain was altered by childhood trauma. I suffered many brain-mind changes after mother's smothering attacks, such as loss of early speech and walking, out-of-body experiences, loss of fear associated with heights, epileptic fits with associated blackouts, and a few other changes that I mention in my autobiography.

Programming my dreams with self-hypnosis led me to eventually initiate, direct, and control other altered states. This progression occurred over many years and was not part of a conscious effort. I believe that most normal people can learn these techniques. Time is not a major element if you think of a few weeks, or six months. I think the learning and self-directed use of self-hypnosis can begin in a matter of days for most of us. After we learn the initial steps of how to induce self-hypnotic trance, the real work can be done by the client him or herself.

The right mood, right cultural expectations, and right environment can create visions of Mother Mary, or felt icebergs on which one can play in a matter of minutes during the heat of summer. These are major altered states of consciousness that create visions and trance, and can occur with groups, not just individuals. Consequently, I assume that belief plays a major part of being hypnotizable. How we interpret belief and what we believe is critical to our entering altered states. Culture provides interpretation, and we provide physiology.

SELF-HYPNOSIS VERSUS INDUCED ALTERED STATES

I may be derelict in my research strategies, but I do not find good examples of long-term self-hypnosis use in the literature. The focus always comes from that of the specialist who is inducing trance in others. Therefore, control from outside of one's own brain-mind state is studied, or usually more accurately described as observed. You cannot observe my dreams, although you can observe my dreaming brain. You cannot observe how I create my thoughts; you can only observe the processes that support them.

I find a parallel between the researcher observing my dreams and that of the researcher observing my self-induced hypnotic states. Good luck. Subjectivity can be studied itself, and I think with good results. Control, as I've repeated ad nauseam, is a critical component of understanding dreams, controlling and directing dreams, and studying the effects of these interventions on the dream processes. It is also central to understanding altered states and all aspects of consciousness, in my opinion.

It has often been the practice of the medical community to study subjects as though we were a more sophisticated version of aplysia. I believe we can only maximize our study of consciousness, self, and altered states by combining both subjective and objective methodologies. The human brain-mind is both physiology and mind. And, conscious control of movement in, out and through various brain-mind states provides additional insight into these processes.

Hobson discusses the status of our understanding the relationship between mind, body, and health: "And whether or not one believes in the unity or the separability of mind and body, the evidence is overwhelmingly strong that mental states can be voluntarily changed in order to affect bodily states (1999: 234, 235)."

He then notes that Buddhism offers "… the power to channel consciousness without in any way entailing mystical belief or ascetic practice (Ibid)."

He then references the severe problem of Buddhist practitioners related to the transmigration of souls. The transmigration of souls is based on mystic assumptions, and the Dalai Lama doesn't plan to clarify transmigration of souls until after his 80th birthday, or so.

This mental slippage between testable empirical procedures that can be replicated, and repackaged definitions of un-testable phenomena such as soul transmigration has been common in our religious community. Religious practitioners commonly define unknowns and then treat their definitions as being on an equal par with constructs that can be scientifically tested. This voodoo process is more difficult for the occultist as we come to understand self, conscious, and altered brain states. Self-hypnosis lets one approximate the states of self-control exercised by the Buddhist in a matter of months without all the religious innuendo. One more doctoral thesis: Compare two or more individuals in states of self-hypnosis as they lucidly share their subjective experiences, and simultaneously record what is happening with their mirror neurons.

EFFECTS OF LONG-TERM USE OF SELF-HYPNOSIS

My experience with self-hypnosis over the past fifty some years is that our brains can learn to control its various states in a matter of weeks. Long-term practice of self-hypnosis most likely increases neuronal mass, just as long-term meditation does. This level of control and physiological change is impossible with just a few hypnotic trances induced by an outsider. If practitioners of self-hypnosis are to derive maximum benefit, it must be through maximizing self-control, which is time dependent.

Achieving eight hours of continuous study without even a water break was accomplished in one 12 week university term. By the end of one term, I was free of test anxiety, and depression as well. The behavioral symptoms associated with my negative MMPI elevations were stabilized within the first year of using self-hypnotism, primarily during the first 12 week quarter. Complex methodologies studying consciousness and altered states would seem most fruitful by combining subjective and objective methods with the same study population. One adept at moving through various lucid states of dreams, visions, and trances while being monitored, should shed light on numerous questions about neural circuit functions between subsystems and macro brain-mind functions.

I think a fun Ph.D. thesis might be that of following a promising undergraduate through a process of development similar to my late 1950s exercises. Scanning of meditating monks brains demonstrate changes in neural mass and related electrical activity.

There are many animal studies that demonstrate how dynamic and plastic our brains are. I make many assumptions in this book about brain plasticity and the consciousness levels we exhibit in various altered states. But most fundamentally, I hope we will come to explore the full potential of subjective self-observation, especially with the developing technology of the 21st Century. Let's repeat that Ph.D. thesis study with a schizophrenic personality.

I believe that quasi-medical, philosophical, and religious dogmas of the ancients will cease to exist once we understand the relationship between brain-mind structure and function, and how subjective, altered states are created and maintained. Top-down and bottom-up research can address fundamental questions in physiology, psychology, philosophy, spirituality, and linguistics. At least, these are my working assumptions.

Finally, I believe that the false debate between atheists and theists will cease to exist once we understand the physiology behind our own spiritual natures. These ongoing debates exemplified by Dawkins are equivalent to how many angels can God put on the end of a pin if He is omnipotent? Simple answer, imagination is infinite.

Imagination, what a term! Increase one's neuronal workspace for thought processes in our dreams, and we get creative "aha" results. This is the playground for imagination.

CHAPER 16

DREAM DICTIONARIES

INTRODUCTION

Dream dictionaries go back as far as recorded history. The snake means this, a death means that, and on and on they go. These approaches to dream interpretation seem endless and are usually totally arbitrary. In this respect, I find agreement with David Linden when he says: I have no confidence... that insight into one's mental state can be gained through analysis of dream content with arbitrary symbolic dictionaries (2007: 219)."

The emphasis here is on arbitrary symbolic dictionaries. But, dream dictionaries need not be arbitrary – they can reflect the actual activation processes and functions of the dreaming brain. To be useful, dream dictionaries must represent what is actually going on in the brain-mind both physiologically and cognitively.

Useful dream dictionaries show the reader how to interpret individual meaning in their dreams. Useful approaches that help us interpret individual meaning in dreams generally rely on case histories as evidenced by authors such as Hobson, Delaney, and Brooks-Vogelsong. Approaches that tell us that dictionary items mean something specific are entirely misleading. In my opinion dream dictionaries that offer occult interpretations stand between the dreamer and possible enlightenment.

Linden asks: "Is dream content meaningful (Ibid)?" and answers that it is a nonissue. If content is interpreted with specific meanings, then content is not meaningful.

But content can be meaningful two different ways. First, content tells me something about my memory processes, as I pull dream elements from both external sources and internally generated creations of my own. And content helps me understand a significant part of how my dreaming brain constructs reality. Dream interpretations offered in this book support both positions.

Dream created elements – places, objects, and people, are used over and over again through the years in my dreams. Content analysis helps me focus on modular brain functions being performed in my dreams. Content analysis improves my understanding of consciousness, and the different levels of consciousness operating in my dreams.

Additionally, isolating content as in my reported nightmares permits me to find the critical bridging element that identifies the causative factors behind the nightmares. In my nightmares, fear becomes embedded in memory with specific motor and muscle fixed action patterns. I know from experience it only takes one learning lesson to embed fixed action patterns supported by intense emotions. If I ignore content, it is considerably more difficult to mine my dreams for meaning. For example, facilitated action patterns are identified through content analysis, and the various dream processes that seem clearly to be related to memory integration and consolidation are a major part of my dreams.

Hobson discusses an example of memory priming as he attempts to recall the term: "eucalyptus," and goes through a step-by-step process of identification (1999:86). What I take from his related analysis is the broader scope of how memory works. "In other words, priming is not just semantic, but also sensory, and often represents broad emotional states (Ibid: 87)."

Each act of memory recall is intensely personal, and I don't have to emphasize this for the reader, it is intuitive. However, He says: "The eucalyptus example also shows how my own personal history is interleaved with word recognition, with smell, and with place names (Ibid: 87)."

Memory is individualistic because it is created in each of our own unique social and environmental contexts, which is noted by Hobson's reference to his personal history. The above example is one of memory search and output from neurons to consciousness. In my dreams, I also consider the other direction, that of input.

Initially, memory elements have to move from short-term memory to long-term memory in order for their later retrieval to be possible. In this interpretation, dream dictionaries, to be meaningful, must take this entire holistic, two way process into consideration. I carefully search for the salient emotions and cognitive elements when I identify the key bridging elements in my dreams. Any or all of our senses can be involved in associative memory input as well as associative memory output.

Day-to-day, how I feel is critical to my well-being. If I'm blue, down, I need to identify this feeling state and do something about it. If I'm living in a state of near pathological anxiety, it is critical to identify, correct, and act accordingly.

I use these examples of identifying dream meaning as it is a kind of reverse priming process that seems to be occurring at the point of dream input to future memory. Numerous dream examples that I provided consistently demonstrated the transparency of my dreams, and their relationship to my day-to-day activities, moods, and long-term experiences. Unless you routinely use dream programming or suggestion in your dreams, you will experience a similar pattern. This has been my experience for over fifty years.

A DREAM EXAMPLE

My brain is responsible for maintaining itself, my body, and selectively bringing sensory communication into my consciousness centers where this activity triggers awareness and response. Most of my brain's activity goes on below my awareness whether I'm asleep or awake. I accept Hobson's basic assumptions that dreams are transparent and represent ongoing brain activity. This too is my experience.

Example:
My wife's bed movements woke me at 5:55 a.m. this morning, November 29, 2010, when I was having the following mundane dream:

I'm in a large enclosure, probably a mall, and need to find a restroom. I ask a passerby if he knows where they are, and he replies: "Restrooms are really hard to find." He looks sympathetic and moves on. The scene changes and I find myself in a large room with many other people, but because the room is large, it is not crowded. There are men and women present, but no children. There are no sinks or mirrors, and people are moving about casually without any noticeable purpose.

I locate a toilet near the entrance only to discover that the top is down, but when I lift up the top, there is no seat. Checking carefully, I discover there are two seats hanging down under the toilet bowl. One seat has a large hole in it with an open end, a special feature for men. The other seat has a small opening that seems unusual, but I decide that it is adequate and I'm in need. I rotate the seat and it turns over into a normal ready position. I carefully take down my trousers and sit on the toilet. I sit, and I sit. I become aware that I'm slightly constipated, and this act may take a while.

As I'm waiting, I notice that my trousers are gone, and I'm sitting on the toilet quite exposed. I look around and find there are still many other people present, but no one seems to be noticing me. My discomfort eases. After some time, I decide that I am constipated, and decide to go about my other activities. At this moment, I fully wake up as my spouse begins to dress for the day.

INTERPRETATION

Paying attention to dream content, I first look for its transparent meaning. It is a body maintenance dream. Yesterday my wife received her first check as a part-time teacher at the local Chinese language school. She treated her little family of three to lunch at our favorite buffet. True to form, we all overate; a second Thanksgiving feast of sorts. I was mildly constipated when I got up at 6:05 a.m. to use the facilities.

Activation of this dream was internal and supportive of a normal body function. I don't believe the toilet stimulus entered an ongoing dream, but was the dream's activator, as I spent considerable dream time finding and attempting to use the toilet. I was in a state of discomfort from overeating, and this physical state dominated my dream senses. This dream vignette is very transparent. Body activated senses dominate my dreams until I take corrective action. The reader will recall my dream scenarios of being too hot or too cold as reported in previous chapters.

Symbolic dreams typically require more interpretation, as do dreams activated by emotions. I find analysis of dream content at least as helpful as analysis of dream form. Analysis of dream content for over fifty years lets me quickly categorize dream activation as primarily cognitive, as with thought dreams, representing body states as indicated above, or signaling dominant emotional states. Being naked or semi-naked in my dreams reflects actual body stimuli that I'm experiencing. Giving esoteric meanings to nakedness in dream dictionaries seems absurd to me. Nakedness is of secondary importance in my dreams, and in this sense it is epiphenomenal.

DREAM DICTIONARIES

Dream dictionaries based on modern research are highly critical of Freud. His dream interpretations were bizarre by modern standards. The "Chester Beatty" Egyptian papyrus from around 1350 BCE comes from Thebes, and contains over 200 dream references (Craze: 15)."

"Particularly interesting are the details of three modes of interpretation, which anticipate principles used by Freud centuries later. These are the detection of hidden associations, the use of opposites, and the use of visual or verbal puns (Ibid)."

Almost a thousand years later, Plato added to what would become Freud's approach to dreams with this idea:

He describes the human psyche as possessing 'a lawless, wild beast nature which peers out in sleep: As we no longer exercise rational control while sleeping, our lust and rage can enjoy free and full expression. Centuries later, such a view would be central to Sigmund Freud's ideas about defining human personality and behavior (Ibid: 19).

Freud's folly was basing his model on the thoughts of ancient philosophers instead of hard won physiological research, or even careful analysis of his own dreams.

Most of our brain's activity is non-conscious, but not through repression. Unconscious in this case, and in most of my dreams, means below the level of waking or dreaming awareness. Mundane dreams are transparent to say the least. I'll look at a few dream dictionaries to scan the great variety of interpretations that exist, and to drive the point home that the dreaming brain processes a lot of mundane, moment-to-moment information, which activate dream processes. We are not in contact with the other side, the world of ancient dream interpreters, or Freud's version of these ancient interpretations.

Craze provides the reader with a quick historical review of dream analysis that requires no specific background in physiology or dream research. Some of these ancient dream dictionaries are more sophisticated than many of the popular ones being circulated today:

1)   The five volume 2nd Century BCE dream dictionaries of Artemidorus contains references to over 3000 dreams.

2)   The Atharna Veda of ancient India considers personality differences in dreams, especially in the Upanishads.

3)   The ancient Chinese Taoist manuscripts "Lie-Tsu" describe six types of dreams.

4)   Aristotle believed that dreams revealed problems of our physical bodies.

5)   Or, in the near past Fritz Perls Gestalt techniques: "The Gestalt method involves contacting different 'parts' of yourself and exploring their meaning." According to Perls: "… dreams are a 'message of yourself to yourself (Craze: 76)."

6)   Craze spends considerable time with Carl Gustav Jung, who still remains popular today. Jung is known for his archetypes which he considered to be universals and Craze lays out a simplified explanation for them.

Personally, I find historical interpretations in dreams interesting because most of these explanations still circulate in popular literature. Historical interpretations touch on experiences that we have in our own dreams, and thus seem to possess credibility. In my opinion, one can be thoroughly familiar with contemporary dream dictionaries of the type quoted below, and still not understand dreams.

How can we gain an understanding of dreams from all these resources? I think the answer is fairly simple; only through research. Attempts to find universal meaning in dream content as set forth by historical figures such as Jung and Freud are doomed to failure. They do, however, reflect earlier attempts by the ancients, as well as some direct borrowing from them. The reader can gain insight into Freud and Jung's interpretations by reviewing historical sources.

Let me give you an example of Jung's archetype of nakedness. Jung would probably say that nakedness in dreams has different meanings for different dreamers. However, nakedness is universal in that it demonstrates how our masks, our personas, are removed in our dreams to reveal our true selves. The simple logic of this interpretation is appealing to many. How quickly we go to symbolic interpretations that intuitively seem so logical. Who amongst us is not trying to improve self-understanding? How misleading it all can be.

Nakedness in my dreams has no such meaning. Nakedness is activated in my dreams by sensory stimulation from my skin. I have given a number of examples, which have occurred for decades, and are consistently patterned. In the summer, I often sleep naked, and full-nakedness appears in my dreams. In the winter, I sleep with a nightshirt, and nakedness in my dreams only appears for the bottom half of my physical Self.

Is this an archetype? Perhaps there are three archetypes: being naked, partially naked, and fully clothed. How easily we invent explanations that resonate with particular time periods and cultures. Since archetypes can be derived so easily from common body sensations that arise across humanity; there just seems to be something operating that is common to all of us. Yup!

The non-conscious universals that appear in my dreams reflect common human emotions such as trauma and anxiety, all manner of external stimuli, my state of health, cognitive matters that my brain is busy with, both sleeping and when awake, etc. However, the model that brings these elements into contemporary interpretations that are compatible with research on dreams and consciousness are not found in works such as Craze's. Jung's scheme is interesting for historical purposes, but not informative in terms of my ability to understand my own dreams.

DICTIONARIES: WORLDLY TO OTHER-WORLDLY

I have referenced Delaney elsewhere, but note that she is well known for her dream work, and strongly encourages her followers to seek understanding of their own unique dream interpretations. Brooks and Vogelsong are most helpful in that they consistently marry their own dreams with science-based literature. These two sources have additional credibility for me as Hobson has written the forwards. I have referenced them considerably, because they are contemporary, serious-minded dream explorers.

Today, the mysterious, occult, alien presence, mystic-infused interpretation of dreams is rampant. Some of our best-selling dream books are those that most emphasize other-worldly interpretations. I reject these interpretations, as they fall well outside my own phenomenological experiences as well as research conducted by the scientific community.

Do I know that 95 percent of dreams represent below conscious level processing similar to my body maintenance or FAP dreams? No! I have not quantified them, and I have little motivation to quantify them. The dream research labs are set up for this purpose. My goal is to demonstrate how we can use careful self-observation, combined with contemporary research findings, to better understand our own dreams.

I found it interesting to discover that my dreaming brain informed me, when I was sitting on my dream toilet, that I was constipated, which was a kind of awareness that would eventually enter my daytime consciousness. Dream insights also help me understand how physical sensation enters and are expressed in my dreams. Body sensations entering dreams can be confusing, especially when they take on complex metaphorical symbolism. Body state sensations can activate one's dream, or enter an ongoing dream scenario as a metaphorical element.

It is now December 25th, Christmas Day, and I had another toilet dream this morning. Yesterday my wife and I attended a dinner party at a friend's house, and I stuffed myself using the holiday as an excuse. Uncomfortable? yes; delightful meal? Definitely. About ten days ago, my wife prepared a special meal of Chinese dumplings for these same friends, and surprise, another toilet dream. Pretty transparent stuff, no? What Jungian archetype is this? What aspect of Freud's unconscious is this? Can we agree that one size fits all dream dictionary interpretations can get pretty silly?

GLOBAL THEMES AND SPECIFIC FAPs

I started this chapter by recognizing the individual nature of dreams. My life has been quite different from most of my readers, and my dreams reflect this entire history of being a unique person, as do your dreams.

I have discussed the importance of fixed action patterns (FAPs) in my dreams, meaning specific elements such as honing bike balance in memory. FAP dream elements should be looked for whenever you are learning new motor routines, enhancing specific skills, or digesting large quantities of cognitive materials. Although when confronting complex cognitive materials in your dreams, think of Freeman, not Llinas. When I started cutting stain glass after a twenty year hiatus, I found myself engaged in fictive dream motions of a controlled and sweeping nature. These were new dream elements for me, and I paid particular attention to them. In the morning when I interpreted this dream, I realized I was improving my cutting and drawing glass hobby skills as I slept.

In terms of what I call global themes, the reader will need to think about his or her own lifestyle. I can only generalize my own examples. However, I'm quite sure memory associations in your dreams are going to become more patterned as you mature and age. Auto-created dream elements and scenarios increase, common behaviors become habitual, and with lucid dreaming, higher order consciousness more easily enters our dreams. I suspect that auto-created dream material differs significantly for the occasional lucid dreamer. The same applies to dream creativity.

I've been a teacher, lecturer, and a public speaker most of my adult life. When I wasn't teaching, I administered various programs and performed related duties. I'm very aware during the writing of this three book series that I'm reflecting over my life, reading extensively in the area of neuroscience, and integrating this contemporary language into various chapters. I know that using dated terminology from psychology or dream analyses would be distracting to the modern reader. If you've reached this section, you will have noted how this personal history plays out in my dreams.

I've often found myself giving fictive lectures and engaging in fictive academic dialogue with colleagues in my dreams. Sometimes material such as Hobson's AIM Model will be automatically reviewed in my dreams. The AIM Model dream reviews Hobson's material by having me explain it to a person who felt like a colleague. Known personalities or concerns with dream forms were not the focus in this dream; review of the AIM Model was. If I had focused on the bizarre characteristics of the dream, the morphing characters, or characters that had mixed features of real life people I know, I would have been misled.

The critical or bridging element in these theme dreams is the lecture-like explanation that I'm delivering, or in other case examples, cognitive content may be written on a dream blackboard, or even read from papers or books. Whole nights of dream recall with five or six interrelated thematic scenarios can remain focused on this type of cognitive dream. When I awaken in the morning, I'm oblivious to other mundane dream scenarios that probably also occurred throughout the night.

Many writers, artists, and scientists have gained ideas, inspiration, and insight while dreaming. If the acquired dream gift is of major importance, we remember it. If, as is usually the case, it is mundane and related to everyday activities, we will probably think it unimportant and readily dismiss these dream elements, or not even recall them. If the reader will refrain from focusing on the bizarre elements of their dreams and look for their activation functions, you will discover your unconscious mind at work in a manner that Freud never understood.

BODY AND MIND FUNCTIONS

My body activated dreams are almost always of a mundane nature. They are dreams that one normally doesn't pay attention to. Nevertheless, they do seem to represent attempted communication from our dreaming brains to our conscious awareness. I have given examples of toilet dreams. I tend to overeat for holidays and special occasions, and this habit usually activates dream scenarios of two types. In one scenario, I will search frantically for a toilet in a public place such as a mall or large store. When I find the toilet, it is unusable for any number of reasons. Obviously, my dreaming brain is trying to inform me that I'm experiencing bowel discomfort. .

In the second dream plot, after much searching, I find a toilet that can be made usable, only to discover that I'm constipated. I also find myself sitting on a toilet that is in public view, but observe that no one is paying any attention to me. Note that the consistency of being naked without others observing suggests that one's higher order Interpreter understands the real situation. Eventually, awareness seeps into my conscious brain, and I get up and go to the bathroom. These dreams are so transparent that they need little interpretation. Mundane body dreams remind us that our brain-minds are constantly informing us about our body and environment. Thank you, Aristotle.

Hot or cold sleeping conditions instigate related dreams. In the example of having a cold shoulder, I dreamt of a 1955 tan Chevy which was located in the exact physical spot in my dreaming brain as my cold shoulder's exposure. An entire story developed around my growing discomfort until I reached up in my dream and pulled the blanket down. As I reached up, the Chevy's skirted underside in my dream turned into the blanket, causing a sensory dream-to-waking awareness. The Chevy was in the exact spatial relationships to my cold shoulder.

Dream content often reflects this real spatial element for me. Pay particular attention to dream content as you transition between dreaming and waking states. For me, the bridging element was a 1955 Chevy. If you are routinely sleep-deprived, images in these transitions will probably just seem bizarre, or you may decide to focus on your 1955 Chevy as a fond memory.

You can practice analyzing these bizarre changes in your dreams, and find that quite often, morphing features are of this nature. Mundane, yes; dream instigators, yes; mysterious dream elements, no. But when your dreams tell you to pay attention, do so. Attention getting dream content is typically the bridging element needed to interpret one's dream. Attention getting means spatial cues like my 1955 Chevy flap, emotional tics or unproductive searches, dream elements out of place, like coy Ruby, or cognitive dissonance such as strange use of math functions.

Notice how personal and individualistic my dreams are. Yours are no less personal. I will often dream of being in a public place with a shirt or top on, but with my lower extremities exposed. This pattern between winter and summer has existed for decades. I think you will notice similar changes in dreams that reflect your lifestyle. I'm often naked in my summer dreams, but only partially uncovered in my winter dreams. The pattern is so consistent that I'm not afraid of being overly subjective with this interpretation.

There is so much Freudian dream hoopla in our culture that I suspect many readers will be let down with my mundane examples. If, however, you are a lucid dreamer, I bet you experience nakedness in your dreams too. Oops, guess what? We just discovered another archetype.

Here is a final example about dream activation created by my sleeping environment. My wife will often roll back and forth with me as we cuddle each other in our nightly dream adventures. Body part stimulation will sometimes activate a sexual response in my sleeping brain, but more often, it is an elbow poke or leg-over-leg stimulation that my dreaming brain responds to. I have a large damaged vein in my left leg from a former blood clot, and weight placed on this leg becomes uncomfortable after a few minutes. My response is to physically move. All manner of dream stories can be activated by these physical maneuvers

As with the example of the Chevy above, or the toilet scenarios, you can learn to identify the various types of physical stimulations in your dreams that are part of creating those 25 to 50 nightly dream scenarios. Look for the patterns and identify the feelings attached to characters, scenes, and any element that gets your dream attention. But don't be fooled by a majority of dreams that are mundane, especially as you age, as your dreaming brain-mind will continue to inform you about everyday critical events and feelings. Readers will note that their lifestyle demands, cognitive focus, health, age, and emotional states will be their main dream story instigators.

Emotions and feelings are separated in my analysis this way: Emotions generate a physical state induced by various chemicals that my brain releases to create what is often an immediate and sometimes intense feeling. For example, in waking moments, I may become fearful in a strange, threatening place such as a deserted street. My non-conscious awareness first activates a body-chemical state that begins to flag my conscious attention. My reaction creates a feeling of fear by re-mapping these body activated emotions. Feelings for me have a component of something being valued, of flight or fight, for example. This flight or fight reaction is generally more reflexive than being a conscious decision. The next stage of the emotion to feeling process for me is a fully-conscious interpretation of body-chemistry turned into thoughtful analysis.

OK, so how do we use this simple emotion-feeling dichotomy to understand our dreams? I know that evolutionary survival has created a brain-mind response to my total environment that is automatic. I don't have to think about that huge bear running toward me, because I will react and think later. Survival! But within a fraction of a second, my conscious brain will begin its interpretive process. My dreaming brain is mostly disconnected from this reasoning process, as is yours. Hence, emotional primacy and intensity is to be expected when we dream.

It seems logical to me that paying attention to mundane dream elements or normal feelings associated with one's daily events has little survival value, but paying attention to negative feelings, intense emotions, or body discomfort does. The dream genie that wakes us up at night is telling us to listen.

When I entered the seventh grade, it was my 12th school change. Test anxiety had been a part of my ongoing history, especially since my father did not permit us to bring homework home. I foolishly entered the University of Minnesota from the military as Superman. My workload was 16 credit hours, six additional hours of lab, and an average work week of 33 hours. Test anxiety returned in all its former glory. I was quickly incapacitated to the point where I sat immobile for two-thirds of a blue book test period. I didn't understand then how my school history was impacting performance.

To this day, I still express anxiety in dreams by recreating some kind of negative school setting. My dream reports have already informed the reader of this fact. School anxiety occupies a large room in the mansion of my mind. This is a personal element in my history, and you too should look for your long-term patterns as you age. In my case, I can usually quickly identify what my waking concern is that is being represented by old memory files being played out in my dreams.

Conflict, fear, and nightmares are presented below in a separate section, because these dream elements and patterns are particularly disturbing. Nightmare recall is not vivid for me before the age of five. But this still leaves me with over 70 years of recall and with 50 plus years of active analysis. Long-term patterns stand out over many decades, with tens of thousands of lucid dreams. Let me start from an earlier history with nightmares.

Nightmares become a common part of my dreams about the time the Japanese bombed Pearl Harbor in 1941. I was five years old. Prior to that time, and starting with my mother's attempts to smother me when I was about 18 months old, my sleeping nights were punctuated with night terrors. I have poor recall during these infant days, but remember some of their waking effects. I had to be careful as a crib infant not to wake mother in the middle of her naps. Earaches, for example, were tolerated until she was awake and moving about.

During the Japanese attack on Pearl Harbor, we were living in the Everett, Washington, Area. Later, a local report noted that a Japanese submarine had been sighted in the Sound. This report initiated night dream visitations by the Japanese submariners where I would be captured and taken to their ship. The submariners would start drilling a hole in my back in order to make me into a flag stand. Repeatedly, I would escape by flying bodily into a hole in the submarine, remain suspended, fall asleep, and eventually wake up in my bed. This terrifying nightmare became a 50 year old friend that I suppressed for 20 years through dream programming.

I interpreted the dream many years later when the Japanese drill turned into my mother's hand, which pressed on my back while a pillow blocked out the light and brought on the experience of suffocation. For me, the bridging element in nightmare interpretation has always been associated with a physical act similar to this one. Once I connected the metaphor of these bridging elements to the actual events, the interpretation was automatic, and this awareness immediately eliminated the nightmare.

When I looked inside my mind and its memory boxes, I found the association. Everett, Washington, was awash in rumors of imminent danger from a Japanese invasion. This was big stuff in the mind of a five year old. Mother's attempts to smother me, my resulting near death experience and Heaven-bound vision all came together. Emotions that fire together in context wire together in context. Individually, we must each locate our own wiring diagrams.

Interpreting the dream removed a neuronal block that had existed for decades. Interpretation of nightmares must create neuronal closure as meaning is established in consciousness. It seems unquestionable that higher order human consciousness requires our brain-minds to sort out endless possibilities to locate the one that fits. Meaning and psychic relief is not derived by closing neural circuits; it is derived by closing those circuits that the conscious mind finds acceptable. Pharmaceuticals cannot do this. Only a conscious mind can.

In a number of ways, this type of dream analysis is simple, although in my case, I first suppressed the dreams through dream programming for a couple of decades. This nightmare was instigated by multiple acts of trauma perpetuated by my mother, probably over a period of months. While still crib confined, I learned to cup my hand over my mouth when mother approached my bed. This hand cupping pattern accompanied me to bed until I entered high school, and I consciously interrupted it.

The incident of sexual assault was singular, and the nightmare's resolution also came immediately once a meaningful connection was established. Metaphorical concepts are critical operational units in these interpretations. Lakoff and Johnson are referenced in my bibliography, and I suggest all serious students of dreams become familiar with them.

My two nightmares involve physical attack. The reader should ask: How can the dreaming mind visually represent an integrated image of fear that is combined with physical force? Answer: It uses metaphor. Don't go to the dictionary to find the meaning of metaphor, go to Lakoff and Johnson.

Over the decades of both suppressed and active nightmares, the different nightmare scenarios came to have a life of their own. Our ability to create extensive, convoluted internal stories is endless. Simply note how extensively internal plots can be used to spin an alternate universe in our dreaming minds.

Brooks and Vogelsong's friend Ruth reports an alternate universe that she visits in her dreams. The effort of analyzing one's own dreams is worth it just to discover the many small or large auto-created universes of our minds. You will not fully understand my universes without a working knowledge of metaphor. In like fashion, the accomplished clinician understands this relationship.

The bridging key to this second nightmare was the physical hold executed by the molester, which I eventually re-experienced in my dream. I run, I'm captured, and held immobile by my pursuer. The hold is almost immediately identified in my dream, and resolution followed just as quickly. Muscle memories generated by my own motor responses to being traumatized were used by my dreaming brain to identify the nightmares. These stories, like most dream stories, were creative, contained the usual bizarre elements of morphing scenes and people, but were always accompanied by a strong feeling of fear. Remember that fear has to become associated with an object before we can identify its meaning metaphorically. At least this is my experience.

In my experience, feelings that are not concretely associated with their original referent, those feelings that remain attached to their metaphorical counterpart, are self-perpetuating, and thereby foster dissociation and pathology. Nightmares have these negative-positive attributes. Positively, nightmares permitted me to function day-to-day with my mother perpetrator rather than being incapacitated. Negatively, they exacted a physical and psychic toll month-to-month and year-to-year. Nightmares should never be suppressed or medicated except in the short-term; that is, if you accept my interpretation.

My nightmares were repressed for twenty years through dream programming. I removed the programming for both nightmares after making a commitment to do whatever was necessary to get rid of them. I had studied a fair amount of psychology and analyzed thousands of my own dreams. History of programming my own dreams gave me confidence that I could return to dream suppression anytime I desired. I felt confident in having enough psychic energy to finish the analysis and gain resolution.

Life histories full of trauma may bring forth many different nightmares with their associated bridging elements: This is my experience. Children raised in brutalizing families can experience PTS similar to, or even worse then, military personnel experiencing combat. This was the case with my sister June's diagnosis at the University of Washington.

Don't despair! Resolving each incident of trauma lifts another weight from our tired brains. Subjectively, I experience trauma resolution through dream analysis as re-uniting one more fragment of self into the whole of my Being. Obviously, I'm partial to dream analysis as a quick, effective means of therapy or self-therapy.

Remember that with trauma, memories are not time dependent. My nightmares were still vivid enough to wake me after twenty years of total suppression. Each of us must decide if it is worth the psychic energy to remove these dinosaurs from our past. Saying this, I note that many military personnel and adults with similar non-military traumatizing histories do not enjoy quality life. My personal position is to grow to the fullest extent of my DNA's potential. It gladdens my heart to see the US Military beginning to pay serious attention to PTS. I would be equally joyful to see the same consideration given to America's underprivileged children.

A final comment about nightmares: You can use autosuggestion, hypnosis, or self-hypnosis to redirect your nightmares if you need additional time to eliminate them. This was necessary in my history of discovery. See an experienced counselor or therapist who has an understanding of post-traumatic stress disorder, and if you're lucky, find a therapist who understands both PTSD and dreams. Just any old counselor will not do.

Negative feelings in dreams are frequent and common for most people. Why this is so is not fully explained in the dream research literature. I assume from a personal point of view that my conscious and sleeping brain has a vested interest in protecting me. Hence, any conflict, threat, or disturbing element in my environment will enter my dreams until it is resolved. This seems very straightforward to me, and doesn't require any more esoteric interpretation. My reported dreams, nightmares, and their resolution reflect this interpretation. Nevertheless, job, marital, or social stress will be reflected in our dreams even when we may consciously deny that such stress exists. Leave your interpretation of dreams open, and consider all of these possibilities.

Dream Programming is a technique that I created as a university freshman in the school year of 1957/58. My two nightmares, along with other childhood traumas, were interfering with sleep, contributing to an abnormal amount of anxiety and depression, and generally disrupting my college progress. I used self-hypnosis to quickly change my nightmares into pleasant dreams. I totally pre-programmed dreams with fun characters and plot scenarios while awake. I directed my Interpreter to intercede in my dreams whenever a nightmare appeared, and that way, I didn't have to wake up and disturb a good night's sleep.

Once I had taught my Interpreter to perform this dream role, conscious intervention in dreams became automatic. Neural plasticity permits us these options that few people with PTS realize. Unfortunate!

The dream programming technique worked wonderfully, and I stopped having nightmares within a few days. I maintained this pattern for about twenty years with no ill effects, and many positive mental health effects. Once this dream suppression pattern was established, it was maintained automatically without any additional conscious intervention needed on my part

Decades later, I had to actively intervene to stop dream suppression. Most readers will probably not be practitioners of self-hypnosis, but many of you will use a milder form of auto-suggestion. This milder level of suggestion usually takes the form of telling yourself that the scary dream character will become a friend, or the threatening animal will become a pet dog or cat, and so on. Same effect, as you have taught your Interpreter to change your dream scenarios. But, as I've demonstrated, dream control can go much farther.

The main idea of using waking suggestion before going to sleep is to modify the dream elements that are giving us trouble. The effect may not be immediate, but if you practice giving yourself these suggestions, and learn how to dream lucidly, you can easily master the technique. If you have trouble with early experiments in suggestion, consult a counselor/therapist who understands their use. Also, read Delaney as a start.

I think anyone can master these techniques with a little practice. In my case I established hypnotic control over my body parts, pain, and attention span and then transferred this control to my dreams. Linkages between conscious and non-conscious functions must be established in order to have the level of control that I'm documenting. If you continue having trouble gaining this type of control, go back and first develop smaller control pieces as I have with self-hypnosis.

A final comment about dream programming trauma: I don't know anyone else having suppressed nightmares for twenty years, hence, you are getting advice from a longitudinal experiment of one. But I do think your brain architecture and levels of consciousness are comparable to mine. After twenty years of suppressing nightmares, I noticed an immediate sense of relief when I stopped. Day-to-day, my subjective Self hadn't noticed this energy drain; that is, until I stopped dream programming. Then, relief was immediate, and the rubber band around my head snapped loose.

Obviously, memories stored in my neural circuits that supported my nightmares were still intact. Once I identified the activating elements of the nightmares, the nightmares immediately stopped. Lesson learned, I believe, is that our brains are so constructed as to keep warning us about life-threatening events until we remove them. This protective process does not subside over time or with age. Dream memories and the primordial quest to survive run on their own clock time.

A final comment about dream programming as an ongoing experience: I had a lot of fun with dream programming, and you may too. Read Brooks and Vogelsong and you will find extensive examples of fun dream adventures. But if you get into the habit of dream programming nightly, you will be disrupting the natural exchange that goes on between sleeping and waking consciousness.

The type of carryover I'm discussing that occurs between different levels of consciousness can be sidetracked. Exchanges between core-consciousness and higher order consciousness cannot be automatic, or nightmares wouldn't exist over decades. At least, such exchanges are not as simple as is the case with how fixed action patterns are embedded.

I stopped dream programming in order to let my emotions and feelings flow naturally. I wanted to experience the world the way other people around me seemed to be experiencing it. Dream programming became a form of emotional control which remained under my conscious command moment-to-moment. And I do mean moment-to-moment. When I stopped dream programming, my nightmares returned. Gradually over a few weeks, the intensity of my overall feelings returned to a level I hadn't known for a number of years. Play with these techniques, but watch for their side effects. Note, however, that non-conscious suppression of former trauma exacts a price. One does not maximize their own sensitivity to Self and others until the brain-mind is cleared. Some of us come to experience the progressive fog of a mind cluttered by trauma until it becomes a quicksand of pathology. In comparison, we pay a small price through nightmare suppression.

Cognitive integration and support from dream analysis remains as one of my most important reasons for almost nightly dream interpretation. I interpret my dreams at least a few times each week, but most often I do so nightly. Dream analysis provides me with an ongoing sense of internal cognitive and emotional stability, and lets me follow my brain-mind developmental patterns over time. The discovery process that results is never ending. It is a discovery process not available to the addicts of mass media and entertainment. This subjective experience, dear reader, is comparable to watching Northern Lights or a beautiful sunset over the prairie.

When I was a young and foolish college professor, I used to pride myself on objectivity, especially, objectivity about my mental and physical states. This self-arrogance was corrected after I fell skiing and spent a week hospitalized in traction. After traction, I quickly discovered how well and how consistently I had been lying to myself. My normal state of overwork, and the accompanying tensions associated with too frequent 15 and 20 hour work days, could no longer be ignored. My back muscles let me know that my body was being abused and in an uncomfortable state of tension. A condition that was long-term and, I thought, simply a part of one's every day, normal work experience and lifestyle. I was wrong.

This experience taught me that subjectivity is just that; being subjective. Learning to be objective about one self, what I call self-honesty, is a slow process that comes with maturity if we are lucky. Back twitches that could become very uncomfortable helped make an honest man out of me: Self-lying about overwork and accompanying tension was no longer an option, but it did teach me the importance of body-muscle cues in understanding my emotional state. These cues have been of immense help in understanding what my dreaming brain is telling me. Sensory input and associated memories in dreams are there to inform us if we will only listen.

Once I got beyond this type of lying to myself, it became easier to explore similar bridging elements in my dreams. I am now aware of how much carryover occurs between these two brain-mind states. Dream interpretation helps me better understand my conscious moods and thought processes, and consciousness carried over into my dreams provides a partial framework for dream understanding. I know that much of my understanding this interrelationship has been made clearer as I've aged, and become more knowledgeable about my dreams and consciousness states.

As I became more sensitive to dream elements I also became more sensitive to the conscious elements affecting my mind and body when awake: The feedback loop works both ways. If you have my experience, you will find increasing sensitization in your social relationships. I come to believe that we can only see in others what we see in ourselves. We only feel in others what we can feel in ourselves. Sensitivity to others' physical and emotional states is much like fine tuning our mirror neurons. Mirror neurons duplicate similar neural circuits in our brains that are being activated in those we are observing. When we more deeply feel what others feel, we more fully come to know our place in the human community.

Another person experiencing discomfort from such things as a marital partner engaging in hanky-panky may go unnoticed by everyone in the workplace except you. Over time, we enhance whatever level of sensitivity we have toward others with each new insight and improvement in self-understanding. You may call this effect increased empathy or sympathy, but it is a mechanism that lets us more fully experience what is going on inside the mind of another person. Long-term, this increasing sensitization strengthens what we call our conscience, and further breaks down the interpersonal barriers we call race, sex, and strange. A sensitizing sequence can be actively taught to undeveloped, fragmented personalities entering our criminal justice system and our mental health centers.

Lucid dreaming can be a window to creativity. Many people have claimed that their dreams provide them with publishable stories, with scientific insights, and artistic creations. Some people approach other altered states rather than their dreams for similar inspiration, but their interpretations are usually of an occult nature. Einstein acknowledged similar inspiration riding his bicycle to work. Focused and rhythmic activities can quickly bring us to the edge of altered states. But often, which was probably Einstein's experiences, we open neuronal channels in our brains between conscious and non-conscious levels, thereby permitting expanded neuronal workspace.

There is an expanded phenomenological sense of freedom and control when I dream lucidly, or engage in self-directed and self-controlled altered states of consciousness. Logically and physiologically, brain circuits must be connecting in new configurations when one travels out-of-body when awake or dreaming. And I'm not referring to uncontrolled hallucinations as defined by our local mental health practitioners. Controlled altered states may be using similar neural circuits as those used by the mentally ill, or for those who are experiencing a daytime visit from Mother Mary, but self-control adds an additional element to the phenomenological experience. Self-controlled hallucinations enlighten, but uncontrolled, they terrify.

Learning to dream lucidly must create new associations between brain circuits. Creativity seems to be fostered by opening up new neural circuits, bringing these experiences into self-awareness, and learning how to control these processes.

Increase in self-awareness takes numerous forms. One form is the awareness of body and emotional states as outlined above. Another form is increasing integration of self that permits one to reduce anxiety, feel whole, and at peace. A third form seems to open up dialogue between the conscious part of our brain-minds and the dreaming parts. In this latter sense, we have access to part of the 95 percent of our brain's processing that goes on below our normal level of consciousness.

How much of one's non-conscious brain activity we can learn to access in our dreams or other altered states remains an individual affair. In my experience and observation, anything that opens additional neuronal workspace tends to enhance creativity, even when these processes boarder on debilitating mental illness.

Lucid altered states are another window to self-awareness. Once I learned how to program and control my dreams, it was easy to generalize control to other altered states. Two major factors led to my discovering the visioning process, how to speak-in-tongues, spirit possession, and spirit-projection. One was the out-of-body experience I had as a toddler. The other major factor was mastering self-hypnosis and applying this skill to dream programming. Thereafter, I discovered that lucidity could be transferred to any altered state. Mastering each altered state of consciousness increases our awareness of Self similar to that of lucid dreaming. An integral part of mastering altered states is losing one's fear, which is necessary for us to gain control.

I believe that whenever we understand something about our own brain states, we become better at understanding our fellow human beings. For example, speaking-in-tongues is no longer a mystery to me. Our use of suggestion and acceptance of cultural indoctrination has a different meaning, once we are able to control and direct altered states. Occult interpretations evaporate as our understanding of human brain-mind states becomes clearer as we master related self-controls. And in the end, the chain of dogma frays, and eventually breaks.

I can engage in out-of-body projection of the type I relate in my Genesis Journey. Entering altered states can be abrupt and immediate as it often is for groups experiencing visions. This collective experience can occur with or without the use of drugs such as peyote or other hallucinogens. Transitions between altered states can occur with or without superimposed images, as one's brain moves from one state to another. To appreciate our ability to rapidly transit between brain states, recall how soldiers or accident victims continue to function, only to discover later that they have been seriously wounded or hurt. We can train our minds to turn this mechanism on and off, and in my example, simply journey to the beginning of time.

The vision of a departed spirit such as Mother Mary, or in my personal experience, a deceased brother of an American Indian friend, can be superimposed on one's immediate environment. Or, in the case of my Genesis Journey where a super imposed landscape would be unnatural, one just experiences the other-world vision that is culturally acceptable. And, just like one's dreams, the visioning is entirely realistic. It is even more realistic than most dreams, as we are totally conscious, and the interpretations we give stem from the logical ability of our waking consciousness.

Again acknowledging how visions emerge, we can project entirely into another altered reality, or we can superimpose the two realities as our brain makes state changes. We observe these state transitions for the mentally ill. Unfortunately, we do not teach the mentally ill how to bring them under their own control. Controlling and directing ASC gives one a different perspective on spirituality, shamanism, and major world religions. It changes my perspective on mental illness, and learning how to control brain state changes has considerably improved my mental health.

By mastering altered states of consciousness, I significantly increased control of myself and my social world. Fear of generic unknown sensations is lost; generic unknowns being those spongy sensations that refuse to take on concrete form. As I lost fear producing anxieties, my energy became focused on life objectives that were purposeful. People who have experienced mental illness appreciate what this sense of control means.

I have a fuller appreciation for the processes whereby we create reality in a normal state of consciousness. I more fully appreciate how my brain constructs and maps the outside world when I observe these processes in dreams and other altered states. Comparing these brain-mind processes in waking and altered states enhances my understanding of Self and others. I observe the difference in how values are formed and manipulated, how reality is created, and the fundamental way feelings are attached to all my senses. Observing how body images form in my dreams offers a different understanding of how primary images are integrated and consolidated fictively in dreams. Once this basic, primary imaging is observed, it is a simple matter to extrapolate secondary symbol formation and metaphor as they emerge in our higher levels of consciousness.

My reality is not an objective, value free, "picture taking" reality of the outside world; my reality, like yours, is constructed, dynamic, and evolving. Interpretation of dreams and other altered states requires this awareness. And, associated awareness becomes clearer as one makes these comparisons over decades.

Waking consciousness and dreaming consciousness and the integration of self has a long fifty year history for me. My childhood was very traumatic, and daily life extremely fragmented. I was a confused child plagued by ghosts, confronted by death from my parent's hands, and socially needing major adjustments. The view over my past 75 years contains memory that includes a little more than 73 of these years. I was not able to see these patterns clearly until I was somewhere in my 5th decade. Waking and dreaming states of consciousness were distinct states until I was somewhere near a half-century of living. Now I have a different view of their interrelationship, and this view has been shared throughout this book.

My subjective view is retrospective and can be criticized for its subjectivity. However, the patterns where I'm striving to integrate the fragmented parts of myself seem very clear. As I pass through sequential stages of adult maturity, I'm aware of qualitative changes. For example, I'm able to control anxiety and depression, my MMPI profile has long been normalized, and for many decades, I have increasingly become a nonviolent person with a sense of stable inner peace.

Going back in childhood, I find a very basic coping pattern. I learned to cup my hand over my mouth in the crib to keep mother from smothering me, I learned how to control bed-wetting, I overcame obsessive behavior demanded from sidewalk cracks in the small town of Island City, I stopped nail biting and head-banging, I learned to control and eliminate stuttering by myself, and generally, bring disruptive school outbursts under control. These changes were achieved without support from my parents, other than being told to stop the behaviors.

I learned from the crib to the university classroom that self-control and behavioral changes were strictly my responsibility. I became my own adult therapist and changed my major to psychology as an undergraduate. I developed a life-long sensitivity to my various states of consciousness, altered or not. The reader's history will be different than mine, but for many readers, their history will be no less stressful or traumatic. We all have the resources of draw upon our hidden inner strengths. Sometimes, however, we need a little extra support to find these strengths. We should never stop searching.

Symbolism in dreams occurs at various levels of abstraction for me, as the reader is aware from my dream reviews. The gun of my army years comes to represent my erect penis in a dream, and a contemporary person from last night or a year ago can become a dream character that is only recognized through my dream feelings. In my dreams, a cold shoulder becomes a 1955 Chevy; sleeping with only a nightshirt leaves me semi-naked in many dreams, sleeping nude in the summer leaves me totally naked in other dreams, and so on. Symbols in my dreams are mostly straightforward and not hidden or convoluted. Dream symbols are metaphorical, because that is how our brains create and process concepts. This conceptual process is increasingly clarified by contemporary neuroscience and neuro-philosophy. It is only confusing to those steeped in the Objectivist framework of traditional linguistics.

Symbols in dreams rarely take on forms that one might associate with repressed psychoanalytic interpretations, especially those speculations generated by Freud in *The Interpretation of Dreams*. Sexual themes are highly overrated. You will note that erotica reported in my dreams is straightforward and easily interpreted. If you use self-hypnosis, or what I've called a lighter form called autosuggestion, you can have as much erotica in your dreams as you wish. You can have orgasms while dreaming, or just pleasurable encounters. On the other hand, it is an easy matter to learn how to think one's self to orgasm in normal consciousness without any external stimulation. These are ancient techniques that can be acquired by a quick review of Hindu mythology. Except as an experiment, why would you want to?

Who you are as an individual, who you are trying to become through positive or negative thinking, and what patterns you have taught your non-conscious brain will be reflected in your dreams. What I am about during the day is carried over into my dreaming nights. In this sense, daytime activities, thoughts, and feelings become the priming elements for our dreams. The efficiency of non-conscious brain-mind activities is available for select viewing through lucid dreaming, and conscious viewing of related altered states can be triangulated with our normal dreams. The reader will evaluate from their own experience how well I have constructed this triangulation.

Truth of the matter is that thought is the parent of complex social action. Truth of the matter is that habituation to daytime routines is the shaper of thought. Truth of the matter is that the metaphorical basis of thought emerges from our 95 percent non-conscious brain-mind activity. And for me, I can most clearly view these processes with clarity in my dreams and visions.

A final comparison between daydreams and night dreams before moving on to dictionaries: My daydreams are typically virtual constructions of events that might happen to my waking self. I run daydream scenarios about work, my social life, possible romances, and various situations that could be detrimental to any of these potential happenings. We all do this, as it is a form of brain-mind activity that has survival value.

My dreaming mind-brain continues running and analyzing these possible future scenarios. I daydream about something during my waking hours, and without any conscious suggestion, my dreaming brain creates the whole scenario on its own. I think there is another potential doctoral thesis here.

DELANEY'S DREAM DICTIONARY

Her dream dictionary will be presented with a few random examples and comparisons to my own interpretations. I like much of what Delaney has written and offered some criticisms in Chapter 5. I think Delaney can be a helpful place to start for non-lucid dreamers who want to learn how to become conscious in their dreams. Her book on *Breakthrough Dreaming* is recommended for the beginner. Delaney's *In Your Dreams* dictionary follows a case history approach that encourages individual interpretation of one's dreams.

Delaney introduces *In Your Dreams* with this content item: "How to Interpret Any Theme in Your Dreams." In my experience, themes in dreams are as individual as are our personalities. If you review the dreams that I've shared in this book with Delaney's interpretations, or hopefully your own reviewed dreams, you will quickly be able to compare theme differences. What Delaney offers is a method to begin your dream analysis, a way to keep and review records of your dreams, and many comparisons of other's dreams that can help readers generalize a basic understanding of dreamer differences. Not a bad start!

In support of Delaney's dictionary, she says that "But I don't believe in one-size-fits-all dream meanings (1997: 3)."and, "This is why I have written a new kind of dictionary – one that, like the old-fashioned kind, lets you go straight to the theme or image you are curious about (Ibid: 3)."

It is this effort on her part in my opinion that makes her dream dictionary worth reading.

Many of us become interested in dreams because there are nagging day-to-day themes in our dreams that seem important. Delaney says: "… we can't help but think that our sleeping mind is trying to tell us something important (Ibid: 6)."

In my experience, if you have pressures, conflicts, or past trauma that keeps expressing itself in your dreams, you will find truth in these words. On the other hand, if you are a mature person with a stable lifestyle, you will probably experience a majority of what I've called common or mundane dreams. Most lucid dreamers preferentially pay attention to their more dramatic night movies and ignore the mundane. Watch this!

In Your Dreams contains a section in most chapters called "What Others Have Said." These reviews are interesting asides to dream interpretation that are worth reviewing, if you find these mostly bizarre interpretations swirling through your own thoughts. If you've read interpretations of the ancients, those of mythology, or traditional psychoanalytic ideas about dreams. you will enjoy Delaney's reviews. However, review of Freud or the ancients in the main will not help you understand your own dreams. You will begin to discover that many ancient interpretations of dreams are closer to modern interpretations than a good share of contemporary dream dictionaries.

I'm selecting Delaney stories from the above work at random here. She recounts a woman named Elena who has recurrent dreams of being chased by thugs down city streets, and the woman is terrified feeling that her pursuers want to kill her. Delaney says: "In this case, Elena said that the feelings in the dream described her feelings of vulnerability in the urban environment she lives in as well as her feelings of being threatened more generally in a variety of situations in which she feels unprotected and alone (1997: 19)."

Delaney's use of the subject's own interpretations is generally reasonable, in my personal experience. This specific example represents use of metaphor compatible with my own dream analysis. But note, there is no one interpretation for chase scenes in our dreams.

Now a second example from Section 2 of *In Your Dreams* that relates to movie and TV stars. She provides guiding questions on page 167 to help you interpret these famous dream characters. I will use item number 7 from this guideline to suggest caution.

"7. If the star does not remind you of anyone in your life or of a part of yourself, and if the main feeling in the dream is that you were incredibly flattered to get the star's attention, have you been needing a boost to your self-esteem lately (Ibid)?"

Delaney may be correct in her interpretation, but counselors, therapists, and dream interpreters have all been cautioned not to use suggestion with clients. Suggestion places an idea in our heads that we can easily come to own. Delaney often offers similar suggestions as you proceed through her helpful and insightful book. In my experience once again, one must proceed with caution not to take these examples at face value. To accept case examples of any type at face value can potentially prime their enactment in our dreams.

I prefer to identify as much content, characters, and scenery as possible in my dreams in order to understand where my dreaming brain is pulling this material from memory. In following the sources of content, I discover how my associative memory is operating, how I'm mixing and creating imagery, and to what degree themes are long or short-term.

Let me offer what I consider to be a critical insight. If I mix characters from numerous places and time periods, I search for the common shared element. If I am in a physical setting or space that seems to be without reference, I ask myself what the referent of the dream might be. For example, the physical space in my Hobson AIM cube dream actually had the cube as its referent.

If there is a lot of gobble-de-gook such as that found in my math focused dream, I ask what this metaphorical concretization actually represents. The reader has other similar examples already covered in my reported dream scenarios.

Over time, we can view with increasing clarity core aspects of our personalities because our basic values and beliefs continuously play out in our dreams. Observing these patterns for core values comes with the caution that one also enacts fantasies in his or her dreams. We mentally run the plays, so to speak, before we pick up the ball.

I look for Delaney's bridging elements, anything that stands out and flags my attention, and then identify major feelings that I'm having toward my dream characters, dream props, or overall scene impressions. I look for carryover themes and patterns from my everyday life, as these patterns are consistently represented in my night time movies. However, the emphasis I place on memory consolidation and integration with various dream elements that I've called FAP, or consolidation and integration of cognitive elements that I've called thought dreams, tends to set my dream history apart from Delaney's work for the general public.

Memory maintenance and consolidation is a major activator of my dreams. I suggest that you not look for deeper meanings in every dream, but consider that your brain must perform a number of housekeeping functions related to memory. Your brain-mind is also aware of long-term emotional states such as loneliness, depressed feelings, anxiety, and social conflicts that are expressed in our dreams. I find Delaney most helpful when she is interpreting feeling.

One more example from Delaney: Cars are a common element in most of our dreams; that is if we are drivers. Delaney presents an example of a man's car dream where he decides to let his wife fix the car. He recognizes that the broken car is symbolic of his broken marriage, and that he cannot fix it alone. His spouse is not cooperating, but leaving all the work to him. Delaney sets forth seven different questions for the dreamer to answer. I find the following question's metaphorical interpretation helpful: "Does the malfunctioning in the car match any malfunctioning area in your life (Ibid: 257)."

This is an example of what I've earlier referred to as complex metaphor.

Delaney's examples can help improve one's ability to interpret dreams. As a soft criticism of her approach, which you may find not to be a criticism at all, do not take her example of the car literally. It is the symbolism in the entire dream scenario's context that is most important. In my dream experience, any number of elements can substitute for the car. Conflict between two characters in a dream may represent the same deteriorating situation as the car needing repair; a broken anything can replace the car, etcetera. I suggest that any focus on specific dream elements with the idea that they somehow represent similar meaning from person-to-dreaming-person is misleading. Delaney is very aware of these differences.

Historically, ancient interpretations of dreams took concrete elements and made them into specific meaning items. For example, death in Chinese dreams was meant to foretell the death of a real person in the here and now. This type of historical mythology was carried over by Freud with all of his erotic interpretations of sexual organs. Delaney goes well beyond Freud's simple symbolic interpretations in my opinion, but nevertheless, one should be cautious of how personal or literary suggestions are used in his or her interpretations. And that includes mine.

BROOKS AND VOGELSONG'S DREAM INTERPRETATIONS

Brooks and Vogelsong's dream interpretations

… offer comment on several ways in which interpreters traditionally attempt to derive meaning from dreams, as well as suggest ways in which lucidity can play a part in developing a new interpretive model (1999: 163).

I will skip their presentation of shamanistic and occultist materials as well as their review of unconscious and psychoanalytic constructs. Their model is based on suggestion theory which:

[Asserts] that while the dream state may be determined by physiology, dream content is determined from moment to moment by awareness interpreting and coordinating various suggestion factors through the world-modeling function. And, further "It follows that dreams make convincing sensory experiences not because they represent literal or metaphorical reality, but because they employ the same capabilities the mind uses to create the perception of reality to begin with (Ibid:173).

Simply put, the mind, or I might add brain-mind, is using its architecture, chemical, and neural capacities in dreams as it uses these capacities and functions when we are awake.

I am in general agreement with their interpretation. Our minds use the same capabilities to create the perception of reality when we are awake and when we are dreaming. Physiology may create a dream state, but thought's cognitive elements can too, as I've presented them in my thought dreams. Sensory experiences enter our dreams metaphorically as I've noted in naked or toilet activated dreams. Memory consolidation and integration around primary images also leave me in a partially modified position from Brooks-Vogelsong.

Content is determined by the type of multi-tasking dreams expressed at any given moment. The effects of suggestion on dreams through what Brooks and Vogelsong call the world-modeling function is a common part of dream self-reports. I believe my dreams reflect a more comprehensive dynamic integrated brain-mind system than what they envision. I include cognitive input at higher levels and neural circuit development and maintenance at the level of fixed action patterns, and encourage the reader to identify primary image formation in their dream.

Additionally, primary image formation as observed in dreams such as my bike balancing example offer new insights into our brain-mind's symbol generating processes. This aspect of primary image formation articulates with Damasio's Qualia I and Qualia II, and Lakoff and Johnson's ideas about metaphorical concepts being central to our thought processes.

I have been contending that extensive use of suggestion in one's dreams skews the outcomes. I personally like these authors for their careful, long-term analysis of dreams. But I find suggestion theory offers an abbreviated view of dream functions, content analysis and mental health implications compared to my experiences. Nevertheless, they offer many valuable observations, and their development of world modeling in dreams makes their book worthwhile by itself.

As Foulkes has remarked: 'To the degree that dreaming employs systems whose major function is the apprehension of what the world is like, then any activity in those systems is likely to be treated as if it reflected world events'" and, "In other words, far from being messages from an intelligent external or internal source pertinent to the real world, dreams can be said to result from a certain form of confused perception that mistakes reflexively generated constructs for realities (Ibid)."

Brooks and Vogelsong's view, dreams substitute one image for another in a rather random manner, the dreamer habitually imposes meaning on his or her dreams when there is no such meaning present, dreams become more complex as we mature, and associations playing out in one's dreams may not reflect any logical associations we experience when awake.

I do not find this random image substitution, as dream images are patterned in terms of the type of function being performed. What is random is the selection of associated images from memory, such as a 1955 Chevy. Any number of memory elements could suffice for this metaphorical representation. Yes, we do impose meaning on mental imagery, whether we are awake or dreaming. But I'm contending that the imagery is appropriate for the function being served by the dream. Why would one impose meaning on a fixed action pattern dream other than interpreting it as a FAP?

We can make these distinctions by analyzing content and function together. In my opinion, image substitution can only be considered to be random if we ignore function. I place much greater emphasis on metaphor in dream interpretation than Brooks and Vogelsong do.

If we accept that dreams multi-task around various functions, then we are obligated to acknowledge differences in dream form that we experience. Why in the course of human evolution would the brain restrict the use of dreams to a single function? And how could our dreaming brains reflect thoughts the same way one embeds a FAP?

"The Dream-Specific Nature of Dreaming" section includes this entry: "Dreams remain far from unfailingly applicable to real concerns, feelings and conflicts, since what we think, feel, and believe while dreaming guides dream images, and these mental processes do not always parallel those of our waking lives (Ibid: 177)."

I also find disagreement with this interpretation. My dreams rather closely parallel my real concerns, feelings, conflicts and everyday activities such as bike riding, cutting stain glass, writing this book or experiencing tension with my spouse. I believe that Brooks and Vogelsong have a more narrow view of dreams due to their extensive practice of dream alteration through various forms of suggestion. If I had written this book during the heyday of my dream programming, I would have found myself in near total agreement with them. From my dream reports, the reader is aware of these differences.

Secondly, how many individuals are so in tune with their non-conscious feelings and macro cognitive patterns of brain-mind activity that their dreams would reflect unfailing applicability to real life concerns? My dreams are closer to my feelings in terms of major emotional relationships than are my short term emotional reactions to situational stimuli, moment to moment, during waking hours. I think yours are too. We are often aware that we ignore our emotions during the day until our dreams remind us to pay attention.

I rarely employ suggestion in my dreams. I've used suggestion a couple of times before going to bed for purposes of checking certain effects as I write this book. My Interpreter may not like a dream ending, and change it without any conscious input from my waking self, or I may go back and repeat the exact same dream as though I rewound the tape and played it again, only with a changed and more desirable ending. But these interventions are not planned before I go to bed, and I don't consciously enter my dreams to make these changes. Basically, I stopped dream programming years ago.

Nevertheless, as the reader is aware, my daytime thoughts, cognitive conundrums, and emotional states constantly enter my dreams. In the sense that Brooks and Vogelsong use the term, world modeling is always active in my dreams. And in support of their suggestion model, model selection for the interpretation of our dreams is critical in that it can be a microscope to see more detail, or in the case of Freud's dream model, it can be a method to obscure dream realities.

As I read Brooks and Vogelsong, I'm impressed with the similarity between my twenty years of dream programming and their observations. They cover the usual forms of dream bizarreness presented by dream researchers such as character, scene, and time changes that are incompatible with daytime consciousness, and add in many dream insights from their own experiments. They also present dream elements and behavior of dream-specific personalities that are, in my opinion, age related. For example: "A DSP, dream specific personality, version of ourselves would commonly not only act out impulses without restraint, but take its exaggerated emotions and behavior for granted within the dream state…" and, "… a dreamer's DSP might think nothing of aggressively hurting or killing a fellow character (Ibid: 180)."

My experience is that the more we play with dramatic dream plots and experiment with an extreme range of fictive behavior, the more bizarre all of these elements tend to become. In the sense of our long-term use of suggestion, we are actually training our Interpreter. In my experience, when we dream naturally, mature, and integrate fragments of our conscious Self, the closer dreams come to match our everyday lives.

Normal and natural dreaming must be permitted over an extended period of time, with freedom from suggestive input, in order for us to identify FAPs, primary image formation, and the complexities of metaphorical thought. My programmed dreams were story plots that were as explicit as the words I'm keyboarding at this moment. I cannot commit murder in my dreams when I dream naturally. I could only commit such acts with practiced dream intervention and programming. Even if I programmed a dream to kill a tormentor, my Interpreter might resist. At a certain level, our acts of conscience are equivalent to embedded FAPs.

I agree with Brooks and Vogelsong that dreams can be a major source of insight into one's own character, feeling states, and aspirations, but in their opinion this is not the normal output of our dreams. They debunk much of what psychoanalysts have had to say about dream interpretation, and I agree with most of their debunking. The one area that I think gets distorted in *The Conscious Exploration of Dreaming* is their overemphasis on the use of suggestion. Extensive use of suggestion distorts one's dreams, and consequently, modifies our understanding of the dream process itself.

The reader can discover all sorts of fun ways to create fictive real life dream plots, enjoy bizarre, physically impossible activities such as flying and walking through walls. from Brooks and Vogelsong. These authors are well read, practiced lucid dreamers, and offer many insights for dream exploration.

A final summary comment of areas of divergence from Brooks and Vogelsong:

a) My examples of self-therapy demonstrate how lucid control of one's dreams can obscure the meaning of our dreams and related bridging elements;

b) Dreams perform useful function such as embedding fixed action patterns;

c) Specific content in dreams is important and necessary to identify dream functions;

d) Dreams do supply pertinent information about one's past and present psychological state;

e) Metaphorical language is what our higher cognitive centers use to think with. Note that this last statement builds on the work of Lakoff and Johnson;

f) "Our observations indicate not only that dream generation is largely automatic, driven by personal and perceptual habits, but that the only motivated element involved is one's own directed attention (Ibid: 68)."

As the reader is now aware, my experience differs from Brooks and Vogelsong on this last point.

I move toward the direction of therapy by criticizing the section which states that "…the only motivated element involved is one's own directed attention."

My dreams demonstrate considerable non-conscious activity that is outside of my waking or dreaming attention. It seems reasonable to suggest that the 95 percent of non-conscious brain activity that goes on below our level of conscious awareness plays a similar supporting role in dreams as it does when we are awake. Hence, the non-conscious mind plays a critical and sometimes *the* critical role in our dreams. I think my natural dream reports over the past year as I've written this book demonstrate this point.

I offer a final quote on their behalf: "Dreaming is not automatically symbolic of waking thought – but it involves a kind of thinking which is symbolic (Ibid: 191)."

It is this suggestion that I've elaborated with my interpretation of metaphor and qualia.

Review what I call mundane dreams, FAP dreams, and a majority of dreams that carry over everyday activities, and you will find a major distinction between my experience and theirs. In my opinion, dream dictionaries that exclude everyday mental processes that support memory integration and consolidation are incomplete. Dream dictionaries must also include interpretive sections on the exchange and communication going on between old brain maintenance functions and new brain higher cognitive functions.

Themes and patterns in my dreams represent metaphorical thought and gestalt-like pattern integration. My dreams multi-task and my dreams evolve and change content and patterns with age and dream function, environment, and social relationships. My dreams are as dynamic, or lacking of dynamism, as my life is.

The final word on understanding dreams has not been written. I'm subject to the same criticisms that I've offered above: We all want more closure on understanding our dreams than any one book or article offers. Progress is like that journey of a thousand miles – it starts with the first, and follows with many, many more steps.

DREAM DICTIONARY BY DEREK AND JULIA PARKER (1985)

The Parkers approach to dream interpretation is a literal dictionary that runs 117 pages, A to Z. This is preceded by 35 pages of symbolic interpretation.

First, let me quote from the back cover of their book: "With this lavishly illustrated guide by your bedside, you'll never spend another day perplexed about the significance of your night-time visions."

One could say the same thing about any dream dictionary, that all you have to do, is believe whatever scheme is presented. This can range from Aristotle to Freud to the Parkers. However, none of these approaches are supported by modern dream research such as J. Allan Hobson's.

Be careful of similar dream dictionaries and guides, as language is often used rather loosely. For example, with the Parkers: "This book takes up the psychologist's theories and the facts discovered by dream researchers, and offers you the opportunity to test them in your own life (Parker: 8)."

In my experience, their interpretations are similar to those provided by astrologers. I will provide three examples that resonate strongly with Freud's discredited dream interpretations. But first, note that Freud was not a psychologist, but a psychoanalyst whose ideas were based more on philosophy of the ancients than science of the 20th Century. Sexual themes run throughout Freud's work, and are represented frequently in the Parker's interpretation as quoted below:

"One of those dreams that almost everyone has at some time or another is of being naked, often in the company of other people who are quite conventionally dressed. Writers about dreams often ally this dream to sexuality, suggesting that it refers perhaps to sexual inadequacy or guilt. This is by no means necessarily the case. Indeed, such a dream can be a simple suggestion that your clothes need attention: you may unconsciously be bored with the style to which you have to conform… (Ibid: 82)."

"A tunnel, it is suggested, is sometimes a sexual symbol, so maybe the whole dream—since you approached it, as it were, through a tunnel—in some way refers to your sexuality (Ibid: 63)."

"Erections always occur during REM or dreaming sleep, sexual or not, but a man dreaming of an erect penis will usually do so in the course of an overt sexual dream; otherwise, the allusion will generally be symbolic. There could be a reference to fears of impotence. With women, there may be an element of penis envy, though of course, this too may simply be part of a sexual fantasy (Ibid: 127)." Note that penis envy is classic Freud.

"(Almost every giant in fiction is in some way connected with sex, and often depicted traditionally with enormous genitals) (Ibid: 139)."

"If a zip-fastener gives way, a suggestion of insecurity or embarrassment. An obvious possible sexual connotation (Ibid: 215)."

This is an excellent example of dream dictionary interpretation that is presented as being professional. The book is thin on research, and tends to represent outmoded theories of dreams as being factual. The symbolic subjectivity in the quotes, I believe, is self-explanatory. The book is probably as historical in nature as that of the ancients. Their examples are so alien when compared to the works of J. Alan Hobson that I can't restrain myself, but here are a few more belly whackers:
Dream Dictionary Themes:" (Parker: 56-83)

Mazes: A maze in a dream usually relates to the dreamer's descent into the unconscious. It may represent the complex defenses put up by the conscious ego to prevent unconscious wishes and desires from emerging into the light (1994: 63).

The reader will note the classic interpretation, which assumes the reality of Freud's use of Unconscious.

Being chased: Dreams of being chased by an unseen but terrifying presence usually indicate that aspects of the self are clamouring for integration into consciousness. The dreamer's fear usually dissipates if he or she can turn and face the pursuer, and gain clues as to what this symbol represents at the conscious level (Ibid: 67).

Feathers: Feathers, whether or not they appear in the same dream as birds, often represent a gift, expressing the desire to show warmth or tenderness to someone close to the dreamer (Ibid: 73).

Any light touch while dreaming can instigate similar representations in my dreams. This type of symbolic or metaphorical interpretation distorts the meaning of somatic representations in dreams according to my experience.

DREAM INTERPRETATIONS BY TAMARA TRUSSEAU

The back cover of Trusseau's book reads: "An authoritative introduction to the world of dreams precedes an A to Z dictionary featuring hundreds of entries, proffering meaning to the many symbols that emerge in our dreams."
A few examples from her dictionary pages 68 to 125 will give the flavor of her perspective:

Acorn: "Success in business matters." **Comb**: "A craving for greater emotional excitement and stimulation." **Tunnel**: "Denotes constraints and difficulties." **Zip**: "An opening opportunity."

Trusseau interprets various dreams between pages 21 and 63. An example of the meaning of nakedness comes from Paul on page 58: "Naked = to see oneself naked in a dream points to a fear of exposure; it also

348

highlights growing emotional problems due to a lack of confidence; to see others naked implies that certain truths and realities are about to be revealed."

For psychological dreams, she says: "Note that psychological dreams may regularly appear to have predictive undertones. These augural connotations are due to the instinctive observations associated with the subconscious and should not be confused with prophetic information."

"Tamara Trusseau has many years' experience in her field. She runs a psychic studio offering tarot readings, spiritual guidance, and dream interpretation (Trusseau: Backcover).

One can quickly see why subjective approaches are discredited by dream researchers and neuroscientists. Palm reading and astrological signs have a similar level of subjectivity, and depend on the gullibility of the client.

DREAM INTERPRETATIONS BY DAVID FONTANA

In *The Secret Language of Dreams*, Fontana emphasizes the work of Freud and Jung in his use of themes and symbols for dream interpretation. In my experience, Freud and Jung's interpretations of dreams are equivalent to interpretations that I have gotten from playful palm readers when in the mood for parlor games. I will give you a few examples for comparison with other's dream dictionaries.

The majority of Fontana's book is devoted to theme and symbol interpretations based on the assumed reality of Freud's unconscious. However, Freud's interpretation goes back to the ancient Greeks and their predecessors. Hobson and Leonard's *Psychiatry in Crisis* develops this line of thought nicely. A few samples of symbol interpretation will conclude this section on Fontana.

The Body: For Jungians, an emphasis upon the right side of the body in dreams often refers to aspects of conscious life, while the left side represents the unconscious (Ibid: 86).

Hair: In dreams, hair often symbolizes vanity; conversely, the ritual act of shaving the head indicates a renunciation of worldly ways (Ibid: 87).

Dreamer flying unaided: If accompanied by strong feelings of awe and power, flying unaided can be a Level 3, archetypal expression of the dreamer's higher self, his or her sense of immortality, and an element in ourselves that rides high above the space-time constraints of the world (Ibid: 105).

The reader increasingly becomes aware of the subjectivity of dream dictionaries as well as how convoluted and subjective are the concepts of Freud and Jung. Dip into the contemporary findings of neuroscience and confirm this observation for yourself. A final quote from Fontana on shamans to reinforce how this level of extreme subjectivity is maintained:

"Shamans attempt to fix a power object of some kind so firmly in the waking mind that it can even be visualized in sleep, reminding them that they are dreaming (Ibid: 162)."

Fontana goes on to reference Carlos Castaneda and his Yaqui shaman guide to other worlds. His focus is on the reflection techniques used by shamans to develop conscious control over dreaming. He introduces the traditional aura of mysticism surrounding shamans, while, in my estimation, failing to clarify shamans, mysticism or dream control: A writer's technique that is used too often by dream interpreters.

DREAM INTERPRETATIONS BY SYLVIA BROWNE

A quotation from her book flap says it all: "Sylvia Browne's Book of Dreams offers a window into our souls and a doorway to The Other Side." She basically supports a wide range of occult and discredited beliefs from astral travel, remote viewing, ability to visit the past, foresee the future, reunions with deceased others, as well as believing that archetypes are factual. She is a New York Times bestselling author. Clearly, occult beliefs are warm and safe in America. She is a great read for fantasy trips, and a sharp contrast with the findings of science.

DREAM INTERPRETATIONS BY ROBINSON AND CORBETT

The Dreamer's Dictionary is preceded by 17 brief pages of introduction which is then followed by 365 pages of dictionary; yup, 365 pages; A starts with abandon and Z ends with zucchini. The subtitle of the book reads: "3,000 Magical Mirrors to Reveal the Meaning of Your Dreams." Everything you ever wanted to know about the meaning of your dreams is painfully set forth. Even Aristotle would have laughed all the way to the publishers before he got to zucchini. Need I say more?

HOBSON ON DREAM MEANING

I have criticized *Freud's interpretation of dreams* so frequently that I will not go into detail here, even though he remains popular amongst adherents to non-scientific methodologies. He is misleading to say the least. His interpretations are as bizarre as any fictive dream element. Hobson destroys his model as completely as anyone I have read. Thus, you should visit Hobson's works for a neuroscientist's understanding of Freud, especially *Out of Its Mind: Psychiatry in Crisis.*

Hobson has another must read titled *13 Dreams Freud Never Had: The New Mind Science.* His "Author's Note" starts this way:

Sigmund Freud correctly believed that dreams are a key to understanding the human mind. He was also correct in assuming that any scientific psychology needed to be brain-based. But lacking that base, he was forced to speculate, and I have found that his contribution to a science of the mind is, at best, obsolete and, at worst, misleading.

The serious student will include *13 Dreams* on his or her early reading list. I have been tying dream and ASC interpretation to the sciences in this book. Hobson places dreams squarely in the middle of what is going on in our minds. If initially you find him a heavy read, go back to Delaney and Brooks-Vogelsong for starters. If you've seeped yourself in the occult, be prepared for reality shock.

CHAPTER 17

MENTAL ILLNESS, CRIME & BELIEF

EXORCISM

In today's Tri-City Herald there was an article lamenting the fact that the Catholic Church does not have enough trained priests to exorcise all their followers who are possessed by evil spirits. They do, however, have a few hundred capable of this task.

It's a frightening state of affairs to be possessed by the devil or some other evil spirit. I understand this fear well, as my mother convinced me of this possibility when I was a child. Possession has been recognized by religions both large and small throughout recorded history; it has been a universal affliction across cultures, and still persists for the uninformed. A compassionate shaman or priest knows firsthand the terror suffered by their followers under this intense state of anxiety. But most importantly, knows how to remove the evil spirit.

Exorcism in its many forms has always been a quick and fairly inexpensive way to handle spirit possession. If the evil spirit or the devil comes back, one just needs another adjustment; much like seeing the chiropractor when your back slips out of alignment. Logic doesn't work, and why would anyone expect logic to work? The problem is not one of logic, but belief. The human mind simply needs to adjust its internalized, abstract integration of meaning, and, Poof! ...the problem is solved, much like riding oneself of nightmares.

In Hobson and Leonard's 2001 book, *Out of its Mind: Psychiatry in Crisis,* the authors propose a model to reform the treatment of mental illness in America.

For at least the last fifty years, I've read articles about priestly exorcisms and the need for more training in this area, hence the 2011 cry for more trained priests is not new. I have witnessed traditional priests (shamans) in Native American ceremonies alleviating misery of their fellows, often groups of followers attending one ceremony, with equal effectiveness. I have not witnessed Catholic priests performing such group rituals, although I have no reason to doubt that they could be equally effective.

Jesus was popular in his day, along with many other prophets who were adept at casting out demons. Jesus' Disciples were directed to go forth and perform this function. Demons must be real, or else Jesus and the Church would be engaging in magic. And so demons are real, one becomes a True Believer, and the exorcism works.

Belief is a powerful transformer of brain circuits and brain chemistry. Our ability using belief to remove anxiety along with the devil and evil spirits is well documented. Talk therapy doesn't work as quickly or as cost effectively. Drug therapy will mask the syndrome, but the little demons will still reside within.

I'm not making fun of contemporary therapists or priests, but instead, drawing attention to the necessity of addressing the meaning of spirit afflictions to the individual so possessed. I know firsthand from childhood what it feels like to be pursued by demons. It is not necessary to understand the complete mechanics behind meaning transfer mechanisms in our minds in order to use them effectively. In my experience, it's the same mechanism I used to rid myself of nightmares.

So where does this leave Hobson and Leonard's reform movement? Ten years have passed, and we continue to see hard dollars removed from patient care, as much decline in education as improvement, the creeping closure of community centers for the homeless and mentally ill, increasing hardening of public attitudes that promotes the death penalty for serious offenders as young as 13 years, whether they are mentally ill or not, and political game playing at the national and state level that shows no abatement, especially as these debates affect funding for the aged, poor, and mentally ill.

Ignorance will not lie unattended; it demands an explanation. The mentally ill and morally inferior must be restrained, or we just kill them. Problem solved! Yes, I'm jaundiced, because of too many decades of criminal justice system involvement. The CJS is now responsible for most of America's mentally ill. Our prisons and jails are full of them.

Hobson and Leonard set forth a meaningful plan to address the needs of the mentally ill in 2001, but their ideas fell mostly on deaf ears. I commiserate with them, as I too spent decades trying to reform the criminal justice system to provide for this population. I thought over the past 40 years that moving the mentally ill into our prisons from state hospitals was a form of institutionalized brutality. I still think this way.

MAGELLAN AND ZHENG HE

Hobson and Leonard state that:

Right now our principal goal, one we know we can achieve, is to improve the lot of multitudes in urgent need of help. But in addition, psychiatric research seems poised to do more by contributing to fresh discoveries—much as the global navigator Ferdinand Magellan did more than improve the lot of Spain through his research for a new route to the Indies (2001: 266).

What struck me as being so ironic is their reference to Magellan. The Chinese explorer Zheng He made a world tour of discovery between 1421-1423, only to have the Emperor and his Mandarin Court stop exploration and within a few years destroy not only their magnificent fleet, but their boat-works capacity. In this simple-minded act, China left world discovery to the West along with its full force of colonialism. Today, we chose to leave mental health to the exorcists and prison guards.

The destruction of our motivation to use science to solve problems of the mentally ill represents state and federal efforts to destroy the fleet. Prisons now hold more mentally ill than our state hospitals did at their peak in the 1950s. Prison overcrowding and inadequate staffing is intensifying through continuous cutbacks as we enter 2011. Even worse, thousands are being released from prison without mental health services being available, with funds being withdrawn for their pharmaceuticals, and without housing or job preparation. One can imagine how fortunate Americans would be if only a form of Roman slavery were available.

Insurance and pharmaceutical companies and vested stock groups have fought the new healthcare law under President Obama with one of the most vicious negative ad campaigns in recent memory. What we can do for mental health, we chose not to do. To believe that prison incarceration is cheaper than community treatment and education contradicts the logic behind deinstitutionalization of hospitals for the mentally ill.

The public doesn't realize that this population has just been shifted from one institution to another. Most politicians remain equally uniformed or just don't care. Politicians only need to pander to base voter instincts in order to be reelected. I'm afraid the problem is not one of logic. And its solution is not waiting on science.

I have two related stories that I am compelled to relate regarding attempts to overcome the negative campaign against offenders of all types: The trail 'em, nail 'em, jail 'em, and if they're really bad, kill 'em mentality that has grown in support of our initial doubling, tripling, and then quadrupling of prison populations.

I spent ten years lobbying the Minnesota Legislature to make changes in laws related to the criminal justice system. In 2000, with the drive and energy of a local legislature from Rochester, Minnesota, Representative David Bishop, who was head of the House Ways and Means Committee, we pushed through legislation to add an additional 19.3 million dollars to the 31 million dollar community corrections budget.

My staff and I had demonstrated a zero re-offence rate for sex offenders supervised in the community with less than three percent committing any other crimes over a three year period of time. We had also duplicated this model in rural Central Minnesota. This and other offender community programs were realizing savings, as community based programs cost about one-tenth that of incarceration.

And other factors one should consider is keeping offenders employed, paying taxes, and maintaining responsibility for their families with community based programs. Throw in prison support as a major mechanism to support gangs and the progressive destruction of a young offender's mental health in prison, and one begins to get the picture.

Minnesota's Governor was able to rotate all these funds out over the next few years and replace innovative community services with new and remodeled prisons. The public believed in prisons, and the Governor wasn't concerned with their abysmal failure rates compared to our community treatment results. The Governor was hell bent on demonstrating that he was tough on crime. As I write these words, June 1, 2011, he has initiated his run for the presidency. Logical!

In the Governor's words, "there is still work to be done." Minnesota had been one of the leading states offering effective alternatives to prison, until the Governor took one giant step for his political career to bring most community alternatives to a screeching halt. I was appalled to see much of my life's work go down the drain, along with that of all who believed in less expensive, more effective and humane treatment of those incarcerated: That includes the mentally ill sent to prisons, children committed to death row, and three strikes offenders with minor crimes serving life sentences.

Representative Bishop was the driving force and the only legislator to push through this additional funding for community corrections. The Minnesota Department of Corrections, the keeper of prisons, offered only opposition, and no one else in the legislature was willing to go against the mindless tough on crime atmosphere. One of the other key legislators in the Senate at that time summed up the situation nicely to me in private after my presentation on our success with sex offenders: "Who cares, the public doesn't." A position clearly associated with re-election and aspirations for higher offices. He did run for higher office, and was elected.

I recount these experiences because I am not optimistic about our chances of bringing mental health initiatives into the 21st Century. The public doesn't like the cost of jails and prisons, doesn't recognize that they now house most of our mentally ill, and isn't about to consent to new taxes. The public does, however, seem willing to remove safeguards against false imprisonment to execute offenders. Unfortunately, DNA and other tests are finding that up to half of serious offenders on death row did not commit the crimes for which they were convicted, Illinois being a good example.

There has been no debate about superior alternatives to prison, about huge cost savings, or about implementation alternatives that immediately start saving money. California used to offer free higher education, but has shifted these dollars into its prisons. Logical? No, but it is politically correct, if one is pandering for political office.

This leaves, I'm afraid to say, Hobson and Leonard's proposal on the sidelines. The best, I think, we can do is continue to advance brain research, attempt to train a small cadre of experts that can lead in the future, and try to minimize the extent of damage being done. I say this as suicide rates remain painfully high, and homicides are once again on the upturn. I say this in light of the fact that 40 years of these policies have created a gang force nationwide that begins to approximate our troops on the ground, and astronomically larger than the gangsterism of the 1930's from which the term got its name. With luck, we will avoid

Mexico's gang challenge to government.

One final comment about education: Schools controlling education regarding those passing through the criminal justice system, my area of expertise and major concern, are stuck in the pre-scientific era of sociology. Most schools of criminal justice operate with models that have not or cannot be tested, as a quick review of Paul Gendreau's work demonstrates. This means that "tough on crime models" continue to dominate corrections thinking in a fashion reminiscent of our past history of using psychoanalysis for the mentally ill. I wonder, as with the Freudian model, do we wait another hundred years before understanding what witchcraft really is?

Hobson in his various works has taken psychoanalysis and psychodynamic practitioners to task for promoting unscientific models of treatment. His comments could be duplicated time and again in the criminal justice field. Unfortunately, we are both talking about a similar overlapping population much of the time. Talk to any local jailer about the revolving door of crazies that pass through their cellblocks daily, and experience their frustration with the system, their inadequate medical budgets, and the cost shifting that has gone from the federal budget to the state to the county, and finally, to the incarcerated.

You can leave jail today in numerous counties across America with a bill for room and board that might run from $40.00 per day to upwards to $100.00 per day. If you are mentally ill or marginally employable, this is a formula for disaster. Question: How does a mentally ill person who has been removed from his public funded medicines and returns to active hallucinations, going to be employed and pay off the tens of thousands of dollars he or she owes the local jail? Who needs reality testing here? We have numerous alternatives.

BELIEF AND CONTROL

Prison brutality is especially devastating for the teenagers who are incarcerated in adult prisons. Unless they are totally repulsive, their chances of being raped are better than 50 percent, unfortunately, much better. Stress and anxiety generally stops their social-emotional growth, and actual regression to earlier emotional growth stages is the norm, even though we know from research that kids as young as 13 years of age incarcerated in adult prisons have more than an additional ten years of ageing before their frontal lobes reach maturity. Their rates of violence increase upon release, versus rates for community or juvenile incarceration, and the frequency of their acting out goes up as well. The criminal justice system is as broken as Hobson and Leonard say the mental health system is. They are interchangeable.

Research presented directly to county commissioners and state and federal legislators usually falls on deaf ears.

I recall one conversation at the county level when I was the Community Corrections Administrator of DFO in Rochester, Minnesota. I was asking for a budget increase, which was denied, and presenting statistical evidence for increased cost if the funding was not forthcoming. One of the long-term commissioners turned to me and said: "That cost is born by the state, not by us."

Lack of integrated services across the hierarchy of political jurisdictions is a problem. As a taxpayer, I just notice the outflow, and it is meaningless to play the game of cost-shifting: That is, unless one is running for re-election, or the presidency, and claiming cost-saving reforms by cutting programs for the vulnerable.

We have shifted control from science and meaningful applied treatment programs to street drugs as self-medication, to pharmaceutical profits, to politics over performance, and to the maintenance and re-immergence of pre-scientific attempts to handle mental health issues such as exorcism. When political posturing approximates witchcraft while clothed in the trappings of science, our educational efforts become that much more difficult.

I applaud competent professionals who try to bring sanity to the business of craziness, but I do not yet share their hope. The problem is not knowledge as many people believe, but the will to change political game playing.

I have come to hold the view that belief is control. Belief directs the rise and fall of civilizations. Belief guided by science can eventually move us out of the cave of darkness, but it requires better public education and political leadership than America has at present. It requires more, not less, investment, and it requires will, courage, and persistence. Unfortunately, pandering to the public for election or reelection is not part of a success formula for enlightenment. This is more pessimism than I have held for the past forty years.

THE GHOST, THE PRIEST, AND SCIENCE

When I was a child, we lived in many old houses with steep wooden stairs. I came to associate steep wooden stairs with a ghost who nightly tried to get into my body as I stepped into the stairway. I would run up the stairs, quickly jump into bed, and cover myself with blankets to keep the ghost from possessing me. As long as I ran quickly, hid under the covers, and lay quiet and barely breathing, the ghost was defeated.

Mother believed in ghosts and shared this fact with me. I didn't need a lot of convincing, because the ghost was a real, felt, daily presence in my young life. It reappeared when I bought my first house in 1970 at the age of 34, a house with steep wooden stairs.

Science that cannot touch the heart of a small child is no science at all. Politicians who care only about power are no public servants at all.

The upshot of the story is that I eventually came to realize that smothering attacks by mother, attacks that put me in the hospital in a near-death state with an out-of-body vision, was my conditioned association with steep wooden stairs. When mother came up the stairs, I never knew if she would attack or nurture me. I became hyper-vigilant, conditioned, and unaware of the source from which the ghost came. Eventually, however, I got a handle on the matter, and the ghost was put to rest. I also came to understand how fear can be transformed in our psyches from abstract feelings to concrete manifestations, and those manifestations can be ghosts, phobias, amnesia, ticks, depression, immobilizing anxiety, etc. Ah, how we lower-class kids enjoy them without treatment, without pharmaceuticals, and with only the local shaman for support.

INTERPRETATION

A priest could've performed a ritual to protect me from the ghost, perhaps even wearing a special cross that I could hold up as I proceeded up the stairs at night. The cross could protect me while I slept, and I might even come to wear it daily, just in case the ghost got creative. If it got inside of me, and mother said ghosts could do this, I would just have it exorcized. Simple enough, but it doesn't advance mental health practice much. Shamanic practices of this nature probably go back 30,000 to 50,000 years.

In 1970, I was a young university professor in complete control of my life when the ghost returned. Local psychiatrists were dominated by Freudian practitioners. I could have spent multiple weekly sessions in therapy learning about my repressed sexuality and other pathologies, as I had a history of many. If I became a True Believer in Freud's religion, I might even have been cured. I would have had a much smaller bank account, however. I am quite sure If I had engaged therapy of the day that I never would have discovered how the ghost became manifest.

In other words, therapy would have been equal to daily maintenance, not to complete recovery with understanding. I might still be using the latest pharmaceutical elixir. But I would have made a new friend; assuming that I stayed in therapy and that I liked the therapist. Of course, I'm referring to the Freudians of my day.

My third alternative would have been to move into a house without steep wooden stairs. This would be a Skinnerian Behaviorist's solution. I wouldn't need to know why some houses had a ghost; all I would've needed was to find a house that felt comfortable, a house without ghosts. Watch TV for more examples.

Bear in mind that the ghost returned when I was 34 years old. It didn't return in a dream, and it returned at a time when I was still practicing dream programming on a daily basis. The nightmare that eventually revealed my mother's role in creating the ghost was still being suppressed through long-term use of dream programming:

The fourth method that finally worked for me was to discontinue dream programming so that related neural circuits sponsoring the ghost could once again be expressed in my dreams. A little additional luck with some yoga positions in management training, and mother's smothering attacks were revealed. Understanding all of these mind-brain connections required years of study and self-analysis, early rejection of the psychoanalytic model, and learning how to interpret my dreams. Please understand that I support real psychotherapy.

A fifth approach in the 1940s would probably have included a combination of being institutionalized in a state hospital, being sedated for hyperactivity, and if I had been lucky, receiving some kind of Freudian talk therapy. I would not have improved. New medications would have been tried by the 1950s and 1960s. I would be permanently stigmatized as a person with serious mental illness, and spent my life laboring in some obscure job, if I was lucky, for the rest of my life. If I had become self-supporting with some menial job, I would've become a medical success case.

Today, I might receive some type of neuro-dynamic interventions such as those proposed by Hobson. I would be put on medications for hyperactivity, and drugs to control my hallucinations and epileptic episodes. I would probably not receive cognitive-behavioral therapy, with public funds being cut and the national health policy under attack. I would be excluded from military duty and the GI Bill, which put me through college. I would never have discovered dream programming or techniques of self-therapy. If my MMPI profile prevailed, I would've been confronted with the distinct possibility of being incarcerated in an adult prison as a morally inferior person.

If, on the other hand, my self-diagnosis of PTSD had prevailed and I was removed from my parents, I would've been placed in a foster home, received minimum pharmaceuticals, and been allowed normal child development. I might mature to enjoy a quality life. This last scenario would be highly unlikely given our current state of public funding for children. I have observed hundreds of institutionalized and incarcerated versions of myself while working with children and youth in our American Criminal Justice System.

If I were put on medications common to the 1950s or 1960s, with knowledge then available from neuroscience, I doubt that my life would have been as fulfilling as it has been. I suspect that my life would have been one of long-term medication with partially disabling social and occupational behaviors, all accompanied by significant mood swings and trials on various new drugs.

If I could start over with the information and knowledge base currently available to Hobson, my future might be as rewarding as it has been. Self-therapy put all of my pathologies to rest by the time I received my BA degree. Nightmares were banished, MMPI elevations eliminated, and life controls implemented that are shades of the meditating monk. I am quite sure that I have a permanent memory of mother's crib assaults and other traumatic incidents in my young life, but these memories are not bothersome, and they do not require any kind of medications, nor have they required drugs to stabilize my behavior; ever!

This digression has one primary focus: How we construct meaning in our lives is critical to our well-being. How therapists impart belief is critical to our well-being. How the public is educated about Self, consciousness, and mental health is critical to our well-being. And last, political control of medicine by pharmaceutical companies, calloused medical practitioners who put profit above children, and insurance companies who only consider the bottom line must change. Change, that is, if the majority of children with my family history are to have value in American society.

THE HAPPY AMYGDALA

Neuroscience has established that the amygdala permanently records traumatic incidents in one's life. I can recall crib trauma with clarity in this, my 75th year. Crib trauma started at least by the time I was 18 months old. My young brain was still physically maturing, with a lot of growth and future neural pruning ahead. Emotional gyrations to cope with crib trauma through adolescent abuse lasted until I was able to stabilize these effects in my early twenties. Self-directed therapy eliminated nightmares, PTS syndrome, and stabilized my MMPI profile without the use of any drugs or pharmaceuticals. Complete recovery from child abuse occurred when I was able to identify the underlying elements that triggered my various mental and physically manifested pathologies.

Identifying the source of my crib and adolescent traumas immediately broke the cycle of nightmares, and shortly thereafter, led to my banishing anxiety and depression. Experientially, I eliminated the effects of traumatic memories locked away in my amygdale by identifying their source of activation. Steep wooden steps became just steps, and the ghost who used to haunt them disappeared.

Occasionally, old memories come to remind me of my history when I encounter similar physical settings to the steps. I simply reflect a moment to reinforce the therapeutic meaning in my nervous system, and all is well. No drugs and no special living arrangements are needed. If you were with me as I trip this memory switch, you would not detect anything unusual in my behavior. I don't reach for a pill box, or call my doctor either. In my experience, we are never free of our memories, but we can be free of their traumatizing effects. I don't mean to downplay the need for medicating drugs. I believe that as we come to understand natural strategies to help the mind-brain balance itself, the use of drugs will become less, not more, commonly prescribed.

Public agencies and the federal government must play a major role in bringing a comprehensive treatment programs to the country that are research based. Pharmaceutical companies are not going to sponsor programs that decrease drug use, and the church is not going to practice a campaign to downsize the number of priests practicing exorcisms; or support a scientific education that would make exorcism unnecessary.

Altered states of consciousness, the physiology behind dream, vision, trance, and occult experiences must all be brought under the microscope of science. A comprehensive understanding of these various states of consciousness lies behind the magic of stable emotions, freedom to enjoy a full nights rest, control of anxiety and depression, and ability to set and achieve major life goals. One's conscious movement across altered states trips across the phenomena of mental illness, for they are brothers and they are sisters.

Leaving intervention to priests practicing exorcism, or drug companies making profits, is not a comprehensive answer. A rational, scientific research program that incorporates all states of consciousness and their related micro-states must be part of the final solution. The fear of Big Brother controlling society with science and technology is eliminated when therapeutic strategies leave control at the individual level. Ignorance of altered states supports the rampant occult logic embraced by large segments, if not a majority, of Americans. This is not world-level public education.

THE UNHAPPY HIPPOCAMPUS AND YOUNG OFFENDERS

One thing we notice with juvenile offenders entering the criminal justice system is a lot of brain damage. For example, when we look closer, we see bilateral differences in the size of the amygdala, hippocampus, and corpus collossum. Hobson also reviews some of the effects of stress on the hippocampus. If an individual is under stress for a prolonged period of time, bad things happen:

So long as the real or imagined emergency is short-lived, well and good. The Amygdala shuts off, the hypothalamus obeys the hippocampus, and the flows of CRF and stress hormones stop." "In theory, repeated episodes like this could do major long-term harm by shrinking the hippocampus, causing memory problems, producing chronically high levels of circulating stress hormones, actually killing neurons in the hippocampus, and causing the amygdale to become chronically hyperactive (2001: 170).

Now check your favorite university program training undergraduates to work in any branch of human services to see if students are being so educated. These are the professionals, by the way, who provide most of the services, that is, if they haven't already been replaced by paraprofessionals who employ hugs and smiles. And, thank god for hugs and smiles.

In the case of depression: "People … tend to have a smaller than average hippocampus, and the degree of atrophy tends to be greater among those who have been depressed longer (Ibid)."

These are common conditions found amongst young offenders, by the way. The lack of knowledge on the part of the general public, correctional personnel, and social workers continues to punish children and young adults who have been brutalized by their environments. Wealthy, educated individuals who have grown up in stable environments generally believe that they have lucky DNA, and ignore the fact that DNA potential is only realized in a supportive environment. This is a form of class arrogance.

When we work with adolescents and young adults in the criminal justice system we see all of these negative effects. These young people are considered to be morally inferior, and hence, they do not need treatment, just punishment – or so the story goes. It can take up to six months in a well-controlled treatment environment to stabilize brain-mind states for these young people. Once, stabilized their memories work better, they typically make rapid school progress, and demonstrate significantly improved social abilities. If they are returned to pressure-cooker living environments, their downward deterioration spiral starts within a matter of days. If they are incarcerated in pressure-cooker prisons, it never has a chance to recover.

When we throw young offenders in with hardened predators, is it any wonder that we get regression rather than progression? "Sock-it-to-them" politicians should try this routine for about three years and see what it does to their values. Better yet, try putting your teenager in this environment for six months and see what happens.

PTSD is as common in poorly run prisons for young offenders as it is in war zones. Medications offer a little relief for some, but massive doses of narcotics gained by any means offer much more relief.

Insanity at the top of our political structure breeds more insanity at the bottom. Strong families, a hug instead of prison rape, and some compassion would be even more helpful.

Young people treated in this fashion are asked to overcome brain chemical imbalance and unilaterally control their own stress hormones, return brain centers such as the amygdale and hippocampus to normal size, heal their own brain-mind, correct memory deficits, and much more all on their own. Unlikely!

Hobson says:

A 1990 study found that, compared to normal subjects, schizophrenics had substantially fewer neurons in a part of the thalamus called the medial dorsal nucleus—this being the main thalamic nucleus communicating with the prefrontal cortex (Ibid: 195).

A defective relationship between brain structures of serious young offenders and their higher reasoning centers is well documented. Neuroscience is demonstrating through rigorous research the effects that both genetics and environment have on brain structure and function. The hope is that pharmaceuticals will alleviate and/or correct these problems. Education that ignores the brain and how it develops, while stressing political solutions for real physiological problems, is doomed. And what does this say about the societies that support such practices? A society that lives in ignorance pays a horrible price.

Dream research and studies of consciousness have taken us a long way toward understanding the brain-mind connections. Drugs have added greatly to our ability to alleviate misery related to altered brain states. Understanding brain architecture is helpful, but the public's will to comprehensively address the needs of infants, children, and adolescents is most wanting. To some extent this is understandable, as much of our education teaches political philosophy, not science. The priests and most of the mental health professionals of the 20th and now the 21st Century are political science majors.

Those who work with young people in the criminal justice system are aware of the impossible conditions under which most serious offenders come to commit their crimes. I used to tell my criminal justice students: "Imagine anything that can be done to a child or another human being, and if you work in the CJS long enough, you will experience this abuse firsthand." Yet, these young offenders have dreams and visions of what they might become, seek love and companionship like new puppies, and return the respect and concern of their surrogate parents in kind. But this doesn't happen if the damage has gone beyond the breaking point, and the brain looks more like hamburger than steak.

Very few offenders that I have ever known or worked with are from the privileged ranks of pampered parenting. Generally, it is the parents of pampered young people who make the political decisions, and very few of their children enter the criminal justice system, as affordable private services are accessible to them. That is, unless their criminal activity is extremely egregious.

Political policy that treats the brain as a black box that can be modified positively through the pain of harsh punishments ignores most 20th Century science. To assume that punishment works, or the young person is genetically deficient, is a cognitive defense against one's own barbarian thoughts. Those of us who have spent years providing services to America's youth know the difference.

PLACEBO EFFECT

The placebo effect is well understood in medicine, and is strong enough that it must be controlled in most research-based experiments, especially with drug and talk therapies. It is the mechanism of suggestion that activates the brain, mind, and body's ability to bring about real, not just imaginary, change in you and me. The effects of sleep, especially quality sleep representing normal cycles that relax and restore our energy, is well documented as a maintainer and restorer of health. In sleep, we observe cell and chemical changes that can enhance our immune system, and enhance or activate healing throughout the brain and body. Cell functioning can actually be altered through mental activity, as one can easily demonstrate for themselves using techniques of self-hypnosis, or as has been well documented by studying Buddhist meditation.

Meditation helps us maintain a better level of health by keeping our bodies and minds in peak mode to ward off and/or fight diseases of all kinds. I prefer the use of auto-suggestion of the hypnotic type to induce these brain states as it is a less time consuming method. Self-suggestion, without the trance effect of self-hypnosis, can be used to help us think positively in either a dreaming or waking state and is used by athletes, people of different occupations, therapists, and shamans.

One can view self-hypnotic states as a form of trance unto itself, or we can see self-induced states falling along a continuum. I prefer to see it along a continuum, with the high-end offering control over body and brain actions that are normally automatic. Self-hypnosis permits us to access any part of our body, turn pain off, remove anxiety or depression, etc. I compare its use to meditation in that the more often this state is entered, the easier it becomes, and the more effective it becomes. Neuronal mass must increase through frequent practice of self-hypnosis, just as it does with frequent meditation. It is at the accomplished end of this continuum, or its highest practiced states, that positive mental health can be maximized. This is my experience.

Self-hypnosis can be used to embed controlled fixed action patterns which are turned on and off at will. It can direct thoughts, and suppress or eliminate unwanted delusional or hallucinatory brain states. These state changes can be engaged on demand, and preempt the expression of anxiety, unwanted visualizations, and the like. It is from this interpretation that I have used self-hypnosis to go a step further than auto-suggestion, as it is typically used in dream and other forms of therapy. I stress the importance of self-control as being critical to gaining and maximizing positive mental health.

Self-hypnosis is under the control of my active Self, my active Interpreter, my active Controller – whatever choice of words you prefer. I experience self-hypnosis permitting me to access a multitude of normally non-conscious brain cell assemblies and neural networks, and know firsthand how this access can shape and reform network functions that create and support various emotional states, brain chemical outputs, input-output gating across the global brain system, and thereby effect cell functioning as well. I believe this is the central mechanism operating in the placebo effect, and we should all learn to control this mechanism.

Further, I think it is an oversight on the part of medicine and therapists of all types to ignore the development and control of the placebo effect. Or in my words, the mind-brain process guided by our conscious Self that can actively rebalance micro-to-macro states across the brain-mind.

Along with psychiatrists of the modern, non-Freudian, non-psychoanalytic types, I think drug use should be minimized. I say this after watching hundreds of young people withdraw from drugs in holistic therapeutic environments, and then go on to use their new found abilities to make rapid progress in school and behavioral control. Drugs keep the brain from finding its own balance, either street or pharmaceutical, and teach the brain to seek relief from an external source. It is like having a life-long drug for a parent, which amounts to maintenance, but not growth.

Our brains can learn new pathways to health, thereby frequently being able to eliminate dependency on pharmaceuticals or therapists. Hobson says: "We have only recently noticed that brain-mind states are all that we are. Our states control our faculties, yet with consciousness, we can control our states (1994: 218)."

After more than fifty years of tinkering with, controlling and directing mind states, I heartily agree.

COMPLEX SYSTEMS

My doctoral dissertation predicted a specific type of criminal behavior. I spend three years collecting data and studying complex dynamic systems, and came to realize that much of what I had been taught about human behavior in psychology, counseling, sociology, and anthropology was based on linear models, not dynamic models. Much of what I had learned about behaviorism was based on false assumptions about the role of our higher cognitive functions in behavior. Over my lifetime, we've moved away from viewing youth as passively responding to uncontrollable unconscious urges, aka Freud, or behavioral conditioning, aka Skinner.

Manufactured schemes explaining personality and the unconscious were taken as gospel truth for most of the 20th Century, and there were many in the "soft sciences." The differences and distance between traditional philosophy and empirical research has continued to increase. Research based philosophy, neuro-philosophy, and cognitive science are gradually supplanting classical thought. Optimism latches onto the hope that these new ways of thinking will enter the public domain in the next fifty years. Yes, I did say 50 years. If you think that is cynical, review the history of Freud's schemes.

Dynamic open systems are fun to play with as one leaves the world of determinism and enters that of probability. The probability of human behavior depends on an evolutionary perspective where children develop in a social environment that is nurturing. Probability of behavioral outcomes also depends on an environment that permits children's DNA to be fully realized, and an environment that permits full expression of critical brain centers. A brain that is a receptacle into which we can pour anger, hate, and insensitivity in the name of correcting deficits as outlined above, is absurd.

When I discovered complexity theory and chaos, the world of determinism as learned during my university days was killed on the spot. Quantum theory became a heuristic friend as it helped me think about what was going on in my own cellular and chemical processes, and quantum processes shared a dynamic quality with real human behavior.

The human brain is an open dynamic system. Unfortunately, politicians funding prisons and de-funding community mental health are still riding to work in horse and buggy wagons. Political scientists love stability.

At this point in time, it is unreasonable to expect medical doctors or psychiatrists to comprehend and embrace all the dynamics going on in our brains. Brain states and systems are incredibly complex.

Technology does not yet permit fine scale analysis of global brain states, but progress continues.

The patient or client today is still somewhat of a guinea pig. When I develop a prediction equation for behavior, I may be entering 250 variables. In the analysis, I'm using specific statistical techniques to sort out what is critical. But these equations are only predicting that part of behavior that lies within the domain of individual to social interaction.

In contrast, by learning to control my own brain states, I can affect hundreds of brain chemicals and countless neural circuits. An interactive model that marries these two streams of internal and external causation is potentially on the horizon. Drugs tinker with the internal brain-mind, prisons tinker with political causation, and never the twain of head and heart shall meet.

It seems apparent that future practitioners in medicine and neuroscience will be using some rather sophisticated computer programs and scanning technologies to perform diagnosis that adequately gets to the micro-level of brain states. I also think computerized robots will be performing most of our fine-grained surgery by 2050, more likely 2030. In similar fashion, sophisticated computer programs with attached technology will come under individual control for their own diagnosis and treatment. The medical practitioner will be a guide, not a god. We know how many variables most professional people hold in their mind when making decisions; it is just a handful, typically five or less.

Understanding dynamic open systems has freed me from pooh-poohing age-old practices such as acupuncture or ritual shamanic healing. If it works, we need to understand how it works. My experience with hypnosis and the medical community for the first twenty years of my professional life simply led me to believe that I was batting my head against a brick wall of defunct paradigms. Trying to discuss altered states with this community was even more difficult. Hence, my affection for researches such as Hobson, Damasio and Ramachandran and physicist-philosophers like Paul Nunez.

CONSCIOUSNESS, ASC AND THE NORMAL BRAIN

In "… 1998, Fred Gage, a professor at the Salk Institute for Biological studies in La Jolla, CA., along with Swedish researchers, reported the first observed regenerated brain cells in humans (Howard: 112)."

Neuroscience has demonstrated over the past half-century, especially in the past twenty years, how the brain becomes wired, and how it is capable of rewiring itself plastically. Increasingly, we come to identify what is going on within cells, between cells, and at higher levels of mind-brain functioning related to cognitive input and output. The mystery of the mind is slowly evaporating, and an increasingly clear picture emerging.

Researchers, such as J. Alan Hobson, have added considerably to our understanding of dream consciousness and the cycling of various brain chemical states as we move from being awake to dreaming, and as we move through the various stages of sleep. I have attempted in this book to share the limited insights I've gained through self-experiments over the past 50 years. I'm proposing that all brain states can be considered normal in the sense that they just represent micro and macro changes in brain chemistry and related electro-chemical functions. However, it seems self-evident that damaged architecture from the brain's own stress neuro-modulators alters how neural circuitry is maintained and functions. And that psychological intervention can reverse and control malfunctions, if introduced early enough into our development. Further, that altered realities are a natural byproduct of brain circuit rewiring, and lastly, brain circuit configurations can be brought under individual control without the use of drugs.

Zimmer has an interesting observation about artificial neural networks that are used to explore various pathologies such as schizophrenia. His focus is on the effects these networks express when a single hub amongst a couple dozen clusters is shut down. "But if they shut down a single hub, the patterns of activity across the entire network changed dramatically (Zimmer: 63)."

What this means to research on the effects of strokes or brain surgery is a potential explanation for the complex effects that are well documented. A sizeable amount of tissue may be removed without any major effect on the individual's behavior, but at other times, a small amount of tissue is affected and major changes occur in the person's behavior. Obviously, this is not a linear, but a dynamic relationship.

This difference is observed in real life strokes and surgery as well. The assumption becomes: Our understanding of how complex systems operate cannot be explained by linear analysis. It can only be explained through an understanding of complex system dynamics.

We note that failure to understand chaotic operations in our brains lies behind our inability to treat more effectively. As we engage in reduction, bottom-up research, our level of ignorance is reduced one hierarchical level after another. I am contending that subjective analysis, self-case studies of my type, can be part of the heuristic modeling that guides developmental methodologies. For example, specific changes in insight, or meaning, can affect both micro and macro state changes in the brain: Nightmare resolution being one example.

Karl Deisseroth is a member of the bioengineering and psychiatry faculties at Stanford University, and conducts research in the area of optogenetics. "Optogenetics is the combination of genetics and optics to control well-defined events within specific cells of living tissue, not just those of the nervous system (Scientific American: 50)."

The significance of this technology is the researcher's ability to control events within specific living cells. Deisseroth states that: "We have found, for example that deep-brain stimulation may be most effective when it targets not cells but rather the connections between cells – affecting the flow of activity between brain regions."

Of interest is the electrical rhythm occurring across groups of living cells using technology that can monitor individual cell events. This is a good example of how technology continues to evolve, and the interesting expansion of related knowledge that results.

Deisseroth's analysis is a little technical, but he bears following in terms of advancing our knowledge of schizophrenia:

We have also learned how to prod one kind of cell, neocortical parvalbumin neurons, to modulate 4-cycles-per-second rhythms in brain activity called gamma oscillations. Science has known for some time that schizophrenic patients have altered parvalbumin cells and that gamma oscillations are abnormal in both schizophrenia and autism—but the causal meaning of these correlations (if any) was not known (Ibid: 54-55).

Hence, pinning down the causal meaning of altered parvalbumin cells and abnormal gamma oscillations has been difficult. He goes on to say that:

In my patients with schizophrenia, I see what clearly appear to be information-processing problems, in which mundane random events are incorrectly viewed as parts of larger themes or patterns (an informational problem perhaps giving rise to paranoia and delusions). These patients also suffer from some failure of an internal 'notification' mechanism that informs us when thoughts are self-generated (an informational problem perhaps underlying the frightening phenomenon of 'hearing voices') (Ibid: 55).

Controlling attention, mood, and behavior modifies our internal relationship to self as it modifies our total environmental relationships. One does not need to understand the technical mechanisms involved to gain control over these mechanisms, in my experience.

At the age of 21 years, my MMPI profile showed critical elevation on the scale of paranoid-schizophrenic. I've already reported the use of self-hypnosis to address anxiety, depression, and concentration, and the subsequent normalization of my MMPI profile. I find Deisseroth's research informative, as the pattern of electrical activity between cell networks appears to be of critical importance for the treatment of schizophrenics. I am speculating, but the self-conditioning exercises I employed resulted in all three critical MMPI areas returning to normal.

I think of the methods I employed with self-hypnosis as a variation of cognitive-behavioral conditioning. My self-therapy must have addressed micro to global brain circuit/network imbalance to have been effective.

I believe we are progressing from the authoritarianism of the Freudians, where the therapist not only insisted on complete control over the patient, and demanded obedience to his dogmatic theories, to new forms of guided treatment, with ever greater participation and self-control exercised on the part of the client-patient. Drug interventions are a major step away from ineffective psychotherapies, but one that clearly is dependent on an improved ability to target specific drugs to specific cells. The question remains, however, what if gamma oscillations are maintained by more than one group of cells? In my personal experience, this seems to be the case.

My main point is that controlling altered states permits me to control any number of neural circuits and their interconnections. I modified control during waking consciousness, dreams, various altered states, and developed control over autonomic brain functions. I followed a natural progression based on behavioral and cognitive needs. I did not follow a manufactured scheme from an outside authority; in my day, that authority was Freud.

I believe the intervention sequence that transfers control to the individual patient is as important as is the treatment strategy. Information processing problems with random events, in Deisseroth's words, were controlled by the routines I self-administered.

Bradley Schlaggar of Washington University in St. Louis can determine abnormal brain development in a child in six minutes using MRI scanning technology. This ability may permit early treatment intervention before dysfunctional neural networks become fixed, and self-poisoning of brain cells proceeds beyond a critical point that necessitates long-term or life-long drug dependence or surgery.

We have come a long way from my youth, when the brain was thought to be non-plastic, incapable of generating new neurons, and mature by our late teens. We have come a long way from believing that dreams can foretell the future, or put us in contact with God. We have come a long way from Freudian dominated beliefs about the unconscious, and how it controls our behavior. We have come a long way from believing that psychoanalysis can effectively treat schizophrenia, etc. We have only taken a very small step in understanding altered states, other than dreams, in terms of their physiological base. I hope we will correct this state of affairs in the early part of this century.

CONTROL

Pierce Howard says:

The principle of control holds that the health of the human (and animal) organism is a function of the degree to which the individual feels in control of his or her situation… (2006: 36).

What does this mean in terms of the main themes presented in this book? I will look at dreams, self-hypnotized states, visions, spirit possession, rhythmic trances, and integrated consciousness, using control as the major factor in the following analysis. I'm suggesting that learned self-control has been inadequately developed by the mental health and medical communities. Control plays a critical role in how we view altered states, including dreams, and various forms of mental illness. From this perspective, it should be fairly clear that authoritarian therapeutic medicine, especially of the pharmaceutical type that does not permit patient interaction, is part of the problem. But first, let me discuss control as a variable that falls along a continuum.

The psychotic in a state of delirium falls at one extreme, where control is beyond the individual's capabilities. At the other end of the continuum is complete control of one's mind-brain state in deep meditation. Somewhere in the middle of the continuum is waking consciousness, which varies around the center of the continuum depending upon the quality of mental health experienced by one's self. A fragmented Self filled with fears, anxiety, and multiple pressing daily problems moves in the direction of the psychotic. An integrated, centered person moves away from the center toward the peace and contentment experienced during meditation.

Using Hobson's three dimensional AIM cube, loss of control places one's state space in the box where, I'm hypothesizing, either internal or external stimuli, or a combination of the two, can be activating dreams and or psychotic behavior. The dreamer experiencing psychotic bizarreness and thinking is in the cube's state space with the psychotic. What I've added in mundane dream analysis is a larger role for external stimuli in dreams and altered states where external stimuli are transformed in my dreams and altered states metaphorically. For example, a cold patch of skin becomes a 1955 Chevy in my dream, or internally, a full stomach from overeating becomes a potty dream.

A hypnotized subject under the control of another, who does not experience self-control, is in the box too. This person does not have a sense of individual control, and the experience has a mystical quality of something out there that is affecting him or her. That something out there can be viewed as Freud's unconscious.

A person practicing self-hypnosis is in a state comparable to the meditating monk who is in control and sits outside the box, thereby determining what happens in the box, or what happens in state space. Both the monk and the self-hypnotist have a sense of control that enhances their desired experiences.

Visions that occur spontaneously while one is awake fall inside the box and at the high end of waking consciousness, with equal input from internal and external sources of activation, although the type of input can obviously vary in terms of percentages. The individual who does not have self-control experiences the vision as coming from the nether world of God, gods, or spirits. Or there is simply a sense of total loss of control for the mentally ill, which is extremely frightening.

Spirit possession is a felt state in the body proper where one is experiencing high end internal sensory input that is not visual. Internally, the body is signaling its Interpreter that something is felt other than normal tissue; a foreign element has entered the mix. Careful reading of Damasio's interpretation of how feelings enter consciousness is helpful here.

We have high end consciousness, high end tissue activation, and a yet to be determined chemical mode. The average person understands this state. We feel it on a dark street in a strange city, when the feel of the neighborhood becomes creepy.

Personally, the 95 percent of the brain's non-conscious activity is always there. I can begin to access its images and feelings in dreams and other altered states, and suspect that this undercurrent emerges to warn me of danger, or call my attention to something I should be paying attention to. When my brain's wiring is faulty and these non-conscious processes break through, I feel the other, God, or creepy.

Trances induced by rhythm, the drumbeat, dancing or flickering lights, can flood our senses with synchronized brain waves through which we come to totally focus on our body proper. We move away from our visual world into a dreamlike state of just feeling. Activation is physical, with either moving body or synchronized brain waves. Visual input is minimized if our eyes are open and we are dancing, and lacking if the trance deepens to the exclusion of our visual world. Various levels of this state space occupation can occur as we move from closed eye rhythm through drumbeat dancing to chanting. In trance dancing, we tend to be in a comfortable brain-mind state where activation is controlled, input focus is internal, and brain chemical states undetermined.

Control always gives us a sense of well-being in any altered state, and the greater our level of control, the greater our sense of well-being. I better understand my various states of altered realities when I use control as a critical analytical variable. Thus, my state space box has the four variables of Control, Activation, Input, and Mode (CAIM). Introducing the control variable brings my higher cognitive functions into the model, which I find indispensable. I apologize to Hobson for this speculative modification.

Hobson, Delaney, and Brooks and Vogelsong all discuss suggestion and auto-suggestion's use in dreaming. Practiced control over body and brain-mind states with self-hypnosis gives me a level of control that I don't find in the reports of the above mentioned authors. I think there is a critical difference in outcome depending on the degree of control exercised. Natural dreaming produces different images, plots, and insights than dreams consciously guided by the individual.

Self-hypnotism can provide total control over dreams, body, and micro-to-macro brain-mind states. The same is true for other altered states. In like fashion, I think we can learn to control much of what passes as waking psychoses in a manner similar to controlling dreams and other altered states. Time will tell.

When we identify the activation source in our dreams as fixed action patterns (FAP), bodily functions, feelings, or being cognitively centered, we can identify the bizarre in daytime psychoses, and either minimize or neutralize the effects. Let me give an example that created a problem for me when I took my first MMPI as a coerced conscript at the University of Minnesota. This was a time when subject rights were totally ignored, but the consequences of the researcher's secrecy were real.

EMBODIED AND DISEMBODIED GUARDIAN ANGELS

Following Damasio and general findings in neuroscience, I accept that my consciousness depends upon the interactive processes taking place between communicating sets of neurons at both micro and macro levels within my brain. This process necessitates a protagonist, a Self that comes to feel what is taking place between me the organism and objects that are either internal or external to my Self. In other words, consciousness is dependent upon an embodied relationship. Sever the connections between this embodied relationship, and we have a comatose person.

Now let's take this normal process of consciousness, and watch what an active Self or Interpreter does with the physical sensations of ghosts or spirits. My mother practiced smothering as a form of infant behavioral control. I associated her footsteps with smothering attacks, and came to connect steep wooden steps with attack. This was a rather classical form of conditioning. My point being that whenever I began to climb steep wooden steps, in multiple locations with dim lighting, I activated associated memories below my conscious level. The feeling would begin in my lower back and gradually spread up my spine into the back of my head. I experienced what my mother taught me was a ghost trying to become embodied. This example makes it easier for me to understand the popularity of current literature on how to keep the Devil at bay.

The ease with which the ghost was put to rest necessitates that we take into consideration our ability to create meaning. The creation of meaning is a cognitive not a purely physiological process, although the creation of meaning is clearly dependent on support physiology.

The critical role of meaning in consciousness moves to center stage in this consideration of therapeutic effect. It is this level of functioning and its conscious control that determined my present state of mental health. I think we are remiss if we leave consciousness under the control of drugs or simple behavioral conditioning. Simple behavioral conditioning is what we find operative in most group homes and related treatment facilities for children, however. As an experiment of one, I can attest to the importance of cognitive-behavioral therapy coming under the guidance of the affected individual.

My mother believed in ghosts and confirmed their reality. I had an explanation for their presence, I felt their presence, and I was terrified by the prospect of a ghost taking control of my body and brain. The physical sensations in my back, lower brainstem, and limbic system told me that the ghost was attempting to enter my mind. Embodiment of spirits seems pretty straightforward to me. Spirit possession and exorcism seems pretty straightforward to me.

Classification of mental illness for a conditioned response that is culturally defined seems to obscure quick and simple intervention therapies. Re-conceptualizing behaviorally induced pathologies as conditioned patterns running on common neural circuits, which use familiar brain chemicals, seems to be a more logical choice: Thus, Occam's razor is accommodated.

A little understanding of non-conscious processes and behavioral conditioning can handle my type of pathology nicely. Imagine how many individuals passed through long-term, expensive psychoanalysis in the 20th Century with similarly simple, easily treatable conditions as this.

Now let me take my Guardian Angel and explain his presence using the same model. I say model, because I used the above sequencing of logical elements to understand and eliminate my ghost.

It appears that as an infant's brain is growing and developing, it is creating new architecture as well as dispersed neural circuits and networks of different sizes and locations. Brain plasticity allows some modification in these processes permitting maintenance of basic functions. In my case, I can attest to the felt presence of my Guardian Angel just as easily as I vividly recall the ghost trying to enter my body and brain: Real feelings must mean real "some-things" out there. This is perfectly logical to a two year old; or maybe even to a 75 year old. If we feel it, it must be real, or love would not exist.

My Guardian Angel was felt and became my companion and protector. Like most children, this spiritual entity brought me comfort and a sense of well-being. It made my traumatic youth a little easier to navigate, as it is a functional psychological mechanism for children's well-being.

Keep it warm, keep it healthy, and don't scoff. He always seemed to be available when I needed him. My Guardian Angel will still appear if I'm under extreme stress of any kind, and that in and of itself is still a comfort. Does my understanding this basic mind-brain state reduce the Angel's emotional value? It does not. Do I know the difference between fictive angels and real angels? Maybe yes, maybe no, as I still cannot explain his confirmed physical presence in my university classroom.

Failure to understand the functions of non-conscious brain processes related to altered states has created a lot of confusion in the understanding of our own spiritual nature. This failure has created a huge impasse to the development of quick and easy therapeutic interventions for many of us; even though many such quick and easy therapeutic interventions have been practiced by shamans for thousands of years. It is a pleasure to see modern mental health efforts beginning to understand and catch up with some of these millennia old techniques. Now if we could just get the placebo effect that is under shamanic control into our everyday therapeutic strategies, we might make another step out of the cave of pathology. Yes, I'm teasing.

THE YOUNG OFFENDER AND THE UNCONSCIOUS

I am always amazed when educated professionals publish second hand accounts of offenders from either interviews with them, or from notes accumulated during their therapy or attempted therapy. One thing we learn as human service workers with serious offenders is that their perceptions and believed interpretations of their own behavior are frequently highly distorted versions of their real life histories. Such stories and biographies titillate more than elucidate. A film such as *Silence of the Lambs* is just such an extreme example.

How many times I've asked an offender why they did something only to hear: "I don't know." Or I hear an explanation that is totally illogical even when the offender's diagnosis falls within a normal range, and I'm quite sure they are not delusional. Most commonly, offenders who have been traumatized and abused just do not understand their own behavior. In this sense, they are mostly like their non-offending counterparts in the community. Let me discuss this phenomenon in terms of unconscious, non-conscious, learning histories and dreaming.

A young man I had in group therapy ducked or flinched every time I raised my arms to gesture; a good example of an unconscious reflex. I followed his nonverbal responses closely. I asked him why he ducked when I raised my hands to gesture, and he gave me the standard answer: "I don't know." He was not being coy or manipulative, because he really didn't know. If I were dreaming, this would be my bridging element, but I'm not dreaming; he is.

His mother was an alcoholic who brought a continuous string of similar drunks home as live-ins throughout his childhood and adolescent years. He was beaten about the head so frequently that he has severe brain damage. His reaction to my gesturing is logical, if not totally normal, under the circumstances. He had difficulty holding a job and left one entrance level job after another. His only explanation for repeatedly leaving employment was that the boss made him feel uncomfortable.

The court system sees him either as a loser and a person who is not willing to tough out a normal work environment; or that it is a simple condition controlled by pharmaceuticals. For me, however, it was a therapeutic bridging element. For the young man, it was a set of conditioned reflexes beyond his conscious awareness.

This young man was from Minnesota, and in a Minnesota treatment program for offenders with behavior disorders, the type of program that was eliminated by Governor Pawlenty in his "get tough on crime, build more prisons at astronomical costs" strategy. My immigrant grandmother with her eighth grade education would've understood this young man.

He was also a very sensitive young man who never had the benefit of loving, knowledgeable parents. He had to be reconditioned to handle hand gestures, verbal criticism, and physical posturing that sent him into panic and withdrawal. Not quite what the criminal justice system offers, yet such an easy reconditioning process; a learning experience so simple I wondered why he had never received help before.

He did have a lot of experience in treatment programs practicing physical take-downs; you know – the kind that teaches these kids a lesson. The kind of physical take downs practiced on the adolescent psychiatric ward at Mayo Clinic, Rochester, Minnesota, when I was the Area's Community Corrections Administrator.

It's easy to understand how children become conditioned by brutal, thoughtless adults, whether they are sober adults in correctional settings, or home drunks. It's much harder to understand the lack of training for untold numbers of human service workers.

A point for consideration is that as one learns to identify bridging elements in dreams that represent implicit memories, or unconscious forms of learning, this sensitivity tends to transfer to our daytime awareness. On the other hand, if the reader has this level of sensitivity, you will probably find it much easier to interpret your dreams.

I use this example to demonstrate how easily we become addicted to words, and in this process of addiction, come to ignore much of the civilized lessons that we have been taught, which the 95 percent that is generally unconscious is. I firmly believe that we must each free ourselves from word addiction, or false paradigms, if we wish to understand our dreams. In doing so, we will understand ourselves better, and in doing so, we will understand others as we've never understood them before. It is not the club, the gun, or steel bars that bring justice; it is love born of interpersonal and self-sensitivity. It is love that is administered with accountability and supported growth.

Studying Delaney's dream bridging elements can be a tool for self-understanding. Keeping a dream journal can be a method by which one can compare their waking and dreaming states of consciousness. Committing oneself to explore the 95 percent of brain activity that goes on below our average conscious day can be an avenue from which we can come to view and understand our fellow beings. Accepting that we are flesh and blood beings with embodied minds is a first step to know this reality we call Self, and I believe we can know others only as well as we know our Self.

Tears are Forbidden

The crib betrays, denies, enslaves.
Softness turned to stone and dust.
Entombed minds a mass of rust.
Steel encompassed minds the same.
Linger not or die in shame.
Only cry and wring your hands.
Tears are forbidden

CHAPTER 18

CONCLUSIONS: SELF, CONSCIOUSNESS, SOCIETY, AND GOD

INTRODUCTION

We humans not only model our world, but interpret all the input from the brain's various modules in the left side of our brains. Gazzaniga's ground-breaking work on split brains confirms this integrative capacity and what happens when the two halves are separated. He says: "The systems that do generate cognitively based inferences are not present in the disconnected right hemisphere. There seems to be a specific brain system committed to making our species the 'believing' species (1992: 132).

Our brain-minds don't just process information, but interpret all the input from our various senses, giving meaning to our own actions, and the actions taking place in the external world.

We know that mirror neurons operate in our brains, creating duplicate chemical states, and neuronal patterns that ape what is going on in others. This gives us social intelligence, ability to predict the behavior of others, and actually feel what others are feeling. Pattern recognition over time creates beliefs about what others are thinking and doing, and we predict their behavior with considerable consistency: A major physiological contribution to understanding the basis of culture and society.

Belief emerges from biology. Belief and prediction written large as the felt Other, can be, and is, projected onto the world. It becomes spirits, gods, or God. In *Mind of the Mystic,* I said this sense of God is written into our DNA. It is part of the brain's architecture. We know where our sense of God comes from, and it is within each one of us. The atheist says this is just the random acts of evolution at work, but the theist says it is the work of an Intelligent Universe.

My point in *Mystic i*s that we cannot resolve the issue of God through argument and polemics; it must be resolved by understanding our biological nature, evolution, and wherever this understanding takes us. Both the theist and atheist must begin their analysis by acknowledging that the origin of belief resides within each one of us as part of our DNA.

LINDEN

David Linden talks about The Religious Impulse, and says that: "I will try to convince you that our brains have become particularly adapted to creating coherent, gap free stories and that this propensity for narrative creation is part of what predisposes humans to religious thought (2007: 225)."

Our brains attempt to create coherent stories whether we are asleep or awake. Vision is a good example of how a modular brain works; we fill in the missing pieces. Our brains fill in the pieces when our senses configure the external world, and our mirror neurons help us predict the behavior of our fellow human beings and their social actions. More nuts get cracked.

The binding together of disparate percepts and ideas to create coherent narrative that violates everyday waking experience and cognitive categories. This function operates subconsciously. We pay no attention to the man behind the curtain (Ibid: 231).

Most of our brain's action occurs below our conscious awareness; it is the man behind the curtain.

Our dreams give us nonnaturalistic experience. [I]t is not an accident that cross-cultural ritual practice often incorporates dreaming, hallucinogenic drugs, trance, dance, meditation, and music (Ibid: 231).

Faith is required, says Linden, as we try to make sense of our world. I totally agree. Faith is that integrative mechanism that takes jerky modular input and creates a sense of smoothness, a sense of flow.

Faith is the byproduct of our ability to reasonably predict the behavior of our fellow creatures. When we combine this faith mechanism of our brains with the felt Other, we have the basis for a religious experience. Generalized, the felt Other becomes written large, and this felt Other can be consciously used to access brain mechanisms that normally operate only at a non-conscious level. As a conclusion to this three book series I'm stating unequivocally that our faith-based nature must be understood, we must understand the god within, before we can even begin to honestly explore the God without. The rest is just polemics and dogma.

The dreaming brain accesses different modular inputs during our sleep cycles than the waking brain does during daytime consciousness. Hobson makes this distinction with the aminergic and cholinergic systems. The bizarreness in our dreams comes from our waking attempt to create coherent, gap free stories, but the input from our logic centers and stabilizing influences from our waking world are lacking in our dreams. Thus, dream experiences seem to morph, characters can have the feeling of someone we know, but with the features of a child's paint by numbers. These processes no longer seem strange to me when I consider how my brain puts sensory information together.

"When scientists claim to invalidate these core tenets of religious faith without evidence to do so, they do a disservice both to science and religion (Ibid: 232)."

I've stated a similar position in *Mind of the Mystic* when I take Richard Dawkins to task for mixing science and philosophical atheistic speculation to imply that he understands first cause. I agree with Linden that by studying the physiology and neuroscience of the brain-mind, we discover our natural inheritance. It seems logical that knowledge of evolution and how the human brain and its functions are built over the eons naturally brings one to this perspective.

The study of dreaming and consciousness continuously brings me to this realization. When we stay too close to the gene and cell, and forget about evolution as a moving force behind complex organisms with dynamic systems and all our cultural byproducts, we are only half out of the cave. I thoroughly appreciate the hard science in neuroscience, as it has contributed to a great leap forward out of this historical cave of antagonism between religion and science. It has helped us bury multiple false doctrines of mysticism, Freudian god-heads, and the false theology of those who assume primary cause. And no, I don't have the answer to primary cause, but neither does anyone else.

369

Glen A. Just

THE GOD GENE

Most damning for proponents of atheism such as Richard Dawkins are the findings of neuroscience. Logical arguments against God or gods fail because spirits are felt, not simply generated cognitively. Pierce Howard in *The Owner's Manual for the Brain,* quotes Dean Hamer:

This variant of the gene—often called the 'spiritual allele ... controls monoamines, chemicals associated with levels of consciousness and interestingly with drugs that lead to mystical experiences (Howard: 893). This is why feelings of spirituality are a matter of emotions rather than intellect. No book or sermon can teach one person to use a different monoamine transporter or another to ignore the signals emanating from his limbic system. It is our genetic makeup that helps to determine how spiritual we are. We do not know God, 'we feel him' (Ibid: 893).

The absurdity of Dawkins' position is made clear by asking one not to feel what is within them. God or no God arguments must address both cognitive and feeling aspects of our biology, or they are illogical.

V. S. Ramachandran presented evidence to The Society for Neuroscience in 1997 that couples temporal lobe activity with religious experience.

This so-called "God module" is common among people who suffer a unique kind of epilepsy that is typically accompanied by visions of God and feelings of being one with the universe. There is apparently a region in the temporal or parietal area that is associated with both epilepsy and intense religious rapture (Ibid: 892).

I can personally verify these feelings. Biology does not confirm the existence of God or primary cause, but it does lead one to question why the feeling of God is so intimately bound into our DNA.

"Separated identical twins show strong similarities, even in their religious feelings and vocational preferences (Ibid: 40)."

We might propose that the debate between atheists and believers is a debate between separate ends of a genetic continuum. If genes can be selfish, perhaps they can debate too. This is the same level of logic, and same level of metaphor.

In *Autobiography of a Ghost,* I discuss my history, and refer experientially to The God Syndrome as the algorithm in our genes made manifest. As we identify the mechanisms behind these feelings, and their range of expression in Homo sapiens, we have different insights into our brains and minds, and a better understanding of consciousness. Clearly, this tendency to feel the Other on the high end of its genetic complexity can readily lead to speaking-in-tongues or the ability to enter trance states with ease. Nothing strange here.

However, those who would see this genetic makeup or expression as a cognitive weakness should perhaps catch up on a little neuroscience. This still doesn't answer the ultimate question of God or no God, but it does increase our current understanding of the phenomena, and how to use this capacity to realize our human potentials in the future.

The arguments of Dawkins and his fellow travelers are vacuous in their unsubstantiated assumptions. But the major loss, in my personal experience, is the stigma that results when one tries to realize their full, emancipated potential possible through the exploration of altered states. As a child and young man, I knew that I would be negatively labeled if I even tried to discuss these feelings and thoughts. Dawkins' academic stature and piercing rhetoric has heaped stigma on people like me.

I know personally that Ivory Chair smugness is not of any help to children who need to discuss their own feelings, visions, dreams and nightmares. Most non-academic folks are afraid to discuss their internal feelings, visions, and strange experiences due to this stigma.

Academically, it has been professional suicide to engage in these discussions. I have trouble forgiving the Dawkin – types who would prematurely close discussions of our innate nature. I personally think Dawkins and Freud would've made great university colleagues: Dogma, dogma, dogma.

Again, I personally attest to the sense of unity that emerges as one matures and brings various misbehaving neural circuits under control. This sense of unity is addicting, and I have little doubt why monkish people are reluctant to give up their lifestyle. I spent three recent years traveling around China, and noted repeatedly that hundreds of Buddhist shrines and temples were being built, and others re-built across that country. Often the motivating force was a monk who had been imprisoned and brainwashed for years by the Communist Party of Chairman Mao. So much for cognitive re-education, even when it is accompanied by brutal environmental conditions. So much for believing that behavior is driven by genes, so much for ignoring the dynamic systems of the human brain-mind and a few million years of complex evolutionary development. What strange behavior this is for a biologist.

The kind of research referenced above, I believe, supports my contention that altered states of all kinds should be brought into the laboratory for analysis. These are normal states reflecting variations in brain activity, and often brain architecture, or wiring. Understanding who we are as a species, and understanding consciousness in all its forms, offers a way out of human misery imposed by semi-educated societies. The religious should become better acquainted with science, and science should become better acquainted with human nature. Leaving religious speculation at the level of ancient philosophy seems a little out of date in the 21st Century. But, it does sell books.

ANTONIO DAMASIO

Damasio is one of the modern researchers of consciousness who has systematically explored the emergence of mind and self in the course of evolution. As with other scientists working in these interrelated areas, he recognizes that any exploratory framework "… must interconnect behavior, mind, and brain events (2010: 19."

Over deep time, the circuits in our brains are gradually changed by selective pressure in evolutionary biology. Selection pressure means that: "The repertoires of neuronal circuitries initially provided by the genome are changed accordingly (Ibid)."

In other words, who we are as a species, as with all other species, is dependent on selective pressure over time that selects adaptive, survival structures within each species. Even evolutionary sociologists acknowledge this mechanism.

Consciousness, minds, and Self are selectively adaptive. The greater the processing power of the organism's brain, the greater is its survival potential. We understand that belief systems help build social groups into functional wholes, which thereby increases their survival potential. The circuits in our brains, and the DNA in our genome, have been selected to generate belief.

In Damasio's understanding, the structure of our brains and minds has a biological value expressed in survival by natural selection. "Consciousness came into being because of its biological value, as a contributor to more effective value management (Ibid: 28)."

Damasio does not agree with those who see that "… our ability to deliberate consciously is a myth "Ibid: 29."

He goes on to say that: "The time will come when the issue of human responsibility, in general moral terms as well as on matters of justice and its application, will take into account the evolving science of consciousness (Ibid)."

From my point of view, the potential of the moral self represents a step from core consciousness of simpler organisms, to autobiographical consciousness, and then to a more complex Self. The moral Self is also subject to socio-cultural selection.

Immoral societies create the brutes of history that pillage and rape, demean and degrade, or arrogantly profess the superiority of a select few. Utopian ideas from ancient Greeks to modern times have addressed these issues piecemeal. Who is the best king, what is the ideal city, the ideal government, governor or civilization.

In modern times of the last two hundred years, it has been conquest, colonialism, racial, social, and class superiority. And don't forget gender. As modern science helps us look deeply into our own psyches and probe the depth of our consciousness, we feel ashamed of our historical ignorance, and we feel ashamed of all the unnecessary pain.

Creating a culture for the general expression of the moral Self becomes a key issue for the evolutionary-dynamic sociologist. In terms of evolution itself, socio-cultural homeostasis in today's world is the highest level achieved by biological evolution. The Self that is aware that it is aware, that has memory of the past and visions of the future, is a Self with a highly evolved conscious mind that overcomes the blind workings of genes and simple cell combinations from deep time evolution.

However this process of mind, consciousness, and Self is originally set into motion, we know that evolution brings us to a state of being in which the ancient selfish gene becomes expressed in the context of evolution's current status as Self, belief, morality, and society.

In my words: To focus on the living cell and not the complexities of the living, conscious, thinking, feeing mind is a mistake. As we come to know mind we experience awe, respect and gratitude for what has been given us. We now know that mind can change matter. And in this knowledge we can no longer support selfish, deterministic and linear ideas of what and who humankind is."

Referencing myself in *Mind of the Mystic*: I am, therefore I think: *ergo cogito sum,* not *cogito ergo sum.* The cell comes before the brain, the brain before the mind, and the mind emerges to believe it can direct both its own and its body's future. And it can. We are directed by belief every living and conscious moment of our lives. Our biological ability to believe and exercise free will is two sides of the same coin.

It is a near-sighted perspective that emphasizes a limited human capacity for free will. Underlying this view of limited capacity are concepts such as Dawkins' selfish gene, regardless of how clever the word usage is. Damasio sums the counterpoint well for me when he says: "If nature can be regarded as indifferent, careless, and unconscionable, then human consciousness creates the possibility of questioning nature's ways (2010: 287)."

Nature is not indifferent, and you and I are living proof of nature's landscape trajectory. I don't see this as a religious issue; instead, I think it's a cheap shot to make it one.

When Dawkins wrote *The Blind Watchmaker*, he claimed that the mysteries of initial conditions and boundary conditions for evolution were solved. Such grand assumptions, but here I will quote Paul Nunez as his sharp tongue drives the nail of absurdity home well.

Nunez quoting Dawkins: "This book is written in the conviction that our own existence once presented the greatest of all mysteries, but that it is a mystery no longer because it is solved (Nunez: 25)."

Nunez says: "I don't believe Dawkins really meant what he said. Assume that evolution by natural selection is both 100% complete and accurate." Also, "We don't know why our universe is the way it is (Ibid: 25)."

Even a casual reading of general physics brings us this awareness. In my opinion, Dawkins takes his reader on an often stimulating path in the country called evolution. However, he is misleading when he makes such sweeping generalizations unsupported by science. As a scientist. this is an especially egregious misstep, as Dawkins thought process encourages his followers to stop thinking and just accept the dogma he presents. Perhaps Dawkins is a closet A-theist. One can enjoy his approach any week by attending one's favorite revival meeting, especially the born-again variety.

Exploration of consciousness, Self, and mind are just as much a part of studying evolution as exploration of genes, cells, and biological processes. Damasio is not afraid to look at the physiological and evolutionary basis of human groups, society and culture, and in doing so, he returns Homo sapiens to a salient and sentient position in the cosmic order. Am I just being anthropocentric? I don't think so.

THE HUMAN CONDITION

I have proposed in my earlier books that we all seek unity, meaning, love, and security in life. Those of us who have known abuse, mental illness, and fragmented selves come to have intense longings for these life elements. I want to slightly modify Pierce Howard's definition of unity when he says: "The principle of unity holds that the body and the mind are one and the same and that a change in one results in a change in the other (2006: 35)."

I am not arguing against this interpretation, but focus specifically on unity as a brain-mind state. My version: Unity is an individual's ability to control brain-mind states by recognizing that the mind and brain are one, and that any component of the brain, including architecture, chemicals, or memories contribute to the states of consciousness and functioning of the brain-mind as one unit. I am arguing that without both a sense of control and actual control, it is not possible for us to reach the highest levels of unity in our brains and minds. Once we have achieved a unified control level over brain-mind processes, we can move rather seamlessly between various states of consciousness at will. Very few people have made this first step, and it is a giant step toward self-actualization.

ON FREE WILL

We recognize that the majority of our brain's activity occurs below our level of awareness. We also recognize that any conscious action we exhibit enters our consciousness a split second after the non-conscious part of our brain has set responding neural mechanisms in action. Once this fact was established physiologically, we were forced to question the degree to which we humans have free will. If our brains decide to act before we are conscious of willing these actions, then do we really have Free Will? Some say no, as effect cannot follow cause. Of course, this response is simple linear determinism.

Secondly, if the brain operates this way physiologically, how can we talk about deliberately making moral choices? The compartmentalized, modular brain's only answer is that we can't. Hence, Free Will and moral choices are illusions. This interpretation is not only simplistic, but unwarranted. It is simplistic because it fails to take into account how our higher cerebral functions control our goal directed behavior.

Let me make a comparison with how I play ping pong. If I think about hitting the ball when it comes barreling towards me, I will probably miss it or hit it badly, so I let my non-conscious reflexes do the work. By non-conscious, I recognize that I've trained my brain to react without reflection; I have trained my brain to react reflexively, as this automatic response gives me some chance of being fast enough to compete. Does this mean that I have no Free Will when playing ping pong?

Obviously not; my conscious brain and all of its higher cerebral functions decided to master ping pong, and did so to a fair degree. When I play the game, I simply access all the learned, memorized fixed action patterns that I consciously acquired. Free Will playing ping pong operates at this higher level, and it occasionally lets me win a game. It permits me to psych out my opposition, plan strategy, and adjust to the evolving game. Lesson: Free Will cannot be interpreted within the limited context of non-conscious brain functions or architecture. Philosophers ignorant of biology appear to misinterpret this process, and they misinterpret it by applying linear reasoning. They should be in the practice of law.

Hobson says this about moral choices:

Part of the reason for believing that moral choice is deliberate comes from comparative and developmental studies. We may learn by natural and human percept, in an entirely unconscious way, but because we can think abstractly, we can analyze both our personal histories and our social context and so make deliberate choices (1999: 82).

Spot on, I think. But let me discuss Free Will starting at our most basic, reflexive level, and then tie this thought progression to consciousness.

Restak uses an example of Ernst Mach suffering a stroke:

When Mach began to recover he "… noticed that his unsuccessful efforts to move his arm and leg were not accompanied by any sense of fatigue or strain. But with additional improvement, things changed: each small gain, ability to move his limbs, brought with it a sense of heaviness and resistance, as if the arm and leg were being held down by enormous weights. The harder he tried to move, the greater his fatigue and the greater the effort required (1994: 37).

The power of will and the mental energy required by our attempts to gain conscious control over functions lost is something that we all experience in different ways. In Mach's case, Will no longer operates, as the embedded circuit memories have been lost and must be regained with considerable effort. It is noted, however, that global brain states are a bit lazy, and just want to access these formerly embedded memories. They too have become habituated.

I watch a baby try repeatedly to reach an object when his coordination has not yet been hardwired into his brain. He repeats and repeats these attempts until finally he has success, which is usually followed by some expression of satisfaction. He has taught his brain a new action pattern. He now has the power of will. Over time, the child will not think about reaching for an object and carefully needing to concentrate on the object's location in space; his action becomes automatic. According to some philosophical discussions, the child has just lost his free will. "Aha," now I understand linear reasoning.

The frustration of losing this automatic ability for a stroke victim is just as obvious. But it is not like the infant learning movement control for the first time.

Most of my physical movements are automatic and effortless. I don't want to think about them, I don't want to have to reassert myself, I just want to have my body parts move as naturally as they always have. Ernst Mach's and my neural circuits work the same way.

Restak says: "'A power of will' – a strange designation when you think about it. Who is doing the willing? What is the cause of the inner resistance? And the origin of the sense of effort (Ibid: 37)."

Equating bodily movement with Will may seem strange to some readers. The body base for Will is intuitive when one reflects on how we initially acquire a skill such as feeding our self. Body-based Will is a relationship that seems natural to us once we accept that the mind is an emergent of our physical brain.

I use an example of Will in my balancing dream where I again come to have fine motor balance on my bicycle. Once my balance was reestablished, all I had to do was will the bike to turn, and it did. This isn't some form of magic willing at all. I simply conditioned my brain to fine tune my bicycle balance and move the bike without conscious input. Yes, I still had control, but I didn't have to think about it. The real use of magic with Will is taking it out of the body and reifying it.

Obviously, accessing habituated patterns riding a bicycle doesn't mean the bike will go wherever my unconscious mind wills it to go. I observe that when I think about turning or swerving around obstacles the bike seems to sense the mental command and acts on it. Oops, the hand of God at work again. Will! This simple example of how we acquire Will in bike riding puts to rest those who argue against it. Ignorance of our modular brain has created a straw man for classical philosophers. Inability to dream lucidly and interpret one's dreams must add depth to this ignorance. Throw in the mystical interpretations of altered states, and the conundrum becomes gigantic.

I have taught myself other forms of Will as well. I will myself not to fall asleep when driving long distances, and so far, I've been successful. Initially, I used self-hypnosis to establish this brain neural circuit response, but later found that it was an act of Will that operated automatically.

How functional not to think of Will as a mysterious something that is part of the non-physical soul that lives in the nether world. Can I relax Will when driving and become tired? Yes I can. Can I relax Will when riding my bike? Yes I can. But why would or should I? My Free Will likes the effects.

I willed myself to stay alert and digest hundreds of pages of university text for up to eight hours without a break when I was an undergraduate student. This usually occurred between after work hours of 10:00 PM and 6:00 AM. After a couple terms, my total attention while reading was so focused that I had to be physically touched to reenter physical space. For me, this represents the same training procedure as that of the infant or Ernst Mach. Attention is a learned-trained neural circuit patterning; I might say it is behavioral structuring of a mental activity as I thought of it over 50 years ago.

Thinking requires me to mentally manipulate encoding within my neurons, and engaging and disengaging various neural circuits as I consciously problem solve. Embedded action patterns are reflexive and don't require conscious attention. They operate on their own, as is the case with muscles when we walk down the street without thinking about foot movement. And triangulation of complex metaphor, or complex FAPs, by my dreaming brain provides insight and problem resolution.

Will is the subjective experience of this end product called learning, and after enough practice, the neural circuits express themselves seemingly on their own. This is the conditioned, practiced brain at work.

I have a secondary abstraction of this overall process, which is part of the normal way my brain encodes memory. I think of this abstraction as conscious Free Will. I know it subjectively, use it, and experience Free Will as something that is just part of my conditioned conscious Self. I just have it, but it initially took a lot of work to acquire. And as a two year old child, much like Ernst Mach, I had to re-learn my initial ability to walk and talk.

Like any other abstraction, Free Will just seems to exist out there in the space of Descartes' dualistic universe. That is, until I stop and think about my mind being an emergent of my brain, and of my mind being a set of processes that creates a sense of unity called Self. Once this Self is created, it gives me a sense of control, direction and purpose. I know this complex set of processes creates Self and consciousness at the same time that sensory processing is going on. And I also know that this awareness doesn't change my subjective Self as a felt object that exists through time. It all seems pretty straightforward.

My sense of Self is as permanent as the Columbia or Mississippi Rivers, and others can know and experience it too. My Self may not be as long lasting as one of these rivers, but it too has a past full of memories and exists through time.

But if I am to be fair to this analogy, my sense of Self is like the water in the river; one can never put his or her toes into the same river water, only the same river. My Self is the river; any moment of Self is the water. Permanence of Self is the river; impermanence is flowing consciousness: Flow, what a nice expression of being.

Free Will as a classical philosophical construction is a shadow on the cave's wall. Moving out of the cave, Free Will as an embedded process is self-directed control of all those encoded patterns in our neuronal circuitry. As I'm not controlled by motor embedded memories, I'm not controlled in the larger sense of my movement through space and time by these micro-processes either.

Neural circuits representing complex reflexive learned patterns of behavior emerge at a mid-stage of animal evolution. Neural circuits representing higher order cognitive processes come later, interact with and guide this earlier neural sensitive architecture. If this were not the case, I couldn't go out Zen driving.

Complex thought emerges in the course of evolution, and thinking permits mastery over older brain structures. My conscious awareness of awareness, secondary consciousness makes nonsense of the unbounded, disembodied arguments surrounding Free Will, or the opposite interpretation that cell behavior in small circuits guides a thinking being of our complexity.

The fact that I can enter my dreams or other altered states and exert control reflects this same relationship. Higher order cognitive processes come into play when needed: What an efficient development from evolution this is, and it's still not over.

I take this position because I experience control over my mind and body in waking consciousness, and I experience and have often practiced this control during dreaming consciousness. Free Will is a subjective state that exists as clearly as my sense of the color red, and both are derived from the same neural processes embedded in my brain and body proper. But note that at our stage of human evolutionary development, there is also considerable thinking that goes on at a non-conscious level. Thought dreams are my example, and creative works being common to others. But this is an area that I've already touched on, and will not further develop here

Quoting Restak: "Today neurologists speak of a 'duality of motor function' when describing the distinction between willed and involuntary action (Restak: 1994: 39)."

For example, stroke patients cannot smile voluntarily when asked, but smile spontaneously. There are different neural circuits activating these motor responses. What I do with self-hypnosis is to consciously take over automatic, reflexive actions such as heartbeat. Or I reverse the process, and let my automatic motor controls lift my arms or legs without conscious input with self-hypnosis.

Why does this process seem mysterious to so many in the medical community? Why not teach stroke victims how to consciously develop the control mechanisms under discussion? I personally do not know the extent of brain plasticity in this area, but I think it is considerable.

In Zen driving, my automatic control system steers the car by itself while my conscious brain relaxes and enjoys the ride. I suspect that opening these neural circuits to alternative controls changes my dreaming consciousness as well, but the process does let me look at dream activation from a different perspective.

I experience a feedback loop between autonomic functions and consciousness that most people don't seem to experience. I experience a feedback loop between thought processes while dreaming and problem solving that most people don't, although artists, writers, and scientists for generations have discussed their use of these mechanisms.

The concept of will and Free Will has been discussed for generations in classical philosophy and semantics rather than as an operational concept that can be researched. Unfortunately, Free Will has been left in the black box of history along with altered states, as the two have much in common. I think we have researchable psychological methodologies to study these mechanisms at a level that articulates with that of the neuroscientist. And I think my discussion of how balance becomes embedded in memory as we practice bike riding is just such an example.

It would be interesting to see how individuals afflicted with apraxia respond to dream programming of the type I've used to establish a relationship between consciousness and motor memory training. For example, can we reestablish a relationship between conceptual apraxia and its connection between knowledge of tools and tool use? What about dissociating iterative loops in neural circuits that drive the electrical storms of the epileptic? Is this relationship any different than that reported by Ramachandran using mirrors to recondition responses to phantom limbs? It's just fun to speculate.

If I can consciously reach into my autonomic nervous system and control outputs that are normally under automatic control, why can't I reach across other neural circuits and change one-way neuronal activity to two-way activity? I knew from practice that the Skinnerian model of behaviorism was incomplete by 1958 as I experimented on myself and my dreaming brain. But these basic paradigm discussions were not possible at the University of Minnesota at that time, nor were they possible at Mankato State University in the 1970s. Today, we no longer deny the reality of the "mental."

ON CONSCIOUSNESS

To wonder how we can be lucid in dreams or altered states, we have to explain consciousness. As my understanding of consciousness improves, I better understand what is happening in my dreams. Like any area of knowledge, when consciousness is confronted, wrestled with, and triangulated through a few disciplines, it comes to take on new meaning. Let me start with dream consciousness and move up from the simplest subjective states I experience to the most complex.

Fixed action (FAP) dreams create sensitivity to the most basic processes in my non-conscious brain. I experience non-conscious brain processes consolidating and integrating dream content through fictive balance rehearsal. For consciousness to exist, my brain-mind must integrate, or bind together, complex sensory elements. To be useful, these elements must reflect an active organism moving through space. This rehearsal, reenactment, fictive movie production requires visuals as an integral part of real life simulation. And in this dream observation I discover how primary images emerge.

The brain-minds of developing fetuses express REM in the womb. Cats and dogs demonstrate REM as we humans do. However, normal adult humans have a fully formed cerebral cortex. Higher order consciousness must add on manipulation of neural mechanisms that I've discussed as Free Will.

The use of suggestion in dreams alone presupposes similar mechanisms. When I can use Free Will across altered states and in complex actions called Zen Driving, I'm quite sure my dream functions have evolved past that of my neighbor's dog. I've been arguing that one does not understand the functions of dreams until these two stage evolutionary neural processes are taken into consideration. A. Damasio gets much of the credit for this reasoning.

Subjectively, the output of these dream generating processes is used to create plots and stories that my conscious brain gives meaning to. Understanding this single task of my multi-tasking brain in my dreams provides me with a small window into my unconscious; a quick look into the black box that sits on my shoulders.

I experience my dreaming brain as it integrates and consolidates memory that becomes part of that vast 95 percent of my collective unconscious, to us a term from Lakoff and Johnson, that supports everyday activity from bicycle riding to reaching for my coffee cup. And I recognize that whatever I can't explain in my dreams appears to be associated with maintenance of non-conscious processes supporting me as an organism.

Second order constructs derived from these basic neural patterns become color, and other representational units of external and internal objects in my environment and brain. I can think of these second order constructs as qualia that include the first derived steps of my most basic memory processes, but I know that value and emotional content is added into, and bound together with, these embedded neural circuits and networks as part of the overall emergence of my core consciousness and higher order consciousness. I naturally experience this subjective hierarchy of consciousness as basic images become qualia such as color or balance, and subsequently experience metaphorical abstraction, as balance is abstractly integrated with other metaphor to become bike balancing, checkbook balancing, and so on.

My passion for a new love is the integration of biological and social longing, which is subjectively real and felt. Free Will in my new relationship of love is an abstraction of circuit integration at ever increasing levels of complexity. But all of this detail is unimportant to my waking consciousness, and mostly goes on below my conscious level of awareness. Consciously, I'm just enamored, and my landscape trajectory is one of consummation.

Third order constructs are at the level of my being aware that I am aware. Second order constructs are combined the way we connect ever larger groupings of neural circuits from species, to family, to genera, to order. This process of hierarchical associational order eventually becomes complex thought. I string constructs derived from various patterns of neuronal circuit combinations into frames of time, movement, relationship to total environment, and relationship of these constructs to self.

I know that this is the process that creates self-awareness and awareness of awareness; the process that creates the sense of my being me. I don't understand all the fine details, nor do I understand all the micro physiology involved, but I can mentally, subjectively, move across this landscape of neuronal elements to understand why I behave and dream the way I do. This is a huge advance over my early school years of Descartes, spirit, soul, Freud, and Skinnerian Behaviorism. Having these additional insights adds more magic to passion rather than less.

Physical passion is one form of rapture, while cognitive-feeling passion driven by understanding adds an additional dimension of rapture on rapture, or psychology added to physiology.

Knowledge is not just power; it is enhanced feeling. Cognitive thoughts as intense as orgasm, when combined with brute nature's physiological responses, explode like Fourth-of-July fireworks in one's journey to the beginning of time.

For a final comparison, let me ask the reader: "When was the last time you had an orgasm that lasted three or four days? Now you subjectively understand my Genesis Journey.

ON SELF

Dream consciousness provides a dream Self; in fact, it provides many selves, as there are many conceptions of Self to be had. Some are bizarre, and capable of actions I would never consider in waking consciousness, like sex with strange, beautiful women, flying as a superhero, or having the strength of a dozen men.

My dream Self is less confined than my waking Self, but my dream Self is created moment-to-moment, as is my waking Self. Knowing this fact permits me to understand how my dreaming Self can morph so quickly, how time can change abruptly, and it also permits me to acknowledge that access to memory is a "now" state.

The memory used by Self is a now state as my dreaming brain pulls stored elements from throughout its library and lets me use them in the construction of dream stories and all other dream elements. This process permits me to mix and match faces and dream characters, as well as permitting me to mix and match any of the physical features of people that I have stored away in memory. Lucid dreaming is access to such wonderful creativity: Never ending fun.

I know that my brain has a concept of me as mind and body. I am two entities or things in one. The terms Subject and Self, or I and Me, that were used earlier represent what I understood from Symbolic Interactionism over forty years ago. The "I" is my nonmaterial Self, and the "Me" is my body Self. There are always two entities in one that I subjectively experience, and I can make them both active agents when I self-talk.

Historical thinkers like Descartes had this awareness and took it to be a logical non-material essence. It is the dual level of Damasio's consciousness, not the dual separation of mind and body by Descartes, which prevails.

In my dreams, as in waking consciousness, I am permitted dialogue between the I and the Me, or Subject and Self. They can interact, but they always occur together. In my childhood days, I literally thought my body flew with me to Heaven or outer space. As I matured, I knew this wasn't the case, but no matter, the feeling is the same. Understanding this relationship in dreams, and as it exists for our waking brain-minds, removed the mystic in mysticism, but it didn't destroy the wonder. In fact, being able to enter, control and direct altered states both increased wonder and understanding.

It is easy for the Subject-Self to talk to the Self-Self (self-talk). We just say that we talk to ourselves, and we do. We do it in dreams and experience the same phenomena in altered states of consciousness. However, we often attribute this other voice to spirits, gods, God, or demons. Craziness is the flip side of normal consciousness, so to speak. And in that my dreaming brain is pretty much disconnected to my motor commands in REM, I don't normally feel fictive dream pain. Things happen I observe, and from these scenarios, I feel all kinds of emotions, especially fear, anxiety, and related negative feelings that these emotions generate.

We come to understand how there can be more than one Self in our dreams. We come to understand why people in some African cultures have more than one soul. How we can even look different and still feel that we are the same I and Me?

I think if you are older, you have the same experience I do when I look in the mirror. The guy looking back at me is older than my subjective Self. My Self as Subject that I carry around moment-to-moment is a composite of all my memories; it must be younger than the image in the mirror. This is one time that I find statistical averaging of self pleasant. But note that we can and do use statistical averaging with our dream characters too, and in this dream process, we often mix and match more randomly.

ON SOCIETY

In the course of our species evolution, we were born into families, and learned to live in multiple family units called clans. Then came tribes, multiple tribal units called nations or states, and so on.

Society in its hundreds of thousands of years has come to be embedded in our brains. Our brains are derived in an evolutionary sense as much from our social as our environmental world. Our increasingly complex social order has given us language, security, and an evolving identity. But the building blocks of all this social order reside in the architecture of our brain. We cannot understand who we are without understanding this architecture and its related functions.

Neuroscience tells us who we are in a manner never possible with classical philosophy or religion. And we become sensitive to the fact that evolution of humankind is not done.

I know that mirror neurons permit me to feel the way you do; to laugh and cry when you do, and know that my brain is duplicating the neuronal expressions taking place in your brain. This is one element in our biological substrate that makes social life possible. I know that by being able to be aware that I am aware, to possess this second order level of consciousness, permits me to communicate with your soul through empathy and understanding. Understanding that is not just thought, but understanding that is based on our brain-mind, brain-body relationship from which consciousness and self are derived. This takes us well beyond the selfish gene.

I know historically that our ancestors have struggled to understand these wonderful achievements of evolution. How do we know what is real? Is life an illusion? Who is God, and all the other questions that are so naturally generated by the emergence of a subjective reality in our brain-minds that we use to experience, as best we subjectively can, the real world out there.

We struggle less now than we did even a hundred years ago to explain all these phenomena. A child in the fifth or sixth grade can know more than the greatest intellects of ancient philosophy; that is, unless he or she lives in a TV centered world.

I know that society, like language, is not just a relative construction of culture. Society, like perception, is built around the architectural parameters established by brains and their emergent minds through millions of years. It's a wonderful sense of belonging to all life that this subjective feeling brings. I have it, the dog doesn't.

My social order is built upon architectural capacity that no other Earth-bound animal possesses, although the dolphin may come close. This capacity has often made my species and me arrogant, and arrogance has been one of the greatest roadblocks to new knowledge. The pompous intellects of history stand like a stone wall against the light of reason. Fortunately, we now have lasers.

ON GOD

Okay, here I go again. The God gene is probably at work. I know that I'm one of those people who feel the Other as a subjective reality. Some of us do and some of us don't.

My near-death experience when I was about two years old opened up a few neural circuits to altered states. I'm happy for this history, even though it made life difficult for me as a child. This capacity has given me an understanding of our DNA-based religious nature. It has improved my sensitivity to the plight of fellow human beings who have not been as fortunate as I have been. It has permitted me flights of fancy that few know or understand. I am thankful to be the person I am. I'm thankful for life.

Brain-mind states that let us experience nothingness, permit us to journey to the beginning of time, bring us to shape shift when awake or dreaming; all these capacities enlarge our sense of unity and belonging. Each altered state I've mastered reaffirms my identity by establishing one more boundary that I control.

But unity and belonging to what? The answer can be the Ultimate Knower, or it can be the natural forces of evolution. In either case, we are the knower, the doer, and an entity that moves through our own creation called time. Self is created for us by evolution, and it becomes our responsibility to direct human outcomes morally and with compassion. No concept of the Blind Watchmaker dictates this view. It is an understanding to be embraced.

Mind

And mind said, let there be matter
And matter became what mind said.

And mind said, let there be evolution,
And evolution became what mind said.

And philosophy said, what is mind,
And mind said, I am who I am.

And philosophy said, mind is not corporeal
And body said, I am what I am.

And man pondered, and man said,
How can the immaterial be body?

And Damasio said, mind feels body,
And Dawkins said, there is no such thing

CHAPTER 19

THINKING ABOUT HYPOTHESES

INTRODUCTION: FINDING MY WAY

V. S. Ramachandran has consistently cut his own path through the wilderness of neuroscience by re-conceptualizing traditional research approaches to the brain and consciousness. His work with phantom limbs is classic with the simple use of mirrors permitting patient's brain to reconfigure their relationship to their missing limb. One can imagine the uselessness of traditional psychoanalytic methods to treat this type of neuronal disorder. I created dream programming for myself over fifty years ago as a similar, simple technique to control nightmares, and then heuristically elaborated my simple paradigm to take control of visions, trances, and other altered states. Generalizing control to altered states provided the insights that I've shared in this book and lend support for the following hypotheses.

My experience with complex, dynamic open systems began in the early 1970s, when I developed my first statistical models to predict criminal behavior. In open systems analysis, we recognize that ongoing input from outside ourselves continuously influences our behavior, and that the total prior shaping of our values, ideas, and beliefs that exist internally at any particular moment in time, our total self of experience, interacts continuously with our external environment. How we think and act changes over time, nevertheless, our ability to maintain predictable relationships within social groups has stable elements that can be found through various statistical methods. Computer programs have taken the labor out of identifying these stable factors. What has not been easy is to get politicians to think dynamically, and they control the purse strings for publicly supported research and treatment programming.

Human behavior is complex, much like predicting the weather, or trying to model what is happening between the sun's core and its atmosphere. These seemingly chaotic and complex relationships are at the core of dynamic processes. In this world of complexity, we deal with probability and not with classical cause and effect, where strict determinism is assumed. And determinism is too often understood as being linear, when it is dynamic and driven by circular feedback loops. What this means in practical everyday terms is that different multiple elements in interaction can create similar effects; that little changes at an earlier point in time can create big changes later on. I've partially addressed this dynamism as similar relationships exist with epileptics, immediate elimination of nightmares through insight and micro to global physiological effects across the brain-mind.

In the first causal scenario, numerous factors can generate hallucinations; and, in the second case, balancing one's brain chemistry can stop neuronal deterioration or destruction and influence multiple behavioral indicators. Let me look at anxiety from a dynamic perspective.

First, I assume that balance and integration of brain-mind activity are critical elements of any dynamic brain-mind model. Complex systems out of balance can be kept out of balance with continuing inputs that influence only a small part of the system. For example, once learned, self-activating fixed action patterns that create anxiety can keep an individual in a state of multiple dysfunctions, unable to work, enjoy life, or even be active socially. Over time, this state can become increasingly debilitating as one's social network collapses, jobs become problematic or disappear, and neuronal mass decreases. We call this a negative, self-perpetuating cycle. A chemical agent may stabilize the individual, or in opposition to desired effects, multiple drugs used experimentally that are derived from the medical or street communities may exacerbate one's anxiety. A downward spiral is not infrequent.

Multiple elements can combine in many different ways to create and maintain a chronic state of anxiety. Interventions too may be of many different kinds and still be effective. When we are dealing with the human brain and mind, the dynamic elements and their related probable outcomes become extremely complex. I can readily see in my own life history how little changes have had major long-term consequences. My decision to control my nightmares through dream programming is an example.

Paul Nunez is Emeritus Professor of Biomedical Engineering at Tulane University in New Orleans, and has this to say in his recent book *Brain, Mind, and the Structure of Reality*.

A central question about any complex dynamic system is this: Is it composed of multiple subsystems with minimal communication, dominated by functional isolation? Or, is it more globally coherent, with all parts acting in almost the same manner. At various times, brains seem to operate over the entire range of this local-global range of dynamic brain states (2010: 130)."

Nunez's specialty is using EEG technology to explore brain structure and function. He offers us a different window into the brain and consciousness, one that permits global pattern analysis and is thus a major tool to analyze the physiology of consciousness. But note the potential problem with pharmaceutical interventions. Even targeted drugs can perpetuate global imbalance.

A critical observation that must be taken into consideration as we learn self-control and gain the ability to move consciously from one altered state to another addresses Nunez's central question. We can learn to control our brain's subsystems, and in my opinion, this control makes all the difference.

Self-control of meta-consciousness directly addresses the integration and control of dynamic subsystems. I don't need to know that I'm impacting my amygdale, hippocampus, or angular gyrus from a neurological point of view; I just know that I'm changing my brain's functioning to achieve certain desired phenomenological and behavioral results. Even my fragmented brain of 1957 understood that what was important was an outcome that created balance and unity through self-control. After all, the black box lived. One doesn't need to understand how aspirin works for it to be effective.

Over the past forty years of work, Nunez says this about consciousness: "A healthy consciousness is associated with a proper balance between local, regional, and global mechanisms (Ibid: 130)."

My autobiography documents how I moved through various states of pathology, from suicidal thoughts, obsessive-compulsive behavior, voices, and other imbalances, to an integrated and balanced me. As I matured from age two, when these patterns started, into my adult years, and with the addition of various educational inputs, I increasingly saw balance and integration as being fundamental aspects of my evolving mental health.

Complex system manipulation has been a formal part of my perspective on mental health for the past 40 years. It is difficult to manipulate complex brain-mind systems with today's pharmaceuticals. Global system effects are too frequently uncontrolled as pharmaceuticals balance one subsystem and unbalance another.

I'm aware of the subjective changes that take place in my brain-mind between the aminergic and cholinergic systems when fully awake and when I'm dreaming. I experienced and controlled these effects before I knew what aminergic or cholinergic meant. But I'm also aware of variations in different altered states as emergent patterns and feelings are forthcoming in visions, speaking-in-tongues, possessing the spirit of an animal, and other shamanic manipulations associated with altered states. The degree of global balance and integration is central to which brain-mind state is being expressed at any given moment.

Visualizing my brain-mind as modular subsystems in dynamic interaction helps me keep this focus as I move from one altered state to another. I argue consistently that altered states should not be simply viewed as being pathological when controlled; conversely, they are a lot of fun and can be health promoting. Controlling nightmares, hallucinations and symptoms of PTS must be considered as health promoting. This is true for conscious visions during waking hours or guided dreams in REM.

In similar fashion, when we continued for thousands of years to see debilitating altered states as the work of evil spirits, we left remediation in the hands of shamans and priests.

Mystery of the mystic variety is not acceptable if we choose to understand brain-mind states from a scientific point of view. Thought experiments and self-experimentation using hypnosis to access non-conscious brain mechanisms are part of my life history. Before I came to consider the mechanisms behind individual cell consciousness in physiology, I had to deal with debilitating mental health issues and all the related dysfunctional behavior. My initial approach to brain-mind functions was global and top down. Thus, I find Nunez both supportive and comforting.

However, when I began to develop controls for autonomic functions such as pain, I had to consider what was happening in subsystems of my brain. When I began to control dreams, visions, speaking-in-tongues, and other altered states of reality, I had to consider subsystems within this dynamic complex. Dynamic Integrated Systems controlled experientially is simply an integrated, balanced consciousness, to paraphrase Nunez.

Dynamic system analysis came together for me in the 1970s, but models that were based on probability didn't sell well to social workers or psychiatrists. Chaos of altered states was just chaos, and the idea that integrated brain-mind patterns could be self-organizing through self-directed, top-down mind control was considered to be too far out.

Psychiatry has assumed pathology when one enters altered states of consciousness, and psychoanalysts have previously attempted to use their interpretation of this dysfunctional assumption to treat unusual neuronal configurations. Failure to understand altered states has focused primary treatment efforts on pharmaceuticals in attempts to achieve balance and integration. However, drugs can impact both global and subsystem mechanisms in our brain-minds. It is difficult to tease out select phenomenological or behavioral effects with drugs.

Fortunately, in areas such as the treatment of depression, cognitive-behavioral strategies, combined with drug treatment, are producing well researched outcomes. Cognitive-behavioral treatment was not only possible, but effective in the 1950s, as my autobiography indicates.

Earlier diagnosis and intervention with depressive and anxious states can probably eliminate most pharmaceuticals if my long-term case study generalizes, especially with early intervention.

Psychologists and psychotherapists are interested in changing their client's behavior and comfort levels, and, must therefore look across various brain states to achieve these purposes. I have been discussing some of the similarities and differences in altered states from dreaming to spirit possession and arguing that our brain-minds can mix and match neural patterns at will to achieve these states. In this mix and match process, we should view ASC as just another expression of neuronal activity that can come under individual control. In support of this general assumption are similarities between daydreams and night dreams, or as I think I've demonstrated with my own dreams, how closely day consciousness is integrated with sleeping consciousness.

I also think the research community makes a major mistake trying to bring about brain-mind end states in one leap, especially with drugs. My experience says that a number of intermediate steps must be employed. First, we need to disconnect some neural circuits and create other patterns that reconfigure or strengthen alternative circuits.

Hobson says: "In dreaming, the world that we are aware of is entirely fabricated, but we do not know it

(2001: 111)."

As a former teacher and student of psychology, dynamic sociology, anthropology, and treatment modalities, I was forced to consider the endless ways in which we construct reality. The study of world cultures historically added tremendous diversity to the extremes of human reality construction. Knowledge of human cultural plasticity enhanced my own sense of normality by removing the narrow interpretations inherited from family and American culture in the 20th Century.

As my university education unfolded, out-of-body experiences, visions, and trances were not just a crazy child's twisted view of life; they became alternate states that a normal brain could entertain, direct, and control. By mixing and matching brain states, I could enter altered states that we call visions, speaking-in-tongues, spirit possession, or dreams throughout the day or night. By the 1960s, it didn't matter that the medical community I knew thought such people were crazy, occult or bizarre, for I knew from world studies how narrowly these minds and models actually were. I enjoyed the world of Zen driving, for example, while those who wanted to explore outside the standard model of consciousness studied Buddhist meditation. To me, my mind was that hungry child looking in a bakery window wanting one of everything.

PHENOMENOLOGICAL SUBTRACTION AND ADDITION

Phenomenological subtraction is a type of experiment repeatedly conceptualized by Ramachandran and others where the brain and consciousness is studied after genetics, disease, or accident destroys or eliminates some working center or set of brain circuits. In my case, I reversed the process with what I call phenomenological addition. I added controlled states to my consciousness, such as speaking-in-tongues or flying out-of-body while awake or sleeping, and then confronted the questions of how, what, and why. I played with out-of-body projections, speaking-in-tongues, cosmic trips to the beginning of time, and whatever altered state interested me at the time. It was both fun and insightful.

I slowly learned that each conquest of altered states permitted advance to the next one. My self-control came in incremental steps. I did not conceive of the end state when I started my historical quest, as dynamic inquiry doesn't currently permit end state knowledge. Linear reasoning with assumed end state findings unduly restricts new discovery. In similar fashion, about one-third of this book has been suggested by non-conscious processes expressed in my dreams.

I have long separated myself from Freudians (1958), and for at least forty years, stopped believing that altered states were other than normal brain-mind expressions of scrambled neural networks. I found anthropological studies of the shaman and shamanism generally devoid of neuroscience research, and therefore greatly lacking. The value of shamanistic practices is their deep time discovery of effective mechanisms to change human relationships with unknowns, whether those unknowns are outside or inside our brain-minds.

Westerners studying altered states of the shaman and shamanism seemed to gain most attention by emphasizing the occult. This I thought was a great loss to interdisciplinary science, as well as a denigration of Native People's capacities. It was a loss that moved shamanic studies a giant step closer to New Age enthusiasts in the muddle of California occultism, and chemically dazzled minds inhabiting parlors of mysticism and illegal drugs.

A. Damasio helped me understand consciousness from a physiological perspective, and Hobson preformed a similar enlightenment with his careful dream research. Ramachandran's unique ways of envisioning research was the single most influential source that removed my sense of being different. Einstein's approach to thought experiments sustained me since my teen years, but Ramachandran made subjective self experiments feel okay. He made them a legitimate part of scientific exploration. Many researchers whom I've referenced have added depth and insight into my own musings, but none more profoundly than these four.

Understanding what chemicals control which brain states has further helped me put mysticism to rest, clarify our religious nature as a species, and understand altered states of consciousness. Altered states seem so natural to me that I have often thought that anyone can develop these abilities. I now think that lucid dreaming is fairly easy to acquire, but I think that brain re-wiring that is as extensive as mine may be required to move across the human rainbow of consciousness. Few people seem capable of controlling as many altered states as I have throughout my life. This understanding emboldened me to put my autobiography, and exploration of mysticism and dreams on paper.

Controlling and experimenting with altered states over 50 years adds interpretive depth to comparisons between these states, as does longitudinal pattern analysis to my case study. My capabilities with altered states, not just lucid dream control, generally include:

1. Being consciously aware while immersed in dreams and other altered states that I am their creator and director. I can enter the body and persona of the bear and become the bear, but still remain the observer.

2. As an extension to (1), by remaining lucid in dreams or other altered states I can change any part of the dream, vision or trance as the scenario unfolds. For example, when I'm in an altered state and I don't like how it's unfolding I just change the characters or outcome along the way. However, I don't make these changes when I'm the shamanic bear or enjoying being the alter ego with the Ghost.

3. I can program a vision, as I have often done with dreams, but I cannot consciously redirect speaking-in-tongues once the process begins. The vocalizations are similar to action patterns embedded in memory that are automatically expressed. Vocalizations occur spontaneously without any conscious effort once the process is set in motion; the pattern is self-reinforcing. The sound system is on but the conscious control switch is off. I can however exercise meta-consciousness and terminate the session when I desire. "Happy" neuro-modulators must be released when one is speaking in tongues. The sense of euphoria builds to the point of rapture; hence, one generally leaves this dramatic level when consciousness is forced. It is much like having a nightmare where dramatic intensity reaches a point that forces wakefulness.

4. Trance states induced by rhythmic dancing, which have included settings at Native American PowWows, are entered progressively. I enjoy the rhythm as I enter the trance state, but conscious ability to observe action around me diminishes as it does when I enter sleep. I'm in the trance and feel its all-consuming power. Primary consciousness is mostly lost and secondary consciousness stays awake at a muted level. The effect is similar to that of moving from sleep to lucid dreaming. Rhythmic trance creates an internal landscape that becomes total. The drum beat goes on, the body moves on its own, and rhythm blocks out all other cognitive processes that one is usually aware of. This is probably why autistics enjoy rhythmic activity at a number of different levels. In native cultures, rhythmic dancing takes the group to whatever expectation they had when the dance began.

5. I continue to be the observer as well as the doer when I project myself into the body of another animal, and at the same time, feel all the emotional intensity demanded of the setting. It is similar to Huxley watching his Self grow from infancy to adulthood. Projecting into the body of another, human or animal, builds my capacity for empathy to an extent that I cannot watch horror movies without considerable pain. I refuse to kill animals for sport for the same reason.

My empathic capacity extends itself, and I actually become the other being. Being two people, or a person and an animal, in an altered state probably employs a broad network of mirror neurons that in their normal, expressive form permit me to feel what you feel, and share your intentions. They permit me to use these same processes to interrogate myself, and allow me to re-create feeling and thought in any other human or animal I choose. Mystics are not mystical.

I have attempted to compare altered states and related brain functions as I've moved from one state to another. In 1958 when I first took control of my dreams, I just assumed that behavior modification created isomorphic changes in the black box we called our brain. I'm a flexible thinker with historical ability to move from one state to another rapidly. This ability was considered to be pathological by the medical community when I was an undergraduate, but I found in graduate school that it offered a strong competitive advantage.

As I've aged, I've come to believe that others miss a lot when they fail to access the full potential of their plastic brains. It took me years to come to this understanding. Paradigm shifts for many of us often just creep up until we can no longer ignore them.

I now find these fifty years of self-experiments and musings very compatible with contemporary neuroscience research. Critical test: Does the reader?

HOBSON'S ACTIVATION-SYNTHESIS HYPOTHESIS

I've borrowed many of Hobson's ideas and compared them with my own dream history. I've not formally expressed these derivatives as a typology, but the option exists. The main differences I report in my dreams, compared to Hobson, are lucid dreams that cover almost 75 years, active dream control and long-term patterns covering 50 years, long-term dream differences with ageing, and my inclusion of other altered states.

Hobson asks what sleep is all about and answers thus:

A behavior as complex as sleep—with all its highly differentiated component non-REM and REM phases—is unlikely to be dedicated to any one particular function, yet folk wisdom has tended to collaborate with scientific reductionism in supposing that one, and only one, function is served by sleep (1988: 285).

In agreement with Hobson, I refer to the functions of dreaming as multi-tasking. The following hypotheses make this assumption: the brain is a complex, dynamic, and integrated system dedicated to multiple functions in either sleep or waking states.

Continuing with Hobson: "Yet, in spite of years of research, science has not definitely established even one function for sleep (Ibid: 286)."

A few years later in *13 Dreams Freud Never Had* (2005), Hobson embraces an expanded view of dream functions. My interpretations that resonate with those set forth in *13 Dreams* follow:

a) Memory is consolidated and integrated;

b) Emotional states are monitored and our consciousness is flagged when these states deviate uncomfortably from our baseline;

c) Cognitive manipulation related to problem solving continues in our sleep; and

d) Body state awareness for extreme conditions is maintained. These are all documented functional manifestations of my dreams.

To have validity, hypotheses must be tested at the same conceptual level as proposed; physiological hypotheses are not tested at a psychological level of analysis.

386

Hobson's example:

[Freudian] functional theory of dreams as the 'guardian of sleep are accepting a physiological answer to a psychological question. Freud's idea that dreaming serves to discharge instinctual energy is similarly problematic. A physiological process might discharge instinctual energy but a psychological process cannot. Freudian theory shifts semantic level. Dreaming is a psychological state, while sleep is a behavioral state. Both are reflections of physiology (Ibid: 286).

Assuming the brain is a dynamic integrated system, cellular maintenance and regenerative processes must be a major activator of visuo-motor expression in dreams. Forms of visuo-motor expression in dreams can appear to be bizarre to our waking consciousness, as they are expressions, not determinants, of the process.

And as Hobson says:

The rest function may well be further elaborated in higher animals with complex brains so as specifically to restore efficiency to such crucial wake-state functions as attention and memory. According to this view, the capacity to concentrate upon and to retain new information would be enhanced by sleep (Ibid: 287).

Sleep deprivation if prolonged can lead to death, thus, there is little question that it's essential. In rats, metabolism keeps ramping up during sleep deprivation until the animal literally dies from over exertion. The rat can't reflect on its internal brain activity, but we can as more highly evolved mammals. Cellular circuit maintenance and the cycles of sleep appear to be closely aligned, as I've discussed fixed action patterns being consolidated in my dreams.

In discussing "Sleep as Rest for the Neurons" Hobson continues:

When microelectrodes were inserted into the cerebral cortex, these investigators, and later Hubel (1959) and Evarts (1960), observed that as many neurons turned on as turned off during sleep, and that almost all of the cells in the brain were spectacularly active during REM sleep. Clearly a general theory of neural rest during sleep can be only partially correct and is particularly controverted (Ibid: 289).

In support of cells resting part of the time in our sleep is the fact that we die if we are too sleep deprived.

Physiologically, cells increase or maintain mass and consolidate memory during sleep. Expanded neuronal mass is evident in studies of brain plasticity and flexibility, which are key aspects of ongoing brain development and change.

One important feature of REM-sleep neuronal activation is its redundancy, its capability of affecting almost every neuron in the brain in a stereotyped way (Ibid: 291).

Everything I experience when dreaming says that "... REM sleep is an active brain-mind maintenance program (Ibid)."

My thought and thinking dreams support a broad exchange of information across my brain's global neural network. I don't know all the intermediate steps, but I do experience the results.

REM sleep is dominant during fetal development, with estimates of upwards to 24 hours of REM occurring around 30 weeks of gestation.

This has led Howard Roffwarg and his colleagues to suggest that REM sleep plays an active role in the structural development of the brain (1966) (Ibid: 292).

We are born with reflexes of sucking and grasping. Genetically driven reflexes expressed at birth come from somewhere. With so many learned motor behaviors and necessary sensory integrations developed after birth, it is highly unlikely that evolution would fail to use night down-time efficiently.

[T]he fixed-action patterns that constitute the sexual act itself have a life of their own (Ibid: 295).

This fixed action pattern (FAP) may be like climbing on a bicycle, but balance can be improved with practice. If you've ever been out of practice, you understand.

Information-Processing Theories, Hobson says, may mean that old information is being compared with new experiences during sleep. And from scratch, "… programming may be developed during the REM stage of sleep (Ibid: 296)."

Insight from neuronal cross-talk is a frequent dream product when my dreams tell me to review CDZs or CDRs; tell me to include new material in chapters for this book or revise others, etc.

Under "Specific Functional Theories" and their creative capability:

It is obvious that our dreams are not simply the reliving of previous experience. On the contrary, we are often actually fabricating wholly novel ones (Ibid).

I interpret this functional sequence of dream expression with this little twist. In my reported nightmares, one central element is always the key to interpretation, and this element represents a physical act performed on my body that had profound emotional impact. My whole nightmare has been built around this element. Once I understand how my dreaming brain uses this element, I can interpret the non-conscious part of the dream to my conscious brain's satisfaction. What I assume is that physiologically, auto-reactive neural circuits are closed through this interpretive act.

This embedded, persistent memory is flagging my waking consciousness, if I will only listen and learn my own dream language. Recall that the human brain is not dependent on our culturally specific primary language. It speaks universally and with metaphor. Language is a derivative; metaphor is built from primary images generated in the body.

To me, this kind of emotional trigger is self-preserving. As an infant, it probably saved my life as I learned to cup my hand over my mouth as my mother approached my crib; not knowing if she would nurse or attempt to smother me. In similar fashion, I never had to be told to run from the Washington mountain lion when I was five years old, for fear activated a complex set of muscle reflexes, and I fled. Why do we need to make dream stories more complex than their simplest explanations? Occam's razor works most of the time. I appreciate Hobson's unified brain-mind view as it resonates with what and how my dreams speak to me.

In summary, I have often used typologies in my professional life to organize complex sets of information. Empirical support for a dreaming brain that operates as a dynamic integrated system comes from Hobson, especially his Activation-Synthesis Model. My dream pattern analysis and long-term self-experiments have comparative value primarily within the research context provided by neuroscience and physiology. Heuristic value exists in my observations to the degree that speculation can be turned into testable hypotheses.

PHYSIOLOGICAL HYPOTHESES

"Brain activation in sleep involves the higher visual centers, a loss of working memory, hyper-associative synthesis (bizarreness) primary activation of the limbic system, organic (physical) amnesia, (forgetting) meaning is transparent or salient, and interpretation is not needed (Hobson: 2002: 18)."

Muscle and balancing dreams that I've discussed in previous chapters involve my higher visual centers and don't need working memory, as the dream is supporting my brain's muscle-balance maintenance, demonstrates activation of the limbic system, and produces bizarre imagery.

Age pattern analysis tells me that physiological functions are especially salient in our younger years; dominating the infant and toddler's life. As I've noted, cognitive dreams become more salient with our older years, and this includes integrative and reflective thoughts. In similar fashion as we grow older, negative feelings diminish as youthful fears and anxiety are replaced by a more tranquil older self. Hopefully!

I used examples of regaining bicycle balance, improving fine motor glass cutting skills, and a fixed action pattern for mowing lawns, and all of these associated behaviors had not been used for decades. These are all skills that are part of my unique history, and reflect the type of homes I've lived in, my hobbies, and how I exercise to remain physically fit.

Reengaging this memory repertoire created a pattern of dream imagery that is unique to me, but reflects individual skills common to most people. Existing dream dictionaries like Sylvia Browne's are totally inadequate to explain imagery from these three dream examples. But most damning is the distortion such dictionaries introduce that lead us away from analyzing real dream functions. However, if occult interpretation of dreams is accepted, this distortion is necessary, or one will stop believing in ancient, occult mental gymnastics.

Recent research that sheds some light on dreaming effects related to memory consolidation and memory forgetting comes from the Stanford University team of Lior Appelbaum and Philippe Mourrain, and their study of zebra fish. Zebra fish larvae are transparent, and neuronal activity can be studied while they are sleeping (Arnold: 26).

Their research lends support for both theories that hypothesize that we can both dream to forget, and dream to consolidate memories. Dreams that reinforce balancing, glass cutting, drawing, and fixed action patterns resonate with these findings.

Hypothesis 1: Acquisition of complex skills can be observed in fixed action pattern dreams, and are positively correlated with measurable increases in neuronal mass. Research demonstrating neural plasticity and changes in neuronal mass have already been demonstrated with animals and meditating monks. Behavioral and physiological skill changes are predicted to co-vary with content related dream time and concurrent increase in neuronal mass.

Dream programming intervention techniques can be used to control and monitor dream content for human subjects. For example, I consistently used dream content to trigger lucid awareness while still immersed in my dreams. Self-monitoring that I've used strongly supports the relationship between dreaming, memory, and skill development.

I'm agreeing with David Linden's basic position on dreams when he states:

"… my own guess is that holistic explanation is more accurate: it's likely that something about the cycling between REM and non-REM stages throughout the night is particularly beneficial in memory consolidation and integration (2007: 201)."

By holistic, he refers to the improvement of memory and its consolidation and integration that occurs in sleep. A research question that I would like to see addressed is the degree to which various stages of sleep express FAP and skill related content. My subjective impression is that earlier stages of sleep perform more of the embedding and strengthening of specific memory elements, while REM puts it all together by incorporating complete visuo-motor patterns. When I'm riding my bicycle over impossible terrain in REM, I'm rehearsing all the components necessary for bike balancing that connect my visual and motor circuits. After a few weeks of practice, my actual balancing is superbly reflected in dream imagery. Thus I assume related neuronal mass changes.

Linden discusses how evolution has cobbled together the brain's working modalities by building new functions on evolving architecture. Kandel traces the development of cells, genes, and neural networks, and how evolution preserves and uses all of this architecture to create functional modules as higher organisms evolve. This fascinating evolutionary history has married a new brain on top of an old brain to create a dynamic integrated system with new functional capacities, but it is a cobbled together functional system that I, too, assume is not perfect.

Dreams are not simply a reflection of higher cognitive processes battered by a Freudian unconscious. Dreams involve dynamic feedback and exchange with our higher cognitive processes. My sleeping brain lectures, processes thoughts, finds solutions to problems, and gives me directions for the next day.

Unencumbered by outside stimuli of daily routines, my sleeping brain often expresses a clarity that I stumble around when awake.

My brain is always multi-tasking, however, it addresses the primary problems I need to solve in any combination from bike riding to book writing. But a significant part of dreaming in my experience must be seen as being devoted to maintaining memory, skills, and physiological capacities necessary to my daily functioning, emotional balance, and cognitive orientation.

My new brain observes my old brain in FAP dreams, and my new brain observes itself in thought dreams. My old brain duplicates real action motion in space, such as bicycle riding, and embeds specific skills in what we experience as bizarre hallucinations, such as riding our bikes over impossible terrain. The new brain handles thought manipulation by employing complex metaphor by turning complex metaphorical associations into ideas. For example, Hobson's state space is metaphorically portrayed as actual physical space in which I physically move around in my dream. These dream associations become ideas and enter my conscious awareness when I wake up. At other times, similar ideas will enter my conscious awareness while I'm still dreaming. Old brain fictive portrayals as visualization of space at hallucinatory levels are abstracted to represent new brain metaphorical concepts such as Hobson's state space cube. One can only observe this process in dreams or some of the other altered states of consciousness.

DYNAMIC FEEDBACK IN DREAMS

I wrote the above section yesterday (3-29-11), and after dropping off to sleep, I had three supportive dreams. The first dream occurred before 2:30 a.m. and the last two followed before 6:00 a.m. when I got up.

I'm at Mankato State University in Minnesota with students. I'm looking for classrooms and searching through class schedules. I'm talking to many different people and wandering through halls and buildings. As I read the class schedules and look up to exchange comments with others, the schedule changes every time I look back. I repeat scanning the schedule a number of times, but cannot find the desired information, as the written pages keep morphing new data. I experience a sense of urgency at not finding the desired data, and an accompanying sense of frustration.

The second and third dreams blend together, as it is now 8:16 a.m. and I've made no effort to separate them. The dreams are of a serial nature, and all of last night's dreams are related to writing this section on hypotheses. I'm in the history department at MSU talking to an old acquaintance about how to generate hypotheses. He seems interested, but critical. The scene morphs, and I'm in a facsimile of my old department talking to a former colleague. He is not helpful, and clearly views my efforts with a jaundiced eye. Another former colleague is also present and observing, but I exchange no information with him. I understand that tests are to be given shortly, and I've not prepared those that I must give.

Next, my role changes instantly from teacher to test taker. I note that the memory associations with my friends and colleagues in the history department all reflect feelings associated with them when we worked together. These associations are not of a cognitive nature.

The third dream is focused on forthcoming comprehensive graduate exams. I move between the two roles of giving and taking the exams. The scene morphs, and I'm observing athletes preparing for some kind of match. I walk through their preparation area and into my office building. I go up two or three flights of stairs, and at the top of the last one, find the step's height is up to my chest. I'm trying to pull myself over, but with difficulty. Two of the athletes behind me push, and I easily gain the top of the step. I thank them, and proceed to the office. Notice that my physical capability in this dream reflects my current age and physical capacity.

The two athletes who pushed me turn into graduate students by the time I reach my office, where we discuss how to format hypotheses for their papers. I'm clearly enjoying leading them down a formatting process, which they are slow to follow. I'm being patient and carefully guiding them in discovery. Next, I'm aware that my wife has risen and getting ready for work. I follow her, and get up for the day.

INTERPRETATION

This is another example of how closely my dreams follow my daily activities. Yesterday was spent running errands to the post office and bank. I spent two hours at the dentists and the rest of the day reading and writing a small section for this chapter. My dream thoughts were struggling with how to present and discuss hypotheses, and when I got out of bed, my dream focused mind was considering whether I should include hypotheses in a separate section, or keep them in each chapter. I realized when writing the first hypothesis that testable procedures must be included for credibility purposes. This had not been my conscious orientation before dreaming. The dreams were fleshing out writing expectations. At this point in time, I realized that self-hypnotic or auto-suggestion is probably necessary to test hypothesis 1, and for credibility purposes, it must be conducted in a lab.

The first colleague mentioned above was a helpful but severe critic of mine. I partially entered university teaching with his guidance, and he was the deciding factor for my mid-year resignation in 1980-81. I was a full, tenured professor at that time, but totally disgusted with my department and trends in education, especially research support from both the state and federal governments.

Jim was a colleague at MSU and a classmate in graduate school. He always seemed to be observing and judging my behavior, and this posture is repeated in the above dream. I supported many different graduate student theses at MSU, and these memories are strongly presented in the dream.

The main characters are real to life in terms of features, emotional reactions to them, and age. The dream physical settings are approximate but none duplicate waking conscious experiences. Cobbled together physical settings are in contrast to true to life age and physical appearance of my dream's characters.

I did not consciously decide to incorporate last night's dreams into this text while I was dreaming, but only made the decision once I sat down at the keyboard. The dreams are an interesting blend of picture-like visuals of characters, while the physical settings are manufactured from different aspects of associated memories.

My dreaming brain puts me back in the classroom at MSU after an absence of thirty years, and justifies my presence by creating teaching obligations. Hypothesis building discussions takes place with real dream graduate students, but I do not generate hypotheses about dreams in the dreams. In fact, I just talk about the process with my dream students. This reflects my current state of thought as I do not have a clear vision of the specific hypotheses I'll be including, or how to test them, although I do have a general outline that I'm following for physiological and cognitive dream hypotheses. As I write these words, I'm still in a discovery mode, which is strongly reflected in and supported by my dreams.

LLINAS FIXED ACTION PATTERNS (FAPs)

Hypothesis 2: Dream content analysis will reflect statistically significant differences for athletes and "couch potatoes" in motor activities versus thinking dreams. Intellectually oriented individuals will have significantly more cognitive dreams while new skill learners will have physical activity dreams. My dreams clearly reflect these differences, especially with ageing.

Hypotheses testing for these two groups should compare individual extremes of physical and cognitive activity and control by age. In my experience it is not Hobson's form expressed in dreams that is the key unit of analysis, but the type of activity being represented. It seems obvious to me that form reflects function. For example, riding a bicycle over impossible terrain in my dreams calls attention to form, while the activity of riding a dream bike is integrating balance in my neural circuits that can be measured during daytime activity. I assume the superhuman ability to ride my bike over impossible dream terrain represents memory consolidation and integration.

The elderly should make good dream subjects to explore the relationship between dreams and memory skills. Exercises for the elderly to improve their balance, especially those who have been physically inactive for an extended period of time, should be reflected in their dreams. Statistical correlations with dream content, form and metaphorical imagery and actual performance, I suspect, will rather closely follow my dream and actual bike balancing.

The fetus appears to be laying down neural architecture that will support complex behaviors; hence, devotes most of its dream time to REM. The gradual decrease in REM sleep into old age suggests that basic architecture, embedded patterns, are in place and new skill development and maintenance becomes the primary purpose of REM sleep as the years go by. Reactivating unused neural circuits is one more way to test this particular dream function.

Hypothesis 3: Long-term practice of controlling dreams through suggestion or self-hypnosis alters the dynamic relationship between higher and lower brain centers: Cognitive dream content will increase in proportion to the amount of dream control executed. Professional activity and educational level should be carefully controlled for comparative purposes.

In my case, multiple interlocking dreams that occupy entire nights are often devoted to teaching and processing recent reading materials and ideas, and in the above dream example, processing ideas about how to present hypotheses in this chapter. Using suggestion to teach one's Interpreter to create, direct, and guide dreams is well documented by Hobson and Brooks-Vogelsong.

I taught myself to create entire dreams in the late 1950s with dream programming. I also taught myself to redirect natural dreams and nightmares by changing the story line and characters while I was still dreaming. In my experience, one can develop as much control over dreams as we desire. This suggests to me that over time we extend structural communications between higher and lower brain centers with the active use of suggestion, especially through the use of self-hypnosis.

In my experience, extensive use of suggestion alters the natural expression of dream content, form, and higher order integration of complex thoughts, especially when suggestion is used to create stories and extended narratives. Given hypotheses 1 and 2, it is yet to be determined how active suggestion changes the expression of fixed action patterns in dreams. From my experience, there must be a tipping point where active dream control interferes with normal dream multi-functions associated with memory, cognitive processing of metaphorical thought, and one's need to maintain emotional balance. My removal of nightmare suppression after 20 years, with their complete return, suggests that nightmares are expressions of core consciousness attempting to regain emotional balance.

I can consciously put a nightmare into its memory lockbox the way some people can put their night or day monsters into non-conscious lockboxes. Only my higher order Interpreter can open and remove the nightmare, as core consciousness does not have this capacity, because insight at this level of complexity only resides with the autobiographical Self. From this perspective, core Self operates at a lower level of abstraction than my Interpreter does. However, primary metaphor dominates the core Self, and autobiographical Self levels are dominated by complex metaphor. .

When I stopped suppressing nightmares after twenty years of active control, I experienced an immediate and very noticeable sense of relief. I've referred to this use of hypnotic suggestion to control nightmares as active repression. There should be a tipping point where hypnotic control of dreams begins to interfere with sleep in a fashion that parallels sleep deprivation. Here I'm assuming that dreams have the major functions that I'm outlining. I'm also assuming that programming extensive dream scenarios with self-hypnosis will meet resistance, and organic mechanisms will tend to reassert themselves and terminate the programmed dream after a certain point.

Researchers should be able to follow an individual like myself, who is controlling his or her dreams, for an extended period of time, and observe the effects on neural networks and circuits before and after control is executed. Individual dream researchers duplicating my dream controls with naïve subjects could be a good start. The immediate positive effect of stopping nightmare control after 20 years suggests the above physiological mechanism.

Hypothesis 4: Dream time devoted to fixed action patterns will not change when one engages in lucid dream analysis that does not involve through the night dream programming. It is assumed that the baseline for FAP neural maintenance is related to age and degree of physical activity. Baselines should be established by age, gender, and lifestyle. I'm making a distinction between extensive dream programming compared to lucidity in dreams. It is thus assumed that any activity requiring extensive physical or mental effort by older individuals will support maintenance or increase in neural mass. Obviously this represents easy forms of activity programming for nursing homes that can range from singing, dancing, chess, checkers or reading, and discussion groups. Or, going barefoot, riding stationary bikes, climbing stairs, walking on two inch high balance beams, etc.

Hypothesis 5: If REM is embedding new patterns in our neural circuits, and if hallucinations are critical to the visualizations that accompany FAPs, then the extent of bizarre hallucinations in dreams will directly reflect acquisition of new skill elements and cognitive manipulations like those I report in my thought dreams.

Nightmares can wake us repeatedly throughout the night, leaving us fatigued and irritable. But nightmares also generate intense fear responses and introduce excessive amounts of cell altering or killing chemicals throughout the night. It seems logical, therefore, that pressure cooker environments from the ghettos, to war zones, to highly dysfunctional families, contain the seeds of their own neuronal destruction. My family history is a typical example.

I think there is a natural balance between REM and N-REM dreams as we age. Long-term lucid dreamers can be engaged to explore this relationship as active dream programmers. However, cognitively and physically active elders will probably exhibit a different balance between REM and N-REM activity depending on their physical and cognitive activity levels.

Another effect of extensive dream control for me seems to diminish distinctions between N-REM and REM. I often have lucid dreams that follow me throughout the night, or during afternoon naps. What I seem to experience as N-REM dreams seem more basic, less coherent, and feel more like one's first attempts to acquire a new skill.

There is this raw quality to early lucid dreams in my night's sleep cycle. I assume highly lucid dreamers, myself included, recall more of their N-REM dreams than minimally lucid dreamers.

Hypothesis 6: Testosterone and estrogen levels have a direct relationship to erotic dreams. I'm not referring to clitoral or penile engorgement as physical manifestations, but dreaming as a psychological state. I'm hypothesizing that erotic dreams can be induced by increasing hormone levels for males and females. Abstaining from coitus will create erotic dreams, while erections occur naturally even when one's normal level of sexual expression is maintained.

In like fashion, I note that when I intensify my moods before sleep, I have related dreams. The example with my stepson and the following dreams activated by elevated adrenaline are another example. This suggests a whole range of sleep lab studies designed to tease out factors associated with dream multi-tasking functions. My dreams reflect both micro and global brain-mind stimulation day-to-day, with both physiological and cognitive activation of my dreams.

Hypothesis 7: Brain chemicals representing fight and flight states will be directly correlated with conflict dreams. Conflict dreams involving survival activity can be induced by injecting appropriate chemicals artificially before the subject enters sleep, or time-released after entering sleep. Chemically induced dreams should be potentially activated with any fear provoking stimuli that the individual responds to, such as snakes, horror films, tsunamis, or PTS inducing scenarios. I can induce a conflict dream by spending a couple hours before bedtime discussing or thinking about various aspects of my personal history. Once enough of my brain's own flight or fight chemicals are released into my brain before sleeping, they activate related dreams.

Dream programming can be used to remove nightmares by confronting negative dream characters, beating them up, or totally suppressing them. More than brain chemistry is involved. How global states are changed along with neuro-modulators affecting emotions has direct implications for our mental health.

In my opinion, dream dictionaries that fail to address the physiological, emotional, and cognitive elements that dream researchers such as Hobson, LaBerge, and Cartwright have documented are a waste of time. Insights and support for improved mental health that is possible through dream and altered state research is too important to leave in the hands of occultists.

Hypothesis 8: "Dr. Rosalind Cartwright, who studies dreams at the sleep-disorder clinic of the Rush-Presbyterian Hospital in Chicago, has found that some of the brain waves that occur during night dreams also occur during daydreams. Dr. Fiss and his colleagues have found that both kinds of dreams occur in the rear of the brain that is disconnected from physical activity. This is why they both usually occur without triggering an instant related action (Barth: 77)."

To me, this exemplifies how easily we slip in and out of different states of consciousness. A little shift in attention and we have daytime visions in the works. Research keeps demonstrating how small variations in neural circuitry can alter more global conscious states.

Lucid nighttime dreaming for many of us is achieved almost as easily as shifting consciousness states during daydreams. If one practices dream programming, the shifts occur with increasing ease, and just as easily while sleeping or in other altered states as they do when we daydream. The struggle that many people have to dream lucidly must mean that the natural ease of state-shifting varies considerably between different people. Those of us who have experienced trauma, visions, and ASC in early childhood seem to have an easier time of making these shifts. It appears that greasing one's neural circuits early in life, or through trauma or deprivation, improves individual access to these neuronal patterns.

Psychotherapists such as Barth often look at how day residue is carried on over into one's dreams at night. This becomes part of the methodology to find hidden meanings and patterns being expressed below one's level of daytime consciousness. If you follow many of my dreams, you will find "day residue" written large. In fact, it is hard for me to think of this carryover as residue because it encompasses so much of my daytime activity, from mundane memory pattern reinforcement to complex thinking, lecturing and talking activities. If we accept the term: "day residue," then I think we should have a comparable term called "night residue," with the latter being carryover that emerges in our dreams and is processed the next day or days. My argument is that below conscious level processing is always occurring, as I've noted in my dream analyses.

As we learn to move across our own brain-mind landscape, we experience a different appreciation for the wonderful capabilities of our brains, and the common striving for health and well-being in all our various conscious-non-conscious states. It seems obvious to me that integrative and mental health supporting functions are always occurring, whether night or day. I think it is most fruitful to approach an analysis of this dynamic complexity with a systems model which emphasizes circular causation

Hypothesis 9: Altered states of consciousness that are under the direct control of the individual will exhibit global EEG patterns that are statistically different than global EEG patterns exhibited during altered states not under individual control. Further, uncontrolled altered states will reflect EEG patterns indicative of psychoses and/or epileptic seizures. Nevertheless, the phenomenological experiences will be the same.

I'm assuming that global patterns are more important than isolated patterns as we try to understand how consciousness is modified by altered states. Although I'm assuming circular causation between global and micro-states, I'm also assuming a global state of consciousness is used by our Interpreter to activate micro-states of ASC. A global state of awareness must remain active because I can observe in ASC as I do in lucid dreams. Therefore, it is not the isolated pattern that is critical to understanding these altered states of consciousness; instead, it is the global pattern across the brain and targeted relevant hemispheres that is our key to understanding them. If this assumption is correct, then targeting pharmaceuticals to specific neural circuits will only have moderate effects.

Obviously, I'm making this assumption from personal altered state experiences. When I control an out-of-body flight, I'm relaxed and in a state of joyful anticipation. This is true whether or not I program this fictive flight into a dream, or activate the out-of-body experience consciously when I'm awake, as was the case with my Genesis Journey.

Two thoughts are generated by considering the relationship between global and micro states. First, pharmaceuticals that target specific neural circuits or networks will not have long-term positive effects, if these drugs interfere with a balanced exchange between micro and global states. Secondly, global impact pharmaceuticals are most likely to interfere with micro-network balance with similar negative outcomes. Drug dosage clearly seems capable of overpowering brain chemicals supportive of micro states.

The second thought acknowledges that the mind can and does affect matter. Identifying the causative sources behind my nightmares had to activate immediate change in communication across micro-macro circuits. My interpretation of this effect says it's a natural healing mechanism provided by our evolutionary history. Activating this mechanism is critical to balanced brain-mind functioning. Pharmaceutical interventions must take these micro-to-macro interaction mechanisms into consideration. Otherwise, improved cognitive-behavioral strategies alone would seem to be preferred. I'm aware that some will see this interpretation as wild speculation, as I'm only a case study of one.

I emphasize the importance of control, understanding the role of the Interpreter, or meta-consciousness, in control, as well as the significance of initiating and directing the experiences of ASC one's self. It is critical that we accept the importance of the mind as a causative agent and using one's Interpreter, or mind, as I have over the years. Consciousness is a global state that seems to move across the brain like sheet lightning. It just needs enough active circuits binding sensory input for awareness to emerge.

These networks can remain under conscious control in any altered state. Learning self-control of all conscious states, altered or normal, is necessary for consciousness enhancement in what I've referred to as phenomenological addition.

I'm suggesting that, to a yet to be determined degree, we slide into uncontrolled pathological states because we don't understand what is happening to us the first time or two, and then future expressions become automatic, as belief guides expression, and expression builds the equivalent of fixed action patterns. And no one out there teaches us how to enact control. I learned to control stuttering, bed wetting, and obsessive control by sidewalk cracks. If I had not stumbled upon remedial action, my ongoing pathological responses would have had a major impact on my life history. Again, I thank Ramachandran's case study examples for empowering me to explain this paradigm shift.

Internal brain states that are experienced as being beyond our control have been historically attributed to demons, spirits, or the Freudian Unconscious. All of these historical interpretations emphasize control elements beyond one's higher consciousness, thereby distracting us from bringing the mechanisms of self-control under our direction. If a five or eight year old can teach himself how to use these control mechanisms, it should not be difficult to establish protocols for informed adults.

The onset of pathology can be frightening to the passive individual, who experiences control as being exercised by something other than one's conscious agent. Our individual fear is transformed into and object called ghost, devil, evil spirit, or uncontrollable unconscious urges. From this perspective, fear becomes a concrete entity, and concreteness requires objectifying the equivalent of a fixed action pattern. The shaman only needs to learn historically what the ritual is for the removal of this concretized object. Exorcism by the priest is a good example, and exorcism of my nightmares being another.

The main difference between the shaman and traditional psychoanalyst is the shaman's quick return of control to the client, or in my personal example, immediate elimination of nightmares. Conscious ability to create, direct, and control ASC, even under shamanic control, eliminates the anxiety, and removes one's sense of helplessness when it produces immediate positive effects. One must acknowledge the role of belief in these basic psychodynamic mechanisms.

Treatment approaches that teach the return of control to the client respect these traditional shamanic methods. But most importantly, self-taught or therapist-taught access to our own brain-mind therapeutic mechanisms can provide this immediate relief. Monitoring of brain activity before and after a therapeutic intervention, such as my removal of nightmares, should record immediate changes in global to micro brain-mind system activity.

Interpretive Aside: We can teach individuals with locked-in syndromes to move a computer cursor with their minds. "A patient viewing a computer monitor can 'learn,' by some unknown process, to modify his EEG to move a cursor toward target letters on the screen, eventually spelling out entire words (Nunez: 138)."

This connection of mind to computer is often, if not generally, viewed as a mysterious process. How does the mind move a cursor? I think the explanation is fairly simple, and answers have been much too complicated. First, we demonstrate that at a global level the mind moves matter in simple acts of letting one's mind lift fingers, hands, and body parts with thought, or removing one's nightmares as I have. Second, programming one's dreams or visions demonstrates the ability of our Interpreter to control and direct complex sensory stimuli by exercising control in altered states, much the same way that we exercise control during waking hours. Third, procedurally, we can learn to take conscious control of non-conscious mechanisms through simple techniques that we learn using self-hypnosis.

We gradually teach our brains to control processes that are normally automatic. Autonomic functioning is normally efficient for a brain that is aware that it is aware, but global control over micro-states, or the brain-mind subsystems, sometimes needs Interpreter interventions to control states that are sliding into alteration.

Most of our brain's activity occurs at the non-conscious level. This is functional processing for each one of us, as we do not have to attend to body maintenance activities such as blood pressure and heart beat. Further, we learn routines such as walking or riding a bicycle through practice, by simply doing something, which become embedded in memory circuits, and are later expressed automatically without conscious effort. Most easily understood when we watch a professional sports player perform flawlessly. I can't understand multi-tasking in my dreams or other altered states if I don't take similar mechanisms into consideration.

When I take control of my heartbeat or consciously enter an altered state of consciousness, I'm performing a similar conscious control over a non-conscious fixed action. I don't find bringing non-conscious functions under conscious control mysterious at all, especially since I have practiced similar controls for the past fifty years.

I think a person like Steven Hawkings keeps himself alive and mentally active for decades through similar conscious efforts, especially when most others with ALS succumb after a few short years from the disease. He keeps neural circuits open and connected that would otherwise progressively close down from isolation. I believe we should teach others with similar conditions these techniques, before the disease progresses to the point where such learning is no longer possible. And generalizing, we should do the same for the mentally ill. We frequently spend tens and hundreds of thousands of dollars keeping patients alive for a few weeks or months, when simple techniques like those used by Hawkings can be self-taught.

I assume that once neural circuits are destroyed or become inaccessible to the global network, the condition cannot be effectively altered. Hence, one of the travesties of emphasizing pharmaceutical intervention is that we do not repair the network, or even keep it from deteriorating.

Early intervention in adolescent or early adult onset schizophrenia is probably susceptible to my type of brain-mind control. Between the ages of five and eight years, I learned to control bed-wetting, stuttering, and obsessive behavior on my own. At the same time, I was enlarging the flight distance for out-of-body experiences, and learning behavioral routines to keep ghosts at bay, which resulted in phenomenological additions by micro-steps.

Hypothesis 10: EEG patterns will demonstrate specific source constellations for each altered state. For example, ASC focused on visual elements will reflect similar patterns found in REM. ASC – speaking-in-tongues, will activate speech activation centers, but not circuits correlated with language processing. Nunez uses EEG in various experiments that attempt to understand what he calls the language of the brain. For me, a FAP-like memory consolidation emerging in one of my dreams is part of what I call this "shadow" language. He says:

> The challenge of learning brain language involves the translation of interpretations of spatial-temporal patterns of scalp or cortical potentials, noting that spatial and temporal properties of cortical dynamics are interrelated. Cognitive processing involves widely distributed source constellations, parts of neural networks that form and dissolve on 100 millisecond or so time scales (Nunez: 129).

Cognitive processing is a very fluid process across the brain. "Specific mental tasks occur with increased correlations between some sites and decreased correlations between others, consistent with the quick formation and dissolution of networks needed for specific tasks (Ibid: 129)."

Thinking involves this rapid electrical storm of activity that is shifting across the landscape of one's brain. I envision the visual effect much like the thunderstorms of my Wisconsin youth, where sheet lighting walked across my visual field in a wonderful dance orchestrated by Mother Nature. The dance is ever more wonderful when the steps are mastered, and we control the sheet lightning of our brains. Which pharmaceutical can control the brain's lightning strikes as well as my conditioned Interpreter?

In an ASC state, I simply envision larger networks of circuits being switched on and off, accompanied by chemical states that affect the brain globally, and at select micro levels. I'm just altering the relationship between local and global brain states as I move from one ASC to another, including lucid dreaming. What I experience, and what I think we will find using EEG technology, and hopefully other related technologies, is patterning of brain circuitry that demonstrates the natural, not supernatural, source of all altered states of consciousness. Each altered state creates its own phenomenological experience.

COGNITIVE HYPOTHESES

Hobson says: "The problem is that we don't yet know enough about how ideas and feelings are instantiated in the brain to give an adequate account of the physiological causation associated with them (2001: 302)."

I believe that as we analyze additional altered states of consciousness, we increase the heuristic value of experiential case study as a useful research methodology. Adding self-control over states of consciousness and autonomic functions has given me insight into these states, which I've compared with Ramachandran's phantom limb therapies.

For example, form and lack of bizarre shifts in dreams regarding time, characters, and scenery is different in visions, spirit possession, or dance trances. These altered states must use the same neural circuits as normal waking states do, but activate these circuits in different combinations, and with different levels of neurotransmitters.

Entering any specific ASC must close down select neural circuits while engaging others. Visions are totally real, feel totally real, and captivate our belief systems for this reason. With self-control in altered states, as in dreams, one's conscious Self agent is involved, usually in charge, and in possession of other general characteristics we associate with consciousness. Hobson's analysis of how differently aminergic and cholinergic systems are expressed in dreams calls my attention to the myriad combinations available as I move from one altered state to another.

We have hundreds of brain chemicals at our disposal, but very little knowledge about their differential expression as we move across altered states. Our contemporary, but rather crude, popular pharmacological interventions do not address the complexities of how individuals can control neural network patterning and related brain chemistries. It seems apparent to me that an entire area of research is being neglected. If I had signed on to this mindset, I would still be stomping cracks in the sidewalks of Island City.

Various forms of altered states can be self-activated or occur spontaneously, as is the case with lucid dreams. The process of activation, time involved, and physical inducement, with or without self-control, can all offer insights that can be monitored physiologically. I'm guessing that mirror neurons are just as active when the shaman takes on the persona of the bear as they are when we empathize with our sick friend. And that vocalization in glossolalia entails the same neural nets as normal speech, minus the activation of higher language centers, and with a significant increase in the brain's natural narcotics.

I'm also assuming, much like Ramachandran's discussion of "aha" moments, that the brain experiences a special moment of accomplishment that peaks with a sense of transcendence and special insight after unique altered states of consciousness have been experienced. I experience this effect as I do with cognitive dreams that solve problems, or provide long sought connections that terminate nightmares. The dynamic relationships going on in my brain between neural circuits and neural modulators is always at play. I can't even think about qualia without feelings being a major component. How is it possible for many cognitive scientists to discuss consciousness or Self, let alone language, from a single dimensional perspective that excludes feeling? This is like discussing the structure of matter, but totally ignoring force fields.

In "Treatment Implications: Changing the Brain by Changing the Mind" in *The Dream Drugstore,* Hobson states:

If dreams are caused by chemical mechanisms in the brain, then both our genetic and our personal histories must be encoded there. That is to say, both the form (genetically determined) and the content (experientially determined) of our minds are physically instantiated in our brains and can be read out in the peculiar language of the dream simply by going to sleep. The same brain systems that mediate this mix of genetic and epigenetic information can be tweaked by drugs in the interest of producing altered states of waking with some features of dreams hybridized into them or they can be tempered by medical drugs in the interest of hybridizing some of the features of dreams out of them. To complete our picture, we would like to know how we can alter such a system with purely psychological interventions (Ibid: 307).

My experience altering the brain-mind system through purely psychological interventions provides what I believe to be corroborating evidence. As I've contended in previous works, we should exhaust this line of research in order to minimize mind altering drugs that have both immediate and long-term negative effects. My experience is that psychological interventions can be easily taught and easily learned. I'm a self-taught example, and my interventions have lasted a lifetime without the use of any pharmaceuticals.

In my experience, drug companies as well as drug company beneficiaries, the stock holders, will continue to ignore behavioral alternatives for the pursuit of profit. Behavioral alternatives thus become a great place for a foundation to support the public good for purely humanitarian goals. I personally know the power of psychological interventions to reduce anxiety, remove depression, dramatically increase attention, and all the benefits that are accrued, as well as self-directed dream control, and dream programming to assuage nightmares. I believe these techniques should be taught to military personnel suffering from PST. Civilians suffering from PST, especially traumatized youth, can enjoy the same benefits. Drugs do not address our need to create and maintain a sense of unified consciousness and self. Drugs mask symptoms; they do not repair.

Psychological intervention addresses our comprehensive needs as highly evolved simians. This comprehensive address has been practiced by shamans throughout history. We now have the tools and research of neuroscience and physiology to make the modern shaman live. Fifty years ago when I attempted to address these issues, I was considered a freak. Thanks Hobson.

We promote Olympics for the body, but offer only little finger exercises for the mind.

Merzenich, for one, has begun a movement to correct part of this imbalance. In order to move beyond a Spartan city state conception of the whole individual, it has been necessary to shuck the shackles of early 20th Century ideas about brain plasticity and brain development. Included were the retarding effects on mental health progress supported by Freudians and related psychoanalytic perspectives. Marrying a new paradigm of neurological capacity with Eudaimonics promotes different approaches to child development, education, and enhanced mental health.

Whether or not conscious experience is itself causal, the brain's activity associated with it certainly can be. I can thus change my brain and change my brains relationship to my body by changing my mind (Ibid: 308).

Controlling the negative impact of one's own brain chemistry to stop and then reverse the damage to cells and dendrites is no small matter. The brain that can poison itself with its own chemicals receives only partial support when artificially created chemicals are used to re-establish the brain's chemical balance. Rather, I am contending, we should first employ psychological interventions designed to stabilize brain chemistry and integrate neural circuits, while carefully controlling drug withdrawal for many who are being over or improperly medicated. I arrive at this conclusion after a lifetime of affiliation with America's Criminal Justice System.

I was diagnosed as having three critical elevations on my MMPI in 1957, including schizophrenia. My traumatized childhood with all the symptoms of PTS and clinical disorders were alleviated by self-interventions. Self-interventions included control of nightmares, which permitted full nights of sleep, removal of anxiety and depression, controlling wide emotional swings, and significant enhancement of focused attention. At 21 years of age and with three years of military service behind me, I decided to take charge of my fragmented Self. When one grows up with a fragmented Self, unity is the Holy Grail.

As a small child, and through adolescence, I was never permitted to discuss the inner worlds of altered consciousness swirling through my mind. I learned to think independently, create my own solutions to whatever problems were confronting me, and believing, as my father did, that one could use their mind to control their emotions and behavior. At age five, I stopped bedwetting and head banging on my own, and reversed and controlled stuttering. At age eleven, I conquered mind controlling sidewalk cracks. At age thirteen, I stopped nail biting. At age sixteen, I rejected suicide. By 21 years of age, I stopped being violent and taught myself dream programming, etc.

Throughout these years from toddler to adulthood, I explored OBE, kept the ghost from entering my body, and maintained dialogue with my Guardian Angel. Each conquest was self-taught and implemented, thus, I became a believer in the power of my own mind. Shamans are not mystical; they just use more of what evolution has given them.

In effect, the fragmented Self that emerged from my childhood looked like a collection of parts masquerading as a drivable vehicle. This fragile profile of parts consumed huge quantities of energy to move my educational and social world from point A to point B. It needed to be reassembled.

I immersed myself in the literature of psychology and psychiatry, and went about the task of remaking who I wanted to become. Unfortunately, in the 1950s, the brain was still a black box, and the key was in the hands of traditionalists. All the basic questions of self, consciousness, and in the 1950s, the Unconscious, were dripping in psychoanalytic terminology. A muddled perception of pathology meant that it was necessary to extricate oneself from the muddle of mud before driving down the road of recovery.

Blind Skinnerian psychology only needed an active agent in order for me to proceed. I proceeded in what seemed like the only logical way, by taking the most pressing dysfunction, which were my nightmares, and an inability to get a good night's sleep, eliminating them, and proceeding to the next issues of anxiety and depression.

The question of how the brain instantiates self is intriguing, to say the least. To me, it looks something like this: Sensory input occurs through a modular sensory architecture, which must be brought into balance; the old brain, which underlies the 95 percent of our learning that is unconscious, was the primary driver behind my nightmares. I taught my Interpreter Self to control my nightmares, thereby empowering my new brain with its higher cognitive powers to take control over all major affected brain functions. I called this aspect of self my Controller; others use the terms Autobiographical Self or Interpreter.

I am aware that I am aware. I am conscious of being conscious. Thus, my higher level of awareness, my autobiographical Self, learns to control the old brain and all of its functions.

Higher order consciousness requires a sense of Free Will, that we are our own Agent, directing our own life. My 8th grade educated father always insisted that this was the case, and as a young university student, I continued to accept the challenge. Achieving unity and enhancing one's self permits improved social, educational, and professional opportunities. In effect, the full benefits of culture open up to us. The muddy ruts of the soggy byways become paved highways.

When we humans add language to the capabilities of self organization, thought processes become more complex, and we manipulate our inner world as no other creature can. The new brain communicates with second and third order images and emotions that are not only felt, but interpreted.

This is a quantitative emergent level of functioning based on evolving brain architecture and higher order functions. We are aware that we are aware, with secondary consciousness added on top of primary consciousness.

As I manipulated my Controller, I consciously experienced these interrelationships as a university undergraduate. I not only came to experience unity, but a sense of mastery over Self and environment that was often transcending. I came to believe as an undergraduate that mental health did not mean maintaining minimum functions for work and social life; it meant moving ever closer to one's maximum innate capacity. Hence, I rejected self-help routines that emphasized maintenance. The type of self-help strategies promoted by 12th or seven strep strategies, for example. It is this background that makes it difficult for me to accept models of drug maintenance.

I came to completely control my nightmares and dreams, discovered my capacity to create and control numerous altered states of consciousness, and learned how to control pain and autonomic brain functions. My behavioral landscape became a gardener's dream that offered flowers, fruits, and the promise of gourmet delights. States of consciousness were no longer pathological. They were states to be explored, explained, and used to create visions of what the human potential offered. My autobiography discusses this progression in detail.

Here I note the outline as my argument for joint exploration and understanding of all the major psychological states of consciousness, in support of a comprehensive interpretation of Self and consciousness.

I can dream or have experiences in many different states of consciousness, and recognize that there is a continuum of how input reaches my Controller, and how I then consciously create output into each state of consciousness, whether altered or normal states. This circular process of causative interrelationships is incredibly liberating once it is brought under personal control.

Cognitive control at a meta-consciousness level exists across all of my various states and levels of consciousness. This is the fulfillment of unity we call good mental health. This operational ability has permitted me to create, direct, and control ASC, and in this process, greatly enhance my personal understanding of the psychology involved. My life-long primary goal has not been to just understand the machinery of the black box, but to comprehend and use its capacity. I thank neuroscience and researchers in physiology for providing the base that sustains this psychological road to recovery.

Hobson says:

The human brain is a complex, dynamic system whose equilibrium depends upon a delicate balancing act between modules within different states of consciousness and whose unity depends upon a well orchestrated integration across those states. As yet we cannot give an adequate account of how a brain comes to instantiate a self, but this still obscure integration process clearly involves memory and emotion, the two modules of the brain-mind that have always been of greatest interest to psychodynamic psychology. Now that we know how memory and emotion are altered in a state-dependent way, we can use that information to generate new approaches to their access, interpretation, and manipulation in the interest of personal satisfaction and social success (Ibid).

We have considerable insight at the macro level as to how conscious control over mind-brain activity can direct and control various states of consciousness. It is exciting to watch, as science continuously reveals the contents of evolution's most marvelous creation; the human mind.

In the section titled "Changing Our Minds—and Bodies—for Comfort and for Health," Hobson notes:

Now that we understand how priming of the brain-mind can occur via exposure to words or visual images and how it can create an unconscious propensity to think and/or act according to the prescription of suggestion, we are in a stronger position to begin to answer some of the questions that have long baffled theorists and healthcare professionals. An important dimension of the processes that we will now consider is the connection of the brain-mind to and from the body. Because our model specifies participation of the brain even in transactions like hypnosis and lucid dreaming, it is easy to see how the body might be used to contribute to the desired changes of brain-mind state (e.g., muscular relaxation and eye closure). And if a change in brain-mind is induced by any means, including purely psychological means, it follows that the body may well be its beneficiary (e.g., by saving energy, reducing blood pressure, releasing growth hormones, etc.) (Ibid: 114).

For me, the body and the brain are huge beneficiaries when the mind-brain is more fully involved. I've played across these frontiers for fifty plus years, and can't imagine what my life would have been if I had continued to live in the standard model of Freudian mysticism, or the shadows of early Skinnerian Behaviorism.

I think we have neglected mind-brain control models of mental health and their related physiological effects, because we were enamored with people like Freud, and then became unduly attached to pharmacological intervention. Psychological manipulation of my brain without specifically understanding all that goes on at the micro-circuit level worked for me.

Transcendental meditation physically changes the brain, as does playing the piano, or the development of complex skills of any kind. Hypnosis, especially hypnosis controlled by the individual, I contend, and think that I have demonstrated such, is an invaluable aid in learning to exercise this level of self-control. Once control is learned, one can turn control on and off – be it at the dentist's, doctor's office, or potentially, a specific trauma site in the brain.

Hobson focuses on reducing muscle tension in order to improve memory, directed action, and creativity, as anxiety has a negative effect on all of these desirable factors. He then goes on to compare relaxation techniques with transcendental meditation, stating that the two are similar (Ibid: 314-317).

Individual differences determine how well we meditate, enter hypnosis or trance, or become lucid dreamers.

Hobson says: "… the zones of the state space that we can or can't enter are more or less accessible on and individual basis … and that individual basis … is both genetic-constitutional-trait bound, as well as environmental-cultural-state determined (Ibid: 317)."

I have reviewed a number of Hobson's positions in order to compare them with my own self case study insights. Sleep and physiological research have paved over the ruts in the old psychoanalytic road. Knowledge convergence in many interrelated areas of science now gives us an enlarged road map to a fuller understanding of dreams, ASC, Self and Consciousness. And I'm contending that the role of self-case study has not been fully exploited as a meaningful psychological partner to neuroscience. Consciousness and altered states must both be studied as separate and interrelated units of analysis. Reduction approaches are necessary, but not sufficient in and of themselves to explain consciousness and meta-to-micro levels of brain functions. The subjective self is a study unit in and of itself.

Cognitive Hypothesis 1: Therapist guided self-therapy will produce enhanced positive outcomes compared to traditional therapies, or therapy provided by therapists using pharmaceutical interventions, when there is minimal damage to the client's brain.

It is my experience that chaos in neural circuitry and related disturbances in brain chemistry can be more effectively controlled by the individual. I am not suggesting, nor do I think it is possible, to remove or eliminate the role of the therapist. Treatment routines and monitoring are too complex at this time for the removal of a trained practitioner, but the practitioner's role should be further shifted in the direction of guide, and not as that of controller, as was the case in the older, standard model of psychiatry. Crudely stated, drug therapy alone is the work of a mechanic who doesn't know how to build the car.

My point is that we are individually able to monitor and control brain states from an internal perspective that is beyond the reach of science's current status in technology and medicine. This situation may change in twenty or thirty years, but the reduction approach to understanding all of the complex mechanisms involved takes time. A second point which I think is demonstrated by my case history is the ability of a recovering brain to heal itself through meta-awareness, and the impact of self-control at this level of brain functioning can enhance balanced brain chemistry and positively integrated neural circuitry. Crude pharmaceutical interventions offer much in stabilizing a client-patient's behavior once conditions have become extreme, but side effects can be almost as debilitating. Proactive medicine requires more than drug reflex actions for extreme conditions.

Cognitive Hypothesis 2: Deterioration of neural circuitry will be interrupted and reversed for adolescent or young adult onset pathologies, such as schizophrenia, by modifying brain chemistry as specified in cognitive hypothesis 1.

Cognitive Hypothesis 3: Speed of individual recovery and maintenance of positive mental health is significantly enhanced quantitatively, to the degree that self-control is taught to, and taken over by, individual patients.

Cognitive Hypothesis 4: Long-term positive mental health gained through guided self therapy alone is superior to chemical pharmacological interventions regarding both short and long-term negative side effects.

A common problem with the current crude level of pharmaceuticals is subsequent refusal to stay on mediations by patients who abhor the side effects. A promise of drug withdrawal may keep a sizeable number of clients on their pharmaceuticals, with reduced dosage as their control increases. In my case, doctor prescribed drugs were never an option, thus, I believe my recovery was quick, because it was drug free. I also had no personal experience of being therapy-doctor dependent. Hobson cautions us to be vigilant about drug overuse. As one who only uses aspirin occasionally, I very much agree.

Psychiatry has assumed pathology when one enters altered states of consciousness, and psychoanalysts have previously attempted to use their traditional dysfunctional approaches to treat unusual neuronal configurations. Failure to understand altered states has transferred primary treatment efforts to pharmaceuticals in attempts to achieve balance and integration, and sent millions of people to pop culture gurus. However, pharmaceuticals have both general and specific effects on the brain. Fortunately, in areas such as the treatment of depression, cognitive-behavioral strategies, combined with drug treatment, are producing well researched positive outcomes. Cognitive-behavioral treatment was possible in the 1950s, as my autobiography indicates. And in that era, global approach therapies were assumed to be under the control of Freudians and their bed fellows.

Psychologists and psychotherapists are interested in changing their client's behavior and comfort levels, and, must therefore look across various brain-mind states to achieve these purposes. I've discussed some of the similarities and differences in various altered states from dreaming to spirit possession, and argued that our brain-minds can mix and match various neural patterns at will to achieve or alter these states; and in this mix and match process, we should view ASC as just another expression of neuronal activity that can be brought under individual control.

CONCLUSION

In the language of mystics, the God within is meta-consciousness, especially when we can use mirror neurons and other brain capacities to experience the feelings and thoughts of others, and then project these wonderful images of the Other onto the universe at large. As we come to understand Self, consciousness, and altered states of reality, we come more fully to appreciate how wonderfully evolution has constructed thought, the brain's ability to image that leads to qualia and Self, and our beginning ability to tease out how feeling emerges from atoms and chemicals. This, for me, is the true mystery of life that we must master, if

Homo sapiens are to have a future free of chaos and destruction, or a future of sustained personal and cultural growth.

At this point in our understanding of Self, consciousness, and our awareness of being conscious that we are conscious permits Theory of Mind, or how others think and feel, by duplicating their brain-mind states in our own brain-minds. We can no longer think of the mind as a separate thing disconnected from our body. And in this transformation of knowing ourselves, we come to appreciate our evolution-given capacity to create ghosts, spirits, and gods. In this three book series, I have taken the position that fundamental scientific understanding of human nature must become widespread throughout humanity, if we are to persevere as a species.

Triangulating dreams, other states of altered realities, and consciousness, has given me the ability to self-heal and grow that is central to the objectives of good mental health. If I had remained at the level of game playing with altered states and dreams that has been common with many using suggestion and lucidity in dreams, I would not have made the next step. The critical step for me was learning how to control, to turn on and off, altered states. This required reifying neural networking called Interpreter, and teaching it to take control of altered states. Over the decades, I have come increasingly to appreciate my Interpreter's ability to control both global and micro brain-mind states.

My experience supports the position that control must be learned top-down. Brain chemicals such as oxytocin have different effects on males and females, as Churchland notes (2011: 71-81).

Intra-species variability between males and females takes on new significance as physiological studies are married to psychological research. Control across brain-mind states becomes a major problem for pharmacological interventions, and highlights the importance of conducting joint research across related disciplines. It speaks directly to the simple, elegant research designs of Ramachandran. It is my contention that a whole series of experiments similar to mine are in order, regarding the extent to which control of the relationship between global and micro brain-mind states can be used to treat and control mental illness.

Mine is a case study of one, but the effects I've achieved with brain-mind control must at least apply to a sub-population of individuals with a broad range of disorders, from obsessive-compulsive disorder, to anxiety, depression, and possibly, early stages of schizophrenia. In my history, first controlling global states permitted me to bring micro-states under control and into balance.

Pharmaceutical interventions tend to affect one or a limited number of micro-systems, but with major negative global effects. Our brains have the capacity to override sub-systems in emergencies, such as pain. Pain is a global state that can be totally turned off when the right brain switch is tripped. My personal history says anxiety and depression are subject to similar system controls.

I didn't have our current knowledge of neuroscience when I began self-experiments in 1957-58; I just treated my brain-mind as a whole unit of operation that could be behaviorally modified. Although I'm usually highly critical of Freud, he was a major contributor to my self-healing approach. In fairness to his historical efforts, he just journeyed down the wrong road. Unfortunately, he did not realize an alternative highway existed that he could follow in his dreams.

I looked for global keys that I could use to enter my psyche. The primary key centered on self-hypnosis, which I used to gain control over unwanted psychological states. Conscious control of global functions necessitates control over micro-conditions such as localized pain and heart rate, and larger brain-mind states associated with Zen driving and daytime visions. Pharmaceutical targeting of gears in the black box does not address mechanisms supporting these outcomes.

Global brain-mind states are isomorphic with behavioral expressions that we label as psychological or pathological. Our brains can switch to flight or fight with the same threat, depending on our brain's interpretation of confronting stimuli. Our mind's interpretation significantly changes what happens to attention, muscle, and adrenaline output. Self-control of global states necessitates top-down control over specific brain-body activities. Artificially altering smaller neural networks, as with medical drugs, can lead to imbalance in the global system. Logically, if the global system is directing one's rebalancing, we have the prospect of both necessary and sufficient neural and chemical inputs coming under global control.

Initially as a young adult, I rebalanced my psychological self according to my awareness of what the world required of me. Then I moved on to empower expanded brain-mind functions.

I'm aware that my brain seeks balance, strives to minimize physical and psychic pain, strives for sociality, and abhors unbalanced states that unduly demand constant energy be it psychic or metabolic. There is a macro-consciousness built into the architecture of a genetically prepared brain that demands attention. All levels of consciousness from both our old and new brains, speaking in evolutionary terms, should be at our conscious disposal. We humans are not only capable of considerable plasticity regarding learning and culture, but possess incredible resilience in our ability to rebalance our own brain-minds.

I have not tried to address all the implication behind these stated thoughts, nor have I exhausted or refined hypotheses that could run into the dozens. That is a project I'm not yet committed to. My goal in this three book series has been given. I leave the reader with my hope that this self-study and history of self-experiments have been of benefit to those who wish to transcend their current level of emancipation.

EPILOGUE

LOOKING BACK

My intimate familiarity with lucid dreams and other altered states began before the age of two. I started active experiments programming my dreams and learning how to control altered states in the academic school year of 1957-58. In those years, my views on these subjects were in conflict with mainstream medical practitioners and psychotherapists.

The beginning of the 21st Century finds the media market flooded with bizarre and occult interpretations of altered states, as dream dictionaries exemplify. My autobiography discloses my initial out-of-body experience before the age of two, and then goes on to explain discovery and control of most major altered states.

Learning how to create, direct, and control dreams and other altered states has enabled me to compare these inner realities with both scientific findings, and the ongoing musings of ancients and their modern occultist counterparts. At 75 years of age, I have decades of this history to put in context. From this long-term perspective, I've made many assumptions. Organizational analysis that moves across this landscape of altered realities focuses on dynamic integrated system processing information in terms of circular causation. The referenced authors have each made their own special contribution to my interpretations.

Brain cell regeneration, life-long brain plasticity, and conscious control by one's Self over altered states without the use of drugs, were quaint and easily dismissed points of view in the 1950s and '60s. As a case study of one, I've tried to demonstrate that we can learn to heal ourselves of childhood trauma. Not just heal ourselves, but come to understand and access a larger part of our true potential, and grow beyond the expected norms of society and popular mental health models.

Entering and controlling various altered states gives one a different slant on historical shamanic and world religions. In *Mind of the Mystic,* I took the stand that humanity has failed to understand its own spirituality by putting the scientific study of religion off limits. By this, I mean that we study derived social products of human groups, which we call religions, and not their biological and neurological roots. This, in turn, leaves human spirituality at the mercy of ancient dogmas, and a lot of kooks. I used my own case history of discovering and experimenting with altered states to present their natural origin in *Mystic.* Altered states that support religious dogma such as speaking-in-tongues and visions, have taken their place alongside the exploration of lucid dreams for me. They are no longer mysterious or of supernatural origin. I defined the shaman and shamanism in *Mystic,* and took anthropology's sub-schools, and sociology's standard model to task for perpetuating occult interpretations.

In this work, I argued that dreams, altered states, Self, and consciousness are so intertwined that understanding how they arise and are expressed depends on our comprehension of how macro integration and functioning occurs across the brain. One must tease out these interrelationships in order to understand the contribution of parts to the whole. By manipulating the whole, we come to better understand the parts. This book is longer than I wanted it to be, as there are many interrelated elements with dreams, altered states, and consciousness. I'm compelled to treat this complex as an interrelated whole, in order to avoid the arguments from various disciplines that any one part of this book is their exclusive domain. Fragmented bits of knowledge cannot stand alone in the modern world, contrary to the practices of isolated historical disciplines.

I documented general findings from prominent researchers in physiology, neuroscience, and related fields in an attempt to circumvent vested interest criticisms that have followed me throughout my professional life: Questions challenging one's professors as an undergraduate or young professor still don't sit well. I felt compelled to explore global neural operations, both from bottom-up and top-down, in order to explain my own dreams and various altered states. This included an appreciation for the position that "The architecture of the network itself shapes the pattern of activity" in various models of the brain (Zimmer: 60).

I have argued extensively that self-modification of brain function and structure, or architecture, is potentially available to all of us; at least under the guidance of a qualified professional.

I believe a paradigm shift is necessary in medicine and the therapeutic community. Specifically, our increasing pharmaceutical drug addictions promoted by mass media should be reconsidered. Profit for the sake of profit, instead of for the common good, is not free enterprise at its best.

I have emphasized multi-tasking functions of dreams. Part of this larger systems perspective incorporated evolutionary differences between our old and new brains. I think failure to note specific functions going on at these two levels in our dreams leads to considerable confusion.

My dreams address memory and motor skills, closely track emotional states, enhance thinking processes and the integration of complex conceptual patterns, and encode primary images as the initial step in concept development that leads to complex metaphor. In effect, my dreams are not the same as my neighbor's dogs. I assume that a more complex brain leads to more complex dreams. There is a qualitative difference as we move up the evolutionary ladder.

In terms of other altered states besides dreaming, I argued that normal brain architecture and functioning that supports dreaming also supports altered states. The gods of ancient belief do not come to play at night. Nature develops functions by cobbling together previous workable brain architectural units to create new functions. Our being conscious of being conscious, the one level of our cognitive ability that seems more advanced, but not exclusive of other mammals, being a good example. This supporting architecture lies behind all the shamanic capacities documented across human history. Altered states are epiphenomena in the sense that small alterations in neuronal networks produce these many wonderful and varied experiences. My history of self-observation-experimentation speaks directly to this assumption.

Common misinterpretation of altered states encourages the stigma felt by untold thousands of people who practice and/or experience visions, automatic writing, etc. A significant penalty paid for failing to study altered states, as we do any other set of neural processes, is paid by the mentally ill. Therapeutic self-control of brain states that I've experimented with for fifty years are not available to them. Discomfort with pharmaceuticals drives thousands of these individuals to use street drugs, and they then remain uncomfortably closeted. This is no surprise to the medical community. Failure to acknowledge this inadvertent medical support for street drugs and pharmaceutical greed has terrible outcomes for the mentally ill. And the mentally ill come to be defined as morally inferior, and in huge numbers, languish in our jails and prisons.

We are aware of being aware, and we should relish this most human capacity. I have offered my subjective history with meta-consciousness, and the role my Interpreter plays at our most advanced cognitive level of complexity. Maximizing human potential means to me that I've extended my concentration from twenty minutes to eight hours without a break, controlled my own nightmares and dreams, eliminated depression and anxiety, and enjoy activities like Zen driving.

Lesson learned: We should never seek to be normal, when normal is based on a statistical average of contemporary world populations. I'm especially pained to see most high school students taking on and acting out role models from the mass media. It is globally painful to watch this process creep into developing nations like China.

I've set forth 15 assumptions about self, consciousness, dreams, and altered states at this book's beginning. I leave it to the reader to decide how well I've made my case. I could've formalized these and other assumptions into a typology, but felt this is premature. Besides, my reported list is not complete or comprehensive enough.

OBSERVATIONS:

Physiological and neuroscience research is continuously refining our understanding of the brain at both the global and micro levels. The brain-mind is an integrated whole, and I find it impossible to consider consciousness, Self, and altered states by considering philosophical, religious, or purely psychological elements separately. I'm privileged to live in the 21st Century, when cross-discipline integration is fast becoming a reality. Application of this century's new scientific base should truly bring to light new therapies that extend the thousands of year old methods of the world's shamans, meaning that non-evasive therapies envisioned through guided self-therapy can emerge from unfolding research and be brought under the looking glass, pharmaceutical profit motives and the lobby might of huge corporations notwithstanding. I believe this will require a paradigm shift in medicine and psychiatry.

Further, my self-therapies that have stood for over fifty years open a window to understanding the placebo effect in terms of causation, not just correlation. Interpreting the crude kinds of self-healing that occurred with the Jesus Movement, and shamanic cures throughout history, still remains mostly in contemporary medicine's black box. Self-control of conscious and non-conscious brain states has been a salvation for me. I understand the placebo effect as stemming from active participation on the part of my Interpreter. Balancing emotions by removing anxiety and depression, while learning self-control over micro brain states, has much to offer clinical therapies.

We now understand that neural networks supporting positive mental health can be strengthened or weakened in our brains, and in doing so, our well-being improves or deteriorates. We understand that our own states of anxiety and cognitive dysfunctions matter, and that mind can, and does, alter cellular processes and structures. My experience supports the position that adding control over normal as well as altered states of consciousness improves brain-mind balance, and further improves our total emotional and social functioning.

I've referred to my methods of self-intervention as brain-mind enhancements. This position is in contrast to medical research that analyzes subtraction of brain capacity that occurs with physical brain damage, trauma, or defective DNA. There has been an entire fleet of therapeutic ships launched by shamans historically that has never been brought home to dock. But the fleet commander knows that how the fleet is organized determines win or loss.

Dreams and other altered states can be used to explore basic image formation; what I've referred to as primary symbols, or perhaps, what some mean by proto-language. Qualia at the symbolic level represent higher order cognitive representations of proto-symbols, such as those discussed in my bicycle balancing dream. Philosophy, cognitive science, and linguistics that seek causative relationships without intimate knowledge obtainable from neuroscience are doomed to failure. One cannot study the atom by focusing on molecules. One cannot study the subjectivity of Self without treating subjectivity as a separate unit of analysis. Human subjectivity, the ability to be aware that we are aware, is a qualitative emergent given us by evolution.

We openly and actively study religion as social, psychological, and philosophical phenomena, but neglect its physiological and neural base. When one comes to control and direct altered states, this oversight seems to be monumental. The physiological study of altered states should become scientific meat. Jesus engaged in rhythmic dancing and glossolalia with his disciples before his crucifixion. Suggest to True Believers that this is not communion with God, and watch the backlash. In the 21st Century, this is an absurd situation.

I've taken the position in this three book series that we will never understand our spiritual nature by living in the cave of dogma. When we bring altered states under our control and direction, the absurdity of historical interpretations becomes clear. My brain shifts its states, and I experience the products of new neural configurations. They are often mind-blowing, but almost always fun! Cultural interpretations of where our self or soul goes in altered states comes into play, and biology is ignored. It is difficult to think of nuclear weapons in the hands of ignorant True Believers as an improvement over their being in the hands of a Hitler.

Dream researchers have moved interpretations of this altered state into the light of day, and outside the cave of dogma. Nevertheless, many still prefer ancient interpretations of dreams as having divine meaning. But when it comes to other altered states, the occultists thrive. Embodied consciousness has changed philosophy, and is changing major world religions as well as returning the soul to body. Embodied consciousness should be brought home to all altered states.

We are unquestionably a spiritual creature. It is hard to imagine any evolved species possessing mirror neurons and Theory of Mind to be without faith and active concern for fellow group members. Disembodiment of soul placed God out there, and not within. The God within demands responsibility that is different from killing abortion doctors or detonating body explosives to kill indiscriminately.

Eudaimonia, harmony in society, cannot be achieved without individuals realizing their innate potentials. This will require broader, targeted education that rids one of mind controlling dogmas. The march of Truth does combat with Ignorance. A more complete understanding of Self and consciousness is required for us to finish this journey. Science must take the final step. Fortunately, researchers no longer fear loss of tenure and university positions when they study consciousness, or even the inside of black holes, for that matter. Why do we still fear the physiological study of spirituality?

As Hobson has so poignantly noted, psychodynamic quackery of the Freudian Era has been positioned under the sun's lamp. But in terms of destroying human lives, garments have been changed in the name of medicine, and the medicine bag has come to replace the couch: Drugs versus talk therapy.

Our culture is populated with self-help books of all kinds. Most of these books attempt to return one to normal functioning or normal behavior, which means one should become like the person down the street. A few approaches such as meditation attempt to teach new capacities, and open up one's brain-mind to additional options. It is to this latter movement that I speak.

In my last five years as a university professor, I encouraged my students to conduct simple experiments and observe their own reactions: Stop using electronic media, including TV, for thirty days, and see what happens. Stop using alcohol for a similar period, and see what happens. Only engage in recreational activities that involve personal interaction with others, etc. Out of classes of 50-60 students, one might take me up on the offer. But when they did, the responses were: "Oh, my!" My life has been filled with self-experiments with most altered states, and the view from Olympus grows ever more amazing.

Learning how to direct and control dreams expands one's sense of Self and consciousness. Learning how to control other altered states expands this expansion. We discover rather quickly that brain plasticity never stops with age. Use it or lose it has a simple ring of truth; exploring music of the universe within our minds brings forth the full orchestra.

Learning Chinese in one's 70s is not easy, but doable. Most aged language learners give up after a few attempts. One needs to understand the intermediate steps required for mind control and expansion. The steps I've outlined using self-hypnosis provide such an outline for me. Brain plasticity does not cease with age, it just changes.

New technology has given us an understanding of mirror and canonical neurons. We possess new understanding of how we can feel and think as others do. We know that DNA is not simply expressed, but what and how DNA is expressed depends on our interaction with our total physical and social environments. If we have a supportive environment, we thrive, and without a positive environment, we stagnate, or become less than fully human.

Incorporating this awareness into the processes of education, re-conceptualizing how Americans operate their criminal justice system, and providing minimum support for medical, nutritional, and social needs of children is my hope for the 21st Century.

Mine is a top-down, phenomenological approach that employs self-observation and self-experimentation. It is subjective, but all human thought is subjective; it is how we manage our subjectivity that qualifies this methodology as being worthwhile. Any one moment in history does not qualify as an objective experience. A lifetime of practicing Freudian psychotherapy does not qualify as an objective experience. A thousand years of religious dogma does not qualify as an objective experience. And the point is made.

One of my favorite students went on to develop a model treatment program for sex offenders in Minnesota. Speaking to groups about working with his fellow human beings, he would say: "All we have to offer our fellow beings is a relationship." This was in the 1970s. It is now 2011, and I sincerely hope I have done the same.

BIBLIOGRAPHY

Ackerman, D. (2004). An Alchemy of Mind: The Marvel and Mystery of the Brain. New York: Scribner.

Adams, F., Aizawa, K. (2010). The Bounds of Cognition. Chichester, UK: John Wiley & Sons.

Alcock, J. (2001). The Triumph of Sociobiology. New York: Oxford.

Andrews, D., Bonta, J. (1998). The Psychology of Criminal Conduct. Cincinnati: Anderson Publishing Company.

Aristotle. (1996). The Nicomachean Ethics. Hertfordshire: Wordsworth Classics of World Literature.

Arnold, C. (January, 2011). Why Sleep Is Good for You. Scientific American (63).

Barasch, M. I. (2001). Healing Dreams: Exploring the Dreams that Can Transform Your Life. New York: Riverhead Books, Berkeley Publishing Group.

Barkalaja, A. Shamanism as Information Design (21-55)) in Leete, A., Firnhaber, R.P., eds. (2004). Boca Raton: Brown Walker Press.

Barrett, D. (2001). The Committee of Sleep. New York: Crown Publishers.

Barth, F. D. (1997). Daydreaming: Unlock the Creative Power of Your Mind. New York: Viking Penguin.

Begley, S. (2007). Train Your Mind Change Your Brain: how a new science reveals our extraordinary potential to transform ourselves. New York: Ballantine Books.

Black, I. B. (2001). The Dying of Enoch Wallace: Life, Death, and the Changing Brain. New York: McGraw-Hill.

Bloom, F.E., Beal, M.F., Kupfer, D.J. (2003). The Dana Guide To Brain Health. New York: Free Press.

Brooks, J. E., Vogelsong, J. A. (2000). The Conscious Exploration of Dreaming: Discovering How We Create and Control Our Dreams. Bloomington, IN: 1st Books Library, The International Online Library.

Browne, S. Harrison, L. (2002). Book of Dreams. New York: Dutton.

Butz, J. J. (2005). The Brother of Jesus: And the Lost Teachings of Christianity. Inner Traditions: Rochester, Vermont.

Carter, C. (2010). Science and the Near-Death Experience: How Consciousness Survives Death. Rochester, VT: Inner Traditions.

Casti, J. (1994). Complexification. New York: Harper Collins.

Chalmers, D. J. (1996). The Conscious Mind: In Search of a Fundamental Theory: New York: Oxford.

Churchland, P. S. (2002). Brain-Wise: Studies in Neurophilosophy. Cambridge, MA: The MIT Press.

Churchland, P. S (2007). Neurophilosophy at Work. New York: Cambridge University Press.

Churchland, P. S (2011). Braintrust. Princeton, NJ: The Princeton University Press.

Clark, A. (2011). Supersizing the Mind: Embodiment, Action, and Cognitive Extension. New York: Oxford University Presss.

Cohen, J.B. (1985). Revolution in Science. Cambridge, Massachusetts: Harvard University Press.

Collins, F.S. (2007). The Language of God. New York: Free Press Paperback.

Craze, R. (2005). Interpreting Dreams: A History of Dream Analysis. London: Southwater, Annes Publishing, Ltd.

Csikszentmihalyi, M. (1997). Creativity: Flow and the Psychology of Discovery and Invention. New York: Harper Perennialu.

Darby, J. Shamanism in Science (14-20) in Leete, A., Firnhaber, R.P., eds. (2004). Boca Raton: Brown Walker Press.

Damasio, A. R. (1994). Descartes Error: Emotion, Reason, and the Human Brain. New York: Grossman/Putnam

Damasio, A. R. (1999). The Feeling of What Happens. Orlando: Houghton Mifflin Harcourt Publishing.

Damasio, A. R. (2003). Looking for Spinoza: Joy, Sorrow, and the Feeling Brain. Orlando: Harcourt Publishers.

Damasio, A. R. (2010). Self Comes to Mind: Constructing the Conscious Brain. New York: Pantheon.

Damasio, A. (December, 2010). The 12 Steps to Consciousness. Discover (66-70).

Dawkins, R. (1989). The Selfish Gene. Oxford: Oxford University Press.

Dawkins, R. (1995). River Out of Eden: A Darwinian View of Life. New York: Basic Books.

Dawkins, R. (2006). The God Delusion. New York: Houghton Mifflin.

Deisseroth, K. (November 2010). Controlling the Brain with Light. Scientific American (49-55).

Delaney, G. (1991). Breakthrough Dreaming: How to Tap the Power of Your 24-Hour Mind. New York: Bantam Books.

Delaney, G. (1997). In Your Dreams: Falling, Flying & Other Dream Themes. New York: HarperCollins, Publishers.

Dennett, D. (1991). Consciousness Explained. Boston: Little, Brown & Company. Diekelmann, S., & Born, J. The memory function of sleep *Nature Reviews Neuroscience* 11, 114–126 (1 February 2010) | doi:10.1038/nrn2762.

Doide, N. (2007). The Brain that changes Itself: Stories of Personal Triumph from the Frontiers of Brain Science. New York: Viking.

Edelman, G.M., Tononi, G. (2000). A Universe of Consciousness: How Matter Becomes Imagination. New York: Basic Books.

Ehrman, B. D. (2003). Lost Christianities: The Battle of Scripture and the Faiths We Never Knew. New Oxford: Oxford University Press.

Evans, P. (1983). Landscapes of the Night. New York: The Viking Press.

Firnhaber, R. P. Mapping the ASC: A Cultural-Physiological Construct (84-119) in Leete, A., Firnhaber, R.P., eds. (2004). Boca Raton: Brown Walker Press.

Flanagan, O. (2009). The Really Hard Problem: Meaning in a Material World. Cambridge, MA: A Bradford Book, MIT Press.

Flavell, J. H. ((1965). The Developmental Psychology of Jean Piaget. Princeton: D. Van Nostrand Company, Inc.

Foulkes, D. (1985). Dreaming: A Cognitive-Psychological Analysis. Hillsdale: Lawrence Erlbaum Associates, Publishers.

Freeman, W. J. (2000). How Brains Make Up Their Minds. New York: Columbia University Press.

Freud, S. (1997). The Interpretation of Dreams. Hertfordshire: Wordsworth Classics of World Literature.

Gackenach, J., Basveld, J. Control Your Dreams. New York: Harper & Row.

Gardner, J. (2007). The Intelligent Universe. Franklin Lakes: New Page Books.

Gazzaniga, M.S. (1992). Nature's Mind: The Biological Roots of Thinking, Emotions, Sexuality, Language, and Intelligence. New York: Basic Books.

Gazzaniga, M.S. (2000). The Mind's Past. Berkeley: The University of California Press.

Gazzaniga, M.S. (2011). Who's In Charge: Free Will and the Science of the Brain. New York: Harper-Collins.

Gendlin, E.T. (1986). Let Your Body Interpret Your Dreams. Wilmette, IL: Chiron Publications.

Grafton, S.T. Embodied Cognition and the Simulation of Action to Understand Others, published online: 25 MAR 2009, DOI: 10.1111/j.1749-6632.2009.04425.x.

Green, B. (2000). The Elegant Universe. New York: Vintage.

Green, B. (2004). The Fabric Of The Cosmos: Space, Time, And The Texture Of Reality. New York: Vintage Books.

Griffin, D. R. (1989). Archetypal Process: Self and Devine in Whitehead, Jung, and Hillman. Evanston: Northwestern University Press.

Guth, A. (1997). The Inflationary Universe. Reading: Perseus.

Hare, R. (1993). Without Conscience: The Disturbing World of the Psychopaths Among Us. New York: Guilford Press.

Harris, S. (2005), The End of Faith: Religion, Terror, and the Future of Reason. New York: W. W. Norton & Company.

Hawking, S. (1988). A Brief History of Time. London: Bantam.

Hobson, J. A. (1988). The Dreaming Brain. New York: Basic Books.

Hobson, J.A. (1994). The Chemistry of Conscious States: How the Brain Changes Its Mind. \New York: Little, Brown & Company.

Hobson, J. A. (1999). Consciousness. New York: Scientific American Library.

Hobson, J.A. (2001). The Dream Drugstore: Chemically Altered States of Consciousness. Cambridge, MA: A Bradford Book, MIT Press.

Hobson, J. A., Leonard, J. A. (2001). Out of its Mind: Psychiatry in Crisis. Cambridge, MA: Perseus Publishing.

Hobson, J. A. (2002). Dreaming: An Introduction to the Science of Sleep. New York: Oxford University Press, Inc.

Hobson, J. A. (2005). 13 Dreams Freud Never Had: The New Mind Science. New York: Pi Press.

Hoeller, S. A. (2003), Gnosticism: New Light On The Ancient Tradition Of Inner Knowing. Wheaton: The Theosophical Publishing House.

Holland, J. (1998). Emergence: From Chaos to Order. Reading: Addison-Wesley Publishing Company, Inc.

Hooper, D. (2006). Dark Cosmos: In Search of Our Universe's Missing Mass and Energy. New York: Smithsonian Books, HarperCollins.

Humphrey, N. (2002). The Mind Made Flesh: Frontiers of Psychology and Evolution. Oxford: Oxford University Press.

Johnson, M. (1987). The Body in the Mind: The Bodily Basis of Meaning, Imagination, and Reason. Chicago: The University of Chicago Press.

Johnson, M. (2007). The Meaning of the Body: Aesthetics of Human Understanding. Chicago: The University of Chicago Press.

Just, G. A. (2009). Autobiography of a Ghost. Eagle Entertainment USA: Mankato, MN.

Just, G. A. (2011). Mind of the Mystic. Eagle Entertainment USA: Mankato, MN.

Kaku, M. (1994). Hyperspace. New York: Oxford University Press.

Kaku, M. (2005). Parallel Worlds: A Journey Through Creation, Higher Dimensions, and the Future of the Cosmos. New York: Anchor Books.

Kandel, E. R. (2006). In Search of Memory: The Emergence of a New Science of Mind. New York: W. W. Norton & Company.

Kauffman, S. (1993). The Origin of Order. New York: Oxford University Press.

Kirsch, J. (2005). God Against The Gods. Penguin Books: New York.

Kuhn, T.S. (1962). The Structure of Scientific Revolutions. Chicago: The University of Chicago Press.

LaBerge, S., Rheingold, H. (1990). Exploring the World of Lucid Dreaming. New York: Ballantine Books.

LaBerge, S. (2009). Lucid Dreaming: A Concise Guide to Awakening in Your Dreams and in Your Life. Boulder, CO: Sounds True.

Lakoff, G., Johnson, M. (1980). Metaphors We Live By. Chicago: The University of Chicago Press.

Lakoff, B., Johnson, M. (1999). Philosophy In The Flesh: The Embodied Mind And Its Challenge To Western Thought. New York: Basic Books.

LeDoux, J. (1996). The Emotional Brain: The Mysterious Underpinnings of Emotional Life. New York: Simon & Schuster Paperbacks.

LeDoux, J. (2003). Synaptic Self: How Our Brains Become Who We Are. New York: Penguin.

Leete, A., Firnhaber, R.P., eds. (2004). Shamanism in the Interdisciplinary Context. Boca Raton: Brown Walker Press.

Lescot, T., Galanaud, D. and Puybasset, L. (2009), Exploring Altered Consciousness States by Magnetic Resonance Imaging in Brain Injury. Annals of the New York Academy of Sciences, 1157: 71–80. doi: 10.1111/j.1749-6632.2008.04120.x.

Linden, D. J. (2007). The Accidental Mind: How Brain Evolution has Give Us Love, Memory, Dreams, and God. Cambridge, MA: The Belknap Press of Harvard U. Press.

Llinas, R. R. (2002). I of the Vortex: From Neurons to Self. Cambridge, MA: A Bradford Book, The MIT Press.

Martin, P. (2002). Counting Sheep: the science and pleasures of sleep and dreams, New York: St. Martins Press.

McElroy, M. ((2007). Lucid Dreaming for Beginners: Simple Techniques for Creating Interactive Dreams. Woodbury, MN: Llewellyn Publications.

Mero, L. (1998). Moral Calculations: Game Theory, Logic, and Human Frailty. New York: Copernicus.

Moffett, S. (2006). The Three-Pound Enigma: The Human Brain and the Quest to Unlock Its Mysteries. Chapel Hill, NC: Algonquin Books.

Noe, A. (2009). Out of Our Heads: Why You Are Not Your Brain, and Other Lessons from the Biology of Consciousness. New York: Hill & Wang.

Ouspensky, P.D. (1931). A New Model of the Universe. New York: Alfred A. Knopf.

Parker, J, & Parker, D. (1985). Dreaming: Remembering, Interpreting, Benefiting. New York: Sterling Publishing Company.

Penrose, R. (1994). Shadows of the Mind: A Search for the Missing Science of Consciousness. New York: Oxford University Press.

Piaget, J. (1962). Play, Dream, and Imitation in Childhood. New York: Norton.

Picknett, L. (2004). Mary Magdalene. New York: Carroll & Graf Publishers.

Pierce, J.H. (2006). The Owners Manual for the Brain: Everyday Applications from Mind-Body Research. Austin: Bard Press.

Powell, R. (2008). The Essentials of Dream Interpretation. London: Southwater, Annes Publishing Ltd.

Prigogine, I. (1980). From being to becoming: time and complexity in the physical sciences. San Francisco: W. H. Freeman and Company.

Radin, D. (2006). Entangled Minds: Extrasensory Experiences in a Quantum Reality. New York: Pocket Books.

Radin, P. (1957). Primitive Man as Philosopher. New York: Dover Publications.

Ramachandran, V.S. (1998). Phantoms In The Brain: Probing the Mysteries of the Human Mind. New York: Harper Perennial.

Ramachandran, V.S. (2004). A Brief Tour of Human Consciousness. New York: Pi Press.

Ramachandran, V.S. (2011). The Tell-Tale Brain: A Neuroscientist's Quest for What Makes Us Human. New York: W. W. Norton & Company.

Restak, R. (1994). The Modular Brain: How New Discoveries in Neuroscience are Answering Age-old Questions about Memory, Free Will, Consciousness, and Personal Identity. New York: Scribners.

Restak, R. (2006). The Naked Brain: How the Emerging Neurosociety Is Changing How We Live, Work, and Love. New York: Harmony Books.

Rock, A. (2004). The Mind at Night: The New Science of How and Why We Dream. New York: Perseus Book Group.

Robinson, J.M. (1990). The Nag Hammadi Library. New York: HarperCollins Publishers.

Robinson, S., Corbett, T. (1974). The Dreamer's Dictionary. New York: Warner Books, Inc.

Rosenblum, B., Kuttner, F. (2006). Quantum Enigma: Physics Encounters Consciousness. New York: Oxford University Press.

Satinover, J. (2001). The Quantum Brain: The Search for Freedom and the Next Generation of Man. New York: John Wiley & Sons, Inc.

Schneider, L. C. (2008). Beyond Monotheism: A Theology of Multiplicity. New York: Routledge.

Shapiro, L. (2011). Embodied Cognition. New York: Routledge.

Smolin, L. (1997). The Life of the Cosmos. Oxford: Oxford University Press.

Spinoza. (1955). The Ethics. New York: Dover Press.

Stanford, C. (2001). Significant Others: The Ape-Human Continuum and the Quest for Human Nature. New York: Basic Books.

Star, C. G. (1991). A History of the Ancient World. New York: Oxford University Press.

Steltenkamp, M. (1993). Black Elk: Holy Man of the Oglala. Norman: University of Oklahoma Press.

Tart, T. (ed). (1969). Altered States of Consciousness. Garden City: Anchor Books.

Toomey, D. (2007). The New Time Travelers: A Journey to the Frontiers of Physics. New York: W. W. Norton & Company, Inc.

Thuan, T. X. (2001). Chaso and Harmony: Perspectives on Scientific Revolutions of the Twentieth Century. New York: Oxford.

Tipler, F. (1994). The Physics of Immortality. New York: Doubleday.

Weatherford, J. (2004). Genghis Khan and the Making of the Modern World. New York: Three Rivers Press.

Trusseau, T. (2008). The Key to Your Dreams: Unlock the Power of Your Dreams. UK: New Holland Publishers.

Varela, F.J., Thomson, E., Rosch, E. (1993). The Embodied Mind: Cognitive Science and Human Experience. Cambridge, MA: The MIT Press.

Verdal, V. (2010). Decoding Reality: The Universe as Quantum Information. Oxford University Press.

Walker, M. P. (2009), The Role of Sleep in Cognition and Emotion. Annals of the New York Academy of Sciences, 1156: 168–197. doi: 10.1111/j.1749-6632.2009.04416.x.

Wilhelmi, B. Differentiations: A Shamanic Reading of the Gospels (142-148) in Leete, A., Firnhaber, R.P., eds. (2004). Boca Raton: Brown Walker Press.

Wilson, E. O. (1999). Consilience: The Unity of Knowledge. New York: Vintage

Zimmer, C. (January, 2011). 100 Trillion Connections. Scientific American (58).

Lightning Source UK Ltd.
Milton Keynes UK
UKHW051107231120
373921UK00011B/962